PRACTICE AND MANAGEMENT OF PSYCHIATRIC EMERGENCY CARE

PRACTICE AND MANAGEMENT OF PSYCHIATRIC EMERGENCY CARE

Edited by

JACQUELYNE G. GORTON, R.N., M.S., C.S.

Clinical Director, Quality Assurance Program,
Community Mental Health Services, City and County of San Francisco
Department of Public Health; Assistant Clinical Professor,
School of Nursing, and Lecturer, School of Medicine,
University of California, San Francisco, California

REBECCA PARTRIDGE, R.N., M.S.

Nursing Consultant, San Franscico, California;
Doctoral Student, University of California,
Berkeley, California

Illustrated

The C. V. Mosby Company

ST. LOUIS • TORONTO • LONDON   1982

MOSBY

A TRADITION OF PUBLISHING EXCELLENCE

Editor: Alison Miller
Assistant editor: Susan R. Epstein
Manuscript editor: Lois Brunngraber
Book design: Nancy Steinmeyer
Cover design: Suzanne Oberholtzer
Production: Carolyn Biby

Printed in the United States of America

The C.V. Mosby Company
11830 Westline Industrial Drive, St. Louis, Missouri 63141

Library of Congress Cataloging in Publication Data

Main entry under title:

Practice and management of psychiatric emergency
   care.

   Bibliography: p.
   Includes index.
   1. Psychiatric emergencies. 2. Crisis inter-
vention (Psychiatry). I. Gorton, Jacquelyne G.
II. Partridge, Rebecca.
RC480.6.P7   616.89′025   82-3514
ISBN 0-8016-1936-X   AACR2

GW/VH/VH 9 8 7 6 5 4 3 2 1   01/B/093

Contributors

MARGARET ALBRIZIO, R.N., M.S.

Psycho-Social Nurse Consultant, Department of Psychiatry, Seattle Veterans Administration Medical Center, Seattle, Washington

GAIL M. BARTON, M.D., M.P.H.

Associate Professor of Psychiatry, Department of Psychiatry, University of Michigan, Ann Arbor, Michigan

MARY SWANSON CROCKETT, R.N., D.N.Sc.

Assistant Professor of Nursing, University of Texas at Austin School of Nursing, Austin, Texas

MELVIN S. GALE, M.D.

Director, Psychiatric Emergency Service, Department of Psychiatry, University of Cincinnati Hospital, Cincinnati, Ohio

MARTIN E. GLASSER, M.D.

Associate Professor of Pediatrics and Psychiatry and Director, Child Study Unit, University of California, San Francisco, California

STEPHEN M. GOLDFINGER, M.D.

Assistant Clinical Professor, Department of Psychiatry, University of California School of Medicine, San Francisco, California; Director, Northeast Project, Department of Psychiatry, San Francisco General Hospital, San Francisco, California

JACQUELYNE G. GORTON, R.N., M.S., C.S.

Clinical Director, Quality Assurance Program, Community Mental Health Services, City and County of San Francisco Department of Public Health; Assistant Clinical Professor, School of Nursing, and Lecturer, School of Medicine, University of California, San Francisco, California

CORRINE L. HATTON, R.N., M.N., C.S.

Psychiatric Clinical Nurse Specialist in Private Practice, Los Angeles, California

ROBERT HAUSNER, M.D.

Director of Training, Westside Crisis Clinic, Department of Psychiatry, Mt. Zion Hospital and Medical Center, San Francisco, California; Assistant Clinical Professor of Psychiatry, Department of Psychiatry, University of California School of Medicine, San Francisco, California

ART HOM, M.S.W.

Assistant Director, Psychiatric Emergency Services, Department of Psychiatry, Mt. Zion Hospital and Medical Center, San Francisco, California; Assistant Clinical Professor, Department of Psychiatry, University of California, San Francisco, California

JAMES P. KRAJESKI, M.D.

Psychiatrist in Private Practice, San Francisco, California

VALLORY G. LATHROP, R.N., D.N.Sc., F.A.A.N.

Deputy Director for Nursing, Saint Elizabeth's Hospital, Washington, D.C.

MARIANN P. MONTELEONE, R.N., M.S., C.S.

Assistant Director of Psychiatric Nursing and Psychiatric Clinical Nurse Specialist, Department of Psychiatry, San Francisco General Hospital, San Francisco, California

REBECCA PARTRIDGE, R.N., M.S.

Nursing Consultant, San Francisco, California; Doctoral Student, University of California, Berkeley, California

BARRY B. PERLMAN, M.D.

Director, Department of Psychiatry, St. Joseph's Medical Center, Yonkers, New York; Assistant Clinical Professor of Psychiatry, Mt. Sinai Medical School, New York, New York

FREDRIC J. PHILLIPS, M.D.

Staff Psychiatrist, Phoenix Programs Inc., Concord, California

GAIL PISARCIK, R.N., M.S., C.S.

Psychiatric Clinical Specialist, Emergency Ward, Massachusetts General Hospital, Boston, Massachusetts

MARK W. RHINE, M.D.

Associate Clinical Professor of Psychiatry, Department of Psychiatry, University of Colorado School of Medicine; Associate Director, Emergency Psychiatric Service, University of Colorado Health Sciences Center, Denver, Colorado

MICHAEL J. RICE, R.N., M.S.N.

Doctoral Student and Research Associate, College of Nursing, University of Arizona, Tucson, Arizona

ARTHUR H. SCHWARTZ, M.D.

University of Medicine and Dentistry of New Jersey—Rutgers Medical School, Piscataway, New Jersey

JOAN F. SCHWARTZ, Ph.D.

Clinical Psychologist, Mission Mental Health Center, San Francisco, California

RICHARD B. SEYMOUR, M.A.

Director, Haight-Ashbury Training and Education Projects, Haight-Ashbury Free Medical Clinic, San Francisco, California

LEO S. SHEA, Ph.D.

Director, Crisis Stabilization Program, Central New Hampshire Community Mental Health Services, Concord, New Hampshire

DAVID E. SMITH, M.D.

Medical Director, Haight-Ashbury Free Medical Clinic, San Francisco, California

ZIGFRIDS T. STELMACHERS, Ph.D.

Chief Psychologist and Director, Crisis Intervention Center, Psychiatry Service, Hennepin County Medical Center, Minneapolis, Minnesota

RICHARD B. WARNER, M.D.

Assistant Professor of Psychiatry, Department of Psychiatry, University of Colorado School of Medicine; Director, Emergency Psychiatric Service, Denver Health and Hospitals, Denver, Colorado

MICHAEL P. WEISSBERG, M.D.

Associate Professor of Psychiatry, Department of Psychiatry, University of Colorado School of Medicine; Director of Clinical Affairs, University of Colorado Health Sciences Center, Denver, Colorado

ALINE WOMMACK, R.N., B.S.

Assistant Director of Psychiatric Nursing, Department of Psychiatry, San Francisco General Hospital, San Francisco, California

ELAINE WUSTMANN, R.N., M.N.

Psychiatric Clinical Nurse Specialist, Evaluation and Treatment Unit, Neuropsychiatric Institute, University of California, Los Angeles, California

Foreword

When crisis intervention theory was first introduced, it encountered much skepticism from psychiatrists because the theory did not fit the standard medical model of long-term, in-depth analysis of the client. Now skepticism has changed to acceptance. Today crisis intervention is recognized as an effective and viable therapy modality. It is no longer considered a "second-best" form of therapy or a "Band-Aid" but a very effective form of brief psychotherapy.

The acceptance of the concept of crisis intervention has contributed considerably to the growing importance of psychiatric emergency care. Public awareness of the broader concepts of mental health and the mental hospital deinstitutionalization movement have further contributed to the development of an increasing number of psychiatric emergency units.

The time has come for a comprehensive text dealing with the clinical components of psychiatric emergency care and crisis intervention as well as the administrative issues of unit management. Jacquelyne Gorton and Rebecca Partridge address this need with great skill and sensitivity. They have synthesized their extensive experience in psychiatric emergency care and administration, enabling them to compile a volume of practical, vital, up-to-date information. Recognizing that the most effective care is provided by the multidisciplinary team, they sought contributions from respected members of the fields of nursing, psychiatry, psychology, and social work. These contributions present the diverse perspectives inherent in this team approach.

Realizing that appropriate care can be provided only when the management of the unit allows it, the authors offer practical suggestions and guidelines for effective and efficient administration. The discussions of unit maintenance and functioning in today's complex institutions will prove invaluable to the novice as well as the experienced administrator or manager.

Gorton and Partridge have succeeded admirably in their intent to meet the needs of all professionals currently engaged in or wishing to enter the field of psychiatric emergency care or crisis intervention. This should be a valuable text to all professionals interested in modern methods of treatment of the mentally ill.

Donna C. Aguilera, Ph.D., F.A.A.N.

Preface

The purpose of this book is to offer theoretical information and practical advice for professionals currently engaged in or wishing to enter the field of psychiatric emergency care or crisis intervention. Most books on psychiatric emergency care and crisis intervention focus on the clinical components of care and rarely discuss issues related to unit management. This book provides comprehensive discussions of clinical psychiatric emergency care and crisis intervention as well as administrative issues of unit management in one volume.

Part One, Practice of Psychiatric Emergency Care, describes the crisis intervention approach that provides part of the theoretical basis for psychiatric emergency care. The assessment process is reviewed in detail, and separate chapters are devoted to the most common psychiatric emergencies. Diagnostic criteria, treatment and intervention strategies, and disposition alternatives are presented for clients experiencing organic disorders, seizure disorders, schizophrenic disorders, affective disorders, borderline conditions, suicidal behavior, homicidal behavior, assaultive behavior, and substance abuse problems. Some unique needs of special clients in crisis are examined as they relate to children, victims of rape and battering, homosexuals, ethnic minorities, and the bereaved.

Part Two, Management of Psychiatric Emergency Care, offers practical suggestions and guidelines that are useful to the novice and the experienced staff leader, unit manager, or administrator. Unit organization and structure are analyzed with regard to theories and strategies for unit management, leadership, and use of the multidisciplinary team. Discussions of unit maintenance and functioning include the potential and actual impact of standards of care, legal rights and responsibilities of staff and clients, budgeteering, and interagency and intraagency collaboration.

Since psychiatric emergency care and crisis intervention involve clinicians representing a variety of disciplines, we have included among our contributing authors representatives from each of the following professions: nursing, psychiatry, psychology, and social work. The diverse perspectives presented by these different disciplines reflect the dynamic processes inherent in the use of the multidisciplinary team approach. Our intent was to prepare a book that would meet the needs of a wide audience, and we anticipate that this volume will be of interest to graduate students, faculty, and clinicians in many health care professions. In particular, those working in psychiatric emergency units, crisis intervention clinics, and medical emergency units will find that this book specifically addresses clinical and unit management issues they regularly confront.

Selecting the terminology that would provide structure and clarity for this volume was a difficult task. Particularly in the health care field, "it is well known that professional jargon helps to unite a group and to set it apart from strangers."* We have attempted to use terms that are understood by and are acceptable to most health care professionals. There were three issues of termi-

---

*From Blau, P.: Dynamics of bureaucracy, Chicago, 1963, University of Chicago Press, p. 106.

nology that required editorial fiat on our part, and we would like to take this opportunity to explain our decisions. The three issues concerning terminology were (1) the use of the phrases *psychiatric emergency care* and *crisis intervention,* (2) reference to individuals who seek or receive care as *clients* or *patients,* and (3) the use of gender-neutral pronouns or gender-specific pronouns.

First, the issue of psychiatric emergency care versus crisis intervention. Obviously, the term *psychiatric emergency care* suggests an illness-oriented medical model approach, whereas *crisis intervention* connotes a mental health approach to situational problems. The popular distinction is that *crises* refer to situations in which relatively healthy individuals are subjected to great environmental stress and that *psychiatric emergencies* are those in which the individuals have psychopathological conditions and in which socioenvironmental factors are less important precipitants.

The crisis intervention approach originally developed as a lay effort to help people with special problems (youths with drug problems, rape victims, suicidal people) who were not being adequately dealt with by the professional community. Today crisis units remain community based but usually employ health care professionals to serve as clinicians. Psychiatric emergency units are usually affiliated with hospitals and urban medical centers but often solicit and maintain considerable community involvement.

Although the impetus and development of crisis units and psychiatric emergency units differed in their original perspectives and settings, in recent years the two approaches have begun to converge. No longer are the distinctions obvious. Some of the crisis intervention literature continues to assume a target population composed of relatively normal healthy individuals undergoing extreme stress; in actual practice crisis clinics often serve clients with marked preexisting psychopathological conditions. And conversely, persons without these conditions often seek help with situational crises in psychiatric emergency units.

We have chosen to use the term *psychiatric emergency care* as a generic one encompassing

crisis intervention, and to this end we have included chapters that deal with helping people in crisis with problems of rape, battering, bereavement, homosexuality, and ethnic minority status. We define a psychiatric emergency as a crisis situation precipitated by an intrapsychic, intrapersonal, biological, or environmental change that potentially impairs the general functioning of an individual.

We recognize that the label of *psychiatric emergency* may not be preferred by all, but we found *crisis intervention* too limiting because of its emphasis on environmental precipitants and the narrow scope of the assessment process implied by a problem-solving approach. The primary shortcoming of the term *psychiatric emergency* is the social stigma it has traditionally carried. The phrase *psychiatric patient* has been particularly stigmatizing, which leads us to the issue of referring to recipients of care as *patients* or *clients.*

In keeping with the view that health care consumers have rights, responsibilities, and a participative role, we refer to individuals seeking or receiving care as *clients. Patient* has been the traditional term in medicine, but in recent years the nursing and social service literature commonly has used the term *client,* especially in reference to community-based health services. *Patient* conveys a proprietary attitude by the provider and generally assumes that the consumer is passive and relinquishes responsibility, that is, the role of the patient is subordinate to that of the care provider. We prefer the use of the term *client,* which suggests a reciprocal relationship between consumer and provider.

And finally, the issue of gender-neutral versus gender-specific pronouns should be considered. Many authors and publishing companies (including The C.V. Mosby Company) have adopted policies regarding the avoidance of the sexist connotations implied by the generic use of masculine pronouns. We wholeheartedly agree with this position. Using feminine pronouns promotes reverse discrimination and is therefore no remedy. So we have used the gender-neutral plural pronouns wherever possible. Writing in the plural form may seem awkward at first, but the process of changing old habits is always a bit uncomfortable. Strict grammarians may occasionally object to the slight deviations from traditional literary customs that using the plural forms necessitates, but we believe that language is dynamic and its use should reflect the emergence of the gender-neutral values of our culture.

We wish to express gratitude to the many individuals who have directly or indirectly contributed to this book. To each of the contributing authors we owe a special thanks. Our appreciation also goes to the staff at Mosby: Mike Riley, in the early stages of the book, and more recently, Alison Miller and Suzi Epstein, who have been very helpful in guiding us through the later stages of the production of this volume. We also wish to thank Audrey Fitzgerald for ably handling our correspondence and typing many drafts and much of the final manuscript.

Jacquelyne G. Gorton
Rebecca Partridge

Contents

PART ONE

PRACTICE OF PSYCHIATRIC EMERGENCY CARE

SECTION A

The theoretical basis of psychiatric emergency care, 2

1 Crisis intervention, 3
   Mark W. Rhine and Michael P. Weissberg

2 An assessment process, 13
   Richard B. Warner and Michael P. Weissberg

SECTION B

Common psychiatric emergencies, 24

3 The client with an organic disorder, 29
   Fredric J. Phillips and Joan F. Schwartz

4 The client with a seizure disorder, 49
   Robert Hausner

5 The client with a schizophrenic disorder, 70
   Mary Swanson Crockett

6 The client with an affective disorder, 86
   Melvin S. Gale

7 The client with a borderline condition, 100
   Stephen M. Goldfinger

8 The client with suicidal behavior, 124
   Corrine L. Hatton and Elaine Wustmann

9 The client with homicidal behavior, 138
   Vallory G. Lathrop

10 The client with assaultive behavior, 149
    Aline Wommack

11 The client with a substance abuse problem, 161
    Richard B. Seymour, Jacquelyne G. Gorton, and David E. Smith

SECTION C

Some unique needs of special clients, 181

12 The client who is a child, 185
    Martin E. Glasser

13 The client who is raped or battered, 205
    Mariann P. Montelone

14 The client who is homosexual, 227
    James P. Krajeski

15 The client who is a member of an ethnic minority, 244
    Art Hom

16 The client who is bereaved, 256
    Margaret Albrizio

PART TWO

MANAGEMENT OF PSYCHIATRIC EMERGENCY CARE

SECTION D

Unit organization and structure, 283

17 Unit management, 285

Zigfrids T. Stelmachers

18 Leadership, 306

Rebecca Partridge and Jacquelyne G. Gorton

19 The multidisciplinary team approach, 318

Barry B. Perlman and Arthur H. Schwartz

SECTION E

Unit maintenance and functioning, 330

20 Standards of care, 333

Gail M. Barton

21 Legal issues, 345

Michael J. Rice

22 Budgeteering, 365

Leo S. Shea

23 Interagency and intraagency collaboration, 392

Gail Pisarcik

PART ONE

Practice of psychiatric emergency care

PART ONE OF THIS BOOK deals with clinical issues of the practice of psychiatric emergency care and consists of three sections. Section A deals with the theoretical basis of psychiatric emergency care and includes two chapters on crisis intervention and assessment. Section B includes nine chapters devoted to the assessment and treatment of the most common psychiatric emergencies: organic disorders, seizure disorders, schizophrenic disorders, affective disorders, borderline conditions, suicidal behavior, homicidal behavior, assaultive behavior, and substance abuse problems. Section C consists of five chapters dealing with some of the unique needs of special clients: children, women who are raped or battered, homosexuals, ethnic minorities, and the bereaved.

SECTION A

The theoretical basis of psychiatric emergency care

There are two chapters in this initial section. The first chapter, Crisis Intervention, discusses the utilization of crisis theory in psychiatric emergency care. The composition and characteristics of the crisis state are discussed in detail, and very practical guidelines and techniques of intervention are suggested. Step-by-step advice is offered to the clinician on strategies for developing a therapeutic alliance, gathering information, and problem solving. The authors point out some common pitfalls that should be avoided.

Chapter 1 offers very practical and clinically relevant information. The reader is reminded that although a theoretical distinction is sometimes made between crisis intervention and psychiatric emergency care, in reality clinicians in both settings are faced with the task of helping clients with and without psychopathology.

Chapter 2, The Assessment Process, offers clinicians a practical approach to the complex task of assessment. The authors remind the reader that it is important to guard against the common tendency to dismiss threats of violence or self-destructive behavior as idle talk. Because one of the paramount concerns in assessment is the determination of the potential for dangerousness, several other chapters are devoted specifically to assaultive, suicidal, and homicidal behavior. The assessment process is reviewed sequentially and includes realistic clinical strategies for assessing a client's appearance, psychomotor activity, affect, speech, thought processes, thought content, perception, consciousness, intellectual functioning, and availability of resources. The chapter concludes with a discussion of treatment planning.

CHAPTER 1

Crisis intervention

Mark W. Rhine, M.D.
Michael P. Weissberg, M.D.

Refuse to directly treat the presenting problem. Offer some rationale, such as the idea that symptoms have 'roots,' to avoid treating the problem the patient is paying his money to recover from. In this way the odds increase that the patient will not recover, and future generations of therapists can remain ignorant of the specific skills needed to get people over their problems (Haley, J., The art of being a failure as a therapist, Am. J. Orthopsychiatry **39**:691, 1969).

No aspect of mental health care is more demanding than the psychiatric emergency. Clinicians are required to deal with severely disturbed clients* whom they have never seen before and to take action with a minimum amount of information under severe time constraints, never knowing who may come in the door next. Anxiety levels are high in the client and the clinician. Additionally, the clinician may have to deal with friends, family, and health care providers as well as a variety of community resources. There is a common misbelief that because crisis therapy is shorter than long-term therapy, it must therefore be easier. Nothing is further from the truth. Clinicians must be able to work fast; they cannot be passive listeners but must be active in gathering information, knowing what to look for and what is irrelevant. They must be able to formulate hypotheses quickly, sorting out potential medical problems from psychological problems, and then take steps to help clients solve their problems,

---

*NOTE: Although the authors of Chapters 1 and 2 prefer the use of the word *patient,* the word *client* is being used in keeping with the terminology of the other chapters.

often with a minimum of training and support.

In the past it has been customary to put the most inexperienced personnel into the psychiatric emergency clinic and then to provide them with minimal supervision. This may have been a reflection of the medical custom of putting the junior intern into the emergency room, of viewing emergency care as a service obligation, and of the anxiety of the more experienced staff who wished to avoid working in this setting. This practice was curious, because the psychiatric emergency clinic represents the chief link of mental health with the public and other health systems. This is where the tone is set for treatment. In fact, treatment can begin and end here. Fortunately this tradition of understaffing emergency services is changing, and now the best psychiatric emergency and crisis services use experienced clinicians. The more experienced staff bring the personality characteristics best suited to crisis work: confidence, ability to work independently yet to recognize when they need help and to seek it out, resourcefulness, activity, ability to function in an unstructured situation under stress, assertiveness, flexibility, and a healthy sense of humor. There has been a move away from the mere "disposition" and triage of clients to active treatment. The value of the emergency clinic for training has become appreciated, and it has been recognized that with proper support the emergency clinic, though stressful, can provide a magnificent learning experience for all health professionals (Zimet and Weissberg, 1979). Crisis theory has provided the framework for this shift in psychiatric care.

WHAT IS A CRISIS?

Among the important psychological needs of every human being are the needs to feel loved, worthy, and appreciated, to feel strong and secure, and to feel that one is good, not bad. Life is a succession of crises, a series of problems that must be overcome lest they threaten these important psychological needs. If these crises are mastered, then self-esteem is bolstered, whereas failure leads to self-doubt. Sometimes the stresses of life seem overwhelming: the woman who has been raped at knife point, the father of

five who has been laid off his job, the couple whose child has developed a life-threatening illness, or the soldier entering combat are all experiencing threats to their psychological homeostasis. Often overlooked, however, are the stresses that are involved in less dramatic, more joyful situations such as marriage, pregnancy and birth, promotion, or a move to a new city. For some, a crisis may be as small as a broken dishwasher or television, especially if the latter is used to occupy the children.

Crises occur to everyone, no matter what their previous level of psychological functioning. As important as the crisis event itself is the nature of the person who is experiencing that event; a stress that may be readily handled in a better-adjusted individual may be overwhelming to someone who is only marginally compensated. Incidentally, some of the crisis intervention literature assumes the clients are relatively normal and healthy individuals undergoing extreme stress, whereas in actual practice crisis clinics tend to receive individuals with marked pre-existing psychopathology, making the therapeutic task more difficult and the goals more limited than some of the literature may imply.

When one is unable to handle a particular stress, a variety of unpleasant symptoms develop which characterize the crisis state. Gerald Caplan (1961), a pioneer in crisis intervention, described crisis as a state that occurs when one's usual ways of coping are inadequate to deal with the stress. A period of disorganization and upset ensues during which abortive attempts at resolution may be made until a new equilibrium is reached. The solutions to crises may or may not be in the best interest of the individual or the environment. The following vignette illustrates some of these principles:

Case vignette #1

A couple who had recently celebrated their fortieth anniversary consulted a divorce lawyer and were referred to a crisis clinic for counseling. At the interview their frustration was obvious as they hurled complaints and accusations at one another. They were at a loss to explain why things had gone so sour, because they agreed they had long enjoyed an "ideal marriage." Insistent questioning by the clinician clarified that their troubles had begun only 6 months earlier when the husband had retired from his railroad job. No longer did he travel 5 days a week but spent all his time at home in their small trailer, dirtying the ashtrays and, as the wife put it, driving her "crazy." The clinician recognized that the couple had established an equilibrium over the years which had been disrupted because the retirement had forced them into an unaccustomed closeness. Therapy was directed toward reestablishing the old equilibrium, with the husband being encouraged to take up pursuits that would get him out of the home for most of the day. At follow-up a year later the couple was again enjoying their marriage, and the husband was devoting his time to a model railroad club and to fishing and hunting.

This couple had functioned comfortably for years until they encountered a stress that they were unable to master in their usual manner. The wife took pride in having everything in order and maintained a meticulous household, a feat that she achieved by virtue of having her husband out of the home for most of the week. Now he dirtied the ashtrays and strewed the newspapers around the living room, and the wife's sense of orderliness and mastery over her environment was upset. A period of disorganization ensued in which the couple, not really understanding the source of their intense feelings, yelled and screamed at one another in futile attempts to solve their problems. Finally they went to a divorce lawyer, another unsuccessful attempt at resolution that, in view of their 40 years of marriage, could be considered a maladaptive one. Ultimately, through therapy, they were helped to utilize their usual methods of coping, namely, to keep distance from one another. A new and more adaptive equilibrium was reached.

Interest in crisis and in crisis intervention began to flourish in the 1940s. In 1943 Dr. Erich Lindemann had the opportunity to work with the survivors of the tragic Coconut Grove nightclub fire (Lindemann, 1944). As he worked

with these people, he discovered that some were more able than others to deal with their grief. This led him to formulate the concept of emotional crisis and to develop an interest in studying what enables some individuals to successfully master a stress while others succumb and develop chronic difficulties.

At the same time the military was interested in the rehabilitation of troops with combat neurosis. During World War II and the Korean War the military developed for such casualties the concept of immediate treatment close to the battlefield so as to return the soldier to his unit and prevent chronicity. The value of abreaction, support, and reassurance in the rapid resolution of these traumatic neuroses was recognized. When these military psychiatrists returned to civilian life, they continued their interest in the short-term treatment of clients.

CHARACTERISTICS OF THE CRISIS STATE

When individuals are unable to solve some significant problem in their lives, they begin to experience tension and anxiety. They can feel helpless and unable to take action on their own, which may lead to depression. Overall functioning decreases. They develop a variety of somatic symptoms, including various aches and pains, dizziness, easy fatigability, and difficulty sleeping and eating. They may experience intense feelings, perceptual changes, sometimes even hallucinations, which make them feel that they are "going crazy." There is a sense of urgency and immediacy, which may lead the individual to contact the clinic at all hours. There may be a frantic search for new solutions. There is an impairment of impulse control, which may be further compromised if the individual turns to drugs or alcohol to help alleviate the intense feelings. Behavior may appear childlike and regressed. They are frequently isolated from their usual sources of help. These feelings may be infectious, and friends, relatives, even therapists, may become caught up in the panic.

It is relatively easy to recognize clients in crisis when they enter the clinic with characteristic symptoms of anxiety or depression and when they can readily relate a significant stress. In many cases, however, things are not so clear. It may be a relative, friend, clinician, or policeman who brings the client to the clinic. In fact, they may be the people in crisis. Some clients have disguised ways of asking for help: the man who enters a medical emergency unit with a headache may not connect this with the fact that his wife has just left him; the woman who has been battered by her husband may "make up" a story to explain her symptoms. The clinician must be alert to covert presentations of crises. For example, child abusers often appear at the clinic with vague somatic complaints (Weissberg, 1977).

Certain characteristics of the crisis state are particularly beneficial to undertaking successful crisis therapy. Clients in crisis may feel an immense degree of trust toward caretaking people; they have almost magical expectations of what the clinician may be able to do for them, much as a child in pain turns to a parent to get rid of the hurt. Such clients immediately establish a positive relationship with the clinician on whom they rely to get them out of their chaotic situation. At times of crisis, clients' defenses are much more mobile than usual, and they are more able to work productively on changes than at other, more defended, times in life. The time of crisis is a true therapeutic opportunity and potential time for growth. Clients may experience lasting positive changes with marked impact on overall adjustment from relatively short periods of therapy.

THE TECHNIQUES OF CRISIS INTERVENTION

There are three phases in the crisis interview: (1) developing the alliance, (2) gathering information, and (3) problem solving. These phases overlap, but for convenience have been separated here.

Developing the alliance

Individuals in crisis are feeling hopeless and helpless and tend to approach the clinician in a dependent manner, looking to the clinician to make everything all right for them. It is impor-

tant to counteract this tendency to regression and dependency by making the client an active partner in the treatment process, or to use a technical term, to develop a "working alliance," whereby client and clinician work together on the problem. Such an alliance develops from the clients' perception that they have been understood and accepted by the clinician and from the clients' conscious intent to resolve the current difficulties. The best way to develop an alliance is to begin where clients want to begin. If they prefer to talk about headaches or belly pains, it is best to start there. As mentioned previously, the client in crisis is ready to attribute almost omnipotent powers to the clinician. It is reassuring to the client to have a clinician who is calm, confident, and hopeful. Clinicians must be active; they cannot wait passively for the story to unfold, but must be gently intrusive, knowing what questions to ask and what areas may be avoided.

Empathy is as important in crisis treatment as in longer term therapy. The following example shows the value of empathy, not only in developing an alliance but also as a major technique in treatment:

Case vignette #2

A 42-year-old woman was brought to the emergency unit the day after the death of her mother with whom she had been living. She was markedly regressed at home, sitting silently in the corner and refusing to eat. In the emergency unit she was motionless, staring at the floor and saying nothing. A psychiatric resident thought that she must be a catatonic schizophrenic or be in a psychotic depression and would require long-term hospitalization.

His supervisor suggested a different plan, and the woman was put into an overnight bed. Each hour until he turned in, the resident would visit her and tell her how sorry he was to hear that her mother had died. The client did not acknowledge his presence until the following morning when she greeted him by stating that, "My mother has just died. I need to go home and help with the funeral."

This also illustrates "meeting the client where they are," evaluating previous level of functioning, and trying to understand the meaning of the precipitating stress.

The clinician must not underestimate the value of empathic listening. It is immensely valuable to confused and panicked clients to have someone listen. They then feel that they are being taken seriously, and their self-esteem, which has been seriously shaken is bolstered. The clinician's attempt to understand makes the clients feel that this craziness may make sense after all, and they may begin to identify with the clinician's attitude toward this seemingly incomprehensible material.

In developing an alliance, it is also useful to pay attention to the client's feelings about being in the crisis clinic and seeing a "psychotherapist." If the client feels weak, out of control, or humiliated, one can counter with comments such as "it takes a tremendous amount of strength to come here, considering how afraid you are of this place," or "I know things feel out of control to you, but I'm sure that we'll be able to make sense out of them."

Gathering information

Gathering information goes on concomitantly with developing the alliance. With so much chaos going on around them, crisis interviewers must know how to keep their bearings. The following are useful areas to cover.

FOCUS ON THE PRECIPITATING EVENT. One of the most useful questions to keep in mind is "why now?" What makes this client susceptible to this event at this time? Clients may prefer to talk about the past in an attempt to avoid what has brought them to the clinic, but the clinician must not be misled. One should look for situations that represent a loss, a threat of a loss, or a change that represents a challenge to the client. One must be alert for medical or organic conditions that may be contributing to, or causing, the client's confused speech or behavior. It is also important to know whether the client is in treatment currently with any clinician, taking any medications, or using any alcohol or drugs. The following diagnosis was almost overlooked:

Case vignette #3

An inexperienced trainee asked his supervisor to interview an emergency client whom he characterized as "the most oppositional and infuriating client I've ever met—she refuses to answer my questions." The supervisor encountered a similar response and found himself becoming irritated until it occurred to him that perhaps the client was unable to answer the questions, rather than simply being stubborn. Further examination proved the woman to be aphasic (unable to talk because of organic brain damage).

HAS THE CLIENT EVER HAD SIMILAR SYMPTOMS IN THE PAST? Clinicians can ask, "Have you ever felt this way before?" If it is discovered that the client has indeed felt this way in the past, it is then important to determine what may have precipitated these past symptoms, because a similar precipitant may well be active currently. For example, if it is learned that a client who was depressed 3 years ago because a woman left him is depressed now, it is highly likely that he has experienced another loss. Although emphasis is placed on the "here and now" in crisis treatment, the interview content is not limited to the present, and it is important to search for common denominators between the present crisis and past experiences. One need not take an exhaustive past history but should explore the past as it appears dynamically relevant to the present crisis.

HAVE YOU EVER EXPERIENCED A SIMILAR STRESS IN THE PAST? If, for example, a client's present crisis appears related to a move to a new city, it would be important to know if the client has made moves in the past and, if so, how the individual dealt with them.

HOW DID YOU COPE? Questioning previous coping ability follows from the previous question. How an individual copes with a past crisis will give us clues as to how to deal with the present crisis. The goal of crisis intervention is to return clients to their precrisis level of equilibrium, and the secret to doing this rests in using whatever has worked for the client in resolving past crises. Psychiatric emergency care is not going to change a client's personality. The goal of psychiatric emergency treatment is to utilize whatever coping mechanisms clients already possess to help them get back to their previous level of equilibrium.

WHY IS THIS INDIVIDUAL SUSCEPTIBLE TO THIS STRESS AT THIS TIME? What elements are there in the client's present circumstances which provoke past vulnerabilities?

Case vignette #4

A 38-year-old man came to the crisis clinic depressed and suicidal after the breakup with a woman with whom he had been having an affair. Initially he was quite tearful and he finally apologized for acting like "a 17 year old." The clinician made a mental note of this unusual comment and also wondered to himself why this man was feeling suicidal. The clinician recognized that anyone would be upset under the circumstances, but wondered why this individual was so upset that he contemplated taking his life. By the end of the interview the clinician had learned that the patient's mother had died of cancer when he was 17 years old.

This past loss made him particularly susceptible to the present loss. His apparent overreaction to the loss gave the clue that he was reacting not only to the present loss but also to one in the past.

As shown in this vignette, crisis therapy need not be limited to dealing with the present when such opportunities as this arise to deal with unresolved past material.

RESOURCES. Crises do not occur in a vacuum. Social systems are involved, as well as "significant others" such as friends, relatives, people at work, and health professionals. These individuals may be at the heart of the problem, and the client may neglect to mention them unless you question actively. These significant others also may be a good source of additional information. We have found it useful not to continue an interview beyond 30 mintues if we are no clearer about the dynamics of the case than at the beginning of the session. At this point it is useful to pursue other sources of information or to allow someone else to help with the interview. In crisis work a somewhat broader definition of confidentiality may be used than may be followed in other settings. When information from outside sources is needed, it is useful not to ask for the client's permission, because if the client refuses permission, the clinician is then in a bind. The clients are told that plans include contacting the family, boss, probation worker, and so on. Then clients are asked whether they would be interested in listening in on the conversation. This circumvents the confidentiality problem, makes clients active participants, and allays the fears of suspicious individuals regarding what's going on behind their backs.

Case vignette #5

A 45-year-old chronic schizophrenic woman became floridly psychotic after discontinuing her medication. Since she had taken the medication faithfully for almost 10 years, the clinician wondered "Why now? Why was she discontinuing it now?" She had no idea. The husband was contacted and said that she had stopped the medication after she had received a letter from her son whom she had not seen in 15 years and that he would be visiting for Thanksgiving.

Case vignette #6

A 33-year-old woman complained of symptoms of anxiety. She had been hospitalized 2 years earlier following a breakup with a boyfriend. Suspecting a similar precipitant this time, the clinician followed that lead, but the client denied being involved with any men at the present time. Meanwhile, another staff member who was looking after the client's 8-year-old daughter in the waiting room, learned from the child about the mother's new boyfriend.

WHAT WAS THE CLIENT'S PREVIOUS LEVEL OF FUNCTIONING? What was the client's level of functioning before the crisis? This will be important in setting realistic goals for the treatment.

The following cases illustrate these points in more detail.

Case vignette #7

A psychiatric consultant to a rural clinic was asked to see a 32-year-old woman with multiple sclerosis and suicidal thoughts, which the client felt were related to the fact that her husband was drinking and having an affair. This looked like an obvious cause-and-effect relationship until the consultant learned that the husband had been having affairs and drinking repeatedly throughout their 13 years of marriage, yet this was the first time that the client had ever felt suicidal. The consultant then reasoned that the multiple sclerosis must be responsible for the suicidal feelings, but learned that although she had been depressed a year earlier when the diagnosis was first made, her symptoms were now improving. In fact, her driver's license had recently been reinstated. The consultant was puzzled; he asked, "Why now? Why was she now unable to deal with the stress of her husband's alcoholism and infidelity when she had been able to in the past?" The woman pondered and was able to answer: in the past she had been active and busy, which always sustained her until her husband returned. Now, however, she was unable to leave their ranch as her arms were too weak to open the heavy gate. Consequently, she was unable to keep herself busy; dwelling for hours on what her husband and the other woman might be doing, she became more depressed and ultimately suicidal in the process. Rather than try to change this woman's long-standing masochistic character structure, an attempt was made to support her previous successful defense mechanism (keeping herself busy to prevent herself from thinking about her problems). The consultant needed to help her find a way to get her off the ranch. This was discussed with the client, who thought that she might be able to get the county commissioners to replace the gate with a cattle guard, a ditch crossed by ties spaced to prevent cattle from crossing but which would permit her to drive off the ranch. She was successful in doing this, her symp-toms abated immediately, and she did not feel the need to keep the follow-up visit.

Case vignette #8

A 47-year-old woman came to the psychiatric emergency unit with the chief complaint, "I've killed someone." Four days earlier a fellow worker had been killed in an industrial accident for which the client felt responsible. The client had turned on a shredding machine while a repairman was in it. The repairman was new and had violated all safety regulations by not informing the client, whose job it was to start the machine each day, that he was in the machine. He also did not shut off the outside power source to the machine. Nevertheless, the client appeared excessively guilty. She had slept and eaten poorly since the accident, and had the feeling that everyone in town was talking about her. She felt like getting a new job (although she had worked at this plant for years and held a responsible supervisory position). She had attempted to talk with her husband who dismissed her by saying, "Accidents will happen." Her husband was asked to come for the next appointment; at this time it was learned that he had experienced similar traumas while working during the war at a munitions plant and seeing several co-workers killed in occupational accidents. He had been interfering with the client's attempt to work out her feelings, and it took very little education for him to see his wife's need to ventilate. He became a helpful ally in the treatment after this session. The clinician wondered why this woman had such excessive guilt over an accident that was indeed tragic and sad, but for which in reality she was not being blamed by others and for which there was no need to be so harsh to herself. The clinician conjectured that this incident might have revived old feelings that had not been completely worked through about some incident in the part for which she felt guilty. In the fourth therapy session, as the client was recalling the scream of the fellow worker just before he was killed, she remembered the scream of her own mother just before she was killed crossing the street when the client was 12 years old. The girl and her mother had been out collecting laundry; the girl had offered to pick up the laundry at the house across the street, but the mother had commented that the door was hard to open and she would go herself. The mother was killed, and apparently the father was unable to help the daughter deal with her feelings. The current incident was a carbon copy of the tragedy nearly 30 years earlier. In the course of her therapy the client had the opportunity to work through, for the first time, the feelings around her mother's death.

Problem solving

The elucidation of the crisis, making a chaotic story make sense, is by itself therapeutic. During a successful interview it becomes clearer why the client is in the emergency clinic now, what the precipitating stress is, and what its dynamic ties to the past are. Helping clients find adaptive solutions to their present difficulties involves certain principles.

EARLY FORMULATION. One does not need to delay developing a formulation with the client about the present situation. This should begin with the first interview, but the clinician should be flexible enough to modify hypotheses as further information is collected. It is useful to describe the situation to the client in a way that appears solvable, maintaining hope but not utilizing empty reassurances.

SET REALISTIC GOALS. Perhaps the biggest problem for the beginning crisis worker is the inability to set realistic goals. Such clinicians may be overcome by therapeutic zeal, attempt too much, and consequently become frustrated and unable to recognize when the treatment is over. The only realistic goal is to attempt to return clients to their previous level of functioning, though many people may go beyond this. The clinician is not responsible for ending the crisis; such a notion will result in overactivity and frus-

tration on the part of the clinician. A better guideline is to help maximize the client's chances for an adaptive outcome of the crisis. In other words, the clinician's job is *not* to resolve the crisis but to help the client find ways to do so.

WHAT DOES THE CLIENT WANT? The client's wants, although seemingly obvious, are frequently overlooked in setting treatment goals. Lazare et al. (1972) wrote an interesting paper entitled "The Walk-In Patient as a 'Customer.'" They point out that it is hard to organize client requests that occur in emergency clinics into traditional categories. Four types of requests are suggested: (1) be a supportive person, (2) be a psychotherapist, (3) be an authority figure, and (4) other ("Tell me what resources are available for me to get help" or "I want nothing").

FOCUS ON TERMINATION FROM THE START. Since many clients come to emergency clinics because of a loss, it is important that they begin to deal immediately with the impending loss of the clinician. Termination issues often are central to brief treatment. Undue dependency and regression are decreased by such a focus.

SUPPORT POSITIVE STRENGTHS. It is important to counter the helplessness that the client feels. An important rule is "never do for clients what they can do for themselves." If they are able to make phone calls to the boss or to the spouse by themselves, by all means let them do so. Reminding clients of their strengths, accomplishments, and capabilities serves to bolster their self-esteem and encourages their active participation in treatment.

AVOID ADVICE. Again, to avoid giving advice is important to counter the client's feelings of helplessness. It may be useful to suggest tentative solutions, but direct advice is generally counterproductive and indicates an overidentification with the client.

TEAM APPROACH. Psychiatric emergency work is very demanding and anxiety producing. It is useful to have colleagues with whom to share the anxieties as well as the work load in interviewing family members, contacting the agencies, and so on.

SPECIFIC TECHNIQUES. Coleman (1960) has written an article outlining a number of specific techniques of value in emergency psychotherapy:

clarification, interpretation, use of transference, supporting defenses, and environmental manipulation. Clarification means pointing out connections, such as the relationship of the current symptoms to the precipitating stress. For example, a young woman appeared markedly better when the clinician pointed out the relationship of her depression of 2 weeks' duration with the fact that she had delivered a stillborn baby 2 weeks earlier. Frequently such connections, though obvious to the clinician, are not so clear to the client. An interpretation connects present events with the past. This woman was later helped to understand that her reluctance to see the significance of her present loss was related to her inability to deal with the death of a sibling many years earlier.

PITFALLS IN CRISIS TREATMENT

The following, although not an exhaustive list, are typical of problems encountered in emergency psychotherapy:

1. *Making a hasty, premature diagnosis.* Clinicians may insist too early that the problem is either medical or psychological; they do not keep an open mind and consequently are unable to "hear" new information that may conflict with their initial hypothesis (Weissberg, 1979).

2. *Not getting information from as many sources as possible.* The clinician fails to contact enough people to confirm the client's story. Frequently, clients in crisis are anxious and confused; sometimes they consciously or unconsciously withhold information. This is overcome by speaking with others.

3. *Feeling certain that the precipitant is identified.* The multiple sclerosis case illustrates how one might have been misled into thinking that the client's symptoms were caused by her husband's drinking and affair, or, if not that, by her multiple sclerosis. Beginners have a tendency to jump at the first possible precipitant they hear and not to question further.

4. *Being frightened of what the client might say.* The clinician may not allow clients to discuss symptoms with their accompanying affect, preferring to give empty reassurances such as "it isn't that bad," especially if the clinician is frightened about what the client might say. The client consequently feels increasingly isolated and misunderstood, leading to increased feelings of helplessness, frustration, and exacerbation rather than to relief of symptoms.

5. *Being misled by chronic psychopathology.* It is important to remember that even schizophrenics and sociopaths can have crises, as the following case illustrates:

Case vignette #9

A 62-year-old man was sent to the emergency unit from a nursing home before being returned to the state hospital where he had spent 20 years after a diagnosis of schizophrenia and epilepsy. He had been living in the nursing home for the past 2 years without any problems, until 3 days before admission, when he had begun to show increasingly bizarre behavior, culminating in an attempt to burn down the home. Rather than return him immediately to the state hospital, he was admitted to the psychiatric emergency unit. There the question was raised, "Why now, after 2 years, was he trying to burn down the home?" Because of this man's religious preoccupations, history taking was arduous, but eventually the following story evolved: he had always felt protected at this home by a certain nurse who was something of a "guardian angel" and who protected him against another nurse whom he regarded as a "witch." The "guardian angel" had gone on vacation 3 days earlier, and he became terrified of what the "witch" would then do to him and subsequently set the fire. The psychiatric emergency team began to work with the nursing home staff, and eventually he was able to return to the home, as he wished.

6. *Doing too much.* Some staff members identify with clients, get caught up in their anxiety, and offer unnecessary advice, which only serves to reinforce the client's sense of helplessness. Clinicians must keep in mind that there are limits to what can be done, and that in the final analysis the problem is the client's, not theirs.

7. *Wanting to "rescue" the client.* Some clinicians attempt too much, try for a "complete cure," take over for the client, and are simply unrealistic in their goals. When these attempts fail, these clinicians get angry with the client.

8. *Disposing rather than treating.* The nature of the clinical setting and of the problem puts pressure on the clinician to move the client on, to make a "disposition." Because of these pressures, it is very easy to focus on the disposition and to forget what treatment may be provided in even one emergency session using the above guidelines. Beginners especially find it hard to realize what very useful therapy may be accomplished in a very short crisis encounter, and they tend to deal with their own anxieties by focusing on "disposing of" the client.

OUTCOME

One can anticipate several outcomes from successful crisis therapy. First, the client will get through the crisis. All emergencies end, and clinicians will serve their clients well if they utilize interventions that will mobilize clients' strengths and adaptive coping mechanisms toward an adaptive resolution. Many clients will be able to anticipate problems better in the future as the result of their treatment, and many others will be able to solve problems more successfully, using techniques that they have learned.

BIBLIOGRAPHY

Caplan, G.: An approach to community mental health, New York, 1961, Grune & Stratton, Inc.

Coleman, D.: Emergency psychotherapy. In Masserman, J., and Moreno, J., editors: Progress in psychotherapy, vol. 5, New York, 1960, Grune & Stratton, Inc.

Harris, M.R., Kalis, B.L., and Freeman, E.H.: Precipitating stress: an approach to brief therapy, Am. J. Psychother. 17:465, July 1963.

Lazare, A., et al.: The walk-in patient as a "customer": a key dimension in evaluation and treatment, Am. J. Orthopsychiatry 42:872, Oct. 1972.

Lindemann, E.: Symptomatology and management of acute grief, Am. J. Psychiatry 101:141, Sept. 1944.

Rhine, M., and Mayerson, P.: Crisis hospitalization within a psychiatric emergency service, Am. J. Psychiatry 127:1386, April 1971.

Rusk, T.: Opportunity and techniques in crisis psychiatry, Compr. Psychiatry 12:249, 1971a.

Rusk, T.: Psychiatric education in the emergency room setting, Can. Psychiatr. Assoc. J. 16:111, 1971b.

Weissberg, M.: The somatic complaint: ticket of admission for child abusers, Primary Care 4(2):283, 1977.

Weissberg, M.: Emergency room medical clearance: an educational problem, Am. J. Psychiatry 136:6, June 1979.

Zimet, C., and Weissberg, M.: The emergency service: a setting for internal training, Psychotherapy: theory, research and practice, vol. 16, no. 3, Fall 1979.

CHAPTER 2

An assessment process

Richard B. Warner, M.D.
Michael P. Weissberg, M.D.

Most people do not take heed of the things they encounter, nor do they grasp them even when they have learned about them, although they suppose they do (Heraclitus).

A young woman walks quietly into an emergency unit where she encounters a triage nurse who asks, "May I help you?" Without speaking, the woman methodically rolls up the sleeve of her shirt to reveal an arm mutilated by several thin, bleeding lacerations. The nurse asks her to step into a nearby room so that her wounds can be examined, but the woman shakes her head. She says angrily, "No one can fix what's wrong with me." When the nurse presses her to "allow us to help you," the woman responds, "No one wants to help me, no one cares."

A middle-aged man is brought to an emergency unit by an ambulance; he is disheveled and stuporous. The paramedics report that they were called to the man's apartment by a friend, and they found there several empty whiskey bottles and some empty pill bottles. The man has been unable to talk with them coherently and by now is barely able to be aroused.

A young man, dirty and eccentric in appearance, is brought to the emergency unit by police, who say that they picked the man up after several merchants called to complain that he was bothering customers in front of their store. The young man had been yelling at people that they were Satan and that it was his mission to avenge the Lord. He is dressed only in a white T-shirt, which, instead of being worn in the usual manner, is wrapped around his waist and under his genitals. When the clinician asks him about this garb, he says that he has girded his loins to do battle for the Lord.

A middle-aged woman is brought to the hospital by her son who says that she has been awake for the past 2 nights and has been accusing the neighbors of skulking around her bushes and peering at her through the windows. Her son says that although she has been in psychiatric treatment, she has never before acted in this agitated and paranoid fashion. In the emergency unit she paces the floor and talks in a flippant, angry manner and will not answer questions directly.

A middle-aged woman, complaining of a pain in her chest, calls an ambulance and is brought to an emergency unit where she is evaluated for a possible myocardial infarction as well as the several other medical disorders that could cause her chest pain. Her electrocardiogram is normal and there are no abnormalities in her physical examination. The intern who is examining the woman notices that she seems sad and comments on the fact, whereupon the woman openly sobs.

These five examples are typical of the variety of ways in which people can report to an emergency setting and draw attention to their need for psychiatric evaluation. They often evoke in the clinician a sense of foreboding because their behavior is not readily explainable nor predictable, and the usual set of mind in which symptoms are investigated will not be sufficient. Emergency unit personnel, particularly physicians and nurses, are usually most comfortable with individuals who present a definable physiological problem. With such physical problems, a symptom picture is elicited, and then further data are collected and evaluated to reach diagnostic conclusions. Having made a pathophysiological diagnosis, the clinician has some idea of what to expect, what complications to prepare for, and what treatment to implement. Implied in this scheme is that recipients of care are either actively cooperative or are rendered passive by their condition to a degree that their behavior will not interfere with the diagnostic and therapeutic procedures.

The person in need of psychiatric intervention on the other hand often presents a bewildering picture of contradictory motivations, secretiveness, bizarre or danger-threatening behaviors, intense emotions, or lack of emotional relatedness which challenges the clinician's own sense of expertise and evokes anxiety (Weissberg, 1979). This anxiety is often handled by the clinician through psychological maneuvers that further interfere with being able to work effectively with the client. For instance, clinicians may respond with hostility and disparagement toward clients who threaten their sense of professional competence. The clinician may readily label the client as "psychiatric" and refer the person to a psychiatric service with a sense of relief that the problem now belongs to someone else. Also, clinicians may deny the presence or importance of clues of a psychiatric disorder and confine their attention to questions of pathophysiology. Clinicians may recognize the presence of an emotional disturbance, but instead of exploring its dimensions, may find themselves readily advising clients what they should do and how they should feel.

FRAMEWORK FOR ASSESSMENT: THE CRISIS

An effective psychiatric evaluation will depend on clinicians' abilities to broaden their perspective and keep in mind the following areas for assessment:
1. Precipitating crisis
   a. External events
   b. Meaning to the client of events
2. Potential for destructive behavior
   a. Suicide
   b. Homicide

c. Spouse abuse and other assaultiveness
d. Child abuse
3. Formal psychiatric and medical diagnoses
   a. Initial complaint and history of the current disorder
   b. Past psychiatric disorders
   c. Medical history, physical examination, and laboratory examinations
   d. Alcohol and other substance abuse
   e. Mental status examination
4. Availability of resources
   a. Family, friends
   b. Current psychotherapist or physician
5. Working relationship with the patient
6. Treatment planning

In making a psychiatric evaluation, try to imagine situations in which clients find themselves. First, how is the person experiencing the series of encounters in the emergency room? Is the clinician perceived as a person who may be helpful, or does the client regard the interviewer with indifference, hostility, suspiciousness, or fear. Does the client seem emotionally engaged or distant? Does the client speak with some spontaneity or does the individual give only short, vague, or idiosyncratic answers to questions? In assessing the way in which clients relate, clinicians form a judgment about what sort of working relationships they have with the person and they try to determine factors that are affecting the relationship.

> The young woman with the lacerated forearm conveys a feeling of anger and hostility as she refuses the nurse's offer of help. Yet her presence in the emergency unit indicates a wish to get some help. Her complaint that no one cares is probably a global reaction to her feeling that someone important to her seems not to care, a reaction that widens to include anyone who might offer help. It is a common reaction to either argue with the person or profess that "we do care what happens to you." It is often more helpful for clinicians to differentiate themselves from the client's transference reaction by saying something like "I think you must be very disappointed with someone who is important to you, and we should talk about that as soon as we have had a chance to attend to these cuts." In this way the client's entitlement to her feelings is acknowledged, while the clinician's concern is demonstrated.

More broadly, what is the situation that has precipitated the sense of crisis, and why now has the client come to the emergency unit? One of the most important tasks for the evaluator is to try to gain a picture of what recent event has led to the person feeling overwhelmed. More often than not, people in the midst of an emotional crisis do not have a clear idea of how they have come to feel as they do. In a crisis one's thinking tends to constrict and a sense of distinct past or future is lost. Rather than past events being perceived as history, they weigh on the present as painful losses or insults. Anxieties about future possible events are experienced as certain and current catastrophes. In short, the present is all consuming and painful. Clients will need the help of the clinician to identify, and place in time, events and expectations to which they are reacting. As events are identified, some attempt should also be made to understand their meaning to the person. How do they affect the way they feel about themselves and the important people in their lives? As the clinician comes to understand the external events and their meaning to the client, this also helps bring some sense of order and definition to the person's life. The extent to which the client can share in this process is also therapeutic.

> Allowing the sobbing woman with chest pain to talk about her distress resulted in her telling of the loss of her husband, who had died one year previously of a heart attack. For the past year she had been withdrawn, disinterested in old friends and activities, and sleeping poorly. Her somatic symptoms represented an identification with her husband, for whom she had not been able to mourn.

POTENTIAL FOR DANGEROUSNESS

Beyond an empathic exploration of the client's crisis, there are several other dimensions to be evaluated. A judgment of the person's potential for destruction, either of self or others, is an essential element. Later chapters of this book provide discussions in depth of the assessment of suicidality and assaultiveness. However, the basic elements of such evaluations are mentioned here because they should be considered in the evaluation of any client in crisis. Often violent syndromes overlap, and they should all be evaluated. The natural inclination to avoid looking into these difficult areas must be overcome to identify clients at risk.

In considering suicidal potential the client should be asked if any plans of suicide have been entertained, and if so, by what specific means. Also, does the person have thoughts of a particular time and place or set of circumstances in which to commit suicide? Any prior history of attempts should be elicited, along with questions about the circumstances in which the person attempted suicide and how they happened to survive. Family history of suicide is important in that models for such action may be an influence. The presence of psychosis, whether functional or organic in origin, will aggravate the person's impulsivity and unpredictability. In this regard alcohol or drug intoxication must especially be noted. Lack of resources or any overt or covert encouragement toward suicide on the part of family should be recognized. Finally, a sense of hopelessness and unwillingness to plan for the future are particularly ominous.

> The man who arrived in the emergency unit stuporous from an overdose was evaluated when he regained consciousness. It was learned that he had been despondent for several months since his wife had divorced him. His business was failing and he had greatly increased his drinking habit. The night of the overdose a younger woman, whom he had met at a party 2 weeks earlier, told him she did not want to continue seeing him. Although he had been entertaining thoughts of suicide for several months, the overdose was an impulsive action, facilitated by his drunkenness. The man was considered a further danger to himself because of his depression, uncontrolled drinking, and verbalized feelings of worthlessness and hopelessness.

The assessment of homicidal or assaultive potential involves consideration of historical factors that are associated with a character disposed to violence as well as acute factors that place the person at greater risk for such behavior in the immediate future. Among the chronic factors the most important area for inquiry is the person's history of violence, including fighting, violent crimes, or murder, as well as experiences in military service. People with a tendency toward violence have often been victims of physical abuse in their childhoods or have witnessed considerable violence in the home. Childhood histories often reveal poor socialization with other children as well as episodes of cruelty to animals. A history of poor job and school performance should raise the question of a person having a chronic conflict with authority.

Whatever a person's characteristic tendency toward violence may be, acute factors raise the probability of violent impulses being enacted. One of the most important is intoxication with alcohol or other drugs, especially amphetamines, cocaine, and phencyclidine. Similarly, psychosis of either organic or functional origins will lessen a person's impulse control and may further aggravate assaultiveness because of paranoid delusions or frightening hallucinations. Manic people in particular can be quite unpredictable and assaultive. The extent to which a person is dominated by certain emotions such as rage, fear, humiliation, or a trapped feeling should be gauged, because one who has little ability to tolerate these feelings will be more prone to resort to a physical action to lower the tension such emotions induce.

The clinician should pay attention to threats of violence and guard against the common tendency to dismiss threats as idle talk. The client should be questioned about the specifics of any plan to harm someone, and the accessibility of weapons must be determined. If there is a particular person who is identified as a likely victim, the role of the victim in provoking an assault should also be evaluated. This is often best accomplished by seeing the two people interact, and that is one reason for including other important people at some point in the interview.

Finally, clinicians should learn to recognize their own range of feelings and psychological reactions to violent people. Often an early and important clue to the client's potential for violence is the clinician's own sense of uneasiness while talking to that person.

The possibility of child abuse should also be

considered (Weissberg and Dubovsky, 1977). If there are children in the home, a series of questions can be asked to yield information about such a problem: (1) How do you feel when the child cries? (2) What do you do? (3) Do you ever feel overwhelmed with responsibilities for the child? (4) Are you ever frightened by thoughts of hurting the child? (5) Do you ever get so frustrated with the child that you hit him? (6) Have you ever hurt the child? In asking these questions it is again important to be as nonjudgmental as possible and mindful of the state of the working relationship with the client. These questions will be more truthfully answered if the person feels the clinician is trying to be understanding rather than trying to conduct a cross-examination.

FORMAL DIAGNOSIS

In addition to attempting to understand why the client is in the emergency unit now and evaluating the potential for destructive behavior, it is also important to draw a series of formal diagnostic conclusions. At the first level, the clinician must discern the presence of psychosis. Second, psychopathology of organic origins must be differentiated from that which is functional. The further differentiation of schizophrenic from affective psychoses, while ultimately essential in proper treatment planning, is not usually as important in the initial emergency evaluation. The emergency management of the functional psychoses does not depend on such differentiation but rather involves structured treatment settings and antipsychotic medications in most such cases. The detection of an organic mental disorder is much more important because of the implication of an underlying medical illness that awaits further diagnosis and specific treatment. Therefore, any emergency psychiatric evaluation should include a consideration of the role of physical illness and alcohol or other substance abuse in the etiology of the disorder.

Several components of information are needed to make a diagnosis. The first of these is the initial complaint of the client. In the usual approach to interviewing, the person's subjective report of the ailment is sought very early in the examination. The clinician pursues the history of development of the symptoms, asking about the time course, association with other symptoms, and factors that seem to aggravate or relieve the symptoms. By confining the early phase of the interview to the client's initial complaint, the clinician not only gathers valuable information but also conveys that the person is being taken seriously, which is important to the development of a working relationship. In psychiatric interviewing, the initial complaint is often not a somatic one, but an expression of thinking, feeling, or behaving in a way that is troublesome to the client or to someone else who has brought the client in. As an early organizer of information, it is important to determine who is being troubled by what, and what is the nature of the client's distress. The clinician then proceeds to get a history of the current distress, tracing its development in time, its relationship to circumstances in the client's recent experience, and its associated symptoms.

In gathering the history of the current disorder the clinician should also consider the client's recent level of functioning in several spheres. Inquiry should be made about personal relationships and any changes that have occurred in recent times. A work history should be gathered with attention paid to levels of skills, productivity, and relationships with people at work. Some attempt should be made to compare the person's highest level of achievement with the current situation and with the potential level of functioning. Changes in functioning should be considered in a time course, noting dramatic change or evidence of a slow but steady decline. The clinician should also try to relate changes in functioning with symptomatic disturbances, getting a picture of the extent to which symptoms are reactive to changes in functioning and the extent to which functioning has deteriorated because of the interference of symptoms.

Another informational component of the diagnostic process is the past psychiatric history. The client should be asked if any symptoms of the current disorder are a repetition of something experienced in the past. The clinician should also specifically ask about prior psychiatric treatments, including modalities of treatment, types of medications, and whether or not the person was hospitalized. Such information will give some idea of the severity of previous disorders and may also help in making a specific diagnosis. Adults tend to suffer the recurrence of the same disorder rather than to develop different disorders as the years pass. The client may even be able to tell the clinician what has been diagnosed in the past and what sort of treatment has been helpful. Such information can be of varying reliability but is useful to consider.

In pursuing a formal diagnosis the clinician should consider the range of physical disorders that may be contributing to the client's current crisis or response to external events. For example, thyroid and parathyroid disease may initially show insidious changes in the person's reactivity to the environment. Occult carcinomas can manifest themselves through symptoms of depression. Cancer of the pancreas is particularly notorious in this regard. Gradual weight loss and disinterest in food may seem to represent a classical case of anorexia nervosa, only to be diagnosed on further careful consideration as a tumor impinging on the hypothalamic appetite center. Various atypical paralyses have been prematurely labeled hysterical conversion reactions but later were found to be the result of neurological disease, such as cerebrovascular accidents, peripheral neuropathies, or Guillain-Barré syndrome. Careful questioning about physical illness, particularly about medications the person is taking, should be combined with a review of physiological systems and physical examination in a spirit of finding what may be there, rather than providing a cursory "medical clearance." The avoidance of an either-or mentality in terms of medical and psychiatric diagnoses will help the clinician keep from prematurely closing diagnostic possibilities (Weissberg, 1979; Weissberg and Friedrich, 1978).

Laboratory examinations should be considered in the light of clinical impressions gained from history taking and physical examination. When careful thought has been given to possible organic disorders that could be affecting the person, specific as well as screening tests (chest x-ray film, ECG, basic metabolic blood and urine tests) can help to evaluate clinical hypotheses.

Such tests in themselves, however, do not answer the question of whether or not an organic disorder is present. Too often routine screening tests are returned as normal and it is then concluded that the person is "medically cleared" without considering the range of possibilities that lie outside the particular screening tests. The diagnosis of an organic mental disorder is based initially on clincial impressions gained from observation and mental status testing, which will be discussed briefly later. When screening tests are normal, it is not necessarily cause to doubt the impression of an organic disorder but reason to consider further possibilities of the etiology of the organic disorder.

The role of alcohol and other drugs must also be considered in both their acute and chronic contributions to the clinical picture. A diagnosis of alcoholism is appropriate when the person demonstrates a pattern of uncontrolled drinking that results in adverse consequences. Alcoholics frequently deny their difficulties and either minimize reports on how much they drink or maximize their estimates of what it takes to affect their behavior. Many alcoholics suffer "blackouts" and are amnesic for behavior that people around them find loathsome. A good screening question that invites the person to reflect on the use of alcohol without seeming judgmental is to ask, "Has there ever been a time in your life when you were drinking more than was really good for you?" (Crowley et al., 1974). Clients who answer affirmatively can be asked to elaborate and compare to the present. If persons are intoxicated at the time of evaluation, it is usually prudent to allow them time to sober up before attempting any sort of detailed interview. An intoxicated person is likely to remember little of the conversation on its completion and is also less likely to follow through with any plans that are made. At the same time it is important to remember that an intoxicated person is impulsive and unpredictable, and steps may need to be taken to protect the individual who has been hinting or threatening suicide or violence.

The ability of amphetamines and cocaine to produce a psychosis indistinguishable from paranoid schizophrenia is well known. Phencyclidine, commonly known as PCP or "angel dust," also is a frequent cause of toxic delirium, with the client manifesting hallucinations, delusions, and bizarre behavior. Likewise, a variety of medications ranging from across-the-counter sleeping preparations to antiparkinsonian medications are abused for their anticholinergic properties. However, the peripheral effects are not invariably present and laboratory tests of blood and urine specimens are sometimes helpful, particularly if specific intoxicants are sought, based on clinical impressions.

> The psychotic young man who insisted that he was a soldier of the Lord gives an appearance that would often be presumed an acute schizophrenic psychosis. However, laboratory examination revealed the presence of amphetamine in his urine, and it was later determined that he had been chronically abusing amphetamines, with a recent escalation to intravenous injections.

The final component of information necessary to diagnose the presence of psychosis as well as to consider its etiology is the mental status examination. Much of the mental status examination is observational and consists of a disciplined evaluation of the person's appearance and behavior, affect, and thought and speech processes throughout the interview. The examination also includes direct inquiry about unusual mental phenomena (illusions, hallucinations, delusions, and suicidal and homicidal thoughts) as well as specific testing of several cognitive functions. The following is a listing of categories of information in the mental status examination and discussion of the relevance of these categories to the diagnosis of psychosis and differentiation of organic from functional etiologies.

Appearance

Clients should be observed for signs of deterioration in ability to groom and care for themselves. Also, any bizarre peculiarities in the person's appearance should be noted, as these may be evidence of psychosis. Facial expressions that suggest suspiciousness, hypervigilance, or lethargy may also be evidence of a state of mind altered by organic or functional illness.

Psychomotor activity

The client's motor movements should also be observed for agitation or retardation. Agitation commonly accompanies states of intoxication with stimulant medications as well as major affective disorders. Retardation is a frequent symptom of major depressive episodes but may also result from a clouding of consciousness that accompanies an organic disorder. Bizarre posturing may be a sign of psychosis, either functional (as in catatonic schizophrenia) or organic in origin. Unusual movements, such as tics and tremors, often are found in neurological disorders.

Affect

Throughout the interview the clinician should be paying attention to the client's affect, noting the range and intensity of emotions. There should also be some evaluation of the appropriateness of the person's manifest feelings in relation to speech content. An organic mental disorder is often manifested by an emotional lability, in which the person cries or angers readily in response to changing stimuli, the emotion often being appropriate in kind but not in intensity to the subject being discussed. Severely depressed people usually show a marked narrowing of range of affect, showing only dysphoric emotions. Manic people on the other hand will often show a volatile set of emotions ranging from euphoria to irritability and anger. An acutely psychotic person will often demonstrate an intense emotionality that seems bizarre or inappropriate given the topics being discussed. The "flat" affect, in which the person seems to have little emotional reaction to topics or affective relatedness to the interviewer, is a common finding in chronic schizophrenic people. As with many of the examples given in this discussion of the mental status examination, this discussion represents a sampling of typical findings, and none of the descriptions can be considered pathognomonic for any particular condition.

In evaluating affect the clinician should also inquire about clients' own subjective awareness of mood, both to get a history of the recent development of particular feelings and to gauge the extent to which they are attuned to their own emotions.

Speech and thought processes

Spontaneity and rate of speech are often disturbed in psychotic disorders, particularly in affective illnesses. The psychotic person may also reveal a formal thought disorder through such phenomena as flight of ideas, loose associations, blocking, or rambling speech. The clinician should listen to how directly the person can answer questions and to how well the story hangs together. When details are heard that sound vague or unusual, the client should be asked to amplify on these, which can provide the opportunity for the person to provide structure and logic to the story or to demonstrate the inability to do so.

Thought contents and perceptions

The clinician should listen for particular themes that run throughout the client's talk. Common themes encountered in an emergency setting are somatic concerns, guilt, loss, fear of losing control, and fear of some external force. The clinician must attempt to judge the extent to which these concerns are based in reality or are exaggerated. The presence of frank delusions, that is, fixed irrational ideas, is a common manifestation of psychosis, but does not reliably help to distinguish organic from functional etiologies. Many people who chronically entertain delusions have learned to keep these to themselves and will not mention them spontaneously. Therefore, it is a good practice to ask the client questions that would prompt the reporting of any unusual thoughts. Similarly, it is important to inquire directly about suicidal and assaultive thoughts.

Disordered perceptions, that is, illusions and hallucinations, are also common symptoms of psychosis, and if not spontaneously reported, their presence should be determined by direct questioning. The character of hallucinations can be helpful in strengthening hypotheses about etiology. Functional psychoses more commonly appear initially with auditory hallucinations, particularly with multiple voices arguing or commenting on the person's behavior, whereas organic disorders more commonly manifest visual, olfactory, or tactile hallucinations. However, these are not strict diagnostic criteria as there are many exceptions to these general rules.

Consciousness

Fluctuating alterations in consciousness are a hallmark of delirium and tend not to occur in functional psychoses. Consciousness can be considered to be composed of levels of arousal and attention. Levels of arousal range from a normal state of alertness, in which the subject is able to be aware of information coming from multiple environmental and internal sources and to focus attention on relevant information, to various stages of somnolence, the most extreme of which is coma, a state of unconsciousness from which the individual cannot be aroused. Delirious persons most often show a fluctuating level of lethargy or stupor, in which they lapse into unconsciousness when not stimulated. Assessment of the person's level of arousal is observational and includes notation of the sort of stimulus needed to keep the person awake. The evaluation of attention span is accomplished through observation of the person's ability to keep a particular line of thought in mind. It can be measured more objectively by testing the client's digit span, that is, the ability to repeat a series of random digits spoken by the clinician. In a normal state of alertness an individual should be able to repeat a series of six digits in order and a series of four digits in reverse order. Inability to do this bespeaks of some interference of attention that may well have an organic origin.

Intellectual functioning

The most reliable part of the mental health examination in diagnosing organic mental disorders is the direct testing of cognitive abilities of orientation, memory or new learning, calculations, and abstract thinking. When cerebral tissue suffers insult, whether toxic, metabolic, infectious, or traumatic, it is the later acquired, more sophisticated and abstract mental operations that are most impaired. Therefore, those with organic disorders are most often disoriented to time and less often to place and rarely to person, which is a fairly primitive operation of memory. Similarly, organic insults most often affect limbic structures necessary to new learning, so that testing of ability to learn three unrelated compound items is a standard feature of the mental status examination. In this test the subject is asked to immediately repeat three items, such phrases as mahogany table, green Chevrolet, and 756 Broadway, and then to recall the items after 5 minutes. A person with a clear sensorium should be able to recall all the items correctly.

The test of serial subtraction of 7s or 3s requires the subject to attend to several memory tasks at the same time as well as to perform simple arithmetic. Organic impairment usually results in a slowing down of the ability to perform the subtractions as well as more serious errors of losing place, perseverating certain numbers, or forgetting the number that is being subtracted. Ability to think abstractly is tested by asking the subject to interpret the moral of several proverbs. Psychotic patients typically can only give a concrete response to the proverb. For example, the proverb "people who live in glass houses shouldn't throw stones" will elicit a response such as "the glass will break" rather than the more abstract answer "if a person has faults of his own, he should not judge others." The interpretation of proverbs is not usually helpful in distinguishing organic from functional psychopathology except that schizophrenic people often give very bizarre, idiosyncratic responses that bear little resemblance to the original proverb.

Throughout the formal mental status examination the clinician must determine the extent to which the client is really trying to answer the questions. Functionally psychotic people can do quite poorly on the examination, but this is usually because they are not trying or because they are too preoccupied, and their answers seem more like random thoughts than mistakes made in a real attempt to answer the questions.

For a variety of reasons direct testing of formal cognitive abilities is often erroneously omitted from interviews in the emergency unit.

This may be because of feeling self-conscious about asking such "silly" questions or from being afraid that the client will be offended or embarrassed. However, experienced clinicians have learned how easy it is to overestimate a client's ability to pay attention, understand, and remember the content of the interview in the absence of formal testing of these abilities. Likewise, the extent of the person's psychopathology in terms of hallucinations, delusions, or destructive feelings can be easily underestimated without direct inquiry.

The examination can be made more palatable, and cooperation better secured, by introducing the questions in a way that explains what the interviewer is looking for and that invites the client to also be curious. Instead of saying, "I'm now going to ask you some questions that may seem silly, but I ask them of all clients," the examination is better introduced by saying, "sometimes when people are under a lot of stress (or feeling ill or taking medications—whatever fits), they have some trouble concentrating, remembering things, or have other difficulties thinking. Have you noticed yourself having these problems?" This question draws clients' attention to helping assess their own possible cognitive difficulties and is followed by the statement, "I'd like to ask you some questions that will help me determine if you might be having any difficulties of which perhaps you haven't been aware." As the various parts of the examination are explored, the client can be told what is being tested, such as ability to concentrate on a task (digit span, serial subtractions), recent memory and new learning (three items, orientation), and ability to think abstractly (proverbs and similarities).

Summary

To summarize this section, the clinician should arrive at formal diagnostic conclusions only after a consideration of the client's initial complaint, history of the development of the current disorder and past psychiatric disorders, a mental status examination, and a thorough evaluation that includes medical history, physical examination, and relevant laboratory examinations. It should be added that often the client is not able or willing to provide the necessary information, and an effort should be made to gather data from any available sources. These will include family, friends, psychotherapists, and other health professionals who have known the person long enough to observe the development of the current disorder.

> The agitated, paranoid woman who accused her neighbors of spying on her was thoroughly evaluated in terms of her medical and psychiatric treatment. Consultation with her physician revealed that she was being treated with a tricyclic antidepressant, an antipsychotic drug prescribed for anxiety, and an antiparkinsonian drug. The dosage of the antidepressant had recently been raised. The findings on mental status testing that she was distractible, disoriented, and unable to perform memory and calculation tests accurately substantiated the conclusion that the client was delirious because of the combined anticholinergic effects of her medications.

AVAILABILITY OF RESOURCES

Another major dimension to be assessed while the client is in the emergency unit is the status of possible resources, people who can help support the person through the crisis. Often the availability of caring, responsible family or friends can help a person avert the need for hospitalization by providing shelter and companionship at a time when the person should not be left alone. However, relying on family and friends requires consideration of how the client regards them and how they relate to the client. Destructiveness of suicidal individuals may be aggravated if the family harbors covert death wishes for them (Rosenbaum, 1970). A person undergoing a psychotic decompensation will regress if returned to a hostile, undermining environment. The attitude of friends and the family toward the client can be surmised from the manner in which they mobilize at the time of the emergency unit visit. The clinician should observe such patterned reactions as a reluctance to become involved, a tendency to deny the seriousness of the person's difficulties or motivations, or an overly solicitous manner that prevents the client from ventilating

any angry feelings. Such behavior can be more important than stated intentions to take care of the troubled individual.

Another important resource for many people is a therapist with whom they are currently in treatment. Early inquiry about past and current psychiatric treatment often yields helpful information, both in understanding the current crisis and in making a formal diagnosis. A visit to the emergency unit may be a reflection of a crisis in an ongoing psychotherapy, a particularly common phenomenon with clients who have difficulties modulating their dependence on the therapist and who are sensitive to occurrences that they interpret as abandonment. Chronic schizophrenic people who have unilaterally decided to stop their medications represent another significant portion of the population in psychiatric treatment who need emergency care. At times, the problem lies with a change in a relationship with a medical physician, an often overlooked precipitant. In all of these cases, consultation with the clients' primary therapist should illuminate the emergency and help determine the proper handling of the situation. In many cases it will be appropriate to abbreviate the interview and encourage the person to talk further with the therapist, particularly when a problem in the therapy is the crisis. This choice, of course, depends on the therapist's availability to the client.

TREATMENT PLANNING

Throughout the interview the clinician should be weighing possibilities for treatment planning, and in this process the status of the working relationship is again an important consideration. Lazare (1972, 1975) recommends trying to learn from the client early in the interview what the client wants and expects from the emergency visit. This wish may be entirely appropriate to the client's needs and the hospital's resources or it may be something that has to be negotiated through the course of the interview. As the crisis is defined and its meaning explored, the clinician will have the opportunity to monitor the client's sense of involvement in that process and the extent to which the client seeks to master and resolve the crisis. The extent to which the person does this is one factor to consider in recommending further outpatient therapy.

Hospitalization or a brief stay in a holding bed in a psychiatric emergency unit will usually be indicated for those persons who remain psychotic, destructive, or unable to care for themselves. In addition, hospitalization may be indicated to further evaluate people who present diagnostic dilemmas or those with whom there seems to be no movement toward resolution of the crisis. In some cases the most prudent plan will be for an extended evaluation by the psychiatric emergency team with the client returning to the emergency unit the next day or remaining in an observation area overnight. Although in an emergency unit it is necessary to process clients efficiently, the pressure for time and space should not be allowed to force premature closure on understanding the person's needs. Extended evaluations in which the person can be seen again at a later time can reduce this pressure.

Whatever treatment planning is considered, it is helpful to spend some time with the client talking about specific problems to be worked on in further therapy and to help the individual anticipate the nature of the therapy. People usually enter treatment with magical expectations of what will be done to or for them, and if these matters are not talked about at the outset the person will inevitably be disappointed (Adler, 1973). In considering these matters the clinician widens the area of concern beyond disposition to actual treatment planning.

SUMMARY

The individual who arrives at an emergency setting in need of psychiatric evaluation may exhibit a large variety of behaviors, ranging from overtly psychotic behavior or straightforward requests for psychiatric help to more disguised or latent psychological distress. The clinician should keep in mind a multidimensional framework that includes evaluation of (1) the precipitating crisis, (2) the potential for destructive behavior, (3) formal diagnosis, (4) availability of resources, (5) the working relationship with the client, and (6) a range of treatment options. Although an emergency unit sets a premium on expeditious handling of people, the clinician must at the same time resist premature closure of these other areas, because each contributes to an effective evaluation.

BIBLIOGRAPHY

Adler, G.: Hospital treatment of borderline patients, Am. J. Psychiatry **130**:1, Jan. 1973.

Crowley, T.J., et al.: Drug and alcohol abuse among psychiatric admissions, Arch. Gen. Psychiatry **30**:13, Jan. 1974.

Lazare, A., et al.: The walk-in patient as a "customer": a key dimension in evaluation and treatment, Am. J. Orthopsychiat. **42**:872, Oct. 1972.

Lazare, A., et al.: The customer approach to patienthood: attending to patient requests in a walk-in clinic, Arch. Gen. Psychiatry **32**:553, May 1975.

Rhine, M., and Mayerson, P.: Crisis hospitalization within a psychiatric emergency service, Am. J. Psychiatry **127**:1386, April 1971.

Rosenbaum, M., and Richman, J.: Suicide: the role of hostility and death wishes from the family and significant others, Am. J. Psychiatry **126**:1652, May 1970.

Weissberg, M.: A case of petit-mal status: a diagnostic dilemma, Am. J. Psychiatry **132**:11, Nov. 1975.

Weissberg, M.: Emergency room medical clearance: an educational problem, Am. J. Psychiatry **136**:6, June 1979.

Weissberg, M., and Dubovsky, S.: Assessment of psychiatric emergencies in medical practice, Primary Care, **4**(4):651, Dec. 1977.

Weissberg, M., and Friedrich, E.: Sydenham's chorea: case report of a diagnostic dilemma, Am. J. Psychiatry **135**:5, May 1978.

SECTION B

Common psychiatric emergencies

The chapters in Section B provide information and case vignettes on common psychiatric emergencies. The assessment process in these chapters emphasizes the psychiatric emergency framework, in that underlying psychopathology is investigated and traditional psychiatric diagnostic labels are applied. The sequencing of Chapters 4 through 7 models the steps followed by clinicians when they diagnose a psychiatric disorder. First, organic disorders must be identified or ruled out and differential diagnoses need to be made, such as the distinction between schizophrenic disorders and major affective illnesses. Chapters 8 through 11 discuss the signs, treatment, and dispositional considerations of the psychiatric emergencies experienced by clients with suicidal, homicidal, assaultive, or substance-abuse behavior.

Chapter 3, The Client with an Organic Disorder, provides a comprehensive and wide-range description of various organic disorders with thorough reference to definition, signs, etiology, and course of disease. Special emphasis is given to the dementias and substance-induced organic mental disorders, with guidelines for using the mental status examination, psychological testing, and medications in psychiatric emergency work.

Chapter 4, The Client with a Seizure Disorder, offers extensive information on forms of epilepsy, neuropsychiatric disorders associated with seizures, psychiatric disorders and seizures, epilepsy and psychiatric medications, and anticonvulsant medications and psychiatric complications. The principle types of epilepsy are discussed with a focus on their relation to psychiatric phenomena. General treatment approaches appropriate to a psychiatric emergency unit are also outlined.

The first section of this chapter describes the signs, symptoms, and treatment of generalized tonic-clonic seizures, generalized absence of seizures, and partial seizures with complex symptomatology. Such neuropsychiatric disorders as alcoholism, post-trauma states, withdrawal syndromes, and toxic states caused by ingestion of phencyclidine (PCP) or amphetamine are examined as causes of seizures in the second section. Schizophrenia, pseudoepileptic conversion reactions, and the behavioral syndrome of epilepsy are discussed from historical, theoretical, and therapeutic perspectives.

In Chapter 5, The Client with a Schizophrenic Disorder, the author discusses treatment considerations inherent in psychiatric emergency work with clients suffering from schizophrenic disorders. The opening paragraphs sensitize the reader to the fragility, hesitation, and tension experienced by the schizophrenic person seeking treatment. Similarly, the difficult task of assessing these clients is noted by the current classification system. A description of the features that may be seen in a schizophrenic client is provided, which includes delusions, altered modes of thinking, perceptual disturbances, disturbances of affect, confusion about ego boundaries, inadequate motivation, withdrawal, disturbances of motion, and impaired presentation of self. A multifactorial point of view is discussed regarding the predisposing factors of schizophrenia. These factors include the genetic base, sociological variables of immigration and growing up under severe and dangerous conditions, impaired sensory function, psychological and neurological variables, and schizophrenia as a learned disorder.

The complexities of working with clients who have schizophrenic disorders are elaborated on in the second half of this chapter. The author describes how to gather information from schizophrenic people and collateral persons, the relationship between exacerbations and life events, frequent emergency unit problems with schizophrenic clients, and dispositional issues of hospitalization or referral.

Chapter 6, The Client with an Affective Disorder, explains that this illness, which causes mood change, is divided into three well-defined categories: major affective disorders, other specific affective disorders, and atypical affective disorders. Genetics, biogenic amines, and psychodynamics are discussed as the three factors of etiology. The clinical presentation, differential diagnosis, and case vignettes of clients experiencing a manic or depressive episode are described.

This chapter ends with a thorough review of interview techniques and treatment approaches as well as advice on how to manage interviews with manic clients, threatened violence, and difficult countertransference issues. The emergency treatment focuses on the use of psychotherapy and chemotherapy. The author concludes by pointing out that the initial interaction will often determine the degree of clients' willingness to continue in the mental health system.

Chapter 7, The Client with a Borderline Condition, presents a chronological overview of how the diagnostic category "borderline" was established and a description of the unique features of borderline clients. The author discusses the theoretical framework that defines the borderline condition. A developmental framework is then proposed which contrasts normal development with the development of persons later diagnosed as borderline. The borderline client as an adult is in a conflict over fears of maternal abandonment versus fears of maternal engulfment and fusion.

An integrated model of the borderline's dynamics and defenses which addresses problems of diagnosis, evaluation, treatment, and disposition is derived from the developmental framework. Information regarding the assessment and diagnosis of borderline conditions centers on use of the structured interview to evaluate the nature of the client's responses. Issues of identity diffusion, reality testing, and defensive style can be explored in three sequential steps: clarification, confrontation, and interpretation. The task of differentiating borderline personality disorders from schizophrenic disorders and behavioral problems is explained.

Since the clinician's response to borderline clients may seriously impair the clinician's ability to properly evaluate and treat these clients, the author provides an extensive description of how therapeutic interactions can be maintained. A comprehensive review of treatment plan considerations includes information on the use of medications, overnight hospitalization, indications for admission, and alternative treatments. The chapter ends with a recommendation that alternative models of mental health programs be designed to meet the specific needs of borderline clients.

Chapter 8, The Client with Suicidal Behavior, discusses people who consider suicide as a way to solve their problems. How psychiatric emergency staff can listen to these people and assist them to find alternatives is addressed. Four ways that individuals communicate feelings of suicide are described: the ambivalent cry for help, the symbolic cry for help, the resistant cry for help, and the unheeded cry for help. The authors explain how legal and philosophical implications will affect the management of these people. Then information on the assessment of suicide risk is given. Areas for assessment include aspects of demographic data, certain clinical characteristics, and identified high-risk factors.

The remainder of the chapter discusses treatment issues for three populations at suicide risk: preattempt, postattempt, and chronically suicidal. Characteristics of each population, techniques for assessment, interventions, and frequent staff responses are elucidated.

Chapter 9, The Client with Homicidal Behavior, offers definitions and statistics regarding homicidal acts. A composite description of convicted murderers outlines a portrait of the offender and the motivation to kill. Also, the relevance of the victim's relationship to the murderer is explained. The author points out that the difference between homicide and assault lies with the outcome.

A detailed assessment process is offered for the clinician to follow in determining a person's potential to kill. It includes environmental conditions, the clinician's response, the expressed intent to kill, the relationship with the victim, and the perceived "benefits" of murder. The immediate goal of clinical intervention is to decrease or eliminate the urge to murder, but the clinician's responsibility to inform the potential victim is also discussed. Psychological, environmental, pharmacological, and physical intervention techniques are explained. The criteria for privileged communication are also provided as a guide for clinicians dealing with clients who are potentially homicidal.

Chapter 10, The Client with Assaultive Behavior, focuses on the process of assault from a behavioral perspective and describes the stages of the assault cycle. Often the precipitant for homicidal behavior, such as frustration and conflict, is the same as that for assaultive behavior. The author discusses the social context of violence and the theory that aggression is a learned response. Assaultive behavior is described as an extreme and socially unacceptable behavior at one end of a continuum of possible behaviors. It is conceptualized as a cycle consisting of five stages: activation, escalation, crisis, recovery, and stabilization. Behavioral changes experienced by the client and recommended interventions are listed for each of the five stages. To assess the client's potential for violent behavior, the author recommends that current and historical functioning be evaluated in the following areas: life stress and resources, family, interpersonal and social relationships, psychological functioning, and biological functioning. For those times when clients become assaultive in the health care setting, information on how to manage such crisis behaviors is offered. Three types of crisis behaviors, fear, frenzy, and uproar, are defined. Case vignettes are included to demonstrate these various presentations and the appropriate clinical management techniques. The chapter ends with a discussion on how to use the specific interventions of medication and physical containment.

Chapter 11, The Client with a Substance-Abuse Problem, begins with an overview of the magnitude of the substance-abuse problems, offers definitions of terms, and describes some general therapeutic approaches. Descriptions of substances commonly abused are presented in alphabetical order beginning with a discussion of alcoholism and ending with a discussion of PCP. In each of these discussions, the authors also provide guidelines in differential diagnosis, and medical and psychological treatment recommendations. Case vignettes of clients suffering from abuse of amphetamines, barbiturates, and PCP illustrate the chapter.

CHAPTER 3

The client with an organic disorder

Fredric J. Phillips, M.D.
Joan F. Schwartz, Ph.D.

"But what did the Dormouse say?" one of the jury asked. "That I can't remember," said the Hatter. "You must remember," remarked the King, "or I'll have you executed" (Carroll, 1949, p. 75).

The Mad Hatter in *Alice's Adventures in Wonderland* was suffering from an organic brain disorder. He, as did many of the hatters of his day, used mercury in blocking or cleaning hats. The mercury was absorbed either through the skin or nose and caused him to become "mad."

Organic brain disorders must be distinguished from functional disorders. Functional disorders are likely to be found where delusions and hallucinations occur in the presence of clear sensorium and intact orientation (to person, place, and time). The absence of disorientation is often the single most persuasive piece of evidence in establishing functional illness.

Organic brain disorders by definition are caused by an organic factor, for example, a drug or chemical, an infection, a blow to the head, physical changes in the cerebral circulation, or changes in the brain itself because of a disease process. The organic causal factor may or may not be known, and the organic disorder may or may not be treatable. The causal factor results in observable changes in cognitive and emotional functioning and in behavior.

Affective disorders change the rate of intellectual production, accelerating or slowing it, but intellectual function itself is for the most part spared. Schizophrenia presents a thought disorder (for example, concrete interpretation of proverbs) but intact orientation. A previous history of earlier manic episodes is indispensable in establishing the diagnosis of bipolar disorder. Often in the case of youthful clients, the picture may be clouded by the simultaneous presence of drug ingestion with intoxication, or acute organic brain disorder with schizophrenia; however, as with most intoxications, the clearing of symptoms over time usually differentiates the organic from the functional component.

In this chapter organic brain disorders and the methods by which they can be treated in a psychiatric emergency unit will be discussed. This will be followed by descriptions of neurological evaluation, mental status examination, and psychological testing for organicity, and a case vignette.

MEDICAL CLEARANCE

The purpose of medical clearance is to determine the immediately treatable and life-threatening conditions in emergency situations to rule out toxic substances or physical causes as factors in the clinical picture, to exclude these factors or treat them, and thereby to clarify the medical and psychiatric symptomatology.

Intoxication, whether alcohol- or drug-induced, is always a medical emergency first and a psychiatric emergency second, since a client may succumb to the effects of respiratory or cardiac depression. Thus medical clearance is obtained at a medical unit before the client is evaluated psychiatrically, or a physicain on the unit must take the responsibility for examining and clearing the client medically before other staff members evaluate the client. Failure to do this may result in permanent injury or death.

An important distinction is the determination of dementia and pseudoretardation; in major depressive states, a slowing of mental functions occurs as a consequence of depression and may masquerade as a true dementia. However, careful psychiatric evaluation and psychological testing soon reveal the slowed but intact menta-

tion that accompanies depression. Dementia is, on the other hand, usually not a reversible condition, and testing demonstrates a real impairment and not merely a slowing of mental function. Pseudodementia is a reversible state; as the depression clears, normal mental function returns and the pseudoretardation disappears.

LEVELS OF CONSCIOUSNESS

The various levels of consciousness are described as follows (see Table 3-1):

obtundation The client responds to stimuli and obeys commands but usually only for as long as the stimulation continues. Confusion may be noted during response and arousal.

stupor Painful stimuli produce withdrawal and bodily movement, often with groans; spontaneous movement is present. Some prolonged intervals of responsiveness are brought about by painful stimuli.

semicoma Painful stimuli produce withdrawal response away from stimulus; no spontaneous movement is noted.

coma No response to painful stimuli is seen, and any psychologically understandable response to external stimuli or inner need is absent (Denny-Brown, 1954, p. 9).

coma-vigil (akinetic mutism) Comalike state exists, in which reflex activity, such as swallowing, sucking, and chewing, may be released by lesions to mesencephalon and in which eye movements may be seen in the absence of other bodily movements and in the presence of unconsciousness.

DELIRIUM: DISORDER OF ATTENTION

SYMPTOMS. Delirium is fundamentally a disorder of attention. Although delirious clients may appear acutely ill, their main difficulty is a compromised ability to attend to environmental stimuli. The result is a state of disorientation, in which confusion and global memory impairment ensue, involving further disturbances in thinking, perception, and judgment. Frequent and abrupt fluctuations in mental status can be noted as well as emotional lability.

Delirium is a waking state. Clients in delirium can usually attend and respond to simple direct questions; however, reality testing may be poor. Clients may be disoriented as to time and place and may misidentify unfamiliar people and places as familiar or may misinterpret environmental cues. Delusions, illusions, and hallucinations, usually visual but sometimes auditory or tactile, may be present. Clients may experience the hallucinations as quite frightening and, in attempts to protect themselves, may hurt themselves or others. Hallucinations and delusions are shifting and poorly organized. Deficits in short-term and long-term memory may be present. Delirium may be accompanied by fear, panic, anxiety, depression, irritability, apathy, anger, euphoria, and silliness. Involuntary tremors and movements may occur. Perseveration in speech and behavior may be seen.

Delirious persons may be drowsy or stuporous. They may be restless and suffer from insomnia. Changes in psychomotor activity can be observed. Tachycardia, sweating, flushing, elevated blood pressure, and dilated pupils may be present in delirious clients. Mild delirium involves confusion, bewilderment, disorientation, and difficulty in concentration.

COURSE. Onset of delirium is usually rapid and lasts generally no longer than 1 or 2 weeks. It is usually more severe at night. While complete recovery is the most common outcome, delirium can also lead to stupor, coma, dementia, and even death.

ETIOLOGY. Delirium, by definition, must have a known organic cause. Causes are head injury (most common cause); infectious diseases, especially febrile and debilitating varieties (pneumonia, tuberculosis, typhoid); meningitis (meningococcic and tubercular); encephalitis (viral, malarial, rheumatic); brain abscess; seizure disorders (postictal, psychomotor, petit mal); metabolic disorders (diabetic acidosis, hypoxia, porphyria, hypoglycemia, uremia, vitamin deficiencies, liver or kidney disease); collagen disorders (systemic lupus erythematosus, or SLE); postoperative state; sensory deprivation; drug intoxication, overdose, or withdrawal (hallucinogens, alcohol, levodopa, belladonna alkaloids, bromides) congestive heart failure, emboli, or hypertensive encephalopathy; respiratory insufficiency (pickwickian syndrome, nitrogen narcosis); or endocrine disturbances (hyperthyroidism, myxedema). Febrile delirium is common in chil-

dren with high fevers caused by infectious diseases. Elderly clients and clients with a history of brain damage or previous delirium are at risk for developing delirium episodes.

TREATMENT. Decision on the therapeutic approach is based on etiology. For example, head injuries may require surgical intervention, and infections may require identification of the pathogen and antibiotic therapy.

DEMENTIA

SYMPTOMS. The major symptom in dementia is memory loss. Remote memory, including recognition, recall, and retention, is generally more intact than recent memory; however, there is marked impairment in both types of memory in advanced stages of dementia. Judgment is impaired. Demented clients may use obscene language or exhibit inappropriate sexual behavior. Early signs of dementia include absentmindedness, carelessness, concentration difficulties, mild tremor and incoordination, irritability, and silliness. Personal appearance and hygiene are often neglected. Clients have difficulty processing complex and new information and coping with novel tasks, especially under pressure of time. Consciousness is usually unimpaired, except in extreme and advanced cases. Often clients will fail to complete a task if interrupted. Learning, comprehension, calculation, reasoning, problem solving, ability to think creatively and abstractly, planning, ability to read and understand printed material or spoken instructions, orientation, and speech may be impaired. Confusion, incontinence, disturbed gait, agnosia, apraxia, personality change, anxiety, paranoia, depression, and social isolation may be present. Performance of demented people usually does not vary with motivation, whereas in depressed clients lack of motivation will adversely and variably affect performance.

A client who had Alzheimer's disease first manifested difficulty in balancing the family checkbook. This was most unusual for him since he was a bank teller.

Senile dementia, by definition, occurs in clients over 65. Onset is insidious. The disorder is progressive. Presenile dementia includes Alzheimer's, Pick's, and Jakob-Creutzfeldt disease.

COURSE. Onset of dementia is sudden in brain hypoxia, meningoencephalitis, and head trauma. Onset is relatively gradual when dementia is the result of brain tumor, subdural hematoma, or metabolic disorder. The most common causes of dementia are cerebral arteriosclerosis and other cerebrovascular disease.

ETIOLOGY. The causes of a variety of dementias are unknown or obscure, for example, senile dementia, Pick's disease, Parkinson's disease, and Huntington's chorea. Treatable causes of dementia are normal pressure hydrocephalus, multiple sclerosis, head trauma, subdural hematoma, and traumatic encephalopathy of boxers (punchdrunk syndrome). Also, occult and postsubarachnoid hemorrhagic hydrocephalus are amenable to treatment.

Dementia can also be caused by prolonged alcoholism and drug abuse; carbon monoxide and heavy metal poisoning; anoxia; cerebral arteriosclerosis and other cerebrovascular disorders; brain tumor; thyroid, parathyroid, or adrenal dysfunction; hypoglycemia; porphyria; Wilson's disease; inappropriate antidiuretic hormone secretion; hyponatremia; hepatic, renal, and pulmonary insufficiency; pellagra; hypovitaminosis B; Wernicke-Korsakoff (WE-KS) syndrome; sustained hypertension; SLE; general paralysis of the insane (GPI); brain abscess; meningoencephalitis; recurrent seizures; remote effects of carcinoma; and hematological disorders.

The nature and pattern of memory loss in dementing diseases and the relationship of the loss to impairments of other cognitive functions can help define the origin of the dementia.

Clinical effects: Loss of recent memory with relative preservation of remote memory and the ability to use stored information in solving problems is characteristic of axial or limbic dementia, such as that seen in WE-KS. On the other hand, a deficit in both recent and remote memory plus a greater difficulty in problem solving and other cognitive functions suggests cortical dementia, such as Alzheimer's disease or senile dementia (Karp, 1980, p. 48). In contrast, emotional lability, such as involuntary laughing or crying, points to vascular disease and not to presenile or senile dementia (Haase, 1970, p. 180).

Laboratory results: Blood levels of trace metals may be useful for differentiating the diagnostic categories of dementia. Calcium and copper levels are lower in clients with arteriosclerotic dementia than in alcohol (WE-KS) dementia, which has lower levels than in senile dementia (Anath, 1979).

Testing: X-ray films of the skull, EEG, lumbar puncture, and computerized tomography (CT) scan are helpful procedures. CT scan may demonstrate cortical atrophy and loss of brain substance. Psychological testing (see later discussion) can sometimes be helpful.

TREATMENT OF SENILE DEMENTIA. In senile dementia, the onset is insidious, so that only a fairly dramatic event or worsening of an already existing condition will prompt the client or concerned relatives to seek advice. These events are usually behavioral, such as violent or unreasonable behavior at home.

In these cases the individual can be examined in the emergency unit, the suspicion of senile dementia entertained, and sedation prescribed. A follow-up appointment is given, often for the next day, or referral is made to another facility for definitive treatment.

Agitation is often worse at night, so that the concerned relative is often interested in obtaining help to get the client to sleep or quieted at bedtime ("sundowner syndrome"). This condition of disorientation is often seen when the elderly person is moved to an unfamiliar setting, and is found in incipient dementias as well as in the general elderly population.

Sedatives or minor tranquilizers are often beneficial when used in conjunction with other treatment strategies, such as a light in the client's room to provide a source of orientation or a ticking clock. Useful medication with elderly clients are minor tranquilizers, such as diazepam and flurazepam; these are safe and generally present few hazards.

Major tranquilizers are indicated in those cases where agitation is so marked that the danger of injury to self or staff is imminent; however, it must be noted that the use of medications with sedating properties by clients of advanced years is not without risk.

Oversedation, because of poor renal function

resulting from diminished renal clearance, can be a serious problem, resulting in a stuporous or obtunded state, which may persist for several days, even after all medication has been discontinued. To avoid these difficulties, renal function studies (blood urea nitrogen, or BUN) should be obtained as well as a previous history of drug sensitivity or oversedation.

Haloperidol, a major tranquilizer, can be given in liquid form, which may be better tolerated than the administration of tablets orally. Dosages in the range of 0.5 mg to 2 mg two or three times a day can be effective, but care must be taken to start at the lowest dose to prevent oversedation. Preexisting thyroid conditions, such as thyrotoxicosis, may contraindicate the use of haloperidol. Evidence of goiter or hyperthyroidism should be noted before the administration of major tranquilizers is begun.

Geriatric clinics are often the referral of choice if the staff members are experienced in the assessment of elderly clients with organic problems. If the client's behavior cannot be tolerated in the home no matter what the nature of medication prescribed or behavioral program instituted, admission to an observation or treatment unit is indicated. It should be emphasized that this step can be avoided if good rapport is set up between client, family, and emergency unit staff person and if the concerned relative is instructed in methods of intervention.

Elderly clients are often maintained on a variety of powerful medications simultaneously. It is extremely important to assess the amounts and dosage strength of each drug, possible contributions to the picture of dementia, and the combined effect of all drugs administered, including any additional medication used to calm or sedate the client. Attention should certainly be paid to potential drug interaction, since these present special problems and great care must be exercised in their management. When dementia is becoming an increasing problem, restructuring the client's routine and daily activities can help.

Attention must also be given to the emotional hardship that the client's family is undergoing during the course of the evaluation and early search for treatable causes of dementia.

Depression is a frequent concomitant of pre-senile and senile dementia. It is often the first manifestation of the dementing process, and when successfully treated, there is a dramatic reversal of the picture of dilapidation and relentless disintegration. Because the antidepressants in current use have a lag time of 2 weeks before any significant remission of symptoms is evident, they probably will not be used by the emergency unit staff member but by the person offering definitive treatment after the evaluation has been completed. Insomnia, loss of appetite, bowel disturbance, and decreased libido are all symptoms of depression which occur in the presence of dementia and which can be successfully eliminated by the proper use and selection of appropriate antidepressant medication.

AMNESIC SYNDROME

DESCRIPTION. Clients with amnesic syndrome have short-term but not immediate memory deficits. They can repeat sequences of digits forward and backward but cannot remember what was presented 25 minutes or more before. Anterograde amnesia is always present, and retrograde amnesia may be present. There is no clouding of consciousness or general loss of major intellectual abilities.

A client with amnesic syndrome was seen in an inpatient unit after she had wandered away from her husband at a restaurant and was later picked up by the police. She was unable to remember her therapist's name or the fact that her husband had visited her an hour before, but she was able to remember her mother's telephone number in another state.

Common additional symptoms are disorientation, impaired perception, lack of initiative, emotional blandness, long-term memory impairment, and confabulation. The client may deny having a memory deficit. Clients are usually aware of themselves and their surroundings. They are often friendly, agreeable, and usually apathetic but not overtly depressed. They can be affectively serene or irritable and sometimes are mildly facetious. They may be affectively shallow. They may forget they are cooking food and burn it. Their ability to function socially and occupationally is impaired.

ONSET AND PREVALENCE. Onset is usually sudden. The syndrome tends to persist. However, this syndrome rarely occurs.

ETIOLOGY. The amnesic syndrome can result from head trauma, surgical intervention, anoxia, infarction of posterior cerebral arteries, and herpes simplex encephalitis. Most frequently, it is caused by thiamine deficiency and chronic alcohol use.

ORGANIC DELUSIONAL SYNDROME

In organic delusional syndrome occurrence of delusions in a state of full wakefulness and alertness is the most prominent symptom. An organic causal factor must be present. The complexity of the delusions ranges from those caused by brain tumors which can be simple and poorly formed to highly organized delusional states caused by amphetamines which are often indistinguishable from acute paranoid schizophrenic episodes. Well-developed delusions of persecution have been reported in clients suffering from Huntington's chorea.

SYMPTOMS. The symptoms that may accompany the delusions include hallucinations (usually visual or tactile), mild cognitive impairment, incoherence, tangentiality, abnormalities of psychomotor activity (for example, pacing, rocking, apathetic immobility), ritualistic or stereotyped behavior, magical thinking, and dysphoric mood. Clients may appear to be perplexed, disheveled, or eccentrically groomed or dressed. Clients suffering from Huntington's chorea may manifest personality changes in their fourth decade, poverty of thought, mood swings, irritability, poor judgment, and sensorial defects.

Social and occupational functioning is usually severely impaired. Clients may attempt to harm themselves or others in reaction to their delusions.

ONSET. Onset may be sudden (as when drug induced) or insidious (as in Huntington's chorea) or occur when an organic agent is present, disappear, and subsequently reappear when the organic agent is no longer present (flashbacks).

ETIOLOGY. The organic delusional syndrome can be caused by hallucinogens such as cannabis, amphetamines, brain tumors, Huntington's chorea, and the interictal syndrome in clients who have temporal lobe epilepsy.

TREATMENT. Treatment is specific to the causation. For example, cannabis delusions usually last 4 to 6 hours and seldom require active intervention, whereas amphetamine psychosis with delusions may respond to phenothiazines.

ORGANIC PERSONALITY SYNDROME

SYMPTOMS. In organic personality syndrome there is change in the enduring pattern of relating to the environment. This is usually associated with frontal lobe damage. One common pattern includes emotional lability, impaired impulse control or social judgment, belligerence, temper outbursts, unprovoked crying spells, and socially inappropriate behavior including sexual indiscretion. Another pattern is composed of marked apathy and indifference. Less commonly, suspiciousness or nondelusional paranoid sensitivity are observed.

Associated features are irritability and cognitive impairment. When temporal lobe epilepsy is present, there may be interictal personality disturbance with marked humorlessness, excessive emotionality, temper outbursts, and verbosity in writing and speech.

Medication-induced organic personality syndrome is transient. Pseudobulbar palsy will cause permanent personality change. Personality change may be the first sign of dementia. Impairment is variable. Cognitive functions tend to stay relatively intact. Poor social judgment may lead to marked impairment requiring close supervision or custodial care. Socially unacceptable behavior may lead to social ostracism and incarceration. Clients with organic personality syndrome may be harmful to themselves or others.

ETIOLOGY. Organic personality syndrome can be caused by the chronic use of certain drugs (such as steroids), endocrine disorders (as in thyroid disease), structural damage to the nervous system caused by tumors (for example, postconcussion syndrome) or vascular accidents (such as pseudobulbar palsy). If the syndrome is caused by a lesion, the lesion is usually located in the frontal lobes. Sometimes the syndrome is the result of temporal lobe disease (for example, temporal lobe epilepsy).

TREATMENT. Treatment is based on etiology. For example, steroid-induced personality syndrome is treated by gradual withdrawal, and endocrine disorders producing personality syndromes are treated according to the specific disorder. Intoxication and withdrawal are organic brain syndromes that are discussed in the chapter on substance abuse.

Mixed organic brain syndrome is a residual diagnostic category for disorders that do not meet diagnostic criteria for other organic brain syndromes. An example is the neurasthenic disturbance seen in clients suffering from the early stages of Addison's disease.

SUBSTANCE-INDUCED ORGANIC MENTAL DISORDERS

IATROGENIC AGENTS. Perhaps among the most common entities found in the group of organic mental disorders are those conditions produced by self-administered pharmacological agents. These agents are prescribed by a physician, obtained from a well-meaning friend, or purchased illicitly. In a day-to-day emergency room practice, one is frequently confronted with clinical situations resulting from an overdose of medication, whether taken by itself or used in combination with other drugs (polypharmacy). Specific conditions arising from drug overdose and abuse are covered in the chapter on substance abuse.

Substance-induced organic mental disorders are sometimes produced by the prescription or administration by the physician of medication in improper range or in appropriate doses that nevertheless exceed the client's biochemical competence (for example, steroid psychosis).

BELLADONNA ALKALOIDS. The belladonna alkaloids are prominent in their antiparasympathetic or, more familiarly, anticholinergic effects. Properly, they are antagonists of acetylcholine and specifically act to counter the muscarinic effects of this agent. In an emergency unit a client who arrives with conditions of dry mouth, flushed face, fever, and tachycardia should alert the examiner to the possibility of atropine poisoning. Psychological effects are dramatic and range from mere clouding of consciousness to delirium. Hallucinations and delusions occur as well as memory defects and disorientation.

Treatment consists of the administration of physostigmine with judicious use of the minor tranquilizers for the control of excitement and agitation. Phenothiazines are contraindicated.

SCOPOLAMINE. A closely related alkaloid, scopolamine, is similar in its effects to atropine but has greater hypnotic potential. Because of this property, scopolamine is contained in many nonprescription sleep aids commercially available in pharmacies (over the counter). Scopolamine and related alkaloids tend to produce a delirious state when used by sensitive individuals or used in inappropriately large amounts. In the dosage range advised by the manufacturer, scopolamine produces somnolence, euphoria, fatigue, and dreamless sleep, but paradoxical reactions can occur in states of anxiety and pain. Restlessness can be marked and amnesia for events during delirium supervenes. Central nervous system (CNS) depression is more prominent with scopolamine than with atropine and can differentiate these compounds in their clinical effects (Goodman and Gilman, 1975, p. 514).

TRICYCLIC ANTIDEPRESSANTS. Increasingly one is aware of the anticholinergic effects of the antidepressants and the ability of the tricyclic antidepressants to produce organic brain syndromes, especially in the elderly. In the elderly, changes in the level of consciousness including delirium can be observed. As with the alkaloids discussed earlier, tricyclics can cause dry mouth, dizziness, constipation, tachycardia, palpitations, and blurred vision. Treatment of toxicity includes, besides withdrawal and discontinuation of the medication, gastric lavage (especially in cases of overdose) and observation in the emergency room or intensive care unit for convulsions, hypertension, and fever. Physostigmine is a helpful adjunct to treatment. Tricyclics vary in their toxic effects and anticholinergic potential; imipramine and amitriptyline have strong anticholinergic properties while doxepin has weak anticholinergic (especially cardiotoxic) effects (Goodman and Gilman, 1975, p. 17).

ADRENOCORTICOSTEROIDS. Endogenous adrenocorticosteroids and artificial steroids administered to clients systemically may exert profound neurocortical effects. These effects are produced in behavior, mood, affect, and EEG. Manic behavior with motor restlessness can accompany high doses of exogenous steroids (steroid psychosis). Such changes remit with decrease in dosage or withdrawal of medication. Among clients seen with medication-associated changes in mentation are especially those medicated for chronic and severe conditions, such as bronchial asthma and collagen disease (for example, SLE). When treated with steroids over a long period, clients may develop characteristic physical changes. The stigmata found in Cushing's syndrome, moonlike facies, "buffalo" hump, puffy skin, hirsutism, and abdominal striae may occur in the course of extended treatment. Memory changes are not prominent, but hypomanic and frankly manic behavior, as in motor drivenness, can be seen. Delusional thinking, such as paranoid ideation, may be noted, but hallucinations are infrequent. Poor judgment and impulsive behavior occur. Observation and sedation are indicated after withdrawal of the steroid medication on a gradual basis. Sudden withdrawal is contraindicated, since endogenous production of adrenocortical steroids ceases when exogenous agents are given (Goodman and Gilman, 1975, p. 1485).

NUTRITIONAL DEMENTIAS

The group of nutritionally induced disorders of brain function is one of the more interesting and rewarding for study and diagnosis, since once the diagnosis is made, the treatment of these entities is relatively rapid and remission is total and complete.

The chemical constituents necessary to prevent signs and symptoms of disordered mentation can be roughly divided into (1) minerals, including minerals in gross amounts (100 mg/day or more); (2) trace minerals, or minerals in minute amounts (no more than a few milligrams/day); (3) organic compounds, including source of calories (protein, fat, and carbohydrate); and (4) vitamins.

AVITAMINOSES. The avitaminoses producing mental disturbances occurring in persons one might expect to see in an emergency unit are broadly those encountered among alcoholics or food-deprived persons whose disturbance in nutrition has been self-induced. The latter category may well include schizophrenic individuals or simply persons deprived of proper food by poverty or circumstance. Among the alcoholics, avitaminosis is the rule rather than the exception. Niacin deficiency (pellagra) presents a dermatological disorder (as well as raw tongue with scarlet appearance, disappearance of lingual papillae, diarrhea, and dementia).

Thiamin lack (beriberi) presents both a cardiovascular and neurological syndrome, and either component may be present. Nervous system involvement is progressive and ranges from a peripheral neuropathy to cerebral involvement (cerebral beriberi). Both Wernicke's encephalopathy and Korsakoff's syndrome are aspects of brain impairment caused by niacin deficiency. In WE the neurological manifestations are more prominent and include nystagmus (horizontal and vertical), ophthalmoplegia, ataxia; KS emphasizes mental state, such as retrograde amnesia, learning impairment and inconsistency, and confabulation. Both are aspects of a diseased brain, and the signs and symptoms fluctuate depending on the extent and severity of the involvement of the neurological substrate (Harrison, 1980, p. 426). Thiamine deficiency is a so-called psychiatric emergency because permanent damage to brain and nervous system can result.

RECOMMENDED TREATMENT. Recommended treatment is 50 mg/day intramuscularly for 5 days followed by 5 mg orally. Lack of riboflavin (vitamin B_2), pyroxidine (vitamin B_6), folic acid, pantothenic acid, biotin, or vitamin B_{12} can produce mental changes, but neurological impairment proceeding to dementia has not been observed.

ELECTROLYTE DISTURBANCES

RESPIRATORY ALKALOSIS HYPERVENTILATION CAUSED BY ANXIETY. Distinct physical signs and symptoms can be the consequences of anxiety and hyperventilation. When these are combined, clients usually complain of a fear of dying, even though they are in vigorous good health. The fear of dying is focused on the cardiorespiratory and central nervous system, because the client most often fears death by heart attack, stroke, or seizure. Usually, repeated examinations have failed to convince the client that there is no cardiorespiratory or central nervous system problem. Serial ECGs do not demonstrate pathology. A careful past history examination reveals the loss, often recent, of a relative to whom the client was attached, caused by death from heart or cerebrovascular disease. On clinical examination in the emergency unit, the client reports numbness and tingling circumorally and paresthesia peripherally. Dizziness and lightheadedness occur and carpopedal spasm is seen in severe cases. Palpitations are often present, but there are no objective signs of heart disease.

TREATMENT. Treatment is sedation or rebreathing air into a paper bag. Some degree of excitement usually accompanies the attack, and in occasional cases, physical restraint may be necessary. There are no hallucinations present and delusional thinking is restricted to the fear of imminent death. This responds to support and reassurance. Memory is intact.

ENDOCRINE DISTURBANCES

Organic mental disorders may occur in the presence of oversecretion or undersecretion of the endocrine hormones. Since these substances have vast and far-reaching effects in bodily chemistry and physiology, the diagnosis of these states is facilitated by the abundance of systemic signs and symptoms in addition to mental manifestations, and these then will usually be more dramatic and obvious to the examiner than will changes in mentation.

Thyroid disorders

HYPOTHYROIDISM. Any disease that leads to decreased production or synthesis of thyroid hormone can produce hypothyroidism. When deficient hormone production dates from birth, the condition is called cretinism. In adults, an extreme form of decreased thyroid hormone causes a condition called myxedema, so-called because of the peculiar and striking appearance of skin

texture, which is thickened and puffy although firm to the touch. In both the infant and adult conditions, hypothyroidism is accompanied by mental slowing and psychomotor retardation. Myxedema madness, delusions, and hallucinations are not present. General slowing of metabolic processes is evidenced by decreased motor and mental abilities. Neurological examination demonstrates the decreased reactivity of the deep tendon reflexes, and cerebellar ataxia may occur. The skin is cool, and depressed ideation with constipation, anorexia, and menstrual irregularity may be prominent. Definitive diagnosis depends on the demonstration of decreased circulating thyroid hormone.

A common cause of hypothyroidism in recent times is the iatrogenic state produced by the surgical or chemical extirpation of the gland, the procedure being used in the treatment of hyperthyroid states. Treatment of iatrogenic, as well as idiopathic, hypothyroidism consists of replacement with thyroid hormone (Freedman and Kaplan, 1967, pp. 1087 and 1090; Harrison, 1980, p. 1701).

HYPERTHYROIDISM. Excess production of thyroid hormone occurs in Graves' disease (idiopathic hyperthyroidism), toxic multiple goiter, neoplasms, and less frequently, thyroiditis. Mental manifestations are most prominent in younger persons. However, nervousness and hyperexcitability are the most frequent signs. Delusions and hallucinations are not often present (Freedman and Kaplan, 1967, p. 1087; Harrison, 1980, p. 1703).

Adrenal disorders

HYPERFUNCTION OF ADRENAL CORTEX (CUSHING'S SYNDROME). The major and profuse symptoms of adrenocortical hyperfunctioning (Freedman and Kaplan, 1967, p. 1090) may be endogenous or exogenous (steroid psychosis), but whatever the cause, the clinical presentation is often accompanied by dramatic mental manifestations, including psychosis. Physical symptoms include increased body weight, easy fatigability, weakness, hypertension, hirsutism, and amenorrhea. Mental status examination reveals paranoid thinking and delusions with full wakefulness and attention. Treatment is surgical removal of tumor or hypertrophied adrenal glands, with or without irradiation. In exogenously induced steroid disorders, withdrawal of steroids on a gradual basis is the treatment of choice.

HYPOFUNCTION OF ADRENAL CORTEX (ADDISON'S DISEASE). The hypoplasia resulting from disease or idiopathic atrophy of adrenocortical tissue results in hypofunction of adrenocortical origin, or Addison's disease. Weakness, fatigability, and typical hyperpigmentation in skin and mucous membranes is typically found in this state. Mental slowing with depression is often found.

Pancreatic disorders

HYPOGLYCEMIA (DIABETES MELLITUS). Pancreatic hypoglycemia is often a result of insulin-treated diabetic states and occurs most often in poorly controlled clients. Since the vast majority of these are in the younger age group (juvenile diabetes) where age of onset is below 40, a high index of suspicion should be maintained when confusion and disorientation are encountered in a client below the age of 40. Head trauma, delusions, and hallucinations are not present. This type of hypoglycemic response is a consequence of excessive insulin medication, dietary mismanagement, or unexpected exercise. After blood for serum glucose determination has been drawn, prompt infusion of 50% glucose solution will produce dramatic reduction in clouded sensorium, confusion, and symptoms of disorientation, often in a matter of minutes (Harrison, 1980, p. 1703).

HYPERGLYCEMIA. In contrast to the younger age group, diabetic coma without ketoacidosis occurs in mature-onset diabetics, that is, those over 40. Clients in this group, often with other illnesses, are undergoing treatment with a variety of medications, are sometimes confined to home or to a nursing home, and will be brought into the emergency unit in an advanced state of fluid depletion and stupor. Neurological signs are generally prominent, ranging from clouding of consciousness and sensorium to frank coma. Pathological signs and reflexes (grasp, suck) and hemiplegia, in the absence (or presence) of a history of cerebrovascular accident (CVA), can be

seen. Intercurrent infection is often found and must be treated vigorously. Fluid replacement and insulin therapy form the main treatment in this condition, since it is associated with a high mortality.

CEREBROVASCULAR ACCIDENTS (STROKE)

Perhaps the most common vascular disease seen in the emergency unit is cerebrovascular disease. There are dramatic neurological and psychological manifestations when stroke is sudden in onset, and yet the same disease can be insidious and gradual in its presentation but with disasterous and disabling sequelae. In the elderly, gradual cerebral insufficiency can mimic depression and even psychoneurotic states.

STUTTERING STROKE. The stuttering stroke syndrome is characterized (1) by fainting spells (transient loss or disturbances of consciousness); (2) often by carotid artery disease with neurological signs; by (3) rapid return of function; (4) by little or no impairment of function; and (5) by recurrent episodes.

SIMPLE STROKE. The common stroke is characterized by (1) rapid onset; (2) loss of consciousness; (3) loss of function; (4) neurological signs; and (5) permanent impairment, on the basis of cerebrovascular disease.

THROMBOSIS. The characteristic picture of cerebral arterosclerotic thrombosis includes (1) transient ischemic attacks; (2) preservation of consciousness; (3) progressive evolution of neurological signs in stepwise fashion; (4) clear cerebrospinal fluid (CSF); (5) rapid improvement; and (6) onset in sleep.

EMBOLISM. The diagnosis of embolism can be made on the basis of (1) absent ischemic attacks; (2) preservation of consciousness (although extensive neurological deficits are present); (3) embolic focus (heart); (4) recent embolic phenomena in other organs; (5) involvement of other brain regions; and (6) rapid improvement.

HYPERTENSIVE HEMORRHAGE. One can suspect the presence of hypertensive hemorrhage on the basis of (1) hypertension; (2) blood in the CSF; (3) gradual onset; (4) absent ischemic attacks; (5) progressive stupor or coma; (6) onset while awake; (7) headache; and (8) nuchal rigidity.

RUPTURED ANEURYSM. A rupture of a congenital aneurysm in the circle of Willis in the brain (berry aneurysm) is found with (1) sudden onset; (2) loss of consciousness at onset; (3) grossly bloody spinal fluid; (4) absent focal neurological signs; (5) periretinal hemorrhages; (6) Kernig's and Brudsinski's signs; (7) third-nerve palsy; (8) convulsion at onset; (9) absent hypertension; and (10) onset during exertion.

MULTIINFARCT DEMENTIA

Multiinfarct dementia is seen with abrupt onset, dementia, focal neurological abnormalities, pseudobulbar palsy with lability of affect (often), and stepwise deterioration in intellectual functioning with patchy degeneration (leaving some intellectual functions spared while affecting others).

SPACE-OCCUPYING LESIONS
(Harrison, 1980, p. 1951)
Tumors of the brain

Tumors in the substance of the brain may be present for long periods without obvious symptomatology. Headache, often progressing to nausea (in a third of cases of headaches), dizziness, and convulsions of adult onset with localized focus are suggestive of cerebral neoplasms. Increasing intracranial pressure is produced by the growth of tumor in the restricted space of the cranial vault and results in the aforementioned signs and symptoms as well as the particular mental changes that may be first spotted by the emergency unit physician or nurse. Loss or decline in general mental ability, slowness in comprehension, and difficulty in sustaining attention may all or individually accompany brain tumors. Neurological syndromes peculiar to the site or area of spread of neoplasia can alert one to the presence of tumor. Tumor originating in other areas (metastatic tumor) frequently appears in brain tissue. Primary tumors of brain substance include astrocytoma, glioblastoma multiforme, oligodendroglioma, meningioma, and reticulum cell sarcoma of cerebrum. Glioblastoma is a frequent tumor type, heavily invasive and often attaining great mass and volume before it is detected or diagnosed. Astrocytoma is less rapid in growth and may be "silent" for years before it is manifest. CT scan and pneumoencephalography are diagnostic aids in detecting the presence of neoplasms; carotid arteriography may be useful as well.

Pseudotumor

An idiopathic condition that mimics tumors of the brain is pseudotumor cerebri; in this state, cerebrospinal fluid (CSF) pressure is increased in the presence of normal findings on CT scan and arteriogram. No cells or increased protein is found in CSF, but papilledema with scattered and inconsistent neurological signs accompany the findings of increased pressure. Mental status changes also suggestive of decline in mental functioning are found.

INFECTIONS OF BRAIN

Bacterial meningitis (BM, or leptomeningitis) and viral meningitis (meningoencephalitis, or aseptic meningitis) are both accompanied by changes in mentation and consciousness. In the former, meningitis is cerebrospinal and results in headache, stiff neck, and impairment of consciousness. Fever and seizures along with pleocytosis of CSF are most suggestive of bacterial infection. The important differentiation between delirium tremens and BM must be made on the basis of CSF examination.

Viral meningitis produces an aseptic meningitis syndrome (AM); fever, headache, stiff neck, and increased numbers of monocytes and lymphocytes in CSF are concomitants of AM. Mental changes are not as profound as in bacterial infections, but headache is dramatic and severe.

Tuberculosis, syphilis, cryptococcosis, and brain abscess may all be present with the signs of aseptic meningitis; culture and microscopic examination of CSF are often diagnostic. Appropriate antibiotic therapy is the treatment.

Encephalitis viruses that are carried by arthropods (rabies) as well as viral agents that infect the brain directly without intermediate vectors (measles) produce the syndrome of encephalitis. Signs of brain substance involvement accompany signs of meningeal irritation with fever, headache, and change in consciousness. Rabies may produce a picture of psychosis, but characteristic signs of hydrophobia and neurological involvement are seen following animal bites. Equine and Japanese B encephalitis outbreaks occur in seasonal and regional epidemics, with decreased consciousness as the most prominent feature.

TRAUMATIC SYNDROMES
Head injury

The importance of a physical insult to the cranial vault cannot be overstressed, since a history of unconsciousness and change in level of consciousness both may connote serious injury to the brain. There is often a direct and pathological relationship between duration of unconsciousness and severity of brain injury. Vital signs and careful monitoring of neurological findings may well identify the nature and extent of the injury. Paralysis and ocular signs as well as the presence of convulsions point to the site of damage. Nuchal rigidity and otorrhagia may be associated with particular points of fracture and bleeding (Chusid and McDonald, 1964, p. 302).

Head injuries can be classified as closed or open. Closed injuries of the head are those in which the integrity of the cranium has not been compromised. Mild injuries (concussion) occur with little or transient loss of consciousness (seconds to minutes), and there are no neurological findings. Memory defect is also minor (retrograde amnesia). Moderate and severe head injuries (laceration, hemorrhage) cause longer periods of unconsciousness and prominent neurological findings and are associated with more profound damage of the brain.

CONCUSSION. A most frequent consequence of automobile-associated trauma, concussion can represent contusion or laceration of the brain at the site of injury or contralateral to the site (contrecoup injury). Brief or prolonged unconsciousness (coma) depends on the extent of the injury. Amnesia can be for the period following recovery of consciousness (anterograde) or for the period preceding injury (retrograde). Mental confusion often indicates laceration of brain substance. Neurological signs that progress indicate more severe involvement and necessitate observation and hospitalization. Recovery phenomena associated with resolving concussion (posttraumatic cerebral syndrome) often include headache, ataxia, lethargy, and personality changes consistent with a depressive illness. Skull x-ray films are indicated and CT scan is helpful in differentiating concussion from laceration of vessels and hemorrhage. Lumbar puncture may be diagnostic in demonstrating the presence of blood in the CSF, and an EEG may be indicated.

HEMORRHAGE. Injuries that produce lacerations and tears in brain substance often produce bleeding that may well be more dangerous and life threatening than the original insult. Changes in level of consciousness may be the single most important factor in establishing diagnosis. A high index of suspicion is also imperative. Blood in the CSF can be demonstrated.

Subarachnoid hemorrhage. In clients who have periods of prolonged unconsciousness or coma (1 hour or more), one should consider the possibility of hemorrhage into the subarachnoid space. Spontaneous subarachnoid hemorrhage, associated with malformed vessels (berry aneurysm), also occurs in the absence of trauma in young adults. Nuchal rigidity and fresh blood in CSF are prominent findings.

Subdural hemorrhage. Slight injury to the brain may produce subdural vein rupture. Acute hemorrhage may remit spontaneously with no intervention; chronic subdural hemorrhage may produce a hematoma that requires surgery (burr holes) and evaluation. A change in level of consciousness may be characteristic and diagnostic. Initial confusion may yield to clearing of conscious awareness and then proceed again to confusion, with increasing intracranial pressure. Personality changes, confusion, and convulsions may appear weeks after injury. Radiological investigation often demonstrates pineal shift.

Extradural hemorrhage. Bleeding from the middle meningeal artery (or vein) may also produce changes in level of awareness. Increases in intracranial pressure also are associated with initial confusion, clearing, and renewed confu-

TABLE 3-1. The neurological examination

Area examined	Assessments
Mentation	Awareness Orientation (oriented to time, place, and person); level of consciousness (obtunded, stuporous, semicomatose, comatose)
Speech	Normal, dysphasia, dysarthria, dysphonia
General knowledge	Knowledge of current events, vocabulary
Memory	Intact, recent memory impaired, remote memory impaired
Retention and recall	Recall of objects, digits forward and reversed
Reasoning	Judgment, insight, abstraction (interpretation of proverbs, similarities, and differences)
Use of symbols	Calculation, reading, writing
Object recognition	Normal, agnosia
Praxis	Ideational, ideomotor, motor, and constructional apraxias
Perception	Delusions, illusions, hallucinations
Mood	Normal, euphoric, depressed, anxious, agitated
Affect	Normal, flat, inappropriate
Gait, station	Hemiplegic, ataxic, spastic, festinating, hyperkinetic, waddling, apraxia of gait, hysterical gait, steppage gait; Romberg test
Cranial nerves—motor system	Atrophy, fasciculations, tremor, dystonia, involuntary movements, palpation, tone, strength
Coordination	Finger-to-nose and heel-to-shin tests, rapid alternating movements
Reflexes	Superficial reflexes, tendon reflexes
Sensation	Touch, pain, temperature, vibration and position sense, tactile localization, two-point discrimination, bilateral simultaneous stimulation, stereognosis, barognosis, skin writing
Head and neck	Bruises over head and neck, scalp and skull tenderness and deformity, signs of head trauma, cerebrospinal fluid drainage from ears and nose
Spine, skin	Nuchal rigidity, low hairline, shortness of neck, spinal deformity, spinal tenderness, limitation of movement of spine, paravertebral spasm, limitation of straight leg raising, palpation for cervical ribs, pes cavus, peripheral nerve enlargement, adenoma sebaceum, café-au-lait spots, trigeminal hemangioma

sion. Burr holes may be necessary, and X-ray films demonstrating fracture across the meningeal groove may be helpful.

THE NEUROLOGICAL EXAMINATION

The first order of business in making a thorough evaluation of a client in the emergency unit is the determination or exclusion of physical disease. In the population at risk for mental health emergencies, an important source of emotional symptoms is neurological disorder. Of these symptoms, those from intoxication are first, and from cerebrovascular disorders, second. Degenerative diseases of the CNS are not as frequent but occur in the general emergency room population with regularity.

The neurological examination consists of many facets (Table 3-1), one of the first to be examined being speech. Speech disorders are frequently encountered in the emergency unit; often the disorder is a temporary one, on the basis of intoxication, but stroke and cerebral ischemia resulting from other causes may produce interference with speech as well. Dysphagia is impairment in the production of language or the comprehension of language because of CNS involvement or insult. Motor aphasia is the inability to produce speech fluently and does not interfere with the understanding of speech, whereas sensory aphasia affects the ability to understand speech and may produce jargon or many meaningless sounds in a faulty attempt to reproduce normal speech. Testing over time will reveal the extent of the impairment, since dysphagia caused by seizure or intoxication usually clears rapidly. Dysarthria is faulty production of speech resulting from impaired articulation. Stock phrases are used to test articulation, such as "Methodist, Episcopal" and "Peter Piper picked a peck of pickled peppers." Scanning speech is characteristic of cerebellar lesions and is a difficulty in maintaining constant volume and rhythm of speech, resulting in jerkiness and irregularities of sound production. Syllable repetition, such as "ga-ga-ga," "la-la-la," and "me-me-me," are used to test this area.

General knowledge refers to fund of information, and standard questions are useful in testing information items. Identification of the President of the United States, the governor of the state, the mayor of the city, the state and federal capitals, and recent events is in frequent use. Answers such as "I never read the newspaper" and "I broke my glasses" are, of course, not acceptable. "This is my bedroom" or "This is an apartment in my house" are examples of misidentification possibly based on an attempt to integrate the site into the client's home system. Remote memories, which are more intact, may form the basis for present responses and in this manner substitute for perceived deficits in recent information. A discussion of previous living situations and past history may appear off the point, but a leisurely discussion of the past may help the client better discern past from present and thus reduce stess and provide a better interviewing situation.

Performance will certainly be variable on formal memory testing, depending on the amount and severity of stress encountered by the client. The test of five objects in 25 minutes can produce remarkably erratic results, and retesting or representation of objects recalled after 5 minutes is useful in avoiding more extensive and elaborate testing; the probability that a client failing the shorter test will also fail the longer one is quite high. Also a familiar setting will give generally higher performance results than an unfamiliar clinic or emergency room.

Many abilities are subsumed under the category of reasoning, but in general, judgment, insight, and abstraction are the mental functions tested in emergency unit examinations. Judgment is tested by asking the client to give the correct response to a situation, with "correct" meaning the socially acceptable response. "What would you do with a letter you found lying in the street with an uncanceled stamp on it?" An unacceptable answer would be: "I would throw it away." Insight is tested by asking clients to explain why they are in the emergency unit or how they were brought there. Answers such as "I don't know" or "The police attacked me in the street" cast doubt on the client's insight. Abstraction is the ability to interpret a proverb or other metaphorical statements, and acceptable answers re-

fer to the latent meaning, whereas unacceptable (concrete) responses repeat the text or miss this meaning. "Don't cry over spilled milk" implies the uselessness of worrying over the past or unchangeable experience; this explanation would be an abstract response. "Milk is cheap, so don't cry" is concrete, since it adheres strictly to the text. "People often spill milk, so you shouldn't cry" is concrete, since it adherees strictly to the situation and fails to generalize the implied concept to the human condition. Concrete thinking is often found in the schizophrenias and in the amentias as well; although the former often impairs insight, fund of information is infrequently affected in schizophrenic disorders and memory is intact.

Symbolic abilities

Reading. Reading ability is based on acquired knowledge and educational level, as are writing and arithmetical ability as well. Thus testing of these categories should proceed only after some determination of educational status has been made. Questions concerning "special education" are helpful in eliciting some degrees of retardation. The individual is requested to read aloud a newspaper headline; if this is satisfactorily performed, a longer paragraph is read for comprehension. Alexia is the inability to read and may be either acquired (organic) or the result of lack of education (illiteracy). Dyslexia is an impairment in the ability to read discovered during the course of an education and includes skipping words and word and letter reversals.

Writing. The ability to write is a complex motor skill and is affected by brain lesions. Clients are asked to write their name and sentences dictated aloud.

Arithmetical ability. The loss of the ability to calculate is significant but often is the result of faulty education. Memory disorders for remote information are also encountered in the inability to recall multiplication tables. Serial 7s (subtract 7 from 100, then 7 from the result, and so on) is a frequent initial test of calculation ability. The examiner should proceed to addition if subtraction is impaired.

MENTAL STATUS EXAMINATION

A thorough and comprehensive examination of the mental and neurological state of the client entering an emergency unit must begin with an appraisal of the client's appearance. This involves grooming, body habits, choice of clothing, gait, stance, movements, and speech. If the client is accompanied by a relative or the police, the chaperone should be closely questioned as to pertinent information concerning the circumstances before departing. An evaluation of loss or impairment in consciousness is best obtained from a reliable observer (see discussion of neurological examination in preceding section). Level of consciousness is determined first and must necessarily dictate the direction of that portion of the examination devoted to mental status. The client's orientation to person, place, and time is vital information. One should accept no facile rationalizations that attempt to explain away lack or loss of contact with news or television, such as "I lost my glasses" or "Who has time to pay attention to things anymore?" A concerned and gently probing manner is most often productive with distraught and upset clients. Often a glass of water, a cup of coffee, or permission for a trip to the restroom to freshen up produces a miraculous change in a resistant client's level of cooperation. Relatives who have regular contact with the client may know details of the recent and remote medical history, which can save hours of frustrating, futile interrogation. A non-directive, conversational style can often provide the vehicle for the introduction of mental status items, so that the requirements of a formal mental status examination can be met without running the risk of alienating or antagonizing the client (a risk frequently encountered in the emergency unit, which places a great emphasis on speed and efficiency). This is especially true of aged clients in whom competence and adequacy are at issue or in question. A warm, understanding, and sympathetic attitude can avert the catastrophic reaction of protest when memory defects or apraxia-aphasia is uncovered and denial is no longer possible. Memory questions, such as significant dates and places, can also be integrated into the easy flow of conversation. In-quisitions as a rule are neither rewarding nor productive, either to client or examiner. Object-naming tests of memory (five objects after 5 mintues or 25 minutes, whichever seems appropriate to start with) can be interpolated between stretches of conversation, as can digit-span and similar items. The contents of pockets or purse may give the necessary clues to the client's identity and situation, but preceding any violation or intrusion of privacy, the client's trust and permission must be obtained. A request to see family photographs may provide an entry into the process of unraveling the mystery of circumstances. Clients may offer to show the examiner their wallet and then feel free to talk at length about their personal situation and difficulties. The topic of grandchildren and children are often reliable conduits to personal information and may hold pleasant associations for the client under evaluation.

Intoxicated clients are a special problem, in that they can often evoke feelings of hostility or belligerence in the clinician. One can be understanding with such a client, while simultaneously setting limits to the client's behavior. The intoxicated client's behavior is often provocative and attention getting and can be most easily handled in a setting that limits the client's motor activity, for example, a smaller rather than a larger interviewing room, and a setting that limits incoming and distracting stimuli that may tend to further disorganize or antagonize the client.

For hospitalized clients, the criteria for orientation are often different from those ordinarily used in an outpatient or emergency setting. The criteria are different because hospitalized clients are often disoriented because of limited access to familiar sources of information, such as newspapers, radio, and television.

In asking dates, the exact date and day of week is always desirable; however, in the hospital, or indeed in the case of a client just released from the hospital, an acceptable margin of error can be a day's leeway either way (Monday for Tuesday, the 28th for the 29th or 27th). Hard and fast rules are difficult to establish in these instances, so that an impression of vagueness and imprecision must have more weight in establishing disorientation than strict inexactitude.

Since the severely depressed client may genuinely be unconcerned with the external environment, care must be taken to distinguish the pseudoretardation that accompanies depressed states from disorientation that is produced by organic causes. Pseudoretardation implies a state of reduced mental functioning that is transient and superficial and that is found as a consequence of apathy and disinterest resulting from depression. A course of successful treatment with antidepressant medication has often revealed a dull and stupid-appearing ("senile") client to be a person of normal intelligence, sometimes in a most dramatic and satisfying way.

It is important to test memory in both formal and informal mental status examinations. In confabulation, the initial greeting and identification of the clinician can be crucial. The question, "Have you ever seen me before?" can lead to confabulatory elaboration and productions, such as "Of course! You used to live down the block from me!" in WE-KP. Explanations for the place of hospitalization or examination may lead to similar elaboration.

PSYCHOLOGICAL TESTING

Psychodiagnostic testing in a psychiatric emergency unit can be done for the purpose of establishing the differential diagnosis of organicity. Testing can usually establish whether organic brain damage is present and can sometimes indicate what part of the brain is damaged. Testing is done by a psychologist who is trained in the administration, scoring, and interpretation of the particular tests being used. Testing is only rarely done in the emergency unit.

TEST SELECTION. The examiner needs to tailor the selection of tests to the special needs of the client and to the stated purpose of the testing.

TEST PROCEDURE. Referring staff members should clearly state the reason for referral, preferably in writing. Before testing begins, it should be agreed whether the referring staff member or the examiner will be the one to give feedback

to the client. As is true with any testing referral, referring staff members who are not psychologists may need to be educated about test ethics.

SPECIAL TEST ADMINISTRATION. Deaf clients can be given written tests. Blind clients can be given oral tests. Aphasic clients can respond to test items by writing or pointing. Severely cognitively impaired clients can be given children's tests, for example, the Wechsler Intelligence Scale for Children, Revised Form. Intoxicated clients should not be tested because it will be impossible to tell whether test results reflect a substance-induced disorder or a functional disorder. Special test administration procedures may need to be used with brain-damaged clients. It is important to elicit maximum possible test performance to make a valid assessment. This may involve rephrasing test items to test the client's limits. For example, when asked, "How much is 40¢ and 20¢?" some concrete-minded, brain-damaged clients will respond, "40¢ and 20¢," because the phrasing of the question does not tell them to add. Their limits can be tested by asking, "If you had 40¢ and added 20¢, how much money would you have?" and if the client fails this item, ask "How much is 40 added to 20?" Clients with short attention spans may need frequent breaks between tests, subtests, or test items.

Criteria for selection of recommended test battery

In a psychiatric emergency setting, the clinician wants to elicit the maximum amount of information relevant to differential diagnosis in the minimum amount of time. Psychologists working in this setting can be expected to have a general knowledge of psychodiagnostic assessment but do not necessarily need to be specialists in neuropsychological assessment. The Wechsler Adult Intelligence Scale (WAIS) (minus the vocabulary subtest) and the Bender Gestalt Visual-Motor Test are recommended as a basic minimum battery. They can be administered and scored fairly briefly and yield sufficient information to diagnose or rule out organic causes and are available and familiar to most psychologists.

Interpretation of WAIS subtest scores

The Information subtest of the WAIS tests remote memory, verbal ability, and cultural knowledge. The scaled score is a good indicator of the client's original ability. It is one of the WAIS scores least affected by brain damage, even when clients have damage confined to the dominant hemisphere. Exceptions are clients who have recently come to the United States or who are non-English-speaking U.S. residents. Information and Comprehension scores drop when dominant hemisphere damage is present; thus when a brain lesion is present, these scores predict the hemispheric side of the lesion.

The Comprehension subtest tests judgment, remote memory, and verbal ability and is a good predictor of premorbid ability when damage is not localized in the dominant hemisphere. The Arithmetic subtest measures immediate memory, concentration, and quantitative reasoning. The Similarities subtest measures verbal concept formation and ability to think abstractly. This verbal test is the best indicator of brain damage.

Digit-Span is one of the WAIS subtests most sensitive to brain injury. Digit-Span Forward measures immediate auditory memory and auditory attention. These abilities, as well as the ability to mentally reverse the order of digits, are measured by Digit-Span Backward. Digit-Span Forward scores of five or less in adults under 65 who have normal hearing are indicative of severely impaired immediate auditory memory. When there is a point difference of three or more between scores on the Digit-Span Forward and Digit-Span Backward, organic disorder is indicated. An exception is that many clients with Korsakoff's syndrome can perform well on Digit-Span.

The Digit Symbol subtest measures visual-motor coordination, motor persistence, sustained attention, response speed, and sometimes memory and perceptual organization. In nonelderly clients, this subtest is the WAIS subtest most sensitive to brain damage. Scores will be extremely low even when brain damage is minimal. Somewhat lower scores on this and other speeded tests are also indicative of depression and normal aging.

The Picture Completion subtest measures visual recognition and organization, long-term memory, judgment, and general information. Picture Completion scores are not affected by brain damage and are thus a good indicator of premorbid ability.

Visuospatial organization, manipulation, planning, and problem solving toward a known goal are measured by the Block Design subtest. Brain-damaged clients tend to achieve low scores on this subtest. Clients with right hemisphere damage have particularly low scores. The Picture Arrangement subtest measures ability to analyze social situations, social judgment, and sequential thinking. Low scores on the subtest are indicative of brain damage. The Object Assembly subtest measures visual organization, motor response, and ability to solve problems when working toward an unknown goal. Object Assembly scores are relatively vulnerable to brain damage.

Bender Gestalt Visual-Motor Test

The Bender Gestalt Visual-Motor Test is a test used widely in the diagnosis of organicity. This is a pencil-and-paper drawing test and cannot be used with blind clients (the client is asked to copy nine drawings, one at a time). The test can usually be administered in 20 minutes or less. This test can be administered and scored easily and quickly and usually yields definitive information as to whether organicity is present. It also has the advantage of being free of cultural bias. It can be administered in any language, including sign language. Max Hutt (1977) has devised a system for scoring protocols for organic brain damage. The client's copies are scored for marked difficulty in angulation (three or more figures with discrepancies of 15 degrees or more); severe fragmentation (in at least three figures); perseveration; overlapping difficulty; simplification; and line incoordination. The presence of each of the first six factors is scored as two points, and of the last two factors, one point. A total score of nine or more is indicative of organic impairment. Scores of six through eight are marginal and need to be corroborated by evidence from other instruments.

Testing for brain damage in the elderly

"Whatever is characteristic of brain-damaged elderly . . . must be assessed against normal elderly patterns" (Schaie, 1977, p. 700). Elderly people generally do better on the verbal part of the WAIS than on the performance part. Conversely, brain-damaged elderly sometimes do better on the performance part. The classic WAIS profile of non-brain-damaged elderly people resembles the profile of clients with right-lateralized brain damage.

Brain-damaged elderly clients generally do poorly on the WAIS, particularly on the Similarities subtest where their concrete thinking is evident. They generally do worse on Arithmetic and Digit-Span (and sometimes Comprehension) subtests than non-brain-damaged elderly people. Tests recommended for detection of brain damage in the elderly are the WAIS, particularly Similarities and Digit-Span Backward subtests, the Bender Gestalt Visual-Motor Test, and the Background Interference test. Rotation and perseveration on the Bender Gestalt Visual-Motor are often noted on the protocols of elderly brain-damaged clients.

INTERVENTION AND TREATMENT: ORGANIC VERSUS FUNCTIONAL DISORDERS

The assessment of organic conditions, especially as regards emergency care, frequently involves the evolution of the disorder over time. In the case of intoxications, the time scale involved is relatively brief; onset is sudden and resolution (if not recovery) is rapid, as the causative agent is metabolized or excreted.

Case vignette

Mrs. K, a 77-year-old white female, was brought into the clinic by the police. She was well groomed, with newly rinsed silver-blue hair, and was wearing no coat, jacket, or hat on a coolish San Francisco evening. Mrs. K stated simply that she had argued

with her daughter and then had left the house, walking to San Francisco from Colma. She insisted in a calm and good-humored manner that she was in no difficulty but needed only to be shown the way to the bus to San Francisco and would be all right. (Since the unit is located in San Francisco, this last request was a clue to the fact that she was disoriented.)

Mental status testing revealed the client oriented to person, but not to place and time. Mrs. K felt she was situated in a suburb of San Francisco and was completely unaware of day, month, season, or year. She guessed that it might be 1910 or so; she gave her birthdate as 1905. Fund of information was limited. She was unable to state who the President or governor was. Mrs. K gave elaborate information concerning her birthplace and early upbringing in another state, but could not relate how she came to the state of her residence. She knew her daughters' names but not where they lived. Names and addresses were found in the contents of her purse. The client could not state her own address or telephone number; however, there were no indications of psychotic thinking, no delusions or hallucinations. Mrs. K gradually resented probing questions and eventually became angry, insisting she wasn't "crazy." Finally, she was unable to remember names, especially the clinician's name, for longer than 5 minutes or name five objects after 5 minutes. Neurological examination was otherwise unremarkable.

The situation was resolved with the appearance of Mrs. K's daughter who said that her mother had been placed in a nursing home that day. Her mother had stepped out the front door, apparently to get a breath of fresh air, forgot where she was, and wandered off. The client had lived for some 2 years by herself in the suburb of Colma, with frequent visits by her married daughters, who looked in on her at least once a day. When this elderly woman became too forgetful to live alone, she moved in with her youngest daughter who lived in

San Francisco. Her decline had been gradual and her memory failed her by degrees. At first, she would leave pots and kettles on the stove to burn; then, she would omit articles of apparel in dressing each morning; finally, she could not be left alone and needed constant supervision, because she would wander and get lost. The decision to place Mrs. K in a nursing facility was made after it became apparent that she could not tolerate the presence of her daughter's young children. Their playful antics and high jinks made her even more distracted than usual. Mrs. K remained in vigorous good health and had regular yearly medical checkups. She showed no sign of depression but only a growing intolerance of change and unexpected stimuli.

A recommendation was made to the daughter when she came to collect the client that her mother be provided with an identification bracelet, giving relevant information. The nursing home itself was unsure whether it would accept Mrs. K since constant 24-hour supervision was beyond its means.

SUMMARY

The task of the emergency clinician with regard to organic brain disorders is to determine the correct diagnosis and to institute proper treatment. Before emergency psychiatric treatment can proceed, medical clearance must be obtained.

A clinical history as thorough and accurate as possible is completed on the basis of a psychiatric interview by an experienced clinician. Neurological evaluation is necessary to detect acute or chronic conditions that may respond to emergency measures. Mental status examination is performed carefully for every client to distinguish functional from organic disorders. Laboratory and radiological studies should be ordered to determine the presence of toxic substances or trauma. Psychological testing is utilized to clarify the diagnosis and to assist treatment planning. Finally, nothing can replace the careful and detailed evaluation of a client by an experienced clinician.

BIBLIOGRAPHY

Anath, J.: Psych. J. U. Ottawa 4:256, 1979.

Arieti, S., editor: American handbook of psychiatry, pt. 8, Organic conditions, New York, 1959, Basic Books, Inc., Publishers.

Carroll, L.: Alice's adventures in Wonderland, New York, 1949, Harper & Brothers.

Chusid, J.G., and McDonald, J.J.: Trauma to the central nervous system. In McDonald, J.J., and Chusid, J.G., editors: Correlative neuroanatomy and functional neurology, ed. 12, Los Altos, Calif., 1964, Lange Medical Publications.

Costin, F., and Hermanson, C.: Organic brain syndromes in programmed learning aid for abnormal psychology, Homewood, Ill., 1976, Learning Systems Co.

Dementias arising in senium and presenium. In American Psychiatric Association Task Force on Nomenclature and Statistics, editors: Diagnostic and statistical manual of mental disorders, ed. 3, Washington, D.C., 1980, The Association.

Denny-Brown, D.: Handbook of neurological examination and case recording, rev. ed., Cambridge, Mass. 1954, Harvard University Press.

Freedman, A.M., and Kaplan, H.I., editors: Comprehensive textbook of psychiatry, Baltimore, 1967, The Williams & Wilkins Co.

Goodman, L.S., and Gilman, A. editors: Pharmacological basis of therapeutics, ed. 5, New York, 1975, Macmillan Publishing Co., Inc.

Haase, G.H.: Diseases presenting as dementia. In Wells, C., editor: Dementia, Contemporary neurology series, Philadelphia, 1970, F.A. Davis Co.

Harrison, T.R., editor: Harrison's principles of internal medicine, ed. 9, New York, 1980, McGraw-Hill Book Co.

Hutt, M.L.: Hutt's adaptation of the Bender Gestalt Test, ed. 3, New York, 1977, Grune & Stratton, Inc., p. 145.

Karp, H.: Dementia Drug Ther. 10:48, 1980.

Kolb, L.C.: Modern clinical psychiatry, ed. 9, Philadelphia, 1977, W.B. Saunders Co.

Organic mental disorders. In American Psychiatric Association Task Force on Nomenclature and statistics, editors: Diagnostic and statistical manual of mental disorders, ed. 3, Washington, D.C., 1980, The Association.

Pietrowski, Z.: Percept analysis: a fundamentally reworked, expanded, and systematized Rorschach method, New York, 1937, Macmillan Publishing Co.

Schaie, K.W.: In Birren, J.E., and Schaie, K.W., editors: Handbook of the psychology of aging, New York, 1977, Van Nostrand Reinhold Co.

Solomon, P., and Kleeman, S.T.: Organic psychoses. In Solomon, P., and Patch, V.D., editors: Handbook of psychiatry, ed. 3, Los Altos, Calif., 1974, Lange Medical Publications.

Sumner, A.C.: The psychology of aging. In Preparatory workshop for the national and state licensing examination in psychology, San Francisco, 1978, The Association for Advanced Training in the Behavioral Sciences.

Wirth, B., Carlson, B., and Santini, S.: Abnormal psychology. In Preparatory workshop for the national and state licensing examination in psychology, San Francisco, 1978, The Association for Advanced Training in the Behavioral Sciences.

CHAPTER 4

The client with a seizure disorder

Robert Hausner, M.D.

. . . I could not
Speak, and my eyes failed,
  I was neither
Living nor dead, and I knew
  nothing,
Looking into the heart of
light, the silence.
T.S. Eliot, *The Wasteland*

The awesomeness of the seizure, its disregard for time and the nuances of life surrounding it, provides the backdrop against which one must experience the disorder. Likewise, psychiatric emergency staff who treat people with seizures must deal with factors such as these in terms of both their effect on the client and their demand on treatment approaches. The seizure disorder itself may have organic *and* psychogenic components, the interweaving of the two being indistinguishably close at times. In the immediate sense, one may be confronted with the need to distinguish genuine seizure activity from hysterical phenomena or malingering; in a more general vein, one may question the etiology of seizure-related psychiatric phenomena and consider whether they are the result of organic cerebral dysfunction (brain) or of meanings superimposed on the seizures themselves (mind). An attempt will be made in this chapter to address some of these problems of the person with a seizure and to offer pragmatic and theoretical frameworks for treatment. This seems especially important since those working in psychiatric emergency units frequently are caught unprepared when a person has a seizure. The intent of this chapter is to assist the reader in identifying and treating seizures while also laying the groundwork for an understanding of their diverse etiologies.

FORMS OF EPILEPSY

Epileptic seizures may be thought of as the overt manifestations of underlying neurophysiological derangement; those for which a cause is unknown are termed *idiopathic* and represent a large portion of the total. In the disorder there is a sudden and excessive neuronal discharge involving either a limited group of neurons (for example, psychomotor seizures originating in or near the temporal lobe) or a more extensive network (such as grand mal seizures). Local seizures also may develop into more generalized forms, the focal abnormal discharge being propagated diffusely. The EEG is used to evaluate the electrical activity of the unstable neuronal population, with the EEG pattern varying in relation to the overall type and particular nature of the seizure itself. However, the general pattern is of so-called paroxysmal activity involving discharges of very high amplitude and waveforms such as spikes, slow waves and spikes, sharp waves, and so on. The amplitude of the paroxysmal activity tends to increase as the seizure progresses and the pool of abnormally firing neurons increases; as neuronal exhaustion sets in, the amplitude and frequency of the discharges decrease until clinical seizure activity ceases.

There are many varieties of epilepsy; the discussion here will be limited to the principal types with an emphasis on their relation to psychiatric phenomena. General treatment approaches appropriate to an emergency psychiatric setting will also be outlined. The terminology used in this chapter is in accordance with the recommendations of the International League Against Epilepsy (ILAE) with the more common nomenclature parenthetically noted (Gastaut, 1970).

Generalized tonic-clonic seizures (grand mal)

SIGNS AND SYMPTOMS. As with all generalized seizures, tonic-clonic (grand mal) seizures are bilaterally symmetrical and do not have focal onset. In some cases there may be premonitory symptoms, frequently involving dysphoric affective changes (for example, irritability, moodiness, overt despondency, apprehension) but occasionally manifesting as mild euphoria or even hypomania; difficulties with cognition may also be present, particularly regarding decision making, judgmental ability, and organization of thought. This period may last from hours to days and should be differentiated from the aura per se. The aura is actually a part of the seizure itself, generally lasting from several seconds to no longer than a few minutes. Depending on the type of aura, it may provide an indication of focal onset of seizure activity within the brain which then rapidly becomes generalized; thus auditory auras would raise the question of a possible posterior temporal focus (as this part of the cortex subserves hearing and language comprehension). Auras occur in only a portion of those suffering from generalized seizures, however, and apart from the rare individual who has continuous auras without the development of clinical seizures (Scott and Masland, 1953), differential diagnosis with regard to altered mental status during an aura usually presents no major problems. Indeed the clients frequently will volunteer that they feel a seizure is imminent.

As the name implies, this type of generalized seizure involves an initial period of tonic contraction of all voluntary muscles, coinciding with loss of consciousness. The tonic phase lasts for approximately 20 to 30 seconds, and is usually marked by apnea and cyanosis resulting from sustained contraction of the respiratory muscles; it is then succeeded by the clonic phase in which voluntary muscles contract and relax rhythmically. During this period, the clients frequently will bite their lips, tongue, or cheek because of jaw movements, be incontinent of urine as the bladder contracts, and exhibit autonomic irregularities (pupillary dilatation, diaphoresis, and so on). The clonic phase usually lasts less than 60 seconds but may be longer in some cases. Following cessation of seizure activity, there generally is a brief period of light coma (that is, persons breathe on their own but do not respond to deep painful stimuli) in which corneal reflexes are absent, pupils are dilated and sluggishly re-active to light, and extensor plantar reflexes (Babinski responses) are present. This immediate postictal (postseizure) period is followed by a variable length of time of up to several hours during which the person sleeps or is extremely lethargic. If forced to be awake, they usually will evidence disorientation (frequently extending to aspects of their own identity), attention diffi-culties, and general cognitive deficits. Headache and a sense of dullness usually accompany these symptoms and may last from several hours to several days. The person is amnestic for the sei-zure although the aura, if present, may be re-called. Very occasionally, transient violent be-havior may occur postictally as well as paranoid hallucinatory states that accompany the clouding of consciousness (Pond, 1957).

This description should be kept in mind when attempting a differential diagnosis of possible grand mal seizures. Conversion reactions or ma-lingering may produce pseudoseizures that ap-pear to mimic epileptic activity, but careful examination can usually differentiate organic from functional activity (see section on psychi-atric disorders and seizures). On the other hand, actual grand mal seizures are becoming increas-ingly familiar to those involved in psychiatric care as psychoactive drugs are being used more widely and tend, in general, to lower the seizure threshold (see section on epilepsy and psycho-tropic medications).

TREATMENT. One seizure by itself rarely is life threatening; however, certain guidelines that should be observed in emergency treatment of an isolated epileptic seizure are listed here.

1. Do *not* restrain movement.
2. Do *not* put anything between teeth (severe damage to teeth or gums may ensue).
3. Do *not* give anything to drink.
4. Loosen tight clothing during the seizure and protect the person's head with your hands.
5. After the seizure has subsided, turn the unconscious client on the side with the face gently turned downward to avoid aspiration of saliva or vomitus.
6. Remain with the person until consciousness is fully recovered and confusion clears.

If a second seizure occurs, immediate neuro-logic evaluation and treatment in a medical emergency department are necessary. Generally, seizures occur in an isolated fashion and are not dangerous, but continued seizure activity may indicate a variety of underlying disturbances (in-cluding a brain lesion, metabolic disorder, or head trauma). Intravenous medication, such as diazepam (Valium), is not required during an isolated seizure episode. Oral medication should be given after the seizure, and when the client is alert, only if immediately drawn anticonvul-sant levels are low or if a reliable history of omission of medication is obtained. However, acute repetitive seizures (in which consciousness is regained between the episodes) or status epi-lepticus (consciousness not regained) requires ag-gressive management with medication (see Bibli-ography). It should also be noted that a first seizure always necessitates a neurological work-up.

The maintenance treatment in this condition involves the usage of one or more anticonvul-sants on a regular, prophylactic basis. The most commonly employed medications are phenytoin (Dilantin), carbamazepine (Tegretol), and pheno-barbital. Low or excessively high serum concen-trations of anticonvulsants may not only be asso-ciated with increased seizure activity but also with development of psychological disturbance (see section on anticonvulsants and psychiatric complications). Table 4-1 presents a guide to

TABLE 4-1. Guide to anticonvulsant dosage and serum concentration

Anticonvulsant medication	Dosage range (usually in divided doses)	Serum concen-tration (thera-peutic range)
Carbamazepine (Tegretol)	600 to 1000 mg/day	4 to 12 μg/ml
Ethosuximide (Zarontin)	750 to 1000 mg/day	40 to 100 μg/ml
Phenobarbital	60 to 120 mg/day	15 to 45 μg/ml
Phenytoin (Dilantin)	300 to 400 mg/day	10 to 20 μg/ml
Primidone (Mysoline)	500 to 1000 mg/day	4 to 15 μg/ml

usual anticonvulsant dosage ranges and serum concentrations that may be of help in evaluating a client who is known to be taking medication for epilepsy.

Generalized absence seizures (petit mal, centrencephalic)

SIGNS AND SYMPTOMS. Generalized absence seizures are included here because the term *petit mal seizure* seems not infrequently to be applied incorrectly to a variety of minor seizures or to brief abortive grand mal seizures. It should be stressed that this form of epilepsy refers specifically to a clinical and electroencephalographically defined disorder in which there is a brief loss or alteration of consciousness (but with no falling), associated with generalized symmetrical 3 cycles per second (cps) spike-wave discharges on EEG. Hyperventilation may precipitate an attack. Disturbance of consciousness may last from 2 to 15 seconds; the usual clinical presentation involves staring or rhythmical eye blinking, although it has been observed that if the seizure lasts more than 10 or 12 seconds, automatisms such as lip smacking, chewing, or fumbling will almost invariably occur (Daly, 1977). The alteration in consciousness may be minimal or more profound, but on termination of the seizure the client immediately will resume prior activities, or experience only momentary confusion. There is usually a varying degree of amnesia for events occurring during the seizure, with dissociative phenomena (Gastaut, 1954) and the above-mentioned automatisms not that uncommon (Penry and Dreifuss, 1969). These features may present difficulties in clinically differentiating absence from psychomotor seizures (see later), such that the EEG is necessary for diagnosis. This type of epilepsy almost always begins in childhood and rarely extends beyond late adolescence; if facets of the picture just described appear clinically in an adult, then the diagnosis of true petit mal epilepsy would be seriously in question.

TREATMENT. Ethosuximide (Zarontin) is generally the drug of choice, because of its relatively low incidence of side effects compared to the other available drugs.

Case vignette #1

A 17-year-old white man reported with a several-day history of increasing agitation, decreased attention span with poor concentration, and inappropriateness of affect. He had intermittently been a behavior problem in school, but over the past week his teacher noted a drastic reduction in skills and motivation. A diagnosis of petit mal epilepsy had been made years ago, for which he was being treated with ethosuximide in combination with diazepam. In view of the seizure history and relatively rapid onset of the initial symptoms, an EEG was performed and revealed nearly continual 3 cps symmetrical spike waves. He was immediately hospitalized for petit mal status, and with adjustment of medication over the next 2 weeks, he resumed his former level of functioning.

Partial seizures with complex symptomatology (temporal lobe, psychomotor)

Complex partial seizures present difficulties not only for the neurologist but also for the psychiatrist and other health care professionals. Psychomotor epilepsy is generally more difficult to treat than many of the other types, and subtle factors may need to be inquired about and considered in order to make an initial diagnosis. The seizure itself may consist of subtle alterations of consciousness that could easily be construed and treated as a functional disorder. Additionally, brief psychoses or confusional states or both may occur postictally (Stevens, 1975; Pond, 1957), conditions which a psychiatric professional may be called on to diagnose and treat. In the following discussion the author will address the psychomotor seizure itself, with particular reference to sensory and cognitive manifestations. As the formal designation indicates, such a seizure may be quite complex in its initial symptomatology, comprising a cutting edge of neurological-psychiatric disturbance. In the section on psychiatric disorders and seizures, further attention will be focused on the controversy over thought and behavioral disturbances in psychomotor epilepsy.

SIGNS AND SYMPTOMS. Complex partial seizures encompass an extremely diverse group but share the common experience of an altered *content* of consciousness which may proceed to an altered *level* of consciousness; regardless of the intensity or complexity of the experience, however, it tends to remain ego-alien (Daly, 1975). In accord with the ILAE nomenclature, various subtypes based on symptomatology may be encountered. They are classified as (1) psychosensory, (2) psychomotor, (3) cognitive, and (4) affective subtypes.

1. *Psychosensory.* The psychosensory grouping is defined by the presence of hallucinations or illusions or both. Unlike those which the schizophrenic usually relates (and which drug-induced or hysterical states may simulate), visual hallucinations are quite frequent and may vary from simple phenomena such as flickering lights and balls of color to more complex ones involving a detailed sequence of events. Auditory hallucinations may also occur, although they usually will consist of simple noises; occasionally, one or more sentences may be heard (sometimes repetitively), but the affective component so often seen in a psychosis tends to be absent or relatively insignificant (Goldensohn, 1975). This is particularly true if the hallucination recurs with regularity, so that there is an objectifying of whatever fear or anxiety may initially have been associated with it. Other types of hallucinations may occur as well, the most common being olfactory (uncinate fits); when present, they usually occur toward the beginning of the seizure. Unpleasant odors predominate, which may be unidentifiable or not uncommonly described as "something burning."

Illusions also are recounted frequently, involving any sensory modality. Sounds may become distorted, for example, but again generally without the affective elaboration that might be seen in the paranoid psychoses. The size or form of objects may appear altered and parts of one's own body may seem different, which is perhaps another aspect of the depersonalization discussed later. It should be kept in mind that hysteria may also occur with such altered perceptions.

Case vignette #2

A 19-year-old man was initially brought by his parents to see a psychiatrist because of vaguely related periods of feeling "strange." This was sometimes accompanied by visual hallucinations consisting of a witchlike figure in black who always approached him from the left side. He felt fearful, controlled by her, and unable to move. After hovering nearby, she would then disappear. This was perceived by him as real, although he was disturbed by the incongruity of his not believing in witches. The presence of visual hallucinations with unilateral predominance prompted a neurological evaluation, which revealed right anterior temporal paroxysmal discharges on the EEG. Treatment with anticonvulsant medication essentially abolished the EEG spiking and the hallucinations.

2. *Psychomotor.* The psychomotor grouping comprises the automatisms that are so often encountered in complex partial seizures. Classification varies widely, but all automatisms entail a temporary state in which response to external stimuli is impaired, more or less unconscious "automatic" behavior is manifest, and amnesia for the episode is present. The automatisms may appear differently, not only between individuals but also in the same individual under different circumstances. The automatic behavior itself involves repetitive actions that are generally inappropriate to the situation (but may or may not be recognized as such by an observer). Frequently, vegetative or oral phenomena are noted, such as lip smacking, swallowing, chewing movements, and gagging. Additionally, pseudopurposeful gestures may be repeated, such as buttoning or unbuttoning clothing, counting change, or stepping up and down. Verbal equivalents may also be seen, with perseveration of a word or phrase. More complex acts or portions of acts may less commonly be carried out: for example, successfully using various means of transportation or engaging in detailed work activities. States equivalent symptomatically to hysterical dissociative conditions may also occur in which one may wander or travel for a variable period of

time, only to regain full consciousness in a strange environment. Some of this behavior may be due to amnesia for postictal activity rather than to the automatism per se. In such instances, differentiation from hysterical phenomena may be difficult, with the EEG and careful observation over a period of time being necessary for diagnosis.

Automatisms are not diagnostic of complex partial seizures, as emphasized earlier in the discussion of petit mal epilepsy; it may be, as suggested by Penry and Dreifuss (1969), that discharges involving various parts of the limbic system are an underlying mechanism for their occurrence, and may thus be associated with different symptomatic seizure types. It may also be noted that violent behavior during the attack is rare, with most combative behavior resulting from an attempt to restrain or prevent expression of the automatism; hence, if no one is endangered by the nature of the automatic behavior itself, it is best to let the seizure continue unhindered (see Chapter 10 for management of assaultive behavior). Following the automatism there may be amnesia, not only for the events during the episode but also for a brief period postictally during which the person appears to be thinking and acting appropriately. Transient postictal depression has additionally been described (Pincus and Tucker, 1974), although its prevalence is subject to debate. It may last up to several hours and occasionally several days, but no specific intervention is indicated unless suicidal impulses are present (which is very uncommon).

3. *Cognitive.* The cognitive grouping also is extremely varied, with cognition loosely used to convey a disturbance of the content of consciousness, particularly of thought but also of more subtle and complex perceptions. Aspects of this cognitive alteration have been called the "dreamy state" (Jackson, 1931) and involve a complex of thoughts and feelings that intrude on consciousness and may produce either confusion or a subjectively coherent state that to the observer tends to appear as confused or inappropriate. The client may experience phenomena such as *déjà vu* (the unfamiliar seeming familiar) or *jamais vu* (the familiar seeming unfamiliar). Although the former is uncommonly seen in psy-

chiatric emergency settings, the latter might be encountered in hysteria, dementia, or even pseudodementia, so that other facets of the client's condition must be considered in using this as a diagnostic sign. Very commonly, the "sense of reality" is disturbed: A client may experience self, others, or parts of the environment as "strange" although recognizable; a sense of detachment and of the world's seeming awry is prominent. This syndrome of depersonalization is, of course, encountered in various psychiatric conditions, including acute anxiety states, depression, schizophrenia (particularly "first-break" or early stages of decompensation), and drug-induced states. Again, a differential feature in this type of epilepsy is the relative moderation of anxiety, whereas significant secondary anxiety is generally associated with depersonalization in the strictly psychiatric disorders. Furthermore, following the episode of depersonalization (which occurs episodically and provides another cue in diagnosis), there may be partial amnesia for the event, not commonly elicited in the other disorders.

4. *Affective.* Emotional concomitants are a cardinal feature of complex partial seizures, especially the feeling of fear or terror. This is often associated with autonomic signs such as pupillary dilatation, tachycardia, pallor, or flushing and with visceral feelings (perhaps described as gastric distress or "a knot in my stomach"). Although pleasant effects may occur ictally, the vast majority are unpleasant and may be a specifically related or ineffable dysphoria. Ictal and peri-ictal depression have also been reported (Williams, 1956), with the affective state sometimes beginning even before the seizure or at its onset and occasionally persisting for up to several days thereafter. In most cases, the seizure itself lasts no longer than several minutes; the sudden development of affective change, confusion following expression of affect, and some degree of amnesia for the experience all should predispose one to consider temporal lobe epilepsy as a cause. Diagnostic points are that hypoglycemia can produce a similar picture (Dreifuss, 1975) and that reactive hypoglycemia may be seen in alcoholics who are admitted to psychiatric emergency departments. As with all findings, this must be

evaluated in the context of the client's general presentation. In some cases there may be a pronounced affective elaboration of an epileptic hallucinatory experience (see case vignette #2), but in the recounting of whatever is recalled, there is usually much less affective involvement than in the psychoses.

Case vignette #3

A 33-year-old woman was brought to a psychiatric emergency unit by her husband after she was noted to be acting bizarrely (verbalizing out of character, crawling on the floor, openly masturbating, and being encopretic). On examination she was extremely loose in associations, agitated, affectively labile, sexually preoccupied and inappropriate, and engaged in fecal smearing (although able to respond appropriately to some concrete questions and oriented to place and day). There was no prior psychiatric or seizure history, but she was being treated for multiple sclerosis with prednisone 40 mg every day over several months. No antipsychotics were given, and several hours after psychiatric admission her agitation and inappropriate behavior ceased, with no evidence of a thought disorder. She then recounted that she had been walking when her head "began to spin" and she felt strange; she then went to her husband's house where she recalled "losing her bowels," which surprised her in retrospect. She also recalled that her husband appeared to get progressively smaller and that the exterior of the psychiatric emergency unit looked "big and blue." She did not remember any details of the emergency unit stay or of her transfer to the hospital. Prednisone was continued without recurrence of psychosis, but the EEG revealed left temporal paroxysmal activity, and CT scan showed a large left parietooccipital arteriovenous malformation.

This client evidenced a mixed type of complex partial seizure: cognitive elements were present (for example, her subjective apperceptive changes) as well as the sensory components involving visual illusions. The postictal state probably occurred while in the emergency unit, in which there was amnesia and which involved a psychosis that to the psychiatric clinician might be indistinguishable from a functional or drug-induced psychosis. The negative psychiatric history should raise suspicions regarding etiology, although the client's rapid recovery and recounting of events (with EEG findings) were necessary to diagnose ictal and postictal psychosis rather than a steroid-induced condition.

Different types of complex partial seizures may occur in combination with one another as in the case just cited, but on the whole are seen less frequently than petit mal seizures, and "psychomotor status" is considered quite rare in contrast to petit mal status. What have been considered cases of "psychomotor status" were probably petit mal in character (Andermann and Robb, 1972; see case vignette #1). The EEG during a psychomotor seizure frequently reveals paroxysmal activity over one or both temporal lobes (especially anteriorly), although discharges within portions of the limbic system and inferior frontal lobe may also give rise to complex partial seizures. In such cases, or in those in which psychomotor epilepsy is suspected but the interictal EEG is normal (representing a significant proportion of clients), special EEG techniques may need to be requested. These might include a sleep EEG or a sleep-deprivation EEG, both of which conditions may facilitate seizure discharge, as well as placement of specific recording electrodes such as nasopharyngeal, sphenoidal, or tympanic leads.

In summary, there are certain salient clinical features of psychomotor epilepsy which help differentiate it from a psychiatric disorder: (1) History or observation of *stereotyped* behavior or subjective experience. The behavior frequently will be pseudopurposeful. (2) The presence of *brief, episodic* abnormalities, usually separated by periods of "normal" functioning. (3) Partial or total *amnesia* for the episode, with attendant *confusion* (altered sensorium) both during the seizure and afterward. (4) The presence of *fear* or terror during a seizure, including a high association with *visceral* sensations. (5) A general *ego-alien* quality to the seizure experience, with some degree of *objectification* and affective distancing subsequently.

   TREATMENT. Both primidone (Mysoline) and carbamazepine (Tegretol) are widely used as first-line drugs for psychomotor epilepsy. Phenytoin (Dilantin) has also been employed successfully. As noted earlier, this type of seizure is generally more difficult to control, and it is not unusual for an individual to be taking more than one anticonvulsant. This may create its own problems, particularly in terms of an altered mental status (see section on anticonvulsants and psychiatric complications).

NEUROPSYCHIATRIC DISORDERS ASSOCIATED WITH SEIZURES

   Since a seizure disorder is a symptom complex and not a disease entity per se, a spectrum of causes needs to be considered in the evaluation of seizures of unknown etiology; those that might more commonly be encountered in an emergency psychiatric setting are listed in the following outline.

   I. Local causes of epilepsy
      A. Head trauma
         1. Penetrating
         2. Nonpenetrating
      B. Cerebral infection
         1. Meningitis
         2. Encephalitis
         3. Abscess (viral, fungal, bacterial)
         4. Neurosyphilis
      C. Vascular disease
         1. Cerebral infarction (stroke)
         2. Embolic phenomena
         3. Arteriovenous malformation
         4. Hypertensive encephalopathy
         5. Intracerebral hemorrhage
      D. Neoplastic disease
         1. Primary
         2. Metastatic tumors of the central nervous system
      E. Developmental disorders
         1. Sturge-Weber
         2. Tuberous sclerosis
   II. Systemic causes of epilepsy
      A. Metabolic-nutritional states
         1. Hypoglycemia
         2. Hypocalcemia
         3. Hypomagnesemia
         4. Alcoholism
         5. Renal failure
         6. Pathological water intoxication with hyponatremia
      B. Anoxic conditions
         1. Postcardiorespiratory arrest
         2. Cerebral palsy
      C. Degenerative disorders
         1. Huntington's chorea
         2. Presenile and senile dementia (Alzheimer's disease)
      D. Toxic states
         1. Lead encephalopathy
         2. Intoxication with or reaction to corticosteroids, penicillin, caffeine, anticonvulsants
      E. Psychotropic administration
         1. Neuroleptics
         2. Tricyclic antidepressants
         3. Lithium
      F. Drug-induced states
         1. Phencyclidine (PCP)
         2. Amphetamine and related compounds
      G. Miscellaneous
         1. Lupus erythematosis
         2. Multiple sclerosis, withdrawal syndromes
   III. Unknown cause—"idiopathic epilepsy"

Several of the known etiologies interrelate so that it may be difficult to evaluate the cause of the seizure immediately. In the psychiatric emergency unit, clients with the following conditions are not infrequently evaluated, and seizures may develop during this time.

   ALCOHOLISM. Although the ability of alcohol itself to lower the seizure threshold is in dispute, it is clear that too rapid withdrawal of alcohol after chronic usage may produce alcohol withdrawal seizures ("rum fits"). This may be seen as an element in either the full-blown or partial clinical picture of delirium tremens but is noteworthy in that the seizure *nearly always* precedes the onset of delirium (Victor and Adams, 1953), that is, occurs before "classical" delirium tremens. The development of grand mal convulsions in a client with subjective or objective tremulousness and hallucinations would immediately suggest a diagnosis of early alcohol withdrawal syndrome and require emergency treatment in a medical department. The visual hallucinations that predominate in delirium tremens should, of course, alert one to a possible toxic state, although pure auditory hallucinations may occur in both delirium tremens and the alcoholic hallucinoses (Victor and Hope, 1958). In the latter, however, seizures are considered rare.

Unlike people with idiopathic epilepsy, the EEG in those with alcoholic epilepsy is usually normal except for transient paroxysmal activity during withdrawal (Victor, 1968). It might be noted that in chronic alcoholics, focal EEG abnormalities may nonetheless be present (probably resulting chiefly from increased incidence of falls with head trauma) and that seizures may occur independent of withdrawal and even be focal.

POSTTRAUMATIC CONDITIONS. Trauma is a common cause of epilepsy in 20- to 40-year-olds. The seizures may start almost immediately after the trauma or up to several years thereafter; it is not uncommon for the seizures to be part of a "postconcussive syndrome" in which the client had a previous head injury (with or without loss of consciousness) and is now experiencing facets of an organic brain syndrome. Impairment of memory is prominent, especially recall and recent memory, with attention deficits and personality change possibly associated as well. Treatment with anticonvulsants is usually necessary once a thorough neurological evaluation has ruled out a space-occupying lesion. It should be stressed that any focal seizure suggests a focal cerebral lesion, be it traumatic, neoplastic, vascular, or other, and requires an extensive diagnostic program beyond clinical examination per se.

WITHDRAWAL SYNDROMES. Withdrawal states are increasingly seen within emergency psychiatric departments. The most common withdrawal syndromes with seizure activity, aside from those that are alcohol related, involve barbiturates or the benzodiazepines (Valium, Librium, Serax, and so on). In either case the clinical findings are similar: mild withdrawal may be associated with headache, dysphoria, insomnia, anorexia, generalized anxiety or weakness, diaphoresis, and dizziness; in more severe withdrawal, orthostatic hypotension, tremor, agitation, hyperthermia, confusion, and delirium may develop. Psychotic states may also be encountered, particularly of the paranoid type, with visual but also auditory hallucinations included. This clinical picture holds true for both the barbiturates and the benzodiazepines, with grand mal seizures usually occurring in only the moderate-to-severe withdrawal states. It has been reported that about 75% of barbiturate users regularly taking 800 mg or more per day will experience convulsions on abrupt withdrawal (Isbell and White, 1953). It should be noted that the principal clinical difference between withdrawal from barbiturates and benzodiazepines is that symptoms in the latter tend to occur a minimum of several days following withdrawal, probably because of the long half-life of diazepam (Valium) and chlordiazepoxide (Librium) or their metabolites (Editorial, Lancet, 1979). Some of the less-prescribed benzodiazepines with a shorter half-life, such as oxazepam (Serax) or lorazepam (Ativan), may be associated with earlier onset of seizures. Treatment in any case is directed toward the establishment of a controlled withdrawal regimen, the scope of which is beyond the present discussion (see Bibliography).

TOXIC CONDITIONS. Psychiatric professionals working within emergency departments may be expected to encounter seizures as a manifestation of toxicity from illicit or "street" drugs; the convulsions are not due to withdrawal but rather to a direct drug effect. The most commonly implicated drugs are phencyclidine (PCP) and amphetamines or amphetamine-like substances such as methylphenidate (Ritalin).

Phencyclidine. Phencyclidine is known by a variety of names, including "angel dust," "crystal" or "China crystal," and "hog," with associated protean clinical presentations. Seizures may not be that infrequent even though they tend to occur with severe intoxication, since "street" dosages are so unreliable. If a history of PCP ingestion, injection, or inhalation is obtained and seizures are noted, the client should immediately be treated in the medical emergency department according to a specific protocol (Goldfrank and Osborn, 1978). In this case the use of an anticonvulsant would not be recommended, as drug side effects and interaction could further confuse serial clinical assessment.

Amphetamine. Intoxication with amphetamines or related compounds may also be associated with seizure activity. Amphetamine psychosis is a well-recognized entity, usually involving pronounced paranoid ideation and delusions with or without visual-auditory hallucinations. In addition to convulsions, there is generally a variety of other physical findings as well, which may be subsumed under the term "hypermetabolic state," for example, tachycardia, marked hypertension, excessive gastrointestinal activity, and fever (Connell, 1968). In such cases, care must be taken in treating the psychosis to ensure that the seizure condition is not exacerbated: chlorpromazine and certain other antipsychotics are known to lower the seizure threshold (see section on epilepsy and psychotropic medications) and chlorpromazine itself also has been found to increase significantly the half-life of amphetamine, particularly as compared with haloperidol (Lemberger et al., 1970). It thus seems advisable to treat acute amphetamine psychosis with seizures by means of haloperidol intramuscularly or orally (5 to 10 mg every 1 to 2 hours as needed); even if seizures have not occurred, it seems prudent to treat amphetamine psychosis with haloperidol if only as a precautionary measure: it is also among the most potent and specific agents for dopamine antagonism (Creese et al., 1975), which is felt to be the principal therapeutic mechanism in amphetamine psychosis. As with PCP intoxication, treatment of the underlying condition is the primary task unless the seizures become repetitive or status epilepticus develops. It should be stressed that altered mental status during the postictal period may confound diagnosis and proper treatment, so that in some instances careful longitudinal observation is essential.

PSYCHIATRIC DISORDERS AND SEIZURES

There are several psychiatric illnesses that are intimately involved with epilepsy from a histori-

cal, theoretical, and therapeutic perspective. Overall, epileptic persons as a group appear to have a greater incidence of associated psychiatric difficulties than the general population (Small et al., 1962). Moreover, it is commonly noted that psychomotor epileptic clients manifest a greater incidence of psychiatric disturbance than other types, although some investigators do not agree (Standage, 1973) or suggest the association may not be caused by the temporal localization itself. Mental disturbance has also been demonstrated to be a psychosocial effect of the epilepsy, particularly in the psychomotor type (Horowitz, 1970). Certain facets of these problems will be presented in the following sections and are intended as a guide to the more pertinent issues, particularly those which may confront the psychiatric emergency clinician (see Bibliography).

Schizophrenia

Although antagonism of schizophrenia and epilepsy was postulated earlier and served as one of the rationales for electroconvulsive therapy of schizophrenic symptomatology, the syndrome of schizophreniform psychosis of epilepsy is by now well established (Slater et al., 1963), with a thorough review of the literature concluding that schizophrenia-like psychosis is greater in epileptic persons than would be expected by chance (Davison and Bagley, 1969). As the epilepsy generally, although not exclusively, precedes the emergence of the schizophrenic syndrome, it has been proposed that the psychosis is etiologically related to the seizures themselves, either as the result of abnormal discharges in the temporal lobe – limbic system (Landolt, 1958; Symonds, 1962) or of incorporation of the effects of repeated clouding of consciousness into one's perception of reality (Pond, 1962). Nonetheless, schizophreniform psychoses of epilepsy appear predominantly in the psychomotor form (Bartlett, 1957; Rodin et al., 1957; Slater et al., 1963; Flor-Henry, 1969).

It should be obvious from the foregoing that this area is somewhat controversial and understandably complex in view of the multifaceted nature of both the schizophrenic syndrome and the epilepsies. In any case the conditions under which an individual may be seen for emergency psychiatric care are also those associated with emergence of psychosis and increased seizure frequency: that is, intrapsychic "stress" is correlated with both of these factors, so that presentation within the emergency department will frequently involve a history of recently increased seizures as well as the presence of more pronounced schizophrenic symptomatology. The mechanism by which emotional stress lowers seizure threshold is unclear but repeatedly observed. The following illustrates some of the difficulties that may be encountered with such a client:

Case vignette #4

A 28-year-old woman with a history of epilepsy and paranoid schizophrenia came to a psychiatric emergency unit because of progressive intrusiveness of primitive "torturing" auditory hallucinations (mental status examination additionally revealed paranoid ideation and thought-blocking, with flat affect). Her brother, with whom she had her only close relationship, had died within the past year, and 6 months previously she felt it necessary to drop out of school because of exacerbation of her epilepsy; she had been transferred to a psychiatric emergency unit after having been treated for a seizure. Psychotropic medications had not been taken for 1½ years, but her anticonvulsant regimen included phenytoin, phenobarbital, and methsuximide (Celontin), a drug for absence seizures. She returned to the psychiatric emergency unit several times, once brought by ambulance because of a reported seizure that caused her to miss an earlier scheduled session. She was treated with an antipsychotic, which she had initially requested, but responded with anger and noncompliance when she read that it lowered seizure threshold.

This client's seizures and thought disorder not only were exacerbated simultaneously but also presented the psychiatric staff with multiple diagnostic and treatment difficulties. Were all the reported seizures genuine or were "hysterical seizures" also occurring? To what extent would a therapeutic working-through of the brother's death ameliorate the psychosis and the epilepsy? Were the anticonvulsants being taken as prescribed, with corresponding therapeutic serum levels (Table 4-1), or were these being neglected as yet another manifestation of the intrapsychic conflict she was experiencing? And last, what antipsychotic, if any, is the drug of choice for an individual with both epilepsy and schizophreniform psychosis? (See section on epilepsy and psychotropic medications.)

Although case vignette #4 illustrates some association between the two syndromes, it should be emphasized that such an association is not universally accepted. As mentioned earlier, an antagonism between schizophrenia and epilepsy has also been posited; indeed, it is not uncommon for schizophreniform symptomatology to worsen when the seizure disorder is brought under control, and conversely, spontaneously occurring seizures in a schizophrenic individual may be followed by amelioration of psychosis. This finds expression in the hypothesis of Landolt (1958) that "forced normalization" of the EEG (as an aim of anticonvulsant therapy) is related to the development of psychotic episodes. Even if such a phenomenon were to occur occasionally, however, it would not necessarily invalidate the association between schizophreniform psychosis and epilepsy but merely reflect certain conditions under which the psychosis might become evident in an individual with seizures.

Pseudoepileptic conversion reaction

As Rangell (1959) has noted, conversion reactions may occur across the spectrum of psychopathology (and not merely in the hysterical personality), such that an absence of hysterical personality traits should not lead one to rule out pseudoseizures; conversely, hysterical traits in a person with reported seizures might raise the index of suspicion regarding pseudoseizures but should not hinder proper evaluation for seizures of organic origin. Pseudoepilepsy may be mistaken for genuine grand mal or complex partial epilepsy, although mimicking of the grand mal type is much more common. These pseudoseizures, or what Charcot (1881) referred to as hysteroepilepsy and what are frequently termed hysterical seizures, are not that uncommon and may indeed be confused with actual convulsive activity. In a significant number of cases, the person may have a genuine seizure disorder with interspersed pseudoseizures; one would be tempted to consider this a form of "somatic compliance" (Fenichel, 1945), in which a degree of familiarity with an altered state of consciousness may tend to promote its unconscious replication if intrapsychic conflict is present. As might be expected, differentiation between organic and functional seizures may be difficult at times, but certain guidelines should prove useful (Table 4-2).

To all intents and purposes, pseudoseizures involve abnormal motor activity that is an attempt to mimic the movements of grand mal epilepsy; to those familiar with genuine seizures, the movements of pseudoseizures seem generally nonrhythmical and clumsy, although Silverstein (1976) makes the point that health professionals and those involved with clinical medicine or epileptic family members may exhibit pseudoseizures that are more convincing.

For pseudoepilepsy to be considered strictly as a conversion reaction, there must be an unconscious symbolic conflict that is being expressed through somatic channels, although secondary gain may be more apparent. At times the conflict may be difficult to ascertain, and questions of malingering might arise. In any case, an EEG ultimately may be necessary to help rule out a seizure disorder if clinical examination provides insufficient basis for diagnosis; if an EEG cannot be obtained during the seizure itself (for example, by telemetry), an immediate postictal EEG should be ordered.

Case vignette #5

A 25-year-old man was seen in the emergency department and admitted to the medical unit with a history of an auto accident 3 days previously and reportedly six "blackout spells" subsequently. He was observed to have what appeared to be three grand mal seizures in the emergency room, which he stated were preceded by "strange tastes and smells." There was no known prior history of seizures or drug abuse, and he was taking no medications. Anger and uncooperativeness were initially noted, and the remainder of the mental status exam-

TABLE 4-2. Differential diagnosis of epilepsy and pseudoepilepsy

Epilepsy	*Pseudoepilepsy*
Seizures occur independently of others' presence	Episodes tend to occur in presence of others
Evidence of trauma from past or present seizure (for example, tongue or mucosal lacerations, scalp hematomas)	Conspicuous absence of lesions
Frequent urinary incontinence	Rare urinary incontinence
Usually tonic phase followed by clonic activity (rhythmical, nonpurposeful)	Frequently no tonic phase; "clonic" with nonrhythmical, perhaps even purposeful, movement)
Pupils dilated and fixed during an attack with no response to threat visually; corneal reflex absent	Pupils reactive to light and threat during an attack; corneal reflex present
Eyelids may be passively opened during seizure	Eyelids may *resist* being opened
Muscle tone absent immediately postictal	Muscle tone present (for example, arm may avoid head if dropped onto face)
Pathological reflexes may develop (for example, Babinski's, Hoffmann's)	Pathological reflexes absent
Deep painful stimuli or forced change of position does not disrupt course of seizure	Deep painful stimuli or forced change of position may abort "seizure"
Amnesia for episode (except perhaps the aura) is complete	Recollection of all or part of seizure (including movements) may be present
Postictal confusion, headache, and lethargy are notable	Postictal state is often rapidly alert without significant confusion or headache

ination was normal except for the man's erratic shifting from lethargic to alert levels of consciousness. Neurological examination revealed questionable central weakness of the right face and difficulty moving the right arm; there were no other abnormal findings. After admission, a number of seizurelike attacks were witnessed (with more than eight occurring over several hours). There was never cyanosis, urinary incontinence, or tongue biting, and the postictal state was invariably alert within several seconds. Pathological reflexes could not be elicited either during or after an attack. An immediate postictal "hand drop" test was performed eventually in which the client's arm, when held above his head and then released, never struck his face. A postictal EEG was normal and CT scan unremarkable. The diagnosis of pseudoseizures was made in accord with these findings; the client signed out against medical advice before further evaluation could be completed.

The preceding case illustrates some of the difficulties inherent in distinguishing genuine seizure activity from pseudoseizures and some of the means by which they may be differentiated. This client was seen in emergency psychiatric consultation before discharge, and although exhibitionism, impulsivity, and pronounced pseudomasculinity were noted—some of the hallmarks of the male hysterical personality (Blacker and Tupin, 1977), it was nonetheless impossible to diagnose the pseudoseizures definitely either as an hysterical conversion reaction or malingering. Such a task is probably most suitable for those engaged in ongoing psychotherapy with the client, whereas the emergency psychiatric clinician must concentrate on determining whether seizures are genuine or not (see Bibliography).

Behavioral syndrome of epilepsy

Behavioral syndrome of epilepsy represents an extremely controversial area, involving the attribution of various so-called personality traits to epileptic individuals. These personality traits are felt to be interictal (present in between and independently of overt seizure activity). The clinical picture is referred to most often in temporal lobe epileptic persons; it has even been reported that a diagnosis of complex partial seizures was made in several clients on the basis of specific personality changes and confirmed by subsequent EEGs (Waxman and Geschwind, 1975).

Numerous character traits have been assigned to epileptic persons over the years. It has been pointed out (Feldman, 1977) that these traits may be observed in nonepileptic persons as well, and that some of them may be mutually contradictory (for example, shyness-isolativeness and impulsivity-aggression). Nonetheless, a recent body of literature has attempted to delineate a personality profile peculiar to temporal lobe epileptic individuals, with the syndrome consisting of the following: (1) overconcern with religious, philosophical, or moral issues; (2) diminished libido (hyposexuality); (3) a tendency toward prolific and highly detailed writing (hypergraphia); and (4) pronounced "temper" and irritability (Bear, 1977; Bear and Fedio, 1977; Geschwind, 1979). These investigators and others feel that such a pattern is seen in a substantial number of those with temporal lobe epilepsy, although it must be stressed that no systematic study has been able to indicate clearly that temporal lobe epileptic clients exhibit different interictal behavior than other types of epileptics. Indeed, there may be a host of variables involved in the development of personality traits in any given epileptic individual, including untoward effects of anticonvulsants, degree of seizure control, familial and developmental factors, and psychosocial effect of the epilepsy. Some of these caveats are addressed to an extent by the previously cited investigators, and Geschwind (1979) makes a point of terming these traits a "syndrome" and not a "disorder" for which psychiatric attention is necessarily indicated. Indeed, treatment of the "syndrome" with antipsychotic medications has met with disappointing results. Geschwind postulates that a spike focus discharging intermittently into limbic structures (and thus altering emotionality) is probably responsible for the clinically observed pattern. Such an approach may indeed be valid in some instances, but the humorless sobriety, obsessionalism, and dependence noted by Bear and Fedio (1977) in their series of temporal lobe epileptics may just as well be understood as defensive maneuvers unconsciously adopted to cope with the loss of control and secondary shame attendant on a seizure. Although an elaboration of these concepts is beyond the scope of this presentation, the correlation of character structure with seizure disorders remains heuristically valuable and clinically engaging (see Bibliography).

As a final note, it should be added that the personality changes described must be considered separately from the intellectual deterioration that has been well documented in chronic epileptic clients (Rodin, 1968; Tarter, 1972). Higher order cognitive functions, memory, computation, and attention may be variably impaired, particularly in those with major seizures (grand mal or psychomotor) that have early onset, long duration, and relatively poor control. These deficits may be encountered in the psychiatric emergency setting, in which case a thorough mental status examination needs to be performed to determine the extent of impairment and whether particular aspects of it (for example, disorientation) may be indicative of more acute factors such as a postictal state or head trauma.

EPILEPSY AND PSYCHOTROPIC MEDICATIONS

As the number and type of psychotropic drugs increases, their relationship to epilepsy becomes more complex, so that the clinician may be confronted with a disturbing array of side effects, drug interactions, absolute and relative contraindications, and even contradictory theoretical guidelines for treatment of a client with seizures. An attempt will be made in this section to provide brief overviews of the major psychotropic drugs and their relationship to epilepsy; when appropriate, therapeutic guidelines or recommendations will be included.

Antipsychotic (neuroleptic) medications

It is well known that antipsychotic medication, when given to an individual with epilepsy,

may lower the seizure threshold and precipitate overt convulsive activity. Although seizures have been noted to occur in less than 1% of clients taking phenothiazines (Logothetis, 1967), it is generally believed that those with a prior history of epilepsy are at greater risk for developing seizures when placed on an antipsychotic. It has been suggested that the more sedating neuroleptics such as chlorpromazine (Thorazine) and thioridazine (Mellaril) are the worse offenders, whereas the more "activating" antipsychotics, for example, trifluoperazine (Stelazine) or fluphenazine (Prolixin), present fewer problems in this regard (Itil and Wadud, 1975). Such a division appears experimentally unvalidated, however, in that systematic studies in humans of epileptogenic effects of high versus low potency and sedating versus nonsedating antipsychotics have, to my knowledge, not been conducted. Nonetheless, there is significant evidence that chlorpromazine does lower the seizure threshold more than other neuroleptics (Schlichther et al., 1956; Tedeschi et al., 1958) and should consequently be *used with caution* in a client with epilepsy or in one susceptible to seizures. The usage of thioridazine is less straightforward: although it is a low-potency antipsychotic with marked sedative effects largely caused by its pronounced anticholinergic activity, it does not seem to be associated with an increased frequency of seizures in epileptic clients (Kamm and Mandel, 1967) and has been advocated for treatment of psychosis in certain cases of epilepsy on the basis of an anticonvulsant effect of acetylcholine blockade (Remick and Fine, 1979). The greatest drawback for its use concerns decreased gastric motility because of the anticholinergic activity, and hence the effect on anticonvulsant absorption. An increased total amount of anticonvulsant may be absorbed after thioridazine is begun, with peak concentration of the anticonvulsant either reduced or delayed (Shader, 1980). This may significantly affect stabilization of an anticonvulsant regimen and should be considered if thioridazine is being contemplated for use in a client with seizures.

Although all the antipsychotics might be associated with an epileptogenic effect, there is some evidence that haloperidol may be the safest to use on theoretical grounds. Aside from its being relatively nonsedating, it has been found to exhibit GABA-like (gamma-aminobutyric acid) effects within the central nervous system (Collins, 1973; Maruyama and Kawasaki, 1975), and increased GABA activity at specific nerve terminals has been positively correlated with an anticonvulsant effect (Gale and Iadarola, 1980). Valproic acid (Depakene), an anticonvulsant medication, is believed to exert its effect by increasing GABA levels in the brain, so that the ability of haloperidol to do the same may in fact provide some seizure protection for a person with both psychosis and epilepsy. Haloperidol has indeed been found to inhibit seizure development in one study (Roussinov et al., 1974), but further experimental and clinical evidence is needed before it can be considered an "anticonvulsant antipsychotic." Regardless, haloperidol does seem to be preferred on an empirical basis by a number of epilepsy specialists (Stevens, 1975; Blumer, 1977), and because it appears to affect concomitant anticonvulsant administration minimally, is probably a drug of choice in the treatment of psychosis with epilepsy.

Several other salient points may be made with regard to the treatment of a client with both a psychotic and a seizure disorder. They are intended as general considerations to promote safer and more effective therapeutic regimens.

1. Avoid "polypharmacy." The greater the number of antipsychotics administered, the higher is the probability that seizure threshold may be lowered, as well as a range of side effects increased.

2. If a change in neuroleptic medication is necessary, this should be done gradually. Too rapid decrease may precipitate a seizure, although it is also reported that seizures more often occur after a sudden increase in neuroleptic dosage (Ban, 1966).

3. If a client develops a first known seizure while taking an antipsychotic, another antipsychotic should be substituted; if the initial drug was haloperidol, change to a piperazine phenothiazine, for example, trifluoperazine or fluphenazine, might be indicated on an empirical basis (Remick and Fine, 1979). This must be accompanied by a thorough neurological evaluation, including EEG and possibly CT scan, to rule out a structural lesion or other cause of the epilepsy.

4. If a problem with seizure control develops in a treated epileptic person concomitantly being administered an antipsychotic, two courses of treatment are available: either substitute an antipsychotic with equivalent dosage or evaluate with a neurologist the possibility of raising the anticonvulsant dosage. Addition of another anticonvulsant seems unwarranted, and may result in complications attendant on polypharmacy with anticonvulsants (see section on anticonvulsants and psychiatric complications). It should be noted that if an individual is already on an anticonvulsant regimen, the addition of an antipsychotic hardly ever results in the precipitation of a seizure (Rodin, 1975), *provided* medications are being taken as prescribed and therapeutic levels are present. These latter conditions are significant, because clients who take their anticonvulsants irregularly or not at all are not infrequently seen in emergency psychiatric settings. In such cases, seizures *may* develop, and it is clinically wise to monitor serum anticonvulsant levels to ascertain both the degree of compliance and the need for additional neurological consultation.

5. Neuroleptics and anticonvulsants are metabolized by the same general enzyme system (hepatic mixed oxidases). It is thus not unusual for some medication adjustments to be made if they are used concurrently. However, this generally is not encountered as a major problem by emergency psychiatric clinicians but rather by those working with the client over a period of time (see Bibliography for further discussion of drug interactions).

Lithium

Lithium is infrequently used in emergency psychiatric units largely because of both the medical workup necessary before usage and the delayed onset of action (generally at least 7 to 14 days). Grand mal seizures as a side effect of therapeutic lithium dosages are uncommon but do occur (Baldessarini and Stephens, 1970) and may also be encountered on withdrawal from lithium (Wharton, 1969). Paradoxically, lithium has experimentally been found to inhibit seizure formation (Roussinov et al., 1974) and formerly was used in Great Britain (as the bromide salt) for treatment of epilepsy. In the emergency setting lithium-related seizures are most often caused by intoxication or overdose. It is therefore crucial to be acquainted with clinical signs and symptoms of lithium toxicity (fatigue, lethargy, fine or coarse tremor, ataxia, muscle twitching, slurred speech, nausea or vomiting, diarrhea, and so on). The toxic state may also involve progressive development or exacerbation of mental impairment. Psychosis may worsen, or the client may report with disorientation, confusion, memory deficit, and even frank delirium. As the syndrome of severe intoxication might not manifest itself until 3 to 4 days after ingestion of an overdose, early diagnosis is critical, following which the client should be referred to the medical emergency department for intensive treatment (see Bibliography for treatment approaches). A history of lithium ingestion should be sought if this clinical picture is observed, and a serum lithium level should be obtained (most seizures occur above 2 mEq/liter).

If the seizure occurs in an individual with no known history of epilepsy, the dosage may generally be reduced until serum levels fall within therapeutic range, at which point the seizure probably will not recur. As noted earlier, a convulsion may infrequently develop while serum lithium levels are within therapeutic range; in such a case, there may be no recurrence of seizures even if dosage is unchanged, although individual clinical discretion at times dictates addition of an anticonvulsant on prophylactic grounds. In those instances in which the client is known to be epileptic and is also on an anticonvulsant regimen, the danger of grand mal seizure breakthrough appears to be slight when lithium is added (Gershon et al., 1960), although some evidence exists that control of psychomotor seizures may be more problematic (Jus et al., 1973).

Tricyclic antidepressants (TCAs)

Treatment with TCAs is hardly ever begun under emergency psychiatric conditions because,

as with lithium, there is a delayed onset of action (generally at least 2 weeks). Although imipramine (Tofranil) has been found to be moderately effective in experimental treatment of petit mal epilepsy (Fromm et al., 1972), there are various reports of grand mal seizures caused by TCAs, for example, imipramine, amitriptyline (Elavil), and protriptyline (Vivactil). The seizures may occur with therapeutic doses (Leyberg and Denmark, 1959; Dallos and Heathfield, 1969) but are seen more commonly in overdoses (Kiloh et al., 1961). It is in the case of an overdose that TCA-associated seizures are most likely to be encountered in the psychiatric emergency unit, and then usually as part of a syndrome involving the central nervous system (with possible agitation, confusion, visual hallucinations, or even coma), cardiovascular system (with complex abnormalities of rate and rhythm), and diverse manifestations of anticholinergic toxicity (including dilated pupils, blurred vision, dry mouth, urinary retention, or paralytic ileus). Those drugs with the most anticholinergic activity, such as amitriptyline or doxepin (Sinequan), obviously cause a more severe clinical picture, but those with slight anticholinergic properties like desipramine (Norpramin, Pertofrane) may also produce seizures in overdose. If a history of TCA ingestion is obtained as part of a suicide attempt or gesture, immediate treatment in the medical emergency department is indicated. Do not wait to see if the clinical presentation regresses before referring for treatment (see Bibliography for treatment approaches to the toxic state). It has been suggested that convulsions are one indication for usage of physostigmine in TCA overdose, but this is not recommended in a psychiatric emergency unit because of the lack of personnel and equipment necessary for adequate monitoring and support.

In summary, overdosage with TCAs may precipitate seizures in epileptic and nonepileptic clients alike; in therapeutic doses, TCAs may well cause seizure breakthrough in an epileptic client, although this is much less likely if an adequate anticonvulsant regimen has been established. It should be stressed that a history of epilepsy does not constitute a relative or absolute contraindication for the usage of a TCA. TCAs at therapeutic doses may also be responsible infrequently for convulsions in a nonepileptic client; another TCA may need to be substituted if this develops to rule out drug idiosyncrasy, but again, neurological evaluation is necessary to determine if there are other causes of the seizure.

Finally, if a client is taking a TCA and is being evaluated over a period of time in the emergency department, remember to continue administering it: sudden cessation of a TCA may produce convulsions in a seizure-prone individual.

ANTICONVULSANTS AND PSYCHIATRIC COMPLICATIONS

Clients taking anticonvulsants will report periodically to the psychiatric emergency unit and with them will be presented a variety of questions regarding mental symptomatology and the antiepileptic medication. This is a quite convoluted area, forming one of the interfaces of psychiatric and neurological illness. To begin with, problems with epileptic clients may arise regarding noncompliance with medication. A number of conscious and unconscious factors may play a role in this (Gutheil, 1977), none of these peculiar to an individual with epilepsy per se; in those prone to psychosis, delusional-hallucinatory material may contribute significantly (Rodin, 1975). If noncompliance results in undermedication, an increased frequency of seizures tends to occur and clients may bring themselves or be brought to the psychiatric unit because of mental phenomena in the premonitory phase of a seizure or in the postictal period (when psychotic symptomatology not uncommonly is encountered). In addition to the psychiatric history, a good medication history with serum anticonvulsant levels should be obtained; if levels are low, concurrent neurological workup should be performed.

Toxicity

If noncompliance takes the form of an overdose, then signs and symptoms of acute toxicity should be seen. These will vary with the individual and to some extent with the medication, although it has been noted that there is a remarkable similarity of toxic effects among the major anticonvulsants (Booker, 1975). Specifically, vestibulocerebellar signs such as ataxia, nystagmus, and dysarthria are commonly present, in addition to sedation, fatigue, generalized weakness, lightheadedness, and irritability. It is significant to note that seizure frequency may actually increase if anticonvulsant levels are within the toxic range (Table 4-1); this may occur with a number of the drugs, although phenytoin is the most notorious in this regard. It should also be noted that the therapeutic range is only a guideline and that the ultimate determinant of a therapeutic versus toxic state is based on clinical evaluation. As with the antipsychotics, the risk of toxicity increases with the number of anticonvulsants concurrently used. It is likewise well recognized that premorbid character traits or pathological conditions may become accentuated or rigidified in the toxic state, necessitating psychiatric intervention perhaps even before a neurologist is consulted.

Not only may there be acute or subacute toxicity, but also the development of overt or subtle mental disturbances possibly associated with summation or cumulative effects of the anticonvulsant at therapeutic or even low dosage (Reynolds, 1975; Editorial, *Lancet,* 1975). A case of delayed idiosyncratic reaction to phenytoin has been reported (McDanal and Bolman, 1975), in which paranoid thoughts and behavior, somatic complaints, and general anxiety were present at very low serum concentrations. The condition was accentuated with an increase in dosage and dramatically reversed on withdrawal of the drug. I observed a similar case (Rainey and Hausner, 1976); one is led to wonder about the prevalence of such a mechanism in the production of psychosis or more subtle mental alterations during therapeutic dosages of anticonvulsants. Reynolds and Travers (1974) have provided further evidence that brain-damaged individuals may be particularly susceptible to these mental disturbances associated with long-term phenytoin "toxicity."

The impression should not be left that only phenytoin is capable of effecting negative changes in mental status; all the other anticonvulsants have also been implicated, especially when within the toxic range.

Psychotropic effect?

A more controversial area involves the question of whether any of the anticonvulsants may have *positive* psychotropic effects. The principal candidate is carbamazepine. It is the only anticonvulsant with structural similarity to the tricyclic antidepressants and is felt by some to be helpful in the depressed or irritable epileptic client (Blumer, 1977). It has therapeutic potential in manic-depressive illness (Okuma et al., 1979), and may elevate mood, produce a sense of "activation," and perhaps positively affect higher cognitive functions (Dalby, 1975; Dodrill and Troupin, 1977). Such "activation" is far from universally accepted, either because no psychotropic effects could be found on psychological testing (Rodin et al., 1974) or because these putative effects are felt to be more apparent than real, stemming from carbamazepine's lack of sedation and from adverse mental reactions commonly associated with the other anticonvulsants (Dalby, 1975). The major difficulty resides in its hematological side effects, so that more extensive testing and utilization of possible psychotropic activity are being approached with greater caution.

A final word is in order regarding valproic acid, which was approved for use in the United States in 1978. As mentioned earlier, it is an anticonvulsant whose mechanism of action seems to involve enhancement of synaptic gamma-aminobutyric acid (GABA) activity. GABA has been shown to inhibit dopaminergic neurons (Aghajanian and Bunney, 1974), and because the dopamine hypothesis of schizophrenia involves dopaminergic hyperactivity within the mesolimbic system of the brain, the possibility exists of a beneficial effect of valproic acid in schizophreniform psychosis of epilepsy. It previously has been suggested that controlled clinical trials of valproic acid be conducted in schizophrenic clients (Koran, 1976) in response to a report of decreasing withdrawal and greater willingness to cooperate in a group of chronic schizophrenic persons receiving the drug (Linnoila et al., 1976). It is

approved at present only for petit mal seizures but also appears to be effective in grand mal epilepsy (Browne, 1980). Further investigation along these lines might prove fruitful in providing a means of dealing more effectively with the psychoses associated with seizures.

SUMMARY

It is hoped that the foregoing has helped create a fuller understanding of the intricacies involved in treating a client with seizures. There are numerous other ramifications that have not been touched on, if only because of their questionable pertinence to emergency psychiatric evaluation (for examples, seizures secondary to drug interactions other than with psychotropics or seizures associated with metabolic encephalopathies). As indicated initially, psychiatric concomitants of epilepsy implicitly involve an interweaving of biological and psychological factors, which to some extent are inextricable (reflecting in part the unity of the human mind and body). As clinicians continue to attempt to distinguish organic from functional and cause from effect, it must also be emphasized that a comprehensive approach is necessary to expand knowledge and extend the basis for treatment.

BIBLIOGRAPHY

Aghajanian, G.T., and Bunney, B.S.: Dopaminergic and nondopaminergic neurons of the substantia nigra: differential responses to putative transmitters, J. Pharmacologie 5(suppl. 1):56, 1974.

Andermann, F., and Robb, J.P.: Absence status, Epilepsia 13:177, 1972.

Asuni, T., and Pillutla, V.S.: Schizophrenia-like psychoses in Nigerian epileptics, Br. J. Psychiatry 113:1375, 1967.

Baldessarini, R.J., and Stephens, J.H.: Lithium carbonate for affective disorders. I. clinical pharmacology and toxicology, Arch. Gen. Psychiatry 22:72, 1970.

Ban, T.A.: Phenothiazines alone and in combination, Appl. Ther. 8:530, 1966.

Bartlett, J.E.A.: Chronic psychosis following epilepsy, Am. J. Psychiatry 114:338, 1957.

Bear, D.M.: The significance of behavioral change in temporal lobe epilepsy. In Blumer, D., and Levin, V., editors: Psychiatric complications in the epilepsies: current research and treatment, McLean Hospital Journal, special issue, 1977.

Bear, D.M., and Fedio, P.: Quantitative analysis of interictal behavior in temporal lobe epilepsy, Arch. Neurol. **34**:454, 1977.

Blacker, K.H., and Tupin, J.P.: Hysteria and hysterical structures: developmental and social theories. In Horowitz, M.J., editor: Hysterical personality, New York, 1977, Jason Aronson, Inc.

Blumer, D.: Treatment of patients with seizure disorder referred because of psychiatric complications. In Blumer, D., and Levin, K., editors: Psychiatric complications in the epilepsies: current research and treatment, McLean Hospital Journal, special issue, 1977.

Booker, H.E.: Management of the difficult patient with complex partial seizures, Adv. Neurol. **11**:369, 1975.

Browne, T.R.: Valproic acid, N. Engl. J. Med. **302**:661, 1980.

Charcot, J.M.: Lectures on the diseases of the nervous system (1881), New York, 1962, Hafner Publishing Co., p. 261. (Translated by G. Sigerson.)

Collins, G.G.S.: Effect of AOAA thiosemicarbazide and haloperidol on the metabolism and half-lives of flutamate and GABA in rat brain, Biochem. Pharmacol. **22**:101, 1973.

Connell, P.H.: Use and abuse of amphetamine, Practitioner **200**:234, 1968.

Creese, I., Burt, D.R., and Snyder, S.H.: Dopamine receptor binding: differentiation of agonist and antagonist states with ^{3}H-dopamine and ^{3}H-haloperidol, Life Sci. **17**:993, 1975.

Dalby, M.A.: Behavioral effects of carbamazepine, Adv. Neurol. **11**:331, 1975.

Dallos, V., and Heathfield, K.: Iatrogenic epilepsy due to antidepressant drugs, Br. Med. J. **4**:80, 1969.

Daly, D.D.: Ictal clinical manifestations of complex partial seizures, Adv. Neurol. **11**:57, 1975.

Daly, D.D.: Classification of epileptic seizures. Symposium on epilepsy: diagnosis and management, Symp. Reporter, vol. 2, 1977.

Davison, K., and Bagley, C.R.: Schizophrenia-like psychoses associated with organic disorders of the central nervous system: a review of the literature. In Herrington, R.N., editor: Current problems in neuropsychiatry: schizophrenia, epilepsy, the temporal lobe, British Journal of Psychiatry Special Pub. No. 4, Ashford, England, 1969, Headley Brothers Publishers.

Dodrill, C.B., and Troupin, A.S.: Psychotropic effects of carbamazepine in epilepsy: a double-blind comparison with phenytoin, Neurology **27**:1023, 1977.

Dreifuss, F.E.: The differential diagnosis of partial seizures with complex symptomatology, Adv. Neurol. **11**:187, 1975.

Editorial, Lancet **2**:264, 1975.

Editorial, Lancet **1**:196, 1979.

Feldman, R.G.: Behavioral aspects of epilepsy, symposium on epilepsy: diagnosis and management, Symp. Reporter, vol. 2, 1977.

Fenichel, O.: The psychoanalytic theory of neurosis, New York, 1945, W.W. Norton & Co., Inc.

Flor-Henry, P.: Psychosis and temporal lobe epilepsy, Epilepsia **10**:363, 1969.

Flor-Henry, P.: Lateralized temporal-limbic dysfunction and psychopathology, Ann. N.Y. Acad. Sci. **280**:777, 1976.

Flor-Henry, P.: On certain aspects of the localization of the cerebral systems regulating and determining emotion, Biol. Psychiatry **14**:677, 1979.

Fromm, G.H., et al.: Imipramine in epilepsy, Arch. Neurol. **27**:198, 1972.

Gale, K., and Iadarola, M.J.: Seizure protection and increased nerve-terminal GABA: delayed effects of GABA transaminase inhibition, Science **208**:288, 1980.

Gastaut, H.: The epilepsies: electroclinical correlations, Springfield, Ill., 1954, Charles C Thomas, Publisher.

Gastaut, H.: Clinical and electroencephalographical classification of epileptic seizures, Epilepsia **11**:102, 1970.

Gershon, S., and Yuwiler, A.: Lithium ion: a specific psychopharmacological approach to the treatment of mania, J. Neuropsychiatry **1**:229, 1960.

Geschwind, N.: Behavioral changes in temporal lobe epilepsy, Psychol. Med. **9**:217, 1979.

Goldensohn, E.S.: Discussion, Adv. Neurol. **11**:197, 1975.

Goldfrank, L., and Osborn, H.: Phencyclidine (angel dust), Hosp. Physiol. **14**:18, 1978.

Greist, J.H., Jefferson, J.W., and Marcetich, J.: Lithium and the primary care physician, Behav. Med. **5**:25, 1978.

Gutheil, T.G.: Psychodynamics in drug prescribing, Drug Ther. **7**:82, 1977.

Horowitz, M.J.: Psychosocial function in epilepsy, Springfield, Ill., 1970, Charles C Thomas, Publisher.

Isbell, H., and White, W.M.: Clinical characteristics of addictions, Am. J. Med. **14**:558, 1953.

Itil, T.M., and Wadud, A.: Treatment of human aggression with major tranquilizers, antidepressants, and newer psychotropic drugs, J. Nerv. Ment. Dis. **160**:83, 1975.

Jackson, J.H.: Epileptic attacks with a warning of a crude sensation of smell and with the "intellectual aura" (dreamy state) in a patient who had symptoms pointing to gross organic disease of right temporo-sphenoidal lobe. In Taylor, J., editor: Selected writings of John Hughlings Jackson, vol. 1, London, 1931, Hodder & Stoughton, Ltd.

Jus, A., et al.: Some remarks on the influence of lithium carbonate on patients with temporal epilepsy, Int. J. Clin. Pharmacol. 7:67, 1973.

Kamm, I., and Mandel, A.: Thioridazine in the treatment of behavior disorders in epileptics, Dis. Nerv. Syst. 28:46, 1967.

Khantzian, E.J., and McKenna, G.J.: Acute toxic and withdrawal reactions associated with drug use and abuse, Ann. Intern. Med. 90:361, 1979.

Kiloh, L.G., et al.: An electroencephalographic study of the analeptic effects of imipramine, Electroencephalogr. Clin. Neurophysiol. 13:216, 1961.

Koran, L.M.: Gamma-aminobutyric acid deficiency in schizophrenia (correspondence), Lancet 2:1025, 1976.

Landolt, H.: Serial electroencephalographic investigations during psychotic episodes in epileptic patients and during epileptic attacks. In Lorentz de Haas, A.M., editor: Lectures on epilepsy, Amsterdam, 1958, Elsevier/North Holland.

Lemberger, L., et al.: The effects of haloperidol and chlorpromazine on amphetamine metabolism and amphetamine stereotype behavior in the rat, J. Pharmacol. Exp. Ther. 174:1 428, 1970.

Leyberg, J.T., and Denmark, J.C.: The treatment of depressive states with imipramine hydrochloride (Tofranil), J. Ment. Sci. 105:1123, 1959.

Linnoila, M., et al.: Effect of sodium valproate on tardive dyskinesia, Br. J. Psychiatry 129:114, 1976.

Logothetis, J.: Spontaneous epileptic seizures and electroencephalographic changes in the course of phenothiazine therapy, Neurology 17:869, 1967.

Maruyama, S., and Kawasaki, T.: Synergism between gamma-aminobutyric acid and butyrophenones administered micro-iontophoretically in the Purkinje cells of the cat cerebellum, Jpn. J. Pharmacol. 25:209, 1975.

McDanal, C.E., and Bolman, W.M.: Delayed idiosyncratic psychosis with diphenylhydantoin, J.A.M.A. 231(10):1063, 1975.

Okuma, T., et al.: Comparison of the antimanic efficacy of carbamazepine and chlorpromazine: A double-blind controlled study, Psychopharmacology 66:211-217, 1979.

Penry, J.K., and Dreifuss, F.E.: Automatisms associated with the absence of petit mal epilepsy, Arch. Neurol. 21:142, 1969.

Pincus, J.H., and Tucker, G.: Behavioral neurology, New York, 1974, Oxford University Press.

Pond, D.A.: Psychiatric aspects of epilepsy, J. Ind. Med. Prof. 3:1441, 1957.

Pond, D.A.: Discussion, Proc. R. Soc. Med. 55:316, 1962.

Rainey, J.M., and Hausner, R.S.: Exacerbation of psychosis associated with long-term diphenylhydantoin treatment, unpublished research report, Lafayette Clinic Research Unit, Detroit, Mich., 1976.

Ramani, S.V., et al.: Diagnosis of hysterical seizures in epileptic patients, Am. J. Psychiatry 137:705, 1980.

Rangell, L.: The nature of conversion, J. Am. Psychoanal. Assoc. 7:632, 1959.

Remick, R.A., and Fine, S.H.: Antipsychotic drugs and seizures, J. Clin. Psychiatry 40:78, 1979.

Remick, R.A., and Wada, J.A.: Complex partial and pseudoseizure disorders, Am. J. Psychiatry 136:320, March, 1979.

Reynolds, E.H.: Chronic antiepileptic toxicity: a review, Epilepsia 16:319, 1975.

Reynolds, E.H., and Travers, R.D.: Serum anticonvulsant concentrations in epileptic patients with mental symptoms, Br. J. Psychiatry 124:440, 1974.

Rodin, E.A.: The prognosis of patients with epilepsy, Springfield, Ill., 1968, Charles C Thomas, Publisher.

Rodin, E.A.: Psychosocial management of patients with complex partial seizures, Adv. Neurol. 11: 383, 1975.

Rodin, E.A., et al.: Relationship between certain forms of psychomotor epilepsy and "schizophrenia." I. Diagnostic considerations, Arch. Neurol. Psychiatry 77: 449, 1957.

Rodin, E.A., et al.: The effects of carbamazepine on patients with psychomotor epilepsy: results of a double-blind study, Epilepsia 15:547, 1974.

Roussinov, K.S., et al.: Experimental study of the effect of lithium, haloperidol, caffeine and theophylline on convulsive seizure reactions, Acta Physiol. Pharmacol. Bulg. 2:67, 1974.

Schlichther, W., et al.: Seizures occurring during intensive chlorpromazine therapy, Can. Med. Assoc. J. 74:364, 1956.

Scott, J.S., and Masland, R.L.: Occurrence of "continuous symptoms" in epilepsy patients, Neurology 3:297, 1953.

Shader, R.I.: Behavioral changes with temporal lobe epilepsy: assessment and treatment (discussion), J. Clin. Psychiatry 41:89, 1980.

Shader, R.I., Weinberger, D.R., and Greenblatt, D.J.: Problems with drug interactions in treating brain disorders, Psychiatr. Clin. North Am. 1:51, 1978.

Silverstein, A.: Hysterical neurological signs, Hosp. Physiol. 12:16, 1976.

Slater, E., Beard, A.W., and Glithero, E.: The schizophrenia-like psychoses of epilepsy, Br. J. Psychiatry 109:95, 1963.

Small, J.G., Milstein, V., and Stevens, J.R.: Are psychomotor epileptics different? Arch. Neurol. **7**:33, 1962.

Standage, K.F.: Schizophreniform psychosis among epileptics in a mental hospital, Br. J. Psychiatry **123**: 231, 1973.

Stevens, J.R.: Psychomotor epilepsy and schizophrenia: a common anatomy? In Brazier, M.A.B., editor: Epilepsy: its phenomena in man, New York, 1973, Academic Press.

Stevens, J.R.: Interictal clinical manifestations of complex partial seizures, Adv. Neurol. **11**:85, 1975.

Symonds, C.: Discussion, Proc. R. Soc. Med. **55**:314, 1962.

Tarter, R.E.: Intellectual and adaptive functioning in epilepsy: A review of 50 years of research, Dis. Nerv. Syst. **33**:763, 1972.

Tedeschi, D.H., et al.: Effects of various phenothiazines on minimal electroshock seizure threshold and spontaneous motor activity of mice, J. Pharmacol. Exp. Ther. **123**:35, 1958.

Tintinalli, J.E., and Hausner, R.: Status epilepticus, J.A.C.E.P. **5**:896, 1976.

Tong, T., and Benowitz, N.: Physostigmime in tricyclic antidepressant overdose, Bulletin of the hospital pharmacy, University of California, San Francisco, No. 8, vol. 24, 1976.

Victor, M.: The pathophysiology of alcoholic epilepsy, Res. Publ. Assoc. Nerv. Ment. Dis. **46**:431, 1968.

Victor, M., and Adams, R.D.: The effect of alcohol on the nervous system, Res. Publ. Assoc. Nerv. Ment. Dis. **32**:526, 1953.

Victor, M., and Hope, J.M.: The phenomenon of auditory hallucinations in chronic alcoholism, J. Nerv. Ment. Dis. **126**:451, 1958.

Waxman, S.G., and Geschwind, N.: The interictal behavior syndrome of temporal lobe epilepsy, Arch. Gen. Psychiatry **32**:1580, 1975.

Wharton, R.N.: Grand mal seizures with lithium treatment (correspondence), Am. J. Psychiatry **125**: 1446, 1969.

Williams, D.: The structure of emotions reflected in epileptic experiences, Brain **79**:29, 1956.

CHAPTER 5

The client with a schizophrenic disorder

Mary Swanson Crockett, R.N., D.N.Sc.

Since I was old enough to know I was a person, I always felt something was wrong with me. But I didn't get a chance to go to a doctor. When I got to Houston, I started going to doctors, college, and having trouble with traffic laws. People took me to the hospital for paranoid schizophrenia. It's when a person hears voices. It's derived from a nervous disorder. I didn't tell anybody but the doctor about the voices.
I am all right now—I feel good—only trouble I have is with my kidneys. (Research subject from independent living outreach program.)

THE SCHIZOPHRENIC CLIENT'S EXPERIENCE IN THE PSYCHIATRIC EMERGENCY FACILITY

Desperation, hope, secretiveness, and fear are often balanced off against each other as schizophrenic clients decide whether to approach a psychiatric facility and turn themselves over to powerful strangers. These strangers may medicate them or lock them up. Worse still, the strangers may listen only superficially and dismiss the clients without the treatment or the temporary escape to a "safer" place for which their risk was undertaken.

Mary Cecil (1956) recounts hearing persecutory voices inescapably for nearly a week before first approaching a psychiatric clinic. She describes herself as circling the clinic building three times until "an entrance grew up where there had not been one before." She reports conversing with her voices about the first doctor, "a dark sallow man with an extraordinary likeness to Satan himself." She decided not to talk to him. She was then passed on to a doctor whom she describes as "more fortunate with his face. There was a coziness all about him." She reports that the threats from her voices finally stopped their opposition to her being interviewed and says "so I finally did tell the warm doctor, though tactfully and with reserve."

The two persons quoted earlier are describing their tension on an initial visit to a facility where they were not known. Clients who go to psychiatric emergency facilities, either voluntarily or under pressure from others, are naturally wary of unfamiliar staff. Even those clients who are returning to familiar facilities may remain suspicious of staff members with whom they are already well acquainted. These clients bring a wavering, often unstated or unconscious hope of being received with warmth and interest, of having their dignity preserved or increased, and of having their difficulties taken seriously and treated constructively. They also bring a pessimism based on experiences of real or imagined rejections, many of these from associates who intended no rejection but were unaware of the extreme sensitivity of many schizophrenic people. A few of those clients who are more experienced in the "patient role" can approach the psychiatric emergency unit as a comfortable return to familiar people who have become the most trusted of their associates.

THE SCHIZOPHRENIC DISORDERS; CURRENT CLASSIFICATION

For many years the schizophrenic disorders were viewed by experts as all being subtypes of a single disorder. Most current investigators, including the panel responsible for the *Diagnostic and Statistical Manual of Mental Disorders III* (1980), or DSM III, now speak of a cluster of disorders that have some similar manifestations but that almost certainly arise from several different etiologies. Thus the singular noun *schizophrenia* can be used as an analogue to the singular noun *cancer*. Cancer, of course, is generally perceived by scientists as a cluster of similar illnesses with a variety of etiologies, courses, treatments, and prognoses.

Unfortunately, the subtypes of schizophrenia, such as catatonic, disorganized (hebephrenic), and undifferentiated, do not divide themselves neatly into clusters, each of which coincides with one of the known etiological factors. Thus known

etiological factors such as patterns of inheritance, certain abnormalities of blood chemistry, demonstrable neurological deterioration, and environmental stressors such as refugee status each are reported to have appeared in each one of the more common schizophrenic symptom configurations such as paranoid, disorganized, or catatonic.

From this current point of view that emphasizes several etiological factors with considerable overlap of symptoms from one subtype to the next, the DSM III states that no single feature of schizophrenia is invariably present nor is any single feature seen only in schizophrenia and never in other disorders.

The authors of DSM III make the point that although the plural term *schizophrenic disorders* is logically more correct, they are retaining the old term *schizophrenia* when discussing each of the symptom subtypes, for example, catatonic schizophrenia.

Manifestations of schizophrenic disorders

Features that may be seen in a schizophrenic client are described in the following paragraphs, but not all of these would be likely to appear in the same individual.

Delusions. Delusions that may be fragmented, bizarre, single, or multiple may be seen among schizophrenic clients. These may be delusions of being persecuted or of having thoughts inserted or removed from one's mind by some external force. There may be delusions of being controlled. There may be ideas of reference or overvalued ideas. Not every delusional schizophrenic person believes without interruption that the delusion is true. "I'm beginning to feel as if everyone is looking funny at me all the time like I did before I went into the hospital the last time," may be reported by a client who acknowledges some doubt about his ideas of reference or delusions.

Modes of thinking. Modes of thinking may be abnormal. These abnormalities may include associative looseness ranging from moderate to a point of incoherence. There may be poverty of speech with only brief, relatively meaningless answers to questions. Thought processes may be stereotyped or repetitive or both. Either overly vague and abstract or overly concrete thinking may be in evidence. There may be blocking of speech. Neologisms, perseveration, and clanging are less common, but may be seen.

Perceptual disturbances. Perceptual disturbances may be present in schizophrenic clients. Although auditory hallucinations are most common in this condition, tactile or somatic hallucinations may occur. Awareness that hallucinations are symptoms of illness rather than real "voices" does occur in some schizophrenic people just as does awareness of delusions that one's ideas are delusional as described earlier. Occasionally a schizophrenic person who has had effective treatment in the past may respond to the question about hearing voices by saying, "Do you mean do I hallucinate? Yes, I do." Visual, gustatory, and olfactory hallucinations are less common in the schizophrenic disorders than are auditory hallucinations. If one of these first three appear without any auditory hallucinations, the client should be examined for possible organic brain pathology.

Disturbances of affect. Disturbances of affect occur in many schizophrenic clients. The most common manifestations of this among schizophrenic people are blunted or flat affect, severe reduction in intensity and expression of emotion, monotonous voice, expressionless face, and even denial of having any feelings. The emotions displayed may also be very inappropriate for the topic being discussed by the client. In the client who has already been medicated elsewhere before being observed in the emergency unit, it is difficult to distinguish between the flattening effects of tranquilizers and the client's usual emotional qualities. Depression, passive or active anger, worry, and apathy may all occur.

Confusion about boundaries of the self. Confusion about boundaries of the self is frequently found among schizophrenic people. This confusion may be expressed as distortion of body image, uncertainty about one's individuality and self direction, or vague persistent discomfort about what one's existence is about.

Motivation. Motivation is nearly always inadequate for sustaining self-initiated, goal-directed activities. Ambivalence and inadequate organization may contribute to this.

Withdrawal. Withdrawal into fantasy and egocentric or eccentric ideation is common. Both ideas and emotions may be detached from the real world, while the clients may seem to be involved only in an autistic preoccupation with their own "reality."

Disturbances of motion. Disturbances of motion are often seen in schizophrenic persons. The most common of these is marked decrease in movement, but the cause is harder to judge in clients who are heavily tranquilized and thus can tolerate more inactivity than when they are not medicated. Movements may be purposeless, stereotyped, or bizarre. In catatonic clients all movement may be resisted at times, whereas excited and even violent motion may occur at other times with or without apparent external stimuli. Pacing, rocking, foot shuffling, pill rolling with fingers, and other stereotyped motions may occur without tranquilizers, but in some clients these are exacerbated as medication side effects.

General presentation of self. General presentation of self is almost always impaired during a schizophrenic episode or in a residual schizophrenic condition. Clients may appear to be confused or out of contact with their surroundings. Grooming may be chronically very poor or there may be episodes of eccentric overuse of cosmetics, peculiar ornaments, and garments inappropriate to the season and situation, even where limitations of poverty are not a factor.

Onset of schizophrenic disorders

Onset of schizophrenic disorders usually occurs during adolescence or early adult life. If the first psychotic episode that has schizophrenic characteristics occurs after age 45, it is classified as atypical psychosis. To be classified as a schizophrenic disorder there must have been continuous signs of the illness over a period of 6 months or more. Usually the acutely psychotic phase is preceded by a prodromal period, characterized by social withdrawal, peculiar behavior, and impaired role function. Personality changes also may be reported by associates. Flat or inappropriate affect, increasingly poor grooming, difficulties in communicating or relating to others, bizarre ideas, and unusual experiences of perception are often reported. The prodromal phase may vary in length from a few days or weeks to many years. It is often difficult or impossible to date the onset of it, and it is not unusual for the prodomal signs to fluctuate, with periods of apparent return to normal function interspersed with gradual increases in the duration and severity of signs of illness. Clausen and Yarrow (1955) document that there are often long periods of indecision after the first onset of a client's bizarre symptoms before families finally bring their family member to a facility for psychiatric evaluation.

Predisposing factors

Modern informed opinion about the predisposing factors or etiology of schizophrenic disorders is moving toward a multifactorial point of view. The epiphenomena that may develop as a result or a correlate of having a schizophrenic disorder are difficult to extricate from the *etiological or predisposing* factors.

GENETIC FACTORS. There seems to be a hereditary base for some but not all schizophrenic disorders. Since concordance rates for schizophrenic disorders in identical twins range from only 30% to 50% in the studies where careful research techniques were used, it is clear that heredity is only a partial explanation and may not apply to some schizophrenic people at all.

THE SOCIOLOGICAL VARIABLES. The sociological variables have been researched most widely, and those for which some evidence exists include the following two factors:

Emigration, particularly if one is a refugee, can be a predisposing factor.

Living in the slums of a large urban area has been shown by several large American studies to be associated with far higher prevalence of schizophrenic disorders than is found in working or upper class areas. Hollingshead and Redlich (1958) have reported this difference to be three

times as high in the slum as in the remainder of the urban area. Dunham (1980) concurs that schizophrenic disorders are more prevalent in large urban slums but also attempts to show that this discrepancy is caused by "social selection" of persons vulnerable to schizophrenic disorders into slum areas by a variety of economic and social mechanisms that include self-selection in some cases. Miller and Swanson (1959) have shown that even "normal" slum-reared 12-year-old boys with no mental illness reported in their families use denial in fantasy as a problem-solving style much more than do "normal" 12-year-old boys from more secure low-income or moderate-income neighborhoods. The boys from the more secure neighborhoods use more self-blame themes than do the slum children. Thus these authors see the problem-solving style of denial in fantasy as endemic among both the psychiatric and nonpsychiatric children in a given demographic area, even though most subjects in both demographic areas studied will never become psychotic.

IMPAIRMENT OF SENSORY FUNCTION. Impairment of sensory function, especially of hearing, is a combination of physical and social variables which seems to contribute to one's chances of becoming schizophrenic by increasing social isolation.

PHYSIOLOGICAL AND NEUROLOGICAL VARIABLES. Physiological and neurological variables are now being explored by many researchers. In general, the state of this research for schizophrenic disorders is far behind that in cancer research. However, both are moving in the direction of increasing differentiation of subgroups with different physiological, neurological, or anatomical abnormalities. One of several comprehensive reviews of this research was done by Bowers (1980).

SCHIZOPHRENIA AS A LEARNED DISORDER

Mednick and Schulsinger (1970) have published research pertaining to their hypothesis that schizophrenic persons have a learned disorder of thought which they have developed as an attempt to cope with physiological and environmental factors. Mednick, in particular, has worked with the hypothesis that preschizophrenic persons have autonomic hyperresponsivity, in many cases either genetic or congenital in origin. They learn to respond to arousal-producing stimuli by "avoidant" responses (either loose associations or psychotic thoughts). These avoidant responses reduce arousal level and thus reinforce the association between the arousal stimulus and the avoidant thought. The avoidant thought reinforcement is completely internal in the person and thus requires no social or environmental interaction by the person to obtain reinforcement. In fact, the reinforcement works better when the process is autistic and the person is isolated and thus less distracted from these internal coping attempts.

TYPES OF SCHIZOPHRENIC DISORDERS AND DIAGNOSTIC CRITERIA

The types of schizophrenic disorders in the DSM III classification are as follows.

DISORGANIZED TYPE. The disorganized type was formerly called *hebephrenic* type. Clients with this type of schizophrenic disorder manifest more odd behaviors such as grimaces and eccentric presentation of self, more fragmented speech and thoughts, and more incoherence than other schizophrenic people do. Schizophrenics of the disorganized type are usually reported to have had a poor premorbid adjustment. Though medication helps somewhat, their overall course and prognosis remain poor. If there are delusions, these tend to be more fragmented and transient than the fixed and systematized delusions of paranoid schizophrenics. Affect is likely to be blunted, silly, and labile with or without situational stimuli that would be perceptible to other observers.

CATATONIC TYPE. The catatonic type of schizophrenic disorder is becoming increasingly rare among North American and European clients. The diagnostic criteria remain essentially the same as in earlier classifications. The subtypes include catatonic stupor with markedly decreased reactivity to external stimuli; catatonic negativism with apparently purposive and sustained immobility; rigidity; and mutism. Any of these four characteristics may be combined with the other three. Catatonic excitement with apparently purposeless hyperactivity may also appear with or without interspersed periods of immobility. Catatonic posturing in bizarre or inappropriate positions may also be seen with or without any of the characteristics mentioned. There is considerable current research suggesting that there are elevated blood levels of beta-endorphins, the opium-like substance produced by one's body during episodes of catatonic immobility. There are some reports of terminating catatonic episodes by the use of opiate antagonists such as naloxone.

PARANOID TYPE. In the paranoid type of schizophrenia, the most prominent manifestations are delusions. These delusions may be persecutory, grandiose, or predominately jealous. Hallucinations may or may not be present. Paranoid schizophrenia is distinguished from paranoid disorder in that the paranoid schizophrenic typically manifests more bizarre delusions and has symptoms such as incoherence, associative looseness, and prominent hallucinations.

UNDIFFERENTIATED TYPE. The classification of undifferentiated type is used for people with clearly psychotic symptoms that do not meet the criteria for the types named earlier (disorganized, catatonic, and paranoid). This classification may also be used for people whose symptoms fit into more than one of the three types just discussed. In the undifferentiated type, there may be prominent delusions or hallucinations. The client may be extremely disorganized. Incoherence may be present at some times but not at others.

RESIDUAL TYPE. The residual type classification is based on a history of one or more schizophrenic episodes during which the person has been clearly psychotic, but is not psychotic at the present time. It is a difficult diagnosis to make, particularly for persons whose histories of drug abuse might have accounted for prior psychotic episodes. However, the residual type designation is used only when the client still shows signs of continuing illness such as withdrawal, inappropriate affect, odd ideation, or markedly eccentric presentation of self. The subtypes of schizophrenia of residual type include subchronic (6 months to 2 years); chronic (over 2 years); subchronic with acute exacerbation; and in remission and symptom free for a considerable period of time with or without medication.

DISORDERS SIMILAR TO SCHIZOPHRENIA AND REQUIRING DIFFERENTIAL DIAGNOSIS

PARANOID DISORDERS. The paranoid disorders are now classified as including paranoia, shared paranoid disorder, and acute paranoid disorder. The boundaries between the paranoid disorders and paranoid schizophrenia are sometimes difficult to ascertain. Paranoid disorders tend to have a later onset, in middle or late adult life, as compared to schizophrenic disorders, which appear first during adolescence or early adult life. Paranoid people may resemble paranoid schizophrenics in that both may be grandiose, angry, seclusive, suspicious, or eccentric. However, paranoid people often maintain coherence and occupational function much better than paranoid schizophrenic people do. Acute paranoia is defined as a condition which has lasted 7 months or less. Paranoid disorder may be classified as such after an illness of at least 1 week marked by persistent persecutory or jealous delusions if there is no evidence of other schizophrenic, manic, depressive, or organic illness.

A paranoid disorder is often difficult to differentiate from acute toxic syndromes. This is especially true for psychoses associated with amphetamine abuse. Some emergency units have access to laboratory tests that make this differentiation more accurately than do the observations of the clinician unsupported by laboratory findings.

PARANOID PERSONALITY DISORDER. Paranoid personality disorder is the classification used for people who exhibit paranoid ideation but who do not carry their jealousy or ideas of persecution to the psychotic level.

SCHIZOPHRENIFORM DISORDER. *Schizophreniform disorder* is the term used for persons who have appeared schizophrenic for any period of more than 2 weeks but less than 6 months according to the many criteria listed earlier. By the time 6 months have elapsed, some of these people may have developed some kind of anxiety disorder or a toxic disorder. Others may have become more clearly schizophrenic. For the period of less than 2 weeks, the term *brief reactive psychosis* may be used.

SCHIZOAFFECTIVE DISORDER. Even the DSM III states that further clarification of the term *schizoaffective disorder* is still needed. It is still applied to persons in whom a diagnostician is unable to clearly differentiate the schizophrenic manifestations from those of an affective disorder because features of both disorders are evident.

ATYPICAL PSYCHOSIS. *Atypical psychosis* is the term used for psychoses, usually of recent appearance, which do not meet the criteria for any other specific psychiatric disorder. It is often used as a transient diagnosis until a clearer clinical picture emerges, or until the psychotic symptoms disappear, as in the case of some reactive psychoses or psychoses related to factors like transient endocrine imbalances.

Differential diagnosis of schizophrenic disorders

In making a differential diagnosis, the clinician will find "The decision tree for differential diagnosis" in the DSM III (pp. 339-349) is useful in deciding which diagnostic term is most appropriate for a given client at a given time.

ACUTE MANIA. Acute mania is difficult to distinguish from an acute schizophrenic condition unless there is additional information supplied by history or by medications the client had been taking. If the clinician has no such additional information, one source that helps is the content of delusions. The manic tends to have more altruistic delusions (world peace, cure for cancer, and so on), while the delusions of the schizophrenic often have more destructive themes. Length and frequency of past hospitalizations are other clues that the client may be able to supply, with shorter but regular cycles tending to be present more often among manic depressives.

Case vignette #1 □ Substance-induced delusional disorder in a schizotypal personality

Ms. W was markedly upset when she was accompanied to the psychiatric emergency unit by a co-worker. Her first distressed statement was "I am afraid I'm losing my mind. I think I must be going crazy!"

She reported having increasingly vivid delusions during the past 2 months. It seemed to her more and more that various individuals and families in the neighborhood were out to get her for some unknown reason. She had also been having increasingly frightening nightmares about being attacked with axes, wooden planks, rocks, shovels, and other neighborhood-type weapons. Finally she began to hear voices saying "We're going to get you." On that day she had begged a co-worker from her factory to make her come to the psychiatric emergency unit and stay with here there, so that she would get there before she became too afraid to make that decision.

Ms. W seemed more overtly upset and more communicative about her developing psychotic experiences than do most schizophrenic persons experiencing a first break. She also seemed more able to perceive these experiences as very abnormal for her. The mental status examination indicated that she was oriented but was not functioning well on abstraction of proverbs. This latter difficulty might have been associated with relatively low education combined with an extremely high anxiety level at the time of this examination. She reported no severe headaches, no visual disturbances, no ataxia, nor any of the other signs of organic brain lesions as listed in the DSM III section on organic brain syndromes. She did report severe sleep disturbances during the past several months.

In response to questions, Ms. W stated that she was a 34-year-old, divorced childless woman who had been working fairly steadily for over 10 years as a semiskilled electronics assembly line worker. She lived alone in an apartment complex but had some social contacts through a bowling team. There were no relatives nor any close friends in the area.

Ms. W had been on the night shift at her factory job for 6 months and had some angry verbal exchanges with various neighbors during that period about their being noisy during the day and keeping her awake. They did not comply at all with her requests that they be more quiet.

When questioned about what she had done about sleeping when the neighborhood remained noisy, she said she bought over-the-counter sleeping pills at the drug store and had also purchased Dexedrine from a contact at the factory to stay awake at night. She had been increasing the doses of both so she could sleep lightly during the days and stay awake, although with difficulty, through the night. A call by the clinician to the hospital pharmacy supplied the information that one of the main ingredients of her over-the-counter sedative was scopolamine.

She was admitted voluntarily to the psychiatric unit for the 5 days that were required to overcome the effects of overmedication so that she could return home. No antipsychotic medications were required. She decided to forego the extra night-shift pay at the factory and work only days and evenings until she found a safer way to manage her sleep problems.

The predicament of Ms. W was a good illustration of the interacting effects of social isolation and legal or illegal substance abuse. A person who was in real communication with either friends, family, co-workers, neighborhood acquaintances, or other groups would be less likely to go quite so far in her solitary way of trying to solve her sleeping problem by using so much medication. Some close associate, if there had been one, would probably have provided her with feedback about her developing psychosis before it reached the acute stage at which she was admitted.

Although Ms. W appeared on admission to have many of the characteristics of a schizophreniform illness, her distress about the symptoms and the relatively sudden onset led the clinician to the conclusion that the most immediate problem was intoxication from the medications she had been taking. However, she was strongly encouraged to consider making the effort to expand her social contacts as a health maintenance measure, which might later become an enjoyable addition to her life-style.

SETTING UP TWO-WAY COMMUNICATION WITH SCHIZOPHRENIC PEOPLE

There are many theories about communication with schizophrenic people. Most of these theories are probably accurate in accounting for some but not all schizophrenic communication problems. Since there is great variation among schizophrenic people, there is no exact formula that should be applied to every one of them. However, generalities such as making oneself clear, using simple terms, and conveying warmth and respect are probably useful for any communication situation with almost any psychiatric client.

Some schizophrenic clients' ability to receive and send communication is impaired because of organic factors such as neurological inadequacy, neurological deterioration, and chemical autointoxication. There are far more placental abnormalities and severely difficult births among people who later are diagnosed with schizophrenic disorders than among those who are not so diagnosed (Mednick, 1970). Pathological conditions of the brain, especially of the hippocampus of the brain, are found more often among schizophrenics than among the general population. Not all schizophrenics have neurological abnormalities, but the incidence is definitely higher than in the rest of the population (Arieti, 1974). For some schizophrenic clients, anxiety may operate without disturbing body chemistry to produce a functional confusion accompanied by misinterpretation of reality in receiving, interpreting, organizing, and storing incoming information. Either the organic or functional theories can be used to account for some of the characteristics of schizophrenic communication. When interacting with a client who is not already well known, the clinician should remain aware that either organic or functional impairment or both may be causing confusion in the client's communication.

Characteristics of schizophrenic communication include tendencies to do the following:

1. Clients grasp at concrete images and items as a delirious person does, without capacity to organize these or perceive them in their current context.

   If you would take me home with your pretty children and be my mother too, I would be well like they are.

   This is a statement from a 31-year-old schizophrenic woman who had children of her own, to a nurse not much older than herself. This nurse had provided hospital care in a matter-of-fact way that did not overly foster dependency. The statement grasps at a fragmentary idea of being cared for with no recognition of most of the evident contextual information such as their similar ages.

2. Clients express concrete ideas as abstract ones.

   Clinician: What would you like us to help you with here?
   Client: Have peace declared.

3. Clients express abstract ideas as concrete ones.

   Client: If I went to the emergency unit again, they would tear this diamond right off my finger—shred the flesh down to the bone—maybe the bone too—blood all over—I'd never be the same.

   The translation after a half hour of interviewing with the support of free talking was as follows:

   My husband said he won't stay around for any more of my going back and forth to hospitals and emergency units.

4. Clients base logic on similarity of predicates rather than of subjects in sentences (Von Domarus principle).

   She has killed me and thrown away my body.

77

Translation by the end of the interview:

She aborted our child, threw it away.

The subjects of these sentences have been changed, while the predicates remain essentially the same in this client's form of logic.

5. Clients send messages about being psychotic and thus requiring hospitalization or other medication interventions.

Nonverbal message:
Client enters office and starts unplugging lamps, electric clock, and typewriter, rubbing ends of electric plugs against each other. Crawls on floor and over furniture to do this. Answers coherently on items such as name and admits past hospitalizations but does not respond to questions about activity with electric cords.

6. Clients lapse into bizarre ruminations and explanations for repeated failures.

I know it must have been one of the Mafia's children that I pushed off the porch steps one day when I was little. I didn't know who it must have been until years later. Terrible things have happened to me all the time. They will never stop—gets worse—probably they're planning to torture me before they kill me.

7. Clients send messages about rage, despair, and other "dangerous" negative emotions coded in psychotic-sounding phrases rather than expressed directly.

My goal is to survive the coming holocaust, the breakdown of the way we live now. I almost look forward to the holocaust.

There is much "off the top of the head" advice published about communicating with schizophrenic people. There are also several research studies that provide applicable information.

The extensive research of Truax and Carkhuff (1967) shows that a clinician who conveys nonpossessive warmth, genuineness, and accurate empathy is statistically more likely to succeed with schizophrenic clients (as well as with other clients) than is a clinician who lacks one or more of these qualities.

The research of Tompkins (1963) extended by Colby (1975) shows that preserving the dignity of the client in both one's overt and covert com-munication is essential to help maintain a paranoid schizophrenic client's ability to communicate coherently. Tompkins had stated that the major source of distortion in paranoid disorders, including paranoid schizophrenia, was a permanent state of vigilance to maximize the detection of insult and minimize humiliation. Colby has been able to transpose this idea into computer instructions that result in psychotic responses to any statement by the simulated professional interviewer which might conceivably threaten the paranoid client's self-esteem. Colby's computer tapes could not be identified by a panel of experienced clinicians as different from tapes of real interviews with paranoid persons.

Donald Meichenbaum (1977) reports considerable success in teaching schizophrenic people to converse more clearly. In Meichenbaum's method, a clinician-instructor models self-dialogue phrases such as "take your time and answer sensibly" for schizophrenic clients. These clients are taught to incorporate such phrases into their own self-dialogue and to use this wherever they might be called on to answer questions. Meichenbaum reports that with much reinforced practice, these clients did communicate measurably more clearly and directly. Although this entire training program could not be carried out within the time limits of the psychiatric emergency unit, Meichenbaum's technique of encouraging confused clients to take time to compose themselves before answering questions can be started there.

Some psychotic talk does contain communication through use of symbols for realities that the client is unable to convey directly. The use of symbolism by the psychotic person is seldom a sensible or meaningful representation of the essence of a concept or feeling. However, a clinician may often profitably observe schizophrenic verbal and nonverbal communications as if these were attempts to convey meanings, even though awkward attempts. The client's concept or feeling can often be located tentatively through attempting to interpret the precursor for the symbol being used. This hunch can then be checked out and clarified in dialogue with the client.

The deterioration of clear, matter-of-fact communication during acute schizophrenic episodes often leaves the clients' symbolic communications as the only accessible avenues for the clinician to explore in gathering information. The important thing to remember when doing this is to check out with the client any interpretation that the clinician is using to make decisions.

RESEARCH ON LIFE EVENTS AS THESE RELATE TO SCHIZOPHRENIC EXACERBATIONS

When using the crisis intervention model for emergency unit situations, it must be kept in mind that there are many instances in which the client or the exacerbation precipitated the event rather than the reverse. Several investigators have reported an increase in life events during the few weeks or months preceding schizophrenic rehospitalization. Of these investigators, Fontana et al. (1972) have critically analyzed or asked whether the event was precipitated by the clients rather than being merely something that happened to them. These investigators report that many events in the clients' lives did occur as a result of clients' own actions and that these events were directly involved in the process promoting hospitalization. They also report that clients favoring a mental illness explanation for their difficulties report significantly fewer events than do those not favoring this explanation. The clinician in an emergency unit must remain aware that three possibilities, with some overlap among them, need to be considered in working with reports of a recent life event. These three possibilities are described as follows:
1. The event may have caused the exacerbation. In this case, the clinician might help the client make a substitute or restorative arrangement.
2. The client may have set up the event consciously or unconsciously in attempts to reach other goals such as declaration of more autonomy, revenge, or premature withdrawal from some support associated with the "sick role." In this case the clinician should not respond as if the event was the cause of the exacerbation rather than an instrument for attempting to meet other goals. Developing more direct ways to reach these goals in the future might be a focus for a part of brief therapy.

3. The exacerbation may have caused the event. In this case the clinician might attempt to teach the client to come in for help earlier if the same symptoms signal approach of a future exacerbation. These symptoms might be sleeplessness, increased confusion, return of hallucinations, and so forth.

EMERGENCY UNIT PROBLEMS WITH SCHIZOPHRENIC CLIENTS

Although schizophrenic clients may occasionally be combative in the emergency unit, far more common problems are withdrawal, passivity, and incoherence. As stated earlier, some schizophrenic clients will interact better with professional people who convey respect, warmth, and good will. However, even the most skilled professional, even a paragon of warm and respectful support, will not be able to overcome the withdrawal and passivity of every schizophrenic person within the emergency unit time frame.

Simple words, short sentences, clear questions, and clear unambiguous statements help somewhat. Making decisions for ambivalent clients and informing them clearly and warmly why this will be done also may help.

Clear explanations about items such as the limits on wandering about or leaving the unit should be stated before the client guesses incorrectly and has to be corrected. Information about times and types of available meals and snacks should be furnished to the client early in the interview. The location of bathrooms and rules about whether this particular client needs to be accompanied there by a staff member should be made explicit in a courteous, warm, and respectful manner. Rules about matters such as smoking should be explained before the client is able to break one of these rules.

It helps if professionals can at times imagine themselves in a state of severe confusion such as some nonschizophrenic people may recall having felt during a high fever, when emerging from anesthesia, or even when awakened suddenly from a very deep sleep. Imagining this occasionally may make it easier for the staff person to understand how clear, coherent, slow, and repetitious one's communication with a schizophrenic person in an emergency unit may need to be.

For the relatively rare schizophrenic person who may be combative in the emergency unit, one should have both adequate discretion and staff teamwork to prevent either the client or staff members from being injured. This is discussed further in the chapter on the assaultive client.

Interviewing of collateral persons. Many schizophrenic persons who have had good quality psychotherapy or medication or both can provide for the emergency unit personnel an adequate history of their illness and prior treatment. Questioning the client first conveys more respect from the interviewer than does asking the accompanying relative or other companion to answer questions first.

If a family member or companion is present, it is generally useful to verify or supplement the client's account by talking with this other person. It is also important for the clinician to assess probable support for clients in the event of their return to the current living situation if clients are now living with persons who have accompanied them to the emergency unit.

Emergency medication. Parenteral neuroleptic administration is often implemented for prompt symptomatic control of acutely disturbed schizophrenic people. Guidelines for using short-acting intramuscular neuroleptics for rapid neuroleptization can be found in Anderson and Kuehnle, 1974; Ayd, 1977; Donlon and Tupin, 1974; Hollister, 1972; Peschke, 1974; Polak and Laycob, 1974; Sangiovanni, 1973.

It is important to avoid using long-acting parenteral neuroleptics at "normal" dosage levels until the client has been tested for sensitivity to a small dose.

Brief treatment. Brief treatment starting in an emergency unit may have two purposes. It may serve to enable clients to return to a previous level of functioning by using their former style of coping. In brief therapy, a clinician may also convey to clients that there are more ways of viewing the clients' situation than their current or habitual ways of viewing it. This can serve as a motivator for follow-up visits. For example, clients who tend to overuse aversive attempts at

controlling or intereacting with others can be introduced to the idea that they would succeed more frequently if they learned to vary this practice by the use of some reward techniques also (Swanson and Woolson, 1972). Clients can get the idea that their presentation of self as chronically angry—or cold—or walled off from others might be changed to their own benefit (see case vignette #2). They can be given the idea that coping phrases like those researched by Meichenbaum (1978) for schizophrenic clients might help them manage better and might even prevent some of their episodes of confusion more effectively.

The case vignette that follows is an example of using a respectful adult-to-adult approach in an emergency unit interview and several follow-up sessions for problem solving.

Case vignette #2

Mr. R was a tall attractive former high school English teacher who was escorted into the psychiatric emergency unit by two police officers. One of the officers unobtrusively removed ashtrays, a small lamp, and other throwable objects to the far side of the room and then quietly moved to a corner of the room and told Mr. R he could relax and sit down. The police officer conveyed confidence that the crisis was now under control and that Mr. R was not genuinely dangerous. Although Mr. R was disheveled, dirty, and tremulous with anger, his appearance and diction still conveyed the impression of an English teacher who has been miscast in a violent role that did not fit him.

The police had been called to restrain Mr. R as he was throwing merchandise around a men's clothing store and shouting, "I'll show you how to treat me better than that!" He had exploded into this rage when a store clerk, seeing his very untidy and confused appearance, had suggested that the store management preferred not to let him try on new clothing.

Mr. R was now 38 years old and reported that he had three hospitalizations during the previous 5 years with a diagnosis of paranoid schizophrenia. He was already known to the local police because of a similar episode of destructive rage when he felt he had been insulted in a sporting goods store about a year earlier. Also, he immediately described having been arrested several times in another state by "police as mixed up as these two. The police in Pennsylvania didn't know what they were doing either!"

By inviting him to describe his own point of view about the incident in the clothing store an hour earlier, the clinician who interviewed him had little difficulty in getting him to state that he guessed he had become more excited than necessary. The courteous but firm police action in bringing him to the psychiatric emergency unit rather than jail seemed to have calmed him somewhat in advance of the interview. He was now temporarily ready to take the position that mental illness might have made him behave this way.

After the point in the interview at which he could talk about having been overly upset and could also report his former psychiatric history in adequate detail, the clinician inquired whether any medication had ever helped him with his anger and tension in the past. He said Stelazine had helped him but he had run out of it about 2 months earlier. He was willing to try some again in an effort to regain his composure. The prescription was obtained and he swallowed the medication willingly. Although oral medication cannot calm anyone within a few seconds, the placebo effect seemed to take over immediately until the actual medication effect could occur.

Because dignity and respect seemed to be such crucial issues with Mr. R, as they are with many paranoid persons, the clinician reflected warmly to him the observation that he looked and sounded like a person who had probably been managing his own life in the past a good bit better than the present scene would indicate. He responded by talking about 4 years of successful military service in which he had risen to the

level of corporal. This was followed by going through college on his own with the help of the GI bill. Then he had taught high school for 6 years and worked toward a master's degree during part of the teaching years.

He spoke of a difficult and lonely childhood and adolescence in a small northeastern town. His father had been in the state hospital since Robert was 8, and his mother managed the family gas station at that time. This was many years before the women's liberation movement had designated this kind of career as appropriate for a woman. He had felt deeply stigmatized because of both his mother's and his father's behavior. He had been able to relate to other adolescents only when they brought their cars into his family's gas station and he felt that they needed and respected his knowledge of cars. He did not socialize with these same teenagers when they were at school.

In returning to the high school scene in a new locality as a handsome young teacher of English, Mr. R had a period of feeling more accepted in that high school than he had ever experienced as a student. He married, had two daughters, and then began to have ideas of reference that the high school boys were watching him with jealous looks and that some of the girls were in love with him. Although this initially may have been based on some observations about real high school crushes on him which some girls may have been signaling, his feelings progressed to the stage where there were delusions about some of the girls sending love messages to his brain. He acted on these delusions and started responding to the "brain messages" by writing love notes, telephoning girls at home, and even turning up on their doorsteps. Of course, he quickly lost his job.

When he persisted even more fixedly in his pursuits, he was committed involuntarily for psychiatric care. After leaving the hospital he resumed chasing the same girls, whom he admitted were now terrified of him. He was jailed and transferred to a hospital. After the third involuntary hospitalization, he took off alone for the West Coast and obtained a job in the mail room of a large business. He had reverted to his childhood self-image and now again viewed himself as stigmatized and an outcast. He continued to take Stelazine during part of that period.

He agreed to come to the clinic and talk with the same clinician the following day. After that the clinician saw him weekly for seven sessions in the clinic and for 3-month and 6-month follow-up sessions. He continued taking Stelazine throughout that period and for the following year.

Mr. R's therapy centered on how he might become more likable to people. After trying several approaches to give him confidence to change himself rather than continuing to change his perceived reality through delusional thinking, the clinician finally decided to use Mr. R's confidence in computers and other machinery to help him. Because of his trust in machines, and because his unstructured time and high reading skills made him a good candidate for supplementary bibliotherapy between clinic visits, Mr. R was given a book about a computerized research study to read. This book was a copy of the research by Truax and Carkhuff (1967) on the three personal qualities of nonpossessive warmth, genuineness, and accurate empathy as facilitators of clinicians' relationships with clients. When the book was loaned to him, emphasis was placed on the role of videotapes in gathering the data and of computers in analyzing it.

He found the book interesting. He was willing to let his confidence in the accuracy of machine-processed knowledge carry him through a transition period of experimenting with changing his approaches to people. He carried a small card listing the three therapeutic qualities in his shirt pocket as a reminder at first.

The change in how he related to others required him to focus on the effects he was having on others rather than on how others were about to ignore or reject him. He started sending fewer signals of anger and isolation. He started awkwardly to find out how people felt about things, "developing empathy." He practiced first *appearing* and later *feeling* warm and genuine in his approaches to people. He carried out assignments to report back on how his landlady and two men in a neighborhood bar where he spent an hour each day *felt* about at least two items. As his history showed, he really wanted to be liked, so his own unconscious motivations helped him to continue developing.

When last heard from by letter 3 years later, he reported he had a good job in the post office, his own apartment, a roommate, and friends. While this was not a brilliant outcome for so intelligent and persistent a human, he reported that he now felt well.

In a research study, Mr. R might have been counted as a genetic schizophrenic because of his father's illness. Because of his outcome, one could speculate that his disorder had been "learned" because he *expected* to become like his father. If so, it was "unlearned" when an acceptable way to unlearn it was presented to him.

DECIDING WHETHER TO HOSPITALIZE THE CLIENT

As Arieti (1970) states, the presence of even mild psychotic symptoms used to be considered an indication for hospitalizing the client. Today, most clinicians avoid hospitalizing clients who have strengths and supports adequate enough to remain in the community.

There are practical considerations also. Insurance coverage, eligibility for veterans or other special benefits, or incomes not low enough to qualify for some of the publicly supported institutions limit the clinician's options for the best placement of some clients. Also, the best clinical facilities are often the ones that have no available beds on a given day.

Reasons for preferring to hospitalize a particular client are as follows:

1. The client is confused to the extent that su-

pervision is required for the sake of the client and others. This level of supervision may not be available except in a hospital.

2. The client appears to need higher doses of medication than should be tried without very frequent professional observation until medication is stabilized.
3. The family may have reached its limits of tolerance for bizarre or otherwise ill behavior. Unless a period of relief is provided for them, they may progress to more hostile behavior toward the client than they have exhibited earlier.
4. The client may need a structured program and group living to stop drifting away from others into deeper psychosis.
5. The client is currently so bizarre that either the client's future self-image, amenability to treatment, or future neighborhood acceptance might be seriously jeopardized by forcing a return to the community before some treatment gains are made.
6. Family may be pathogenic for some schizophrenic persons; hospitalization is used to evaluate this hypothesis. To test the effects of a temporary removal of a client from the family requires more time and observation than usually can be afforded in psychiatric emergency work. With information regarding the effect of hospitalization on the client and family, a more carefully studied choice between family therapy and removal of the client from the home might be made.

Contraindications to hospitalization include the following:

1. Serious negative changes in one's self-image as a competent person may occur as a result of having been hospitalized one or more times for psychiatric reasons.
2. Psychiatric hospitalizations may cause the client to be perceived less favorably by family members, employers, and other associates.
3. Job, school, or living arrangements interrupted by psychiatric hospitalization may be difficult, sometimes even impossible, to resume.
4. The clinician might be able to modify some stressful aspects of the client's environment by negotiating with or educating family, board

and care operators, or other persons who accompany the client to the emergency unit.

5. Extended outpatient facilities, sheltered residential arrangements, socialization groups, day treatment, and other supports provided by community mental health systems might be used where available rather than hospitalization.
6. The temptation to stop struggling to live in the real world, to live dependently and passively, is a dangerous one for some schizophrenic people. Experienced clinicians who have developed empathy for the conflicts of many schizophrenic people often hesitate to offer the opportunity for withdrawal into the "patient role" without due consideration for its dangers to a vulnerable person. Sometimes it can feel as uncomfortable to a clinician to offer this retreat as it would be to offer a large drink to an alcoholic. Some schizophrenics benefit from brief retreats into hospitals, but not all do.
7. The structured programs required by many inpatient units seem to be negatively correlated with recovery in schizophrenic men who are young in age and also young in years of illness than are less structured programs. These are the findings reported by Sanders et al. (1967). They report less difference for women when outcomes after being in structured and in unstructured programs are compared. Some structured programs seem to be interfering with people's need to think through the issues related to one's breakdown. A busy schedule can promote denial.
8. The client may be able to cope outside of the hospital even with severe symptoms and may have been doing this for some time. Unless there is evidence that bizarre behavior represents an acute exacerbation, there may be no reason to hospitalize the client.

Choosing the referral target

Some of the issues in choosing a particular hospital, or deciding not to hospitalize, are discussed in the previous outline. There are also limitations for the clinician who wants to refer a client to the best outpatient care. Eligibility for insurance, welfare support, or other financial help is one of the limitations. So is availability. As is often true with hospital referrals, the best clinicians are often those who are too fully booked to accept any more clients.

Length of experience in a particular emergency unit increases a clinician's knowledge of referral targets available within that area. One learns with increasing precision which colleagues and programs are best for which kinds of clients and situations. It is important to learn from other staff members all one can about this unofficial level of reality, since referral targets may appear officially to be identical but really are not. It is also important to share this information when one has obtained it through experience.

MAKING THE REFERRAL. The main elements in making effective referrals are using salesmanship, being accurately informative, and being persistent in following up until some kind of bonding occurs between the referral target and the client. Since the best targets usually do not need additional clients, it is often necessary to present the client and situation in such a way that the target agency or target clinician will be interested in working with that client.

If the target agrees to see the client once, accurate information should be sent along in a thorough but concise form. Many referrals are not consummated unless some arrangement is made to have the client or a person responsible for the client call back to the emergency unit and notify the clinician there when an actual meeting between client and referral target has occurred.

INFORMING THE CLIENT OF THE REFERRAL. Informing the client of the referral should be done with clarity about the reasons for the clinician's choice of target. The client needs to be given information about what gains are hoped for. Other people who take responsibility for the client also need this information.

As with clients in other situations, termination should be considered a significant part of the treatment. Emergency unit clients should depart with the feeling that they were seen as important people and that their problems were treated constructively and with due professional seriousness.

BIBLIOGRAPHY

Anderson, W.H., and Kuehnle, J.C.: Strategies for the treatment of acute psychosis, J.A.M.A. **229**:1884, 1974.

Arieti, S.: Interpretation of schizophrenia, ed. 2, New York, 1974, Basic Books, Inc.

Ayd, F.J.: Guidelines for using short-acting intramuscular neuroleptics for rapid neuroleptization, Int. Drug Ther. Newslet. **12**:5, 1977.

Bowers, M.B.: Biochemical processes in schizophrenia: an update, Schizophr. Bull. **6**(3):393, 1980.

Cecil, M.: Through the looking glass, Encounter p. 18-29, Dec. 1956.

Clausen, J.A., and Yarrow, M.: Mental illness and the family, J. of Soc. Issues **11**(4):3, 1955.

Colby, K.M.: Artificial paranoia: a computer simulation of paranoid processes, New York, 1975, Pergamon Press, Inc.

Donlon, P.T., and Tupin, J.P.: Rapid "digitalization" of decompensated schizophrenic patients with antipsychotic drugs, Am. J. Psychiatry **131**:310, 1974.

Dunham, H.W.: Social systems and schizophrenia, New York, 1980, Praeger Publishers, Inc.

Fontana, A.F., et al.: Prehospitalized coping styles of psychiatric patients: the goal directedness of life events, J. Nerv. Ment. Dis. **155**:311, Nov. 1972.

Hollingshead, A.B., and Redlich, F.C.: Social class and mental illness: a community study, New York, 1958, John Wiley & Sons, Inc.

Hollister, L.E.: Mental disorders—antipsychotic and antimanic drugs, N. Engl. J. Med. **286**:984, 1972.

Mednick, S.A., and Schulsinger, F.: Factors related to breakdown in children at high risk for schizophrenia. In Roff, M., and Ricks, D., editors: Life History Research in psychopathology, Minneapolis, 1970, University of Minnesota Press.

Meichenbaum, D.: Cognitive-behavior modification: an integrative approach, New York, 1978, Plenum Press.

Miller, D.R., and Swanson, G.E.: Inner conflict and defense, New York, 1960, Henry Holt.

Myers, J., and Roberts, B.: Family and class dynamics in mental illness, New York, 1959, John Wiley & Sons, Inc.

Peschke, R.W.: Parenteral haloperidol for rapid control of severe, disruptive symptoms of acute schizophrenia, Dis. Nerv. Syst. **35**:112, 1974.

Polak, R., and Laycob, L.: Rapid tranquilization, Am. J. Psychiatry **128**:600, 1974.

Sanders, R., Smith, R.S., and Weinman, B.S.: Chronic psychoses and recovery: an experiment in socioenvironmental treatment, San Francisco, 1967, Jossey-Bass, Inc.

Sangiovanni, F., et al.: Rapid control of psychotic excitement states with intramuscular haloperidol, Am. J. Psychiatry **130**:1115, 1973.

Swanson, M.G., and Woolson, A.M.: A new approach to the use of learning theory with psychiatric patients, Perspect. Psychiatr. Care **10**(2):55, 1972.

Tomkins, S.: Affect, imaginery, consciousness: the negative effects, vol. 2, New York, 1963, Springer-Verlag New York, Inc.

Truax, C.B., and Carkhuff, R.R.: Toward effective counseling and psychotherapy: training and practice, Chicago, 1967, Aldine Publishing Co.

CHAPTER **6**

The client with an affective disorder

Melvin S. Gale, M.D.

> *A profoundly painful dejection, abrogation of interest in the outside world, loss of the capacity to love, inhibition of all activity, and a lowering of the self-regarding feelings to a degree that finds utterance in self-reproaches and self-revilings, and culminates in a delusional expectation of punishment* (Sigmund Freud).

The severe affective disorders exist at one end of a continuum of mood disturbances. Moving along the continuum, one reaches the milder affective disorders, which then merge imperceptibly into the normal changes in mood caused by the vicissitudes of life. There are a variety of methods of classification of these disorders; this chapter will use the classification scheme of the American Psychiatric Association's *Diagnostic and Statistical Manual III*. DSM III divides illnesses that cause mood change into three well-defined categories: *Major affective disorder,* in which a full syndrome of affective disorder has been present for 2 years; *other specific affective disorder,* in which the illness has been present for 2 years but only a partial syndrome has been present; and *atypical affective disorder,* for affective illness that does not fit either of the other categories.

Major affective disorders

The category of major affective disorders is subdivided into two groups. All clients who have had true manic episodes are considered to be in the *bipolar* category, the underlying assumption being that these clients either have had depressed episodes or will have them in the future. Clients who have had one or more true depressive episodes but have not had manic episodes are placed in the other category, the unipolar affective disorders, or *major depressive illness.*

Bipolar affective disorders are subclassified according to the current presentation of the client: *manic type,* for the client who has a 2-year history of affective illness and enters the clinic with a manic episode; *depressed type,* for the client with a 2-year history of affective illness that includes prior manic episodes and who reports with a current depressive episode; and *mixed type,* for the client who is experiencing symptoms of both mania and depression at the same time or alternating every few days.

Epidemiologically, women are reported to have more affective illness than men. The female/male ratio is approximately 1.5:1 and decreases with increasing age. The risk for either sex is greater when there is family history of affective illness (Helgason, 1979). When considering all affective disorders, the overwhelming preponderance are unipolar depressions and only a small minority are bipolar.

Clients with bipolar illness are younger at the date of the first symptom than those with unipolar illness, with the first episode usually occurring before 30 years of age (depressive episodes can occur at any age). They have shorter cycles of illness and remission (both shorter periods of illness and less time between episodes). The overall prognosis is worse in bipolar illness: approximately half of unipolar clients recover in 5 years without treatment, but fewer than a fourth of bipolar clients do (Angst, 1979).

Other specific affective disorders

As with the major affective disorders, a 2-year history is required for other specific affective disorders; the difference is that the severity requirements are less strict. These clients do not show a full syndrome of either mania or depression, but there are some affective symptoms. The category includes clients who had what was called personality disorders in the past and who have a history of long-standing maladaptation to life

dating from early adulthood, as well as current depressive or manic symptoms. There are no psychotic symptoms whatsoever, but the periods between episodes are characterized by poor adjustment to life. There are two categories of this disorder: cyclothymic and dysthymic.

CYCLOTHYMIC DISORDER. Cyclothymic disorder is marked by alternating periods of depression and hypomania, but neither severe enough for the diagnosis of a manic episode or a true depressive episode. Alternating moods are typical, without discrete episodes of illness and health.

The concept of symptom pairs is especially useful in diagnosing cyclothymic disorders. Two symptoms are opposite each other, with one being experienced when the person is in a depressive episode and the other experienced when in a manic or hypomanic episode. The most common symptom pairs are shown in Table 6-1.

DYSTHYMIC DISORDER. Dysthymic disorder is analogous to major depressive illness, except that the severity of the depression is not as pronounced. There generally is a lifelong illness with no more than a few months of normal functioning. This is comparable to the former DSM II diagnosis of depressive neurosis.

The main diagnostic entities to be differentiated from other specific affective disorders are the personality disorders. In the latter the mood fluctuations are less prominent, less se-

TABLE 6-1. Symptom pairs used in diagnosing cyclothymic disorders

Depressive episode symptoms	Manic episode symptoms
Feelings of inadequacy	Inflated self-esteem
Social withdrawal	Uninhibited seeking of social contacts
Excess sleep	Decreased sleep
Lowered work productivity	Increased work productivity
Decreased energy and attention span	Creative thinking—great energy for work
Decreased sexual drive	Increased sexuality
Decreased pleasure in activities; guilt	Increase of pleasure-seeking activity

vere, and less frequent, and they do not significantly interfere with social and work functioning.

Atypical affective illness

Both of the previous diagnostic categories have relatively strict requirements for a diagnosis to be made. Yet there are clients who have affective symptoms and do not fit the criteria for any of the prior categories. These are the atypical affective illnesses. In an emergency setting this diagnosis should rarely be made.

ETIOLOGY OF AFFECTIVE DISORDERS

Affective illness is complex, and it is therefore not surprising that there is no consensus as to etiology. Three approaches to the problem of etiology are described.

Genetics

There appears to be a strong genetic influence, because first-degree relatives of bipolar clients show as much as 50% morbidity in some series. Yet neither bipolar nor unipolar clients always breed true; both illnesses can occur in the same family, which supports an inference of polygenic inheritance.

Zerbin-Rudin (1979) describes three different viewpoints regarding the role of heredity in affective disorders. The oldest idea holds that unipolar and bipolar illnesses are genetically identical, but that in unipolar cases the mania is latent (given enough time, the mania would reveal itself). The second and more recent view postulates great individual variation in vulnerability to affective illness. When the combination of genetic predisposition and life stress causes a crossing of the first threshold of vulnerability, unipolar depressive illness appears. If the combination of genetic and environmental factors is even stronger, the second threshold is passed and bipolar illness shows. This notion is consistent with the predominance of unipolar clients and allows for multifactored inheritance, which appears more accurate than a unitary hypothesis. The third and most recent view proposes a sharing of

genes between two separate disease entities, unipolar and bipolar.

If genes indeed do carry significant force in determining presence or absence of affective illness, then biochemical abnormalities would be expected to be the mediators of these illnesses.

Biogenic amines

Garver (1979) reviews the current status of the biogenic amines hypothesis for the etiology of affective illness: norepinephrine (NE) and serotonin (5-HT), the two major biogenic amines implicated, serve as transmitting agents in certain synapses of the brain. An effective reduction of activity of either amine appears to underlie depressive illness, whereas a disturbance of balance among transmitter agents with net increase in activity may produce mania.

Supporting evidence is to be found in the effects of reserpine and methyldopa. Both drugs can produce depression and both are known to deplete brain supplies of NE and 5-HT.

Further support arises from known effects of antidepressant medications. Monoamine oxidase (MAO) is an enzyme that deactivates NE and 5-HT, thus MAO-inhibiting drugs exert an antidepressant effect by raising effective levels of NE and 5-HT. Similarly, tricyclics exert their antidepressant effect by causing an increase in effective levels of NE and 5-HT. This increase is brought about by prevention of the reuptake of NE and 5-HT into the neurons, which would otherwise render the amines ineffective.

There is evidence of two subtypes of depression, depending on which amine is deficient in action. For those clients with NE deficiencies, desipramine is most effective. Amitriptylene, which has little effect on NE reuptake but major effects on 5-HT reuptake, is most effective with clients who have 5-HT deficiencies. Nortriptyline and imipramine have moderate effects on both NE and 5-HT metabolism.

Psychodynamics

Freud (1957) proposed that depression is the result of loss of an ambivalently held object and subsequent turning inward of aggression felt toward that object to one's self. The reader is referred to Bibring (1953), who has expanded this psychodynamic-developmental viewpoint with the emergence of ego psychology, and to Kohut (1971), who has broadened this further with the understandings of self psychology.

Beck (1963) demonstrated a significantly higher proportion of parental death in seriously depressed clients compared to other psychiatric clients. A similar study by Birtchnell (1970) showed severely depressed clients to have more parental loss than moderately depressed clients, but he did not find more parental death in depressive clients when compared to other psychiatric clients.

The work of Beck (1972) provides further support for the interpersonal viewpoint of depression, in the finding of precipitating stress in 95% of depressive clients (in contrast to schizophrenic clients, who show no such correlation). The precipitating stress is often the loss when a relationship ends. Beck postulates that there are in the general population both a continuum of ego strengths and a continuum of life stresses that may impinge. The combination of degree of stress and strength of the person undergoing that stress determines whether or not affective illness will appear.

Akiskal (1973) argues cogently for a unified hypothesis of depression, including genetic, developmental, pharmacological, and interpersonal factors. Although less simple, such a multifactorial viewpoint appears to be more accurate.

CLINICAL PRESENTATIONS
Manic episode

The predominant indicator of a manic episode is mood elevation. Elation, grandiosity, and increased self-esteem are hallmarks of mania. When these clients are frustrated and cannot get their way, they often become irritable, sometimes severely so, and are capable of lashing out at others who interfere with them.

The associated signs frequently seen include rapid and loud speech, excess motor activity, and diminished sleep. These clients may be quite distractable and are likely to take risks that are unwarranted given the possible rewards. Impaired

judgment may cause a manic client to underestimate risk. There is a voluble sociability well beyond appropriate levels. An intrusive and domineering quality is often noted. Sexuality is typically increased, with greater sexual drive than usual. Delusions and hallucinations, when present, are congruent with the often inflated mood, and consistent with the client's other ideas about himself and his self-worth.

Case vignette #1 illustrates a typical presentation of the manic state.

Case vignette #1

When his name was called, Mr. A jumped up excitedly in the waiting room. He was dressed in a three-piece business suit, yet incongruously: the suit was dirty and wrinkled, the shirt was not tucked in, his hair was not combed, and there was a 2- to 3-day's growth of beard. As he approached, moderate body odor was noted.

He started speaking immediately in a rapid speech that was poorly enunciated so that at times some of his words could not be heard clearly.

His first sentence was "I'm high." Then he changed the subject quickly and discussed the role and training of a psychiatrist, saying he had a number of professional associations with psychiatrists and that he used to practice law. He asked the clinician where he took his training, but continued to speak at a rate so rapid as not to leave time for a response. Mr. A continued speaking rapidly and loudly, completely dominating the brief interaction.

The clinician attempted to take Mr. A from the public waiting room to a more private interviewing room, but Mr. A did not appear to be paying attention to the clinician's directions to follow. He did readily go along after two or three attempts to get his attention.

After a few minutes of uninterrupted speech by Mr. A over a variety of topics whose connections to each other were elusive, the clinician decided to break in to obtain more historical data. Mr. A, becoming upset at the repeated loud interruptions needed to break into the flow of his speech, stood up and pounded the table in anger. At this point the clinician began to worry about possible physical danger to himself. He left the client in the room and sought assistance from other staff members.

Mr. A demonstrated some of the common signs of mania—talkativeness, grandiosity, distractibility, and flight of ideas, as well as an insight into his state of illness (in the brief opening comment that he was high). For such a client irritation at a clinician who attempts to interfere with his flow of thoughts may well rise to a level dangerous to the clinician.

DIFFERENTIAL DIAGNOSIS OF MANIC EPISODES. A number of alternatives for differential diagnosis of manic episodes exist.

Hypomania. The differentiation between mania and hypomania is in degree, without a sharp and objective distinguishing line. Hypomanic episodes show some of the signs just listed, but are much less severe. The client is more likely to maintain the ability to function at work and at home. The risks taken are less severe in that there is little danger to the client, and the elation is intermittent and more controlled, more moderated. These symptoms may escalate with time if they are early indicators of an evolving manic episode.

Schizophrenia versus mania. Schizophrenia, especially the paranoid type, may be very difficult to differentiate from mania. Both may show grandiosity and delusional jealousy. Both can demonstrate extreme rage and risk of violent outbursts.

Schizoaffective schizophrenia. The term *schizoaffective schizophrenia* has had a variety of definitions in the past and now is given in DSM III for the sole purpose of categorizing clients when the clinician is unable to make a differentiation between affective disorders and schizophrenic illnesses. Emergency clinicians will rarely have the time to do enough investigation to adequately diagnose complex cases. It is better to acknowledge an incomplete diagnosis by using terms such as *affective illness versus thought disorder* than using the term *schizoaffective schizophrenia* and thereby implying that a more thorough diag-

nostic attempt had been made without success. If this advice is followed, schizoaffective schizophrenia will have little use in emergency situations.

Organic brain syndrome with mania. An organic brain syndrome (OBS) can produce virtually any psychiatric symptom, and mania is no exception. The diagnosis is based on history as well as current symptom. Those with mania should have virtually no OBS signs, whereas those with OBS-induced mania should have a variety of OBS signs. In OBS the mania is likely to be transient.

Cyclothymic personality. Clients with cyclothymic personalities do have changes in their mood, but when they feel good they will not be as manic as in a true manic episode. The differentiation is a matter of degree.

Depressive episode

As in a manic episode, the hallmark symptom of a depressive episode is the mood: a sadness, a dysphoria, a loss of interest in the usual social and individual activities that provide pleasure (including sex). Energy level is lowered. Associated symptoms include anorexia, and decreased weight may be noted since the anorexia is often long standing and severe. Insomnia is quite common. Two other associated symptoms are psychomotor retardation and psychomotor agitation.

Psychomotor retardation. Psychomotor retardation is marked by a slowness of action and thought. The client is readily fatigued and cannot concentrate well. Clients may take a long time to answer a simple question because they have difficulty organizing their thoughts.

Psychomotor agitation. At times distress is manifested by increased activity, or psychomotor agitation. This can be differentiated from a manic episode because the degree of agitation is not as severe as in mania.

Feelings of worthlessness and guilt are typical indicators of depression, concomitant with the mood. There can be preoccupation with death and frequently suicidal preoccupation or suicidal wishes. Hypochondriacal concerns are common. Just as in the manic episode, if there are delusions and hallucinations, they are congruent with the mood.

Case vignette #2

Mr. B was sitting on a chair motionless and looking toward the floor. His face looked sad. When his name was called, there was no noticeable response at first, but a repeat calling of his name did yield a lifting up of Mr. B's head as he looked in the direction of the clinician. He was asked to accompany the clinician to the waiting room and he slowly followed.

His clothes were unkempt. On his hand a ring, somewhat larger than his finger, was taped to keep it from falling off.

Speech was slow with long pauses. Mr. B needed repeated questions to keep the conversation alive. Each response did correctly answer the question asked, but with little elaboration. After continued encouragement from the clinician, Mr. B began to speak a little more spontaneously. He had lost his wife and his job and believed both of these losses resulted from his recurrent episodes of manic depressive illness, which he had suffered for about 20 years. The rest of his family had lost interest in him. Now, at age 63, he didn't see any chance of returning to work as a lawyer, since his illness recurred every year or two. He felt he should be shot, "just like a horse with a broken leg," to end his misery. He felt he had ruined his life, and now that the results of his imprudent living were with him, he saw no way out.

When asked today's date, he said he didn't know. The clinician encouraged, almost forced him to guess, and he did correctly give the month and year but could offer no guess as to the day of the month.

Feelings of worthlessness, hopelessness, and guilt, all hallmarks of depression, were readily elicited from Mr. B. Given his perspective, suicide appears a logical step to end his suffering. His refusal to guess the date may be more the result of apathy than poor memory, since when he was pushed harder about month and year, he was correct.

DIFFERENTIAL DIAGNOSIS OF DEPRESSIVE EPISODE. An elderly person can appear demented on questioning, when actually an apathy based on an underlying depression prevents the client from responding normally. The depression and apathy cause an inability to concentrate and function at normal capacity on a mental status examination. Wells (1979) has called dementia-like symptoms based on functional illness "pseudodementia," and he describes a variety of features that distinguish true dementia from pseudodementia. The reader is referred there for more detail.

Just as in differentiating mania from OBS, a depression caused by OBS should also show other signs of organic cause. At times this can be difficult to determine, because cognitive testing may be impaired as a result of the depression.

Schizophrenia versus depression. Withdrawal and decreased ability to function are seen both in schizophrenia and in depression. In schizophrenia, the sequence is that the affective component of the illness is secondary to and follows the thought disorder and thus is a later-appearing symptom. In affective illness, in contrast, the affective symptoms are the first to show. Any hallucinations or delusions are not only mood congruent but occur after the affective disturbance has been significant.

Catatonic schizophrenia must be differentiated from affective illness with psychomotor retardation. Waxy flexibility and stereotypy are seen in catatonia but not in affective illness and thus are useful for diagnosis if present.

As in the differentiation of schizophrenia from mania, differentiation between schizophrenia and depression can be difficult with certainty in an emergency setting. See Pope and Lipinsky (1978) for further information.

Bereavement and a reaction to loss will always produce sadness in a normal person. The differentiation between the normal sadness of a loss and the pathological sadness of depression is primarily made on the presence or absence of self-depreciation and self-worth. This will be discussed in greater detail later in the chapter.

DIFFERENTIAL DIAGNOSIS OF AFFECTIVE DISORDERS

A number of other psychiatric illnesses and syndromes must be differentiated from affective disorders. Some common ones will be discussed.

Self-destructive impulses or action without significant disturbance of affect

When in an unpleasant situation, one may consider a variety of methods to change the situation, including a self-destructive act. When this planning is done consciously, the risk to life is generally calculated to be low. People with this conscious manipulation pose little risk of suicide completion, except if the plan is poorly executed, and they do not report to the emergency unit with symptoms of affective illness.

Another group of people perform what appears to be similar behavior, but the motives are unconscious. When evaluating self-destructive behavior in which disturbance of affect is absent, one of the first differentiations is between the rare conscious manipulation and an unconscious attempt to manipulate, in which the client is completely honest in denying any awareness of the goals.

In either of these situations the self-destructive act is likely to be one that, at least in the client's mind, has low *lethality* and high *publicity*. Many people are aware of the act, and often the person who is notified is a key actor in the client's dynamic system.

Some disturbance of affect may be seen in these cases, especially if the attempt to manipulate the environment has failed. When it has succeeded, all may be temporarily well, and no intervention wanted.

In the majority of these situations there is no affective disorder but rather a reactive disturbance to a stressful event.

Case vignette #3

Mr. G has been in a homosexual relationship for about 2 years with the same partner. At 28 years of age he is relieved that he has been able to settle down, his early 20s having been filled with a series of short homosexual relationships that were unsatisfying because of their instability.

On the evening of admission to the emergency unit, Mr. G's lover said that he had found another man and wanted to end the relationship. Mr. G felt that the loss would be overwhelming, and said, "There's no point in living without you." He walked to the medicine chest, took the first bottle of medicine he could find, came back into the room where the lover was and swallowed all the pills in the bottle in front of him.

When the clinician approached the client in the emergency unit, gastric lavage had been accomplished and the lover was at Mr. G's bedside. The lover was saying he would never see anyone else again, his true affection was with Mr. G, and he was sorry he had caused such a disruption to Mr. G.

On examination Mr. G expressed regret for the overdose, saying it was silly to act so impulsively. He recognized the importance of his relationship with the lover but felt that the relationship was sound and that as long as he had the lover he was fine. When asked how he would feel if the lover and he split up, he said he did not want to even think about that and was sure it would not happen.

Affect was bright and he voiced no complaints, only wanting to go home. He denied all depressive symptoms.

In this case the loss was averted, at least for the moment, by the suicide attempt. Although lethality depends on what medication was taken, the event was highly public and the lover had little choice but to call an ambulance to bring Mr. G to the hospital. The fact that the loss is now temporarily resolved, means Mr. G has little wish for any psychotherapeutic work. The suicidal impulse is no longer present, and there may be very little the clinician can do.

Sadness without depression

People who experience sadness without depression are found throughout the general population, and they usually do not feel they have any psychiatric disorder nor do they seek psychiatric help. The main differentiation between sadness and depression is self-depreciation. When a loss is suffered, whether a loss of relationship or a blow to one's pride (a self-esteem loss), sadness including crying is quite normal and appropriate. Other manifestations of sadness beyond crying are also frequently seen, such as insomnia and anorexia. But the degree to which persons feel that they are worthless and do not deserve to live is a major indicator of psychopathology rather than normal sadness (Katz, 1971). Helplessness is another major indicator.

The degree of affect expressed is not a reliable guide. During normal grief reactions, intensity of affect can be exceedingly high. In fact, the person who expresses the greatest degree of affect immediately after the loss is frequently able to completely reconstitute and resolve the loss, whereas the person who was the best defended and showed least affect often fails to resolve the grief reaction and will continue to suffer depressive symptoms.

Adjustment disorders

Severe psychiatric symptoms of any type other than psychotic are typical of adjustment disorders (DSM III), including depression and withdrawal. Adjustment disorders are defined as maladaptive responses to a stress with either severe symptoms or impairment of social or work functioning. The precipitating psychological stress has occurred within 3 months of the current symptoms.

Adjustment disorders are differentiated from affective disorders in that they are not a part of a long-standing pattern but appear as a transient response to specific stress that has a strong psychodynamic meaning. The symptom complex is often mixed. When the stress is removed from the client either through environmental manipulation, through changes that occur naturally, or through psychotherapeutic intervention, the adjustment disorder passes. In almost all cases, adjustment disorders are transient.

Typical diagnoses of the adjustment disorder category include adjustment disorder with depressed mood, adjustment disorder with mixed emotional features, and adjustment disorder with withdrawal. In this last category note that although withdrawal is a common symptom in depression, in the adjustment disorder with withdrawal the prominence of the depressive affect is missing.

Personality disorders

Personality disorders are long-standing patterns that have handicapped clients for most of their lives. They began in late adolescence or early adulthood, and any stress can exacerbate the disorder.

The differentiation between this and affective disorders is based on the fact that in personality disorders, depression is only a secondary phenomenon, the result of the deleterious effects of the personality, and is not consistent over periods of time.

Uncomplicated bereavement

Sadness and distress are seen after any loss, but self-depreciation is typically absent in normal grief reactions. The study by Clayton et al. (1972) of depression in widows showed 35% of widows to have depressive symptoms comparable to those who were diagnosed as clinically depressed. Not surprisingly, the presence of relationships with children was associated with less depression. Parkes (1970) also reviews the depression seen in the first year after widowhood.

Case vignette #4

Mr. and Mrs. C's car was hit head on by another car that crossed over the center line. Mr. C was driving and his side of the car sustained the brunt of the collision, causing serious injuries. Mrs. C only had minor injuries, so she was able to accompany her husband. Although Mrs. C was rapidly treated, Mr. C's injuries were severe and he died shortly after reaching the emergency unit. The driver of the other car was intoxicated and sustained two fractures, which were readily casted.

The psychiatric emergency unit clinician was asked to see Mrs. C shortly after she

93

heard the news that her husband died. She was crying uncontrollably and was enraged that her husband was killed "by that no-good drunk. He should have died, not my husband—it's not fair." Her fury at this other driver was intense and continuous. She prayed loudly, and disturbed other clients in the emergency unit with a piercing scream. She would not stop screaming or stop her rage. All her speech was intermittent, interrupted by loud sobbing.

She asked to see the body again but doing so only further stimulated her feelings and her screaming.

The clinician said little. Indeed there was little room to get a word in, and it was not clear if Mrs. C was listening. About a half hour later, Mrs. C called a funeral home to begin funeral arrangements and notified her brother to let the rest of the family know.

This is a normal case. The strong affect is understandable and appropriate. Little intervention is needed and in fact can be harmful if it does anything to interfere with the evolving grief reaction. Sedation or encouragement to suppress feelings is contraindicated.

The differentiation from affective disease is found in the very short history and clear precipitating event. Although the distress present is not markedly different from an affective illness, there is no self-depreciation in a normal grief reaction. See the chapter on bereavement for more detail.

INTERVIEW TECHNIQUE

In contrast to an initial interview in an outpatient setting in which the purpose is primarily diagnostic, in emergency settings the level of distress experienced by clients means both diagnostic and therapeutic purposes should be served. The diagnostic purpose is to make a clinical diagnosis, to assess suicide or other risks, and to make an appropriate disposition. The therapeutic goal is to have the client feel understood and less alone and thereby to relieve the stress to some degree. Experienced psychiatric emergency clini-

cians combine both these goals into an integrated, cohesive interview with no discrete boundary between them.

The sequence of the interview is critical; if it does not have an early empathic intervention, the client may not feel trust toward the clinician. In cases where there is an empathic failure, not only is there little therapeutic work done, but an accurate diagnostic assessment cannot be made. If clients do not feel they can trust the clinician, there is little chance that they will be open and honest enough to let the clinician know their most important and, of course, most painful thoughts. One of the most common errors made by novices is to gain a thorough history at the expense of the therapeutic relationship (see discussion of working alliance in Greenson, 1965). They may obtain pages of data but find out that the most important information is missing; although the data they have are accurate, they are also useless for their purposes.

Because of the critical importance of an early empathic intervention, the clinician listens to the client and searches for an opening in which to identify some feelings. To understand what is being felt and experienced by the client is the necessary first step, but it is not in itself sufficient. Saying "aha" or "I understand" or "I know how you feel" does not convey to the client the accuracy of that understanding and generally is not useful. The utility of the empathic understanding is the repetition back to clients, in words that are understandable to them, of exactly what it is that the clinician understands.

After a successful empathic intervention the interpretive or explanatory phase can begin.

Case vignette #5

Mr. L says he is likely to commit suicide tonight if he does not get any help. His girlfriend of 4 years has moved out. When asked to describe his relationship with her, he goes on to say how much she helps him. He used to spend money foolishly, and she offered to control the checkbook and asked that he give her his paychecks as soon as he got them. He agreed and then she controlled the finances, in his view effectively ending this problem. He goes on to say how he used to drink too heavily but she helped him with this by telling him that if he wanted her to stay with him he would have to cut down his drinking, and he was able to do so upon her demand.

Clinician: I can see she meant a great deal to you and you'll be missing her badly.

Mr. L (tears welling up in his eyes): I sure miss her. I don't know how I can get along without her. She was everything to me. I feel weak, like I can't make it on my own.

Clinician: It seems that this feeling you have that you are weak has made you feel dependent on her to help you to fill in some of these weak spots, as when she helped you control your drinking or your spending. Since she met these important needs of yours, you feel like you can't do without her.

The clinician's first response was a straightforward empathic comment only pointing out the importance of the girlfriend. As is usual with correct empathic interventions, the client's response showed more affect and gave additional data.

The second intervention explained why she was so important. This interpretive step can frequently be accomplished even in the first session of an emergency encounter. When successful, the therapeutic effect can be great.

With a correct empathic intervention, the client feels understood, rapport is strengthened, and the optimum setting is established for obtaining the full set of required data. After an intervention or two like this, one can ask about suicide risk with a greater degree of confidence that the response will be honest rather than an attempt to cover up to avoid embarrassment. The other advantage of a correct empathic intervention is therapeutic. Clients feel that at least someone else understands them, and this is always the first step toward the possibility of getting some help with their problem. There is now a possibility that their situation can be improved.

INTERVIEW WITH MANIC CLIENTS. Generally speaking, the more disorganized the manic client's thought processes are, the more disorganized the interview will be. The seriously manic person will not be able to provide correct logic or sequence. This individual will start talking on one topic and end up somewhere else, with the clinician able to observe the jumping around as well as the high rate of speech. But clinicians know they will be able to make better diagnostic and therapeutic decisions with certain concrete information if it is available. During these times it may be necessary to supply the structure to the interview that the manic person is unable to provide. This means interrupting clients when they deviate from the topic and bringing them back to the clinician's chosen topic. Clinicians should use questions that require only short answers, rather than asking the client to go through an organizing process to bring together pieces of data. It is just this very organization that some manic clients will not be able to provide.

Obtaining the client's attention may require assertive behavior. One may stand up, speak in a loud voice, or interrupt the client. When doing so, it is best to continue speaking rapidly, pausing only when soliciting a verbal response from the client, because any time the clinician stops, the client may verbally intervene. It is best to formulate the verbal plan of action, or even mentally rehearse ahead of time, to be able to speak without hesitation and with the appearance of confidence.

The assertiveness and control described here is a calculated risk for it may impede the therapeutic relationship and may be dangerous. Thus it is postponed until the clinician is prepared to take such a risk, usually later in the interview. As far as the concern about whether the manic client will tolerate assertiveness without getting irritated and possibly violent with the clinician, the guideline is always the same: *the clinician must subjugate therapeutic goals to the need for the clinician's safety.* No professional person, either in the mental health field or anywhere else, can be expected to function at peak capacity, to think clearly, to react quickly and decisively, when fearful of bodily injury. Because their work brings them in contact with a number of clients who have the potential for violence, psychiatric emergency clinicians must be careful to avoid heroic measures.

THREATENED VIOLENCE. Clinicians must maintain a high level of sensitivity to possible violence. Alertness, along with the concomitant anxiety that comes from being on the alert for signs of physical danger, is the best protection.

It is an unpleasant and sobering thought to realize that in the course of a day's work, one may be subject to violent attack. Because of the unpleasantness of this thought, some clinicians use the defense of denial, saying to themselves that the risk is not really that great, that through either luck or their superior empathic abilities, no client would ever strike them. It is just these clinicians who are at the greatest risk for violence, since they will be least able to make use of the protective mechanisms that are available in case of danger. The greatest and most useful protective mechanism is the anxiety felt when clues of potential assault are perceived. A denial mechanism will prevent that clinician from seeing and making use of those danger signs. This anxiety leads to a willingness to act immediately on the slightest clue to protect oneself (see chapter on the client with assaultive behavior).

Case vignette #6

Mr. D is a 38-year-old man who appears to be having a manic episode. His disorganization prevents any history from being obtained. While speaking, he does mention having been in jail for assault. He completely dominates the interview, so that the clinician is unable to get any questions answered. After a few questions, the client is upset at being interrupted and stands up, looking furious. He expresses anger at the clinician and continues to stare at the clinician. The clinician decides to leave the room to remove himself from danger.

This is a successful resolution of a possibly dangerous situation. One does not need concrete evidence of risk, such as a client saying "I'm going to hit you," before acting (although that evidence is often present). A subjective feeling of discomfort, even if the clinician cannot spell out the exact source of that discomfort, is adequate reason for self-protective measures. In this setting, the staring, the standing up, the history of assault, and the angry facial expression are enough evidence to warrant not continuing the one-to-one interview. Reacting in this manner, a clinician may be abbreviating many encounters in which there is no danger; however, if one continues interviewing in a situation of possible assaults, sooner or later there will be a mistake and the clinician will be hurt.

INTERVIEW DON'TS. With clients who are depressed and considering suicide, there is a temptation to convince the client that their thinking is mistaken, that suicide actually is not the best choice, that there is much to live for. It is a very rare client who can accept this advice. A much greater risk is that the client will feel that clinicians do not understand how bad things are, that if clinicians did, they too would draw the same logical conclusion that the client has, that is, that suicide is the best alternative.

Moralizing. There are a number of clients who have strong moral or religious prohibitions against suicide. For these people, those prohibitions can be effective deterrents to suicide, even if the level of depression would otherwise be severe enough to make suicide a possibility. These clients are lucky. How can one convince clients who do not have such moral prohibitions that they should adopt them? It is not possible. Those who do not have internal moral prohibitions are unlikely to accept them from anyone else. Again, as earlier, the risk is that an attempt to convince the client only makes the client feel misunderstood. Either the client will say yes to be polite and to silence the clinician, or get into an argument over it. Neither outcome is productive.

Interviews with seriously depressed clients. The lowered energy level of seriously depressed clients often leads to very slow interactions. Depressed clients often need extended periods to answer even simple questions because of their slowed thinking. The delays are in no sense oppositional although clinicians do often find this slowness to be very frustrating.

Countertransference

Whenever two humans interact, a relationship develops. If one person feels strong distress and seeks help from the other, the relationship is intensified from the help seeker's standpoint (even if from the helper's standpoint the interaction may be routine). If the topic discussed is the private thoughts and feelings of the client, then that tends to make that relationship even more intense because the client is being more open. In a psychiatric emergency context, the combination of both of these factors tends to make even a brief interaction of great importance to the client.

Viewing the interaction from the clinician's perspective, the manner in which the client deals with the clinician may make the interaction especially intense for that clinician. Clinicians become aware of a variety of thoughts and feelings inside themselves, arising from the client's manner and from their own personality. Usually there is interaction between both these variables, and in the broadest sense, both may be called countertransference.

If not recognized, these reactions usually interfere with the clinician's ability to be objective, whereas an awareness of one's own reaction may help to identify some subtle element in the client which evoked it. To improve clinicians' abilities to identify these reactions, some common ones evoked by emergency clients with affective illnesses will be described.

IRRITATION. The response of emergency department personnel to physically ill people is rapid assessment and short-term intervention. Many findings, especially with the critically ill client, are readily available with no cooperation at all from the client. In psychiatry, however, the client must talk, and one cannot make a client talk more quickly. Yet depressed clients by the very nature of their illness, often think and talk slowly. To wish to speed up a client is understandable, and one may feel irritated and frustrated at the slowness. Clinicians should not express either directly or subtly their irritation, since it is the illness itself that causes the slowness. A clinician should not be angry with a client for demonstrating signs of illness.

When clients are referred to psychiatric emergency units from emergency medicine practitioners, this irritation may have been in some way already expressed. If so, psychiatric clinicians may need to first deal empathically with clients' perceptions that those helping are upset with them. This is especially difficult when clients are embarrassed over their problems to start with.

"If you want to kill yourself, go ahead and quit wasting my time. I've got plenty of other clients who want help to stay alive." Physicians and nurses but also other emergency clinicians are oriented toward preserving life. They expect their clients to feel likewise and to cooperate. They are in a dilemma when the client appears to operate at purposes counter to their goals (Patel, 1975). Clinicians should not be angry with a client for being ill. Their obligation is as always, to do what can be done to protect the client's life, even if the client does not cooperate in this.

FEELING TRICKED. Some clients will make minor self-destructive gestures, unlikely to cause serious illness or injury, for the purpose of effecting a deprived environment. When clinicians fail to keep appropriate distance from these clients, they may feel a strong allegiance to them, feeling that they are truly victims of adverse circumstances. This overinvolvement may create the risk of their feelings being hurt later. If the clinician later discovers that the client was only "using" the emergency unit to cause a change in someone else, this can be disappointing to an overinvested clinician. If clinicians become angry or feel they were taken advantage of, an unnecessary and disturbing response may be provoked.

Clinicians can avoid overidentification by maintaining a professional perspective of the client, without affect. The presence of any affective response within the clinician is an indicator to carefully examine one's self for overinvolvement.

TREATMENT

The two elements of emergency treatment of affective illnesses are psychotherapy and chemotherapy.

PSYCHOTHERAPY. The short time available in a psychiatric emergency setting limits the duration of psychotherapeutic work but not its importance or helpfulness. In fact, the initial therapeutic response may determine clients' willingness to continue in the mental health service system as opposed to coping with their illness on their own. Willingness to follow through with treatment recommendations is rare (Coleman and Errera, 1963). The reader is referred to

Chafetz (1965), who discusses a number of methods for improving follow-up.

Psychodynamically, clients who experience the greatest amount of stress have exceeded their ability to defend against intrapsychic forces. Just as these defenses fail to protect the client from dysphoria, they also are less likely to ward off exploration by clinicians. Thus the client in the most severe distress may be the most amenable to interpretive interventions. After the client feels better, the clinician may find psychotherapeutic work impeded by strong defenses.

The empathic response is the most critical element of the clinician's response. This has been addressed earlier. The second major element is the explanation, or interpretation, of events that are important in the client's life and have a psychodynamic significance, forces that shape the client's current feelings. When there is a precipitating event that exacerbates an affective disorder, clinicians should aim for an understanding of the impact of that precipitating event (empathic understanding), the explanation of why that event is as important as it is (dynamic interpretation), and the explanation to the client of what in their background has made them this vulnerable to these stresses (genetic interpretation). In the majority of psychiatric emergency clients, the completion of this three-part model will not be possible. However, clinicians who aim for these goals will find a number of clients in whom all three parts may be completed in the first interview, or in some cases in the second or third interview of focal psychotherapy. In many clients with affective disorders, precipitating events do not appear; in those cases, the interventions are mainly empathic and supportive.

CHEMOTHERAPY. Antidepressant medication has limited usefulness in the emergency department because of the well-known long time lag (5 days to 2½ weeks) before antidepressant action occurs. Its sedative action, however, is much more timely. The ratio of toxic level of drug to therapeutic level of drug is not particularly high, making suicide relatively easy. Nevertheless, antidepressants do offer the advantage of specific treatment of the primary illness.

Sedative-hypnotics are helpful in symptom removal because their effect is immediate. For the depressed person with insomnia a question arises—should a prescription go home with the client? There is both short-term risk of suicidal overdosage if more than a few day's worth is prescribed, as well as longer term risk of habituation. The clinician is left to choose between overly free prescribing of minor tranquilizers for everyone who does not sleep well or the other extreme of denying soporifics to depressed clients who can benefit from them with little risk of abuse.

Given the previously described problems of poor follow-through with referrals, arranging for a follow-up interview in a few days plus writing a prescription that only supplies enough medication until that appointment will both reduce risk of abuse as well as promote attendance at the next interview.

Dalmane, as a benzodiazepine, is the preferred hypnotic for a client with a significant suicide risk. It offers a therapeutic/toxic ratio that allows greater safety from overdose than the barbiturates or the nonbarbiturate hypnotics. Chloral hydrate has merit also.

A relative contraindication to sedative hypnotics exists for clients with possible OBS, since the decreased functioning of the cerebral cortex because of the medication may exacerbate the OBS. Some clients will feel terribly afraid and upset by this phenomenon and, paradoxically, become more agitated.

Lithium carbonate is the drug of choice for manic illness, yet the combination of required testing before prescribing, the need for excellent client cooperation, close toxic/therapeutic ratio, and delay preceding full effect make lithium unsuitable for emergency prescribing.

High-potency major tranquilizers are indicated for mania, especially haloperidol, but also thiothixene (Navane) and fluphenazine hydrochloride (Prolixin). Older, lower potency phenothiazines possess undesired autonomic effects and are therefore less useful, even though they are more sedating. Rapid tranquilization with high-potency major tranquilizers may be appropriate to rapidly calm the agitated manic person.

Use of injectable amobarbital (Amytal) is another route for sedation of acutely agitated clients, especially when the presence or absence of psychosis has not yet been determined. The only absolute contraindication is acute intermittent porphyria, but in these cases either a history of abdominal pain or multiple scarring of the abdomen will be tipoffs. The risk of giving too much is that respiratory depression results. A prudent prescribing regimen for an agitated client is to start with a low dose of intramuscular amobarbital with an expectation of repeating 45 minutes after the injection. By aiming the dose low there is little risk of overdosage, the most dangerous hazard of any sedative. Initial dosage of 100 mg intramuscular amobarbital is not overly conservative and will keep the clinician from having to rescue oversedated clients. Once a clinician has seen the effect of the first 100 mg, the size of the second injection dose can be determined with much more accuracy.

SUMMARY

Affective disease is at times very painful, and this pain may bring such clients to an emergency department. Accurate diagnosis and effective treatment are necessary not only to reduce the suffering but also to protect manic clients from hurting themselves or others and to prevent depressed clients from committing suicide. These are true emergencies since they are life-threatening illnesses.

BIBLIOGRAPHY

Akiskal, H.S., and McKinney, W.T., Jr.: Depressive disorders: toward a classified hypothesis, Science 182:20, 1973.

Angst, J.: The course of unipolar and bipolar affective disorders. In Schou, M., and Stromgren, E., Editors, Origin, prevention, and treatment of affective disorders, London, 1979, Academic Press, Inc.

Beck, A.T., Sethi, B.B., and Tuthill, R.W.: Childhood bereavement and adult depression, Arch. Gen. Psychiatry 9:295, 1963.

Beck, J.C., and Worthen, K.: Precipitating stress, crisis theory, and hospitalization in schizophrenia and depression, Arch. Gen. Psychiatry 26:123, 1972.

Bibring, E.: The mechanism of depression, In Green-

acre, P., editor: Affective disorders, International Universities Press, 1953.

Birtchnell, J.: The relationship between attempted suicide, depression and parent death, Br. J. Psychiatry 116:307, 1970.

Chafetz, M.E.: The effect of a psychiatric emergency service on motivation for psychiatric treatment, J. Nerv. Ment. Dis. 140:442, 1965.

Clayton, P.J., Halikas, J.A., and Maurice, W.L.: The depression of widowhood, Br. J. Psychiatry 120:71, 1972.

Coleman, J.V., and Errera, P.: The general hospital emergency room and its psychiatric problems, Am. J. Public Health 53:1294, 1963.

Freud, S.: Mourning and melancholia, London, 1957, The Hogarth Press, Ltd.

Garver, D.L., and Davis, J.M.: Biogenic amine hypothesis of affective disorders, Life Sci. 24(5):383, 1979.

Greenson, R.R.: The working alliance and the transference neurosis, Psychoanal. Q. 34:155, 1965.

Helgason, T.: Epidemiological investigations concerning affective disorders. In Schou, M., and Stromgren, E., editors: Origin, prevention, and treatment of affective disorders, London, 1979, Academic Press, Inc.

Katz, M.: The classification of depression: normal, clinical, and ethnocultural variations, In Fieve, R., editor: Depression in the 70's, Amsterdam, 1971, Excerpta Medica.

Klerman, G.L.: Clinical research in depression, Arch. Gen. Psychiatry 24:305, 1971.

Kohut, H.: The analysis of the self, New York, 1971, International Universities Press.

Minkoff, K., et al. Hopelessness, depression, and attempted suicide, Am. J. Psychiatry 130:455, 1973.

Parkes, C.: The first year of bereavement, Psychiatry 33:444, 1970.

Patel, A.R.: Attitudes towards self poisoning, Br. Med. J. 2(5968):426, 1975.

Pope, H., and Lipinsky, J.: Diagnosis of schizophrenia and manic-depressive illness: A reassessment of the specificity of schizophrenic symptoms in the light of current research, Arch. Gen. Psychiatry 35(7):811, 1978.

Wells, C.: Pseudodementia, Am. J. Psychiatry 136(7):895, 1979.

Zerbin-Rudin, E.: Genetics of affective psychoses, In Schou, M., and Strömgren, E., editors: Origin, prevention, and treatment of affective disorders, London, 1979, Academic Press, Inc.

CHAPTER 7

The client with a borderline condition

Stephen M. Goldfinger, M.D.

Emergency psychiatric care hinges on the ability to assess a client's complaints and level of functioning for the purpose of establishing a diagnosis and an appropriate treatment plan and disposition. The client who comes in complaining of being followed by the CIA and who, in a rambling and unconnected way, describes the radio as "talking to him" can be readily diagnosed and appropriately treated. The clinician seeing such a client can on most occasions make fairly accurate predictions about other symptoms likely to be present. The client's reality testing, object relations, coherence of thought, and ability to make appropriate decisions will probably show consistent evidence of severe impairment. A brief history will allow the clinician to confirm a diagnosis; a treatment plan can then be instituted.

Clients with a borderline condition, by the very nature of their pathological condition, pose a tremendous challenge to the emergency room clinician. They may report with "a confusing combination of psychotic, neurotic, and character disturbances with many normal or healthy elements" (Grinker, 1977). Often their description of themselves appears to be inconsistent, their history unreliable, their requests manipulative. Over a series of visits their behavior toward the interviewer may shift from one of infantile dependence to overt hostility. Their affective state may well swing from hopeless depression to rage within a single hour. Begging for whatever help the clinician may offer, they later may disdainfully reject any proposed treatment plan. The inexperienced clinician may feel confused and impotent and frequently responds with anger and rejection. Yet the borderline client is behaving in a consistent and expectable way. Even the clinician's feelings are, in fact, a predictable "symptom" of the borderline syndrome.

HISTORICAL ROOTS

The use of the term *borderline* began with the need to describe a client population in the "no-man's-land between sanity and insanity" (Green, 1977). For many years the term's own borders were stretched to accommodate those disorders with symptomatology clearly too severe to fit within the neurotic spectrum, yet without sufficient evidence to warrant a diagnosis of psychosis. Defined only by what it was *not,* the term was applied to individuals otherwise described as suffering from "ambulatory schizophrenia" (Zilboorg, 1941), an "as-if personality" (Deutsch, 1942), "pseudoneurotic schizophrenia" (Hoch and Polatin, 1949), a "psychotic character" (Frosch, 1960), "latent psychosis" (Bychowsky, 1953), and multiple other psychiatric disorders. Therefore it became impossible to make any a priori assumptions about the symptoms, degree of pathology, level of functioning, or prognosis for a client so labeled. What did emerge, however, was a clear indication that clinicians practicing in diverse settings were being asked to evaluate and treat a group of clients inadequately described by the diagnostic classifications then in use.

In 1968, Grinker and his co-workers published an extensive behavioral study of hospitalized clients with a borderline symptom profile (Grinker et al., 1968). What emerged from their statistical analysis was a picture of a cluster of disorders sharing several common features. Particular symptoms of affective states were markedly variable and fluctuating, but they felt that "the syndrome itself as a process is recognizably stable, giving rise to the paradoxical term 'stable instability' " (Grinker, 1977).

With the publication of Otto Kernberg's seminal paper, "Borderline Personality Organization" (1967), clinicians were offered a potential tool for understanding and interrelating the seemingly disparate elements of borderline phenomena. Descriptive clinical concepts preceding his work had focused on precisely those superficial and behavioral aspects that were the most paradoxical and confusing. Rather, Kernberg proposed that what was needed was a "structural analysis," an attempt to distill out and reconstruct the particular qualities of ego functioning which characterized these behaviors. Through intensive psychoanalytical work with such clients, Kernberg and others (Kernberg, 1975, 1977; Masterson, 1976; Chessick, 1977; Green, 1977) were able to formulate a theoretical explanation of the seeming vagaries of borderline behavior. Through reconstruction of the events of early childhood, the nature of the relationships, affects, and defenses of the adult population became more easily understandable. They now emerged as logical and comprehensible sequelae of the unresolved struggles and conflicts of distinct maturational challenges (Kernberg, 1966; Zetzel, 1971; Rinsley, 1977). Such a theoretical conceptualization is essential to meaningful therapeutic work with these clients.

Concurrent with the research on the dynamics of the borderline personality, others began to further delineate demographic, diagnostic, and prognostic features of this group (Werble, 1970; Gunderson and Singer, 1975; Gunderson et al., 1975; Gunderson, 1977; Perry and Klerman, 1980). Although some essential data have yet to be collected and interpreted, there now exists sufficient evidence that the borderline syndrome is a discrete clinical entity, warranting its inclusion as a diagnostic category in the Diagnostic and Statistical Manual of Mental Disorder (DSM III).

DESCRIBING THE POPULATION

To make a diagnosis of borderline personality disorder, the DSM III requires that the individual be over 18 years of age and show evidence of at least five of the following:

  a. Impulsivity and unpredictability in at least two potentially self-damaging areas
  b. A pattern of intense and unstable interpersonal relationships
  c. Difficulties with intense or uncontrollable anger
  d. Disturbances of identity and sense of self
  e. Affective instability with abrupt and short-lived shifts
  f. Intolerance of being alone
  g. Evidence of self-destructive physical acts
  h. Chronic feelings of emptiness and boredom

These criteria may be seen as manifestations of disturbances in four major spheres: affects (c, e, h), object relations (b, f), the sense of self (d), and behavior (a, g). Each of these aspects of the borderline client will be more closely explored, after which an attempt to explain these characteristics as a function of the client's early development and psychodynamics will be proposed.

Affects

Disturbances of affect are among the most frequently noted features of borderline behavior. In one study every client in the borderline cohort clearly exhibited a major affective symptom at the initial examination (Gunderson et al., 1975). Most commonly reported are anger, depression, and feelings of boredom and emptiness, although hatred, fear, envy, and disgust are also often present.

A predominant presentation of borderline clients to emergency services involves anger and rage as its central features. These clients are frequently hostile, sarcastic, and argumentative. The interviewer is often the target of such behavior (Perry and Klerman, 1980), although it is more frequently directed at important love objects in the client's life. The anger is often dramatically displayed, with shouting and temper tantrums. In some clients, it is striking in its pervasiveness, seeming to engulf everyone and everything in the client's world. In others, it is only expressed as sarcasm or rudeness, seeming to become self-directed and replaced by depres-

sion and helplessness. Grinker et al. (1968, p. 90) contend that "anger seems to constitute the main or only affect that the borderline patient experiences," and, in fact, divide the syndrome into subclasses largely based on how this anger was manifested.

Although depression is frequently cited as a major symptom of borderline presentations, it is usually qualified by such words as *emptiness, alienation,* or *anhedonia.* Rather than involving the guilt so often associated with reactive depressions, the depression seems symptomatic of a sense of alienation from the world, of detachment from sources of pleasure and stimulation. After exploration, it is sometimes possible to identify a precipitant, usually a rejection by a love object. However, the client's lack of acknowledgment of any concern over this loss frequently obscures its significance. Rather than grief or sadness, helplessness and hopelessness are the hallmarks of this depression (Hartocollis, 1977). Although best observed during ongoing therapy, the rapid shifts in affect so characteristic of borderline clients are sometimes strikingly demonstrated in emergency settings. The depressed and dependent client who suddenly erupts into rage when his wish for hospitalization is denied is a common phenomenon in any emergency unit. Although a more complete understanding of this behavior must await exploration of borderline dynamics, it can most simply be viewed as an inability to tolerate painful and conflicting affects.

Object relations

Perry and Klerman (1980) demonstrated specific elements of interpersonal behavior in borderline clients which statistically differ from those of control groups. Their relationships are often transient and unstable and are marked by intense affect. These clients appear demanding, clinging, and manipulative in their close relationships and give evidence of intense hostility, anger, and sadism. Ambivalent feelings are prominent, and there is a tendency both to overidealize and to feel contemptuous of love objects. Central to this is an inability to realistically evaluate others.

In some of the literature (Gunderson and

Singer, 1975; Kernberg, 1967) emphasis is placed on a sense of superficiality and a lack of ability to feel empathy. Although clients are aware of social conventions (Gunderson, 1977) and expectations, there seems to be no central core of true feeling. This is reminiscent of Helene Deutsch's early description: an "essential characteristic is that outwardly he conducts his life as if he possessed a complete and sensitive emotional capacity" (1942, p. 303, 304). However, what is missing in most cases seems to be the reciprocity of feeling which distinguishes mature object relations.

Both of these interpersonal styles can be seen as compromises arising from the clients' discomfort with being alone. Unable to establish mature relations but longing for closeness, they tenuously engage others. Some ventures become intense, conflictual, and short lived; others may last longer but remain superficial.

Many borderline clients continue to live with their families despite "serious reservations about central family figures" (Werble, 1970). Their potential for marriage is not high. In their vocational interactions, they may remain regularly employed but rarely advance in their careers (Gunderson et al., 1975). Their leisure-time activities seem limited or nonexistent and rarely involve social contact.

Behavior

As the DMS III criteria imply, the two seminal features of borderline behavior are impulsivity and self-destructiveness, which are probably the most frequent precipitants for seeking emergency psychiatric treatment. Although no specific behavior is pathognomonic, "virtually every borderline patient is involved in considerable acting out in a variety of ways . . . self-destructive acts, destructive acts toward others, antisocial behavior, and drug or alcohol abuse" (Gunderson, 1977, p. 179). Suicidal gestures and threats are common, as are physically self-damaging acts, often without suicidal ideation, such as superficial lacerations or self-inflicted cigarette burns (Grunebaum and Klerman, 1967). One study of borderline clients reported an average of two prior suicide attempts (Perry and Klerman,

1980); however, destructive acts toward others were not common.

Often, such self-destructive behaviors are coincident with an object loss. After unrealistically relying on a love object for support, clients experience feelings of abandonment and concomitant rage which lead to self-mutilation or impulsive drinking and polydrug abuse. Such behavior is frequent in hospitalized clients as well (Adler, 1973). As noted, neither imposed isolation nor forced compansionship is tolerable to this group.

Many authors (Kernberg, 1967, 1975; Gunderson, 1977; Perry and Klerman, 1980) stress the promiscuous and perverse sexual practices of these clients. It seems as if the more global phenomena of impulsivity, self-destructiveness, and ambivalence which characterize their behavior color the sexual sphere as well.

Sense of self

A sense of identity diffusion and a poorly integrated self-concept often become apparent early in the interview with borderline clients. Contradictory perceptions and behaviors coexist; when questioned, these clients often cannot explain why. No overall, integrated sense of "a self of which these are merely parts" exists. Clients may report a certain feeling only to question whether, in fact, they are experiencing that feeling. Often, they report feeling only bored or empty. This sense of emptiness is often a metaphorical allusion to the absence of any coherent sense of being an ongoing individual with accumulations of feelings and perceptions. Rather, each affect seems to spring de novo from "out there," without the sense of self as a causal entity. Clinicians may, in fact, experience this identity diffusion in their own inability to feel these clients as whole or "real," or to empathize with them (Kernberg, 1977).

Having detailed some of the expectable variations of affect, object relations, behavior, and self-concept of the borderline client, I will now propose a developmental framework that will allow a better understanding of these phenomena. From this may be derived an integrated model of dynamics and defenses of the borderline condition, addressing problems of diagnosis, evaluation, treatment, and disposition.

A DEVELOPMENTAL PERSPECTIVE

The peculiar nature of borderline phenomena is best understood as an outgrowth of a unique pattern of mother*-child interaction. It can be seen as a failure in the process of separation-individuation, a maturational sequence that characterizes the first 4 years of life. This process, first fully formulated by Margaret S. Mahler (1965, 1968, 1975), serves as a model against which the vicissitudes of borderline development can be examined.

Normal development

During the first 3 months of life, infants remain in an autistic, dreamlike state. At about 3 months, they "hatch," entering a stage in which their image of themselves and their mother is as a symbiotic unit. Their experiences of the world are mediated by and experienced with their mother. Her emotional state is perceived and experienced as their own. Through her mothering, their own needs are met, their discomforts are corrected. Together, they encounter new objects and experiences. The work of separation-individuation starts as the infant begins to differentiate between self and mother and to form the earliest precursors of a sense of self. Through interactions with mother, the infants are stimulated to widen their scope of exploration. Her responsiveness implies a whole world that will provide comfort and support. Acting as a buffer between the child and the world outside, she provides the rudiments of ego boundaries and self-identity. During this period of "differentiation," the child must actively master an ever-widening repertoire of physical and interactional skills. A successful mother is gradually taken for granted—she has provided for her child a base of security from which to expand.

---

*The term *mother* is used here in place of the more cumbersome *primary nurturing object*. For an overview of the role of the father in separation-individuation, see Goldfinger (1976).

During the second half of the first year, the infant enters what Mahler calls the "practicing" subphase of separation-individuation. During this period, thrust on by the ability to crawl and thus physically distance themselves from the mother, children begin to experience their separateness in many other ways as well. Psychomotor maturation and new widening spheres of exploration provide for a growing sense of mastery and further separation.

Increasing realizations of "I can do" and "I can go," coupled with perceptions of mother as a separate being, augment a nascent sense of individual identity. During the height of this subphase, the child may at times seem almost oblivious to the mother's presence, content to try out new skills and elated perhaps by a freedom from the sense of fusion with the mother. Appropriately supporting increased independence, she may still serve as an "auxiliary-ego," helping the child modulate and develop a growing repertory of adaptive and regulatory functions. Through identification with the mother and her ego functions, the child's own ego is strengthened. More sophisticated defense operations and enhanced frustration tolerance, impulse control, and reality testing become available. In an environment with "good enough mothering" (Winnicott, 1965), the child's growing sense of autonomy and mastery have been encouraged and rewarded.

Having "flexed its wings" during the practicing subphase, the toddler must now reapproach mother and establish a new level of interaction consistent with this newfound sense of self as a separate individual. The quality of the mother's response to this challenge is critical. She must be able to lend emotional support to efforts at independence and freedom, yet be almost instinctively aware of when, in fact, reassurance and assistance are needed. The successful mother is "quietly available" (Mahler, 1968), able to share the child's exploits and growth, remaining neither distant nor engulfing.

One of the critical tasks of this subphase of development is the establishment by the child of the beginnings of "object constancy." The discrete part-object "memory islands" of infancy continue coalescing into integrated internalizations. Bits of disparate experiences of the mother in different situations must begin to fuse. In infancy, experiences with "her breasts," "her smile," "her arms," gradually become integrated as experiences with "mother." The challenge of the rapprochement subphase is, in part, achieving the ability to recognize this mother as continuous over time. Multiple, discrete experiences with mother in various activities and affective states must become integrated into a whole-object representation. Through her continued availability, the mother aids this process. Relatively consistent in her behavior despite her own changing moods, she fosters the child's integration of good-mother (rewarding, feeding, accepting) and bad-mother (punishing, denying, rejecting) images. Thus the child will become able to maintain a sense of the mother as an ongoing, whole person despite temporary fluctuations in level of frustration or satisfaction.

Similarly, the child of this subphase should be actively establishing a more consistent and integrated self-image. A sense of "*me* that stays the same despite what *they're* doing" must find its place beside a "*they* that are the same despite how *I'm* feeling."

Thus, normal mother-child interactions serve to foster the growth of autonomy, healthy curiosity, and positive self-identity. The child becomes able to integrate changing internal feeling states, as well as varying behaviors and feelings in others, into generally stable images of self and others. The development of these skills is ultimately tied to the mother's capacity to promote them. The consequence of a failure during this critical period can have a profound impact on later functioning.

Borderline development

Certain specific variations of mother-child interaction during separation-individuation seem to lead to the development of a borderline personality as the child matures. A model for this process has been offered by Kernberg (1975), Masterson (1976), and Rinsley (1977). What follows is a simplified version of their proposals.

The mother of the borderline client frequently exhibits borderline dynamics herself. Unable to tolerate separation, she responds to her child's

maturation as a threat to her own stability. "She depersonifies the child, cannot see him as he is, but rather projects upon him the image of one of her own parents or of a sibling; or she perceives him as a perpetual infant or an object and uses him to defend herself against her own feelings of abandonment. Consequently, she is unable to respond to his unfolding individuality and he early learns to disregard certain of his own potentials in order to preserve his source of supplies (approval) from the mother" (Masterson, 1976). The child, therefore, is faced with a critical dilemma. To continue growing and individualizing, the child is dependent on mother's support and encouragement. However, movement in this direction now entails loss of precisely those "supplies."

The child's affective response to this dilemma involves a complicated set of varying emotions. Potential loss of mother evokes depression and fear, since she is felt both as a part of oneself and as necessary for one's very survival. To maintain continued support, however, the child must sacrifice a growing sense of independence and self. Such considerations may evoke feelings of passivity, helplessness, and emptiness. Rage at the mother, whose demands cause so much pain, may become a central focus of the relationship. In response to abandonment of positive self-images and incorporation of the mother's negative attitudes, the child may feel guilty and hopeless.

To protect the child's fragile ego, multiple defenses come into play. Unable to tolerate threatening negative images and affects of the mother and self, the child uses splitting to separate these from such positive images as exist. Images are split—good-mother loves and rewards but only a passive and clinging self. Bad-mother rejects and punishes a part-self representation that feels bad, guilty, empty, and inadequate. There cannot exist a sense of good-mother-good-self, of rewards and love for independent identity and autonomous functioning. Object constancy cannot be achieved, for part representations of self and mother cannot be integrated.

Other defense operations—denial, primitive idealization—are needed by the child to protect the immature ego from the conflict between love and hate. The price paid for survival is a sacrifice of basic ego maturation with widespread use of primitive defenses and areas of failed reality testing. Rather than an integrated world view, the child's internal reality reflects isolated fragments of experience actively kept separate. "Clinically, the child who is going to become a borderline patient lives from moment to moment, actively cutting off the emotional links between what would otherwise become chaotic, contradictory, highly frustrating and frightening emotional experiences with significant others in his immediate environment" (Kernberg, 1975, p. 1965).

The child as adult

The characteristic affects, behaviors, and object relations of the adult borderline client can all be viewed as sequelae of these infantile conflicts and defenses.

The borderline client as a child felt threatened with maternal abandonment. With an immature self-identity still ultimately linked to mother, such a loss would have entailed a loss of part of self as well. Being alone meant being without resources, without support—being empty. Intolerant of being alone, the child fared no better by approaching mother. Instead of depression, the child then faced engulfment and fusion.

This conflict, unresolved in childhood, is reenacted in the adult client. Still needing to be with people, they cling to others as if their very existence still depended on them. For a time, the other person may become an idealized object, a substitute for the all-good-mother lost in childhood. Such a relationship, however, is usually short lived. Perhaps the threat of engulfment reemerges; perhaps the fear of abandonment becomes too great. The relationship becomes unbearable—for the moment, being alone seems preferable.

This, too, is of course unsatisfactory. The old ambivalence cannot be escaped. Trapped by conflicting needs and fears, the client rages against a universe that cannot provide satisfaction.

The adult client attempts to deal with these conflicts by using the primitive defenses fixed in childhood. Gross splitting and denial follow some of these experiences; the affects related to them appear to be banished from consciousness. Such

an internal restructuring, however, has other consequences as well. The client's sense of being a continuous self, existing over time, falls victim to these defenses. Causality and continuity are sacrificed as experience is parceled into discrete "memory islands." To the external observer, therefore, the behavior may appear impulsive, contradictory, or disconnected. To the client, with a memory that specifically excludes various past experiences, life may seem chaotic, confusing, or somehow incomplete.

Although these conflicts are present in all borderline clients, the extent to which they compromise functioning is extremely variable. Depending on the extent and degree of maturational failure, the client will have developed a more or less successful ability to cope with external stressors. In some clients, the underlying pathology of self- and object-representations may only emerge during intensive therapy or catastrophic loss. Many clients successfully maintain equilibrium by establishing a life-style that avoids or protects against these potential threats. By frequent changes of job or location, they may avoid exposing themselves to intimate relations and their inherent dangers. Group living situations or membership in a cult or religious sect may provide both a sense of identity and a diffusion of the intensity of any single relationship.

The most severely impaired clients often reflect a succession of inadequate and futile attempts to master basic interpersonal and vocational survival. Chronic alcohol or drug abuse, in an effort to medicate their rage or depression, further compromises their inadequate coping skills. They may have a history of multiple suicide attempts, psychiatric hospitalizations, or petty arrests—testaments to prior failures of their ability to maintain themselves in any sort of equilibrium.

CRISES AND THEIR PRESENTATIONS

Clients request emergency psychiatric treatment when some external event threatens the homeostasis at whatever level of functioning they have established. The nature and severity of the stress will, of course, reflect the individual's personal dynamics and coping skills. The particular events that precipitate crises in borderline clients are intimately related to the conflicts previously examined. Under some circumstances the client may sense an impending loss of affective or behavioral control. In other cases the clients' loss of control brings them to the attention of friends or police who bring them to the emergency unit.

The most frequent precipitant of crises in borderline clients is undoubtedly the real or threatened abandonment by a love object, a source of support. Depression, suicidal ideation or gesturing, and a frank suicidal attempt are common. In other clients the clinical picture is dominated by rage against the object, often accompanied by impulsive behavior. Reality testing and other major ego functions may appear grossly impaired, as the client struggles to defend against further fragmentation. Alcohol or psychoactive drugs, originally used by the client to moderate the affective flood, may serve instead to augment it. Borderline clients whose functional incapacity is most severe may be able to establish only the most marginal of social and vocational adaptations. Their impaired interpersonal skills and chaotic affective life may preclude their establishment of any stable jobs, relationships, or living situations. A vicious cycle frequently ensues in which depression and rage at their external environment and their characterological deficits mutually exacerbate each other. Such individuals may seem *always* in crisis and utilize emergency psychiatric services with disarming frequency. Often unwilling or unable to effectively engage in residential treatment or ongoing psychotherapy, they represent a significant segment of the chronic recidivist population (Schwartz and Goldfinger, 1981).

Many individuals with borderline character structure are able to maintain adequate functioning for extended periods. Adaptive choices of vocation and life-style may effectively mask or minimize the effects of their impairment. Avoiding conflictual decisions and sidestepping choices that would upset their equilibrium, they are well defended against the emergence of dysfunctional behaviors. Many of these individuals will thus successfully avoid developing symptoms severe enough to require professional intervention. However, the price exacted by such rigid and re-

strictive life-styles may be considerable. Others will function well until some life event forces them to confront their difficulties with separation or individuation or both. High school or college graduation, leaving home for work, marriage, parenting, or difficulties with intimate or work relationships may serve as precipitants for the reemergence of early conflicts. Clients who may have previously coped quite well may come to the emergency unit for help at these times. Terrified or overwhelmed by intense affective states, they may be unable to connect these to the external events from which they arose.

Other clients, having previously recognized aspects of their personal or interpersonal difficulties, may have already sought psychiatric treatment. It is well recognized that psychotherapy with borderline clients often pursues a tumultuous course (Masterson, 1976). As the conflicts and fears of childhood reemerge in the transference, powerful affective responses to the therapist may ensue. It is not uncommon for clients already engaged in outpatient therapy to seek crisis intervention for feelings that will, on examination, be recognized as manifestations of their transference fantasies. Third-party interventions (in the crisis service) can often help to elaborate and resolve these "crises" to a level where the client may return to ongoing therapy.

To better illustrate some specific examples of borderline behavior and dynamics, two case vignettes will be presented. These clients exemplify many of the common features of borderline pathology yet differ markedly in their level of functioning and severity of pathological condition. Their presentation and history will be described, followed by a brief discussion of dynamics. Following this, further examples of their behavior will be given to illustrate aspects of the assessment process and the formulation of a treatment plan.

Case vignette #1

Ms. A is a 23-year-old woman who came into the emergency unit looking anxious and somewhat tearful. When asked why she had come, she begins to cry and says, "I blew it, I really think I blew it. Oh, God, why?" She explains that she has been living with a man named Bill for 2 months. "I love him, I mean, I know he's the one for me . . . and now I think its all over."

She says that she was waiting in their apartment for Bill to come home from work. Although he usually left the office at six, it was after seven and he hadn't arrived. She had phoned the office, but there was no answer. As the time passed, she became anxious and then angry. "I just started pacing around the flat. At first, I thought he might have gone for a drink with his friends, but then I just knew. I just felt it inside—he was probably out with his secretary. I should have known. It was too good to last." She began to feel she "was exploding." She turned on the TV set, but was too preoccupied to watch. "I just kept thinking about Bill—he didn't care, I knew it now. I started pounding the sofa, like it was him. 'Damn it,' I thought, 'What have I done?' The voices on TV, it was some silly show with a young couple, they almost seemed to be taunting me. I started to cry, then picked up a paperweight Bill had given me. It was like it was just part of his lie. An then . . . I don't know, I just sort of screamed inside and threw the paperweight at the TV. That smashed it; the glass flew all over. That was like a shock, like I woke up. I got scared at what I'd done and what I might do, so I came in. I really need to talk to someone."

Ms. A relates that she was the youngest of four children. Her parents were professionals in the small town in Illinois where she grew up. She remembers little of her childhood, "though it was sometimes lonely when my brothers were in school." She finished high school with good grades. "It came easily for me." When asked, she says she had few close friends, "but that didn't matter." She enrolled in the state college, but dropped out after her first year, saying she just wasn't happy there. It was a 2-hour drive from her home town and felt "cold and unfamiliar." She went home to live with her parents, taking a job as a salesgirl "until I could figure out what I wanted to do."

During the next 2 years, she had several boyfriends. One, whom she "really loved," broke off the relationship because he felt she was wasting her time as a salesgirl and wouldn't grow up. Another had asked her to marry him, which scared her. She couldn't see herself as a housewife. After another year, during which she felt she "just vegetated," some old high school friends who had gone to school in California returned to Illinois. They described it in such glowing terms that she decided she was bored with Illinois and moved to San Francisco.

On her arrival she lived off her savings until she found a job as a bank teller. It was at work that she met Bill, a customer. "I just felt attracted to him immediately. We used to talk when he came to the window—I'd wait for him all week. When he asked me out, I thought I'd die." They dated for six weeks, during which time she says she felt like she "was floating." When the lease on her apartment ran out, Bill offered to let her stay at his place until she could find another. She has been there since.

Discussion. Ms. A's presentation reflects her temporary loss of impulse control over the threat of abandonment by Bill. Her relationship with him exemplifies many of the characteristic features of borderline object-relations. Her instant attraction to him initiated a process of over-idealization which seemed to have continued until the evening she came to the psychiatric emergency unit. From the start, Ms. A related to Bill more in response to her own projections of what she wished for than in response to his innate qualities.

Alone in San Francisco, she must surely have been longing for a figure on whom she could depend. Her description of "floating" during the time they were dating seemed to evoke images of the satisfied infant blissfully secure in her mother's arms. Bill's offer of his apartment, at a point where Ms. A's need for protection and help was about to increase, surely strengthened her idealization of him. He had become the good-mother; through identification and merger with him, Ms. A could feel safe and whole.

Overall, Ms. A seems to have been able to cope

with the challenges of adolescence and early adulthood moderately well. Until this point, her response to stress had been reasonably adaptive—relying on her family for support, choosing jobs below her level of intelligence. Although she described some examples of impulsive behavior (for example, moving to California), she had managed to remain stable and functional for extended periods.

The intensity of Ms. A's fear of abandonment by Bill seems directly related to the importance he had for her at that time. Further from her family than she had ever been, she was in a new city without either friends or another place to live. Although the clinician might see Bill's lateness as a minor problem, to Ms. A it evoked overwhelming terror and rage. Just as his mere presence had once allowed her to "float," even the slight possibility of abandonment by him called forth fear of devastating isolation.

Case vignette #2

Mr. H is a 31-year-old man brought into the psychiatric emergency unit by the police. He is unkempt, angry, and appears intoxicated. Some dried blood on his clothing and hands calls attention to a superficial laceration on his left wrist. The police report that they were called by a shopkeeper who saw Mr. H sitting on a nearby doorway crying and bleeding. He denied any problems when they approached him, angrily telling them to mind their own business and leave him alone. Concerned, they brought him in.

When approached, Mr. H yells, "Just leave me alone. OK?" He is asked what happened. "I cut myself, yeah. So, big deal. Now are you happy?" Although he refuses to answer any further questions, he accepts a cup of coffee and a chair in one of the interview rooms.

Mr. H is already well known to the staff. He has been seen 10 times in the past year and has been hospitalized 4 times during that period. He is known to be a hostile, sarcastic client who rarely follows through on any aspect of his treatment plan. He has, on most visits, been brought in by the

police after some impulsive suicide gesture or minor destruction of property.

Mr. H is a bitter, angry man. He feels that the mental health system doesn't want to help him. He points to the times he has been seen but not admitted to the hospital or discharged after only a week to prove his point. He feels no one can understand him, accusing the clinicians of being "little do-gooders in fancy clothes" who cannot relate to his life-style. "All you know is 'lock him up, dry him out, and throw him out.'" His own failure to follow-up with outpatient appointments is "just to show you how dumb your whole little system really is."

Mr. H has a psychiatric history dating back to his childhood. He was labeled a juvenile delinquent during junior high school and was a runaway at age 16. Supporting himself by panhandling and petty theft, he hitchhiked from city to city. At age 18 he was arrested as part of a barroom brawl that resulted in one man's accidental death. During his hearing he became overtly psychotic and was sent to a state mental hospital. After 4 years, he was discharged and moved to San Francisco.

Mr. H has described his years in San Francisco in the late 60s as the only truly happy period of his life. He said: "Living with various groups of hippies in the Haight-Ashbury district, I felt like I was home. Lots of drugs. Lots of love and loving people. You could just do your thing; someone always had money for food or grass." He became sexually involved with several women and even two of the men in a large apartment where he lived for several months. He also began to experiment with amphetamines, LSD, and heroin.

With the dissolution of the hippie movement during the 70s, Mr. H became depressed and isolated. After several suicide gestures, he began to receive federal disability. Forced to move to the central city by economics, he lived in a single-room occupancy hotel. As his old friends began to disperse, his source of drugs dropped off and he turned to alcohol. Living a marginal

109

existence in Salvation Army missions or cheap hotels, his world consists of the fellow alcoholics, drug abusers, prostitutes, and deinstitutionalized state mental hospital residents.

Discussion. Mr. H is clearly a severely disturbed individual. His history and presentation evidence a long-standing pattern of impulsive and self-destructive behavior. With the possible exception of his experiences in the Haight-Ashbury district, his life seems devoid of any stable living situation or object-relations. His story seems to be one of failed attempts to flee from overwhelming feelings of rage and depression. Running away or escaping into drugs or alcohol, he still cannot avoid these feelings. Unable to ask for help directly, he engages in self-destructive behavior that, when discovered, will ensure him access to emergency intervention. However, his basic lack of trust and fear of intimacy preclude his following through on any voluntary treatment options. Angry and disappointed, he denies his own contributions to the problem, accusing and chastising the very clinicians whose help he has secured (albeit indirectly).

ASSESSMENT AND DIAGNOSIS

Careful assessment and diagnosis are the foundations of sound psychiatric care. Warner and Weissburg have outlined the fundamentals of this process in Chapter 2. However, the borderline client presents some unique challenges for the clinical evaluator. The client arriving at the emergency unit is, almost by definition, a client in crisis. One of the central features of borderline personality organization is the tendency under stress to regress to more primitive states of functioning. During crises, therefore, the client may well appear to have elements of psychotic behavior. Without a detailed assessment of the client's history, prior functioning, and object relations, the clinician may mistakenly see the client as schizophrenic. A common error with these clients is to formulate a diagnosis of chronic psychosis based on history alone. Two factors contribute to such a mistake. First, older clients may well have had their first contact with

psychiatry before the borderline personality was widely recognized as a clinical entity. Misdiagnosed as schizophrenic, they have carried the label ever since. Second, these clients have an impaired ability to integrate their experiences. Frequently the history they give is inconsistent or incomplete. During a period of depression, for example, they may omit the description of periods of high functioning, depriving the interviewer of data that might mitigate against a diagnosis of schizophrenia.

The second major pitfall in work with these clients revolves around the nature of their interactive style. Because of their early experiences, they are mistrustful of a world they feel cannot meet their needs. Later adult object relations only serve to augment this feeling. In an attempt to find a substitute for the good-mother they lost, they cling to new objects of dependence. Since these clients come to psychiatric emergency units during periods of greatest need, clinicians are often seen as the object of this longed-for support. Depending on their unique personal history and their history of previous psychiatric contacts, this view may evoke a wide range of behaviors. The clinician often becomes the target of a storm of intense affects and contradictory demands, and feelings evoked by the client may hinder the ability to make an objective assessment. Every clinician is trained to be aware of responses to clients and to keep them from interfering with clinical work. Borderline clients, however, seem uniquely able to evoke powerful feelings in even skilled and experienced clinicians. Awareness and understanding of the nature of these responses are essential to any successful work with them. This problem is of such clinical significance that it warrants discussion in a separate section.

The structural interview

In an attempt to remedy the potential for error in a purely phenomenological-descriptive assessment, Kernberg (1977) proposed the use of a "structural interview." In addition to the usual history and mental status examination, this technique offers a tool for evaluating the client's conflicts with particular reference to how they are demonstrated in the interaction with the interviewer. Issues of identity diffusion, reality testing, and defensive style are perhaps best evaluated in this manner.

As the client begins to discuss particular difficulties, the interviewer is asked to pay close attention to any areas that appear contradictory, vague, or incomplete. This material is then approached in three sequential steps: clarification, confrontation, and interpretation. The client's ability to observe, explain, and understand his conflicts and behaviors is thus more fully explored.

In *clarification,* the clinician simply asks for further details about the areas that remain unclear. It serves to assess the extent of the client's awareness or confusion regarding the material. Confrontation involves pointing out statements that remain contradictory, particularly those of which the client seems unaware. With the assumption that such incongruities result from defensive operations, this intervention attempts to bring these to consciousness. The client's capacity to recognize the presence and significance of these conflicts, to integrate these perceptions, and to respond to the clinician are observed. Can the client alter perceptions when faced with their incongruities? Is the client able to empathize with the interviewer's observations? Can the client connect the issues being discussed with related problems in other areas?

Interpretation involves linking the client's statements or behavior to some hypothesized unconscious or preconscious process. It may use material from the client's history but is perhaps most effective when focused on the current interaction with the interviewer. Interpretation can serve several functions. It allows the clinician an opportunity to assess the extent of the client's ability to recognize causal relationships and to identify recurrent behavioral patterns. It may help to validate useful hypotheses that explain the client's behavior. It is perhaps the single most valuable indicator of the client's potential to engage in intensive or exploratory psychotherapy.

The use of the structural interview may appear to be unnecessarily stressful to the client and may be likely to elicit defensiveness and distrust. Rather, these interventions should be made in a manner reflecting genuine interest, concern, and mutual "working together to understand." Many clients respond quite favorably to the unusual degree of care and attention this technique requires. Some clients may recognize, for the first time, repeated patterns of behavior. Some clients will, as a result of new understanding gained during the interview, attain mastery over areas that previously were sources of confusion and conflict.

To clarify the details of the structural interview, brief exerpts from the interviews with two clients are presented here.

Interview After Ms. A had described her problem with Bill and the incidents of that evening, the interviewer began to explore these events more specifically.

Clinician: . . . and then you just threw the paperweight at the TV?

Ms. A: Yeah, it just sort of happened. Like I wasn't even part of it, I didn't control it. OK, I was angry and scared, but I just lost it, went crazy for a minute.

Clinician: Crazy?

Ms. A: Yeah, I mean, why do a dumb thing like that? It just doesn't make any sense. It isn't like me at all.

Clinician: Or, since it *was* you, or a part of you, that part must have felt awfully angry and frightened.

Ms. A (tearfully): I guess so. I love Bill and I thought he loved me. And now I just don't know . . .

Clinician: What's more, I think you feel you need Bill now. Losing him would be scary—and it's hard to recognize how much you feel you need him.

Ms. A was frightened by what she considered a "crazy" outburst and was unable to recognize the underlying fear that motivated this action. By being asked to clarify the incident, she confirmed this suspicion. Confronted with her wish to split off this behavior, Ms. A was forced to focus on just the material she was struggling to avoid. To understand the intensity of her reaction, Ms. A had to recognize the extent of her feelings of dependence on Bill. This process was begun with the clinician's preliminary interpretation that ends the example.

Through further discussion and interpretation, Ms. A began to show some understanding of why Bill's lateness was so threatening. Her fear that she was crazy diminished as she became able to integrate her behavior into a more complete view of what the evening had meant to her.

Sometimes the client's level of anxiety or rage precludes the exploration of any major areas of conflict. The format of the structural interview can, however, be useful in even a condensed form around seemingly insignificant areas.

Interview

Mr. H: Look, I'm not interested in talking to you or any other self-righteous, sadistic, dumb shrink! Just leave me alone!

Clinician: Wow! I just asked you if you wanted more coffee! I haven't said 10 words to you. I kind of get the feeling that that wasn't really all meant for *me!*

Mr. H: You're just like all the rest. You guys are all the same.

Clinician: Sounds like you've had a pretty hard time with people who promised to help, huh? Do you want cream and sugar?

Hardly a formal psychodynamic intervention, the clinician has, however, clarified Mr. H's anger, confronted him with how it didn't seem to be generated by this particular situation, and interpreted its source. By asking about "cream and sugar" and ending further verbal entanglement, the interviewer hoped to provide some initial foundation from which Mr. H could work at separating the current situation from projections of prior interactions. The structural interview can, when properly used, serve the interviewer both as a diagnostic and a therapeutic tool.

In addition to the interpretative work, the clinician working with these clients will frequently find it useful to make other interventions that will help the client recognize or correct various inappropriate perceptions or responses. Simply by providing information and reassurance, the clinician may facilitate the client's ability to approach specific difficulties in a less personalized and maladaptive manner. Areas of reality testing which have been compromised as a defense against painful conflicts may be modified by frank and concerned offers of alternative views and perceptions. When a client is helped to recognize and label a previously frightening affect, a sense of mastery and control may be afforded. During the interview with a client who

comes in complaining of a "groundless" sense of dread and depression, it may emerge that the client's psychotherapist is on vacation. Simple interventions might be offered to help the client recognize this possible source of depressed feelings. With reassurance and discussion of how common, in fact, such feelings are, sufficient support may be provided to allow the client to comfortably await the clinician's return.

Differential diagnosis

The problem of differentiating borderline personality disorders from other diagnostic classifications has given rise to numerous research studies (Gunderson et al., 1975; Carpenter et al., 1977; Gunderson, 1977; Perry and Klerman, 1980). These studies focus on discrete areas of symptomatology and behavior, comparing borderline clients with schizophrenic and other diagnostic cohorts. Although variations in the criteria for inclusion and the nature of the phenomena studied make comparison difficult, at least one distinguishing characteristic emerges. In distinction from the schizophrenic group, borderline clients are consistently noted to have fewer, if any, psychotic symptoms. Hallucinations were notably absent. When present, delusional material was of a paranoid or depressive nature. When psychotic symptoms are present, they are frequently transient and felt by the client as ego alien.

Although individual studies seem to provide additional differentiating features, no pathognomanic symptoms or symptom clusters are discerned. By focusing on phenomenological criteria, frequently limited to behaviors occurring at the time of interview, one misses the enduring *patterns* of behavior that are the foundation of borderline character structure. As Gunderson points out, "the more enduring characterological traits have stronger diagnostic power than the relatively transient and multidetermined sign and symptom data popularly emphasized in diagnostic systems" (1977, p. 191).

Although there is much evidence to support the existence of a borderline personality disorder as a unique diagnostic entity, many issues remain unresolved. Specific clinical descriptions, laboratory studies, uniform exclusion criteria and genetic, prognostic, and follow-up studies have yet to be carried out (Guze, 1975). This is not, however, to imply that the diagnosis of borderline personality cannot be a useful and accurate clinical assessment. The DSM III, by providing consistent criteria for making this diagnosis, will also serve to establish a relatively uniform data base for further research.

In the DSM III, borderline personality disorder is offered as an Axis II diagnosis. This should help to underscore the notion that such a diagnosis represents an enduring pattern of behaviors and symptoms. By providing for multiple concurrent diagnosis on Axis I, the clinician is able to acknowledge both the current, predominant symptomatology and the persisting character structure. Axis I diagnoses of substance use, anxiety, and psychosexual disorders and disorders of impulse control will frequently be associated with an Axis II diagnosis of borderline personality.

Clients with borderline disorders may well come for treatment with behavioral problems that will *appear* to be classified by a V code diagnosis on Axis I (conditions not attributable to a mental disorder). Such a choice is, in almost all cases, an inappropriate one. Behaviors noted in the V codes such as "adult antisocial behavior," "noncompliance with medical treatment," or "marital problem" are intimately related to borderline pathology. Viewing such difficulties as independent phenomena is a frequent and serious clinical error.

Clinicians working with borderline clients often feel that their complaints are exaggerated and goal directed. They may be seen as overly melodramatic or manipulative and thought to be malingering or reporting with a factitious disorder. Such a view may seriously impair the clinician's ability to properly evaluate and treat the client. Once again, such inaccuracies result from an incomplete understanding of borderline dynamics. The therapeutic relationship is no less subject to defensive and pathological distortions than any other in the client's life. In fact, it is uniquely vulnerable to such distortions. These must be analyzed and understood to avoid clinical decisions arising from the clinician's own un-

conscious or preconscious needs or responses (Racker, 1957). Often, this is the most difficult and challenging aspect of work with borderline clients.

THE THERAPEUTIC INTERACTION: THE CLINICIAN'S RESPONSE

Borderline clients frequently arrive at the emergency unit with feelings of hopelessness and despair. They feel abandoned and betrayed by the people on whose support they feel totally dependent. Depressed and overwhelmed, they act and feel incredibly needy and helpless. They may see the emergency unit clinician as their only source of support and relief. Unable to recognize the possibility of change, they are often convinced that if the clinician cannot help, suicide is the only alternative. Other borderline clients may seem to have already decided that the therapist cannot help. When they arrive at the emergency unit, the clinical picture may be dominated by their rage at a world that cannot meet their needs. From the start, the clinician is seen as merely another representative of that world and is treated with sarcasm and contempt. Often during an interview a single client will shift from one of these positions to the other. As in childhood, the wish for support and protection is counterbalanced by the fear of abandonment and isolation.

Buffeted by this intense and fluctuating affective storm, the clinician may begin to respond with equally intense and vacillating emotions. The client's fantasies of help and protection may evoke complementary fantasies of being able to rescue and comfort. Anger and hostility may leave the clinician frustrated, challenged, or frankly infuriated. In the face of a realistic view of what can, in fact, be offered, the clinician may feel overwhelmed and impotent. Faced with the potential threat of suicide should the client not feel sufficiently provided for, the clinician may respond by feeling fearful or manipulated. To work successfully with borderline clients, one must be able to understand these responses and keep them from affecting clinical decisions.

The very nature of emergency psychiatric settings tends to evoke certain feelings in clinical staff. Clients are usually seen during their periods of lowest functioning. Although crisis intervention may result in rapid improvement, many clients are evaluated and referred to another facility for further care. Emergency unit clinicians are, therefore, deprived of the opportunity to observe the client's improvement; should they see the client again, it will usually be in the context of another crisis. Thus although the client may, in fact, have functioned for some time at a considerably higher level, the clinician sees only the worst. With borderline clients who, as noted, are frequently unable to relate to any emotional state other than their current one, this problem is augmented.

Despite the hopefulness that many clients evidence, experienced clinicians recognize that many psychiatric disorders involve a chronic course. In the case of psychotic or organic disorders, both client and clinician have often become comfortable with this knowledge. During periods of stability and low stress borderline clients may *appear* "perfectly normal." Faced with such behavior, the clinician may fall into the trap of becoming overly optimistic, only to become terribly disappointed when another crisis ensues; thus, the dilemma. Should the clinician focus only on the chronic, relapsing nature of the disorder, the result may be depression and feelings of futility. If the clinician becomes overly invested in evidence of progress or stability, disappointment is inevitable. Only by recognizing that borderline disorders are chronic, with periods of decompensation but also the possibility of gradual but sustained improvement, can the clinician avoid either extreme.

Countertransference

Countertransference may be defined as the whole of the clinician's unconscious reactions to the individual client (Laplanche and Pontalis, 1973). It is helpful to think of countertransference as arising from three sources. Objective countertransference involves feelings "in reaction to the actual personality and behavior of the patient, based on objective observations" (Winnicott, 1949, p. 69). Personal countertransference arises from specific identifications and ex-

periences on the clinician's own part. Projective counteridentification occurs when the clinician "is unconsciously and passively 'led' to play the sort of role the patients hand over to him" (Grinberg, 1963, p. 436).

Objective countertransference becomes a particular problem when dealing with clients whose basic style is obnoxious, provocative, or offensive. Although the public may shun such people, and private therapists may decline to work with them, clinicians in emergency units do not have these options. Borderline clients who may be viciously abusive and hostile or appear hopelessly selfish and self indulgent may be justifiably loathsome. It may at times be therapeutically useful to share *some* of these feelings with the client, although the phrasing, timing, and non-recriminatory content of such an effort are essential (Winnicott, 1949). Ordinarily these feelings are probably best dealt with through simple acknowledgement that they exist. A staff attitude that encourages open, frank discussion of these reactions with co-workers will usually provide sufficient support.

Personal countertransference responses will, of course, depend on the unique dynamics of each clinician. Borderline clients do, however, tend to resonate with specific sorts of individual dynamic issues. Moreover, mental health professionals as a group frequently share common personality characteristics. A recognition of certain typical countertransference reactions may help beginning clinicians recognize their own unconscious material when it begins to interfere.

With their tendency to split good-objects and bad-objects, borderline clients tend either to overidealize or degrade the clinician. The idealized transference is usually manifested by the client's fervent belief that the clinician will understand all of the client's difficulties and be able to offer some form of "treatment" that will relieve the pain and suffering. "I feel like no one else has understood me before," "You're making me feel better already," "I can tell you're not like all of them!"—such phrases should alert the clinician to the client's unrealistic and aggrandizing transference. Since clinicians do, of course, wish to help, such "idealization appeals to residuals of the infantile narcissism of the beginner therapist, and heightens his omnipotent self-expectations to perform the therapeutic *tour de force* that the patient so confidently expects from him. The magical expectations of the patient excite the magical expectations of the tyro" (Maltsberger and Buie, 1975, p. 131). The clinician must come to understand that the client is, at the core, asking for the nurturance and total support missing during childhood. Disappointing the client is not a matter of poor technique; it is inevitable. Although it may be possible to help the client repair the intrapsychic damage of the past, such a task is clearly outside the domain of crisis work.

Some clinicians may begin to notice that they feel cold and indifferent despite the client's portrayal of a life replete with external stresses and experiences that would ordinarily evoke pity, horror, or sympathy. Sometimes the clinician may feel that the client is exaggerating or lying. Often the client will be labeled as manipulative and the behavior seen as sociopathic, an attempt to gain something from the staff, perhaps medication or a hospital bed. Such feelings should alert the clinician to a possible countertransference response. Genuinely (albeit unconsciously) concerned for the client's welfare, the clinician may also realize that nothing can be offered which would alleviate these difficulties. In an unconscious attempt to relieve their own feelings of guilt and impotence, clinicians may avoid sympathizing with just how awful the client's objective situations are by viewing them as bad or manipulative. This response is especially likely to occur in work with borderline clients. The widely varying levels at which they may function in different spheres seems to provide the clinician with a justification for denying the extent of their own incapacity.

Case vignette #3

A young clinician described to his supervisor a case he had seen earlier. He was surprised at the intensity of his own anger and hostility toward the client.

"Mr. J obviously had a borderline condition. He had come to this city from the Midwest about a month ago, after being discharged from an inpatient unit there. He demanded that we take total care of him.

It's not even just that he wanted to be hospitalized. When I offered him lunch, he insisted that I feed it to him. God, the nerve! O.K., he had broken his leg 2 days ago, but just how helpless did he want me to think he was? He had money and a hotel room. I was furious—we had a full waiting room, no inpatient beds available and *he* expects me to *feed* him!"

When asked what he had done for the client, the young clinician sheepishly admitted that he had abruptly told the client that he could do nothing for him, gave him the name of an outpatient clinic, and "threw him out." Although he felt that the client could, in fact, manage as an outpatient, his own rage at the client frightened him. The clinician admitted that he had initially felt quite positively toward this client. It was only later in the interview, when he "realized that the client acted so helplessly, even though it was clear that he could, in fact, hold his own" that the anger emerged. He felt as if the client was trying to manipulate and exploit him.

On discussion the clinician became able to realize that the client's helpless behavior reflected true internal feelings. He had, after all, been in the city for only a brief time and *did* have a broken leg. Gradually the clinician began to talk about his own feelings of helplessness as he struggled to provide meaningful and appropriate dispositions for the many clients he had been seeing. "I mean, he didn't need hospitalization. O.K., so he may have needed more support. I knew that there were no half-way house beds available, and it was too late at night to get any of the social service agencies. What was I supposed to do, take him home with me?"

As he began to explore these feelings, the clinician recognized how he had felt impotent and useless to the client. It was suggested to him that perhaps by labeling the client "manipulative" and able to "hold his own," he could feel more comfortable about his own inability to provide any tangible help. By accusing the client of, in essence, being "unworthy" of help, he could avoid his guilt at how little he felt he could actually

115

offer. He agreed that he was feeling frustrated and depressed by a sense of futility and seemed greatly relieved to have gained some understanding of his feelings and behavior.

Projective counteridentification is perhaps the most insidious of the countertransference responses that borderline clients evoke. Burdened by contradictory and painful split-off aspects of their identity and self-view, they may project these motivations or characteristics onto the clinician. Should clinicians not be sufficiently aware of this process, they may unconsciously accept these projections and behave *as if they were their own.* For example, a client may be engaging in some illicit activity with no conscious feelings of guilt or shame. Instead, these opposing feelings, unconsciously split off, are projected onto the interviewer. Although usually tolerant and nonjudgmental, the clinician may begin to find himself feeling disgusted or reproachful by the client's activities. Unlike personal countertransference (as, for example, might occur if the clinician were also struggling with some unconscious guilt), projective counteridentification originates in the *client's* dynamics.

This sort of response is particularly hazardous since it is not limited to any one clinician. In the client for whom projective mechanisms are particularly active, a number of staff members may respond in a similar fashion. Strengthened by what appears to be mutual validation, such distortions can seriously undermine an entire clinic's ability to work effectively with the client. Such unconscious staff countertransference responses are well documented as being particularly frequent and perilous in work with borderline clients (Adler, 1973, 1977).

Coping with countertransference can present a significant problem in work with borderline clients. Left unacknowledged and unresolved, such feelings can seriously impede appropriate and effective therapeutic decision making. Eventually, intrapersonal and interpersonal conflicts evoked by these clients may result in a staff-wide attitude of depression, anger, and frustration.

It is essential that clinics dealing with these clients establish a milieu in which emotional reactions to clients can be acknowledged, shared, and discussed. Since countertransference reac-

tions are frequently unconscious and unnoticed by the primary clinician, they may perhaps be most effectively managed by a general policy of regular case discussions and ongoing clinical supervision. The expectation that cases will be presented and dynamics, disposition, *and* personal reactions discussed in a systematic way should become a part of the "ethic" of all emergency units. Clinicians given responsibility for case supervision ideally should be senior personnel with significant experience in the care of borderline clients. Aware of the significance of countertransference responses and alert for their presence, they must also work to establish an environment of rapport and mutual support conducive to the discussion of these difficult feelings. More formally scheduled ongoing meetings in which individual supervisors and clinicians can develop closer working relationships are a useful adjunct to "on-line" discussion.

In addition to such dyadic work, the value of regular staff meetings and case conferences cannot be overemphasized. A portion of such meetings may be set aside specifically to deal with affective "process" issues. Senior clinicians, by sharing their own experiences and responses, can help encourage less experienced staff to become more open and willing to acknowledge their difficulties. Case presentations that focus on countertransference reactions can provide a forum for collective exploration and enhanced understanding of these phenomena. Indeed it may be only in such a context that evidence of projective counteridentification can be recognized and remedied.

The special problem of suicidality

The evaluation and treatment of self-destructive behavior is discussed in Chapter 8. The assessment of suicidal behavior is, however, fraught with the potential for countertransference distortion. The client who makes a first suicide attempt after an overwhelming loss is generally met with great sympathy and concern by the clinician. The client who has made several dozen gestures, and who perhaps has been seen in the same crisis unit just as many times, may elicit scorn, anger, or a wish to avoid further therapeutic involvement. Borderline clients, with their chronic impulsive and self-destructive behavior, frequently arrive at the emergency unit following suicidal gestures or other self-destructive acts. In evaluating such clients, even greater care must be taken to avoid allowing countertransference to overshadow clinical considerations.

Many unconscious factors elicited by such clients impede objective evaluation. Identification with the client's basic feelings of helplessness and despair increase the wish to become the omnipotent, protecting good-mother. Guilt and shame over the realistic limitations of one's ability to provide such support are frequent responses. To avoid such uncomfortable feelings, one may wish to avoid or minimize contact with the client who evokes them. The recognition, however, that clinical errors with such clients may in fact be fatal serves to counter this impulse. What may result instead is a growing sense of rage and aversion toward the source of these feelings. One *must* deal with such clients; one must also recognize and deal with the reactions they evoke (Lowental, 1976). Although a complete discussion of the particulars of such responses is beyond the scope of this chapter,* familiarity with their prevalence and manifestations is essential. Labeling self-destructive behavior as manipulative does not obviate the need to evaluate its potential lethality, recognize its dynamics, and institute appropriate therapeutic measures.

TREATMENT CONSIDERATIONS

The choice of how best to help a client in crisis involves consideration of multiple contributing factors. Naturally, the central focus of any treatment plan is a thorough understanding of the client's immediate problem, overall level of functioning, ego strengths, and environmental supports. Against these must be weighed the extent of the client's current regression, the denial or exaggeration of real difficulties, and the possibility of potentially violent or self-destructive be-

---

*See Maltsberger and Buie (1974) for a more complete review and bibliography.

havior. In crisis work, attention must be paid to those issues that demand or may be amenable to immediate treatment. Problems that, though perhaps more severe, are not contributory to the current situation are best dealt with in another setting.

Borderline pathology is of a characterological nature, involving enduring patterns of behavior. Although it is necessary to understand the genesis and vicissitudes of such behavior to properly evaluate these clients, overall character structure will not be changed by brief treatment. Rather, it provides the background against which current difficulties must be understood. The task of effecting lasting "structural" changes in these clients can only be carried out in the context of long-term treatment. Crisis intervention must have as its focus the reduction or elimination of the immediate stress, the protection of clients from responses that might harm themselves or others, and the inauguration or suggestion of a plan to help alleviate the more long-range difficulties.

Assessing the environment

After establishing a dynamic formulation of the client's central conflicts, behaviors, and defenses, the scope of inquiry must widen to include environmental factors. To most effectively formulate a treatment plan, both the client's difficulties and the environmental context in which they occur must be assessed. With borderline clients, special care must be taken to evaluate the objective extent of external supports. Given the propensity of such clients to distort their perceptions in response to internal states, their view of their environment is frequently unreliable. The roommate who the client feels certain will be available for solace and support may, in fact, be unwilling to participate in any treatment plan. Parents, seen as rejecting and unreliable if not malevolent, may in reality be anxious to help the client follow through on outpatient appointments or other treatment. Every effort should be made in encouraging clients to allow the clinician to contact significant people in their lives. Such direct contact may serve to provide valuable information as well as be useful in establishing a more accurate appraisal of the clients' support systems.

The therapeutic alliance

Objective criteria for deciding on a treatment plan must be balanced against the acceptability of such a plan to the client. Clients' cooperation with any suggested course of action will depend to a large degree on their relationship with the person proposing the plan. The intense transferences with which the borderline client views the clinician frequently mitigate against any true therapeutic alliance. As long as the clinician is viewed as either omnipotent or impotent, or totally loving or rejecting, any plans or suggestions offered to the client will be subject to parallel distortions. It is hoped that by remaining aware of such transference issues as they emerge and by curtailing their own countertransference responses, the clinicians will help maximize the alliance.

The client who feels accepted by and able to trust the clinician has perhaps received all that one can offer during a crisis intervention interview. Although further therapeutic measures may well be needed, these can now be presented as extensions of the current process. If the client is to voluntarily participate in treatment, the quality of experience in this first encounter may well be critical.

Many clients, of course, will be so regressed, affectively charged, or internally preoccupied as to require more acute, perhaps involuntary, treatment. Nonetheless, within the restrictions imposed by their impaired ability, every effort should be made to nurture such threads of a therapeutic alliance as may be possible. For such clients the primary goal of crisis intervention is to provide the client with a level of external protection and support until they are able to provide for themselves.

The treatment plan

Although the primary focus of ongoing treatment is often outside of the emergency unit, it is there that the treatment plan must begin. Naturally, the local availability of particular facilities and services will have a profound impact on the form of this plan. Certain global considerations will, however, be universally applicable. Will the client be able to maintain himself outside of a structured setting? How significant is the risk of self-destructive behavior or dangerous acting out? If admission to some structured setting is indicated, will the client be best served by hospitalization or some less restrictive placement? Is the client so out of control or overwhelmed by anxiety, rage, or fear that medication is indicated? Although these questions are addressed in the evaluation of most clients, their application to work with borderline clients involves some special considerations.

Kernberg (1977) discusses some of the difficulties inherent in evaluating borderline clients during periods of crisis. Although a long-range treatment plan must eventually be decided on, "under conditions of acute crisis, crisis intervention is indicated" (p. 120). Such treatment is, in many cases, directed toward allowing the client to be reconstituted to a condition where a more thorough assessment is possible. Given the borderline client's potential to undergo rapid shifts in level of functioning, many clients will present a markedly different clinical picture after such interventions. The treatment plan, therefore, should strive to bolster the client's rapid reintegration and, where possible, postpone an ultimate disposition until this has occurred.

Some clients may respond quite favorably to the clarifications and confrontations of the structural interview. To the extent that their reality testing remains unimpaired, they may be able to use the interviewer's comments to correct their perceptions. With such insights some clients will begin to become somewhat more realistic in their assessment of their present crisis (Kernberg, 1977; Stone, 1980). For such clients the response to the interview alone may be sufficient for them to reestablish some measure of homeostasis. Work with such clients can begin immediately to help solidify these gains, and a referral for outpatient psychotherapy may be all that is indicated.

In many cases, however, more extensive interventions may be necessary.

MEDICATION. The efficacy of pharmacological

agents in the long-term treatment of borderline pathology has only recently begun to be rigorously evaluated (Klein, 1975a, 1977). When used judiciously in the emergency setting, however, they can be an effective adjunct to other supportive measures. For many clients the degree of anxiety, psychotic ideation, or rage may preclude extensive verbal interaction. Such behavior will often respond quite rapidly to low-dose neuroleptic agents, allowing the clinician to proceed with a more thorough diagnostic assessment. Klein (1975b) cautions against the use of neuroleptics until an appropriate diagnosis has been made. Although such treatment may, in fact, be ideal, it is a luxury that many community-based facilities can hardly afford. What is essential, as Klein points out, is continued assessment beyond the initial interview.

The pain of borderline clients on arrival frequently generates a wish in the clinician to provide immediate relief. Minor tranquilizers may seem to be an effective remedy in such situations. Prescribing them for such clients "just for a while until they're feeling better" is a therapeutic error. The pain the client feels is part of a longstanding character disorder that cannot be cured by a benzodiazepine. Although short-term use of these drugs has its place in outpatient therapy (Kernberg, 1975), as a method of crisis intervention it is generally more effective in putting the clinician at ease than in helping the client. Pharmacological agents should be used with borderline clients for the relief of specific target symptoms. In the emergency setting, their use should be further restricted to those instances in which the symptoms preclude further evaluation and disposition planning.

OVERNIGHT HOSPITALIZATION. Ianzito et al. (1978) studied the use of overnight (less than 24 hours) hospitalization as a treatment modality. Although they did not include borderline character disorders as one of their diagnostic classes, their findings seem applicable to this group. They suggest that "overnight admission is a useful modality in the treatment of psychiatric illness. It is most suitable for emergencies where there is diagnostic uncertainty or intermediate severity of psychopathology, but can also be effective when the patient might benefit from simple sup-

portive maneuvers" (p. 73). Their data indicate that approximately half of the people admitted overnight were able to be discharged the next day.

Overnight admission can be a particularly effective treatment modality with borderline clients. A substantial number of clients show a marked reduction of suicidal and homocidal ideation and anxiety or depressive symptoms after 12 to 24 hours. Many of these clients may then be discharged or more appropriately placed in halfway houses or other structured settings (Havassy et al., 1980).

Occasionally, crisis work with these clients become a struggle over hospitalization. Feeling unable to take care of themselves any longer, they view admission to the hospital as their only hope. The clinician who questions this becomes the rejecting bad-mother. The client's behavior may escalate, perhaps with suicidal threats, if admission is denied. Frequently, an overnight admission provides the ideal treatment. Because of the short duration of treatment, the client may avoid the behavioral regression frequently associated with inpatient admissions (Adler, 1973). The clinician, suddenly transformed into the good-mother, may use the time to further a therapeutic alliance and establish some ongoing treatment program.

INDICATIONS FOR ADMISSION. Inpatient hospitalization is occasionally an effective and appropriate treatment for borderline clients. During periods of overwhelming stress or incapacitating symptoms, it can provide a safe "holding environment" in which the client may safely be reconstituted. Hospitalization is indicated "for those borderline patients whose chaotic life situation and incapacity to provide meaningful information to the psychotherapist make the diagnostic process itself (particularly distinguishing the condition from schizophrenia) extremely difficult and consequently hamper the planning of treatment. Short term hospitalization is also indicated when acute life threatening or other crises have potential damaging long range consequences for the patient . . ." (Kernberg, 1973, p. 35).

It is often difficult to objectively assess the need for hospitalization for many clients in the face of their overwhelmingly needy and support-seeking presentations. Suicidal threats or gestures must be carefully explored in an empathic manner in an effort to clarify their underlying meaning. On many occasions hospitalization will indeed be appropriate. At other times, both client and clinician may come to recognize such behavior as a simple (if dramatic) request for help that may be better provided by other treatment modalities. Severe acting-out behavior must be similarly assessed, particularly on those occasions in which law enforcement agencies have requested the evaluation. Was an otherwise stable client impulsively acting in the throes of an acute decompensation? Does the client give evidence of sociopathic features; were there clear and gainful goals to the behavior? Has the client by the end of the interview regained sufficient self-control to manage outside of a protective environment?

Perhaps the single most important determinant of the need for hospitalization is the extent of the client's regression. During severe regressions many borderline clients become so impaired that they are able to exert little control over their reality testing, affects, and impulses. Such states (particularly common during alcohol or other drug intoxication) will be readily assessed during an interview. On these occasions, hospitalization can be lifesaving. At other times it will be more difficult to determine the degree of regression. A review of previous contacts, consultation with current or recent therapists, or interviews with family or friends can be extremely helpful in establishing baseline behavior. Brief hospitalizations during which more background information can be obtained will often foster rapid recompensation. When there remains significant doubt about clients' ability to maintain control of their impulses, it is generally advisable to use brief admissions as a means of both assessing and re-establishing levels of internal control.

ALTERNATIVE TREATMENTS. In many communities, there are few treatment options available at an intermediate level between hospitalization and outpatient therapy. Many borderline clients not in need of hospitalization are unwilling or unable to tolerate the intimacy of individual psychotherapy. Their difficulties in dealing with authority and intimacy may preclude their effective use of halfway house or other residential treatment facilities. This group of clients, seen during acute crisis and noncompliant with follow-up treatment, is a phenomenon familiar to most emergency psychiatric clinicians (Schwartz and Goldfinger, 1981). Although innovative, "open-door" drop-in and day treatment programs (Crafford, 1977) are becoming more common, for many clients the emergency unit remains their primary treatment source. Open 24 hours a day, it may be seen as providing comfort exactly when needed. Although the staff is familiar, no one person is always there, thereby allowing for some diffusion of the transference. Having perhaps been frequented by clients during a period of extreme rage yet still open and functioning, it reassures clients that it can survive their own destructiveness (Winnicott, 1971).

Although every effort should be made to help such clients find more effective sources of treatment, it is likely that the local psychiatric emergency unit will, for many, continue to serve as primary source of therapy. When staff members begin to identify clients for whom this is happening, the formulation of a written history and treatment plan, available to all of the staff, can be a valuable asset. It is sometimes most convenient for a single clinician to formulate such a plan. However, a case conference focused on such clients, with the task of jointly drafting a plan can be a valuable clinical and educational endeavor.

Treatment plan for Ms. A. During the interview Ms. A became aware of how the evening's events were part of a larger context of her expectations from Bill. She responded to the interviewer's noncritical questions and concern by becoming less anxious and frightened. In fact, she appeared genuinely grateful for the opportunity to gain some understanding of why she had been so agitated.

Ms. A had functioned relatively well before the current crisis and had been able to use the interpretations offered during the interview to regain a sense of mastery over her impulses. The interviewer therefore began to introduce the possibility of further exploration in outpatient treatment, presenting it as a means of resolving some of the questions raised during the interview.

Recognizing that her return to the apartment would involve some difficult explanations to Bill, the interviewer discussed with Ms. A possible ways of explaining her behavior. They agreed that she would call him from the clinic, which she did. His supportive tone and obvious concern helped allay her fears of returning home.

The clinician working with Ms. A recognized that although she seemed to benefit from the interpretations during the interview, she might not yet be motivated for further treatment. By offering it as a strictly voluntary option, the clinician was attempting to further support the fact that Ms. A was *not* "crazy," as she had been worried about earlier. Rather it was hoped that she might at some future point consider further treatment more seriously if later difficulties developed.

It was also made clear to Ms. A that she was welcome to call or come in to the unit at any time she *began* to feel out of control again.

Treatment plan for Mr. H. In response to Mr. H's numerous previous contacts the staff had already formulated an ongoing treatment plan. Since he had demonstrated minimal improvement with hospitalization, it had been decided that he would only be admitted if significant suicidal or homocidal ideation were present. In their absence he was to be offered various treatment alternatives but was free to reject any services offered.

When questioned about his lacerated wrist, Mr. H replied, "Hah, I wasn't trying to kill myself, if that's what you mean. Hell, if I wanna die, I know how to do it." Further questioning seemed to confirm that although frustrated and depressed, Mr. H was in fact unlikely to kill himself at that time.

Mr. H seemed genuinely shocked when the clinician asked, "So, what do *you* want to do?" After several caustic comments about being "led on" and "tortured," he was finally able to recognize that the clinician was indeed serious. Caught without an adversary against whom to struggle, he seemed genuinely confused.

Several possibilities were offered, including the option of an overnight stay, "no strings attached." After some further questioning, Mr. H admitted that he had been sleeping in the park for several nights and could use a bed, "but nothing else, ok? No drugs, no shrinking." It was agreed that at nine the next morning he could leave. If at that time he wanted any further help, he would have to ask for it.

Although this treatment plan may at first seem overly harsh and rejecting, it grew out of a sincere effort to help the client. A review of his previous contacts made it clear that prior interventions had had little impact on his behavior. Each presentation was viewed as a discrete entity; treatment decisions were being made with no overall consideration of how they might best impact on his chronic recidivism. Until he could begin to respond to interventions as something other than external constraints *forced* on him, any therapeutic engagement seemed futile. Thus, unless it were absolutely essential for his safety, Mr. H could freely choose the level of therapeutic involvement. In this way an effort was made to avoid engaging with him only around issues of control. It was hoped that Mr. H might eventually be able to gain some ability to trust that the staff would neither reject him when he asks for help nor impose restrictions on his freedom. Perhaps one day he might feel comfortable enough to come in on his own, without police escort or impulsive gestures.

ISSUES FOR FURTHER CONSIDERATION

Borderline pathology has only recently come to be recognized as a discrete clinical entity. Demographic data and research on its prevalence, clinical course, and response to treatment are only now beginning to be collected. Clinicians throughout the country, however, are gradually becoming aware that it represents a mental health problem of significant proportions.

Traditional therapeutic modalities are often less than successful in working with these clients. Community mental health programs that may deal effectively with chronic psychotic or affective disorders are often inappropriate for borderline clients (Schwartz and Goldfinger, 1981). The nature of their symptoms and lifestyle often precludes their acceptance into existing nonhospital programs. Hospitalization—necessary in some instances—may, however, induce regression and dependence; gains achieved during admission may evaporate in the face of exacerbations at time of discharge. Their impulsive behavior, frequent alcohol and drug abuse, and tendency to test all rules and limits often preclude residential placement. The frequent history of self-destructive acts, frank suicide attempts, or forensic involvement eliminates many of these clients from such programs as they might accept. Ongoing psychotherapy is perhaps the only effective treatment that might address their underlying character disorder. Such a course, however, is subject to such intense transference (and countertransference) phenomena that it may be impossible for many clients to tolerate.

Clearly, alternative models of service delivery designed to address the specific needs of this population should be established (Segal and Baumohl, 1980). Social service agencies, case management systems, and residential programs must be made aware of the expectable interactional patterns. Outpatient clinics may, perhaps, be forced to alter existing patterns of service, offering drop-in groups or unscheduled visits. Until such programs can be implemented, these clients may well continue to use psychiatric emergency units for their primary care. It is incumbent on such services, therefore, to address the specific needs of these special clients and to recognize the unique challenges they pose.

BIBLIOGRAPHY

Adler, G.: Hospital treatment of borderline patients, Am. J. Psychiatry 130:32, 1973.

Adler, G.: Hospital management of borderline patients and its relation to psychotherapy. In Hartocollis, P., editor: borderline personality disorders, New York, 1977, International Universities Press, Inc.

Bychowski, G.: The problem of latent psychosis, J. Am. Psychoanal. Assoc. 4:484, 1953.

Carpenter, W.T., Gunderson, J.G., and Strauss, J.S.: Considerations of the borderline syndrome: a longitudinal comparative study of borderline and schizophrenic patients. In Hartocollis, P., editor: Borderline personality disorders, New York, 1977, International Universities Press, Inc.

Chessick, R.D.: Intensive psychotherapy of the borderline adult, New York, 1977, Jason Aronson, Inc.

Crafford, C.: Day hospital treatment for borderline patients. In Hartocollis, P., editor: Borderline personality disorders, New York, 1977, International Universities Press, Inc.

Deutsch, H.: Some forms of emotional disturbance and their relationship to schizophrenia, Psychoanal. Q. 11:301, 1942.

Frosch, J.: Psychotic character, J. Am. Psychoanal. Assoc. 8:544, 1960.

Goldfinger, S.M.: The role of the father in separation-individuation, thesis, New Haven, Conn., 1976, Yale University.

Green, A.: The borderline concept. In Hartocollis, P., editor: Borderline personality disorders, New York, 1977, International Universities Press, Inc.

Grinberg, L.: On a specific aspect of countertransference due to the patient's projective identification, Int. J. Psychoanal. 43:436, 1963.

Grinker, R.R.: The borderline syndrome: a phenomenological view. In Hartocollis, P., editor: Borderline personality disorders, New York, 1977, International Universities Press, Inc.

Grinker, R.R., Werble, B., and Drye, R.C.: The borderline syndrome: a behavioral study of ego functions, New York, 1968, Basic Books, Inc, Publishers.

Grunebaum, H., and Klerman, G.L.: Wrist slashing, Am. J. Psychiatry 124:524, 1967.

Gunderson, J.G.: Characteristics of borderlines. In Hartocollis, P., editor: Borderline personality disorders, New York, 1977, International Universities Press, Inc.

Gunderson, J.G., Carpenter, W.T., and Strauss, J.S.: Borderline and schizophrenic patients: a comparative study, Am. J. Psychiatry 132:12, 1975.

Gunderson, J.G., and Singer, M.T.: Defining borderline patients: an overview, Am. J. Psychiatry 132:1, 1975.

Guze, S.B.: Differential diagnosis of the borderline personality syndrome. In Mack, J.E., editor: Borderline states in psychiatry, New York, 1975, Grune & Stratton, Inc.

Hartocollis, P.: Affects in borderline disorders. In Hartocollis, P., editor: Borderline personality disorders, New York, 1977, International Universities Press, Inc.

Havassy, B., Goldfinger, S.M., and Mariacher, D.: Unpublished data, Psychiatric Emergency Services, San Francisco General Hospital, University of California School of Medicine, 1980.

Hoch, P.H., and Polatin, P.: Pseudoneurotic forms of schizophrenia, Psychiatric Q. 23:248, 1949.

Ianzito, B.M., Fine, J., and Pestana, J.: Overnight admissions for psychiatric emergencies, Hosp. Community Psychiatry **29**:11, 1978.

Kernberg, O.F.: Early ego integration and object relations, Int. J. Psychoanal. **47**:236, 1966.

Kernberg, O.F.: Borderline personality organization, J. Am. Psychoanal. Assoc. **15**:641, 1967.

Kernberg, O.F.: Discussion of: Adler, G.'s "Hospital treatment of borderline patients." Am. J. Psychiatry **130**:1, 1973.

Kernberg, O.F.: Borderline conditions and pathological narcissism, New York, 1975, Jason Aronson, Inc.

Kernberg, O.F.: The structural diagnosis of borderline personality organization. In Hartocollis, P., editor: Borderline disorders, New York, 1977, International Universities Press, Inc.

Klein, D.F.: Psychopharmacology and the borderline patient. In Mack, J.E., editor: Borderline states in psychiatry, New York, 1975a, Grune & Stratton, Inc.

Klein, D.F.: Who should not be treated with neuroleptics, but often are. In Ayd, F.J., Jr., editor: Rational psychopharmacology and the right to treatment, Baltimore, 1975b, Ayd Medical Communications.

Klein, D.F.: Pharmacological treatment and delineation of borderline disorders. In Hartocollis, P., editor: Borderline personality disorders, New York, 1977, International Universities Press, Inc.

Laplanche, J., and Pontalis, J.B.: The language of psychoanalysis, New York, 1973, W.W. Norton & Co., Inc.

Lowental, U.: Suicide—the other side, Arch. Gen. Psychiatry **33**:838, 1976.

Mahler, M.S.: On the significance of the normal separation-individuation phase. In Schur, M., editor: drives, affects and behavior, vol. II, New York, 1965, International Universities Press, Inc.

Mahler, M.S.: On human symbiosis and the vicissitudes of individuation, New York, 1968, International Universities Press, Inc.

Mahler, M.S.: The psychological birth of the human infant, New York, 1975, Basic Books, Inc., Publishers.

Maltsberger, J.T., and Buie, D.H.: Countertransference hate in the treatment of suicidal patients, Arch. Gen. Psychiatry **30**:625, 1974.

Maltsberger, J.T., and Buie, D.H.: The psychiatric resident, his borderline patient and the supervisory encounter. In Mack, J.E., editor: Borderline states in psychiatry, New York, 1975, Grune & Stratton, Inc.

Masterson, J.F.: Psychotherapy of the borderline adult, New York, 1976, Brunner/Mazel, Inc.

Perry, J.C., and Klerman, G.L.: Clinical features of the borderline personality disorder, Am. J. Psychiatry **137**:2, 1980.

Racker, H.: The meanings and uses of countertransference, Psychoanal. Q. **26**:303, 1957.

Rinsley, D.B.: An object relations view of borderline personality. In Hartocollis, P., editor: Borderline personality disorders, New York, 1977, International Universities Press, Inc.

Schwartz, S., and Goldfinger, S.M.: The new chronic patient: clinical characteristics of an emergency subgroup, Hosp. Community Psychiatry **32**(7):470, 1981.

Segal, S.P., and Baumohl, J.: Engaging the disengaged: proposals on madness and vagrancy, Social Work **25**:5, 1980.

Stone, M.H.: The borderline syndromes, New York, 1980, McGraw-Hill, Inc.

Werble, B.: Second follow-up study of borderline patients, Arch. Gen. Psychiatry **23**:7, 1970.

Winnicott, D.W.: Hate in the countertransference, Int. J. Psychoanal. XXX, 1949.

Winnicott, D.W.: The maturational process and the facilitating environment, New York, 1965, International Universities Press, Inc.

Winnicott, D.W.: The use of an object and relating through identifications. In Winnicott, D.W.: Playing and reality, New York, 1971, Basic Books, Inc., Publishers.

Zetzel, E.: A developmental approach to the borderline patient, Am. J. Psychiatry **128**:867, 1971.

Zilboorg, G.: Ambulatory schizophrenia, Psychiatry **4**:149-155, 1941.

CHAPTER **8**

The client with suicidal behavior

Corrine L. Hatton, R.N., M.N., C.S.
Elaine Wustmann, R.N., M.N.

> *Sometimes only a dramatic gesture like suicide can unleash the resounding echo of pain* (C. Hatton).

Within recent years there has been an increasing recognition of suicide as a major health problem. In the United States suicide is the tenth leading cause of death, and among adolescents it ranks second (Mont, 1975). Suicide deaths are still underreported, and statistics vary from county to county, state to state, nation to nation. The reported rate for the United States has ranged between 10.0 and 12.6 per 100,000 during the past decade (Allen, 1977). Many theorists and clinicians offer a variety of explanations for this phenomenon. However, it is not the intent of this chapter to discuss such theories but rather to examine the identification, assessment, and management of clients with suicidal behavior or ideation.

Frequently, people who feel miserable and think of suicide will share that feeling with someone. They are often amenable to intervention and eventually find alternative means to structure their lives. However, this process may be interrupted by any one of four complex dilemmas, or cries for help.

AMBIVALENT CRY FOR HELP. The ambivalent cry for help (Farberow and Shneidman, 1961) is made by the client, yet the client resists help.

This resistance emanates from a variety of internal sources, for example, feelings of hopelessness, a need to manipulate, or a belief system (cultural or personal) that makes seeking professional help ego dystonic, that is, it conflicts with their normal self-concept. Such resistance may evoke in others feelings of anxiety, irritation, or frustration. Thus frustrated family members and friends frequently request advice and assistance from professionals in handling such situations.

SYMBOLIC CRY FOR HELP. The symbolic cry for help occurs when the client cries for help but is not heard. Either the message is too obscure or the person to whom it is directed does not want to hear or does not know how to listen. For example, an individual may make vague statements about not being around in the future or may suddenly begin giving away all valuable possessions. The recipient may fail to recognize the significance of such behavior.

RESISTANT CRIES FOR HELP. Resistant cries for help are given frequently by the client, and helpful interventions are frequently provided. However, the client continues the suicidal behavior. This category refers to the chronically suicidal individual whose behavior often reflects a personality disorder. Although the suicidal behavior is symptomatic in nature, it becomes ego syntonic (part of the recognized self—"the way I am") and a generalized mechanism to manipulate and cope with the environment.

UNHEEDED CRY FOR HELP. People who hear a cry for help and do not respond to it appropriately do so either because of a lack of knowledge or because of countertransference issues. In response to hearing an individual's suicidal ideation, friends may become afraid of getting involved. To avoid feelings of helplessness and depression, they decrease contact with the suicidal person, thereby withdrawing a much-needed support system. The clinician, too, may feel helplessness or hopelessness, which may be conveyed to the client or acted out in the treatment approach.

LEGAL AND PHILOSOPHICAL IMPLICATIONS

Additional factors influencing the clinician's management of suicidal clients are the responsibilities and restrictions placed on clinicians as stated by law and the clinician's beliefs regarding clients' right to commit suicide. Society's answer to the philosophical and moral question of whether an individual has the right to kill himself is reflected in the laws regarding assessment and management of suicidal clients who refuse treatment. The lack of consensus regarding this issue is indicated by the differences in laws from state to state, and ambivalence is reflected in the ambiguity of the language of these laws. So it is the responsibility of clinicians to be knowledgeable about their state's legal position regarding the criteria under which individuals can be held for treatment against their will, who has the authority and responsibility to make that decision, and the procedure required to implement such action.

In California, for example, only police officers or selected staff members of a county-designated facility have the authority to transport an individual involuntarily to a treatment facility. This type of involuntary detention is based on the criterion that the individual is a "danger to self or others or gravely disabled" and may be continued for a period of 72 hours for purposes of evaluation and treatment (California Mental Health Progress, 1968).

Because of the limited availability of police officers and county-designated psychiatric staff, concerned family members frequently use coercion to get a client to an appropriate facility for treatment. Clinicians frequently encounter suicidal clients in locations that legally restrict their authority, for example, general emergency rooms, private offices, and "nondesignated" treatment facilities. Therefore each clinician must be prepared with a procedure specific to the setting which allows for emergency assessment and management of suicidal clients. Also individuals may refuse to be detained long enough for the assessment, necessary for legal detection, to be completed. Such short-term detention, based on just cause for suspicion of suicidal intent and done in good faith, is thought to be in the client's best interest, but this type of detention is controversial.

In addition, California law states that a person who is a danger to himself must be "imminently suicidal" to justify involuntary detention. Although "imminently suicidal" is generally interpreted as the prediction that a person will commit suicide within 24 hours if intervention is not forthcoming, such a statement is vague and open to a wide range of interpretation. For example, the police generally interpret it to mean an individual must take specific action, and they will detain a person only after he has seriously attempted suicide. Some clinicians require only suicidal intent stated by the client, whereas others may rely on reports of family and friends. Thus the interpretation of the law and information received from the client and significant others is highly influenced by the clinician's personal philosophy regarding clients' rights and the clinician's role and responsibility in intervening.

It would seem appropriate at this point to explain our position regarding clients' right to kill themselves. It is our long-held belief, based on clinical data in the field of suicidology, that most people with suicidal ideation are ambivalent, that is, the wish to die is counterbalanced by a wish to live. Studies indicate that in greater than 50% of successful suicides, the victims sought professional help 6 months before the suicide (Litman, 1966). Health care professionals can often be the force or influence that tips this balance and can assist the suicidal person to determine alternatives to death. Also, persons who feel suicidal are often overwhelmed by feelings of dread and misery and view suicide as a means of escaping this horrible feeling of despair, which is usually time limited, varying from hours to months. Lastly, suicidal persons are frequently grateful for another chance at life and a new opportunity to deal with problems that they had previously found overwhelming. Clinicians cannot assess and manage suicidal clients until they come to some philosophical and moral decisions about the right of human beings to end their own lives. The ethical position of this chapter is that human beings have the right to do with their lives as they choose. However, as has been previously mentioned, suicidal people are ambivalent about living and dying. Often their desire is to rid themselves of the psychic pain of misery and depression and they may not wish to be dead at all. Therefore, if everything has been done by mental health clinicians to help people with their pain and distress, then the professional responsibility has been fulfilled and it is the clients' right to choose what they want to do with their lives.

GENERAL ASSESSMENT OF SUICIDE RISK

Assessment of suicide risk is a process that clinicians undertake in an attempt to reasonably predict the suicide potential of a particular person. Usually this potential is predicted on a low (not likely to commit suicide) to high (likely to commit suicide) continuum. Some clinicians and theorists identify this assessment process as *lethality assessment* (Hoff, 1978). Others argue for the use of the term *suicide risk assessment,* reserving the term *lethal* to mean *deadly or fatal* (Beck et al., 1974). At the present time both terms seem to be used interchangeably to refer to this assessment process. In this chapter the term *assessment of suicide risk* will be used throughout. This process is based on specific data (often called a scale) that has been collected and used over the years. Although the data base for scales has not been scientifically established (Brown and Sheran, 1972; Beck et al., 1974; Hatton et al., 1974; and Neuringer, 1974), an assessment process based on clinically validated data is necessary for clinicians who are in a position to offer evaluation and assistance.

A thorough and perceptive assessment of this problem forms the foundation of any care-giving relationship and is the basis on which intervention is determined. In *People in Crisis* Lee Ann Hoff (1978, p. 117) points out the following:

> The importance of lethality assessment can be compared to the importance of diagnosing a person's cough before beginning treatment. Effective assessment of lethality should accomplish the following:
> - Cut down on a guesswork approach in working with self-destructive people.
> - Reduce the confusion and disagreement that often occur among those trying to help suicidal people.
> - Provide a scientific base for service plans for self-destructive people.

• Increase the appropriate use of hospitalization for suicidal persons.

Failure to assess the degree of suicide risk may result in unnecessary problems. An example is given in the following case vignette.

Case vignette #1

Ms. J, a 30-year-old woman, was taken to a psychiatric emergency unit by a friend because she threatened to take an overdose of Nembutal and a pint of alcohol because "no one cares for me." She was angry and verbally abusive, felt people had let her down, was specific in her plan to kill herself that night, and had Nembutal and alcohol at her disposal. The psychiatric emergency staff were anxious and frustrated by her anger and hostility and hospitalized her because of the detail of her suicidal plan. However, a more thorough assessment of the precipitating event (hazard) might have revealed that Janet was presently in outpatient treatment and that her suicidal feelings were precipitated by an argument with her clinician which she had interpreted as termination of treatment. Thus a call to her clinician clarifying her misperceptions and scheduling an appointment within the next few days might have promoted resolution of the crisis and avoided hospitalization.

The components of the assessment process listed here are summarized from the published works of Shneidman and Farberow (1957), Tuckman and Youngman (1968), Maris (1969), Breed (1972), Brown and Sheran (1972), Beck et al. (1974), Buglass and Horton (1974), and Farberow (1975).

Components of the assessment process
A. Demographic data
  1. Age
  2. Sex
  3. Race
  4. Socioeconomic factors
  5. Living arrangements
B. Clinical characteristics
  1. Hazard
  2. Crisis
  3. Depression
  4. Coping devices
  5. Significant others
  6. Personal resources
  7. Past and current psychiatric history including suicide attempts
  8. Life-style
  9. Suicide plan
    a. Method
    b. Availability
    c. Specificity
    d. Lethality
C. High-risk factors
  1. Multiple high-lethality suicide attempts
  2. Alcohol and drug abuse
  3. Isolation and withdrawal
  4. Disoriented or disorganized behavior

Demographic data

AGE, SEX, AND RACE. The patterns of suicidal behavior have been analyzed according to age, sex, and race. More women than men attempt suicide. Men accomplish suicide more often than women and use more lethal methods. The persons at greatest risk of suicide as measured by age and sex are men in middle and old age. However, there is an alarming rise of suicide among adolescents and college-age youth. There are ethnic variables in the suicide rate since ethnic groups have their own special problems and risks. For example, there is a rise in the suicide rate of native Americans, blacks, and Mexican-Americans and the suicide rate is highest for those under the age of 30 (Hoff, 1978, p. 123).

SOCIOECONOMIC FACTORS. Socioeconomic factors such as unemployment, lack of financial resources, family chaos and disorganization, forced retirement, and disruption in living conditions increase a person's risk of suicide. Suicide exists in all socioeconomic groups. There are no statistical data that identify religion or education as a major variable in suicide potential.

LIVING ARRANGEMENTS. In general, the rate of suicide of married individuals is lower than that of single, separated, widowed, or divorced people. The questions that need to be answered by the data gathered are: What is the quality and quantity of these living arrangements? How satisfying are they to the client? The greater the satisfaction, the lower the risk of suicide.

Clinical characteristics

HAZARD. A *hazard* is defined as an external event in the life of an individual which may pose an actual or potential threat to that person's otherwise steady state of functioning. This event may be maturational (occurring along the developmental sequence from infancy to old age) or it may be situational (loss of loved one, physical illness, role change, and so on). It always represents some kind of loss to the individual, and the more significant the loss, the greater the risk of suicide.

CRISIS. *Crisis* refers to the internal emotional disturbance (symptoms) such as anxiety, fear, sadness, anger, and physical illness. The degree of disorganization demonstrated will probably be proportional to the individual's ability to adapt to the feelings prompted by the crisis situation. The less ability to adapt, the higher the risk of suicide.

DEPRESSION. There is an obvious association between depression and suicide. The degree of the depression can be evaluated by examining the severity of the symptoms. Vegetative signs (that is, decreased appetite with weight loss, decreased libido, and insomnia) may indicate a higher degree of depression than symptoms of overeating or oversleeping. Other symptoms include anhedonia, decreased concentration, decreased energy and motivation, social isolation, psychomotor retardation or agitation, flat affect, poor personal grooming, feelings of helplessness and hopelessness, excessive crying, and change in level of functioning. Severe symptoms of depression indicate a higher risk of suicide.

COPING DEVICES. Coping devices are the ways an individual usually manages various stressful situations. The more destructive or maladaptive (drinking, drugs, isolation, and so on) the devices, the greater the risk of suicide.

SIGNIFICANT OTHERS. Significant others are the persons in an individual's world who are or could be available for support and reassurance. The more support, both in quality and quantity, a person has nearby, the lower the risk of suicide.

PERSONAL RESOURCES. Personal resources are basic daily necessities of living (housing, food, time, physical and mental abilities, job, hobbies, and so on). The more resources available to the clients, the more likely they will be able to cope with the crisis and thus the lower their suicide risk.

PAST AND CURRENT PSYCHIATRIC HISTORY, INCLUDING SUICIDE ATTEMPTS. In general, if an individual has a past history of suicide attempts and subsequent psychiatric treatment with poor response to and dissatisfaction with that treatment, then the higher the current suicide risk. However, if psychiatric treatment was viewed as beneficial, then perhaps the individual can use treatment again as a coping device.

LIFE-STYLE. A person's *life-style* may be defined as the quality and maintenance over a period of time of the person's job, interpersonal relationships, and coping strategies. If a person feels fulfilled and satisfied and can maintain and manage personal conflicts and problems in a fairly constructive way, one could say that this person has a stable life-style. If a person has had a number and variety of ungratifying jobs, friends, and social situations and copes with problems and conflicts in a destructive way, this person could be said to have an unstable and dissatisfying life-style. Obviously the more unstable the life-style, the higher the risk of suicide.

SUICIDE PLAN. In general, the more specific the plan and the greater the lethality of the method, the greater the risk of suicide. Guns, hanging, drowning, and prescribed medication are more lethal than wrist cutting, nonprescribed medication, and gas poisoning. Someone with a definitive suicide plan and the means available is at a higher suicide risk than someone who is just considering the possibility.

High-risk factors

MULTIPLE HIGH-LETHALITY SUICIDE ATTEMPTS. If a person has a history of multiple high-lethality attempts, the risk of suicide is even higher than usual. The probability is that one of these attempts could be successful.

ALCOHOL AND DRUG ABUSE. The correlation between substance abuse, particularly alcohol, and suicide is high (Litman and Wold, 1976). It is uncertain whether the relationship is one of cause or effect (Soloman and Arnon, 1979). Drinking increases loss of control and in combination with other drugs can be lethal. The statistics on other forms of drugs are incomplete.

ISOLATION AND WITHDRAWAL. Many people, either by design or accident, are painfully isolated and alone. Some individuals have alienated their last support system and withdrawn into a state of aloneness to which suicide seems like a welcome alternative. Such persons are at high risk even in the absence of any other positive assessment factors.

DISORIENTED OR DISORGANIZED BEHAVIOR. If an individual is expressing suicidal ideation and if thought processes seem to be disorganized, fragmented, or distorted with little orientation to reality, then that person is at greater risk for suicide. The ability to think clearly and plan effectively is in jeopardy. The disorientation and disorganization may be caused by psychological stress, physical illness, alcohol abuse, or drug reaction or may be symptoms of a chronic mental disorder.

DIAGNOSIS

Suicidal behavior is not a diagnosis but a symptom present in a variety of diagnostic categories. According to the DSM III, acute suicidal intent as a crisis indicates a diagnosis of adjustment disorder with depressed mood. However, suicidal ideation and behavior can be secondary symptoms of other mental disorders and relate most closely to the affective disorders in which a dysphoric mood is prominent. In schizophrenia there occasionally are depressive symptoms, but suicide is most frequently an unpredictable consequence of the psychotic process often present. Chronic or repeated suicidal behavior bears a particularly close relationship to the borderline personality disorder, the criteria for which include impulsivity, rapid and marked mood shifts, and physically self-damaging acts—specifically, suicidal gestures (DSM III).

Preattempt population

The preattempt population consists of those individuals who seek help because of suicidal ideation or threats before carrying through the action. Those complaining of suicidal ideation often seek help themselves because they are plagued with recurrent thoughts of self-destruction which are often frightening and indicate concrete evidence of the severity of their depression, which they may have denied previously. However, there are individuals who maintain a strong denial of feelings or an inability to express these feelings directly and thus present a myriad of other complaints or symptoms, for example, requests for medication, somatic distress, anxiety, restlessness, and fear. Further exploration and direct inquiry are required to reveal an underlying depression and possible suicidal ideation. It is common for clinicians to misinterpret the symptoms of depression, that is, insomnia, anorexia, lethargy, anhedonia, and fatigue, as indications of physical illness requiring medical attention.

Suicidal threats, as defined previously, may have a quality of manipulation involved, whereby persons see this as their only method of obtaining what they want, for example, a change in environment or relationship, attention from significant others or health care professionals, or hospitalization. Threats may be identified by the way individuals express their suicidal ideation either in the interview or to significant others, for example, comments such as, "If you do or do not do such and such, I will have to kill myself." Also, assessment by the clinician as to what life changes the individual hopes to effect by attempting or talking about suicide may give indication of motive. There are those situations in which suicide is viewed only as a removal from pain, and any potential changes in others will not affect the client's dismal view of life. For others, a change in another "will make everything all right again," and this may be the desired consequence of the threat.

ASSESSMENT. Whether ideation or threat, the suicidal risk must be assessed. Most people have thoughts of suicide at some point in their lives, but this does not mean that they will ever carry such a thought through to action. Furthermore, a threat gone unattended without exploration of other alternatives may force an individual with such coping strategy to attempt suicide to achieve desired ends. It is in this population that the concept of ambivalence, which is involved in every suicide, becomes apparent. That even the most suicidal of individuals may make their needs known to someone reveals at least an unconscious wish or hope for help.

A number of factors are involved in every assessment of suicidal risk, as discussed previously in this chapter. Those relating to the preattempt population include the nature of the ideation, the plan, and the thought processes. Again, this is not to say that the other factors, for example, precipitating event, crisis situation, support structure, past history, and use of drugs and alcohol, are not critical in making an assessment and planning intervention.

For some people suicidal ideation may be only a periodic fleeting thought. Those at greater risk find a large amount of their time consumed by thoughts of suicide or an increase in frequency of such thoughts. However, if these frequently occurring thoughts are ego dystonic because of religious beliefs, personal philosophy, life circumstances, or dependency on others, then the suicide risk decreases. For example, a mother who believes her three dependent children would not do well if she were dead may be deterred from suicide even though she wrestles with the throughts frequently.

Those who spend time to carefully plan the attempt are at greater risk than those individuals who act on impulse. However, the poor planning inherent in impulsive behavior can make an otherwise nonlethal gesture (where the goal is not to die) exceedingly lethal. An example is given in the following case vignette.

Case vignette #2

J.F. is a young man who impulsively takes pills frequently to gain parental attention. One day he inadvertently dies because his parents don't arrive home as scheduled.

This example shows that the individual's history must be evaluated in terms of patterns of behavior and impulsivity. The suicide plan is highly significant and must be assessed in terms of specificity, availability, and lethality. Some people with suicidal ideation have never thought of how they would go about it. Others can tell

you by what means they would like to die but have no idea how to obtain the means. Still others may have the means available but have chosen a method that is highly unlikely to result in death. In general, the longer the period of time for ambivalence to operate and thus rescue to occur, the less lethal is the method. For example, starving, walking into the ocean, wrist slashing, and taking pills are less lethal than hanging, use of a gun, or jumping from a tall building or bridge. Therefore, each of these factors must be carefully assessed and specific questions asked. It is the suicidal plan that discusses each of these factors in detail which is the most seriously lethal.

Case vignette #3

A 52-year-old man who had recently lost his job in management had been thinking of suicide with increasing frequency in the previous 2 weeks. Although he had not written a suicide note, he had planned what he would say in it to his son and wife and had decided that he would take pills when his wife was at work and his son at school. He had taken inventory of what medications were available and had researched them to make certain of their lethality. Although taking pills is not the most lethal of methods, it was clear that this man's detailed plan was highly lethal.

Frequently clients themselves are able to tell you the likelihood of a future attempt and the time span in which they are considering it, as in statements such as, "I won't do anything today or tomorrow, but if things don't change soon I will" or "If my girlfriend breaks up with me, I will definitely kill myself." However, for individuals in whom thought processes are not clear but disorganized and out of contact with reality, as in those with psychosis or drug or alcohol intoxication, assessment becomes more difficult and suicidal risk increases. Because of distortion of reality and an inability to control behavior, auditory command hallucinations are the most lethal of suicidal ideation.

Case vignette #4

A 20-year-old girl had the delusion that she was the cause of the auto accident that killed her mother and voices told her she must be punished by killing herself. Unfortunately, she stopped all psychiatric treatment, discontinued her medications and eventually hung herself.

INTERVENTION. The first decision to be made is determining the severity of the problem and the need for hospitalization. Recommending hospitalization is not only a treatment of choice but also a professional responsibility for those working with clients in whom suicide potential is so high and imminent that other alternatives are unsafe. Voluntary hospitalization is preferable and an effort should be made to enlist clients' participation in their treatment. However, when that is not possible, 72-hour involuntary hospitalization must be employed when legally available. Hospitalization may also be indicated in treatment of depression or psychosis in which suicidal ideation is a secondary symptom. It should be noted that at no time should an imminently suicidal person be left alone while arrangements are being made for hospitalization, whether voluntary or involuntary.

Frequently, hospitalization may be avoided through detailed and imaginative intervention and planning, which should be done whenever possible. Even with persons in whom the suicide risk is low, clinicians are still dealing with individuals who are significantly depressed and possibly in crisis and who view suicide as one means of coping with their present situation. Crisis intervention techniques (discussed in Chapter 1) are geared toward clear identification and understanding of the hazards and the assistance in developing alternative methods for coping. Outpatient treatment is the ultimate disposition as an alternative to hospitalization. Such treatment consists of either short-term crisis intervention, short-term therapy, or long-term therapy in cases of more chronic and pervasive illness. However, treatment arrangements must be based on factors related to the clients' needs and limitations, for example, motivational, financial, and geographical factors. Also, contrary to usual psychiatric referral procedure in which client participation and responsibility is fostered, in crisis cases with concomitant client disorganization

and decreased problem-solving skills, it is often helpful to make treatment arrangements for clients, thereby providing them with a specific plan to use. It should be noted that clients who have had a negative experience with treatment may have less confidence in its ability to help them and thus may not receive the same degree of hope from such intervention.

Even in optimal situations, suicidal ideation or threat rarely dissipates immediately and intermediary measures detailed to the specifics of each case must be employed, allowing and encouraging as much independent functioning as the client can tolerate. Mobilization of a support structure is one such measure. Some clients with a severe level of depression and decreased problem-solving skills often require assistance to identify and elicit help from significant others. For those presently in treatment, their therapist should be contacted and incorporated into the treatment plan. Frequently the therapist is involved in the crisis, since the client has found it necessary to employ additional external support. It is helpful to assist the client in identifying the feelings and motivations for such behavior. Arrangements should be made to have a responsible person stay with a client with high suicide risk both for comfort and safety. In situations where there are truly no significant others, it may be necessary for clinicians to utilize themselves in that capacity on a temporary basis by being available for crisis telephone calls. Arranging a schedule whereby the clinician will call the client at certain intervals provides structure, hope, and a sense of concern for the client.

Planning for removal of the client's intended means of suicide attempt is another critical intervention. This may be accomplished through significant others or, in situations where rapport has been established, through contracts with the clients themselves. Although such action appears elementary and sometimes not effective, it significantly decreases the likelihood of an immediate impulsive attempt.

Further intervention may consist of assisting the client in planning concrete activities and in setting priorities as to what to do to decrease stress. Medication may be prescribed for relief of symptoms such as insomnia and anxiety. Of

131

course, it must be prescribed in small nonlethal dosages with an explanation of its temporary effectiveness. It is inappropriate to have antidepressants prescribed on an emergency basis, since the effectiveness of such medication will not be apparent for at least 2 weeks and should be prescribed by the physician seeing the client on a regular and longer term basis.

Finally, the client must be able to contract with the clinician to make telephone contact with the clinician or come to a prearranged available facility before any suicidal action, in case of acute suicidal ideation in the future. An inability to make such a "no-suicide contract" may indicate hospitalization as the only alternative.

STAFF RESPONSE. There are certain general responses to this client population experienced by all staff members—psychiatrically trained or not. Everyone at times may feel anxiety and an overwhelming sense of responsibility when dealing with the life-and-death matters of these clients. Even many physicians who are generally accustomed to making life-and-death decisions feel more comfortable and in control in the medical setting than in dealing with the emotions and behavior of others. Periodic feelings of inadequacy are inevitable for even the most knowledgeable and experienced. Sometimes in an attempt to establish empathy, clinicians may overidentify with the client, which results in feelings of powerlessness and diminished problem-solving ability. Depression may develop from an inability to immediately change the client's plight. Also, a clinician can become extremely angry at being manipulated if the clients' incapacity for dealing with their environment constructively is diminished. Furthermore, it is critical to be able to view the crisis situation as the client sees it, or it may appear insignificant or irrelevent when viewed in personal terms, thus hindering the establishment of empathy and rapport.

Postattempt population

The postattempt population consists of those individuals who seek help after making a suicide attempt or gesture—the difference being in intent. The goal of self-injury as a gesture is not to kill oneself but, as in the case of threats, to

manipulate one's environment. These people are frequently brought in by paramedics or significant others who have found them or in whom they have confided. Thus they may or may not have come in voluntarily.

The first priority is medical treatment to save their lives or avoid permanent disability. Those who have taken overdoses are usually induced to vomit, and gastric lavage may be necessary. Depending on the type and amount of material ingested and on the time since ingestion, it may be anywhere from minutes to days before such a client is ready to be evaluated psychiatrically. However, as soon as the mental status is clear of drug effects, suicide risk should be assessed. Similarly in trauma cases where self-infliction is known or suspected, psychiatric consultation should be available as soon as the client is medically treated and stable.

Frequently these individuals are angry and hostile for a number of reasons. First, they may be angry they were not successful. Also, they may be angry at receiving uncomfortable medical care that they did not want. There is also a displacement of anger at significant others. However, in many situations such behavior is representative of their usual style of interaction. Finally, the disorientation and confusion experienced while coming off drugs may create a paranoia with associated hostility and belligerence. In general, although these individuals have gone so far in the suicidal process, ambivalence still remains and must be evaluated.

ASSESSMENT. The goal of assessment remains the same as in the preattempt group. However, for the postattempt population there are two aspects for which the client must be assessed— the lethality of the attempt and the client's present level of suicidality immediately after the attempt. In evaluating the lethality of an attempt there are a number of detailed factors to be ascertained.

The method. In addition to recalling previously mentioned facts regarding the lethality of method, it is important, as an indicator of the seriousness of intent, to determine the client's perception of the lethality of the means used. Even though the clinician may know the lethality of a method, the unsophisticated lay person may have a different perception. For example, an individual may believe that because aspirin or Tylenol are over-the-counter drugs, an overdose will not result in death, not knowing that large enough amounts of Tylenol can cause irreversible liver damage and death. In the same respect it often appears likely to the general public that an overdose of Valium alone will surely result in death. Valium alone does not cause respiratory depression and only when accompanied by alcohol or a similar depressant will it result in death. Therefore, an assessment of the client's experience with and knowledge of the means used is necessary. Furthermore, a comparison of the attempt method to what was actually available to the client may also indicate ambivalence. For example, in the case of overdose the clinician must ask, "Did the client take all the pills or were some left in the bottle?" Using a less lethal means than what was obviously available may indicate conscious or unconscious ambivalence.

Circumstances. Specific details of the attempt as to where, when, and in whose presence it occured and what the realistic expectations of the client were not only indicate the degree of planning and ambivalence, but also may provide clues about the desired target of a gesture. For example, an attempt made at a time and place in which it is unlikely for the client to be found by others is more lethal than one made in the presence or with realistic expectation of the arrival of others. Furthermore, in the latter situation one must question why the client chose those particular persons to be present.

Means of obtaining assistance. In addition to the preceding facts, how the client happened to come to the treatment center is important information. Even in situations of well-planned suicides, ambivalence may be evidenced by clues that the client gives. A suicide note, which in certain situations can indicate a high degree of planning, may also be left as a clue indicating that the individual is not just sleeping. Frequently, if frightened by the actual prospect of death, a person may make a phone call, subtly alerting others or actually soliciting assistance. Obviously, there is less lethality involved with clients who come to the treatment center by their own

volition than with those who were accidently found and brought in.

One cannot assume postattempt level of suicide risk based on the lethality of the attempt. Although assessment of the lethality of an attempt indicates the degree of risk, the very act of committing an attempt and the resultant consequences of such may increase or decrease the suicidal risk. The degree of suicide risk may be decreased because of any one of several factors. Frequently a gesture results in achieving the desired ends, such as the alerting of others to the degree of distress, the gaining of attention from significant others, or the mobilization of resources and assistance. Even in situations where such consequences are unexpected, the response of others can have a profound effect on changing individuals' perception of their world. Making an attempt may also bring to awareness an individual's ambivalence and true desire to live. Furthermore, although there is no change in an individual's life situation, at times one observes a certain sense of relief or acceptance in such people. It appears to be related to a feeling of having taken control and having tried all alternatives for solution available to the individual. Now they are willing and able to accept the assistance of others with full cooperation.

Conversely, an individual may feel more intensely suicidal after a gesture that does not obtain an expected response. Furthermore, an unsuccessful suicide attempt may augment previous feelings of despair with embarrassment and further feelings of failure exhibited in such statements as, "I can't even do that right." Frequently a difficult work, school, or social situation is only compounded by the suicide attempt. In addition, it may provide the individual with experience so that next time, more knowledgeable, he will "do it right."

Therefore assessment of postattempt suicidal ideation is critical. Questioning clients' feelings on realization of their lack of success may indicate relief or disappointment. A detailed exploration of future plans is necessary for evaluation of problem-solving skills. Those clients who are vague or unrealistic indicate a greater suicidal risk. A flat denial of suicidal ideation after an attempt may be a manipulation and should not be trusted. One must question why there has been a change in thinking or feelings and the degree of reality orientation.

INTERVENTION. As stated earlier, medical intervention is the initial priority. However, frequently in an attempt to provide appropriate physical treatment, medical staff members lose sight of the potential suicidal risk in such clients. Keeping a safe environment that is free from potential means of further attempt and maintaining continual close observation are necessary during physical recuperation. Furthermore, an individual's feelings after the attempt, as described earlier, may be highly influenced by the response of those around them. Usually medical staff members are the first persons with whom the client has contact after a serious attempt. A lack of understanding, hostility, or ridicule may establish negative expectations for future responses from others and a lack of trust of health care professionals.

Further psychiatric intervention based on the assessment does not differ significantly from that previously stated for preattempt clients. However, when planning intervention, one must remain aware that in addition to emotional distress, such clients may be suffering physical discomfort as well, and thus coping skills may be further debilitated. Therefore, discharge should be planned at a time that will produce the least amount of stress and when the support system is fully available rather than at the convenience of the staff or the hospital. For example, frequently a client may be medically cleared and ready for discharge in the middle of the night, and emergency centers, being geared toward efficiency, will plan discharge to make space available. However, there are few supports available at night, and the interruption of sleep for both client and significant others places added stress on the system as a whole. Thus coordination of services is an integral part of such intervention. This is true for follow-up as well. Frequently, clients will obtain medical follow-up while ignoring emotional needs. Therefore, psychiatric assessment should be included in medical follow-up of suicide attempt cases.

STAFF RESPONSE. In addition to the previously stated response to suicidal ideation, the postattempt population frequently evokes a particularly negative response from health care professionals. Having a goal of health maintenance, professionals devote their time, energy, and emotions to caring for the involuntarily sick and in many cases to keeping them alive at all cost. By attempting to take their own lives, these individuals violate the very purpose of the clinician's work. Thus the clinician is forced to provide optimal care to frequently hostile, uncooperative clients. Anger and frustration are manifest in the thought, "Why should I try to keep them alive when they don't want to live anyway?" Therefore, it may be difficult for clinicians to identify and empathize with such despair and particularly with the use of such means of communication. These feelings are understandable; however, at times such feelings are acted out and communicated to the client as hostility or less than optimal treatment. This is often the situation for both medical and psychiatric staff. Such feelings must be recognized, understood, and controlled, so that they are not acted out unconsciously.

THE CHRONICALLY SUICIDAL—THE SUICIDAL CHARACTER

The preceding discussion of suicidal behavior and management is based on the view of suicide as a response to a crisis situation. As stated previously, it is a means of obtaining relief from intense emotional suffering that is time limited, and thus clients require temporary protection and nurturance until they regain adequate coping skills and can resume full responsibility for their lives. In such clients the suicidal state is ego dystonic; by conflicting with their normal self-concept, it is experienced with anxiety and emotional pain.

However, for those individuals who are unable to obtain such nurturance in other ways, suicidal behavior becomes an adaption response or a generalized coping mechanism. The attention and concern given to suicidal behavior provide much secondary gain when contrasted with the emptiness of the individual's usual existence. Although it is symptomatic in nature, it also becomes characterological and ego syntonic. In such situations suicidality is chronic, and although the immediate short-term risk may be low, the long-term risk is high and at times inevitable.

The assessment of such clients can only be made by looking at their behavior over time. This can be difficult on initial contact and requires extensive history taking, which generally reveals an increase in frequency and severity of suicidal behavior. Furthermore, careful observation and exploration usually elicit the aspect of secondary gain.

Treatment of such clients creates a dilemma, since it is the nurturance inherent in the crisis approach that serves as a reinforcer and functions to shape and increase suicidal characteristics. Thus the standard procedures of such an approach are both ineffective and countertherapeutic. However, such clients are truly suicidal and the immediate risk must be dealt with.

Case vignette #5

Ms. M, age 32, had an unstable life-style history as evidenced by multiple ungratifying relationships and jobs, poor interpersonal rapport, and destructive ways of coping such as drinking, drug use, or low-lethality suicide attempts. She was well known to the local suicide hotline because she frequently called when she was feeling lonely and hopeless. When she ingested a small amount of pills, her family was called. They responded by attending to her immediate need for attention and nurturance. Occasionally she had not ingested pills at all, and then the family would become annoyed at their previous reinforcement of her secondary gains (attention and nurturance) for the primary behavior (pill ingestion). The tragedy occurred the one time Marsha ingested a lethal dosage of medication, called her family, and they didn't believe her. She was dead before rescue could be instituted.

Focusing on the suicide crisis and the client's will to live only leads to power struggles in which such clients must strive harder to prove their need to be taken care of. Expressed empathy and concern are necessary to bring such needs to the clients' awareness and to enlist their involvement in taking responsibility for their own life. A treatment plan that balances the client's responsibility with professional support is optimal.

Case vignette #6

Ms. N. had a history of chronic suicidal behavior, and with anger and hostility, she stated she was feeling suicidal. Exploration revealed that in her therapy session the previous day, she became extremely angry at her therapist's lack of attention and ultimately walked out, leaving her a note that she would continue to try if the therapist would. Since the therapist had not called or responded to her note, she felt no one cared. Identifying and empathizing with such feelings created the basis to further explore how her use of suicidal behavior was a means of obtaining caring and how her behavior was ineffective in meeting her needs. It was clear she needed and wanted the help and support of her therapist, but she placed the responsibility for getting it on the therapist, whom, however, she eventually decided to call to make another appointment as soon as possible.

Since hospitalization is the ultimate in situations fostering dependency, for such clients it should be avoided whenever possible and alternative treatments providing support and structure, for example, day treatment, should be explored and utilized. In those situations of acute suicidal crisis, hospitalization should be planned with the client to be as brief as possible. Again, it is critical to return control and responsibility to the client as soon as possible, thus fostering internal rather than external controls.

It is the fine balance of management of the immediate short-term risk weighed against the long-term development of the suicidal character which challenges the clinician.

STAFF RESPONSE. One can easily imagine the degree of frustration and anger that such individuals evoke in the staff. The negative response of staff members to suicide attempts can only be increased by the number of repeated attempts of such clients. The hope of assisting individuals in learning new and constructive means of coping with a crisis with resultant gratification gradually diminishes as clients repeatedly reappear exhibiting the same behavior. However, such hopelessness in the clinician can be dangerous if communicated to clients (thus validating their already existing feelings) or if acted out in inappropriate treatment based on an attitude of, "What's the point—they're going to do it some day anyway." However, a defense against such feelings may result in an overreacting to the immediate crisis at the sacrifice of promoting responsibility and growth.

The clinician must recognize that the goals of treatment for this population are different from those in a clear crisis state.

Case vignette #7

Ms. C, a 23-year-old single, obese, neatly dressed, licensed vocational nurse, seeks help. She says she feels "helpless—afraid I might hurt myself—it's hopeless—I've been through all this before and nothing helps. No one loves me—my mother threw all my clothes away and my sister hates me. I have no place to go—no job—no money. No one can understand my dilemma."

She states she is not now in any immediate danger to herself or others. She is alert, articulates well, and is in control of herself. Currently Ms. C says she vacillates between feeling well and put together and having periods of confusion and anxiety in which she feels extreme psychic pain and panic. In the past during these difficult periods, she would overdose to decrease the pain and confusion. She is unable to identify any trigger or predisposing factors for the confusion states. She denies excessive use of drugs or alcohol except when she overdoses.

The onset of suicidal ideation and attempts began 3 years ago after a breakup with a male friend who was also a co-worker. Subsequently, she made multiple suicide attempts and had multiple hospitalizations. She reported making many elopements from hospitals where she was admitted for therapy. She lives with her mother and younger sister and experienced the loss of her father years ago when her parents were divorced.

She thinks her family has given up on her, and she feels guilty for hurting them and letting them down. She believes she has no resources available in friends, family, religion, profession, co-workers, and so on. Her greatest strength has been in her work, which she is able to do competently and enjoyably when she is not in a confused and anxious state.

This example demonstrates well the life-style and behavior pattern of the suicidal character. A pattern of utilizing suicide and hospitalization as a reinforced coping mechanism with an externalization of responsibility has begun to develop. The concomitant response of friends and family to withdraw from the client is also a common result of the individual's ineffective and inappropriate means of manipulating others to care for her, leaving her more "starved" than ever. Ms. C is at low immediate risk for suicide since she has no specific plans, is in control of impulses, and seeks help. She is capable of working and has some family who have helped her in the past and may offer support again. However, she demonstrated poor involvement in and commitment to treatment symptomatic of her difficulty in relating to others in general. If she continues to sever connections with others, her long-range suicidal risk will be high. The goal of emergency treatment then is to intervene in the previously reinforced pattern of behavior by avoiding hospitalization and encouraging her participation in further long-term treatment, pointing out the ineffectiveness of her present behavior.

BIBLIOGRAPHY

Allen, N.: History and background of suicidology. In Hatton, C., Valente, S., and Rink, A.: Suicide: assessment and intervention, New York, 1977, Appleton-Century-Crofts.

Beck, A.T., Resnick, H.L.P., and Lettieri, D.: The prediction of suicide, Bowie, Md., 1974, Charles Press.

Breed, W.: Five components of a basic suicide syndrome, Life Threatening Behavior 2:3, Spring, 1972.

Brown, T., and Sheran, T.J.: Suicide Prediction: A Review, Life Threatening Behavior, **2**:67, Summer 1972.

Buglass, D., and Horton, J.: A scale for predicting subquent suicidal behavior, Br. J. Psychiatry **124**:573, June 1974.

California mental health progress: Lanterman-Petris-Short Act, Sacramento, Calif., Oct. 1968, Department of Mental Hygiene.

Farberow, N.L., editor: Suicide in different cultures, Baltimore, 1975, University Park Press.

Farberow, N., and Shneidman, E.S.: The cry for help, New York, 1961, McGraw-Hill Book Co.

Hatton, C.L., Valente, S.M., and Rink, A.: Suicide assessment and intervention, New York, 1977, Appleton-Century-Crofts, p. 40.

Hoff, L.A.: People in crisis: understanding and helping, Menlo Park, Calif., 1978, Addison-Wesley Publishing Company, Inc., p. 117.

Litman, R.E.: Acutely suicidal patients: management in general medical practice, Calif. Med. **104**:168, 1966.

Litman, R.E., and Wold, C.I.: Beyond crisis intervention. In Shneidman, E.S., editor: Suicidology: contemporary developments, New York, 1976, Grune & Stratton, Inc.

Maris, R.E.: Social forces in urban suicide, Homewood, Ill., 1969, Dorsey Press.

Mont, M.: Epidemiology. In Perlin, S., editor: A handbook for the study of suicide, New York, 1975, Oxford University Press.

Neuringer, C., editor: Psychological assessment of suicidal risk, Springfield, Ill., 1974, Charles C Thomas, Publisher.

Shneidman, E.D., and Farberow, N.L., editors: Clues to suicide, New York, 1957, McGraw-Hill Book Co.

Solomon, J., and Arnon, D.: Alcohol and other substance abusers. In Hankoff, L.D., editor: Suicide: theory and clinical aspects, Littleton, Mass., 1979, PSG Publishing Company, Inc., p. 278.

Tuckman, J., and Youngman, W.F.: A scale for assessing suicide risk or attempted suicides, J. Clin. Psychol. **24**:17, 1968.

CHAPTER 9

The client with homicidal behavior

Vallory G. Lathrop, R.N., D.N.Sc., F.A.A.N.

*Let no feelings of caveman
    vengence influence us.
Let us rather help him who
    did so human a thing.*
Anatol Hold

Ever since Cain slew Abel, man has grappled with the painful fact that one human being is capable of willfully killing another human being. Recent statistics show that a murder occurs every 24 minutes in this country (U.S. Department of Justice, 1980). Trends indicate that more murders occur in the southern states, in suburban areas, and in large core cities of 250,000 or more and that a higher frequency of offenses occurs in December than in any other month.

From supplemental information on murder gathered by the Uniform Crime Reporting Program of the U.S. Department of Justice (1980), a profile of the murderer and the victim can be drawn. The offender is most likely to be a male, probably white, between 20 and 39 years of age, who killed someone he knew as the result of an argument. The victim is very likely to be male (3 out of 4 times), white, between 20 and 34 years of age, and acquainted with the assailant. The similarities between these two profiles should not be overlooked.

Murder as a symptom of a larger social problem is reflected in the data concerning the circumstances of the crime and the motive. In 1979 nearly half of the murders committed were the result of arguments, and over half of the victims knew their assailants. Murder by a stranger clearly occured in connection with other actual or suspected felonies.

It is the person attempting to cope with violent and homicidal impulses toward family or friend who is likely to seek out help from an emergency unit. For this reason it is helpful to have some knowledge of who kills whom and for what reasons, based on offenses already committed. The Uniform Crime Reporting Program provides information regarding the circumstances of murder.

The probability that a wife will kill her husband is almost as great as that of the husband killing his wife. The differences rest in the motivation of each spouse. Husbands are more likely to kill their wives over romantic triangles. Wives are considerably more likely to kill their husbands as the result of arguments over money or property. Overall, arguments, other than those just mentioned, are the major motive for murder among spouses.

When a child kills a parent, the act probably is committed during an argument and it is twice as likely that the victim is the father. Sons are more apt to be victims than daughters. Brothers are victims more often in arguments over money or property. Sisters are less apt to be murdered in any of the circumstances described.

When an acquaintance is the victim, the major reason is an argument over money, property, or a romantic triangle. Friends are killed as a result of arguments over money or property more than any other reason. If the victim is a boyfriend, the murder is the result of a general argument or romantic triangle. However, a girlfriend is far more likely to be killed as the result of a romantic triangle. Neighbors are just as likely to be victims as the result of romantic triangles and the commission of other felonies as they are as a result of arguments.

These data point out some of the many factors that come into play when one person willfully deprives another of life. Family roles, responsibilities, perceptions of self, concepts of masculinity and femininity, communication patterns within families, as well as the psychological status of the client and ability to maintain self-control are all factors to be considered in the management and treatment of the person who is homicidal.

The homicidal individual is likely to be an isolated person incapable of establishing meaningful relationships with others. These individuals see themselves as inadequate, powerless, helpless, and frequently hopeless. Their profile is not unlike the suicidal person. The dynamics of destruction, whether to self or others, bear great similarity to each other. This person may also exhibit signs of paranoid ideation.

The single most compelling factor in drawing a clinical picture of homicidal persons is their previous behavior patterns. Is there a history of homicide, other violent acts, or suicidal threats or gestures? How they coped with stress and conflict in the past is the best indicator of how that individual will respond in the future.

HOMICIDE VERSUS AGGRAVATED ASSAULT

Aggravated assault is described by the Uniform Crime Reporting Program, as the unlawful attack by one person on another for the purpose of inflicting severe or aggravated bodily injury, usually accompanied by the use of a weapon or by means likely to produce death or great bodily harm. In terms of definition, *what separates homicide from aggravated assault is not the intent but the outcome.* If the victim dies as the result of an assault, the assailant becomes a murderer.

Differences between these two violent crimes lie in the frequency with which each is committed. Between 1975 and 1979, the number of murders committed increased by 5%; the number of aggravated assaults increased by 23% (U.S. Department of Justice, 1980). In the past 15 years the number of victims of aggravated assault has nearly tripled. Whereas the rate of murders has apparently leveled out to some extent, the rate of aggravated assault is steadily increasing.

The similarities that exist among the offenders and the victims of these two violent acts are well documented in the literature. The assailant and the aggravated assault victim are very likely to be male, white, about the same age (between 20 and 39), argue in a dwelling, and know each other. A firearm, knife or other cutting instrument, or other weapon is used in the commission of the crime.

The origins of dangerous behavior have often been studied with varying results. Parental abuse has been cited as a predisposing factor as has the presence of the triad of enuresis, pyromania, and cruelty to animals. Alcohol has also been indicted as predisposing to violence. Unfortunately, as Stone so ably stated, "Much of this scattered clinical wisdom about violence has never been proved valid in controlled studies" (1975, p. 30).

Consideration must also be given to neurophysiological indicators when one reviews the possible origins of violence in the homicidal or assaultive person. Monroe has defined these episodic behavioral disorders as "precipitously appearing, maladaptive behavior that interrupts the life-style and life flow of the individual" (1978, p. 1). The behavior is generally out of character for the individual and out of context for the situation. The interruptions are described as either one abrupt act (or a short series of acts) motivated by fear or rage or as more sustained behavior, characterized by multiple acts and accompanied by other psychological symptoms. One thing is clear: whatever predictive, predisposing, and prognostic factors are used, they pertain to the potentially dangerous assaultive person as well as to the homicidal individual.

THE ASSESSMENT PROCESS

The question facing the clinician is simple and blunt. Will this person kill someone? The task of trying to make this determination can be difficult, frightening, and at times distasteful. Murder, or attempting it, is socially repugnant, and viewing it from an objective clinical perspective is not a simple undertaking.

The environment

The potentially homicidal person may seek assistance at any emergency unit. The emergency unit in the suburban private hospital is viewed as much by some as a haven for help as the unit in the large city public hospital is by others. Clinicians frequently overlook the violent potential of some individuals simply because of an underlying assumption they have made regarding those individuals who may contemplate or commit these kinds of violently dangerous acts. For example, it is not safe to assume that the well-dressed person, the middle-class professional, or the civil servant needs a less thorough evaluation than the cab driver, the construction worker, or the unemployed auto worker. The examination should not be altered because of the person's attire, occupation, or other similar external variables.

Ordway (1967) has stated that it sometimes seems the criteria used by the same clinicians for evaluating dangerousness vary when they work in different settings. He goes on to say it is possible that a clinician gives active conscious attention to the concept of danger much more in one clinical setting than in another. It is the externally oriented mind-set the clinician in the psychiatric emergency unit must judiciously try to avoid.

The clinician

The idea that murder is an available option for solving a problem is foreign to most persons. When listening to responses, clinicians can rapidly come up with numerous solutions to the stated problem and postulate what they would have done had they been in a similar situation. Some might even inquire why certain other alternatives were not tried. Although interesting, the responses offer little meaningful data with which to make an assessment and may be perceived by the client as avoiding the real issue.

The major concern must be focused on how clients see themselves and the environment rather than how they look to others. It is extremely important to determine how the client feels and why, what is important to the client, and what is threatening to the client and not to make any assumptions just because it is the opinion of the interviewer.

The client

The objective collection of pertinent data from the client is the single most important step in the assessment process. The information provided by the client serves as the essential foundation on which judgments will be made. Whether the client overtly threatens to kill someone or impresses the clinician as a high risk for some homicidal behavior, a comprehensive, in-depth social history and responses to direct questioning about killing someone must be obtained to the extent possible.

Few clients seek emergency care with overt statements that they are going to kill someone. They generally assume that the clinician will find out why they are there. The question "Why are you here?" seldom evokes the true reason. Many times the client considering homicide appears to be seeking some kind of medical attention but hopes the real emotional problems will be discovered in the interview process.

Case vignette #1

W.P. was a 30-year-old man, married, living with his wife and three children. He began to feel despondent and helpless after losing his job as a janitor. After a period of time, his ideas became paranoid in nature and he began believing his wife was having an affair with his best friend. He started to complain that he had contracted a veneral disease and accused his wife of giving it to him. He bought a pistol, which he placed in their top dresser drawer along with open notes on how he wanted to kill his wife. Although he had no clinical symptoms of a venereal disease, he continued to complain and finally went to an emergency unit for treatment. He told the staff he had contracted a venereal disease from his wife and he wanted something for it. He was told he had no overt symptoms to support his claim but they would give him an intramuscular injection of an antibiotic as a prophylactic measure. No further inquiries were made regarding his wife, his feelings, or other social history that might have indicated serious emotional problems. Approximately 2 weeks later, W.P. shot his wife five times,

killing her as she lay sleeping. He told the arresting officer he was tired of her playing around and giving him a veneral disease that made him impotent.

The question this case raises is obvious. Could the murder have been prevented if a clinician in the emergency unit had asked some questions about the feelings of W.P. and not dealt exclusively with the initial complaint? Did the clinician for some reason assume that W.P. was correct in his assumption that he had contracted something from his wife? Investigation could not validate any extramarital affairs by the wife. Would the emergency unit clinician have been able to discover the emotional turmoil being experienced by the client? Although these questions can never be answered, the very fact that one can speculate demonstrates the incomplete nature of W.P.'s contact with the emergency unit staff.

During the interview clients must begin to feel that the clinician is interested in them as individuals and is willing to listen and hear what is said and that the clinician can accept what is told regardless of how "bad" or personally distasteful it might appear.

The clinician needs to ask straightforward, direct, often blunt questions and to avoid the temptation to digress into less emotionally laden topics. For example, when the client says he got so angry he wanted to choke his wife, the clinician may respond by asking questions about the status of the marital relationship. The message given to the potential offender should not be "I don't want to hear what you're saying." The client's feelings, perceptions, plans, and previous behavior patterns are of paramount importance and should provide the primary information.

Most authors agree past behavior is the single best predictor of future behavior and therefore the social and psychological history should be gathered first. Although the client's responses indicate specific directions to take, the use of a general guide or assessment tool might prove helpful to ensure that certain areas of importance are covered.

A guide to use in gathering information should include the following factors:

Factor I: Demographic data
  Age, race, sex, marital status
  Place of residence
  Employment status
  Occupation
Factor II: Social history
  History of violent behavior
    Involvement with someone's violent death
    Cause of someone's death
    Arrest record
    Engaging in fights
    Homicidal thoughts
    Homicidal plans
    Threats to kill someone
    Use of a knife or gun
    Tying up someone with a rope, strap, and so on
  Psychiatric history
    Diagnosis
    Hospitalizations
    Course of treatment
    Type of admission and discharge
    Medications
    Alcoholism
  Family history
    Parental abuse
    Violent behavior
    Parental seduction
  History of enuresis, pyromania, and cruelty to animals
Factor III: Current intent to kill
  Does the client want to kill someone?
  What plans have been made?
  Who is the intended victim?
  What weapons are accessible?
  Have arguments or fights occurred already?
  What exactly happened in these altercations?
  Does the client feel other family members approve?
  What is the current drinking pattern?
  Is the client anxious or depressed?
  Does the person feel provoked?
  What are the conditions under which the client might resort to homicide?
Factor IV: The "benefits" seen by the client
  Will clients perceive themselves as more powerful or stronger or feel others will view them with respect?

Will attention be gained from someone now considered remote and unattainable?
Is physical force the only way they think they will be "heard"?
Will there be a resolution to a perceived threat to sexual identity?
Will it provide the final mastery or control over a long-standing emotional conflict?
Does it offer freedom from some perceived frustration, anger, rage, or oppression?
Factor V: Neurophysiological aspects (Monroe, 1977)
  Has the client ever experienced confusion even in a familiar place?
  Does the client feel fully responsible for actions?
  Has the client ever experienced slurred speech?
Factor VI: The family
  How do they measure the client's potential to kill or seriously harm the intended victim?
  Is blame being placed on the intended victim, thereby giving tacit approval for the action being contemplated?
  Does the client have a "tough guy" reputation?
Factor VII: The victim
  How is the victim known to the potential assailant?
  What is their actual relationship?
  How does the intended victim communicate with the client, for example, sarcastic, condescending?
  Is the victim provocative?
  Is the victim helpless in the situation?
  Has the intended victim previously been a victim of this person or others? (This information should be gathered not only from the client and family but also from the intended victim if possible.)

These factors are certainly not all inclusive, and the client's responses will open other avenues that should be explored. They do provide an initial guide for use in an assessment of the extent of the risk present in the homicidal client. The list appears long and the task will necessarily be a lengthy one, but the seriousness of the consequences to both potential offender and intended victim mandate that full attention be given to all areas possible.

Determining the potential to kill

Assessments regarding the client's homicidal intent are made by analyzing the information obtained from these seven major factors. If client's demographic information places them in a higher risk category, a positive potential exists. The social history contains crucial assessment factors. When present, a history of violent behavior significantly increases the client's risk potential. The seriousness of the person's current intent to kill is reflected in what has actually been done thus far in carrying out the decision to kill. This too deserves close consideration.

The benefits the client sees as a result of murdering someone should not be overlooked. They tell the clinician a great deal about why individuals want or need to kill and what process they followed to reach that point. It helps to determine whether the client sees any alternatives to murder.

The family's perceptions of the current situation as well as the way the client views the family are aspects worthy of consideration. Often the family can provide information regarding the availability of weapons. Family members frequently provide approval of clients' actions through actual statements, support of the person, or hiding previous threats or activities from police or intended victims. Statements such as "If my wife did that to me, I'd kill her" or "You know, if he had killed you, I wouldn't blame him one bit" seldom fall on deaf ears.

The role of the victim in a homicidal incident cannot be underrated, especially since more than half the victims know their assailants. That relationship takes on added importance when trying to determine the potential risk in the homicidal client. As in any social interaction, it is best to have the contributions and perceptions of both concerned parties.

Murder has taken place with the sanction of the victim. At times the victim has been the first to exhibit a dangerous weapon. Sometimes the intended victim will actually challenge the individual to kill: "Go ahead, you might as well shoot me right now, because if you don't, I'm leaving."

In the determination of the homicidal intent of a client, an assessment of neurophysiological signs is an essential component. Dysfunction of dorsolateral convexity of the frontal lobes is behaviorally characterized by impulsivity, disinhibition, euphoria, distractibility, reduction in concentration and motivation, reduction in abstract reasoning, and inability to predict consequences of one's actions. Dysfunction of the orbital surface (limbic projection) of the frontal lobe is behaviorally characterized by lack of self-control, emotional outbursts, changes in personality, lack of guilt and remorse, increase in sexual and aggressive drives, more psychopathic-type behavior, affective disorders, and an increased sensitivity to alcohol (Yeudall, 1977; Yeudall and Wardell, 1977). These signs will alert the clinician that further neurological examination may be necessary to evaluate and treat the client as a potential sufferer of an episodic behavioral disorder.

The final aspect is the unmeasurable quality and ability the clinician brings to the setting. It is that unnamed intuitive skill that develops with time and experience which also provides insight into the evolution of some kind of risk profile. Perhaps it is the intensity of a particular response, a certain look, an expression that briefly crosses the client's face, the posture or movement whenever certain areas are discussed. Possibly it is a combination of all these and others. Still, it is not infrequent to hear clinicians state, "I don't know what it is, but there's something about this person that bothers me and makes me think he's really dangerous." These feelings should be evaluated.

If the clinician is experiencing some kind of response to the client in the interview setting, these responses should be examined closely. The practitioner must determine whether these reactions are a response to some stimulus emanating from the client or whether they are a personal bias emerging because of the topic being discussed, for example. Nevertheless, these feelings must be considered by the clinician whether or not a label can be applied.

Beyond the point of analyzing each of the factors there are no set procedures or predictable tables to rely on. There are no rules to use in determining dangerousness. In fact, there are no guarantees that the person who has never committed a violent act in the past will not do so in the future, any more than there is a guarantee that the person who has committed a violent act in the past will do so again.

What is known is that those who have used violence as a "successful" solution to a problem are prone to use it again. However, it is recognized that for many murderers the elimination of a specific troublesome person removes the conflict and the person never kills again.

Case vignette #2

T.M. was a 19-year-old woman, single, living at home with her parents and an older sister who was bedridden with muscular dystrophy. T.M. was given the responsibility of providing total care for her sister since she did not work and both parents were employed. She also did most of the cooking and housekeeping. As a result she spent most of her time at home with little, if any, social life. She began to complain to her mother of vague physical problems, which the family doctor found to be groundless. Her father felt she was just trying to get out of doing work around the house. Her mother thought maybe there was some other reason and took her to see a psychiatrist. After several sessions, T.M. stopped going, saying she saw no reason for it. The psychiatrist made no further contact with the family. Approximately 1 month later, T.M. killed her sister by stabbing her to death. Since that time, T.M. was charged, convicted, and sentenced for murder. She completed the prison sentence and has lived in the community for over 10 years without incident.

Emphasis must be given to the problems of prediction of dangerous behavior and specifically homicidal behaviors. Ultimately the decision regarding the client must be highly individualized to the life of the client. It must take into consideration all information obtained from as many sources as possible. It must give added attention to any prior history of violence. It must take heed of the interviewing clinician's inner thoughts and reactions. The way this is all balanced out and the opinions and judgments reached rest with the clinician responsible for making the final assessment.

INTERVENTION

The process of intervention with the homicidal client is not one that can be completed in a short period of time. It may take several hours of intense interaction before the clinician begins to clearly establish a rapport with this client. The immediate goal is to significantly decrease or eliminate the urge to commit murder. In addition, the next and almost as immediate a goal is to try to engage the client in finding ways to prevent such potential situations from recurring in the future.

Psychological intervention

To decrease or eliminate the immediate urge to kill someone, the clinician must begin to "defuse" the potentially explosive client. The best method for this is through verbal interactions between clinician and client, encouraging ventilation of feelings rather than acting them out. By allowing the client to shout, pace, pound fists, curse, or express feelings in other acceptable ways, the clinician can see that the energy and rage that has built up can be expended without harm to others. During this sometimes noisy and active time, the clinician should remain calm, attentive, and in full control of the situation. Situations should be fully explored and consensual validation offered where appropriate. The major thrust, though, should be in seeking alternative solutions the client has ignored, overlooked, or is unaware of. The question is, "What could you do instead?" Once the client begins to more adequately engage in problem-solving processes, the question of what can be done in the future will also need to be answered. Immediate intervention with the homicidal client can essentially be reduced to four steps:

1. *Listen* to the anger, the rage, the cry for help to gain self-control
2. *Validate* the appropriateness of responses when they arise
3. *Confront* the urge to kill and point out alternatives, consequences
4. *Support* the client's efforts to learn better methods of self-control, to learn from this traumatic situation, and to learn how to solve problems in socially acceptable ways

After deliberation, it may be determined that the homicidal client, because of previous history, family resources, emotional status, and willingness to participate, could be helped by psychotherapy. Rosenbaum and Beebe (1975) emphasize that the key to controlling homicide is control of impulsivity. They speak of taking the necessary steps to help the client separate the thoughts of homicide from the act. Therapy should proceed in a systematic fashion, avoiding impulsive decision making on the part of the client, fully exploring all homicidal thinking, and operating on the premise that the client is free to feel but not necessarily to act. It should be implicit in the relationship that the ultimate responsibility for homicidal behavior rests with the client. The client also should be made aware that the clinician will communicate to law enforcement agents and intended victims any danger to prevent the loss of life.

Confidentiality of relationship

The question of confidentiality in the client-clinician relationship and the issue of privileged communication are especially sensitive issues when a potentially homicidal person is involved. For over 20 years, the following factors have been accepted as essential in judging the merit of a particular relationship and its protection by privilege:

1. The communications must originate in a confidence that they will not be disclosed.
2. This element of confidentiality must be essential to the full and satisfactory maintenance of the relationship between the parties.
3. The relationship must be one which in the

opinion of the community ought to be sedulously fostered.
4. The injury to the relationship imposed by the disclosure of the communications must be greater than the benefit thereby gained for the correct disposal of litigation (Wigmore, 1961).

At the present time, over 40 states have physician-patient privileged communications laws. More than 20 states also recognize by statute a psychologist-client privilege. Some states specifically recognize the psychiatrist-client relationship. All statutes on privileged communication have certain exceptions. For example, physicians are required to report certain communicable diseases and gunshot or knife wounds and to testify in cases in which a client is being prosecuted for homicide. Since all states exercise some form of control over the confidentiality of the relationship between clinician and client, there is a clear obligation for clinicians to become aware of all relevant laws and statutes pertaining to that aspect of their practice.

Manipulation of environment

Intervening in the environment includes taking those actions that separate the potential assailant from the victim. This could include advising spouses to live apart to avoid danger. It may mean trying to dissuade provocative family members or friends from visiting the client. Managing the environment also includes confronting significant others regarding provocative or condoning behavior and helping intended victims to see their willingness to be victims or to recognize how it fulfills their need to be punished. Intervention in the environment might mean teaching concerned family and friends how to pick up clues to the client's behavior and to identify prehomicidal actions so that potentially heated situations can be consciously cooled.

Involuntary commitment of the potentially homicidal client also changes the environment. Although it does remove the client from the immediate stimulus, it has been noted that it provides only brief protection for society.

If the decision has been reached that the client is a danger to others and all efforts aimed at voluntary admission to the hospital are refused, then involuntary commitment must be considered. The variety of ways one can be admitted to a psychiatric facility for treatment reflect great activity on the part of state legislatures.

Psychiatric facilities can admit people to inpatient units by applying a variety of admission criteria as mandated by state, county, and institutional policy. Individuals can be admitted on an involuntary basis or on an informal involuntary basis, as in the states of Pennsylvania, Illinois, and New York. In Florida, Georgia, and Minnesota, persons can be admitted on a pretreatment status, such as during an emergency when more diagnostic information is necessary to complete the assessment. Moreover, some states, such as New York, Florida, and Georgia, promote voluntary admissions or admissions made on an informal basis by asking officials to encourage individuals to select such admissions standards.

Procedurally, involuntary commitment may be accomplished through the courts or through medical certification by a psychiatrist. Emergency commitment for a specific period of time may be done by state or local officers. To accurately carry out the duties and responsibilities to the client and the community, it is essential that the clinician be aware of current statutes governing these activities. Mental health law is an ever-changing and evolving field that requires vigilant monitoring by clinicians who are subject to the impact of its movements.

When readmission is contemplated for a person who has been previously hospitalized in a psychiatric facility, consideration should be given to whether this readmission might discourage the client from seeking assistance when the next problem arises and whether this potential consequence could increase the chance of homicidal activity. If hospitalization is the treatment of choice, the client should be encouraged to voluntarily enter a psychiatric inpatient facility. Assistance should be provided in finding a suitable facility and direct support be given in gaining admission there. Clinicians should accompany homicidal clients to the facility or unit, see that they are properly admitted, and provide the unit treatment team with adequate and accurate information; these important steps are necessary

to decrease the risk that these individuals may not seek help with future problems.

Pharmacological agents

When psychotherapeutic efforts are not sufficient in helping the homicidal client regain sufficient self-control, it may be necessary to administer some type of medication. The type of tranquilizer used depends on the response of the client to initial interventions. If agitation, irritability, and tension have decreased to some extent, the use of lorazepam or even diazepam may be indicated to further assist in defusing the situation. If a more rapidly acting tranquilizer is indicated, hydroxyzine may be the drug of choice. Severely agitated, angry, and minimally controlled individuals may respond successfully to trifluoperazine and haloperidol as well as phenothiazines. The administration of tranquilizers is an adjunct to, not substitute for, other psychotherapeutic interventions. Since drug therapy is an ever-changing component of the physician's armamentarium, it is essential that current literature on available drugs be reviewed periodically to assist in determining the appropriate form of medication.

Physical control

It may be necessary to physically restrain a violent homicidal client. This restraint may take the form of separation in a locked room away from stimulating individuals. It allows the person an opportunity to be alone and regain sufficient self-control. It also affords the client an avenue in which to "blow off steam," curse, shout, and if not under restraint, pace the floor without disturbing or frightening others.

Physical control can also be exerted by virtue of the strength represented in the physical presence of a number of staff members who appear as a coordinated, efficient, and effective team capable of providing the control a client needs. These staff members—four or five is usually sufficient—may not even need to do anything other than arrive and be visible to the client.

If it is necessary to provide the client with some degree of control, it should be done decisively, firmly, coolly, and without harm to the client or staff. Chapter 10 discusses techniques of managing an assaultive client.

SUMMARY

Homicide and aggravated assault are becoming increasingly more serious problems in this country. It is estimated that a murder occurs every 24 minutes and an aggravated assault every 51 seconds. These crimes often involve persons who know each other. The major difference between assault and murder is in the outcome of the violent act—if the victim dies, assault becomes murder. This chapter has discussed the process of evaluating a client's potential for homicide.

The assessment process is crucial in determining the risk potential of homicidal clients. The clinician must carefully assess clients' potential for violent behavior no matter what their occupation or economic status. The clinician must also be willing to ask blunt and direct questions and be ready to listen to direct and possibly repugnant answers.

There are seven essential factors in gathering information from and about a potentially homicidal client. They are as follows:

Demographic data
Social history
Current intent to kill
The "benefits" seen by the client
Neurophysiological aspects
The family
The victim

These factors are certainly not all inclusive, but they do provide a guide for predicting the homicidal risk potential of the specific client. In the end the final decision about the client's potential for homicide must be made without precise measures since none exist. What is known is the probability that once individuals have used violence as a successful solution to a problem, they are prone to use it as a solution again in the future.

Interventions for the homicidal client include psychotherapy, manipulation of the environment, administration of pharmacological agents, and physical intervention through the use of restraint or confinement or both. Finally, legal issues that directly and indirectly affect the practice of the clinician and the future of the client and possibly the intended victim must be reviewed for their impact on each situation.

BIBLIOGRAPHY

Allen, R.C., Ferster, E.Z., and Rubin, J.G., editors: Readings in law and psychiatry, ed. 2, Baltimore, 1975, The Johns Hopkins University Press.

Barnhill, L.: Basic interventions for violence in families, Hosp. Community Psychiatry **31**:8, 1980.

Duncan, J., and Duncan, G.: Murder in the family: A study of some homicidal adolescents, Am. J. Psychiatry **127**:1498, 1971.

Fromm, E.: The anatomy of human destructiveness, New York, 1973, Holt, Rinehart & Winston, Inc.

Gulevich, M., and Bourne, F.: Mental illness and violence. In Daniels, D., Gilula, M., and Ochberg, F. editors: Violence and the struggle for existence, Boston, 1970, Little, Brown & Co.

Hellman, D., and Blackman, N.: Enuresis, firesetting and cruelty to animals: a triad predictive of adult crime, Am. J. Psychiatry **122**:1431, June, 1966.

Henry, A., and Short, J.: Suicide and homicide, New York, 1968, The Free Press.

Kinzel, A.: Body-buffer zone in violent prisoners, Am. J. Psychiatry **127**:59, July, 1970.

Lanzkron, M.: Murder and insanity: a survey, Am. J. Psychiatry **119**:754, 1963.

Lathrop, V.: Aggression as a response, Perspect. Psychiatr. Care **16**:5, 1978.

Lion, J.R.: Evaluation and management of the violent patient, Springfield, Ill., 1972, Charles C Thomas, Publisher.

Macdonald, J.M.: Psychiatry and the criminal, ed. 3, Springfield, Ill., 1976, Charles C Thomas, Publisher.

Monroe, R., et al.: Neurologic findings in recidivist aggressors. In Shagass, C., Gershon, S., and Friedhoff, A., editors: Psychopathology and brain dysfunction, New York, 1977, Raven Press, Appendix A.

Monroe, R., et al.: Brain dysfunction in aggressive criminals, Lexington, Mass., 1978, Lexington Books.

Mowat, R.R.: Morbid jealousy and murder, London, 1966, Tavistock Publications, Ltd.

Ordway, J.A.: Experiences in evaluating dangerousness in private practice and in a court clinic. In Rappaport, J.R., editor: The clinical evaluation of the dangerousness of the mentally ill, Springfield, Ill., 1967, Charles C Thomas, Publisher, p. 35.

Physicians' desk reference, ed. 35, Oradell, N.J., 1981, Medical Economics Co.

147

Rappeport, J.R., editor: The clinical evaluation of the dangerousness of the mentally ill, Springfield, Ill., 1967, Charles C Thomas, Publisher.

Rosenbaum, C., and Beebe, J.: Psychiatric treatment: crisis/clinic/consultation, New York, 1975, McGraw-Hill Book Co.

Silver, L., Dublin, C., and Lourie, R.: Does violence breed violence? Contributions from a study of the child abuse syndrome, Am. J. Psychiatry 126:404, Sept. 1969.

Stein, J., editor: The random house college dictionary, rev. ed., New York, 1980, Random House, Inc.

Stone, A.: Mental health and law: a system in transition, Washington, D.C., 1975, National Institutes of Mental Health Center for Studies of Crime and Delinquency, DHEW Pub. No. (ADM) 75-176.

U.S. Department of Justice: Crime in the United States, Washington, D.C., Sept. 1980, U.S. Government Printing Office.

Wigmore, J.H.: Evidence in trials at common law, vol. 8, Boston, 1961, Little, Brown & Co.

Yeudall, L.T.: Neuropsychological correlates of crimnal psychopathy. I. Differential diagnosis, paper presented at the Fifth International Seminar in Comparative Clinical Criminology, Montreal, 1977.

Yeudall, L.T., and Wardell, D.M.: Neuropsychological correlates of criminal psychopathy. II. Discrimination and prediction of dangerous and recidivistic offenders, paper presented at the Fifth International Seminar in Comparative Clinical Criminology, Montreal, 1977.

CHAPTER 10

The client with assaultive behavior

Aline Wommack, R.N., B.S.

When aggression builds up in us, it feels, at a certain point, as though a switch has been thrown, and we become violent . . . we swing wildly, hitting whoever is within range. One's mind becomes foggy, and perception of the enemy becomes unclear; one loses awareness of the environment and wants only to act out this inner compulsion to do violence, come what may (May, 1972).

Assault can be defined as an unlawful violent attack on another, which may or may not include battery (Stein, 1967). Assaultive behavior in the clinical setting is frightening for the client losing control, for others viewing the incident, and for staff members who must manage the situation. Assaultive behavior is a psychiatric emergency that occurs for a variety of reasons, but it always represents a failure in communication and a failure of the client's ability to cope with intense stress. General functioning is severely impaired by fear, anger, and uncontrolled rage, which renders the client incapable of making rational choices.

This chapter focuses on the process of assault from a behavior perspective and describes the specific stages of the assault cycle. Assaultive behavior is cyclical and therefore cannot be maintained for extended periods. The behaviors of each stage of the cycle increase in intensity and are clearly observable. Frequently, assaultive behavior can be prevented if clinicians are alert to the early cues of the process and have a planned, rational approach. With this approach staff members maintain their confidence and can intervene to assist the client experiencing dyscontrol (difficulty with control) to achieve a higher level of functioning, and others viewing the incident will remain calm. Prevention, planned action, and teamwork are essential to the successful management of assaultive behavior.

SOCIAL CONTEXT

Many of the scientific investigations of violence focus on the social unrest of the 60s: race riots, freedom rides, student rebellions, and antiwar protests. History shows that such attempts to change the social order are often accompanied by violence. Some societies, especially those experiencing rapid development of change, frequently sanction or legitimize violence because violence can be a forceful tool for change when it receives popular support. Arendt (1970) noted that power and violence often appear together, but she suggests that power and violence are opposites; one cannot rule absolutely in the presence of the other. Wolfgang (1969) observed that violence takes many forms and is a response learned through socialization. Violence can be legitimized depending on the agent, target, goal, and the context within which it occurs.

Following the assassinations of President Kennedy and Martin Luther King, the National Commission on the Causes and Prevention of Violence (1969) was formed. It concluded that societies often organize and legitimize violence to preserve themselves. Violence occurred when individuals or groups were unable to achieve the quality of life they sought. Violence and protest occurred when demands were not met or the "system" was unresponsive, and counterviolence occurred when others felt threatened by social reform.

Wolfgang, Arendt, and the National Commission on the Causes and Prevention of Violence contend that violence occurs when a threat is perceived, power is lost, or a system remains unresponsive. Violence, or assaultive behavior, in the clinical setting occurs for similar reasons.

AGGRESSION

Aggression is an act intended to harm the object or person perceived to be causing frustration or threat, and it results from a complex interaction of biological, psychological, social, and environmental factors. The focus of this chapter is the management of the behavioral process of assault, so only a brief discussion of the concept of aggression as a learned response will be presented. Pavlov's theory of conditioning and the stimulus-response theory of personality of Dollard and Miller are useful in illustrating how aggression may be learned.

Classical conditioning demonstrates that a conditioned stimulus paired with an unconditioned stimulus produces an unconditioned response. A conditioned response is produced when the pairings are repeated many times and the conditioned stimulus becomes the stronger influence.

An instigator (activator) is an "antecedent condition" that produces a predicted response. Instigators can be internal or external, with several instigators operating simultaneously to produce a response. A "goal response" reinforces the behavior preceding it and terminates a predicted behavior sequence. Frustration occurs when there has been interference of an activated goal response and the predicted behavior has been prevented. The behavioral response to frustration is learned to be effective in reducing the strength of the "frustration-induced activator," but does not reduce the original activator (Dollard et al., 1939).

An early Pavlovian experiment demonstrates how aggressive behavior can be shaped. A dog placed in a training harness was conditioned to give a salivary response to the secondary stimulus of a card with a circle. The dog was further conditioned to have the salivary response inhibited in the presence of a card with an oval. The cards were then designed to have an increasingly similar appearance, so that the oval became more circular. The dog, unable to distinguish the difference in the cards, responded to the conflict with aggressive behavior by barking, biting at the harness, and finally refusing the training situation (Scott, 1975). In this experiment and in subsequent experiments aggression occurred when there was a high degree of motivation, conflict, inability to adapt, and no means of escape.

Similarly, Dollard et al. (1939), heavily influenced by the early works of Freud, developed a

150

theory of personality based on "stimulus-response" concepts, which integrated the experience of frustration and aggression as a response to conflict. Personality, molded by the experiences of early childhood, is a collection of habits, or links between a cue and response. Learning occurs when a cue evokes a response, the cues are strengthened, and the learner is driven to make a response. Drives, present at birth (primary) or acquired (secondary), activate behavior (Hall and Lindzey, 1970). Dollard et al. suggest that acquired drives such as anxiety, shame, or pleasure motivate behavior. Conflict experienced during infancy and early childhood is repressed and is later expressed as emotional distress in adult life. Conflict has its roots in the following principles (Hall and Lindzey, 1970):

1. The wish for goal completion increases the nearer the goal becomes.
2. The wish to avoid a negative stimulus increases the nearer the stimulus comes.
3. Avoidance elicits a greater response than does the capacity of approach.
4. Increase in the drive of avoidance or approach increases its capacity to elicit a response.
5. When two responses are competing, the stronger will occur.

Frustration and aggression are response sequences that share a causal relationship. Aggression follows frustration, effectively reducing the intensity of the secondary (frustration-induced) activator. Aggression, which is not always overt, can occur in dreams or fantasy, can be directed toward self, or can be displaced onto an innocent substitute. Regardless of how aggression is expressed, it leaves the intensity of the primary activator unaffected.

Aggression as a goal response is based on the perception of the object producing threat or frustration. Perception is a process in which unorganized sensations from internal or external sources are structured and organized. If the process is successful, the integration (by the ego) produces a feeling of safety (Sandler, 1960). When the process of perception is not successful, the ego is exposed to excitation that can be neither mastered nor controlled, producing the feeling of danger. The feeling of danger produces an arous-al state precipitating the act of aggression (approach) or flight (avoidance).

In summary, aggression is an act perceived as a threat to harm object or person. As a goal response, aggression is based on the process of perception, which can produce the feeling of safety or danger. When a goal is blocked, frustration can occur. Depending on the strength and type of stimulus-producing interference, the individual may choose avoidance or goal completion. When frustration continues, aggression, which may be repressed, displaced, or enacted, can follow.

Learning theory is one of many models that can be used to explain individual aggression. Violent behavior occurs when a threat is perceived, a sense of powerlessness ensues, communication and adaptability fail, and the system is felt to be unresponsive to an individual's needs.

CONTINUUM OF BEHAVIORS RELATED TO ASSAULT

Assaultive behavior is part of a continuum of related behaviors. Most behavior occurs within the middle range of the continuum between the two extremes of withdrawal and assault. Behavior, characterized as fluid and ever changing, is based on perceived internal or external life events.

Fig. 10-1 illustrates that most behavior falls within a "normal" range. The individual maintains control, communicates effectively, moves between passivity and aggression, but remains largely within an assertive range, acting and reacting to life events within socially acceptable limits.

The extremes of the continuum represent areas of dyscontrol and severe response to frustration and conflict. For example, a client may become increasingly disorganized and unable to cope, experiencing inaction, passivity, immobility, and finally, withdrawal. Clients experience frustration as being painful; unable to cope, they react with avoidance, a rewarded self-protective response that they have learned to be effective at reducing the frustration-produced pain.

Similarly, the client moving toward the assault stage experiences frustration and an inability to cope with intense internal feelings. Mobilized to action, this person perceives events as intrusive. The individual becomes increasingly aggressive as inhibitions weaken and impulsiveness heightens and moves rapidly through threat of injury to physical contact. The goal response to frustration and conflict is disinhibition, increased aggression, and assault. This is a learned response that has been reinforced and is perceived to be self-protective and pain reducing.

For both clients choices were made based on life experiences and the successful reduction of pain. Whether avoidance or aggression, the style (habit) was developed over time, was rooted in childhood, and is specific to given stimuli (activators).

The conditions that preclude violence seem to be very specific to each individual and cannot be generalized, as noted by the lack of accurate clinical predictions of violent behavior. Despite

various attempts at classification (Rappeport, 1967), no adequate pattern emerges. This is resulting in the "deweighting" of expert testimony in the courts regarding psychiatric predictions of dangerousness. Pfohl (1978) conducted a study of professionals charged by the courts to assess the "immediate dangerousness" of prisoners with indeterminate sentences at Lima State Hospital in Ohio. Pfohl reports that 12 multidisciplinary teams used inconsistent criteria between teams and among subjects. Decisions were often subjectively based on "negotiated interactions," having little to do with the subject's mental status. Diamond (1974) concludes psychiatrists overpredict dangerousness, erring on the side of conservatism and safety. The psychiatric community posits that dangerousness is neither a medical nor psychiatric diagnosis but rather an issue of legal judgment and definition, established and dictated by social policy (American Psychiatric Association, 1974).

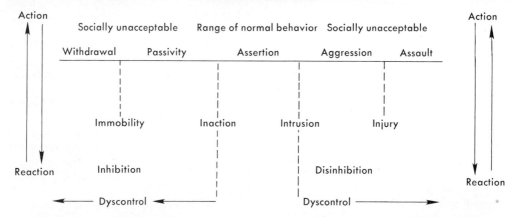

FIG. 10-1. A continuum of behaviors related to assault. *Passivity* is characterized by withdrawn behavior. *Assertion* indicates the socially accepted ability to say, "Yes, this should be done" or "No, I will not do that." Examples of *aggression* are spitting, swearing, yelling, refusal to comply, and verbal threats with no threat of physical injury. In *assault* there is a phsyical consequence and the crisis phase is uncontrolled, for example, hitting, kicking, scratching, biting. Note that if proximity is close, then a threat should be considered an assault because it could be carried out.

Adapted from Smith, P.: Management of assaultive behavior (training manual), Sacramento, Calif., 1977, California Department of Developmental Services.

ASSAULT CYCLE

Predicting the probability of future violent behavior in society is difficult, but predicting assaultive behavior in the clinical setting is less difficult and more reliable. Assaultive behavior follows a cycle that can be interrupted at various points to prevent escalation to the stage of actual assault (Fig. 10-2).

Assaultive behavior can be conceptualized as having five stages (Smith, 1977). The stages vary in time and intensity based on the client's tolerance for stress. The five stages of the assault cycle are as follows:

I. *Activation* is the first stage of the assault cycle, in which an "antecedent condition" is present and a predicted behavior response is produced. A stimulus causes stress, which is experienced internally. Clients at this stage remain in control and perceive that they have alternatives.

II. *Escalation* is the second stage of the assault cycle, in which stress remains and frustration increases. The client experiences feelings that descend from helplessness, fewer alternatives, and despair to ensuing panic. With decreased tolerance to frustration, the client has physical symptoms of severe anxiety: respiratory changes, increased heart rate and blood pressure, as well as increased movement and agitation. As agitation increases, behavior intensifies (escalates) to the point of total dyscontrol, and interactive communication fails.

III. *Crisis* is the third stage of the assault cycle and is characterized by autonomic nervous system influence, particularly of the sympathetic (thoracolumbar) division. In the client's state of "fight or flight," epinephrine is secreted by the adrenal glands, glucose is released from the liver, and the blood supply is diverted to skeletal mus-

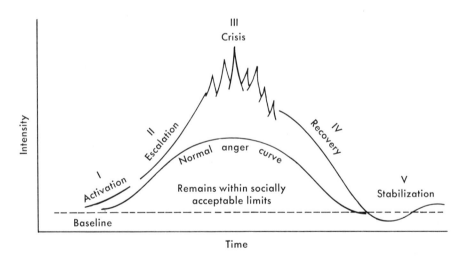

FIG. 10-2. The five stages of the assault cycle. *Stage I*—Activation. Stress occurs, but there are no signs of agitation. This phase will not necessarily end in a fight. *Stage II*—*Escalation*. Intervention is used here with most success. *Stage III*—*Crisis*. Assault and battery occurs (series of peaks and valleys). *Stage IV*—*Recovery*. Client still agitated, less emotional, with fewer physical manifestations. *Stage V*—*Stabilization*. Client feels guilt and remorse. Most success in therapy here if drugs have not been given. The client is ready to listen to therapeutic intervention now.

From Smith, P.: Management of assaultive behavior (training manual), Sacramento, Calif., 1977, California Department of Developmental Services.

cles. Heartbeat is strengthened and accelerates, blood pressure is elevated, and breathing is easier as bronchial muscles relax (De Coursey, 1968). The client, out of behavioral control, is unable to make rational choices and needs external constraints. The intensity of rage is disproportionate to the frustration-induced activator. The resulting assaultive behavior serves only to reduce the immediate frustration and has no effect on the primary activator. The crisis stage, while the most intense, is the briefest stage, lasting from a few seconds to a few minutes.

IV. *Recovery* is the fourth stage of the assault cycle and is characterized by decreased agitation, fewer physical symptoms of anxiety, and increased communication. The intensity of mood decreases as the client masters external behavior, and gradually containment is no longer required.

V. *Stabilization* is the fifth stage of the assault cycle and is characterized by the client's ability to be in complete control of external behavior. Agitation, anxiety, and impulsiveness have been replaced by feelings of guilt, atonement, and remorse, often manifested in a "postcrisis depression." It is during this stage that the client is most receptive to therapeutic intervention. Exploration of the assaultive incident can be useful in changing patterns of behavior and prevention of future incidents.

Throughout the assault cycle, the clinician should be cognizant of behavioral changes in the client. As the client's behavior changes, so must the clinician's. Initially, the clinician takes a less active role in the interview, supporting the client's strengths and problem-solving abilities. Through effective listening, the clinician identifies, clarifies, and interprets issues while reinforcing the client's ability to make choices.

As the client's behavior becomes increasingly agitated, the clinician should become more directive, providing plans, directions, and decision. In a nonpunitive manner, verbal interactions should be concise and focused on decreasing threat, providing limits, and lowering frustration.

ASSESSMENT

Careful assessment of the client's history in the clinical interview may reveal the potential for violent behavior. Clients who are "at risk" are provoked to violence in certain settings and specific situations (Armstrong, 1978). Frequently suicidality is assessed without careful attention to the potential for violent behavior. This potential, once recognized, can often be rechanneled into more appropriate outlets of expression.

To understand the context of violent behavior, one must assess current and historical functioning in the following areas (Menninger and Modlin, 1971; Barnhill, 1980):

1. Life stress and resources
2. Family, interpersonal, and social relationships
3. Psychological functioning
4. Biological functioning

Interpersonal or family violence may be predisposed to or precipitated by life stresses that the client cannot adapt to over time. Frequently these life stresses involve significant others in the client's system, are erosive to self-esteem, and frustrate efforts to gain or maintain security, status, or reputation. Stresses can occur outside the family system and include financial, occupational, academic, or legal difficulties. Stresses can occur within the family system and include life-cycle transitions, interpersonal conflicts, or relationship alterations. The initial complaint may be expressed directly or indirectly as the desire to harm someone or something. Frequently the client has diffuse fears of losing control but expresses the anxiety and tension somatically. In an effort to mediate the stress, the client often has been looking for assistance—calling friends or family, making frequent medical appointments, contacting clergy or lawyers. When resources are inadequate or fail, violent behavior often serves as a final attempt to meet one's needs.

Assessment of the familial relationship assists the clinician in evaluating the value of conflict within the client's system and the level of violence within the client's family. Which family members were violent, to whom, and how frequently? When violence occurred, was it goal directed or cathartic? The client's childhood history may suggest disturbed parenting, resulting in the child's distorted perception of self in relation to those in the immediate environment. This perception is later carried into adult life. The clinician should look for evidence of parental seduction, battering, emotional deprivation, rejection, or foster home placement. Hellman and Blackman (1966) cite enuresis, firesetting, and cruelty to animals as childhood indicators for violence in later life.

The quality of the client's current interpersonal relationships needs to be assessed. Frequently, assaultive clients perceive others as strong and themselves as weak or inferior, thus leading to ambivalent, shallow, or stormy relationships. The degree of symbiosis between the client and the potential victim as well as the current reality factors capable of triggering rage reactions should be examined. There appears to be a greater incidence of violent behavior in lower socioeconomic classes, which is thought to be related to the stresses of survival. An assessment for potential violent behavior should include questions to determine whether the client belongs to a subculture that values violence.

Violent behavior can occur in most of the psychodiagnostic categories. Therefore the clinician needs to evaluate, in addition to the intensity and degree of aggressive impulses, the level of control over these impulses, the provocativeness of the potential victim (including the clinician), and the client's sense of powerlessness.

Clients may be psychotic, experiencing command hallucinations telling them to harm someone, or the client may be endangered and in need of protection. Clients may report altered states of consciousness with "amnesia" for events or periods of time. Family members may report having observed moodiness with "personality changes," actions suggestive of violence (for example, purchasing or carrying weapons), or reckless driving and recent auto accidents. Previous history may reveal suicide attempts or arrests or convictions for assaults inflicting injury or for homocide. These actions suggest chronic low thresholds for anxiety, anger, and frustration with poor impulse control.

Clearly these symptoms occur in a variety of psychiatric conditions and are not solely indica-

tive of violent behavior. Their importance in the assessment of the assaultive client relates to degree, intensity, and control over aggressive impulses that clients may be experiencing. Violent behavior often occurs when clients experience overwhelming feelings of powerlessness and despair.

Two areas of biological functioning should be assessed: pathology and toxicity. While the presence of pathological conditions may not contribute directly to poor impulse control, it can indicate vulnerability. These indicators include recent head trauma, infection, seizure activity, blackouts, and cerebrovascular, neurological, hormonal, or metabolic disorders.

Toxic factors are substances used nonmedicinally to alter mood or behavior. Toxicity is noteworthy because it often causes labile behavior and irritability, lowered impulse control, released inhibitions, and impaired judgment. These clients are at higher risk for erratic, irrational, and violent behavior that is disproportionate to environmental stimuli. Substances commonly found to produce limited impulse control and erratic behavior include alcohol, barbiturates, amphetamines or similarly acting sympathomimetics, phencyclidine, and hallucinogens. The assessment should include pattern of use, duration, and impairment of social or occupational functioning. The intoxicated client is unable to reason. The therapeutic task is prevention of injury to the client and others in the immediate area until the client regains appropriate control of behavior.

As previously noted, accurately predicting violent behavior is difficult. A careful exploration of the client's history is useful in establishing patterns of assaultive behavior and the circumstances under which it occurs.

CRISIS MANAGEMENT

When the client enters the crisis stage of the assault cycle, the focus of intervention is no longer prevention but management. The clinician must accurately assess the type of behavior and provide the necessary external control. Crisis behavior is best conceptualized as an arousal state in the emergency response system (Armstrong, 1978). The client's behavioral presentation can change, in which case the clinician's response must be altered as well. Three of the most common types of crisis behavior are *fear, frenzy,* and *uproar* (Smith, 1977).

FEAR. The fearful client is threatened and frightened, often sitting in a defensive posture, scanning the environment, hypervigilant, and looking for a place to flee (avoidance). The client may be experiencing command hallucinations or may be influenced by psychoactive drugs but clearly believes this is a life-threatening situation. There are a number of physical signs. The client is usually pale (vasoconstriction), fists may be opening and closing, and muscles are rigid and tense in preparation to fight, though generally avoidance and flight are preferred. Pupils are often dilated (sympathetic nervous system), taking in the greatest field of vision. The client remains hypervigilant and distrustful. Breathing which initially is irregular, rapid, and shallow, becomes deeper, slower, and rhythmic. The therapeutic task is to decrease the threat, build trust, help the client feel in control, and allow choices. Allowing time is important because it decreases the threat. Slowly approaching the client diagonally from the front (a position of indirect control), the clinician should speak clearly in a well-modulated tone and inform the client of the choices and the proposed actions of the assembled staff. Haste will confuse the client, increase fear, and may cause interventions to fail. Giving the client alternatives, time, and space to respond gives control back to the client and can have a calming effect.

Case vignette #1

Mr. J, a disheveled 25-year-old man, was brought to the psychiatric emergency unit by police, who found him crouched near some garbage cans in a downtown parking garage. Entering the unit, Mr. J was in handcuffs, appeared tense and frightened, and made no direct eye contact with the clinician, though he clearly was visually scanning the immediate area. He was assessed to be in the end of the *escalation* stage and near *crisis*. The clinician attempted to calm him and reduce his fear by

having him taken to an office away from the crowded, confusing waiting area. Explaining to Mr. J that he was safe and unharmed, the clinician allowed him time to assess his surroundings and build trust. Adopting a calm, nonintrusive manner, the clinician explained the handcuffs would be removed when he appeared less tense and less prepared to fight. During the next hour the handcuffs were removed without an assaultive incident.

Case vignette #2

Ms. V, a 23-year-old college student, was brought from a party to the psychiatric emergency unit by her boyfriend. On arrival, she was agitated, frightened, and afraid to have people come near her, believing "they were after her." Efforts to calm her failed, and she alternately clung to her boyfriend or attempted to run away. The clinician was informed that Ms. V had been using "speed" and "suddenly went crazy." The psychiatrist ordered 5 mg of haloperidol injected intramuscularly. Still frightened, Ms. V began to strike out at staff members in an attempt to flee. Her behavior was quickly contained by the assembled staff, and medication was given. The clinician continued to work with her until her agitation decreased and she eventually fell asleep.

FRENZY. The frenzied client is extremely frustrated, is unable to solve problems or make rational choices, and manifests behavior that is increasingly uncontrolled. The frustration is diffuse, as is the resulting aggressive behavior. The experienced loss of control is as frightening for the client as was the activator of the cycle. The client maintains an attack posture, will focus on an object, and then move in to attack. Physical signs of frenzy usually exhibited are flushed skin, squinting, constricted pupils, and tunnel vision (parasympathetic nervous system), which focuses vision on the object of attack. Hyperventilating, the client is prepared for rapid action. Often the client makes facial grimaces and has an almost grotesque, "bigger than life" appearance.

The therapeutic task is to restore immediate and firm control. The clinician should approach the client from the front, the position of direct control, and stay out of reach of arms and legs. Other staff members should approach simultaneously in a "fan" position (semicircle) around the client. The clinician's voice should be commanding and clear, taking all decision making from the client. Medication, seclusion, or physical restraint may be needed until the client regains control of external behavior. The client must be reassured that violent impulses will be controlled.

Case vignette #3

Mrs. M, a 45-year-old woman looking tired, worn, and disheveled, was brought to the psychiatric emergency unit by the police. They had been summoned by the apartment manager because Mrs. M was throwing bricks and belongings out of her fourth-floor apartment window, flooding the apartment with water, and keeping the neighbors awake by knocking on their doors. On arrival in the unit she was argumentative, intrusive, agitated, and unable to respond to verbal limits. Frustrated and frightened, Mrs. M knocked books and papers from desks. Her behavior was immediately contained by the staff, and she was placed in restraints until she responded to medication by becoming calmer.

• • •

The crisis behaviors *fear* and *frenzy* are responsive to internal stimuli. They are most often seen in psychosis. The client's boundaries are fragile, and control is tenuous. The loss of behavioral control increases environmental misperception and heightens assault potential.

UPROAR. The client in uproar exhibits goal-directed behavior in a style that is noisy and confusing to others. This behavior has been successful in the past and rewarded by completion of desired goals. This client is usually not psychotic and is often willing to "up the behavioral ante"

to attain the desired goal. Underlying the client's behavior is an insatiable dependency conflicting with the fear of merger with the care giver. The attempts to have these needs met are often self-destructive, intense, and contradictory. The client in uproar is likely to arouse negative feelings in the clinician. The countertransference is such that the clinician feels angry and helpless, because the ideal of "good therapist" is being challenged and taxed. When this occurs, the client may be inappropriately confronted, unconsciously punished, or transferred to an alternative care-giving system. Perceived as being rejected and abandoned, with goal completion frustrated, the client becomes assaultive. Groves (1978) describes a similar phenomenon occurring in a medical emergency setting.

Physical signs of uproar include the ritual of "verbal garbage" (so many questions or demands in a short time span that the interviewer is confused and unable to respond), motor activity, and quick escalation from object violence to person-oriented violence (self or others). This client is often known to the clinic staff and may have developed the reputation of being a "systems abuser." The client in uproar is demanding and uses the "bully" role because it has previously provided goal completion by attention and manipulation of the staff. The therapeutic task is to set limits on the dependency and maintain clear boundaries in the therapeutic relationship. The clinician should avoid being caught up in the content by keeping the interview focused on process. Aberrant behavior should not be reinforced with eye contact. It should be clearly stated that the client is both responsible and accountable for the behavior. The client should be assured that the staff members wish to help, but this cannot be adequately communicated until behavior is controlled. The staff must remain consistent, the client must be held accountable for behavior, and the clinician must be aware of the countertransference issues of anger, rejection, and unconscious punishment of the client.

Case vignette #4

Mr. R, a 29-year-old man, was referred to the unit by the Salvation Army because he had no money and no place to stay. He was well known to the crisis staff and had previously exhibited self-mutilating and assaultive behavior. Efforts to engage him in treatment had repeatedly failed. Mr. R would sign out against medical advice, would be AWOL from the inpatient unit, or would smuggle contraband into the halfway-house, causing immediate discharge. He would not follow up with outpatient therapy. On arrival at the unit he was tearful, angry, argumentative, frustrated, and demanded to be admitted. In front of an audience, his behavior escalated. He produced a razor blade, which he placed on his tongue or manipulated with his fingers. He refused to give up the razor blade and challenged the staff to "take it away." The clinician responded to his behavior in a cool, calm manner, expressing to him the desire to assist because it was evident he was distraught, but that nothing could occur until he removed the razor from his mouth. The clinician reminded him that he was capable of acceptable behavior and that was the expectation. Mr. R was offered the choice of behaving in an acceptable manner (relinquishing the razor blade) or leaving the clinic. He calmed down, gave the razor to the clinician, and the interview proceeded without incident.

Case vignette #5

K.R., a 34-year-old woman, had darted into a police station, left a suicide note, and then ran away. The police gave chase, which ended with a scuffle, and she was placed on a 72-hour involuntary hold for psychiatric evaluation. She arrived by ambulance in four-point restraints, screaming, spitting, agitated, and prepared to fight if given the chance. K.R. was transferred to a bed, where the restraints were continued.

K.R. was familiar to the unit's staff, because episodes like this one had occurred when her therapist of 4 years was on vacation. The clinician discussed her angry feelings and fear of abandonment until she was calmer, in control of her behavior, and then the restraints were removed.

The crisis behavior *uproar* is a response to intense feelings of dependency and fear of merger with the care giver. The client often reacts to this conflict with suicidal thoughts and destructive behavior directed toward self or assaultive behavior directed toward others.

MEDICATION AND PHYSICAL CONTAINMENT

Medication to improve the symptoms of tension, hyperactivity, combativeness, hallucinations, or acute delusions may be ordered by a physician based on the client's behavior and medical history. Medication should be given when these symptoms preclude verbal intervention and the clinician is unable to deescalate the client's behavior. Medication used early in the escalation stage often prevents an assaultive crisis from occurring.

Physical containment is a way to prevent injury to the client and the clinician through the use of the assembled staff working as a team. The principles of physical containment are to *deflect* and *evade* blows directed toward the clinician and to *contain* the client's movements within safe limits (Smith, 1977; Rouslin, 1978).

Staff members should be assembled (usually five people will be sufficient). One staff member is designated as the leader, and each of the other four staff members is responsible for a specific limb. The staff approaches the client in a fan (semicircle) position, giving verbal cues as to desired behaviors, and allowing space and time for the client to respond to the cues. In most instances, seeing five staff members, who are calm, organized, and controlled, provides the needed external control for the client. It is necessary to always assemble enough staff to carry out a procedure safely. Staff members can use verbal and nonverbal cues to their advantage, assuring the client that violent impulses will be curbed and that the staff is in control.

Should physical containment become necessary, the closest wall or the floor can be used to contain thrashings until the client is more self-controlled. Using their body weight against the client's strength, staff members should grasp the client by the clothing at the waist and above the joints on the limbs. Using the shirt, belt, or waistband permits a strong grip with good leverage, which restricts movement of the client without impeding circulation or causing undue pain. Grasping above the joints on the limbs reduces the chance of injury or pain to the client. To further contain movement, the staff should place the client prone against the wall or floor (with the front of the body turned toward the supportive surface), with palms up away from the wall or floor, feet spread apart, and each staff member containing the movement of one limb. This position prevents injury and decreases client's leverage while still allowing some movement.

Directions to the client must be specific and concise. The goal is to provide external control until the client can resume self-control of behavior. Assaultive behavior is managed best when the staff *knows* and *practices* a predictable, rational procedure that provides needed control for the client.

In certain instances seclusion and mechanical restraint may be necessary. They are not justified because of staff shortages or as a punishment for an infraction of the rules, but they are necessary for clients with extreme dyscontrol. In some states seclusion and mechanical restraint are viewed as a denial of the client's rights. If mechanical restraint or seclusion is used, formal papers justifying the denial of rights must be completed. The reason for and the desired effect of the restriction imposed should be explained to the client and assurance should be given that the restriction will be discontinued when behavior is less dangerous and calmer. A staff member should be assigned to monitor the client who is in seclusion or restrained. Only rooms specially prepared for seclusion should be used. If the client is in restraints, all skin areas that may become sore must be padded and protected, circulation to the distal portion of the restrained limbs should be checked often, clothing should be loosened, and the client should be made as comfortable as possible. Restraints on limbs should be loosened and limbs massaged. It is wise to loosen only one restraint at a time. An hourly rotating schedule should be used to ensure each limb is massaged and exercised at least once during each 4-hour period. Liquids, food, and toileting should be offered hourly. The goal of seclusion and restraint is to provide needed external control in a structured environment for the client unable to provide internal restraint of violent behavior. The restrictions are discontinued when the client regains mastery of external behavior. Following each assaultive incident, restraint, or seclusion procedure, the staff should review and discuss the incident to improve their skill and express their feelings. It cannot be emphasized enough, however, that assaultive behavior is best managed through prevention, observation, and sound clinical judgment. Thorough documentation of precipitating crisis behaviors and successful interventions should be written in the chart and communicated to the staff.

SUMMARY

Assaultive behavior results from the complex interaction of social, environmental, and psychological factors. This chapter focused on the process of assault from a behavioral perspective. The assaultive process is conceptualized as falling within a continuum of behavior common to all. The assaultive process occurs under intense stress when culturally prescribed adaptation fails. The assaultive cycle has five stages with observable behaviors increasing in intensity at each stage. Through identification of crisis behaviors and the careful exploration of the client's history, the clinician may avoid an assaultive incident or manage one successfully. Sound clinical judgment, prevention, planned action, and teamwork are the keys to the prevention and management of assaultive behavior in the psychiatric emergency unit.

BIBLIOGRAPHY

American Psychiatric Association Task Force: Clinical aspects of the violent individual, Washington, D.C., 1974, The Association.

Arendt, H.: On violence, New York, 1970, Harcourt, Brace Jovanovich, Inc.

Armstrong, B.: Handling the violent patient in the hospital, Hosp. Community Psychiatry 29(7):463, 1978.

Barnhill, L.R.: Clinical assessment of intrafamilial violence, Hosp. Community Psychiatry 31(8):543, 1980.

De Coursey, R.M.: The human organism, ed. 3, New York, 1968, McGraw-Hill Book Co.

Diamond, B.: The psychiatric prediction of dangerousness, University of Pennsylvania Law Review, **123** (2):439, Dec. 1974.

Dollard, J., et al.: Frustration and aggression, New Haven, Conn., 1939, Yale University Press.

Edelman, S.E.: Managing the violent patient in a community mental health center, Hosp. Community Psychiatry **29**(7):460, 1978.

Fawcett, J., editor: Dynamics of violence, Chicago, 1971, American Medical Association.

Gordon, J., Petrick, J., and Wommack, A.: Prevention and management of assaultive behavior (trainees' workbook) San Francisco, 1980, San Francisco General Hospital Department of Psychiatry.

Groves, J.E.: Taking care of the hateful patient, N. Engl. J. Med. **298**(16):883, 1978.

Gutheil, T.: Observations on the theoretical basis for seclusion of the psychiatric inpatient, Am. J. Psychiatry **135**(3):325, 1978.

Hall, C., and Lindzey, G.: The reinforcement theory of Dollard and Miller. In Hall, C., and Lindzey, G.: Theories of personality, New York, 1970, John Wiley & Sons, Inc., p. 421.

Hellman, D., and Blackman, N.: Enuresis, firesetting, and cruelty to animals: a triad of adult crime, Am. J. Psychiatry **122**:1431, 1966.

Lion, J.R.: Evaluation and management of the violent patient, Springfield, Ill., 1972, Charles C Thomas, Publisher.

May, R.: Power and innocence: a search for the sources of violence, New York, 1972, Dell Publishing Co., Inc., p. 183.

Menninger, R.W., and Modlin, H.C.: Individual violence: prevention in the violence threatening patient. In Fawcett, J., editor: Dynamics of violence, Chicago, 1971, American Medical Association.

Monroe, R.R.: Brain dysfunction in aggressive criminals, Lexington, Mass., 1978, Lexington Books.

National Commission on the Causes and Prevention of Violence: Progress report to President Lyndon B. Johnson, Washington, D.C., 1969, U.S. Government Printing Office.

Pfohl, S.J.: Predicting dangerousness: the social construction of psychiatric reality, Lexington, Mass., 1978, Lexington Books.

Rappeport, J.R., editor: The clinical evaluation of the dangerousness of the mentally ill, Springfield, Ill., 1967, Charles C Thomas, Publisher.

Rouslin, S.: Perspect. Psychiatr. Care, vol. 16, no. 5-6, Sept.-Dec., 1978.

Sandler, J.: The background of safety, Int. J. Psychoanal. **41**:352, 1960.

Scott, J.P.: Aggression, ed. 2, Chicago, 1975, University of Chicago Press.

Smith, P.: Management of assaultive behavior (training manual), Sacramento, Calif., 1977, California Department of Developmental Services.

Smith, P.: Learning to manage assaultive behavior, Innovations, Spring, 1979, p. 35.

Stein, J., editor: The random house dictionary of the English language, New York, 1967, Random House, Inc.

Wolfgang, M.E.: Violent behaviour, Cambridge, England, 1969, W. Heffer & Sons, Ltd.

Wolfgang, M.E., and Ferracute, F.: The subculture of violence towards an integrated theory in criminology, London, 1967, Tavistock Publications, Ltd.

CHAPTER 11

The client with a substance abuse problem

Richard B. Seymour, M.A.
Jacquelyne G. Gorton, R.N., M.S., C.S.
David E. Smith, M.D.

Drug abuse clients are not stomachs to be lavaged, or central nervous systems to be kept functioning or respiratory systems to be maintained. They are individuals with a host of psychological, social and environmental problems all of which have played some role in bringing these clients to this critical point in their lives (Jacobs, 1975, p. 47).

The intent of this chapter is to provide the reader with information regarding the extent of various substance abuse problems, the manifestations of different substance abuse patterns and initial signs, multiaxial evaluations and diagnoses according to DSM III, and recommended interventions. The chapter begins with an overview of the magnitude of the substance abuse problem, definitions of terms, and a description of some general therapeutic approaches. Descriptions of substances commonly abused are presented in alphabetical order starting with alcohol and ending with phencyclidine (PCP), and diagnostic criteria are given for the various substance abuse problems. It is hoped that this information will facilitate the diagnosis and treatment of substance abuse clients who seek help from the emergency unit staff.

There are approximately ten million alcoholics, two million polydrug abusers, and a half million opiate abusers in the United States alone. These substance abusers are not isolated in urban ghettos; demographic studies show that addiction and abuse have no boundaries. What this means is that every health professional who sees clients will at times encounter substance abuse.

161

Substance abuse defined

Substance abuse is defined as use of a substance to the extent that it interferes with one's health or social, personal, or economic functioning (Meyers et al., 1968; Schick et al., 1970). Differentiating between use and abuse depends on an evaluation of the frequency, duration, and intensity of the use relative to anticipated consequences and outcomes of such use (Schick and Freedman, 1975). Thus clients who have used a drug only once may be assessed as substance abusers if they experience a lasting consequence, for example, a specific organic brain syndrome after taking a substance just one time.

Duration of the disturbance is usually assessed on evidence of a pattern of use over a month's time. Both daily use and sporadic use over 30 days apply. Episodes of binge drinking resulting in family and work problems throughout the month would satisfy this criteria even though the client functioned adequately between binges.

Substance dependence defined

The DSM III defines *substance dependence* as a more severe form of substance abuse because of the requirement of physiological dependence as demonstrated by tolerance or withdrawal. Also, there is usually a pattern of pathological use that causes a disturbance in social or occupational functioning or both.

TOLERANCE. *Tolerance* refers to the physiological phenomenon in which progressively larger amounts of the substance are necessary to achieve the desired effect or in which there is a diminished effect with regular use of the same dose.

WITHDRAWAL. *Withdrawal* is defined as the "development of a substance-specific syndrome that follows the cessation of or reduction in intake of a substance that was previously regularly used by the individual to induce a state of intoxication" (DSM III, p. 123). Characteristics of the withdrawal syndrome vary with the substance. Frequently observed symptoms are anxiety, restlessness, irritability, insomnia, and impaired attention (DSM III, p. 122).

When two substances are used compulsively (National Commission on Marijuana and Drug Abuse, 1972; Schick et al., 1970; Schick et al., 1972), either concurrently or at different times, it is defined as *multiple substance abuse*. When the client's symptoms represent more than one substance abuse disorder, multiple diagnoses should be made except when the specific substances cannot be identified, or when there are too many substances to identify each of them individually, or when the substances used are from different nonalcoholic substance categories. In the above three conditions, the diagnostic category "Other, Mixed or Unspecified Substance Abuse" is applied in the DSM III. Multiple abuse is a common practice of many drug abusers, and the resultant spectrum of symptoms often makes diagnosis and treatment of these clients difficult for psychiatric emergency unit clinicians. However, there are some general guidelines staff members may find helpful when dealing with substance abuse clients.

General approaches with substance abuse clients

Success in working with clients who are experiencing a substance abuse crisis depends on developing a strong rapport by presenting a reassuring, nonjudgmental attitude and by providing immediate, tangible help. Usually at some point during the interview clients are asked if they wish a referral for ongoing treatment. This referral is routinely offered because after a substance abuse crisis chronic abusers may be unusually motivated to seek help and this motivation sometimes provides the impetus for clients to engage in an aftercare program (Wesson et al., 1974).

The goal of the four approaches listed in the following paragraphs is to achieve an alteration or favorable resolution of the substance abuse crisis. Judgment must be used in the selection of the most appropriate approach in response to the circumstances of the crisis.

Assistance. The involvement of another individual or authority in the substance abuse crisis often provides enough support for clients so that they can endure the crisis and evolve a personal solution. This gives clients an opportunity for growth by having mastered the crisis. Psychiatric emergency clinicians often directly involve others or ask clients to recommend someone they are comfortable with to reassure and guide them during the substance abuse crisis.

Taking over. Some cases require the complete management of the substance abuse crisis by the clinician, for example, active treatment of overdose clients. This approach is direct and often necessary, but the client does not actively participate in the resolution of the crisis.

Education. In some instances clinicians provide additional information or resources so clients may resolve their own substance abuse crisis.

Relabeling. In this approach the clinician defines the major problem, which may not be the substance abuse crisis itself but the way the client and those who brought the client to the psychiatric emergency unit are reacting to the situation. How clients label their problem greatly affects their response. For example, parents who bring their adolescent children to a psychiatric emergency unit after discovering substance use may state that their entire problem is the child's substance use. However, the most immediate crisis is the parents' reaction to the discovery as manifest in statements such as, "How could my child do this to me?" The perceptive clinician can relabel the crisis as a disruption in how the family functions as a unit and focus on the discovery of substance use as an example of how the family copes with the crisis (Wesson et al., 1974).

Guidelines for assessment and treatment of substance abuse clients

1. History of substance use
   a. Length of time client has been taking substance
   b. Route of application (inhaled, ingested, insufflated, injected intravenously or intramuscularly)
   c. Effect on client's life (cost, appearance, and so on)
   d. Physical infirmity that could exacerbate problem
2. Instance of use leading to crisis
   a. Type of drug
   b. Availability of sample for testing if not readily identifiable

c. Self-medication because of physical, mental, or emotional problem
   d. Concomitant use of prescription or over-the counter medications
   e. Drinking by client—kind, quantity, length of time
3. Pattern and circumstances of use
   a. Substance taken alone or with groups
   b. Crisis precipitated by identifiable events, such as loss or celebration
   c. If habit, pattern of development and method of maintenance
4. Extent of potential support system
   a. Family or friends available to help client follow through on treatment
   b. Community groups of agencies specifically addressing client's abuse pattern
5. Client's treatment and motivation for following through
   a. History of previous treatment
   b. Willingness to change abuse habits
6. Informing of the client
   a. Assurance of confidentiality
   b. Explanation of rationale for treatment and what to expect
7. Observation and symptomatic treatment until precipitating substances are identified
   a. Close observation of client and monitoring of vital signs
   b. Only symptomatic treatment before substance identification
   c. No medication if there is any question

ALCOHOL ABUSE
Definition and diagnosis of alcoholism

Alcoholism is described as alcohol dependence in DSM III and has all the qualities of substance abuse and substance dependence. The impairment may involve physiological, psychological, or social dysfunction. As tolerance for alcohol increases, it is common for alcoholics to engage in polydrug use, usually with barbiturates and other sedative drugs. Alcoholism is progressive, often to the extent that alcoholics organize and orient their life around drinking, and it should be treated as a disease (American Medical Association, 1977).

Diagnostic criteria for alcohol abuse and dependence

A. Pattern of pathological alcohol use
   1. Need for daily use of alcohol for adequate functioning
   2. Inability to cut down or stop drinking
   3. Repeated efforts to control or reduce excess drinking by "going on the wagon" (periods of temporary abstinence) or restricting drinking
   4. Binges (remaining intoxicated throughout the day for at least 2 days)
   5. Occasional consumption of a fifth of liquor (or a more-than-intoxicating amount of wine or beer)
   6. Amnestic periods for events occurring while intoxicated (blackouts)
   7. Continuation of drinking despite a serious physical disorder that the individual knows is exacerbated by alcohol use
   8. Consumption of alcohol not intended for drinking
B. Impairment in social or occupational functioning because of alcohol use
   1. Violence while intoxicated
   2. Absence from work
   3. Loss of job
   4. Legal difficulties (for example, arrest for intoxicated behavior or traffic accidents while intoxicated)
   5. Arguments or difficulties with family or friends because of excessive alcohol use
C. Additional criteria for alcohol dependence
   1. *Tolerance* (need for markedly increased amounts of alcohol to achieve the desired effect, or markedly diminished effect with regular use of the same amount)
   2. *Withdrawal* (development of alcohol withdrawal, for example, morning "shakes" and malaise relieved by drinking, after cessation of or reduction in drinking (DSM III, p. 169)

It is important to note that clients who demonstrate behavior that meets the criteria for a diagnosis of alcohol dependence represent less than 5% of the total number of people who abuse alcohol. Appropriate treatment for clients with alcohol dependence is more physiologically oriented than for those clients who are treated early under the diagnosis of alcohol abuse (Becker, 1974).

Intoxication

The relationships between the ingestion of alcohol, the blood ethyl alcohol concentration, and the signs of intoxication vary and depend on the rate of ingestion, alterations in absorption, metabolism, and excretion, and history of use. Alcohol is fully absorbed within 30 minutes to 2 hours depending on the beverage ingested and food intake. The signs of progressive blood alcohol levels are summarized in Table 11-1.

A diagnosis of alcohol intoxication is not made when there is evidence that the quantity of alcohol ingested was insufficient to cause intoxication in most people, as in alcohol idiosyncratic intoxication.

TABLE 11-1. Signs of various blood alcohol levels

Blood alcohol level (mg/100 mg)*	Signs of intoxication
20-99	Muscular incoordination
	Impaired sensory function
	Changes in mood, personality, and behavior
100-199	Marked mental impairment
	Incoordination
	Prolonged reaction time
	Ataxia
200-299	Nausea, vomiting
	Diplopia
	Marked ataxia
300-399	Hypothermia
	Severe dysarthria
	Amnesia
	Stage I anesthesia
400-700	Coma
	Respiratory failure
	Death

From Becker, C.E., et al.: Alcohol as a drug, New York, 1974, Medcom Press.
*Lethal dose varies. Adult dose is 5 to 8 gm/kg of body weight. Child's dose is 3 gm/kg of body weight. If there is no food intake, lethal dose occurs before above doses are absorbed. Signs of intoxication are more apparent when blood alcohol level is rising than when falling.

Diagnostic criteria for alcohol idiosyncratic intoxication

A. Marked behavioral change (e.g., aggressive or assaultive behavior resulting from recent ingestion of an amount of alcohol insufficient to induce intoxication in most people)

B. Behavior atypical of the person when not drinking (DSM III, p. 132)

Fructose has been found to be effective in reducing the blood alcohol level in intoxicated clients who can tolerate this simple sugar. Fructose is converted to D-glyceraldehyde, which is metabolized to nicotinamide-adenine dinucleotide (NAD), which is needed to oxidize more ethanol. It is believed that fructose increases the elimination rate of alcohol from the blood by as much as 80% (Becker, 1974).

Signs of alcohol-drug reactions

Since approximately 60% to 70% of the adult population consume various amounts of alcohol, it is predictable that other drugs, whether prescribed or not, will be taken with alcohol or while there is still alcohol present in the blood. Whenever considering a possible alcohol-drug reaction, clinicians should remember that there are many over-the-counter drugs containing high concentrations of alcohol, including cough remedies, mouthwashes, tonics, and liquid vitamins. These over-the-counter drugs, as well as sedative-hypnotics, tranquilizers (particularly the phenothiazines), antihistamines, tricyclic antidepressants, and narcotics, have potent additive depressant effects when taken with alcohol.

Psychiatric emergency staff may also frequently have to assess clients who have taken ethanol with methyl alcohol (methanol; also called wood alcohol). Methyl alcohol is often consumed as a cheap substitute for other alcoholic beverages or accidentally as an ingredient in household or industrial chemical preparations. Methanol is toxic but its metabolites, formaldehyde and formic acid, are even more toxic, causing metabolic acidosis and damage to the CNS and retina. Hyperventilation, which is precipitated by the acidosis, and visual loss within 12 to 24 hours after methanol ingestion are the primary signs of methanol poisoning. The client with methanol poisoning is given ethanol because alcohol dehydrogenase, the enzyme that metabolizes ethyl alcohol and methyl alcohol, has a greater affinity for ethanol. If an adequate blood concentration of ethanol is maintained, alcohol dehydrogenase will combine with ethanol so that methanol is not metabolized; it is safely excreted into the urine. Table 11-2 presents a summary of alcohol-drug combinations and resultant reactions that may be used in the assessment of clients who appear to have combined drugs with alcohol.

TABLE 11-2. A summary of selected alcohol-drug combinations and resultant reactions

Concomitant drugs	*Resultant reactions*
Alcohol-sensitizing agents	
Disulfiram (Antabuse)	Blockade of the metabolism of alcohol results in flushing of face, dyspnea, hypotension, tachycardia, nausea, and vomiting. Believed to be caused by accumulation of acetaldehyde.
Calcium carbimide (Temposil)	
Analgesics	
Aspirin	Potentiation of gastric irritation; alcohol-induced thrombocytopenia; lactiacidemia produces hypercemia.
Propoxyphene hydrochloride (Darvon)	Potentiation of CNS depressant effect of alcohol.
Opiates	Potentiation of CNS depressant effect of alcohol.
Anticoagulants	
Warfarin (Coumadin)	Half-life of warfarin decreased by chronic use of alcohol, but anticoagulant effect may be enhanced in the presence of liver disease. Occasional moderate doses of ethanol unlikely to interfere with warfarin therapy in patients with normal liver function.

From Becker, C.E., et al.: Alcohol as a drug, New York, 1974, Medcom Press.   *Continued.*

TABLE 11-2. A summary of selected alcohol-drug combinations and resultant reactions—cont'd

Concomitant drugs	*Resultant reactions*
Anticonvulsants	
Phenytoin (Dilantin)	Half-life decreased with chronic ingestion of large doses of alcohol because of induction of microsomal enzymes.
Phenobarbital	See sedative-hypnotics.
Antidepressants	
Amitriptyline (Elavil)	Potentiation of CNS effects. Deaths have been reported with amitriptyline.
Imipramine (Tofranil)	
Nortriptyline (Aventyl)	
Doxepin (Sinequan)	
Monoamine oxidase inhibitors	Hypertensive crisis precipitated by alcohol beverages containing tryamine. Potentiation of CNS effect of alcohol.
Antihistamines	Potentiation of CNS depressant effect of alcohol. Sedation and decreased psychomotor performance.
Antihypertensives	
Guanethidine (Ismelin)	Potentiation by alcohol of postural hypotensive effects. Increased CNS depression. Potentiation of side effects of reserpine.
Hydralazine (Apresoline)	
Methyldopa (Aldomet)	
Rauwolfia alkaloids	
Anti-infective agents	
Chloramphenicol (Chloromycetin)	Disulfiram-like reaction.
Ethionamide (Trecator)	Psychologic abnormalities reported when use associated with heavy alcohol consumption.
Furazolidone (Furoxone)	Disulfiram-like reaction.
Griseofulvin (Fulvicin; Grifulvin)	Possible disulfiram-like reaction.
Isoniazid (INH)	Chronic alcohol abuse may enhance metabolism.
Metronidazole (Flagyl)	Mild disulfiram-like effect.
Quinacrine (Atabrine)	Disulfiram-like effect.
Sulfonamides	Possible mild potentiation of CNS depressant effects of alcohol.
Tetrachloroethylene (Perchloroethylene)	Potentiation of CNS depressant effects of alcohol.
Antipsychotic agents	
Chlorpromazine (Thorazine)	Potentiation of CNS depressant effects of alcohol. Significant impairment of psychomotor function. All phenothiazines have some potential.
Hydroxyzine (Atarax; Vistaril)	Probable potentiation of CNS depressant effects of alcohol.
Central nervous system stimulants	
Dextroamphetamine (Dexedrine)	No significant or constant antagonism of CNS depressant effect of alcohol.
Hypoglycemic agents	
Sulfonylurea drugs:	Potentiation by alcohol of hypoglycemic effect. May also see disulfiram-like effect, particularly with chlorpropamide and tolbutamide.
Tolbutamide (Orinase)	
Chlorpropamide (Diabinese)	
Acetohexamide (Dymelor)	
Tolazamide (Tolinase)	
Phenformin hydrochloride (DBI)	Potentiation of hyperlactacidemia caused by chronic alcohol abuse.
Sedative-hypnotics	
Barbiturates	Additive effects with enhanced sedation, respiratory depression, and occasionally death.
Chloral hydrate (Noctec)	Potentiation by all of CNS depressant effects of alcohol. Psychomotor function impaired. Additive effect may be fatal.
Ethchlorvynol (Placidyl)	
Glutethimide (Doriden)	
Meprobamate (Equanil; Miltown)	
Methyprylon (Noludar)	
Benzodiazepines (Valium; Dalmane; Librium)	
Sympatholytic drugs	
α-adrenergic blocker:	Disulfiram-like effect.
Phentolamine (Regitine)	
Vasodilators	
Nitroglycerin	Potentiation by alcohol of hypotension; may cause cardiovascular collapse.

Alcohol withdrawal

Alcohol withdrawal tremor and seizures. The most widely known neurological sign of withdrawal is tremor. However, the tremor of alcohol withdrawal must be differentiated from that of anxiety, thyrotoxicosis, or "essential" or familial tremor. Clinicians need to study the client's history and follow the tremor course. The tremor from alcohol withdrawal is an exaggeration of a mild tremor that many people have after being frightened, after drinking too much coffee, or after "a night on the town." This tremor is usually benign but slowly worsens as the client continues to drink over time. It is important that psychiatric emergency unit staff members ask the client if drinking alcohol eliminates the tremor, because alcohol "cures" this tremor. Some alcoholics claim that the immediate effect of alcohol in stopping their "shakes" is the reason that they continue to drink. Tremors may be so severe they cannot walk or bring a glass to their lips. After several days of withdrawal, the tremor ceases.

The "rum fit" seizure is generalized and nonfocal. It may be single but is usually followed by one or more additional seizures with interim recovery of consciousness. The postictal period is short, and though multiple seizures and even status epilepticus occur in 3% of the cases, most of the seizures are over within 6 hours. It is prudent to include a lumbar puncture, electroencephalogram, and skull x-ray films in the initial evaluation, but further tests, such as pneumoencephalogram, cerebral angiogram, or brain scan, are generally unnecessary if the seizures are clearly a result of withdrawal and the neurological examination is negative for anything else.

Diagnostic criteria for alcohol withdrawal

Cessation of or reduction in heavy prolonged (several days or longer) ingestion of alcohol, followed within several hours by coarse tremor of hands, tongue, and eyelids and at least one of the following:

1. Nausea and vomiting
2. Malaise or weakness
3. Autonomic hyperactivity, for example, tachycardia, sweating, elevated blood pressure
4. Anxiety
5. Depressed mood or irritability
6. Orthostatic hypotension

Clients entering unit with symptoms of alcohol withdrawal should be referred to proper treatment on the basis of symptom severity (DMS III, p. 133).

Alcohol hallucinosis

Clinicians may group hallucinations as a result of withdrawal according to content and according to the mental state associated with them. Becker (1974) claims alcoholics have visual, auditory, or a mixture of both visual and auditory hallucinations during withdrawal. Although auditory hallucinations are typical of functional psychosis or schizophrenia, a definite diagnosis should not be made on the basis of hallucinatory content or until all signs of alcohol withdrawal have disappeared. In addition, the usual age (about 40 years old) at onset of alcohol hallucinosis is later than in schizophrenia, and neither family backgrounds nor preillness personalities are similar to those for schizophrenic clients.

Hallucinations with a clear sensorium except for time (the client is fairly oriented and alert) are indicative of alcoholic hallucinosis. Hallucinatory behavior is likely to be transient and intermittent, and it usually increases in the evening. The mental status examination shows disorientation only to time, with clients able to converse rationally and often aware that they are hallucinating, as opposed to the hallucinations of psychotic clients.

Clients with atypical delusional-hallucinatory states may have relatively secure orientation but also marked paranoid ideation and obvious hallucinatory behavior that they often deny. The different behaviors demonstrated by these clients can be explained by evaluating the client's premorbid personality, the abruptness of withdrawal, and the meaning of the hallucinations for the client. Those clients who have had hallucinations during previous periods of withdrawal may be familiar with this experience and seem to largely ignore them. Other clients never seem comfortable with their hallucinations and fear for their sanity.

Transient hallucinosis, like withdrawal seizures, tends to occur during the first 24 hours after the client stops drinking and is self-limiting. Many withdrawing alcoholics know that a few drinks, diazepam, or other sedative drugs will stop or diminish these hallucinations. However, most experienced alcoholics also know that alcohol or other sedative drugs will only temporarily alleviate their hallucinations, and will, therefore, seek medical help once the hallucinations start. Clients having alcoholic hallucinations are usually not a danger to themselves or others except for the often unexpected but very dangerous few who may try to hurt themselves in response to the frightening internal voices.

Diagnostic criteria for alcohol hallucinosis
A. Organic hallucinosis with vivid auditory, visual, and tactile hallucinations developing shortly (usually within 48 hours) after cessation of or reduction in heavy ingestion of alcohol in an individual who apparently has alcohol dependence
B. Response to the hallucinations appropriate to their content, for example, anxiety in response to hallucinatory threats (DSM III, p. 136)

Two basic guidelines should be considered by clinicians when assessing clients demonstrating possible alcoholic hallucinations. (1) It is important to rule out a diagnosis of paranoid schizophrenia. (2) After the diagnosis of alcoholic hallucinations is established, the client should not be treated with phenothiazines or other antipsychotic drugs. Phenothiazines lower the seizure threshold, and antipsychotic drugs, in general, can exacerbate the situation.

Once hallucinations have started, seizures rarely begin; however, a series of withdrawal seizures are often followed by transient hallucinosis or delirium tremens.

Alcohol withdrawal delirium

There is a clear difference between the signs of delirium tremens (DTs) and the signs of alcohol hallucinosis. The clients experiencing DTs have hallucinations but they are also greatly disoriented and agitated, unlike clients with alcohol hallucinosis who have clear sensorium. Clients with DTs are disoriented in all three spheres—time, place, and person. The characteristic hallucinations are constant, and these clients have no awareness that they are hallucinating. There is no means of determining which clients will experience serious DTs and which will have no more than several days of tremulousness with or without transient hallucinosis.

Diagnostic criteria for alcohol withdrawal delirium
A. Delirium occurs within 1 week after cessation of or reduction in heavy alcohol ingestion
B. Autonomic hyperactivity, for example, tachycardia, sweating, elevated blood pressure (DSM III, p. 135)

Alcohol amnestic disorder

At times psychiatric emergency staff may meet clients who claim that they do not remember how they arrived in this "strange location." These clients may have developed enough tolerance to the effects of alcohol that they can complete complex tasks and travel many miles but yet have no recollection of doing so. This amnesia results from a thiamine deficiency and the first stage is called Wernicke's disease. Wernicke's disease is a neurological disorder manifested by confusion, ataxia, and eye-movement abnormalities (gaze palsies, nystagmus, and other neurological signs). If Wernicke's disease is not treated with massive doses of thiamine, the memory impairment can be permanent. Clients who suffer from a confirmed diagnosis of alcohol amnestic disorder usually do not recover but only experience a slight degree of improvement with time.

Diagnostic criterion for alcohol amnestic disorder
Amnestic syndrome following a prolonged heavy ingestion of alcohol (DSM III, p. 137)

Clinicians should take a careful history from these clients, particularly regarding their drinking habits, and help these clients reorient themselves. Since amnestic periods caused by drinking are indicators of severe alcohol abuse, continued drinking jeopardizes brain functioning, and it is important that these clients seek further on-going treatment for their drinking problem.

AMPHETAMINE ABUSE
Patterns of amphetamine abuse

Amphetamine is sometimes used, either orally or intravenously, to counteract effects of other drugs, and frequently once a pattern of continued use is established, it is used to ameliorate the effects of amphetamine abstinence. It may be taken in low oral doses to enhance physical or emotional performance, or it may be taken in high doses, either orally or intravenously, to produce euphoria and a rush. Many people are occasional amphetamine users who take low oral doses to study for an examination or for "treatment" of their obesity. Obese clients are often under medical care, but they are not always carefully supervised, and some of these clients may actually abuse the drug (Schick et al., 1972).

Cocaine and other stimulants. In recent years a number of amphetamine substitutes or analogues have been developed as a result of the effort to discover a nonaddictive stimulant. These tend to follow the patterns of abuse seen in amphetamines and can be treated similarly.

Currently the most popular recreational stimulant is cocaine. Usually insufflated, cocaine can irritate and in time damage the nasal mucosa and septum. An alarming turn is the growing practice among the affluent of "free basing." This is the practice of refining street cocaine to the point where it can be vaporized and taken directly into the lungs, thus greatly increasing the drug's toxicity and potential for damage.

Properties of amphetamines

The primary mood-elevating properties of amphetamines are caused by augmentation of norepinephrine, whereas amphetamine psychosis is mediated through amphetamine effects on dopamine receptors. Antipsychotic medications, for example, phenothiazines and butyrophenones, are potent blockers of CNS dopamine receptors, and phenothiazines also possess some capacity to block the effects of norepinephrine. More has been written on the catecholamine-releasing and reuptake blockade effects on behavior and psychosis by Snyder (1973) and Wesson and Smith (1978).

The amphetamine psychosis results from prolonged high-dose amphetamine abuse, often in association with sleep deprivation. The clinical manifestations of full-blown amphetamine psychosis resemble those of a functional paranoid schizophrenic reaction but are dose related and have a much shorter course as demonstrated by the following case vignette seen at the Haight Ashbury Free Medical Clinic.

Case vignette #1

A 28-year-old Asian-American came to the clinic after injecting approximately a gram of methamphetamine each day for 3 weeks. This pattern included multiple injections each day with periods of sleep deprivation for up to 2 or 3 days. The client was hearing voices and had some visual hallucinations. In addition, he had a paranoid delusional system that involved specific members of his church who he felt were trying to kill him. In fact, church members were part of his support system and referred him to the clinic. The client accepted that his fears might not have a reality base and agreed to enter into treatment. He was given 2 mg of haloperidol twice a day in association with supportive counseling. Approximately 6 hours later he entered into a prolonged sleep lasting 12 to 14 hours, and on arising, found that hallucinosis and paranoia were reduced somewhat; however, they persisted for over a week. The medication was continued during this time period and then slowly reduced. The hallucinosis and paranoia faded completely, and it became apparent that the individual had some degree of residual depression but no other major underlying psychopathological condition that contributed to the amphetamine psychosis.

Amphetamine abuse clients usually appear at psychiatric emergency units in such a state of amphetamine psychosis. Staff members need to carefully record the client's presentation and response to interventions so that proper diagnosis and referral can be expediated the next time the client returns. Unfortunately, these clients do not seem to respond well to phenothiazines, lithium, or antidepressants and they often resume amphetamine use.

Difficulties in diagnosing acute amphetamine toxicity

In some cases the amphetamine use is concealed and the clinician will be presented with an acutely agitated, anxious, paranoid, sometimes belligerent client, in whom the cause for the abnormal behavior is not readily apparent. The differential diagnosis (Wesson and Smith, 1979) includes the following:

1. Paranoid schizophrenia
2. Manic-depressive illness during the manic phase
3. Psychoneuroses, especially anxiety neurosis and phobic states with panic
4. Amphetamine-precipitated psychotic reaction
5. Drug intoxication with psychedelics, phencyclidine, as well as other sympathomimetics—ephedrine, cocaine
6. Hyperthryoid crises, including ingestion of thyroid preparations
7. Pheochromocytoma

History from friends or relatives of the client may provide important clues. A history of recurrent episodes of hyperactivity and paranoia treated for long periods with antipsychotic medication suggests paranoid schizophrenia; however, the possibility of chronic amphetamine use, accounting for the recurrent episodes, must still be considered. Urine testing for amphetamines may be useful; however, the urine tests may be negative for amphetamines if the urine is alkaline, because urinary excretion is markedly reduced. Blood testing for amphetamines would be most helpful in confirming the diagnosis; however, several days may lapse before results are available.

On physical examination pupils are usually dilated and heart rate and blood pressures increased; however, any psychological state that produces an epinephrine or norepinephrine response can also dilate pupils or increase heart rate and blood pressure. If the behavior is not outside of tolerable limits for a psychiatric ward and if blood pressure is not dangerously high, a period of observation is frequently helpful in establishing the correct diagnosis. Antipsychotic medications are effective in reducing agitated, hostile behavior but may further obscure the diagnosis, especially when toxicological analysis is not undertaken. For this reason benzodiazepine sedatives are initially preferred for behavioral control. If the individual is suffering from amphetamine toxicity, the abnormal behavior will subside over 1 to 3 days as the level of amphetamine in blood falls. An individual who remains actively psychotic after blood and urine amphetamine levels are negative has a psychiatric disorder instead of, or in addition to, an acute toxic reaction to amphetamines.

Treatment of clients in acute toxicity

While the intravenous abuse of amphetamines is most pernicious and likely to result in acute toxicity, high-dose oral use can also produce psychotic reactions. Even moderate dosages of amphetamines in conjunction with physical exertion at high environmental temperatures may contribute to heat stroke through interference with the body's temperature regulation. Deaths of several bicyclists have been attributed to this phenomenon (Williams, 1973).

Massive overdoses of amphetamines occasionally occur in suicide attempts, intravenous users who obtain unusually potent preparations, and children by accident. Clients may be unconscious following seizures and with hypertensive crises or even cerebrovascular accidents. Treatment strategies are largely determined by the initial signs and symptoms. Strategies to reduce the amount in the client's system include inducing emesis in conscious clients, gastric lavage with an acidic solution (ion trapping) in unconscious individuals, and acidification of the urine with ascorbic acid or ammonium chloride to enhance excretion. Hypertensive crises are treated with an α-adrenergic blocking agent, such as phentolamine. The current antipsychotic drug of choice in treating amphetamine toxicity is haloperidol.

Experimental studies substantiate that sufficiently large doses of amphetamines will induce a paranoid psychosis in all individuals (Griffith et al., 1969). Methylphenidate (Ritalin) produces a similar reaction (Lucas and Weiss, 1971). Unless the individual suffers from schizophrenia, the psychotic (or methylphenidate) reaction is dose dependent and will resolve as the amphetamine is excreted from the body.

When amphetamines are withdrawn, these clients become depressed and anxious and their sleep difficulties intensify. Clinical experience has demonstrated that they do not respond well to phenothiazines, lithium, or antidepressants.

Clients arriving at the clinic with ongoing amphetamine dependence should be referred to outpatient treatment.

Amphetamine precipitated pyschotic reactions

Amphetamines can also precipitate latent psychotic reactions that do not necessarily subside on cessation of drug use. It is important to carefully distinguish between acute toxic reactions that are dose related and drug-precipitated psychotic reactions that continue after blood and urine tests are negative for amphetamines. The prognosis, as well as the long-term treatment, is quite different. Usually a period of observation (24 to 48 hours) will be necessary to differentiate between the two conditions. With a drug-precipitated psychotic reaction, long-term maintenance with antipsychotic medication in conjunction with psychotherapy is the treatment of choice (Wesson and Smith, 1978). Therefore, these clients are usually hospitalized.

Diagnostic criteria for delusional disorder from amphetamine or similarly acting sympathomimetics

A. Recent use of amphetamine or similarly acting sympathomimetics during a period of long-term use of moderate or high doses
B. A rapidly developing syndrome consisting of persecutory delusions as the predominant clinical feature and at least three of the following:
  1. Ideas of reference

  2. Aggressiveness and hostility
  3. Anxiety
  4. Psychomotor agitation (DSM III, p. 149-150).

Diagnostic criteria for intoxication from amphetamine or similarly acting sympathomimetics

A. Recent use of amphetamine or similarly acting sympathomimetics
B. Within 1 hour of use, at least two of the following psychological symptoms:
  1. Psychomotor agitation
  2. Elation
  3. Grandiosity
  4. Loquacity
  5. Hypervigilance
C. Within 1 hour of use, at least two of the following physical symptoms:
  1. Tachycardia
  2. Pupillary dilation
  3. Elevated blood pressure
  4. Perspiration or chills
  5. Nausea or vomiting
D. Maladaptive behavioral effects, for example, fighting, impaired judgment, interference with social or occupational functioning (DSM III, p. 148)

BARBITURATE ABUSE
Patterns of barbiturate abuse

Barbiturates fit within the general category of CNS depressants that includes ethyl alcohol, minor tranquilizers, phencyclidine, phenothiazines, and benzodiazepines. These drugs can produce sedation, sleep, and coma preceded by a period of disinhibition. Cross-tolerance and dependence exist with most sedative-hypnotics.

As with amphetamine abuse, high-dose barbiturate abuse experienced an epidemic in the late 60s but seems to have decreased since then. Street users usually combine barbiturates and alcohol, which is a potentially lethal combination. Use is often part of a complex polydrug pattern, although fast-acting barbiturates, methaqualone, or benzodiazepine can also precipitate crises.

Detoxification is usually attempted on an inpatient basis because of the danger of life-threatening seizures and consists of substitution, usually with phenobarbital, and a stepdown withdrawal. Vital signs need to be monitored.

Action of most frequently prescribed barbiturates

In usual clinical doses the primary site of action of barbiturates is the central nervous system. Barbiturates produce CNS depression ranging from mild sedation to coma, with the degree of depression dependent on the particular barbiturate, the individual's barbiturate tolerance, the dose, the route of administration, and the state of excitability of the nervous system. Individuals in the manic phase of manic-depressive illness tolerate large amounts of barbiturates without sedation (Sapira and Cherubin, 1974) as do individuals who have taken amphetamines (Greenwood and Peachey, 1957; Smith et al., 1979).

Critical nature of diagnosing and treating barbiturate overdoses

BARBITURATE INTOXICATION. Clients who have overdosed on barbiturates or other sedative-hypnotics arrive at emergency units with a variety of signs and symptoms that must be interpreted quickly and accurately. A sedative-hypnotic overdose is a life-threatening emergency that cannot be treated definitively by nonmedical personnel.

Signs and symptoms of sedative-hypnotic overdose include slurred speech, staggering gait, sustained vertical or horizontal nystagmus, slowed reactions, lethargy, and progressive respiratory depression characterized by shallow and irregular breathing leading to coma, and in sufficient dosage, death. Fig. 11-1 outlines the ways in which an acute sedative-hypnotic overdose can be treated in an emergency unit setting.

The majority of clients who are treated for an overdose of sedative-hypnotics are acutely intoxicated or in coma following the ingestion of a single large dose, but, they are not usually phys-

ically dependent. Unless the sedative-hypnotic has been used daily for more than a month in an amount equivalent to 400 to 600 mg of short-acting barbiturates, a severe withdrawal syndrome will not develop (Smith and Wesson, 1976).

Diagnostic criteria for intoxication from barbiturates or similarly active sedatives or hypnotics

A. Recent use of a barbiturate or similarly active sedative or hypnotic
B. At least one of the following psychological signs:
   1. Mood lability
   2. Disinhibition of sexual and aggressive impulses
   3. Irritability
   4. Loquacity
C. At least one of the following neurological signs:
   1. Slurred speech
   2. Incoordination
   3. Unsteady gait
   4. Impairment in attention or memory
D. Maladaptive behavioral effects, for example, impaired judgment, interference with social or occupational functioning, failure to meet responsibilities (DSM III, p. 140)

Diagnostic criteria for abuse of barbiturates or similarly acting sedatives or hypnotics

A. Pattern of pathological use
   1. Inability to cut down or stop use
   2. Intoxication throughout the day
   3. Frequent use of the equivalent of 600 mg or more of secobarbital or 60 mg or more of diazepam
   4. Amnestic periods for events that occurred while intoxicated
B. Impairment in social or occupational functioning for example, fights, loss of friends, absence from work, loss of job, or legal difficulties (other than a single arrest because of possession, purchase, or sale of the substance)
C. Duration of disturbance of at least 1 month (DSM III, p. 170)

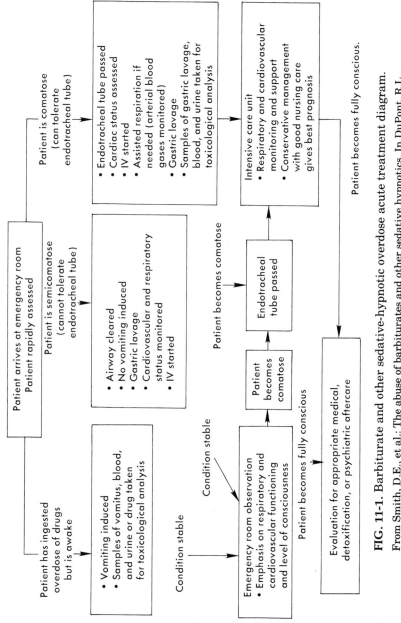

FIG. 11-1. Barbiturate and other sedative-hypnotic overdose acute treatment diagram.

From Smith, D.E., et al.: The abuse of barbiturates and other sedative hypnotics. In DuPont, R.L., Goldstein, A., and O'Donnel, J., editors: Handbook on drug abuse, Washington, D.C., 1979, National Institute of Drug Abuse, Office of Drug Abuse Prevention.

Diagnostic criteria for dependence on barbiturates or similarly acting sedatives or hypnotics

A. Tolerance (need for markedly increased amounts of the substance to achieve the desired effect or occurrence of markedly diminished effect with regular use of the same amount)

B. Or withdrawal (development of withdrawal symptoms after cessation of or reduction in use of barbiturates or similarly acting sedatives or hypnotics (DSM III, p. 171).

BARBITURATE WITHDRAWAL DELIRIUM. Delirium because of barbiturate withdrawal may include disorientation to time, place, and situation as well as visual and auditory hallucinations. The delirium generally follows a period of insomnia. Some individuals may have only delirium, others only seizures, and some may have both delirium and convulsion.

During the first 1 to 5 days of untreated sedative-hypnotic withdrawal, EEG may show a paroxysmal burst of high-voltage, "slow-frequency" activity that precedes the development of seizures.

Diagnostic criteria for withdrawal delirium from barbiturates or similarly acting sedatives or hypnotics

A. Delirium within 1 week after cessation of or reduction in heavy use of a barbiturate or similarly acting sedative or hypnotic

B. Autonomic hyperactivity, for example, tachycardia, sweating, elevated blood pressure (DSM III, p. 141)

Amnestic disorder from barbiturates or similarly acting sedatives or hypnotics

The essential feature of an amnestic disorder caused by prolonged heavy use of a barbiturate or similarly acting sedative or hypnotic is an amnestic syndrome (DSM III, p. 141). It should be stressed that both the barbiturate and nonbarbiturate sedative-hypnotics can produce physical dependence for the duration of withdrawal sequelae, determined in part by the differing metabolic properties and duration of action of the primary drug of abuse, for example, physical dependence on large doses of a short-acting barbiturate produced when the drug is abruptly stopped and a peak seizure liability around the second day (Wesson and Smith, 1976). Conversely, with a longer acting nonbarbiturate sedative-hypnotic, such as diazepam, a large or even clinical dose over a long period of time produces physical dependence, and abrupt cessation can cause withdrawal seizure as well as withdrawal psychosis with the peak danger time being the fifth and sixth day. All of these withdrawal syndromes from sedative-hypnotics can be managed by the phenobarbital substitution and withdrawal technique described by Smith and Wesson (1976). Often, however, it is required that such individual's tolerance to the sedative-hypnotics be tested before the initiation to the phenobarbital substitution and withdrawal technique. This can either be done by 100 mg doses of a short-acting barbiturate such as secobarbital or 100 mg of a longer acting barbiturate such as phenobarbital, with the latter having both diagnostic and therapeutic usefulness. Substantial tolerance occurs with chronic sedative-hypnotic abuse and can produce diagnostic confusion in the treatment of the emergency situation as demonstrated by the following case vignette seen at the Haight Ashbury Free Medical Clinic.

Case vignette #2

A 22-year-old white woman came to an emergency room after recent injection of a total of 1,000 mg of secobarbital. She had slurred speech, staggering gait with other signs of acute intoxication, and was semicomatose at the time of arrival at the emergency unit with her friends. Her vital signs remained stable, however, and she did not lapse into a full coma. After an observation period of approximately 3 hours she was discharged with the advice that she should see a psychiatrist. In 2 days she came to a community clinic with a barbiturate withdrawal seizure. In retrospect, it should be emphasized that if an individual can inject up to 1,000 mg of secobarbital without becoming comatose, substantial sedative-hypnotic tolerance exists and there would be substantial seizure liability on withdrawal. A more appropriate course after observation and management of the overdose is to hospitalize the client and initiate medication for detoxification from the barbiturate dependence. A sedative-hypnotic that has been taken at high dose level over a long period of time should never be abruptly stopped. The drug itself can be reduced in a graded fashion or a longer acting sedative-hypnotic such as phenobarbital can be substituted and then withdrawn.

HALLUCINOGEN ABUSE
Patterns of hallucinogenic use

There are three general categories of psychoactive drugs—uppers, downers, and hallucinogens. Hallucinogens are represented mainly by LSD, with some incidental use of mescaline, peyote, psilopcybin, and a few synthetics like methylene dioxyamphetamine (MDA) and phencyclidine (PCP). PCP will be discussed later in the chapter.

While use of LSD continues, it has changed to a low-dosage recreational pattern, and increased knowledge of how to deal with "bad trips" has greatly decreased the incidence of hallucinogenic crises in the emergency room. Problems will occur, however, from adulterants in street preparations and from drugs given deceptively such as PCP. Generally, hallucinogens are not habit forming and, with the decline of countercultural use, are rarely used serially.

In the cases evaluated there is little physical danger to the client from low dosages of the drug. This is also true of the occasional cases of cannabis use that appear.

In acute hallucinogenic toxicity, clients are aware of having taken a drug but are in a state of severe anxiety and panic, feel they cannot control its effects, and want to be taken out of their state immediately (Smith and Seymour, 1980). There are four recognized chronic reactions to hallucinogens or psychedelics: (1) prolonged psychotic reactions, (2) depression severe enough to be life-threatening, (3) flashbacks, and (4) exacerbation of preexisting psychiatric ill-

ness (Wesson and Smith, 1978; Whitfield et al., 1980).

Diagnosis and treatment of hallucinogen abuse

Correct diagnosis is based on a thorough understanding of the stages of a hallucinogenic experience. The course of a hallocinogenic reaction, or acid trip, based on an ingestion of 100 to 250 μg of LSD can be described in the following three phases, the precise duration of each phase being dependent on dosage, individual idiosyncrasies, set, and setting:

Phase I. Sensory (ingestion to fifth hour)
Sensory changes (visual, auditory, tactile, olfactory, gustatory, kinesthetic)
Awareness of internal bodily functions
Phase II. Symbolic: recollective/analytic (second to eighth hour)
Visual imagery: vivid colors, "hallucinations" (illusions), altered visual perceptions
Mood affect changes
Altered communication
Phase III. Insight/integration/transformation (second to tenth hour)
Heightened suggestibility
Concern with philosophy, religion, cosmology
Magnification of character traits and psychodynamics
Exaggerated emotion
Feelings of psychological perception, heightened insight

Diagnostic criteria for hallucinogen hallucinosis
A. Recent ingestion of a hallucinogen
B. Perceptual changes occurring in a state of full wakefulness and alertness, for example, subjective intensification of perceptions, depersonalization, derealization, illusions, hallucinations, and synesthesias
C. At least two of the following physical symptoms:
  1. Pupillary dilation
  2. Tachycardia
  3. Sweating
  4. Palpitations
  5. Blurring of vision

6. Tremors
7. Incoordination
D. Maladaptive behavioral effects, for example, marked anxiety or depression, ideas of reference, insanity anxiety, paranoid ideation, impaired judgment, and interference with social or occupational functioning (DSM III, p. 154)

Diagnostic criteria for hallucinogen delusional disorder

A. Recent hallucinogen use
B. Development of an organic delusional syndrome that persists beyond 24 hours after cessation of hallucinogen use (DSM III, p. p. 155)

Diagnostic criteria for hallucinogen affective disorder

A. Recent use of a hallucinogen
B. Development of an organic affective syndrome that persists beyond 24 hours after cessation of hallucinogen use
C. Absence of delusions (DSM III, p. 156)

A quiet room in a supportive environment that includes individuals whom the client can trust provides the best site for a "talk-down" to occur and is vastly superior to a busy, noisy emergency unit where the client may feel threatened by a variety of people, objects, and situations. A nonthreatening physical setting also helps clinicians to avoid presenting themselves in an authoritative or threatening style. Sitting on pillows on the floor is recommended for both client and clinician. External stimuli such as bright lights, loud music, or strangers coming and going through the room all may be interpreted as hostile by the client experiencing a bad trip.

Empathy toward the user and self-confidence on the part of the clinician are essential qualities for dealing with a hallucinogenic crisis. Anxiety or fear emanating from the clinician is almost certain to be communicated to the client, who may perceive the fear in an amplified manner. Physical contact with the individual often is reassuring but also can easily be subject to misinterpretation. The clinician must often rely on judgment.

Psychotic reactions usually occur in clients who are already disturbed. These are similar to schizophrenic reactions and can be both severe and prolonged. Appropriate treatment often requires residential care and then outpatient counseling.

Flashbacks are transient spontaneous recurrences of drug effects well after the hallucinogenic intoxication. These instances fade in time but in extreme cases should be referred for medication and outpatient therapy.

OPIATE ABUSE
Patterns of opiate and opioid abuse

In the late 60s and early 70s, heroin use reached epidemic proportions in the United States. Its use is still widespread. Generally it is taken intravenously or intramuscularly. Drugs in this category produce euphoria, sedation, analgesia, sleep, and in overdoses, coma and respiratory arrest. Street preparations usually contain a low percentage of heroin. Detoxification is not life threatening and can often be accomplished on an outpatient basis with symptomatic medication or even without drugs in therapeutic communities. Methadone, a synthetic opioid, is used to maintain opiate addicts who seem unable to give up drugs. This opioid can precipitate heavy use of alcohol. Propoxyphene hydrochloride in high dosage can produce overdose crises.

Two ominous recent developments are the spread of high-purity southwest Asian heroin to affluent, previously unaffected populations and the appearance of "china white." Persian heroin is smoked by people who are then horrified to discover that opiates are just as addictive when smoked as when injected. "China white" is the street name for a synthetic opioid, developed in clandestine laboratories, that is many times more powerful than heroin. An analogue of fentanyl, this new opioid has a high overdose potential and also carries the implication that potent street narcotics no longer depend on opium production outside the United States. Overdose treatment is the same as that for any opiate or opioid.

Only the diagnosis and treatment of opioid overdose will be discussed in this section. The reader is referred to DSM III for further information regarding opiate organic mental disorders.

Diagnosis and treatment of opiate overdose

The combination of pinpoint pupils and a declining level of consciousness is presumptive evidence of overdose of an opiate, for example, heroin or morphine, or an opioid, such as methadone, pentazocine, or propoxyphene hydrochloride. While pinpoint pupils are an important diagnostic sign, in advanced coma pupils may be dilated as a consequence of hypoxia. Fortunately, overdose with both opiates and opioids can be reversed by the administration of a single narcotic reversal agent, naloxone (Narcan).

Diagnostic criteria for opiate intoxication
A. Recent use of an opiate
B. Pupillary constriction (or pupillary dilation as a result of anoxia from severe overdose)
C. At least one of the following psychological signs:
   1. Euphoria
   2. Dysphoria
   3. Apathy
   4. Psychomotor retardation
D. At least one of the following neurological signs:
   1. Drowsiness
   2. Slurred speech
   3. Impairment in attention or memory (DSM, III, p. 143)

Naloxone treatment is usually accomplished in the emergency unit. The preferred route of initial administration of naloxone is intravenous; 2 to 3 ml of naloxone should be given intravenously unless the client is in shock and has low blood pressure, in which case 1 ml can be given under the tongue and repeated sublingually or intravenously to gain a response. If this is done, the injection site must be carefully watched for oozing blood, which, if aspirated, can be extremely serious.

If the overdose is the result of an opiate or opioid, pupillary dilation and an elevation in the level of consciousness will occur within 20 seconds to 1 minute of intravenous administration

of naloxone. If the preceding response to naloxone is obtained, a second injection of 2 ml intravenously should follow for a prolonged effect.

For overdose caused by methadone or propoxyphene napsylate (Darvon-N), both very long-acting preparations, repeated doses of naloxone will be required every 1 to 2 hours, because naloxone is a short-acting narcotic antagonist and the opiate effect will outlive the antagonist effect of a single dose.

The availability of a specific reversal agent must not be substituted for general supportive measures such as clearing an airway, maintaining respiration, keeping the client warm, and elevating the feet.

PHENCYCLIDINE (PCP) ABUSE
Patterns of PCP abuse

PCP and its analogues, including ketamine, have become the "bogeyman" drugs of the present. Curiously, about 95% of their users experience no crisis. PCP is a dissociative drug that, depending on dosage, can be a stimulant, a depressant, or a hallucinogen. These drugs can be produced cheaply and easily with readily accessible ingredients. Use has increased among minority persons and less affluent or educated young people, but is rare among substance-sophisticated populations. The 5% of users experiencing PCP intoxication are hard to deal with for several reasons. The client may go from a comatose to violent condition and vice versa without warning. The chemical itself can be stored in various tissues, including fat cells, for long periods of time, as well as being subject to reabsorption from the intestine. Clients who abuse PCP and its analogues should continue with treatment and be monitored for recurring symptoms. The PCP syndrome can be seen in the following four behavioral stages that may be successive:

Stage I. Acute PCP toxicity: Reactions of acute PCP toxicity are a direct result of PCP intoxication. Their onset may be minutes to hours following PCP ingestion.

Stage II. PCP toxic psychosis: Stage II is apparently not related to toxic blood levels of PCP and does not inevitably follow stage I.

Stage III. PCP-precipitated psychotic episodes: In some individuals PCP may precipitate a psychotic reaction lasting a month or more, which clinically appears to be much like schizophrenia.

Stage IV. PCP induced depression: PCP can produce a depressive reaction in some individuals. This may follow any of the previous stages and last from a day to several months (Smith and Wesson, 1980).

Diagnostic criteria for PCP or similarly acting arylcyclohexylamine intoxication

A. Recent use of PCP or a similarly acting arylcyclohexylamine
B. Within an hour (less when smoked, insufflated, or used intravenously) occurrence of at least two of the following physical symptoms:
   1. Vertical or horizontal nystagmus
   2. Increased blood pressure and heart rate
   3. Numbness or diminished responsiveness to pain
   4. Ataxia
   5. Dysarthria
C. Within an hour occurrence of at least two of the following psychological symptoms:
   1. Euphoria
   2. Psychomotor agitation
   3. Marked anxiety
   4. Emotional lability
   5. Grandiosity
   6. Sensation of slowed time
   7. Synesthesias
D. Maladaptive behavioral effects, for example, depersonalization, belligerence, impulsivity, unpredictability, impaired judgment, and assaultiveness (DSM III, p. 151)

Case vignette #3

At a rock concert in the San Francisco Bay area, six adolescents who had previously experimented with a variety of psychoactive drugs, including PCP, ingested an unknown quantity of PCP in tablet form. Although they had experience with PCP, they had been primarily smoking it in a form called "crystal joints," and this was their first exposure to the tablet form of PCP. All six became acutely intoxicated;

one, a 17-year-old, white, male high school senior, became comatose. Friends took him to the emergency unit of a local hospital after observing the young man for a couple of hours and becoming concerned over his extreme muscular rigidity and shallow respirations. He was hospitalized and maintained on a respirator for over 3 days. With this supportive management he recovered fully, but there was a period of cerebral dysfunction with poor memory and depression lasting over a week following the acute PCP toxicity.

This case vignette also demonstrates that a client can go from stage I acute PCP toxicity to stage IV cerebral dysfunction and depression without going through the psychotic stages II and III.

Treatment of stage I clients

COMATOSE CLIENTS. As in the management of any comatose client, the first level of consideration is stabilization of the cardiovascular and respiratory systems and protection of the individual from bodily harm, such as during convulsions.

Cardiovascular system. Treatment of the hypertension with diazoxide (Hyperstat) has been recommended (Eastman and Cohen, 1975).

Convulsions. Convulsions may occur and are not necessarily limited to one or two. Therefore, recommended treatment is administration of intravenous diazepam over a period of 2 minutes following the seizure.

Respiratory depression. Occurrence of respiratory depression is unusual with pure PCP except in very high dosages. However, respiratory depression may be marked when combined with alcohol, other sedative-hypnotics, or opiates. If the client is sufficiently depressed, respiratory assistance on a respirator is necessary.

CONSCIOUS CLIENTS. Clients in acute toxicity may also report to psychiatric emergency units with symptoms of paranoia, agitation, thought disorder, negativism, hostility, and grossly altered body image. Assaultive and antisocial behaviors often result in the individual's coming to the attention of treatment personnel. In the management of such clients, Luisada and Brown (1976) have delineated the immediate goals of treatment as (1) prevention of injury to the client or others, (2) assurance of continuing treatment, (3) reduction of stimuli, (4) amelioration of the psychosis, and (5) the reduction of agitation. The reduction of external stimulation through the use of seclusion or a "quiet room" is of prime importance. Clinicians disagree as to the most appropriate pharmacological intervention. Luisada and Brown (1976) recommended chlorpromazine for phase III, although Smith et al. (1978) prefer diazepam for symptomatic or behavioral control. Haloperidol has also been used successfully for all phases (Showalter and Thornton, 1977).

ELIMINATION OF PCP FROM THE BODY. Although many clinicians prefer conservative supportive management, Aronow, Miceli, and Done (1978) have successfully utilized continuous gastric suction, acidification of the urine with vitamin C and cranberry juice, and a potent diuretic such as furosemide to enhance elimination of the PCP.

PCP is recycled through the enterohepatic circulation, and introducing a slurry of activated charcoal into the intestine may decrease reabsorption of PCP from the small intestine. This should *not* be used instead of gastric suction in a comatose client; however, 100 ml of activated charcoal slurry should be inserted into the stomach just before the nasogastric tube is removed or may be given orally to a noncomatose client.

Treatment of stage II clients

After the acute PCP toxicity phase has passed, some individuals develop a prolonged toxic psychosis. Most clinicians recommend the use of nonphenothiazine tranquilizers such as haloperidol. Some clinicians use sedative-hypnotic medication. There is no sound research basis for the use of either of these medications, nor is there any indication that these medications shorten the course of acute PCP toxic psychosis. It does appear, however, that they make the client more manageable in a ward, which is probably the major reason that these medications are used.

Treatment of stage III clients

The characteristics of the PCP-precipitated psychotic episode are of the schizoaffective type with paranoid features and a waxing and waning thought disorder. A majority of the individuals in stage III have psychotic or prepsychotic personalities, and this is the major prognostic indicator. Immediate goals of treatment are the same as those described for acute PCP toxicity, including prevention of injury and reduction of stimuli.

Treatment of stage IV clients

PCP-induced depression is a very frequent condition, the diagnosis of which many clinicians miss, particularly when it comes after a stage III PCP-precipitated psychotic reaction. In this depression the individual has high suicide liability or may use other types of drugs to alleviate the depression. If antidepressants are prescribed on an outpatient basis, dosages for only 2 or 3 days should be dispensed at one time. The client should be cautioned about possible interaction of tricyclic antidepressants with PCP, alcohol, and other drugs and advised to discontinue the tricyclic antidepressants if PCP usage is resumed. The underlying basis of a PCP-induced depression is unknown, and disagreement exists among experienced clinicians as to what constitutes the most appropriate treatment.

SUMMARY

In this chapter, the authors have attempted to describe the most common substance abuse problems and indicate interventions appropriate for psychiatric emergency treatment. The content on substance abuse is intended to facilitate the work of clinicians in identifying the problem, providing emergency treatment, and arranging disposition of the client. Aside from indicating disposition, treatment issues regarding detoxification have been excluded. It is suggested that clinicians who want a broader knowledge of current substance abuse problems and treatment avail themselves of the variety of publications and continuing education programs in the field of substance abuse.

BIBLIOGRAPHY

American Medical Association: Manual on alcoholism, ed. 3, Monroe, Wis., 1977, The Association.

Aronow, R., Miceli, J.N., and Done, A.K.: Clinical observations during phencyclidine intoxication and treatment based on ion-trapping, National Institute of Drug Abuse Research Monograph 21:218, Aug. 1978.

Becker, C.E., Roe, R.L., and Scott, R.A.: Alcohol as a drug, New York, 1974, Medcom Press.

Done, A.K., Aronow, R., and Miceli, J.N.: The pharmacokinetics of phencyclidine in overdosage and its treatment, National Institute of Drug Abuse Research Monograph 21:210, Aug., 1978.

Eastman, J.W., and Cohen, S.V.: Hypertensive crisis and death associated with phencyclidine poisoning, J.A.M.A. 231(12):1270, 1975.

Greenwood, R., and Peachy, R.: Acute amphetamine poisoning: an account of 3 cases, Br. Med. J. 30:742, March, 1957.

Griffith, J.S., Cavanaugh, J., and Oates, J.: Schizophreniform psychosis induced by large-dose administration of d-amphetamine, J. Psychedelic Drugs, 2(2):25, 1969.

Jacobs, J.E.: Emergency room drug abuse treatment, J. Psychedelic Drugs, 7:1, 1975.

Lucas, A.R., and Weiss, M.: Methylphenidate Hallucinosis, J.A.M.A. 217(8):1079, 1971.

Luisada, P.V., and Brown, B.I.: Clinical management of the phencyclidine psychosis, Clin. Toxicol. 9(4):593, 1976.

Meyers, F.H., et al.: A review of medical pharmacology, Los Altos, Calif., 1968, Lange Medical Publications.

National Commission on Marijuana and Drug Abuse: Problem in prospective, Washington, 1972, U.S. Government Printing Office.

Sapira, J.D., and Cherubin, C.E.: Drug abuse: a guide for the clinician, Excerpta Medica 109:494, April, 1974.

Schick, J.F.E., and Freedman, D.X.: Research in nonnarcotic drug abuse. In Arieti, S., editor: American handbook of psychiatry: new psychiatric frontiers, ed. 2, vol. 6, New York, 1975, Basic Books, Inc., Publishers.

Schick, J.F.E., Smith, D.E., and Meyers, F.H.: Patterns of drug use in the Haight Ashbury neighborhood, Clin. Toxicol. 3:19, 1970.

Schick, J.F.E., Smith, D.E., and Wesson, D.P.: An analysis of amphetamine toxicity and patterns of use, J. Psychedelic Drugs 5(2):113, Winter, 1972.

Showalter, C.V., and Thornton, W.E.: Clinical pharmacology of phencyclidine toxicity, Am. J. Psychol. 134 (11):1234, 1977.

Smith, D.E., and Seymour, R.B.: The dream becomes nightmare: adverse reactions to LSD—their nature and treatment. In Cohen, S., and Krippner, S.: LSD into the Eighties, Santa Cruz, Calif., 1980, Unity Press.

Smith, D.E., and Wesson, D.R.: PCP abuse. Diagnostic and psychopharmacological treatment approaches, In Smith, D.E., et al., editors: PCP problems and prevention—selected proceedings of the National PCP Conference, J. Psychedelic Drugs, 12(3):293, July-Dec., 1980.

Smith, D.E., and Wesson, D.R.: Barbiturates: their use, misuse and abuse, New York, 1976, Behavioral Publications, Inc.

Smith, D.E., Wesson, D.R., and Seymour, R.B.: The abuse of barbiturates and other sedative-hypnotics. In DuPont, R.L., Goldstein, A., and O'Donnel, J., editors: Handbook on drug abuse, Washington, D.C., 1979, National Institute of Drug Abuse, Office of Drug Abuse Prevention.

Smith, D.E., et al.: The diagnosis and treatment of the PCP abuse syndrome, National Institute of Drug Abuse Research Monograph 21:229, 1978.

Snyder, S.H.: Amphetamine psychosis: a "model" schizophrenia medicated by catecholamines, Am. J. Psychiatry, 130(1):61, 1973.

Wesson, D.R., and Smith, D.E.: A clinical approach to diagnosis and treatment of amphetamine abuse, In Smith, D.E., et al., editors: Amphetamine use, misuse, and abuse: proceedings of the National Amphetamine Conference, 1978, Boston, 1979, G.K. Hall & Co.

Wesson, D.R., Smith, D.E., and Lauren, K.L.: Drug crisis intervention: conceptual and pragmatic consideration, J. Psychedelic Drugs, 6(2):135, April-June 1974.

Whitfield, D.C., Smith, D.E., and Seymour, R.B.: Psychedelics. In Whitfield, C.L., editor: The patient with alcoholism and other drug problems: a clinical approach for physicians and helping professionals, Chicago, 1980, Year Book Medical Publishers, Inc.

Williams, M.H.: Drugs and athletic performance, Springfield, Ill., 1973, Charles C Thomas, Publisher.

Some unique needs of special clients

T his section examines issues of psychiatric emergency care for clients in situational crises as a result of their status as children, ethnic minorities, or homosexuals. These clients are viewed as having unique needs because of their developmental stage, cultural practices and beliefs, or sexual preferences. The needs of victims of rape and battering and of the bereaved are also examined within the context of psychiatric emergency care.

Chapter 12, The Client Who Is A Child, delineates specific situations in which children may experience crisis. The author explains that conditions of youth in crisis resemble adult crises but are unique in that the young are in a position of dependency. Because of this dependency, treating the child as a member of a dynamic system that includes both family and society is emphasized. How to evaluate initial complaints, how to structure the family interview, and how to use special interviewing techniques are explained. Circumstances for treatment that are best handled with and without parental involvement are discussed along with the observation that parents may be excluded when youthful clients seek help with problems related to substance abuse, venereal disease, or pregnancy.

The remainder of the chapter provides a discussion of treatment approaches with clinical examples to illustrate such clients as the child who is a danger to self, the child who is a victim of sexual assault, the emotionally abandoned child, and the child who is a danger to others. The chapter ends with an explanation of how community supports can be utilized during treatment planning and referrals.

Chapter 13, The Client Who Is Raped Or Battered, acknowledges that female victims of criminal assault are frequently referred to psychiatric emergency units. The chapter presents important background information on the psychology of women as it relates to rape and battering. The social conditioning of women to fill certain roles is identified as the basis for the victimization of women. The stresses of role change experienced by women who attempt to break away from traditional standards is explored as one reason why women are the primary consumers of mental health services and antianxiety medications. The author points out that although women are frequent recipients of mental health care, mental health services do not always appropriately address the problems of women.

Historical attitudes toward women and the power relationship of men over women are examined. Appropriate interventions with battered women are discussed, including careful questioning about family violence, legal considerations, safety issues, and use of crisis intervention techniques. Historical and current issues regarding rape are compared and contrasted with the syndrome of battering. Four different types of rapes are defined, and the necessary support that should be given during the physical examination, during questioning by police and legal authorities, and throughout the clinical interview are detailed. In addition, the effect of the attitude of the staff is described, and recommendations for educating staff members are made.

Chapter 14, The Client Who Is Homosexual, provides useful information for clinicians working with individuals regarding the emotion-laden area of sexuality. Definitions of terms and the results of research on homosexuality are presented. A selective review of the literature examines the extent of the homosexual population, the basis of a homosexual orientation, the relationship of homosexuality and psychopathology, and the stereotypical view of homosexuals.

A description of the stages of identity development is recommended as a framework for the assessment process. The section on evaluation and treatment issues asks staff members to identify their attitudes, fears, and beliefs about homosexuals as well as to understand the feelings the homosexual client may bring to the emergency situation. A discussion of common clinical presentations focuses on issues of relationship breakups, crises in "coming out," worry over exposure, aging, illness or death of a lover, and the stress of holidays. The author ends on a positive note by pointing out how clinicians can therapeutically direct homosexual clients in the interview and through community or individual referrals.

Chapter 15, The Client Who Is A Member of An Ethnic Minority, is intended to heighten the consciousness of "majority culture" staff members to the special problems of minorities and to provide information and techniques clinicians may use in helping ethnic minority clients. The chapter presents a brief summary of the cultural barriers to psychotherapy, a discussion of the need for a transcultural perspective, and suggestions for ways psychiatric emergency units can better provide culturally relevant care. Vivid case vignettes demonstrate some of the problems of miscommunication and varying cultural views of illness.

A method of intervention is presented that explains how various goals and techniques of crisis theory can be implemented depending on three variables: the ethnic minotiry group membership plus individual differences of the client, the degree of client acculturation into the dominant culture, and the source of stress. Crisis support mechanisms and brief crisis treatment are recommended as appropriate interventions.

Chapter 16, The Client Who Is Bereaved, also explains how crisis intervention strategies can be used. The author emphasizes use of crisis theory in conjunction with the bereavement model to support healthy coping patterns and to foster an uncomplicated bereavement. The concept of loss and its relationship to stress are discussed. Then the concept of death is examined in the context of modern technological society. References to the works of Freud, Lindemann, Bowlby, and Kübler-Ross illustrate the development of psychiatric theories in these areas. Each phase of bereavement is examined with attention to pertinent behaviors and issues germane to that phase, suggestions for intervention, and examples to illustrate major points.

Related topics, such as factors that affect the character of grief, atypical grief syndrome, and the application of the bereavement model to other types of loss is briefly described in the latter portion of the chapter. Systems theory is applied to family bereavement and specific attention is given to childhood bereavement, the "identified patient" in the family, and infant deaths. Finally, special consideration is focused on the needs of the clinician when a client dies.

CHAPTER 12

The client who is a child

Martin E. Glasser, M.D.

The task of each family is the task of all humanity (Margaret Mead).

Young persons who come to psychiatric emergency units in crisis appear with conditions that initially resemble adult crises but differ because they are still in a position of dependency to family and society. For this reason, youth in crises can rarely be dealt with as autonomous individuals but, in fact, must be seen as members of a dynamic system that includes both family and society (Ackerman, 1966) (Fig. 12-1). Children not only have a need but a legal right to have their dependency needs met, as well as to have available support mechanisms that can be utilized for the preservation of their developmental growth, physical safety, and protection (Goldstein et al., 1973).

Crisis for the child is the result of a maladaptive state in the child or the family, with the child seen by others as the "identified patient." In reality, however, the child client may be a vehicle for communicating the problems found within the entire family (Kanner, 1957). This chapter will highlight specific areas in which children may find themselves in crisis.

Adolescents often arrive at emergency units with problems that are seen as self-destructive. Frequent examples include substance abuse, suicide attempts, and psychotic states. The approach

185

to these clients differs in the inclusion of family members and some special legal and dispositional guidelines that will be discussed in this chapter.

Children who come to the emergency unit in crisis often have problems that are the result of family dysfunction or are the aftermath of being a victim of exploitation. Various approaches utilizing the individual and family members are discussed with clinical examples to illustrate the situation.

The initial task of the emergency assessment team must be to engage the "identified patient" and the family in a dialogue. A prerequisite for assistance is acknowledgment of the reported problem, while attempting to interview both the family and child in a nonthreatening, nonblaming, and understanding manner. The developmental age and level of the child determine the method of interview of the child individually as well as the manner in which the family can be seen and interviewed as a unit.

When a child is the identified patient, the interview, either with or without family mem-

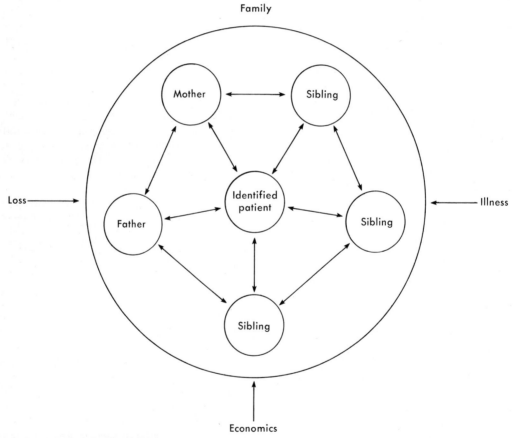

FIG. 12-1. Forces and interactions with the identified patient.

bers present, should ideally start with the child (Montalvo and Haley, 1973). The child interview should have a goal of establishing communication with the child with consideration of developmental stage, as well as the goal of gaining a perspective as to the child's own conceptualization of the problem.

The teenage years bring many opportunities for young people to experiment in life without parental knowledge or approval. Therefore, their arrival at emergency units is often without the knowledge or approval of parents and family. The notification of a parent or guardian or the acquisition of a temporary legal guardian is required for the initiation of treatment for minors. This requirement serves as recognition of an existing family system in which the child is an active participant, with the child's problem related to the family system by its origin or by the fact that it soon will affect the family.

The logical exceptions to the immediate en-

gagement of the family system include conditions in which teenagers would feel that informing the family would be a compromise to the requested care, for example, in situations involving pregnancy, drug abuse, venereal disease, rape, or incest. Federal law does grant a child over 13 years of age temporary emancipation status when dealing with these special circumstances. These exceptions to parental involvement will be more fully explored later in this chapter (De Francis, 1974). The absence of a visible family unit may also lead the psychiatric emergency unit clinician to the decision to treat a child as "emancipated," depending on local laws that define this special status.

Permission to intervene without parental knowledge

Fig. 12-2 is a flow sheet elucidating the clinician's options for possible intervention with or

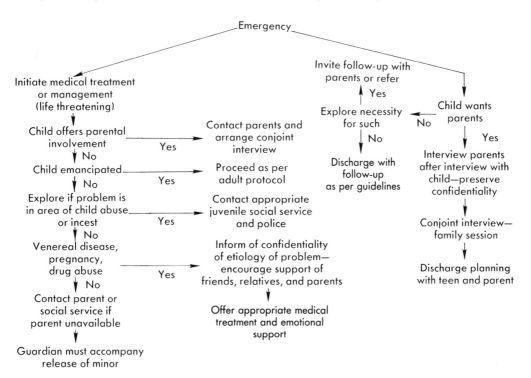

FIG. 12-2. Flow sheet of the clinician's options for possible intervention with or without parental involvement.

without parental involvement. The preservation of health in an emergency situation does not require parental permission, although attempts for such should always be sought, that is, when a child has a life-threatening health problem, hospital authorities can authorize emergency care if the child may die without such immediate care.

The "emancipated minor" status varies in its definition in each community, although the general theme behind this status is that if minors are emancipated by means of marriage or have demonstrated the ability to live independent of family economic supports and away from the family's residence or with family permission and sanction have lived away from home for an extended period of time, they are functioning in an independent manner. The ability of emergency unit personnel to confirm the status of emancipation is often difficult. For this reason it is advisable for each emergency facility to thoroughly evaluate the laws and regulations concerning this status and develop a protocol that is accepted by all members of the staff and administration so they know when the emancipation status can be utilized.

Clinicians are often perplexed with child clients as to whether or not to treat them against their will or without parental involvement. In the case of self-destructive acts, exploitation, or homicidal behavior the clinician must initiate assessment of the child, with appropriate administrative sanction (permission from the legal authority in the community relating to care of minors). This approach differs from that used with the adult client in that minors are not allowed to be "released back to the street" when they are in potential danger, without the clinician clearly identifying the appropriate adult who will assume responsibility for the monitoring and care of the minor. The clinician hence assumes a dual responsibility of assessment as well as protection of the minor when existing support resources from the parent or guardian are either unavailable or insufficient. When the child is a victim of exploitation resulting in abuse, is neglected, or is without appropriate supervision for developmental age and functioning, reported to state youth authorities is

mandated for all health professionals (De Francis, 1974). Although reporting laws differ in each state, the general theme is to give responsibility for the child's care and safety to youth authorities when parental involvement is not sufficient. However, once suspicion of abuse or neglect is seen, failure to report places the clinician and treatment facility in legal jeopardy.

When the child has limited functioning because of mental illness, developmental state, substance abuse, or a significant impairment in judgment, the child is in a position of possible vulnerability or exploitation. If the family is unavailable, unwilling, or unable to assist, the clinician is responsible for locating a resource that will protect the child client.

Clinicians have a further responsibility to look beyond the reported behavioral problem if the client is an infant or school-age child, that is, it must be considered whether the child may be a symbolic representation of the mental health problem of the parent or family.

Infants who are brought to an emergency unit or mental health facility are totally dependent on their environment. An infant may be withdrawn, malnourished, or perhaps even physically exploited. The responsibility of the evaluating clinician is to ensure during the assessment phase that the minimal needs for the infant's health and safety are currently being met. The health team cannot leave the standards of health and safety solely to the judgment of the parents but have the mandate to enforce minimal survival standards on behalf of the child.

Case vignette #1

A mother came to the emergency unit with her 9-month-old infant and asked to see a psychiatrist. The initial complaint was that her infant was so irritable that he was "driving her crazy." Although the mental status examination of the mother revealed no thought disorder, it was clear that she was quite apprehensive over the care of her infant and somewhat ambivalent about meeting the infant's demands. The child appeared to be small and developmentally younger than the stated age with a suggestion of marginal nutritional adequacy. The infant was indeed quite irritable but also had a diaper saturated with urine. After the clinician encouraged the mother to change the diaper, it was noticed that the infant had a significant and probably chronic diaper rash. With the mother's permission, a pediatric consultant was called in who confirmed the marginal health and nutritional status of the child; the child was approximately the weight and development of a 6-month-old infant. The mother did not appear motivated to participate in mental health services and insisted the problem was in the infant; she had no awareness of her own involvement or of problems in the infant-parent relationship. Because of the clinician's concern that the infant's minimal emotional and health needs were not being met, the suggestion was made to the mother that the infant be hospitalized, thus acknowledging the mother's concerns. The mother agreed and the infant was placed in the pediatric unit.

The preceding example demonstrates how a child can be brought to the emergency unit as the "problem." Although the mother was not giving permission to fully explore her own ambivalence over care of the infant and appeared unmotivated to do this, it was clear that the severity of the problem in the infant-parent emotional relationship was leading to a compromise of the minimal physical survival standards of the infant. Accepting the mother's concern as she defined it—as the infant's physical problem—allowed the emergency personnel to further assess the possible strengths and supports needed for the physical and emotional survival of the infant and to engage the mother in a treatment intervention.

School-age children rarely seek help without a parent or a guardian, although these children may be brought to the attention of emergency unit staff members by schoolteachers, neighbors, or relatives. Yet, when children do ask for assistance from staff members without parents accompanying them, it suggests that there is significant conflict in the relationship between parents and children. For this reason, it is important to speak to these children directly to assess their perspective of the problem. When the school-age child requests hospitalization or removal from home, clinicians should be alert for the possibility of abuse, neglect, or some degree of exploitation by the family in the parent-child relationship.

Case vignette #2

A mother and father came to the psychiatric emergency unit accompanied by a reluctant, negativistic 8-year-old boy. The initial complaints by both parents included a long list of examples of how the child was not responding to their limits or suggestions. It quickly became evident that some of the demands placed on the child were either excessively harsh or developmentally inappropriate. It was also clear that there was an undercurrent of dissention and disagreement between the parents concerning their child and their own relationship. During one point in the parental interview the father suggested that "even spanking doesn't help any more." When the child was interviewed alone, he appeared depressed, withdrawn, and made no attempt to deny or negate the problems his parents described. This prompted the clinician to further investigate the possibility of previous physical abuse of the child.

This example should raise questions for the assessing clinician: (1) Is the situation a danger to the child or to the safety of others? (2) Is the occurrence of the problem caused by a precipitating event or is the problem a recurrent one? (3) Why has the family sought attention for the problem at this time? (4) Does the child need to be in a protective environment (hospitalization or shelter) to assess the risk to self or others? (5) Can resources be brought into the family that can temporarily alleviate the intensity of the problem? (6) Can use of crisis intervention techniques for the family and identified patient with appropriate follow-up alleviate a need for hospitalization?

In adolescence the developmental stage can

lead to an anticipated emotional withdrawal from parents and family supports with subsequent developmental depression and anxiety in the adolescent years. Although the influence of the family is always a factor in dependency needs of the adolescent, the family may not appear during the initial interview as a significant influence but indeed is usually "reacted to" rather than acknowledged.

Case vignette #3

A 15-year-old girl was brought to the emergency unit by her adolescent boyfriend. She was initially seen by the physician in the emergency facility because of superficial, self-inflicted lacerations over her right wrist. Appropriate medical attention was given, and the adolescent was referred to the psychiatric emergency unit. On initial interview the adolescent appeared cooperative and stated, "I don't want my parents to know about my suicide attempt. They don't even know I'm here." The adolescent revealed that she had had a verbal disagreement with her parents earlier that evening over whether or not she would be allowed to go out with her boyfriend to a movie. After her request was denied, she went into her room and inflicted the lacerations to her wrist with a sharp object. Without her parent's knowledge, she phoned her boyfriend who met her outside of her home and accompanied her to the hospital. Exploration of the adolescent's fantasies revealed she believed that if her parents found out they would be shocked, guilty, and remorseful about not letting her go to the movie. Despite the initial reluctance of the girl in informing her parents, it became clear that her preoccupation and fantasies were all in the area of the parents' reaction to her "suicide attempt." She agreed to allow the clinician to phone her parents in her presence.

It was clear that the problem existed with the adolescent and her family. The protest, in the form of self-inflicted injury, was a desperate attempt to engage the family so they could understand her desires and needs and the intensity of her rage when she felt inappropriate limits were set. When the adolescent realized the clinician was able to understand her plight and empathize with her situation, she was willing to allow the clinician to bring the family into the psychiatric emergency setting.

Family interview

When the child is a client in the psychiatric emergency setting, the evaluation is incomplete without a survey of the world in which the child exists. This must include not only an individual interview with the child but also input from parents regarding educational status, peer involvement, health status, and current level of developmental functioning. The interview with one or more parents may be the only initial access to the family system, but can often lead to the invitation of all family members to the unit so that a complete family assessment can be made with all members of the family present.

Techniques for carrying out the initial interview (Montalvo and Haley, 1973) as well as approaches to use with the entire family (Ackerman, 1966; Cox, 1975; Howells, 1968; Minuchin, 1974; Satir, 1964; Skynner, 1969) are discussed extensively in the literature. All approaches, despite their variations in methodology, have a common goal of allowing the clinician to examine the family system with a focus on identifying the dynamics within the family as well as their strengths and weaknesses. The clinician should be alert as to covert messages given by the family to the identified patient as well as other obstacles that may prevent the client from receiving the needed emotional supports from the family. The family session during a crisis situation also allows the clinician to help communicate to the family members the despair of the client, while it simultaneously helps the client identify supports in the family previously not recognized.

The initial complaint of the client may offer some insight into "family secrets" that may be identified in the family session; examples include threatened loss of a parent by death, divorce, or emotional abandonment; severe emotional problems in parent or sibling; or exploitation of the client by sibling or parent. At times secrets that the client has held become intolerable. The family session gives an opportunity to share such secrets as promiscuous sexual activity, pregnancy, breaking of past family mores or rules, school failure, or incest. Other times the client may be creating a crisis to divert attention away from a family member in an attempt to rescue the family member. As the family works toward a clarification of the problem, the ability for the family to solve the problem must be assessed. The clinician may share the family's perceptions or, on the other hand, may see that the client and family differ as to the problem and approaches that will lead to a resolution of such. Ideally the client, family, and clinician will be able to agree on an effective intervention plan, with the clinician able to act as both a facilitator and a locator of appropriate resources.

Case vignette #4

A 13-year-old girl came to the emergency unit after inflicting lacerations on her wrist. Medical care was given and she was referred for a mental health assessment. The initial interview revealed that a boyfriend at school had found a new girlfriend. Her anger at being rejected was her stated conflict and the cause of her "wanting to die." With the client's permission the mother, father, and younger brother were invited to participate in the family interview. It became apparent by the client's interaction with her parents that the "secret" that her mother and father were getting divorced because of father's girlfriend was no longer tolerable for the client to keep and was indeed a significant underlying conflict that resulted in her self-destructive act.

Interview techniques for children

The traditional direct interview style utilized with adults is often unworkable with young children and preadolescents (Conn, 1939; Levy, 1933). The preadolescent and younger child often rapidly become noncooperative in the face of direct questioning, progressing to responses of "I don't know" or "I don't care." Hence, indirect techniques must be utilized to reduce the anxiety of the child, engage the cooperation of the child, and elicit information from the child (Simmons, 1974). Techniques of the child interview are shown in Fig. 12-3.

Younger children in crisis must have the availability of a setting that can be experienced as nonthreatening and, if possible, familiar. Individual assessment and engagement of the child can best be accomplished by separating the child from the parents and engaging in an interaction that allows the child to feel less anxious while starting an initial dialogue with the clinician. Offering children an opportunity to walk to an area where they may receive a snack or to engage in an activity such as a game, is one method to accomplish this task. Younger children may need further distance, initially from the clinician, thus necessitating utilization of a playroom or toys to accomplish these goals (Edinburgh, 1975). Many times a child is more upset by parental reaction than by the actual circumstances precipitating the crisis. If the parents' presence appears to be increasing the anxiety state of the child, separating parents from the child by means of a separate and simultaneous interview with the parents by a colleague often leads to a catharsis for the parent by diminishing parental anxiety and also provides a separate dialogue with the child (Skynner, 1969).

The adolescent frequently assumes an initial attitude of distance from the clinician, giving the clinician an opportunity to initiate the interview. This passive position of the adolescent can be experienced by the clinician as "resistance" but often is the adolescent's way of testing the clinician's intent to see if a trusting relationship could evolve. Because the crisis frequently has placed the adolescent in a state of feeling vulnerable and isolated, any opportunity for the adolescent to initiate topics of discussion or make choices should be utilized to diminish the potential struggle for control that can develop between a youthful client and clinician. Even such choices as to where the adolescent and clinician should sit, where the interview should be held, or later during the intervention, whether or not the adolescent should be present when the parents are in-

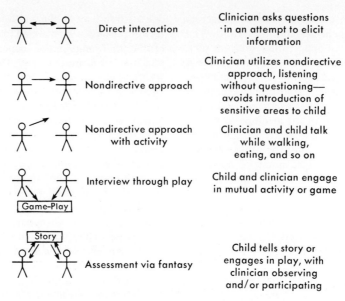

Direct interaction	Clinician asks questions ·in an attempt to elicit information
Nondirective approach	Clinician utilizes nondirective approach, listening without questioning— avoids introduction of sensitive areas to child
Nondirective approach with activity	Clinician and child talk while walking, eating, and so on
Interview through play	Child and clinician engage in mutual activity or game
Assessment via fantasy	Child tells story or engages in play, with clinician observing and/or participating

FIG. 12-3. Techniques for interviews with children.

terviewed can be utilized to allow adolescents to feel that they have some control or choice in the situation.

Case vignette #5

A 14-year-old girl was brought to the emergency room after threatening to ingest pills found in the medicine cabinet. When the clinician asked if the adolescent would prefer to be interviewed with or without her parents, she nodded her approval of being interviewed alone and joined the clinician in the interview room. The initial moments of the interview were characterized by the client's lack of spontaneous speech with attempts on the part of the clinician to engage the adolescent in some topic that was not threatening. As the clinician inquired about the grade level and location of the adolescent's school, she started to respond by brief answers, graudally talking about her peers, school activities, and interests. After approximately 15 minutes the clinician was able to question the teenager as to why her parents brought her to the emergency unit. A dialogue ensued re-

garding the parent-child conflicts from the teenager's own perspective, indirectly validating her feelings of comfort with the clinician as a person both interested and willing to listen to "her side of the story." This led her to invite her parents to join the session. A family therapy session followed, lasting for about an hour and a half, during which time the clinician was able to initiate a crisis intervention plan that engaged the adolescent and her family.

EXCEPTIONS TO PARENTAL INVOLVEMENT
Substance abuse

Many adolescents experiment with mind-altering drugs in an attempt to have a pleasurable experience without the fear of physical addiction. Although multiple substance abusers may indeed have knowledge of the pharmacological effects of the drug which they hope will accomplish the desirable pleasure of a mood-altering experience, one must appraise the judgmental deficits or misinformation regarding psychopharmacology of the teenager. Also to be explored is the possible preconscious self-destructive component involved in the behavior, as well as the possible use of drugs as a form of protest or rebellion. In other words, the appearance of a teenager in the emergency unit with psychological or pharmacological undesirable drug side effects does not in itself rule out the possibility of underlying crises in a given youngster. Only with careful exploration of the knowledge, judgment, and details of "abuse" of particular mind-altering substances and exploration of the fantasies concerning parental reaction can the clinician truly assess the motivating factors for drug use in a given individual.

Case vignette #6

A 15-year-old boy was admitted to the emergency unit of a city hospital after ingesting PCP at a rock concert. During the hallucinogenic period he spoke of a strong desire to die and revealed multiple conflicts concerning his parents and peers. As the PCP cleared, the youngster remained depressed and revealed to the staff a history of numerous examples of high-risk behavior that resulted in several accidents, including a fracture of his hand and of his leg during the previous year. With the assurance from the clinician that his use of PCP would not be mentioned to his parents, the client agreed to the participation of the clinician with the family members in a joint therapy session in an attempt to develop an approach that could assist the teenager in the resolution of his problems.

The chapter on substance abuse (Chapter 11) discusses approaches that can be utilized for teenagers as well as adults. In the assessment of the child or teenager who is using mind-altering drugs, the psychiatric approach would be the same as it is for adults with the exception of special concern for confidentiality regulations of the federal government, as well as a simultaneous exploration of adolescent perceptions of their own behavior and its impact on the family constellation.

The intent of the laws concerning confidentiality for youthful drug users is to enable pro-

fessionals to treat the complications of mind-altering drugs while allowing the development of rapport and dialogue with youth. The health professional also has an opportunity during this dialogue to correct the distortions or misinformation that the teenager might have. This dialogue is free from the threat of criminal prosecution to either the clinician or the minor and allows a rare opportunity for the teenager to speak to a nonjudgmental adult who can assist in clarifying the perceptions and preferences concerning the use of drugs.

Venereal disease

Although mental health professionals are not usually involved with the treatment of venereal disease, there are times and situations in which mental health consultants are asked to assist with these problems among teenagers. One example is when an adolescent female is told that she is in need of treatment for pelvic inflammatory disease which requires hospitalization. The conflict and fear of potential discovery of her problem by her parents, as well as the risk of potential infertility if treatment is not initiated, can leave the adolescent immobilized. Her concerns can be diminished by reassuring her that the information concerning the etiology of the problem will not be shared with her family if she desires to preserve the confidentiality of the clinician-client relationship. It is, indeed, a controversial ethical issue as to whether or not a teenager should be hospitalized for several days without notification of the parents, even if the reason is venereal disease.

Although each state has different guidelines, the ideal situation would be to facilitate adolescent utilization of family supports. This can frequently be done by exploring adolescent concerns and fantasies as to why they would not want their family to be involved and then offering assistance in utilizing the family supports without revealing the underlying cause of the condition. This may then lead to the clinician being involved in clarifying the level of psychosexual development of the teenager to the parents. When this involvement is invited by the teenager, it can be extremely helpful to the adolescent and family in redefining, reassessing, and clarifying the current level of psychosexual functioning.

Pregnancy

The indications for mental health consultation or intervention in teenage pregnancy are limited. Most states recognize the pregnant teenager as emancipated with free choice of termination, progression of pregnancy, or of subsequent adoption. Most pregnant teenagers are assisted by health care professionals in these decisions. When a teenager is (1) placed in a position of being coerced, (2) immobilized with indecision; (3) in a psychotic state or severe emotional turmoil, or (4) "unloved" and feeling abandoned with no emotional supports available, the mental health consultant should be called to assist the young woman in resolving her crisis (Pasnau and Glasser, 1975).

When active coercion of a pregnant teenager becomes apparent to the health professionals involved, it is important to include a mental health clinician as a consultant for the pregnant teenager and significant others in an attempt to reduce the coercion. If a teenager is not allowed free choice, multiple studies have confirmed that emotional turmoil or a repetition of the pregnancy will occur within a relatively short period of time after a teenager has been "forced" to go along with an unacceptable plan, such as abortion or adoption.

Another indication of the need for psychiatric assistance is the statement of an adolescent accepting the news of pregnancy that she cannot tolerate the thought of the pregnancy continuing but also cannot tolerate the thought of the termination of the pregnancy. This at times can reach the point of the teenager becoming suicidal because of the immobilized state and conflict of feelings. In this situation, crisis intervention is indicated to engage the teenager (initially alone, but ideally with the family's participation at a later time) to resolve her ambivalence and fears, with the goal of removing her from a state of immobilization.

When a teenager is in a state of psychosis or has a history of severe depression and self-destructive behavior, the concern of the health professionals treating her frequently calls on the mental health consultant or crisis team to assist in an evaluation. It is important to realize that a preexisting psychotic disorder is not an indication in and of itself to terminate or to progress with pregnancy, with no predictable sequelae over and beyond the preexisting emotional state. The need for clarification of the adolescent's psychiatric state is often very beneficial to the teenager and staff, thus enabling the staff to help with the desired option or decision of the teenager. When the severely emotionally disturbed teenager desires to continue her pregnancy, however, this is still another indication to develop a mental health support team that can work closely with the obstetrical team to plan for the needed services during the pregnancy and the extensive support services that must be available to the disturbed teenager after the birth.

There are some teenage women who have a history of extensive emotional deprivation during their youth and preadolescent years. Their isolation from the family frequently precedes the pregnancy by months or years. The announcement of the confirmation of pregnancy might at times elicit a response such as "I've never been loved, but now I will have someone to love and someone who will love me," or "The baby's father is not important and he will, I'm sure, vanish when he hears of my pregnancy. In fact, I don't really want him around." The isolated, emotionally deprived adolescent who is pregnant presents another crisis in which the mental health team might be called for evaluation and assistance. The "unloved" teenager's emotionally deficient background has ill prepared her for a nurturing role. She should understand that a baby will not solve her problems of loneliness and may actually increase her sense of isolation. The engagement of the adolescent in a noncoercive manner into a dialogue frequently can be continued during the pregnancy in an attempt to facilitate the teenager's involvement in parenting classes as well as to provide needed supportive psychotherapy to deal with her own problems. This can be an effective way to prevent possible neglect and abuse of the unborn child (Glasser, 1980).

THE CHILD AS A VICTIM

Although many programs that specialize in assessment of children who have been victimized by abuse, neglect, and exploitation are located within the pediatric medical setting, there are times when it is helpful and appropriate for the psychiatric emergency clinician to assist in these situations.

Physical abuse

In cases of the physical abuse of children by their parents, the intervention has initial goals, primarily, of assessing the extent of physical injury, providing necessary emergency medical treatment, and guaranteeing the child's safety from further physical injury. The concern for the parents and their motivations for the abuse are frequently a low priority in the emergency setting. It is often confusing to emergency unit staff members when the child's reactions appear somewhat paradoxical, in that despite the reported injury the child appears to be willing to go home with the parent once again. Although psychiatric emergency clinicians are not always called in to assist in these situations the crisis mental health evaluation of the child and parents is often advisable (Schultz, 1972).

When an adolescent is a victim of physical abuse, the presentation is often disguised. The behaviors that lead to the teenager being brought to the emergency unit may not initially be seen as a result of physical abuse, but as the interview is directed to the environment in which the adolescent is living and functioning and the types of restrictions and discipline experienced by the teenager are explored, the history of adolescent abuse may be elicited.

Case vignette #7

A 15-year-old boy was brought to the emergency unit after jumping out of a third-story window. Because of the fortunate presence of an awning below, the fall was broken and injuries were minor and limited to soft tissues. The history revealed that the father had been physically abusive in the past and was in the room at the time of the jump, verbally reprimanding the child. A family meeting revealed a history of suicide attempts in three out of four siblings during theie adolescence resulting from the father's harsh physically and verbally abusive disciplinary techniques. The interview with the client elicited a plea for someone to intervene in the family situation that the client felt was intolerable. The interview with the family initially dealt with the severity of the adolescent's frustration and depression. The family responded by agreeing to participate in family therapy during the adolescent's hospitilization.

Sexual abuse

The child victim of sexual abuse also experiences the emotional trauma of being sexually exploited. Effective treatment of sexually abused children is contingent on several variables. Because of the emotionally charged nature of the abuse, the anxiety over the situation is experienced not only by the victim but also by all hospital staff members who attempt to initiate emergency treatment for the victim. Staff members and parents are often more concerned with their own feelings of outrage and are unable to support the youngster. This places abused children in a position of seeing significant others in a state of turmoil which amplifies their own anxiety and confusion over the situation (Landis, 1956).

The role of psychiatric emergency staff in cases of sexual exploitation is to assess the severity of the circumstances involving the act, as well as to reduce the tensions of the situation to minimize emotional trauma and sequelae. The variables that must be assessed in each case include (1) the degree of physical harm or pain experienced by the victim during the act, (2) the identity of the perpetrator, (3) repetition of the act, (4) the reaction of significant others, (5) the developmental stage of the victim, (6) the timing and rapidity of the intervention, and (7) the ability to allow simultaneous catharsis to the victim and parents (Glasser, 1979; Steele, 1979). The psychiatric team also has an opportunity to assist other health professionals in the emergency assessment and intervention of a child victim of sexual abuse.

Preschool children frequently show a minimal degree of physical harm and trauma. When the perpetrator is a stranger and the incident is an isolated act, the developmental level of the preschool youngster allows parents and others to minimize the emotional sequela by offering support and comfort. Frequently the reaction of others is that of outrage, and this anxiety of others affects and influences a child's perception of the act. When a psychiatric emergency clinician is available at the time of the emergency assessment of a preschool youngster, there is an opportunity to allow simultaneous catharsis for the parents and their children which promotes a rapid resolution in the family system of the emotional reaction that inevitably results from the child having been exploited sexually (Glasser, 1979).

Case vignette #8

A 4-year-old girl was in the park playing with a group of children. Although the mother was watching from a nearby bench with other parents, the young girl disappeared from view for a short time. When she returned, she came to the mother and complained that a man had removed her pants and placed something sticky on her "bottom." It quickly became apparent that the girl had not been physically harmed but had been fondled by an unknown perpetrator who had rubbed Vaseline on her buttocks and fondled her genitals. The girl was primarily reacting to her mother's distraught state and, when offered toys and a snack, was able to relax and engage in a conversation with her pediatrician. Simultaneously, the mother was taken into another room and allowed to express her rage and concern over the incident. The mother spoke to the police giving all the necessary information to locate the perpetrator. During the interview with the pediatrician and victim it was explained to the child that the man was confused and should not have done what he did. She was reassured that no harm had come to her and

that her mother would soon be back to take her home. After a great deal of support was given to the mother about her need to continue the child's normal daily routine, the child and mother were rejoined and they returned home with minimal emotional distress being observed in either the child or her mother.

School-age children are more vulnerable to sexual exploitation than preschool children because of their independent travels to and from school and unsupervised play on weekends and after school. When school-age children are sexually exploited, there is a higher incidence of attempted penetration and other sexual acts that can elicit pain and trauma. When the sexual exploitation is discovered, the child is frequently brought to the emergency unit by the police, with parents either accompanying the child or joining them when notified. Although the prepubescent developmental level of these children is such that they are more aware of the taboo nature of the act than a preschooler, they still frequently conceptualize their genitalia as an "undifferentiated" area. The availability of a psychiatric clinician who will be accepted by the family during the physical evaluation seems contingent on whether or not the clinician is present at the time of the initial assessment.

When a child is first brought to an emergency unit, a support team can coordinate any needed interviews by others, as well as postpone examinations and interviews until the child and family are emotionally available for such. Both the health examination and interviews can be conducted in a manner and in an environment that can minimize further emotional trauma to the child and the family. This can be accomplished by interviewing the child in a playroom setting while the parents are dealing with representatives from other agencies. At times, allowing the child to sleep overnight in the hospital with family members present may be necessary before any extensive physical evaluation is done or interviews are conducted.

Case vignette #9

A 7-year-old boy came home from school an hour later than usual. He shared with his mother that he had been offered candy by an older man who took him to a car and attempted to "put something into his bottom." The boy appeared somewhat embarrassed to share this information with the mother and fearful of punishment for being late from school and for having taken candy from a strange man. The mother became quite upset and immediately phoned the police who brought the mother and child to the emergency unit. An initial examination revealed that the youngster was not in any significant physical distress but had some reddening around his anal area. Initial attempts to obtain forensic material were delayed because of the child's significant anxiety and agitation at being examined. The mother was not able to offer emotional support to her son as a result of her frantic attempt to contact his father and to give any information she could to the police. It became apparent that there was minimal physical harm to the child but that his emotional turmoil was the result of both the man hurting him and his mother's distress. After support services were offered to the parents and the child, the parents were allowed to sleep overnight in the room with the child and to share with their son that the reason for their emotional upset was not anger toward him for being late in coming home from school or for accepting candy from a stranger. The psychiatric clinician was able to oversee the crisis intervention and to coordinate the medical services as well as the needed interviews for the child and the parents. Appropriate follow-up services were arranged for the child's discharge the next morning.

Teenage victims of sexual exploitation are well aware of the sexual implications of the act and frequently are enraged when they come to the emergency unit. Adolescents' awareness over their vulnerability, assault to their body integrity, and subsequent rage make adolescents difficult people to engage in dialogue. Adolescent victims' loss of control over the situation frequently causes them to be overwhelmed by feel-

ings of vulnerability and rage with the potential of experiencing any medical intervention as assaultive, painful, or intrusive. For these reasons the initial contact in the medical setting should be with someone with psychiatric training who can help to diminish the victim's rage and vulnerability and so facilitate the appropriate medical intervention.

Timing of the introduction of the psychiatric clinician is critical. Ideally when victims are first identified and brought to the receiving facility, the psychiatric clinician is there to meet them (Glasser, 1979). After a brief screening physical to determine that the teenager is not in a state of medical emergency, the interview can continue between clinician and victim to establish rapport and to ensure a supportive empathic approach to facilitate the expression of feelings. Concerns are frequently raised at this time by victims over whether or not they want their parents, boyfriends, spouses, or loved ones to be notified. It is indeed an option for teenage victims to notify family or friends. Usually teenagers desire the support of these people, but their fear of rejection places them in an ambivalent state. Once rapport has been established, the clinician can be available, with permission of the victim, to have joint sessions with the teenager and family and, at times, significant others. The clinician can also play an important role as advocate in supporting the teenage victim during the necessary interviews with the police and other agencies as well as being present, when invited, during the medical examination.

Case vignette #10

A 16-year-old girl had recently come to an urban setting to visit her older sister. She had been raised in a rural community with no previous exposure to a large city. The young woman had been in the city for a few days when she met another girl the same age, and they proceeded to explore the city on foot. When a car stopped with several teenage boys, the girls conversed with them awhile and decided to join the boys for a "ride around the city." Shortly thereafter, the teenage boys raped both girls and abandoned them on the street. When police brought the victims to the receiving hospital, the visiting teenager was most distraught. She was able to give a description of the boys in the car but was preoccupied with her loss of virginity, reaction of boyfriend back home, fear of telling her sister, and a desire to not have her parents know what had happened. The psychiatric clinician was available at the time of her entry into the hospital and after a brief screening medical examination took the teenager into a safe, quiet setting and was able to explore her many concerns and feelings after the rape incident. Later that evening the teenage victim was able to invite to the hospital her sister who with the help of the clinician became very supportive of the victim. The victim's request not to notify her parents was honored.

When the perpetrator is from the family, and the sexual exploitation has been repetitive, the emotional sequelae of this situation is more intense and serious. Incestuous activity can victimize children as young as 4 years old. Frequently sexual exploitation continues through adolescence until teenagers become aware that the parent or sibling has been sexually exploiting them. This usually occurs when teenagers become involved with peers and "move away" from the family emotional ties. The subsequent rage that teenagers experience is intensely felt but also leaves teenagers in a double bind as to how they can express their feelings.

If adolescents go to the authorities and reveal the history of sexual exploitation, their fear is that "no one will believe them" and the family will totally reject them. On the other hand, if the authorities do believe them, they fear that the perpetrator will be arrested, the family will fall apart, and all family members will blame the victim for this disintegration. Because of these conflicting fears, teenagers feel extremely ambivalent about whether or not to reveal the ongoing sexual exploitation and become preoccupied and concerned with the sequelae of their disclosure. Hence, when victims reveal to the receiving facility that the perpetrator is within the family, this should be an indication for a psy-

chiatric clinician to become immediately available. The clinician should not only be aware of the current legal requirements and protocol of reporting incest but also should be able to assist the teenager in resolving the double bind. Since most states have mandatory reporting laws for professionals in cases of incest, the clinician has no choice but to report the incident to the specified agencies.

The prognosis for effective intervention with incest appears to be related to the timing of supportive services offered to the victim, the immediate involvement of the police in confronting the parent, and removal of the perpetrator so that the teenager will be no longer vulnerable to repercussions of the exposure or to repeated incest. When the perpetrator admits guilt and enters a treatment program utilizing a combination of parent-peer counseling groups, family therapy, and individual therapy for victim and perpetrator, the prognosis appears quite good for the family to reconstitute, with the teenager being neither emotionally abandoned nor forced to carry the burden of family disintegration.

If immediate psychiatric support and agency involvement is not obtained within the first 24 hours, the ability for any effective intervention remains limited. The end result of nonavailability of support services to the victim is usually a family reorganization, leaving the victim emotionally abandoned. This then fulfills the worst fears of the teenager, that not only "no one believes me," but "I've been thrown out" with no support system and no place to go. Perhaps this is one of the reasons that a number of studies show that 60% to 80% of teenage prostitutes report an incestuous relationship, with no attempts at intervention once exposed (Silbert, 1980). Similar statistics are found among those teenagers who are in juvenile detention facilities.

Case vignette #11

A 15-year-old high school girl was appearing increasingly depressed and withdrawn in the school setting. When a counselor approached her, asking about her behavior and apparent depression, she reluctantly and tearfully stated that her father had been sexually exploiting her since she was a child and that during the last 3 years had been forcing her to submit to sexual intercourse. She stated that she had attempted to tell her mother but her mother did not appear interested nor did she seem to believe her. The teenager continued to state that she now had a boyfriend at school and could no longer tolerate the situation with her father. The counselor notified police who came to the school and subsequently brought the girl to the community receiving facility. By the time the girl had arrived at the facility her ambivalence and fears had peaked. The psychiatric clinician was able to establish a rapport with the girl and speak with her at some length about her fantasies and fears and reinforce her right to be able to have body integrity and not to have to continue with an exploitative relationship. Although the clinician could not guarantee that her fears of family disintegration and emotional abandonment would not take place, the clinician offered to remain with the girl during the needed interviews with police and other agencies. Later during the assessment period the girl volunteered to allow her mother to join the session. When the mother arrived, she established a dialogue with the clinician and after a brief period of denial and disbelief, became very tearful and revealed that she herself had been sexually abused by her father and shared with her daughter that she had been afraid of this happening in her own family. Because of the fears of the mother and her own unhappiness, she had been unable to believe her daughter's earlier story. Both the mother and daughter agreed that the father must be confronted and "needed help," but neither wanted the father to go to jail. By contacting appropriate agencies and gaining the mother's and daughter's support, the specialized team working with sexual abuse was able to continue to work with the entire family and help them through the legal process to enter a treatment program. The mother and daughter agreed that the initial contact was probably

the most important in establishing a dialogue and allowing for effective intervention.

The emergency response to sexual exploitation can be a significant factor in the presentation and intensity of a posttraumatic neurosis or "rape trauma syndrome." The seven assessment variables described at the beginning of this section will also be extremely relevant in the development of a traumatic neurosis. The follow-up after emergency intervention for all victims must be well planned and at times can last for several months or longer.

THE CHILD AS A DANGER TO SELF

Although children do not usually use their life as a "vehicle of expression" before age 12, one must be constantly alert for the school-age youngster's use of their life as "protest" (Ackerly, 1967). In evaluating the youngster, one must not only utilize guidelines described in Chapter 8 but also carefully assess the child for impaired judgment from organic causes. Family dysfunction and scapegoating can also promote and encourage self-destructive behavior in the youngster.

Case vignette #12

A 12-year-old boy after a minor verbal altercation with his mother went to the bathtub and placed his head under the water. When the mother heard the choking of her child, she came to the bathroom to find him gasping for air. He stated at the time that he intended to kill himself. When the history was elicited, it was discovered that the child had a severe case of meningitis 2 years previously, leaving the child with significant mood liability and a judgmental deficit. Although the potential lethality of the act was low, the child's judgment was significantly impaired, with the mother feeling that he was "unpredictable and out of control." The child was hospitalized for further evaluation of his condition and for his physical protection.

199

A psychiatric disorder is different from "a call for help" in that there is a total inability to predict behavior of the psychotic child. When the child is unable to sort out reality and responds only to the voices in his head, he consequently presents a real danger to self and others, requiring hospitalization.

Case vignette #13

A 15-year boy came to the emergency unit with ruminations of killing the downstairs neighbor. He claimed that the neighbor was "plotting to get him and his family and that either he must kill himself or kill the neighbor." A history revealed that there was no recent ingestion of mind-altering drugs but in fact the adolescent's behavior had dramatically deteriorated both in school and at home over the preceding month. A closer evaluation in a mental status examination revealed that the teenager had a thought disorder with a diagnosis of acute paranoid schizophrenia. For his own protection, he was hospitalized.

When a youngster speaks in an emergency unit setting of taking "a few pills" the clinician must be reminded that this history is frequently unreliable. For this reason any suggestion of an ingestion should be treated with full medical treatment (ipecac, lavage) rather than with an attempt to determine the number of pills by taking the history with the child as informant. A review of guidelines described in Chapter 8 appears especially appropriate to evaluate the degree of self-destructiveness in the child in adolescence.

Case vignette #14

A 14-year-old girl was raised in a single-parent home. Her mother and she had a loud and intense verbal altercation because the mother would not allow her to go out on a date with a boy. The girl went into the next room, slamming the door and stating that she was going to kill herself. The mother could hear the medicine cabinet opening in the bathroom with the girl shaking pills out of a container. When the

mother walked into the bathroom, the girl took the pills in hand and swallowed approximately 15 of them. Mother and daughter both came to the hospital where the daughter was immediately lavaged. Although the lethality of the girl's attempt seemed low, her perturbation was quite high. Mother and daughter were engaged in crisis intervention, with a significant diminishing of the anxiety of the girl; both agreed to continue in outpatient therapy.

Despite the culturally variable range of experience, adolescence in American society is a developmental phase in which depressive affect becomes a part of teenage life because of their movement away from the family constellation and support system. It is also a time in which adolescents become aware of the possibility of using their own life as a vehicle of expression along the continuum from reckless explorative behavior to a preplanned suicide attempt. For these reasons, evaluation of lethality should not be solely related to the medical dangers or the drug ingested but to the fantasies of adolescents as to what the potential danger might have been in their own mind. Several factors to explore in the assessment of self-destructive acts among adolescents are as follows: (1) adolescent's knowledge of the effects of the ingested substance or act; (2) premeditation of plan and presence of suicide note; (3) discovery of action determined to be planned or accidental; (4) amount of pills left in bottle, if bottle is found; (5) notification of self-destructive act—planned versus accidental; and (6) the state of reality testing, the impaired or altered state of consciousness because of medication or organicity (Schneidman and Farberon, 1957; Teicher, 1967).

The self-destructive act may be a signal to outsiders to look more closely at the stage in development as well as at the functioning of the family or peer support system available to youth. The "cry for help" is also an ambivalent message for someone to examine the child's world with an exploration of family, peer, school, and community interaction in an effort to clarify the current stresses that the youngster is declaring as "intolerable" (Teicher and Jacobs, 1966).

The clarity of the child's thinking may be significantly altered by judgmental deficits, mind-altering drugs, or the presence of an emerging thought disorder, but on the other hand, the first cry for help "in reality" is to alert society of an intolerable situation in which the child is dependent on the family supports, which the child experiences as exploitive or insensitive.

Fig. 12-2 clarifies the legal rights of youngsters in relation to involvement of parents or agency representation. The category of "minor" however increases the responsibility for the mental health professional to explore and identify support services available to youth before the client can be released (Adams 1971).

The teenager is in a developmental phase that leads to an increased interaction with peers but also leads to experiences that may trigger past unresolved conflicts within the family in which the child was raised. Losses of a boyfriend or girlfriend might lead to a self-destructive act that on further exploration can be related to a previous loss of a parent or to past suppressed feelings from previous family turmoil. The tendency for teenagers to recreate family conflicts in peer groups enables the assessor to identify themes of loss or conflict that may give a hint as to the underlying conflict (Choron, 1972).

The indications for hospitalization as a result of self-destructive behavior include not only a careful assessment of suicidal potential but also whether or not the adolescent has available family supports. In the case of a teenager who has no significant family supports, a relatively minor self-destructive act (low lethality and low perturbation) can rapidly escalate if the adolescent is discharged into an environment in which there are no supports. When it is clear that the adolescent's attempt or level of suicidal ideation is high, the adolescent should be hospitalized, with or without their cooperation. Notification of parents should be attempted after the hospitalization. When an adolescent experiences an altered state of consciousness because of an underlying organic deficit or ingestion of drugs, hospitalization should be considered until the judgmental deficit is thoroughly evaluated or the effect of the mind-altering drug has diminished.

When a teenager appears to have a life-style of prostitution or of being "on the run," the clinician must evaluate the self-destructiveness of the behavior as well as carefully assess the amount and availability of emotional supports of the client, allowing additional supports to be utilized when necessary. The guidelines for discharge are related, as previously discussed, to the state of emancipation of the youngster; however, the self-destructive aspect of behavior must be explored with attempts to offer voluntary programs that will assist teenagers with their life support system and alternatives.

THE CHILD AS A DANGER TO OTHERS

Assaultive school-age children who are brought to the emergency unit with a history of threat of assault or of behavior leading to the injury of another must be evaluated as to their capacity for reality testing and judgment. Although children can become extremely agitated and "strike out," it is unusual for a child to physically injure a peer or an adult with intent to harm them. When this is the case, one must question the presence of impaired reality testing because of some insidious psychotic process. Although in the child an underlying fear of bodily harm to self is frequently present, the obvious symptom may well be of a counterphobic nature, that is, striking out or fearless behavior. When in the assessment phase of a school-age youngster this type of ego fragmentation is suspected, hospitalization is indicated to protect the youngster and others from this behavior. Or similar concern is the appearance of the symptom of fire setting in the school-age child, which should also be treated as a serious threat to others, usually necessitating an inpatient assessment (Kaufman et al., 1961).

The intervention of adolescent assaultive behavior should follow guidelines similar to the treatment of adult assaultive behavior. It is unusual to reveal a history of an adolescent having physical confrontations with parents. However, when this confrontation appears with the adolescent and parents, one must be alert for underlying homicidal ideation on the part of the youngster.

201

EMOTIONALLY ABANDONED CHILDREN

In certain dysfunctional family situations (for example, presence of incest or significant marital discord), the child is rejected from the family support system. This can be a very hurtful and confusing situation for a child who has no one to turn to.

Case vignette #15

A 15-year-old boy accompanied his mother to the West Coast following his parent's divorce. Shortly after their arrival, the mother became romantically involved with a man and moved in with him. The child was given the living-room couch as his sleeping place and within 3 weeks found himself locked out of the house. After wandering the streets and being approached by a number of men, the boy walked into an emergency unit in a state of high anxiety, asking for assistance.

These children may come to a psychiatric emergency unit with a multitude of cryptic complaints, but after an assessment of the children and their environment, it becomes apparent that these children are functioning in the community without the needed supports appropriate to their developmental level and capacities. Although attempts to reengage the family are certainly appropriate, at times these attempts will be totally unsuccessful. For this reason, psychiatric emergency unit staff must be able to utilize community resources to help the emotionally abandoned child or adolescent to find temporary support systems and shelter while a team approach can be initiated to help reestablish needed supports.

UTILIZATION OF COMMUNITY SUPPORTS

The clinician is at times faced with the need to protect the youngster from potential dangers in the environment resulting from immaturity, judgmental deficits, drug-induced altered sense of reality, and impulsivity. Community resources found within a department of social services,

shelter facilities, community youth shelters, church resources, and homes of extended family members can be used at times in lieu of hospitalization to offer protection to the youngster, while the assessment of the child's environment continues, delineating factors that contribute to the state of crisis. The situation leading to the symbolic cry for help may be a result of (1) intolerable living situation because of exploitation, (2) expectations of adults far exceeding developmental and judgmental resources of the minor, and (3) absence of supervision and emotional support necessary for the minor's growth and security. When these problems are discovered, shelter and protection might be indicated as the initial intervention.

Although the first attempt to find support services for youth should be an exploration of family and extended family, there are many situations, such as those discussed above, in which the child is emotionally abandoned or a victim of physical or sexual abuse or in which the return home jeopardizes the safety of the child. In these situations, depending on the immediacy of the agency support systems, the child may need to be hospitalized as an administrative emergency until the clinician is confident that the appropriate support system can be made available to the child.

Case vignette #16

A 14-year-old girl was brought to the emergency unit in a state of acute anxiety. She stated that it was the result of having several drinks and smoking marijuana. It became clear to the emergency team that her anxiety was somewhat of an exaggerated nature and not related to a history of drugs. As rapport was developed between the teenager and staff, it was learned that the child had run away from home 8 months before and had recently engaged in prostitution. An attempt to reach the parent was sanctioned by the teenager, but the mother's response was one of apathy and rejection. Although the teenager was ambivalent about entering a shelter facility, she agreed to do so if she could meet the new worker from the Department of Social Service and have the resources explained to her as well as an opportunity to visit the shelter before she entered it. Because of these circumstances and the fact that it was a weekend evening, the girl was offered hospitalization until the appropriate social worker could see her on the next working day. During the hospitalization, it was discovered that she had gonorrhea and other significant health problems that were treated.

Referral of client

When the clinician, client, and family or guardian reach a point of understanding regarding the problem situation, the following components of the treatment plan must be considered:

1. The need to utilize hospital or community resources for the safety of the minor.
2. Quality of family supports and engagement of them, with consideration of developmental stage of the minor.
3. Availability of appropriate treatment resources within the community willing to accept the minor or family or both.

Suggestions for increasing the probability of the family and client to carry out treatment suggestions are as follows:

1. Clarification of initial problem with minor and family participating in development of treatment plan, need for professional help, and location of resources.
2. Reinforcement to client and family that self-destructive act and emergency assessment must be seen as *initiating* involvement with professionals with a clear statement of agreement of appropriate treatment plan.
3. Initial contact with appropriate treatment resource should be made, ideally, at time of crisis intervention or as soon as possible within next working day. Delays in availability of treatment resources lead to a high rate of noncompliance with youth and families. Follow-up visits by the emergency assessment team may be necessary after interview period to ensure that unacceptable delay in making referral does not occur.

4. Statement of need for confirmation of implementation of accepted treatment plans must be made at time of emergency assessment with plans made as to time of follow-up contact and method of such.
5. Notification of community resources of minor at risk with attempts for treatment outlined. If implementation of treatment plan is not carried out, follow-up contact can reveal loss of motivation of client or family, with client remaining at risk. Outreach of this type to community agencies when a minor's life is at risk because of family dysfunction or neglect for needed treatment to prevent further life-threatening behavior is frequently mandated by local laws set up for protection of minor (De Francis, 1974).

SUMMARY

Every child has a right to have emotional and physical survival needs met. If survival needs cannot be met in the family or if such a support system is lacking, the responsibilty for youth in crises lies with the evaluating clinician.

When a child is the client in crisis, the clinician is placed in a special situation with regard to methods of evaluation. Children must be seen as part of a dynamic system of social structure. With this in mind, the clinician must ask: (1) What are the underlying circumstances causing the child to be in the emergency unit *now?* (2) What are the developmental resources of this child and how does this child measure up to expectations of normalcy? (3) Why is the child's current support system inadequate to resolve the crisis? (4) Looking at both the child's mental state and the environment, what kind of interaction is taking place between the two? (5) How can existing supports be maximized or what outside resources, such as social services or hospitalization, can be brought in to achieve homeostasis in the family system? Timing is a crucial element; the immediate availability of a supportive clinician in the emergency room situation can minimize emotional sequelae despite the nature of trauma that places a child in crisis. Indications for hospitalization for children differ from that of adults in that the hospitalization may be used not only as a treatment and assessment, but also as a resource for the protection of the child while community supports are being explored.

BIBLIOGRAPHY

Ackerly, W.C.: Latency age children who threaten or attempt to kill themselves, J. Am. Acad. Child Psychiatry 6:242, 1967.

Ackerman, N.W.: Treating the troubled family, New York, 1966, Basic Books, Inc., Publishers.

Adams, P., et al.: Children's rights, New York, 1971, Pragaer Publishers, Inc.

Choron, J.: Suicide, New York, 1972, Charles Scribner's Sons.

Conn, J.H.: The play interview, Am. J. Dis. Child. 58: 1199, 1975.

Conn, J.H.: Child reveals himself through play; method of play interview, Ment. Hyg. 23:49, Jan. 1939.

Cox, A.: The assessment of parental behavior, J. Child. Psychol. Psychiatry 16:225, 1975.

De Francis, V.: Child abuse legislation in the 1970's, Denver, Colorado, 1974, American Humane Society.

Edinburg, G.M., Linberg, N.E., and Kelman, W.: Clinical interviewing and counseling principles and techniques, New York, 1975, Appleton-Century-Crofts.

Glasser, M.E.: Retrospective study—600 cases of sexual exploitation of children. Unpublished paper presented at 1979 winter meeting of the Regional Organization of Child and Adolescent Psychiatry, Monterey, Calif.

Goldstein, J., Freud, A., and Solni, A.: Beyond the best interests of the child, New York, 1973, The Free Press.

Howells, J.G.: Theory and practice of family therapy, Edinburgh, 1968, Oliver & Boyd.

Kanner, L.: Child psychiatry, Springfield, Ill., 1957, Charles C Thomas, Publisher.

Kaufman, I., et al.: A re-evaluation of the psychodynamics of fire-setting, Am. J. Orthopsychiatry 31:123, 1961.

Landis, J.T.: Experiences with 500 children with sexual deviation, Psychiatric Q. 30:91, 1956.

Levy, D.M.: Use of play techniques, Am. J. Orthopsychiatry, 3:266, 1933.

MacKinnon, R.A., and Michels, R.: The psychiatric interview in clinical practice, Philadelphia, 1971, W.B. Saunders Co.

Minuchin, S.: Families and family therapy, Cambridge, 1974, Harvard University Press.

Montalvo, B., and Haley, J.: In defense of child therapy, Fam. Process 12:227, 1973.

Morrison, G.C.: Emergencies in child psychiatry: emotional crises of chldren, youth, and families, Springfield, Ill., 1975, Charles C Thomas, Publisher.

Pasnau, R., and Glasser, M.E.: The unwanted pregnancy in adolescence, Journal Fam. Pract. II, 2:91-94, 1975.

Stair, V.: Conjoint family therapy: a guide, Palo Alto, Calif., 1964, Science & Behavioral Books.

Schneidman, E., and Farberow, N.: Clues to suicide, New York, 1957, McGraw-Hill Book Co.

Schultz, L.G.: Psychotherapeutic and Legal Approaches to the Sexually Victimized Child, Int. J. Child Psychother. 1:115-128, 1972.

Silbert, M.: Sexual assault of prostitutes. Unpublished study, National Institute of Mental Health. No. IROINH 32782, Nov. 1980.

Simmons, J.E.: Psychiatric examination of children, Philadelphia, 1974, Lea & Febiger.

Skynner, A.C.R.: Indications and contraindications for conjoint family therapy, Int. J. Soc. Psychiatry 15: 245, 1969.

Steele, B.: Maltreatment of children: physical and sexual, dialogue, J. Psychoanal. Perpsect. 3(1):3, Summer 1979.

Teicher, J.D., and Jacobs, J.: Adolescents who attempt suicide, Am. J. Psychiatry 122:1248, 1966.

Teicher, J.D.: The enigma of predicting suicide attempts, Feelings, vol. 4, no. 4, Columbus, Ohio, 1967, Ross Laboratories.

Truax, C.B., and Corkhoff, P.R.: Toward effective counseling and psychotherapy: training and practice, Chicago, 1967, Aldine Publishing Co.

CHAPTER 13

The client who is raped or battered

Mariann P. Monteleone, R.N., M.S., C.S.

Testimony: About five years ago when I lived in Chicago I awoke one night gagged with my hands pinned down by someone who was wearing leather gloves and holding a razor to my throat (Brownmiller, 1975, p. 392).

This chapter focuses on women as a group of individuals with unique problems and needs. Aspects of the psychology of women have been included to provide the clinician with a review of this psychology and its influence on the development of rape and battering of women. In society, women have frequently been ignored, devalued, and relegated to an inferior status, resulting in the formation of stereotyped responses to them. Despite the woman's suffrage movement at the beginning of the century, the passage of the Nineteenth Amendment in 1920, and ratification of the Equal Rights Amendment by a number of states, the inequalities between the sexes remain largely unresolved.

Societal change has been slow because the attitudes that have evolved about women limit rather than enhance their interactions with others. The Women's Movement of the 1960s encouraged women to free themselves from conventional views. They sought help and support from each other in the form of self-help groups, called consciousness-raising groups. The expectations that roles would change allowed women to anticipate and to experiment with better conditions for themselves.

This expectation has been slow to be realized, but women-to-women support has continued to encourage this shift. As women began to feel entitled to fuller life experiences, women's groups began exploring the problems of violence against women. Initially, the investigation focused primarily on the violence of rape but grew to include other types of battering. The treatment of the woman who has experienced rape or battering is a primary concern of the psychiatric emergency clinician. The numbers of women seeking professional assistance after being attacked are increasing. Coping effectively with these emergencies can help women to develop adaptive problem-solving skills and to learn to mobilize available resources, thereby reducing the impact of rape or battering.

GROWING UP AS A WOMAN

For better understanding of the dynamics of rape or battering of women, it is useful to examine the socialization process of women. Socialization refers to societal preparation of individuals for their role. It is a complex process, accomplished over time and by a variety of means. Although there have been some shifts in the responsibility for socialization to both parents, it has been primarily the responsibility of mothers. In today's more isolated society, women have lost the support of "kinswomen" to lend help in mothering. They have been asked to accept total obligation for the care of their infants (Rossi, 1968).

Socialization affects sex role behavior through reinforcement, modeling, identification, and cognitive development (Williams, 1977). Reinforcement theory explains that the child learns behavior as the result of direct reinforcement from the environment. Modeling theory states that the child learns sex role behavior by simulating the behavior of others. Identification is a phenomenon similar to modeling with the precondition of an affectional bond between the child and adult (Katz, P., 1979). Cognitive development teaches the child to experience a positive sense when acting in a gender-appropriate manner. It accentuates children's increasing understanding of their sexual identity and the meaning of the

sex roles as society views them (Williams, 1977).

Through this process, which begins at birth, children are shaped into fulfilling certain roles. "When the appearance of the external genitals is unequivocal, the infant is assigned to the appropriate sex; whether the parents are pleased or not, they do not question the assignment, and while their pleasure or displeasure may contribute to the intricacies of the child's developing masculinity or feminity, the child does not question if its body is that of the assigned sex" (Stroller, 1977, p. 63). These sex role differences are supported by interactions with others and by the educational system, the occupational world, and the media. For example, a well-received educational television program for preschool children consistently depicted girls playing with dollhouses and following after boys. Therefore, it taught children both how to spell and how to behave in culturally approved sex roles (Williams, 1977).

"In our society, females are supposed to be unaggressive physically and sexually, nurturant and caring toward others, expressive and friendly and attentive to their appearance. Males are expected to be physically and sexually assertive, independent, competent and emotionally tough" (Williams, 1977, pp. 171-172). From childhood, females are expected to be passive, unassertive, and compliant. This behavior is rewarded; deviance from it is not. However, the reward of success or accomplishment goes to men whose behavior is active, assertive, and autonomous.

Children develop their gender identification during their second year of life, and sex role behavior follows through the mechanisms of reinforcement, modeling, identification, and cognitive development. Parents socialize girls and boys to standards that are assigned by society. Boys are encouraged to function in an instrumental manner, to be achievement oriented with a love of competition. Girls are taught to function with an expressive focus, to be understanding, warm, and concerned about the welfare of others (Williams, 1977). Girls are urged to be nurturant, obedient, and responsible while boys are rewarded for achievement and self-reliance (Barry et al., 1972). "They (women) had been prepared since childhood for a life of unqualified giving, in a framework of stable, protective relationships" (Ehrenreich and English, 1979, p. 308).

Young women's role development is influenced by early experiences in the family. Achievement and competition are often seen as unfeminine goals and girls are encouraged to be sensitive to approval. This burden may hinder the development of self-confidence. Women are promised rewards for attractiveness, not for academic excellence. Social pressure often forces young women to conform to the feminine aim of finding a spouse and making a home (Williams, 1977).

Horner's research (1972) provides striking proof of this phenomenon. In a study of middle-class and upper-middle-class white female college students she found a motive to avoid success in response to the perceived negative consequences the young women expected success to bring. "It seems apparent that most, otherwise achievement-motivated, young white women when faced with a conflict between their feminine image and expressing their competences or developing their abilities and interests adjust their behavior to their internalized sex role stereotypes" (Horner, 1972, p. 67). Horner went on to state that these women in an effort to feel or appear more feminine, disguised their capabilities and retreated from the mainstream of thought, nontraditional aspiration, and accomplishment in society.

Thus by the time a young woman reaches her early teens she probably has been molded by her parents, the educational system, and the media. She is likely to be passive, unassertive, compliant, nurturant, and pleased to help others. As she matures, her education is chosen to support and intensify these characteristics. She strives to find a good husband, settle down, and raise a family or choose a traditional female occupation such as teaching or nursing. This shaping of women's behavior to passive and dependent roles explains one of the reasons why many women are passive victims of rape or battering.

As women become more aware of this conditioning and the myths and biases to which they are subject, patterns of submission will continue to change. One change is noted by women's challenge of male supremacy and the subsequent feeling of loss of power for many men. This feeling of loss of power may be a result of women's

employment because of personal interest or financial need and their demand for salaries, status, and promotions equivalent to those of men. Men's sense of powerlessness may be a result of women taking a more active role sexually and rejecting the double standard of sexual morality. Or men's feeling of powerlessness may be a result of increased educational opportunities for women and their adoption of additional professional roles.

There are other changes threatening the traditional balance of power. As more parents share child care, the result is children who are not socialized entirely by one parent. This change in parenting with more contact with the father may provide girls with rewards for achievement-oriented and assertive behavior. And as women continue to join the workforce, children are provided with other role models in addition to mother as housewife. Children of working mothers experience mother not only as nurturing parent but also as professional person or career woman who demonstrates assertion and ambition as positive qualities.

Today the educational system and the media are more sensitive to a variety of life-styles and cast women in different roles. There are more women attending graduate and professional schools than ever before. Although the message of "find a good husband and settle down" is still being promulgated, women who deviate from this model receive increased support and acceptance by society in general. Television now portrays women in nontraditional roles. They are portrayed as ambitious, achievement-conscious, and appropriately sexually assertive individuals. As a result of these influences, a woman can choose alternatives to the outdated stereotypical sex roles.

Another aspect of change is that women are redefining their relationship with their own mothers. The mother is the first same-sex person with whom a young girl has contact and through whose modeling and identification she learns what is feminine behavior. "The quality of the mother's life—however embattled and unprotected—is her primary bequest to her daughter, because a woman who can believe in herself, who is a fighter, and who continues to struggle to create livable space around her, is demonstrating to her daughter that these possibilities exist" (Rich, 1976, p. 204). Young girls who have mothers who are assertive, take initiative, maintain a career, and value academic success, learn that these characteristics are also part of feminine behavior.

To develop and support the growth of such characteristics as components of the feminine image, women are using individual and collective friendships with each other. The spread of consciousness-raising groups is an example of how women are utilizing collective friendships. The experience with consciousness-raising groups taught women that they could be as supportive of each other as they had been in traditional modes. In these groups women can help each other with events such as reproduction and menopause, as well as with physical illness, care of the sick, and provision of emotional support in times of crisis (Seiden, 1976). Networking constructs a support system by building on relationships with friends, acquaintances, and friends of friends. Women are using network systems to their advantage in seeking employment, in child care, and for assistance and encouragement. "The most important thing one woman can do for another is to illuminate and expand her sense of possibilities" (Rich, 1976, p. 204).

The change in women's view of their relationships with other women as important and useful is the result of women thinking more highly of themselves and each other. Networking used formally and informally has become very popular. The practice of women helping each other in times of crisis forms the basis for self-help groups in which women can explore multiple concerns including rape or battering directed against them.

Even though progress has been made in the advancement of women's self-image, there is a carryover from the customary value system in that institutional inequalities still exist. This is highlighted by the fact that many women as mature adults choose the role of mother and housewife. Millet (1970) examines the male-female power structure, which she contends is the basis for the exploitation of the female by the more powerful male. Dixon (1972, p. 189) extends this theory to include marriage: "the institution of marriage is the chief vehicle for the oppression of women, it is through the role of wife that the subjugation of women is maintained." The role of housewife is low-status unpaid labor. It is a 24-hour-a-day, 7-day-a-week job. There are no paid vacations, no holidays, and no uniform way of evaluation performance. However, in the realm of deferring personal needs, limiting potential, and depriving liberties, the combined role of housewife and mother cannot find an equal.

On the other hand, women who work outside the family are encumbered by other burdens. Women are paid low wages in comparison to men for the work they do, 59¢ to each dollar that men earn. Women average 40% less than men in the same occupations (Straus, 1979). The women who work both inside and outside the home must become "superwomen" handling the responsibility and pressure of two or three full-time jobs: housewife, mother, and paid employee. Often these women refuse to ask for assistance with their jobs of wife and mother because they believe that they should be able to handle these responsibilities or because they believe that they are following their husbands' wishes. The stress of work load and role change causes many women to be in conflict over what has priority among the roles of wife, mother, and employee. As women struggle to choose appropriate priorities and to complete their work load, they find that the end result is not efficient accomplishment of the work but rather emotional and physical turmoil. The men who are their lovers, husbands, colleagues, and supervisors may feel the effects of this turmoil and may fear that alleviation of women's struggle will result in a change in the power structure. To cope with this fear and their uncomfortableness with distressed women, men often react by attempting to impose rigid control over their wives, lovers, female colleagues, and subordinates.

THE MENTAL HEALTH OF WOMEN

As indicated in the preceding discussion, women are subjected to many pressures. Women are trying to cope with attempts to limit their roles, their work overload, and their own ambivalence over their role change and expansion. However, many women who were socialized to be passive, dependent, and nurturing are discovering that these behaviors are not effective in reducing these pressures or the stress of change. As would be expected, women are the primary consumers of mental health services and antianxiety medications. They are more accepting of the sick role and more likely than men to report somatic illnesses, depression, and suicidal thoughts (Chesler, 1972). Chesler maintains that the line between socially dictated feminine behavior and psychiatric pathology is a thin one. If a man possessed the personality traits that women have been encouraged to develop, he would be considered to have psychiatric difficulties.

Broverman et al. (1972) highlighted this problem by studying the attitudes of mental health clinicians. When they were asked to describe a mentally healthy man, woman, and adult, they indicated that their description of a mentally healthy man was identical to their description of a healthy adult, while a healthy female was defined by opposite descriptions. Therefore, their idea of a healthy man does not differ from their idea of a healthy adult, but in the case of women, their idea of a mature healthy woman differs from their adult health concept. These preconceived attitudes have significantly influenced the type of mental health care that women have received.

Women are taught to be more expressive and emotional than men. Their self-respect may depend on the quality of their interpersonal relationships, from which they receive admiration, appreciation, and affective rewards. Many are taught not to be interested in achievement or competition and the focus on the need for emotional protection makes them unlikely to take risks or allow themselves to be in conflict. While many women strive to accept competition, ambition, and accomplishment as feminine characteristics, institutions are often unprepared to recognize these behaviors as feminine and are often unwilling to understand the difficulties women experience in attempting to change the feminine image.

An example of institutional archaism and resistance to the changing needs of women can be illustrated by the manner in which women are often treated by the mental health system. It is perhaps doubtful that the interpretations and the process of transference as provided by Freudian therapists can build women's sense of self. The reason for this doubt is that the Freudian tradition fosters the domination of women. "The Freudian theories are based on the assumption of male superiority. They imply that the most fear provoking and disorganizing concept to the male concerns the possible loss of his masculinity; and the female, likewise acknowledging the supremacy of the phallus, is beset by feelings of inadequacy and resentment" (Bosselman, 1972, p. 251). With this basis, traditional psychotherapy has reproduced and strengthened the view of women as lacking in power because they will never possess the "desired" phallus. "The Freudian vision beholds woman as essentially warmhearted creatures, but more often as cranky children with uteruses, forever mourning the loss of male organs and male identity" (Chesler, 1972, p. 79). The girl becomes resigned to this fact and according to Freudian theory substitutes the wish for a phallus with the wish for a child. She at first strives to compete with mother for the love of father. This competition then is replaced by an identification with mother as the female child models passive behavior. "This passivity is assumed to stem from three factors: (a) the female is constitutionally less active and aggressive, (b) the female genital organ is not as appropriate as the male's for the expression of active or aggressive impulses and this leads to at least a partial renunciation of this mode, and (c) the social environment exerts pressure on the girl to inhibit activity and aggression" (May, 1972, p. 301).

How are women able to grow psychologically with the encumbrances of the paternalistic psychoanalytic model? How does this model reinforce the oppression of women and the submission to rape or battering? Does it offer the dynamics of feminine masochism and the need for an unhealthy equilibrium in a relationship as the primary reasons why some women tolerate rape or battering?

The mental health system must also change to be able to identify and properly address the problems of women in this society. To explain that the incidence of rape and battering of women is a private problem among selected unhealthy women who have a psychological need to be abused is a product of outdated attitudes about women. In a study of how psychiatric clinicians interact with abused wives, it was found that clinicians were inattentive, condemning, and skeptical in an attempt to prevent the pain of empathy (Hilberman, 1980). "This distancing is achieved by disbelief, labeling, and accusations that the victim 'needs' the abuse or could have controlled or prevented it by being less provocative, and the unfounded assumption that most victims come from poor or black families and are thus different from the clinician" (Hilberman, 1980, p. 1342). Clinicians need to recognize and to be in control of their need to seek distance from "the victim" to adequately treat women who have been violated.

Fortunately women can choose other therapeutic experiences than what is offered by Freudian-trained clinicians who have not yet succeeded in changing their approach toward the abused and toward "women's place." As mentioned, the 1960s saw the development of consciousness-raising groups. These groups began in New York City and were usually composed of 10 to 15 middle-class women from various occupational roles. In these groups different aspects of the feminine condition were discussed. "Consciousness raising is the name given to the feminist practice of examining one's personal experiences in the light of sexism, i.e., that theory which explains women's subordinate position in society as a result of a cultural decision to refer direct power on men and only indirect power on women" (Gornick, 1972, p. 171). Support was gathered as many women realized that theirs was not a unique position and, in fact, that many of the vicissitudes of their lives were directly related to their sex. Gornick feels that it is not one personal emotional history that explains problems but rather the influence of patriarchy. By participating in consciousness-raising groups, women not only can educate themselves about the effects of oppression and submission but also can receive support for changing their feminine identity.

Another example of mental health care appropriate to the current needs of women is feminist therapy. Feminist therapy is a type of treatment that seeks to make changes in mental health by incorporating the values of feminists and attempting to make women aware of the effect social oppression has had on their life. "Major trends in feminist therapy appear to include a grounding in current research about women, a relative priority given to environmental interpretations rather than intrapsychic ones, and a trend toward greater egalitarianism between therapist and patient" (Seiden, 1976, p. 1117). Feminist therapy does not necessarily have to be done only by a female therapist, but the therapist who espouses it should be comfortable with the issues confronting women as a result of their place in society. Feminist therapy seeks to destroy the "more powerful other" role of the therapist and replace it with a more equal balance of power. Autonomy and independence are encouraged. Assertion training, abandonment of sex role stereotypes, and diffusion of guilt are sought. The ability to generate options and alternatives and the process of problem solving are strengthened. In this context, assertive behavior is no longer seen as "castrating," and nurturing behavior is no longer seen as desirable.

In addition to traditional individual and group psychotherapy, therefore, consciousness raising, other self-help groups, and feminist therapy offer help for women in turmoil because of attempts at changing their femininity or because they are victims of violence.

VIOLENCE AGAINST WOMEN

Violence against women often takes the form of rape or battering. The increase in the expression of violence in society and growing attention to women's rights have also encouraged women to seek help in ameliorating their problems and improving their life situation.

The male-female power structure forms the basis of exploitation of females. Women have been socialized to adopt sex roles that reinforce the belief that they are inferior to men. They have been denied rights that have not been denied to men. "The facts of (women) denial were plain enough: they were told their development was less important and should not interfere with men's development: they were, in short, held less important, less valued, less valuable" (Miller and Mothner, 1978, p. 29). Men view themselves as the dominant group with women belonging to the subordinate group. "Mutually enhancing interaction is not probable between unequals. The dominant group is denied any truthful reaction to its action, consensual validation or feedback. With no wholly truthful reactions to guide them, the dominants go on dispensing all knowledge and wisdom for the society, building distortions on top of distortions" (Baker and Mothner, 1978, p. 29). This subservient position makes women feel that they are unable to protect themselves. They may feel that violence is to be expected. They may feel that they are powerless to escape it because it is condoned by society.

In addition to the attitudes their inferior status may engender, women's sex roles have supported passivity, nurturance, and compliance. Women's functioning with an expressive emphasis subjects them to unqualified devotion to others, burdensome responsibilities, and lifetime commitments. Self-esteem is inhibited by the need for approval. The lack of self-confidence and self-esteem prevents the development of assertive behavior. The need for emotional protection makes them uncomfortable when in conflict.

Adoption by women of an unaggressive, passive life-style seems to reinforce the attitude that women are to expect and to accept violence. Some women may feel that their "duty" to their partners is to meet physical and emotional needs. Successful performance of this duty may make some women feel worthwhile and useful. Inability to handle this responsibility can frequently precipitate guilt in women. Often women are identified as the ones who should have insight regarding the dynamics of the relationship and should use this knowledge to facilitate the continuation of the relationship. Unfortunately, in their attempts to maintain relationships, many women neglect or refuse to assert their own needs. Over time the result can be that these women suffer from low self-esteem and are in need of assertion training.

The development of self-esteem and self-confidence underlies the development of assertive behavior. Assertive behavior is defined as the expression of one's own ideas or perceptions without anxiety and without intruding on the ideas or perceptions of others (Withers, 1978). The Women's Liberation Movement has shown that a positive self-image is a necessary prerequisite for assertive behavior (Greenleaf, 1978). Greenleaf points out the circular nature of the relationship between behavior and self-image: if one does not behave assertively, self-confidence is lost; and if self-confidence is lacking, then assertive behavior is unlikely. Assertive training groups help women to build their self-image and to learn how to assert their needs, wants, and values.

BATTERING

As previously mentioned, this chapter will consider the specific problems of battering and rape as separate entities though the two problems often occur simultaneously. Battering transcends cultural, ethnic, and socioeconomic lines. It also occurs among those couples who are living together but who are not bound by formal marriage contracts. However, the institution of marriage has aided in the development of battering. "The married woman's loss of identity begins with the loss of her name. She takes her husband's domicile; she becomes his legal dependent. In most states he has sole financial authority within the marriage. Although the law says the husband must support the wife, if he decides to give her no money or clothing and provides her only with groceries for the table, she has no legal recourse" (Martin, 1976, p. 37). Martin believes that several factors predispose wife abuse. "It has its roots in historical attitudes toward women, socialization of rigid life roles according to one's sex and the power relationship of man over women in marriage and in society at large" (Martin, 1979, p. 10). In her opinion the solution involves changing the power structure. "Until women are on a par with men in the home, on the job, in educational opportunity, and in politics, they will continue to be vulnerable to be abused by the men in their lives" (Martin, 1979, p. 13).

From earliest times women were the property of their fathers and then their husbands. As property, they could be treated as such. "Rebellious women might be beaten privately (with official approval) or punished publicly by the village 'father,' and any woman who tried to survive on her own would be at the mercy of random male violence" (Ehrenreich and English, 1979, p. 11). The view of women as men's property began changing with the Industrial Revolution, which altered the rule of the father to reflect changes in the economy (Ehrenreich and English, 1979). However, since male-female inequality remains, there continues to be undertones of the phenomenon of women as property in sexual mores. Reed (1978) believes that the essence of male sexual control in society is based on the husband's exclusive possession of the wife, who risks serious penalties if she does not restrict her sexual activity to him alone.

Wife battering carries the burden of secrecy, denial, and projection. The power position of males in our society may add credence to the stereotypical view that the man is driven to battering by a nagging wife who seeks to be beaten. "Most battering husbands believe that they have the right to make all the decisions for the family and to mete out punishment if their demands are not met" (Martin, 1976, p. 72). In addition, many men assume that physical violence is an adaptive method of discharging stress and anger.

The man who batters the woman with whom he lives often does not appear to have been able to resolve his dependency feelings toward his own mother and hence all women. He is beset by feelings of low self-worth, incompetence, and weakness. He is angry with himself, frustrated, and disappointed with his life and its insecurity. "Abusers tend to feel weak and powerless, and must resort to violence to assure themselves that they are, in fact, strong and in control" (Fleming, 1979, p. 287). The man who is an abuser is usually unable to maintain his role as primary provider for his family. He displaces these negative feelings in an immature and aggressive manner by maintaining one area of success, the control of his home through beating

his wife. Violent feelings may have a variety of targets, but wife beating is often tolerated as a socially acceptable practice to discharge these feelings. "Many policemen personally believe that husbands do have legal right to hit their wives, providing it does not produce an injury requiring hospitalization—the so-called 'stitch rule' found in some cities" (Straus, 1979, p. 47). It is also probable that the husband who batters his wife either grew up in a family where his mother or siblings were beaten or where he himself was abused. According to Strauss, in this society children are taught that people respond to stress and frustration by aggression.

Women socialized in our present culture may feel in a powerless position. "Perhaps the most fundamental set of factors bringing about wife beating are those connected with the sexist structure of the family and society. In fact, to a considerable extent, the cultural norms and values permitting and sometimes encouraging husband-to-wife violence reflect the hierarchical and male-dominant type of society that characterizes the Western world" (Straus, 1979, p. 51). The longer women remain in these relationships, the longer their self-esteem is assailed. They feel imperfect, inadequate, and unattractive as a consequence of the violence in their lives and often come to feel that they are responsible and even deserving of the beatings (Weingourt, 1979). The culture ultimately continues to see success in marriage as the burden of the wife. Success in marriage means success as a women because marriage is the role to which "properly" socialized women should aspire whether they are beaten or not. Women tend to accept responsibility for the success of the marriage because they do not see themselves as existing separately from their husbands and children. Although, this is a burden it is also the source of pride (Weingourt, 1979).

Men who batter their wives give various reasons for their behavior as noted in the following quote. "His stated reasons for his use of violence vary: he may say it's because of stress at work, because he was worried about money, because she taunted him, because he was drunk, because she was pregnant, because she bought the wrong kind of mustard. The one thing these excuses have in common is self-justification—it was not his fault" (Fleming, 1979, p. 96).

Children are the unfortunate viewers of family violence. Straus (1979) believes that the family is the first setting where most people experience violence. He goes on to state that 90% of parents use physical punishment, which teaches children that those who love have the right to hit. The feelings of children after viewing a beating range from anger with their parents to guilt toward themselves for not stopping or helping to stop the assault. Children become confused especially when family violence is an everyday occurrence. They begin to feel that acting on violent impulses is acceptable and will continue the pattern as they grow older.

Given this picture of aggression and shame, why does a woman stay in such a relationship? The primary motivation to maintain the unhealthy status quo is fear: fear for herself and fear for her children. Other reasons include hope that the man will reform, lack of alternate housing, lack of financial independence, feelings of love toward the man, belief that the man is not responsible because he is ill and needs help, fear of being alone, fear of reprisals, belief that this is part of the marriage contract, and religious or cultural teachings that endorse the continuation of marriage and the avoidance of divorce. Seligman's concept of learned helplessness (1975) also offers an explanation of why women feel trapped in relationships of battering against them. Because of multiple factors preventing action and because of attempts to leave that have failed, the woman beings to feel that no one and nothing can free her from her situation. This lack of hope for change can engender inactivity. "This expectation of powerlessness and inability to control one's destiny, whether real or perceived, prevents effective action" (Hilberman, 1980, p. 1343).

Interventions with battered women

Women who are battered usually come to the emergency unit only when injuries are serious enough to require immediate medical care. When the injuries are thought to be less serious, there is a tendency for the victim to feel too humiliated and embarrassed to seek treatment. Other wom-

en with minor injuries may not seek treatment because they rationalize that this is the final beating because "he will reform," or they may fear his reprisals. Many women blame themselves for causing assaults against themselves and believe that by changing their behavior, they are taking precautions against future abuse. Because many women think that they understand how they provoked the beating, they begin to build hope that the violence will stop as they demonstrate the "right" behavior. This hope that the "right" behavior will be recognized and appreciated by the abuser is reinforced by post-assault expressions of contriteness and affection. Additionally, many women refer to these post-assault reconciliations as evidence that the hurtful situation will improve. However, improvement rarely occurs.

It is important for clinicians to keep these facts in mind during their assessment of battered clients. Initial nondirective questioning and an attitude of concern will foster a willingness in the client to participate in physical and psychiatric assessment.

Battering should be suspected when a woman comes to the emergency unit with soft tissue trauma, lacerations, or fractures. In a psychiatric emergency unit a woman whose chief complaint is depression or anxiety should be questioned about physical abuse. Optimally, a psychiatric clinician should be assigned to clients when there is suspicion of battering. This clinician can act as an advocate by explaining necessary medical procedures and questioning to the client. Before examinations are initiated, it may be important to minimize the fact that the clinician is a member of the psychiatric emergency unit. Psychiatric clinicians can be introduced as counselors, nurses, physicians, or social workers or in other general terms in an attempt to prevent the arousal of the client's negative reactions toward the word *psychiatric*. Many victims may fear that if they are being assisted by clinicians with expertise in mental health care, that they will be viewed as being mentally disordered. These fears and negative associations over receiving psychiatric help can result in a rejection of the psychiatric clinician's skills. Such a rejection would be unfortunate since psychiatric emergency staff are very skilled in crisis intervention techniques and have been called to spend extended time with clients who have been battered.

To offset this potential rejection, clinicians can explain that family violence is a common occurrence and, more importantly, should appear calm, knowledgeable, in control, and nonjudgmental. Reassurance should be offered at every step of the evaluation and physical examination. Clients need to feel that psychiatric emergency clinicians are with them to answer questions, to provide support, and to discuss feelings.

When questioning begins, the victim may give an explanation of how the injury occurred in a manner that shields the attacker from any responsibility. To immediately question this account may threaten the client and force her to defend her story. She is probably feeling frightened and concerned about her safety. The man who battered her may be in the waiting room or on his way to the hospital. She may be confronting her denial of the seriousness of this matter for the first time. It is important that clinicians be sensitive to these concerns and intervene with gentle questioning regarding the existence of these fears.

If the client is not immediately assigned a psychiatric clinician, the medical clinician should proceed with the physical assessment and an effort should be made to establish rapport. After completion of medical treatment, the clinician should ask the client if events before the injury can be reviewed. At this time it may be possible to ask questions to clarify or confirm details. If the client maintains that the injury was the result of an accident, the clinician should begin to question this in as gentle and nonthreatening a way as possible. For example, one might say, "I understand, Ms. Jones, that your injury was caused by a fall. However, I have seen similar injuries that were inflicted during family disagreements." After this first attempt to establish an alliance, the stage is set to begin talking about something the client finds very difficult to discuss. It would then be important to state something like this: "Here at the hospital there are trained people who can help with this type of situation. No woman has to live with that kind of fear." If the client continues to insist that the

injury was accidental, the clinician should not pursue the matter. Perhaps a comment that if in the future the client discovers anyone who experiences family violence, the hospital's psychiatric emergency unit can be contacted. It should be explained that the psychiatric emergency unit is open 24 hours a day and has staff trained to help with difficult family problems.

If the client has continued to refuse crisis intervention, it is important to note in her chart that because of the nature of her injuries that there was some suspicion that she had been the victim of battering. It is useful to document this clearly as a suspicion and not as a fact. The next clinician may then more actively pursue the need for crisis intervention during subsequent emergency unit visits.

The client who is willing to discuss the circumstances of her battering should be referred to the hospital's psychiatric emergency unit for crisis intervention and follow-up. The client should be seen as soon as possible and lengthy delays in the emergency unit waiting area should be avoided. Often the referral can be made while the client is awaiting the results of x-rays or other tests. It is useful for the client to know that the medical clinician and the psychiatric clinician have, with the client's permission, communicated and exchanged information. The psychiatric clinician should interview the client in a private area and address the issue of safety. If the assailant is in the emergency unit, he should not be involved until the clinician has an understanding of what has happened and until the woman has made a decision about how she is going to proceed. It is useful to have police officers on duty in the emergency unit in the event that the situation escalates or the woman decides that she wishes to press charges.

The psychiatric clinician must convey to the client that her situation is not unique and that the clinician will not be shocked or frightened by what she has to say. The clinician should explain that to be helpful it is important to understand what has happened and that the information is confidential and can only be given to others with the client's written permission. The clinician should explain that the violence will not stop unless something is done and, in fact, that the violence will become more serious and more frequent. The clinician must seize this postcrisis phase as an opportunity to provide alternatives at a time when the client's resistance and denial are low and she is more available for interventions.

The client should be asked to tell the clinician what has happened, that is, to describe the battering in as much detail as possible. If the client appears to be having difficulty talking about what happened, the clinician should ask questions that may make it easier to focus on the incident. These may include questions that ask what was happening before the assault, what happened during the assault, and what happened after the assault. There are three phases to the assaultive incident: the building up of tension, the release of tension during which time the assault occurs, and the postassault phase. Information should be gathered about each phase. The more structured and detailed questions are, the easier data gathering will be.

Other important questions include the type of living situation, person with whom the client lives, numbers of children and their ages, the client's previous experience with battering or sexual assault with this man or with another, and who knows about the violence. During the discussion of the incident the clinician should begin to assess how the client can best be helped. This includes an evaluation of the client's support system: family, friends, neighbors, and other people who could be of benefit to the client. The clinician should ask the client if the police were called before her arrival at the emergency room and the details of her interaction with them and her assailant. The clinician should explore with the client whether alcohol or other drugs were used before the battering. Alcohol and drugs release inhibitions and make control of aggressive behavior difficult. The use of alcohol or drugs may seriously complicate the situation. This client can be referred to Al-Anon and the partner to Alcoholics Anonymous or a drug treatment program.

The clinician begins to plan the intervention by asking clients how they want to proceed. Some clients are ready for continued crisis intervention to help them decide what to do and to help them to pursue legal action. However, many women are too frightened to receive assistance with decision making. Clinicians need to first explore these fears and then list the clients' options. The options should include the possibility of crisis intervention or group treatment, a place to live if she decides to leave her home, and information concerning legal action.

The clinician should be concerned about the safety of the woman and her children. No woman should return to a home where she or her children are in immediate danger. The clinician must ask the client if there are ongoing threats to her safety. Straus (1978) states that the largest single category of murder victim relationship is between family members and also points out that more than half of American households contain hand guns. The clinician must question the client to discover if there is a gun or other deadly weapon in the house. If the client is returning to a home where there is a weapon, the weapon should be given to the police.

If the client feels unsafe, alternate housing must be found. The client may have a family member or a friend who will offer shelter. This type of shelter can be used if her attacker will not know where she is. Many cities have temporary shelters for battered women and their children. The advantage of battered women's shelters is that their location is usually not known to the assailant. They are frequently staffed by women counselors, many of whom have been the victims of assault. These women are able to understand the victim's dynamics and can provide assistance from their vantage point of having endured and successfully ended their own injurious life-style.

If the victim says that she can safely go home, a return appointment should be made with the psychiatric emergency clinician for the next day. It is important to see the client again within a short period of time so that the ambivalence that many women experience does not grow. Since child care may be a problem, it should be offered at the hospital so the client cannot use it as an excuse to avoid the appointment. It may be available through a volunteer program.

At the second appointment the clinician should clarify the scope and focus of the crisis intervention. It should be stated that the client and the clinician will meet weekly or twice weekly for 6 weeks to discuss how the client can best deal with her present situation. Crisis intervention theory teaches that intensive discussion of stressful and difficult situations aids in the development of adaptive coping mechanisms and crisis resolution (Aguilera and Messick, 1978). Therefore, in crisis intervention with the battered woman, the client needs to be asked for a description of the details of the assault or assaults. The clinician should inform the client of the availability of the psychiatric emergency unit at the hospital and the telephone number of the unit should another crisis develop suddenly. It is best if the same clinician sees the client each time she comes to the psychiatric emergency unit to provide for continuity of care. However, it is also useful to introduce the client to at least one other clinician in the event that the assigned clinician is absent when the client calls.

The clinician should continue to explore with the client the extent of the problem. "The real and perceived powerlessness of the battered woman is what stands between her and self-determination. Providing her with the support that she needs to retake control of her life is the primary function of the counselor or therapist" (Fleming, 1979, p. 122) Coping mechanisms used by the client should be determined. They may be both adaptive and maladaptive. Statements that she deserved the beating are evidence of a maladaptive coping style. "The extremely low levels of self-esteem found among many battered women allow them to conclude that although they may not be worthy of much, at least they merit the attention of a beating" (Fleming, 1979, p. 85). This low esteem inhibits assertive behavior. Without assertive behavior the woman has difficulty protecting her rights and she cannot make decisions. She may continue to keep her partner's behavior a secret, to make excuses for it, and to hope that he will change. She may not believe that she can escape. Her behavior is influenced by these attitudes.

Adaptive attitudes also affect behavior. The woman must guard against isolation and denial of the violence. She must practice assertive behavior and attempt to get a job to free herself

financially from her partner. Investigating her legal options, she can learn what to expect if she calls the police. For example, she does not have to tolerate any indications that the police are undermining or disputing the seriousness of her report or that the police will not protect her if she decides to leave. She should know her rights regarding police arrest, citizen's arrest, and the restraining orders of her assailant and be sure to get the number of the police report, the officers' names, and their badge numbers. She should request photos of her injuries and save anything that might be considered evidence of battering. By informing her neighbors and friends of the problem and encouraging their help should an emergency arise, she can work out a plan for them to call the police if she is beaten again and unable to call herself. She should make a plan for leaving in an emergency, taking with her any important documents (birth certificates of herself and her children, marriage license, credit cards, bank books, insurance certificates, lease to apartment or deed to house), money, keys, and jewelry but not taking anything that belongs only to her husband. She must learn her financial, emotional, and legal resources.

Children who are exposed to battering have pervasive and often severe reactions that are of concern to the client. It is usually not a secret to children that there is family violence. Children become frightened when adults appear out of control. They may worry that the fighting is their fault or that they are next in line to be beaten. They may identify with the battering and continue it as they mature. A study of children from violent families (Munson and Hilberman, 1978) demonstrated that boys exhibited aggressive, disruptive behavior and girls exhibited withdrawn, passive behavior. If the clinician believes that the child's exposure to battering has caused significant trauma, the child should be referred to a child therapist. Symptoms that indicate a need for a referral include multiple physical complaints, many seemingly unfounded fears, poor school achievement, difficult peer relationships, and separation difficulties.

After several appointments the clinician and client should have reviewed her options and planned interventions to resolve the crisis. The next steps are to implement these interventions (leaving the home, securing a restraining order, telling family and friends of the problem) and to evaluate the results of these interventions.

The clinician must decide at the end of crisis intervention with the battered woman if longer term therapy is needed. If the clinician assesses that the crisis has not been resolved, continued treatment is necessary. Indicators of the need for further treatment are the client's expression of depression, grief, or anger to the point that these feelings impair her functioning. In addition, she may report prolonged periods of sleeplessness, lack of appetite, or listlessness. The client may ask that therapy be continued to help with her immediate situation or to help her mediate between other systems such as legal aid, financial services, or employment counseling. Psychiatric emergency clinicians need to understand the three stages a woman must experience to free herself from the battering relationship (Wiengourt, 1979) if clinicians are to effectively work with these women in continued therapy. These stages are related to mourning and loss. The first stage is "ambivalence." The woman feels a sense of terror and foreboding. This terror changes to guilt and self-recrimination, and she sees herself as failing in the relationship. She gets angry but usually displaces this anger onto the clinician. "Counseling appointments are missed, demands for counseling are made at inappropriate times and shelter rules are broken" (Weingourt, 1979, p. 46). The clinician must focus the anger toward the appropriate object while at the same time helping the client to give up the position of nonresponsible victim.

The client then moves into the second stage called "awareness of the impact." The client begins to realize the immensity of the job if she is to take control of her life. She feels sad, isolated, and fearful of what is to come. Anger is more readily experienced in this stage as is guilt. However, there may also be a positive change. "The woman becomes aware that she does not have to allow this to go on any longer. If she chooses to accept the victim role with all of its positive and negative ramifications then she can also cast it aside" (Weingourt, 1979, p 46).

The final stage is called "acceptance of loss." The client must realign her life according to her new self-image; she must define new patterns of behavior and implement them. Weingourt views this as a stage of readiness and reconciliation.

Hilberman (1980, p. 1345) states that there are beliefs that must be challenged by the clinician working with the battered woman. These include the beliefs that violence is normal, exercisable, and manageable. "These beliefs reinforce the battered woman's tenuous denial and protect her husband and her marriage at the expense of her self-esteem and autonomy and possibly, her life."

Case vignette #1

Mrs. R, a 45-year-old married woman, was brought to the emergency unit by her 18-year-old daughter. She had been cut on the face by her husband in a family argument. The client, who spoke very little English, had been in this country 6 years. The daughter interpreted for the hospital staff and the laceration was sutured. Because of the seriousness of the injury, Mrs. R was referred to a psychiatric emergency clinician.

The daughter, M, reported that her parents had been having marital difficulties for many years. According to M, her father drank a great deal and beat her mother when he was intoxicated. The client agreed with this account, also mentioning that her husband was out of work and that financial problems seemed to make things worse. Mrs. R stated that when not intoxicated her husband was a reasonable man.

Because of the client's religious and cultural background, she was unwilling to consider any therapy for herself. She was given a referral to an Al-Anon group that had been formed by other women with the same cultural and ethnic background. Through her attendance in Al-Anon the client convinced her husband to attend AA. Continued attendance at AA and Al-Anon eventually solved this couple's problem.

Case vignette #2

Ms. G, a 33-year-old divorced mother of a 6-year-old son, walked into the psychiatric emergency unit requesting an evaluation. She stated that she had been living with a man for 2 years who had begun to beat her when they argued. Ms. G had last been beaten 3 days ago but had not come to the emergency unit because she was afraid that people might ask questions. However, she began to fear that her boyfriend might begin to beat her child so she decided to get information from the hospital so that she would know what to do if she were battered again.

The clinician and Ms. G began talking about the details of the beatings. There did not appear to be any specific pattern to them except that they were becoming more frequent. Ms. G's boyfriend felt sorry afterward and would always promise to stop. Ms. G wanted to move out of his apartment but was out of work and did not think that her Aid to Dependent Children payments could support both her and her son.

The clinician and Ms. G reviewed other housing possibilities as options until she found a job. Ms. G throught that a girlfriend might be willing to rent a room in her apartment to her and her son for a small amount of money.

The clinician warned Ms. G that she should not inform her boyfriend of her new address when she moved. The clinician also reminded Ms. G of the possibility of pressing charges should she be beaten again.

The client was seen several days later. She had moved in with her friend and informed her boyfriend of her desire to terminate the relationship by letter. He did not know where to reach her. She had begun looking for work and felt an increased sense of self-respect because she was no longer being beaten. She expressed an interest in continuing to see the clinician on a weekly basis. After six sessions she was referred to her community mental health center for continued therapy at her own request.

RAPE

Women who are raped present a somewhat different clinical picture than women who are battered. Rape is similar to wife battering in that it is a confrontation between male and female, whether strangers, husband and wife, or two people living together. Rape is defined as "forced sexual aggression which results in a disruption of the individual's physical, emotional and sexual equilibrium" (Burgess and Holmstrom, 1979, p. 203). It is not a sexual act but an act of aggression and violence. Brownmiller states that for men who rape, the penis is used as a weapon to subjugate women; that men have the potential to transform their biological tool to a weapon must be forever conscious to women. "Man's structural capacity to rape and woman's corresponding structural vulnerability are as basic to the physiology of both our sexes as the primal act of sex itself" (Brownmiller, 1975, p. 4).

The woman feels herself to be helpless against her attacker in a potentially life-threatening situation. "Rape became not only a male prerogative, but man's basic weapon of force against women, the principal agent of his will and her fear. His forcible entry into her body, despite her physical protestations and struggle, became the vehicle of his victorious conquest over her being, the ultimate test of his superior strength, the triumph of his manhood" (Brownmiller, 1975, p. 5). Rapes between men are occurring with increasing frequency, but for the purposes of this chapter, only male-female rapes will be considered.

The rape of women began in earliest time and Brownmiller points out that historically marriage was a solution to rape. "Female fear of an open season of rape, and not a natural inclination toward monogamy, motherhood or love, was probably the single causative factor in the original subjugation of woman by man, the most important key to her historic dependence, her domestication by protective mating . . . the historic price of woman's protection by man against man was the imposition of chastity and monogamy. A crime committed against her body became a crime against the male estate" (Brownmiller, 1975, p. 6). Woman was man's property and as such was part of the spoils of war. The rapes of women are poorly documented in war and revolution, but they did occur in large numbers. "Rape is the quintessential act by which a male demonstrates to a female that she is conquered—vanquished—by his superior strength and power (Brownmiller, 1975, p. 44).

History reveals the rape of American Indian women and white women by their captors and the rape of black slaves by their masters. In some countries raping a woman was not a crime unless she lived with her husband or father. Her "honor" belonged to them. If she lived alone, she had no "honor" to be stolen through rape; therefore no crime was committed.

Burgess and Holmstrom (1979) describe four types of rape: (1) blitz rape—occurs without any previous interaction between the victim and the assailant, (2) confidence rape—the assailant obtains sex through deceit, betrayal, or violence, (3) accessory to sex—the assailant obtains sex through pressure, and (4) sex stress—the partners agree to have sexual relations but then something goes wrong.

Groth (1979), who studies sex offenders, maintains that rape serves nonsexual needs; he also reiterates the themes of anger and power. The man who rapes is rarely an oversexed individual who is looking for multiple targets to diffuse his sexual feelings. Often, in fact, he is impotent. He is not usually psychotic or bizarre. He does not rape because he is confronted by a woman who is dressed "provocatively." He rapes because he has a need to discharge violent impulses toward another and to subjugate another to his power. "The woman is often a faceless object for the rapist's expression of hostility and the victim feels degraded and used" (Notman and Nadelson, 1976, p. 410).

Women, because of their socialization process, are an accessible target for the rapist. The frustrated, violent man chooses a woman as the object of violence, humiliation, and domination because she is below him in the social strata. For a man who feels he is a failure as a man, often the only group he feels superior to are women. For a woman who is the victim, rape is a terrifying and dehumanizing experience. "The rape victim usually has had an overwhelming frightening experience in which she fears for her life

and pays for her freedom in the sexual act . . . rape involves an overwhelming confrontation with another's sadism and aggression and one's own vulnerability" (Notman and Nadelson, 1976, p. 409).

Unfortunately, in the present social and criminal system, the burden of proof is on the victim. Often she is judged by the amount of struggle that occurred, the number of bruises or injuries that she had, and how hard she tried to flee from her assailant. In no other life-threatening crime with perhaps the exception of wife battering, does society expect that the victim fight and try to get away. Rape is the only violent crime that looks to the victim for responsibility (Katz and Mazur, 1979). The victim is asked by police, by the courts, by her family, and sometimes by clinicians, if she in any way behaved provocatively: in her attire, behavior, or mere presence. In this society being alone at night on the street may be viewed as provocative behavior. A victim of a nighttime street rape will be made to feel that she is responsible for the rape. However, a woman who is raped by a man who breaks into her apartment at night while she is sleeping will get more sympathy and support.

Interventions with women who have been raped

A woman who has been the victim of a rape has the potential of being victimized in numerous ways. She is initially victimized physically and emotionally by the assailant. She may then be victimized by the police and others who may ask difficult and probing questions in a brusque manner. She may be victimized by the hospital staff if they appear judgmental while they complete her examination. She may be victimized by the lawyers if, as they question her about her past life, they state or imply that she played a role in the rape. She may be victimized by her own memories and nightmares.

Because of the potential for continued victimization and the fear of reprisals, many victims do not report rape to the police. In fact, they may not tell anyone what has happened. Victims frequently deny the impact of the potentially life-threatening experience that they survived. However, these victims feel the burden of keeping this secret from family and friends. They may remain distrustful and easily frightened because they have not had an opportunity to resolve this crisis. Many years later, in a similar situation or one that brings back the memory of the rape, victims may experience emotional symptoms.

If the woman decides to report the rape to the police the first action taken by the officers is to take a brief preliminary report of the rape. They will then help the victim obtain medical evaluation and treatment. It is important that the victim not change her clothes, wash, or douche, before the arrival of the police or before the physical examination at the hospital as she may destory evidence. Washing or douching may remove pubic hair or semen, which would be noted by the physician at the time of gynecological examination.

At the hospital the woman should be greeted by a clinician who is experienced in counseling rape victims. This clinician should remain with the victim while she is medically evaluated. The clinician should reassure the woman that she is safe and will not be harmed any further. A history will be obtained before a thorough physical examination is initiated. The results of the examination are recorded to document any injuries in addition to the sexual trauma. A gynecological examination is performed, and specimens are collected to test for venereal disease and the presence of semen.

The clinician should be alert to the psychological impact of the gynecological examination. It is preferable that this procedure be performed by a female physician. If only male physicians are on duty, it is imperative that a female staff member be present during the examination. Procedures may be more uncomfortable and painful because of the trauma that has occurred during the rape. In addition, at a time when a woman is feeling powerless this examination recapitulates the sense of invasion she experienced.

The victim should be questioned as to the type of sexual contact (oral, anal, or vaginal) so that all appropriate specimens may be collected. These specimens will serve as legal evidence during court proceedings and need to be collected according to specific protocol. Penicillin or tetra-

cycline may be given to prevent the contraction of venereal disease. The question of a possible pregnancy must also be addressed. All methods of pregnancy prevention available should be offered such as an intrauterine device, diethylstilbestrol (DES), or other medication. Instead of using preventive measures, the client may wish to wait to discover if she is pregnant. After confirmation of the pregnancy she can request a menstrual extraction or abortion. These procedures need to be explained to the client even if she chooses to use DES because DES is not totally effective in preventing a pregnancy.

Further explanation of the serious side effects of DES should be provided by the prescribing physician. DES allegedly causes problems in children born of the pregnancy during which DES was used. These problems are cancer in daughters and testicular abnormalities in sons. It is believed it may also activate a latent cancer in the rape victim. Since nausea is a common side effect of this drug, antiemetics should also be considered. The client should be informed of the need to be treated for gonorrhea 4 to 7 days after the rape, tested for syphillis within 6 to 8 weeks after a rape, and tested for pregnancy six weeks after the client's last menstrual period.

It is important that each part of this procedure be explained in as much detail as required by the client. These explanations may need to be repeated several times so the victim understands what her choices are and the potential consequences of her chosen course of action. The response of victims may vary appearing upset and shaken to appearing in control (Burgess and Holmstrom, 1974).

The clinician must not forget that no matter how calm the victim appears, she is still distressed at having been in a potentially life-threatening situation. The clinician should be supportive in a direct manner and convey to the woman that there is nothing to fear and that the clinician is in control. The victim may want to ask questions or she may want to begin to tell the clinician what has happened. The clinician should establish a trusting relationship in hope that it will make the victim feel less powerless. This relationship can be strengthened by the clinician's concern for the client and the expertise that the clinician gains in working with other victims.

If the police questioning has not occurred before arrival at the hospital, it should be initiated immediately after the physical examination so that the victim has an opportunity to remember and report as many of the details of the act as possible. It is important for the victim to be as specific as she can: many small and seemingly insignificant details can provide clues. The victim should be advised to write down the details of her attack so that she does not forget and has an outline to refer to in future questioning. If the victim has come to the emergency unit on her own she may reconsider reporting the rape to the police. The clinician should accept the victim's decision and not attempt to influence her. If the police are involved, the victim may also decide not to pursue legal action. The client may need assistance in telling the police that she has changed her mind. The decision whether to pursue legal action can be delayed several days as long as specimens have been collected immediately and according to protocol. If the victim decides not to involve the police, the clinician must inform her that emergency unit staff members are legally bound to make a police report that lists her name, address, the type of assault, and the type and degree of injuries. However, it must be understood that a police investigation will not be done unless she requests one.

After the physical examination is completed, the clinician should assess the client's emotional state. The degree of her distress can be evaluated as she responds to questions regarding the details of the assault. If the client has difficulty describing what happened, the clinician can ask: "Have you ever seen the man who assaulted you before? Where were you when the assault occurred? What happened when he assaulted you? Was a weapon involved? Did you feel that your life was in danger? Have you ever been sexually or physically assaulted? Have you ever been the victim of incest?" Other questions may relate to the specifics of the incident.

The clinician should then review the physical and emotional symptoms that the client may experience. This information should be given to the client in writing so that she can refer to it in the future. An excellent source of information regarding behavioral, somatic, and psychological sequelae to rape can be found in *The Rape Trauma Syndrome* (Burgess and Holmstrom, 1974). The clinician should help the client to anticipate these symptoms so that she will not be surprised or frightened when they occur. The physical symptoms include those related to any physical trauma (soft tissue injury or muscle stiffness). Also possible are gastrointestinal syndromes including nausea, vomiting, diarrhea, abdominal pains, and anorexia. There may be a urinary tract infection because of irritation of the urinary meatus.

Emotional symptoms may include sleep disturbances such as difficulty falling asleep, difficulty staying asleep, or nightmares. These may be a result of fearing a recurrent attack when she is asleep. Other emotional symptoms are depression and phobias subsequent to an intense preoccupation with the details of the rape. For example, the victim could have a phobia of small closed spaces if the attack occurred in a car. The victim can show a marked change in her relationships. She may have great difficulty resuming her normal functioning and may become withdrawn. She may experience a lack of sexual interest.

Compound reactions are defined by Burgess and Holmstrom (1974) in clients who have a past or present history of physical, emotional, or social problems in addition to the rape trauma syndrome. This group includes women who have had previous psychiatric admissions. Former symptoms may be exacerbated by the stress of the rape, and the client may need to be evaluated for psychiatric treatment or for brief hospitalization. Women who abuse drugs or alcohol may also have more complicated reactions to the rape. This may be because they had these substances in their systems when the rape occurred and were therefore at a disadvantage. The stress of the rape may worsen their substance abuse. Another group of women who may have compound reactions are prostitutes. The prostitute may have difficulty convincing the police that a rape has occurred because of her previous contact with them and a possible history of arrests. These victims often do not pursue legal recourse. Prostitutes often respond more to the physical abuse related to the rape than to the sexual abuse. Because of the traumatic effects of being raped and because of her difficulties with the police, the prostitute is at a severe physical and emotional risk when she returns to the street.

Burgess and Holmstrom discuss the silent rape reaction that is manifested in women who have been raped at some previous time and who have not resolved this earlier attack. The reason that the rape has not been resolved is because the woman has not told anyone, has denied her emotional reaction to the rape, and has attempted to handle the situation alone. The second rape brings back the memory of the first attack. The clinician should again question the victim concerning experiences similar to the rape. This will allow her to talk about previous rapes or incest. These previous experiences must be discussed if the clinician is to help the client with the present situation.

After the clinician has reviewed some of the expected symptoms, it is important to ascertain whether the client has any questions about these symptoms or the medical treatment that she has received. The clinician should then give the client an opportunity to again review the incident in full detail if she wishes. At this time the clinician may ask the client questions about her affective state and the nature of her support system. In some cases the victim may be with a friend or family member. If she is not, perhaps she can call someone who will stay with her or can provide the victim with a place to live on a temporary basis. Again, the safety of the woman should be the primary concern. If the rape occurred in her home or apartment she should find another place to stay. She may need to decide if she should move from her present living situation.

As the interview continues, the clinician needs to evaluate the victim's coping style. Does the woman appear to be handling the stress? Has she been able to mobilize her resources and begun to make decisions? As noted, in working with battered women the therapeutic task is to help the victim free herself from constant threats to her safety. This is done through work aimed at increasing trust, improving self-worth, and de-

creasing the sense of alienation that battered women feel.

The woman who has been raped usually does not have to live with the attacker. The threat to her safety is not the same as for the woman who lives with a man who batters. The therapeutic task for the woman who has been raped is to help the victim deal with her sense of powerlessness after this violent and degrading event.

The client who has been raped should be given as much control over her life as possible. In planning the intervention the clinician should ask the client how she wants to proceed. Areas that need to be discussed include where will she stay at present, who will she tell about what happened, will she tell her family, husband, or lover, will she continue to go to work or school, will she pursue criminal investigation. It is the responsibility of the psychiatric emergency clinician to fulfill the advocacy role while encouraging the client to verbalize her feelings about the subsequent change in her life.

In many areas of the country there is a specific rape crisis group, often affiliated with a women's center. It may be of the self-help type composed of women who have been raped. This type of group may be an excellent referral for the client. The rape crisis group may also provide individual counselors who stay with the victim throughout all procedures: the medical examination, the police report, the identification of the assailant, the probable cause hearing, the grand jury hearing, and the trial. Each step of this long and complicated process should be explained to the victim in as much detail as she needs.

Therapeutic interaction with the rape victim should be based on the model of crisis intervention that addresses the present situation and looks at the past only in terms of previously used coping skills. The client must decide to see a psychiatric emergency unit clinician or to see a rape crisis counselor. If she chooses a rape crisis counselor, this person should be called as soon as possible and should meet the victim while she is still in the emergency unit. If the rape crisis unit does not provide 24-hour coverage, the victim should be given a counselor's telephone number and advised to call the counselor. The psychiatric emergency unit clinician will need to secure the client's permission to also report to the counselor. The clinician will need to call the client on the following day to verify that she has contacted the rape crisis counselor.

If the client chooses to see a psychiatric emergency unit clinician, a contract should be made to determine the scope and focus of the treatment. The degree of disorganization and upset caused by the rape and the quality of the support system can give the clinician a yardstick in determining the frequency of the treatment sessions. Frequency may also be affected by the decision to press charges once the assailant is apprehended; resolution of the crisis becomes more complicated when the court process drags the proceedings on for months and years. A general guideline for the duration of sessions is 6 weeks. The clinician must be available to act as an advocate for the client by accompanying her when she meets with the police or goes to court. The client also needs to know the hours of operation and the phone number of the psychiatric emergency unit should she need immediate help with another crisis. Again, it is best if the same clinician sees the client each time she comes to the psychiatric emergency unit to provide for continuity of care. However, it is also useful to introduce the client to at least one other clinician in the event that the client needs assistance when her usual clinician is absent.

At the end of the 6 weeks of crisis intervention, the client and clinician may reevaluate their contract. It may be necessary to refer the client for psychotherapy especially if the situation is complicated by a compound reaction or by a silent rape reaction. The client may also wish a referral to the rape crisis center instead of or in addition to a mental health clinic referral.

Case vignette #3

Ms. T an 18-year-old woman, was brought to the psychiatric emergency unit by the police. She had been raped earlier that evening. She fled from her assailant and walked for several miles before she found help. She refused medical examination but did agree to talk with a psychiatric clinician.

Ms. T had met the man who raped her in the downtown area in a record store. They began a conversation which ended in the man's suggesting that Ms. T come to his apartment for dinner. Ms. T arrived at the apartment, which was on the outskirts of the city. After dinner the man suggested making love, but Ms. T refused. He then overpowered her and raped her. She escaped but was unsure whether to seek police help because the man was someone she knew.

The clinician supported Ms. T's decision to proceed with legal action. The clinician also persuaded Ms. T to have a medical examination so evidence could be collected. After Ms. T had made her statement to the police, she and the clinician reviewed the events of the rape. The client agreed to a follow-up appointment with the clinician and a referral to a rape crisis group.

Case vignette #4

Ms. B, a 20-year-old college student, was knocked down and raped as she jogged alone in the park. She was badly beaten by her assailant and was brought to the emergency unit by ambulance. On arrival she appeared dazed, confused, and in shock. She was bruised on the face and upper torso; there were abrasions and lacerations on her legs and she was bleeding vaginally. There was no loss of consciousness.

Ms. B asked that a clinician call her sister who lived nearby so that she could be with her. The police questioning was deferred until after her medical evaluation. The medical examination was completed and treatment was instituted. There were no fractures, vital signs were stable, and several lacerations were sutured. The client was released to her sister. Since her sister was in the emergency unit, the psychiatric emergency clinician had not been initially called. The police and the psychiatric emergency clinician arrived simultaneously and with the client's permission, the clinician remained.

After the police report was completed, the clinician reviewed the details of the rape with Ms. B. The client appeared to want to continue talking about it. She was angry over her vulnerability and the fact that a woman could not jog alone in the park in the early afternoon without being assaulted. The client's sister appeared very concerned, and support was offered by her suggestion that Ms. B stay with her for several days. It appeared that Ms. B's anger was her way of coping with the rape. Since Ms. B had an adequate support system, the clinician made an appointment for the following day.

The next day the clinician continued to assess Ms. B's coping mechanisms. The client verbalized that it was not fair that a woman's life had to be so restricted. The clinician allowed and encouraged these angry feelings to be ventilated. The client was worried that her parents would want her to live at home again where they could watch her. It was useful for the clinician to remind Ms. B that her parents did not have to be informed of the rape. If she chose to tell them, she could accept their concern without having to return home.

Ms. B decided to press charges when her assailant was apprehended. She continued to see the psychiatric emergency clinician and accepted a referral to a rape crisis group at the university women's center.

ATTITUDES OF STAFF MEMBERS

In working with women who have been battered or raped, the client is best served by female clinicians since the victims have been injured by men. This victimization may make it impossible for clients to feel safe with male staff members. In many emergency units the physicians are men, but female staff members are available to be with victims during examinations.

If the psychiatric emergency clinician is a man, a woman clinician should be provided. Many psychiatric emergency unit teams have male and female members present or call members at home as needed. If there are no female staff members, this should be explained to the client. The male clinician should then proceed with the evalua-

tion at a pace that is comfortable for him and the client. Transfer to a female clinician for follow-up care should be discussed at the end of the psychiatric emergency evaluation.

Assumptions of the staff are reflected in the care delivered to victims. Many staff members maintain that women are "responsible" for both battering and rape. These beliefs are the result of factors previously outlined: the socialization process of women, the role of women in society, and the covert fear that staff members may harbor over their own victimization.

Efforts at consciousness raising and education of staff members have resulted in some positive changes in how women are viewed and treated as victims of battering and rape. However, attitudes and prejudices have been learned and practiced over time and are not easily extinguished. Staff from medical and psychiatric units, police departments, and women's agencies need to be encouraged to attend conferences on the theories and research findings regarding victims' reactions and treatment needs. A useful teaching technique is the case presentation to demonstrate the knowledge and sensitivity required in caring for women who have been raped or beaten. Discussions that focus on staff members' feelings over working with women who have been victimized should be encouraged. In addition, recommendations for staff and interagency collaboration can be used for program planning and the development of procedures.

Emergency units also need written policies and procedures for the treatment of raped or battered victims and for staff training in protection against similar assaults toward staff members. These protocols provide administratively endorsed guidelines for the staff to follow when working in these anxiety-provoking situations.

SUMMARY

This chapter has focused on how psychiatric emergency clinicians can work with women who have been raped or battered. The socialization process of women was reviewed to demonstrate how this process has contributed to mental health problems of women and subsequent rape and battering of women. The chapter ended with explanations of appropriate interventions and case vignettes of raped and battered victims seen in psychiatric emergency units.

BIBLIOGRAPHY

Aguilera, D., and Messick, J.: Crisis intervention: theory and methodology, ed. 3, St. Louis, 1978, The C.V. Mosby Co.

Barry, H., III, Bacon, M., and Child, I.: A cross-cultural survey of some sex differences in socialization. In Bardwick, J., editor: Readings on the psychology of women, New York, 1972, Harper & Row, Publishers.

Bosselman, B.: Castration anxiety and phallus envy: a reformulation. In Bardwick, J., editor: Readings on the psychology of women, New York, 1972, Harper & Row, Publishers.

Broverman, I., et al.: Sex role stereotypes and clinical judgments of mental health. In Bardwick, S., editor: Readings on the psychology of women, New York, 1972, Harper & Row, Publishers.

Brownmiller, S.: Against our will: men, women and rape, New York, 1975, Simon & Schuster, Inc.

Burgess, A.W., and Holmstrom, L.L.: Rape trauma syndrome, Am. J. Psychiatry 131(9):981, 1974.

Burgess, A.W., and Holmstrom, L.L.: Rape: victims of crisis, Bowie, Md., 1974, Robert J. Brady Co.

Burgess, A.W., and Holmstrom, L.L.: Rape: crisis and recovery, Bowie, Md., 1979, Robert J. Brady Co.

Chesler, P.: Woman and madness, New York, 1972, Doubleday & Co., Inc.

Dixon, M.: The rise of women's liberation. In Bardwick, S., editor: Readings on the psychology of women, New York, 1972, Harper & Row, Publishers.

Ehrenreich, B., and English, D.: For her own good, New York, 1979, Doubleday & Co., Inc.

Fleming, J.: Stopping wife abuse, New York, 1979, Doubleday & Co., Inc.

Gornick, V.: Consciousness. In Bardwick, S., editor: Readings on the psychology of women, New York, 1972, Harper & Row, Publishers.

Greenleaf, N.: The politics of self esteem, Nurs. Digest 6(3):1, Fall 1978.

Groth, A.N.: The rapist's view. In Burgess, A.W., and Holmstrom, L.L.: Rape: crisis and recovery, Bowie, Md., 1979, Robert J. Brady Co.

Groth, A.N., Burgess, A.W., and Holmstrom, L.L.: Rape: power, anger and sexuality, Am. J. Psychiatry 134(11):1239, 1977.

Hilberman, E.: Overview: the "wife-beater's wife" reconsidered, Am. J. Psychiatry 137(11):1336, 1980.

Hilberman, E., and Munson, M.: Sixty battered women. J. Victimology: An Int. J. 23/4):460, 1977-1978.

Horner, M.: The motive to avoid success and changing aspirations of college women. In Bardwick, J., editor: Readings on the psychology of women, New York, 1972, Harper & Row, Publishers.

Katz, P.: Development of female identity. In Kopp, C., editor: Becoming female: perspective on development, New York, 1979, Plenum Press.

Katz, S., and Mazur, M.: Understanding the rape victim: a synthesis of research findings, New York, 1979, John Wiley & Sons, Inc.

Korner, A.F.: Sex differences in newborns with special reference to differences in the organization of oral behavior, J. Child Psychol. Psychiatry 14:19, 1973.

Martin, D.: Battered wives, New York, 1976, Simon & Schuster, Inc.

Martin, D.: Foreword. In Fleming, J.: Stopping wife abuse, New York, 1979, Doubleday & Co., Inc.

May, R.: Sex differences in fantasy patterns. In Bardwick, J., editor: Readings on the psychology of women, New York, 1972, Harper & Row, Publishers.

Miller, J., and Mothner, I.: Psychological consequences of sexual inequality, Nurs. Digest 6:27, Fall 1978.

Millett, K.: Sexual politics, New York, 1970, Doubleday & Co., Inc.

Murphy, L.: The widening world of childhood, New York, 1962, Basic Books, Inc., Publishers.

Notman, M., and Nadelson, C.: The rape victim: psychodynamic considerations, Am. J. Psychiatry 133(4): 408, 1976.

Reed, E.: Female biology and the double taboo, Nurs. Digest 6:13, Fall 1978.

Rich, A.: Of woman born, New York, 1976, W.W. Norton & Co., Inc.

Rossi A.: Transition to parent, J. Marriage Fam. 30:26, 1968.

Rubin, J.K., Provenzano, F.J., and Luria, Z.: The eye of the beholder: parents' view on sex of newborns, Am. J. Orthopsychiatry 44:512, 1974.

Schafer, R.: Problems in Freud's psychology of women, J. Am. Psychoanal. Assoc. 22:459, 1974.

Seiden, A.: Overview: research on the psychology of women. II. Women in families, work and psychotherapy, Am. J. Psychiatry 133(10):1111, 1976.

Seligmen, M.E.: Helplessness: on depression, development and death, San Francisco, 1975, W.H. Freeman & Co.

Stoller, R.: Primary femininity. In Blum, H., editor: Female psychology, New York, 1977, International Universities Press.

Straus, M.: A sociological perspective on the prevention and treatment of wifebeating, Nurs. Dimens. 7: 45, Spring 1979.

Weingourt, R.: Battered women: the grieving process, J. Psychiatr. Nurs. 17(4):40, 1979.

Weitzman, L.S., et al.: Sex role socialization in picture books for preschool children, Am. J. Sociol. 77:1125, 1972.

Williams, J.: Psychology of women, New York, 1977, W.W. Norton & Co., Inc.

Withers, J.: Background: why women are unassertive, Nurs. Digest 6(3):68, Fall 1978.

CHAPTER 14

The client who is homosexual

James P. Krajeski, M.D.

The mental health community has become increasingly aware of the need of minority groups to obtain adequate and appropriate services within the mental health system. The advent of the gay liberation movement has brought to the forefront an awareness of a large population of relatively invisible persons identifiable only through their sexual behavior or alternate life-styles that differ from the majority of the population.

Included in a broader group of individuals who engage in sexual behavior or life-styles at variance with the general population are transsexuals and transvestites as well as individuals

labeled as bisexual and homosexual. Just as the members of many minority groups may have little in common, so these individuals may actually have more dissimilarities than similarities. However, their evaluation and treatment do raise certain common issues. Such clients may stimulate anxiety in as well as provoke and test the value systems and attitudes of the clinicians who are trying to assist them. They may bring into question the professional knowledge and expertise of the clinician, often in an emotionally laden area of sexuality with which the clinician may only be marginally familiar or proficient. Many clinicians have had little contact with such individuals on a personal basis and may be unfamiliar with their lives or the issues that they bring to the emergency care situation. In many locations there may be few educational resources available and clinicians may find themselves avoiding or ignoring these clients or being faced with providing suboptimal care.

DEFINITION OF TERMS

Because confusion sometimes exists in the use of the concepts transsexual, transvestite, and homosexual, some clarification of these terms is in order. An understanding of these concepts involves the idea of sexual identity, which can be viewed as encompassing four components: biologic sex, gender identity, social sex-role, and sexual orientation (Shively and De Cecco, 1977). *Gender identity* is defined as an individual's conviction of being male or female, which may or may not be consistent with the individual's *biological sex. Social sex-role* includes characteristics that are culturally associated with masculinity or femininity, whereas *sexual orientation* refers to an individual's physical or affectional preference.

Transsexuals are individuals who believe that they are in essence trapped in a body of the wrong sex. For example, a biological male may feel that he is really a woman. Such a belief is often present from a very early age. This individual is described as having a gender identity disorder or gender identity conflict. Homosexuals do not have a gender identity conflict. Homosexual individuals feel that they have a gender identity that is congruent with their biological sex. For example, homosexual men do not see themselves as being female nor do they wish to be female. Homosexual individuals simply are attracted to an individual of the same sex as a sexual object. The issue is sexual orientation and not gender identity.

A transvestite represents another variation in sexuality. While the term sometimes is used to describe anyone who dresses in clothing of the opposite sex, it usually is used to refer to a man dressed in women's clothes. As a clinical entity described in DSM III, transvestism involves a heterosexual male who engages in recurrent and persistent cross-dressing for the purpose of sexual excitement.

This chapter will primarily deal with individuals who are labeled as bisexual or homosexual, because in view of their absolute numbers they are much more likely to be seen in the psychiatric emergency care facility than are transvestites and transsexuals. However, much of the material presented in this chapter regarding clinical issues will apply in some ways to all these individuals.

While homosexuality has been defined in terms of sexual orientation or sexual interest, a more thorough examination of the term in both theoretical and practical applications is warranted.

One method of defining homosexuals is to do so in terms of physical object choice, and therefore persons who have sex with individuals of the same sex are labeled as homosexual. This definition is often modified in some way to exclude certain individuals who may engage in homosexual acts but are still not necessarily considered homosexual, for example, adolescents or prisoners. A second definition might include a somewhat different group of people; sexual orientation would be defined in terms of erotic fantasy and would include individuals who do not have sex or seldom have sex but whose predominant erotic interest or fantasy is directed to members of the same sex. This would also include individuals who have sex with partners of the opposite sex, but who have a significant degree of sexual fantasy directed to the same sex.

Many times individuals are labeled as homosexual based on self-identification or self-labeling as being homosexual. In some instances individuals do not label themselves as homosexual even though they engage in homosexual behavior. Whether one is evaluating research or dealing with a client in a mental health setting, it is important to clarify what is meant by the use of the word *homosexual.**

Additionally it should be kept in mind that individuals have varying degrees of sexual interest or behavior ranging from exclusively heterosexual to exclusively homosexual. Kinsey's

---

*Terminology raises certain issues. Some persons object to the use of *homosexual* as a noun, believing it identifies an individual as wholly sexual when sexuality is just one aspect of an individual. The term *gay* often implies a more positive healthy image than *homosexual.* More recently there has been increasing use of the phrase *gay men and lesbians* rather than the terms *homosexuals* or *gays.* The scientific and medical literature has no consistent approach to the use of these terms. To avoid the sexist connotation of the generic pronoun *he* and the awkwardness of *he/she* and *gay men and lesbians,* the term *homosexual* is used in this chapter to refer to both men and women. *Gay* is used where *homosexual* does not express quite the same concept as *gay,* such as homosexual versus gay identity or where current usage seems to clearly dictate use of the term *gay,* that is, gay liberation, gay groups, or gay organizations.

seven-point scale* (1953) is a useful measure of the degree of homosexual or heterosexual interest or behavior. Although there is a tendency to view homosexuals and heterosexuals as two distinct polarized groups, there is in reality a continuum of sexual behavior and interest.

RESEARCH ON HOMOSEXUALITY

The idea of a continuum of sexual behavior and interest makes research and data collection on homosexuality ambiguous unless one explains how homosexuality is being defined. For example, a consideration of the percentage of homosexuals in the general population obviously requires defining homosexuality in some manner.

Before the question "How many homosexuals are there?" is examined, a few observations concerning research and homosexuality should be noted. There have been significant problems in past research on this subject. Some of these difficulties have included imprecise definitions of homosexuality, use of prison and patient samples, failure to use appropriate controls, investigator bias, the assumption that homosexuals represent a homogeneous group, and failure to consult with the population being studied. The positive aspects or positive adaptations that have occurred within homosexual groups have been largely ignored. Because no representative sample of homosexual individuals exists the results of any particular study can seldom be reliably applied to all homosexuals. An additional problem has been the lack of studies and investigations of female homosexuality so that much less is known about this subject than about homosexuality among males.

Extent of the homosexual population

It is important to keep the preceding discussion in mind when evaluating the various data

used to describe the incidence of homosexuality. The extensive studies done by Kinsey (1948) reflect a high degree of homosexual contact, with 37% of the total male study sample having at least some overt homosexual experience to orgasm between adolescence and old age. Another finding from the Kinsey study indicated that 10% of males in the study were predominantly homosexual (5 or 6 on the Kinsey scale) for at least 3 years between the ages of 16 and 55.

The accumulative incidence of overt contacts to the point of orgasm among females reached only 13% compared to the 37% figure for males; also in contrast to male experience, only about a half to a third as many females were in any age period primarily or exclusively homosexual (Kinsey, 1953). A review of the incidence of homosexuality in a number of studies was undertaken for a National Institute of Mental Health task force on homosexuality by Gebhard (1972). He estimates that about 4% of white college-educated adult males are predominantly homosexual. For females the incidence of predominantly homosexual individuals is estimated as being between 1% and 2%. Marmor (1980) estimates that more or less exclusive homosexual behavior in Western culture ranges from 3% to 5% for adult females to 5% to 10% for adult males. No matter what data one uses, it is clear that there are at least several million homosexual men and women in the United States and that some will assuredly be seen in psychiatric emergency units.

If the homosexual individual is to be treated and dealt with fairly and effectively, the emergency care staff must have a firm factual basis from which to operate. There has been a great deal of inaccurate information circulated among health care professionals, and unproven theories have sometimes been accepted as fact. The 1970s brought a new look at the traditional concepts and ideas. A significant result of this was the removal in 1973 by the American Psychiatric Association of homosexuality from the list of mental disorders. This occurred after studies indicated that homosexuality failed to meet the criteria of a mental disorder. The APA also adopted a position statement indicating that homosexuality implied no impairment in "judgment, stability, reliability or general social or

---

*The Kinsey scale rates psychological reactions and overt behavior on a scale ranging from 0 to 6. A rating of 0 = completely heterosexual; 6 = completely homosexual; 3 = equally heterosexual and homosexual. 1, 2, 4, and 5 represent gradations between these points. Behavior and psychological reactions are sometimes rated separately using the same seven-point scales.

vocational capabilities." In addition, the group stated that they deplored discrimination against homosexuals and urged the enactment of civil rights legislation to offer protection to homosexual citizens (American Psychiatric Association, 1974).

Origin of a homosexual orientation

What is known about homosexuality from the research literature and from clinical experience? One of the most frequent questions that arises is why does a homosexual orientation develop. There remains no answer to this question, although there are at least three current theories, involving genetic, hormonal, and psychodynamic factors.

GENETICS. Genetic theories regarding homosexuality assume that there is some kind of hereditary transmission or inheritance of homosexuality. The theorized mode of transmission is uncertain but is more often viewed as inheritance of a predisposition toward homosexuality rather than genetics absolutely determining sexual orientation. Studies involving monozygotic (identical) twins and dizygotic (nonidentical) twins have shown conflicting results and have not ruled out environmental factors. Concordance rates for monozygotic twins have varied in studies from 100% (Kallman, 1952) to 40% to 60% (Heston and Shields, 1968) to 0% (Kolb, 1963). Obviously, the answer to the role that genetics has in determining sexual orientation awaits further research.

HORMONES. A rapidly expanding area of research involves the hormonal area. Scientists have attempted to study various hormone levels in adult homosexuals, expecting to find some difference in the levels of sex hormones between homosexuals and heterosexual subjects. However, although hormones have been shown to affect sexual drive, they have not been shown to affect sexual orientation in humans. Recent studies have been focusing on prenatal hormone levels based on data from animal studies which indicate that during critical phases of development of the fetus the brain can be influenced by hormone levels with a resultant effect on sexuality later in life. Tourney (1980) summarizes the results of major studies of hormones in homosexuals showing results that are conflicting and confusing. As one example, in studies of testosterone levels in male homosexuals, two investigators have shown a decrease, five have reported no change, and four have reported an increase. Tourney also summarizes some of the developments in both animal and human studies of prenatal hormone levels which also give no firm answer regarding the role of prenatal hormones in humans.

PSYCHODYNAMICS. The area of psychodynamic theories of homosexuality is characterized by controversy. Often psychodynamic formulations have been offered which were based on work with homosexual clients who were in therapy with clinicians who clearly believed that homosexuality represented some type of disordered development. Because of the population from which these formulations have been drawn, there has been considerable question raised regarding the validity of such constructs when applied to all homosexual individuals. One theory holds that homosexuality is the result of disordered development involving fixation in the separation-individuation process with disturbed self-identity and gender identity, identification with the mother, and disturbed object relations and ego-functions (Socarides, 1979). Another commonly held theory views parental relationships with children, particularly that of a close-binding intimate mother and hostile competitive father, as causative factors in homosexuality (Bieber and Bieber, 1979). This psychodynamic explanation suggests that the male homosexual has a fear of aggressive males who are identified with the father. A psychologically unavailable female is replaced by a male, and at the same time the homosexual is offered mechanisms for dealing with fear of aggression and rejection by men. Bieber and Bieber disagree with the idea that homosexual men fear the "oral castrating power of the vagina" or that they are afraid of women. They also disagree with the idea that a defective separation-individuation process is responsible for the development of homosexuality.

Contradicting the idea of disturbed parental background as an etiological factor in homosexuality is a study by Siegelman (1974). He found in a sample of 307 male homosexuals that both fathers and mothers were more rejecting and less loving than those of a heterosexual comparison group. However, in subsamples of both heterosexuals and homosexuals who scored low on measures of neuroticism there were no significant differences in family relations. This study raises considerable question regarding the influence of a particular family constellation in the development of a homosexual orientation. It also points out the need to consider a number of variables in research on this area including the level of neuroticism of the respondents.

Other psychodynamic theories have abounded. One holds that homosexuality is the result of a phobic avoidance of heterosexual intercourse and another holds that homosexuality is linked to paranoid delusions. The validity of these theories, which were derived from clinical work, is questioned by the research literature. As one example, Freund et al. (1974) measured penile volume changes in response to various sexual situations and found that the results contraindicated the phobic theory of homosexuality. Lester (1975) reviewed studies relating paranoia and homosexuality and found that although more studies have tended to support the position that there was a relationship, several studies have failed to support this and others have been inconsistent in their results.

As with so many areas related to homosexuality, the clinician can have little confidence in following a particular theory when dealing with the homosexual client. This is further complicated by the realization that homosexual individuals, in addition to falling in various places along a spectrum between homosexuality and heterosexuality, also are subject to all the varieties of mental disorders to which heterosexuals are subject. Since these illnesses are often thought of as having diverse dynamic formulations, it becomes even more confusing to attempt to assign a particular theoretical construct to explain the development of homosexual interest and behavior in all people.

The importance of the role of psychodynamic factors in homosexuality awaits further research. Unfortunately, there has been a tendency to equate psychodynamics with psychopathology and, as Mitchell (1978) points out, this has led to a polarization between the view in which a psychodynamic dimension is accepted and pathology presumed and the view in which pathology is denied and any possible psychodynamic contribution rejected. It should be noted, of course, that psychodynamic factors may be present in many of our actions but that they do not necessarily imply pathology.

Homosexuality and psychopathology

Apart from psychodynamic considerations, one can look at the functioning of adult homosexual individuals to determine something of the nature of homosexuality. Here the evidence from research is overwhelmingly in favor of a nonpathological view of homosexuality. Eighteen research studies that contrast homosexuals with other comparison groups utilizing psychiatric interviews, self-report questionnaires, and projective tests are summarized by Meredith and Riester (1980). They find that in 13 studies utilizing self-report questionnaires 85% of the studies challenge the concept that homosexuality is necessarily psychopathological. They also review two studies utilizing psychiatric interviews and three studies using projective tests, finding that all of these challenge the concept of homosexuality as necessarily psychopathological. Another review of the research literature (Hart et al., 1978) also concludes that the findings do not demonstrate that homosexual individuals are less well adjusted than their heterosexual counterparts. An example is provided by Clark (1975) who studied 140 males in matched groups expressing varying degrees of homosexual or heterosexual behavior (0 to 6 on the Kinsey scale) utilizing the Tennessee Self Concept Scale. No significant differences were found in any of the groups on measures of personality adjustment or psychopathology. In another example Adelman (1977) compared professionally employed lesbians and heterosexual women on the Minnesota Multiphasic Personality Inventory (MMPI) and also found no pathological differences. Although some studies may indicate that a group of homosexual individuals has a higher degree of pathology than a similar group of het-

231

erosexual individuals, they nearly always indicate that many homosexual persons are little different than their heterosexual counterparts, thereby dispelling the idea that homosexuality is invariably or intrinsically linked to pathology. There are disturbed homosexuals, but it would not be unreasonable to expect a higher incidence of emotional problems in a population that faces such significant discrimination and prejudice from society at large.

Facts or stereotypes?

Homosexual men and women have been victims of a number of stereotypes, so it is important for clinicians to have some idea as to which commonly held beliefs concerning homosexuals are true and which are not. Only the most common ones will be examined here. It is often held that homosexuals can be identified by their appearance or mannerisms. While this may be true of some, it is not true of the vast majority. Usually lesbians are pictured as being "butch," or masculine in appearance, and male homosexuals are pictured as caricatures of women. While the actual percentage of homosexuals who fit these stereotypes is unknown, the Kinsey statistics indicate that only a small portion are identifiable on the basis of factors such as hand movements, walk, voice, and dress (Gebhard and Johnson, 1979). In this study lesbians are rated as less obvious than homosexual males. A rough summary of the results indicates that for most characteristics less than 15% of the males were quite obvious (Gebhard and Johnson, 1979). Pomeroy, who was extensively involved in the Kinsey studies, reports 5% as the number of lesbians and 15% as the number of homosexual males who can be identified on the basis of mannerisms (1969). The actual percentages of these figures should not be taken literally as being accurate, but they do suggest a generally low percentage of identifiable individuals.

Another common stereotype holds that older homosexuals, particularly males, lead miserable unhappy lives. Kelly (1977) finds in a study of 241 homosexual men that there is little evidence to suggest that being homosexual causes problems in old age. Kimmel (1979) describes a study

of 14 homosexual men that demonstrates the respondents to have a wide diversity of patterns of aging, with many positive aspects as well as satisfaction with life. Although homosexuality per se did not seem to have a negative effect on aging, it was noted that the social stigma of homosexuality did have adverse effects. Because of a paucity of research, little is known of the lives of aging lesbians, but there is no reason to assume that they would be worse off than their male counterparts solely on the basis of their homosexuality. The influence of society's attitude toward women, however, may affect lesbians differently than homosexual males.

It has been commonly stated that homosexuals are unable to sustain relationships and that they are doomed to short-lived tumultuous, and unhappy affairs. In an extensive research project involving nearly 1,000 homosexual men and lesbians conducted by the Institute for Sex Research, over half of the males and nearly three-quarters of the females were involved in a "relatively steady relationship" (Bell and Weinberg, 1978). A number of individuals were engaged in relationships for more than 5 years.

On the other hand, homosexual males in the Bell and Weinberg study report a large number of sexual partners whereas the majority of lesbians report fewer than 10 female sexual partners during their homosexual careers. The high level of sexual contact among many male homosexuals does place these individuals at a high risk for health problems related to venereally transmitted disease and illnesses such as hepatitis. Many states still do not permit consensual homosexual acts, and so individuals are placed under further stress in these areas. In spite of discrimination and stress placed on homosexual individuals by society, less than 6% of the lesbians and 14% of the homosexual males in the Bell and Weinberg study report that they would take a "magic heterosexual pill" that would change their sexual orientation.

It is also commonly believed that homosexuals assume male-female roles in relationships. Over 90% of the respondents in the Bell and Weinberg study report that they share roles equally.

IDENTITY DEVELOPMENT

Since the development of an identity as a homosexual person is often marked by anxiety and emotional turmoil, it is essential that mental health professionals have an awareness of the stages in this process which may have particular relevance to psychiatric emergency care. Various models are available (Lee, 1977; Cass, 1979; Troiden, 1979) to elaborate on the process of homosexual/gay identity formation. While the models are generally similar, different names are applied to parts of the identity development process. For purposes of clinical work the names may be of less significance than knowledge of a general stepwise path followed by most homosexuals in development of an identity. The model and terms proposed by Cass (1979) will be used as a framework. Here the first stage is labeled as "identity confusion." It is during this stage that an individual becomes aware of certain feelings, impulses, actions, or behavior that are related to the individual's concept of homosexuality. At this point questions arise regarding the possibility of being homosexual. This questioning is likely to carry a significant degree of emotional turmoil, confusion, or perhaps panic. During this stage various solutions to defining one's self as homosexual come into play. These may involve increasing denial, inhibition of homosexual interest or behavior, or a redefinition of homosexuality in a way that excludes one's own behavior or interest. During this stage self-hate and negative feelings about oneself may become significant.

If identity development proceeds, then the next stage is viewed as one of "identity comparison." During this stage there is greater acceptance of oneself as being homosexual and an increasing sense of alienation from the rest of society including family and friends. Significant confusion may result from not knowing what the future holds for someone with a homosexual identity. Traditional heterosexual models may not seem applicable and the homosexual individual may feel isolated and alone. Individuals will probably attempt to make themselves appear as heterosexual, and there may be intense emotional discomfort with the increasing sense of being homosexual. There may be attempts to stop any homosexual feeling or behavior, to engage only in covert behavior, or to pass as a heterosexual.

A third stage is labeled as "identity tolerance." Here individuals come to tolerate the idea of probably being homosexual. Contacts with other homosexuals become prevalent with a decrease in the feeling of isolation and alienation. The quality of the contacts determines the way individuals feel about themselves and the homosexual community. Positive contacts lead to a positive self-image making homosexuality seem more acceptable, whereas negative contacts lead to self-criticism and a negative self-image. There again may be an attempt to inhibit or reduce homosexual contacts. However, if there are increasingly positive experiences, this stage ends with the person saying "I am homosexual."

The next stage is that of "identity acceptance." The individual accepts a homosexual identity and has increasing contacts with other homosexuals. The homosexual subculture provides increasing support and begins to play an important role in the individual's life. There may be increasing compartmentalization of one's existence with a homosexual life at home and an attempt to pass as a heterosexual in situations such as work. There may be a movement away from families or others to avoid the increasing gulf between the homosexual identity and the heterosexual world. Many individuals are able to fit into both a heterosexual world and a homosexual world at this stage by keeping two separate identities.

A fifth stage of "gay pride" begins with an increasing awareness of the differences between one's own positive feelings and acceptance of being homosexual and society's rejection of homosexuality. There may be increasing devaluation of heterosexual values and increasing commitment to the gay culture and life-style. The gay activist arises out of this stage, and individuals reveal their sexual orientation to other people. A positive reaction by heterosexuals to this may lead to the sixth stage.

In this final stage of "identity synthesis" supportive heterosexuals come to be trusted more and viewed more favorably while nonsupportive individuals are further devalued. Similarity between homosexuals and heterosexuals becomes more notable, and finally sexual orientation comes to be viewed as a part of one's total identity rather than being seen as one's identity.

Within this framework the process of identity development usually begins by late adolescence but may begin earlier or much later and may proceed at varying rates in different individuals, ranging from a relatively short period of months to nearly an entire life span. Identity development can be stopped in any of the stages. A variety of mechanisms may interfere with the developmental processes with denial and repression being the most common ones for dealing with unwanted homosexual impulses and feelings.

EVALUATION AND TREATMENT ISSUES

The homosexual client in the psychiatric emergency setting is in many ways no different from the heterosexual client. Homosexual clients enter with the same variety of crises as does the heterosexual population. There are schizophrenic homosexuals, manic-depressive homosexuals, and neurotic homosexuals. There are homosexuals who enter with personality disorders, posttraumatic stress disorders, suicide attempts, and assaultive behavior. Many homosexual individuals treated in the emergency unit will have problems totally unrelated to their sexual orientation just as heterosexuals are treated for conditions unrelated to their sexual orientation. Indeed it is likely that the sexual orientation of many homosexuals will be unknown as they pass through the emergency care process.

There is validity, however, in considering special issues that will arise around the treatment of homosexual individuals in the emergency setting which may be different from those encountered in the treatment of heterosexual individuals. These differences will be evident from the perspective of staff members and from the perspective of the client.

Staff issues

It is essential that clinicians be aware of their own attitudes and feelings regarding homosexuals. It is to be expected that the staff will have

incorporated many of the negative beliefs, societal prejudices, or fears concerning homosexuals to which everyone is exposed. Obviously these should not be allowed to influence or exert a negative effect on the treatment situation. When looking at their own feelings, many clinicians will recognize that they in fact have little personal or firsthand knowledge of homosexuals and they will have difficulty in determining which of their beliefs concerning homosexuals are true and which are not. Unfortunately, very few mental health training facilities present comprehensive discussions of homosexuality. Often those that do discuss it do so in terms of narrow theories without presenting a comprehensive view of current research and without the input or participation of homosexual mental health professionals or with no participation of the population being studied.

Individuals who are uncertain of their knowledge of homosexuality might consider ways of expanding their understanding by reading or by participating in seminars or discussions with homosexual colleagues or those who are knowledgeable on the subject. Those clinicians who hold strong negative attitudes toward homosexuals and who are unable to alter these attitudes should avoid working with clients who are homosexual.

Because it is important to move quickly to establish rapport and to care for the client in the emergency unit, it is essential to avoid obstacles to these goals. To assist in doing so with the homosexual client, staff members might ask themselves how they would feel if they were gay and came into this particular emergency setting. Factors ranging from the choice of magazines in the waiting room to the wording of questions on forms to the attitudes of all personnel should be considered as having a possible influence on how the emergency unit will be perceived.

Clinicians should avoid making assumptions about any particular individual's sexual orientation and they should not make assumptions about any particular homosexual person. A slogan of the gay liberation movement has become "How dare you assume I am heterosexual." Since in fact the vast majority of homosexuals and heterosexuals cannot be identified by appearances, any individual who comes into the emergency unit should be viewed as having an unknown sexual orientation. Likewise if the client is known to be homosexual, one should not make any particular assumptions regarding psychodynamics, abilities, problems, strengths, weaknesses, and so on. Homosexual individuals are an extremely diverse group, and just as one would not assume that all heterosexuals are alike, one should not assume that all homosexuals are alike.

The determination of the sexual orientation of a client may rely on the client's own revelation of this but often will depend on the history taken by the clinician. The way in which questions are asked and the way in which the issue of sexual orientation is approached may well set the tone for the entire emergency visit, treatment, and outcome.

A homosexual who is troubled, whether by an issue related to sexual orientation or some entirely different matter, will appreciate the clinician who asks questions in such a way that a response involving a homosexual feeling or behavior could follow. The homosexual client will recognize the greater degree of sensitivity displayed in the question asked of a woman "Are you emotionally involved with any one?" as opposed to the questions "Are you emotionally involved with a man?" or "Do you have a boyfriend?" The latter questions are likely to be viewed as ones that assume that the client is heterosexual. This in turn might suggest that the clinician has little awareness of homosexuality and did not perceive the sexual orientation of the client. The client may question the knowledge of the clinician or the value system.

The clinician should be particularly alert to assumptions and types of statements or questions made in interactions with individuals who fit traditional heterosexual masculine and feminine stereotypes. Rapport will be much more difficult to establish with the adolescent football jock who may be troubled by homosexual feelings if one begins by asking questions that assume heterosexual interest. Some clients will find it difficult to raise the subject of their own homosexual interest if the clinician does not specifically ask about this area. This may be a particular

issue in problems revolving around marital conflicts where the homosexual interest of one of the partners is not recognized by the clinician while other less relevant issues serve as red herrings in the evaluation and treatment process.

Client issues

The homosexual client may bring to the emergency situation a certain set of attitudes, fears, or beliefs that, whether justified or unjustified, may complicate the treatment process. The clinician must be aware of these and have an understanding of the antecedents that bring about such feelings if they are to quickly establish rapport and deal with the emergency situation.

Many, if not most, homosexual clients will be somewhat distrustful of the heterosexual clinician (homosexual individuals may assume that clinicians are heterosexual just as readily as the reverse occurs). Homosexuals are uncertain about the reception that they will receive if they reveal their sexual preference. There are powerful conditioning forces within society which let homosexual individuals know that they are disliked, considered evil, and so on. Additionally, most homosexual men and women have some idea of pathological concepts of homosexuality which have been advocated by some mental health professionals, and they have no guarantee that the clinician in the emergency unit will be understanding, knowledgeable, or empathetic. A homosexual client may expect the staff to respond with disapproval, disappointment, anger, or ridicule. Others may expect the clinician to be an expert in the subject and, when they discover this is not true, may be disappointed because they feel that there is little help that can be offered by the clinician. The homosexual client may be particularly sensitive to discrimination or to subtleties of language and intonation which indicate disapproval, discomfort, or a lack of knowledge on the part of the clinician. Particularly devastating and disruptive of therapeutic work is the overhearing of staff discussions or remarks concerning the client's sexual orientation in the hallway or adjoining rooms. Needless to say, such discussions should not occur.

No matter what the attitude or behavior of the

235

client, the clinician who maintains a professional, empathetic, concerned attitude based on adequate knowledge of homosexuality will work most successfully with the homosexual client.

Homophobia

It should be remembered that both staff and clients bring into the therapeutic situation a set of feelings that have been conditioned by the world in which they live. Because of the strong social stigma concerning homosexuality, it is difficult to imagine that more than a few people could escape having negative attitudes toward homosexuals at least at some point in their lives. The term *homophobia* has increasingly come into usage today. Attempts have been made to bring greater specificity and definition to this term. Hudson and Ricketts (1980) define the word in terms of a negative affective response to homosexual individuals. Commonly the word *homophobia* is used in a broader sense to refer to negative attitudes and feelings as well as irrational fears of homosexuals. The discussion here will utilize the word in its broader context.

Within the clinician, homophobia may manifest itself in a number of ways. These may include a sense of anxiety in the presence of homosexuals, a discomfort in working with them, or a lack of sympathy and understanding. Such an individual may unconsciously be quick to assume negative clinical formulations and fail to differentiate between sound clinical research and societal or personal value systems. Homosexual clients may receive care that is inferior to that given to heterosexuals by virtue of the clinician's inability to accept the homosexual's life-style. Karr (1978) demonstrated experimentally that labeling a male individual as homosexual would result in the individual being rated as more womanly, softer, more tense, less clean, less rugged, more passive, and quieter than the same individual who was not labeled as homosexual. Moreover, in the same study the person who labeled the individual as homosexual within a group setting was seen as being superior by being more masculine and more sociable. This certainly suggests that the clinician must guard against devaluing the homosexual individual and failing to

fairly and adequately assess and treat the homosexual client simply because the client is homosexual.

While some clinicians indicate that they have no negative feelings about homosexuals or that they are "neutral," they may have subtle homophobic attitudes and feelings. Clinicians might become more aware of their own feelings if they personalize homosexuality by asking themselves some of the following questions: How would I feel if a close family member revealed a homosexual identity? How would I feel if someone of the same sex made a sexual overture toward me? How would I feel working with a homosexual colleague?

The homosexual client may be just as likely to suffer from homophobia as is the clinician. Doubtless much of the emotional suffering experienced by some homosexuals would be lessened considerably if they were free of their own homophobic attitudes and feelings. Homosexuals may be more likely to devalue themselves and view themselves and their lives and accomplishments negatively than would a heterosexual in a comparable situation. The self-hatred and despair that is evident in some homosexuals can often be viewed as an internalized homophobic response based on an incorporation of negative societal attitudes. A homosexual individual suffering from homophobia may be insecure, dependent, and depressed and lack self-confidence. These characteristics may interfere with the formation of satisfactory relationships resulting in the confirmation of the individual's homophobic beliefs and self-hatred. Such an individual may complain that "Homosexuals are undependable, they are not interested in anything but sex, and their relationships never last." The clinician who is homophobic or not knowledgeable about homosexuals may accept the client's assessment as an accurate one and fail to note the client's distortions. In so doing, the clinician further reinforces the client's pathology. In contrast, the knowledgeable or nonhomophobic clinician recognizing the client's distortions and self-defeating behavior will be in a far better position to effect positive change within the client.

Closely linked to the concept of homophobia is the concept of heterosexual bias (Morin, 1977).

Heterosexual bias assigns a higher value to heterosexuality and may view it as more preferred than homosexuality. Such a view may be particularly noticeable in the language used by clinicians, and the subtle but clear message will be evident as well to the homosexual client. Researchers who talk about "abnormal" hormone levels or "arrested" development as a reason for the development of same sex interest clearly signify their belief that heterosexuality is preferred. Clinicians who ask clients how they have learned to deal with the "problem of homosexuality" also indicate their value system.

CLINICAL PRESENTATIONS

The psychiatric emergency unit will undoubtedly be visited by many homosexual individuals who present no issue related to their homosexuality. These individuals can and should be treated with regard to the complaint that brought them to the unit. Yet there exist factors unique to the homosexual person and special considerations related to homosexuality of which the clinician must be aware. Proper and successful treatment will require that consideration be given to these issues. Some of the more common clinical situations will be discussed.

Breakup of relationships

Perhaps one of the more common situations in which homosexuality may play a significant role in the psychiatric emergency unit is in the context of the breakup of a relationship. Here, just as in the breakup of heterosexual relationships, the individual may appear in a variety of conditions, for example, depressed, angry, violent, explosive, intoxicated, or suicidal. There may be some unique and potentially complicating aspects as a result of being homosexual. Some homosexual individuals may be particularly vulnerable to losses because of a lack of support systems enjoyed by many heterosexuals. Of particular concern are closeted homosexuals who may have a limited circle of friends as a result of the need to conceal the homosexual aspect of their lives. Heterosexuals may be able to utilize family, co-workers, neighbors, and a variety of

friends as parts of a support system during a crisis. The closeted homosexual may be unable to ask for support or help from family members or fellow employees in the work situation and thus may be extremely isolated. An example follows:

Case vignette #1

M.Y. came to the emergency unit complaining of depression, sleeplessness, and suicidal preoccupation following the breakup of a 3-year relationship with her lover, J.N. She felt that she was too exhausted to continue with her job as the manager of the housewares department in a small department store, a position which she had held for 8 years.

She related that her parents who lived in the same city knew that her "roommate" had decided to move to a larger apartment to be "by herself." M.Y. felt that her parents were secretly relieved by this because she sensed that they wondered about the relationship between the two women and they had always seemed somewhat distant with J.N.

M.Y. was very concerned about knowledge of her sexuality being disclosed at her job, fearing that she would be dismissed if someone were to discover this. She had attempted to cover her depression completely since some of her co-workers knew that she had a roommate "to cut down on expenses" and that her roommate had recently moved. She was afraid that someone would conclude that she was upset because of the move and make some connection regarding her sexual orientation.

M.Y. also indicated that she and J.N. had no real close friends because they had spent most of their time with each other or with their respective families. Part of their relative isolation was related to their fear of being seen with other women couples.

M.Y. typifies the problems of the closeted homosexual. In contrast, the heterosexual individual would likely be able to talk with her family and share some of her grief and loss. Addition-

237

ally, the heterosexual would be likely to share to some degree her breakup of a relationship with her friends and co-workers and there would be some acceptance and understanding of a lowered ability to function at work at least for a short time.

Though it is not specifically addressed in this example, one could speculate that M.Y.'s situation might be made worse by her own homophobia or at least by her own internalized negative homosexual stereotypes. Such a situation as the breakup of a relationship is likely to reinforce a lack of self-esteem and reinforce any doubts or concerns which a client might have about sexual orientation. Thus the inevitable negative images of homosexuality which the client holds either consciously or unconsciously are likely to be stimulated by emotional stress with the client in effect verifying the statement "It is true homosexuals are a failure and I am a failure."

The clinician's role in dealing with the situation presented by M.Y. is to assess the client's strengths, evaluate and bolster the client's support system, and reduce the feelings of alienation and isolation. The clinician should be able to provide reality testing around issues related to homosexuality. An understanding, nonjudgmental approach to the client is essential. A knowledge of homosexually related community resources will also aid both the client and clinician in planning continued treatment and care. Certainly, if it were available, a gay women's rap group could be considered as a possible referral for M.Y.

Gay groups might be particularly useful in situations where individuals are isolated, alienated, or have the feeling "I am the only one." Groups can provide a measure of reality testing around homosexual issues as well as a network of understanding, friendly persons. In such situations homosexuals may be surprised to find that many of their own stereotypes are untrue and recognize a new range of possibilities for themselves in social or occupational worlds.

Crises in "coming out"

Crises that occur in the coming-out process may result in the homosexual individual coming

into the psychiatric emergency care facility. Since the coming-out process begins at various ages and proceeds at various rates, a variety of presentations may ensue.

FAMILY AND CHILD. Parents may bring in one of their children having suspected or determined that the child is homosexual. This may occur at anytime from early childhood through adolescence. It may often follow discovery of a diary, observation of the child in a sexual relationship with a member of the same sex, or a "confession" by the child. Situations that arise because of the parent's perception that the child has "failed" to develop usual interests (the sissy boy, or tomboy girl) might occasionally appear in the emergency unit but are more likely to be seen in an outpatient clinic or by the private clinician.

The concern of the parents must be assessed. Their reaction may vary from anger and disappointment to hopelessness and despair. Frequently they will want to know how they have failed and will be filled with guilt and remorse. They may want to find out if their suspicions are really true or may want the clinician to "do something about it." The child will likely be significantly anxious, depressed, and often resentful and may be compliant or quite uncooperative.

The clinician will need to utilize appropriate family therapy techniques in dealing with the situation. Both parents and child are likely to be impressed and respond more readily to professional intervention if the clinician is able to demonstrate some knowledge about homosexuality. Education in these instances may be the best therapeutic intervention. Some assessment as to the validity of the parent's or child's concerns should take place. Some cases may present fairly clear evidence that the child does or does not have a strong sexual interest in the same sex. However, many situations will result in an ambiguous answer to this question. It is important that the clinician not attempt to allay fears by simply saying that the child is probably just going through a phase and that all children do this. Certainly providing reality testing concerning homosexual contacts among children or adolescents is likely to be appropriate. It is better to admit the possibility of the child developing a homosexual preference and to provide assistance to the family to deal with this possibility. This approach will allow children and adolescents to more comfortably come to terms with their own sexuality as it unfolds. Treating the child as if homosexual interests are something that should or must be changed is not seen as helpful. Both parents and child (depending on age) may be helped by referral to appropriate readings on the subject of homosexuality (see Bibliography). Certainly referral for ongoing family or individual therapy should be considered.

ADOLESCENTS AND ADULTS. As individuals move from childhood into adolescence, the possibility increases that they will come into the emergency unit of their own accord because of some crisis related to the coming-out process. Crises related to homosexuality in the adolescent or adult may result in extreme stress, and the client may exhibit a wide variety of clinicial manifestations ranging from mild depression to suicide attempts and acute stress syndromes. When conflicts over sexual orientation lie behind these situations, it is essential that the conflict be identified and discussed. Taking a thorough history is important in addition to remembering that conflicts over sexual orientation may occur in any individual. Clients may be reluctant to reveal their own feelings and fears.

It should be mentioned that not every individual who reports to the unit with concerns over the possibility of being homosexual can be truly considered to be homosexual. Each situation must be assessed individually. There should be some attempt to assess an individual's behavior and feelings on the Kinsey scale. Obsessive or delusional concerns about homosexuality may be evidence of a significant psychiatric disorder just as obsessive or delusional concerns about any subject may be an indication of a mental disorder.

Once a conflict over sexual orientation is identified as a possible or certain cause of the clinical syndrome, resolution of the conflict can begin. There should be sufficient history taken to determine the degree of sexual interest and behavior. Exploration of the client's specific conflicts should take place. Usually these conflicts will revolve around issues related to traditional

value systems and issues related to inaccurate information regarding homosexuality. Isolation and alienation may play a significant role, with the individual describing the feeling of being the only homosexual in the world. Clients may express a strong desire to rid themselves of this "sickness."

Case vignette #2

Mr. J, a 22-year-old man, was brought to the crisis service following an overdose of tranquilizers at his home. After medical clearance of his condition, an assessment was made of his psychiatric status. He indicated that he had been having pressures in his sixth-grade teaching job that he had started 6 months ago. When questioned in more detail about the precipitating causes, he was vague about precise events, making references to two teachers and a supervisor with whom he had what seemed to be relatively minor disagreements. Feeling that something was missing in this explanation, the clinician explored other facets of Mr. J's life. Finally, when specific questions were asked about his sexuality, he became tearful and admitted that he had been extremely upset recently because he was aware of his increasing sexual interest in a male friend whom he had met at a hiking club to which he belonged.

Although he said he had been aware of "something different about me" during adolescence and had thought at least once that he might be a homosexual, he suddenly felt panicky about his interest in his friend, believing that it was not normal and that he must be homosexual. Because of these thoughts, he became anxious and feared that he would have to quit his teaching career (if he were not fired first) when in fact he liked it very much and had received a great deal of positive feedback concerning his abilities. Other concerns arose regarding his family and their disappointment if they were to guess his secret. How could he explain a career change or what would he say if they found out? The clinician was surprised to find that Mr. J knew only one person who he thought was homosexual and that Mr. J had read very little about homosexuality, most of it in his college texts that had discussed the "causes" of homosexuality. He expressed a desire "to be normal like everyone else."

The clinician discussed Mr. J's concerns openly and nonjudgmentally, conveying an attitude that whether he was homosexual or heterosexual made little difference in whether or not he was happy and successful in life. The clinician corrected some inaccurate stereotypes and ideas that Mr. J had concerning homosexuals during the course of the discussion but no attempt was made to define Mr. J as homosexual or heterosexual. A second meeting was set up for the following day at which time a referral was made for him to be seen by a therapist who was known by the clinic to work well with both homosexual and heterosexual clients.

This vignette demonstrates the necessity for clinicians to be aware of their own feelings and values regarding homosexuality. Though the clinician may at first react negatively to the idea of a homosexual working with young children, it is important to examine the validity of such a feeling, which has the potential for unfavorably influencing the therapeutic situation. For example, the clinician who is opposed to homosexuals working as teachers may consciously or unconsciously encourage individuals to deny or give up their homosexual interests. It is important for these clinicians to have sufficient knowledge concerning homosexuality to recognize whether their opinions are supported by clinical findings or are the result of negative conditioning by society. Recognizing the coming-out process as one that extends over a period of time and involves some degree of turmoil has important clinical implications. Recognition of this will prevent the clinician from stepping in too quickly and inappropriately reassuring clients that they are not homosexual or whisking clients off to the therapist who specializes in attempting to change sexual orientation when clients express dissatisfaction with being homosexual.

In addition, recognizing the diversity of homosexual persons in terms of personalities, lifestyles, and social and career abilities will prevent the clinician from making unwarranted assumptions about individuals simply on the basis of their sexual orientation.

Some adolescents (or adults) may have conflicts over the way in which they fit traditional masculine or feminine roles and confuse this with sexual orientation issues. For example, the adolescent male might perceive himself as insufficiently masculine in appearance, behavior, or interests and conclude that he must be homosexual (based on his stereotype of a homosexual person) even though there is no basis for such a conclusion. An evaluation must be made of the complete clinical picture. In a case such as this the psychiatric emergency unit clinician can provide useful reality testing around these issues, but referral for ongoing therapy may often be necessary.

THE MARRIED HOMOSEXUAL. Another group of individuals who may come to the attention of the emergency clinician are heterosexually married individuals who are at some point in the development of a homosexual identity or who reach some crisis in the equilibrium of the marital relationship and their homosexuality. Approximately one fifth of the males and one third of the females studied by Bell and Weinberg (1978) had been married, indicating that marriage is not a criterion for heterosexuality. The married homosexual (here the fallacy of labeling individuals as either homosexual or heterosexual is particularly relevant) may come to the unit in a crisis because of a decision to tell the spouse or to make a major alteration in the marital relationship or because the spouse has found out about the homosexual interest or behavior. Occasionally couples will come to the unit because of marital discord seemingly unrelated to homosexuality, but one of the pair will secretly reveal to the clinician a homosexual interest or behavior which in fact may have a significant bearing on the situation. In such instances clinicians must be careful not to violate confidences in working toward a solution.

The married individual who arrives at the emergency unit may be guilt ridden and depressed as a result of either homosexual feelings or behavior. If the crisis is the result of the homosexual partner recently becoming involved in an intense homosexual relationship, the degree of emotional stress may be even higher because of the pressure to choose between the new lover and the marital partner and to quickly make a decision. Again, it is important for clinicians not to let their own values interfere in the treatment of such cases. When clinicians feel apprehensive about what to do in cases involving a third party, they might look at the approach that would be taken if the individuals involved were heterosexual and follow these guidelines. If a third party is not involved in the crisis, then some of the general guidelines suggested earlier may be useful for dealing with the crisis situation. Most likely a referral for longer term treatment will be necessary to resolve the conflicts around the individual's "coming out" and the conflicts around the individual's marital situation.

FEAR OF EXPOSURE. A number of other situations involving homosexuality may arise and very often will require referral for short-term or long-term therapy. On arrival individuals may be acutely anxious, depressed, or panic stricken because of fear of exposure of their sexual orientation. The reality factors must be considered since there may be good reason for the anxiety, for example, if the individual is in danger of losing a job or faces legal sanctions. Referral to appropriate community or legal services should be considered in addition to treatment of the reported symptoms.

THE AGING HOMOSEXUAL. The aging homosexual may report problems of depression, loneliness, or despair. The clinician should recognize such symptoms as a result of the client's individual personality makeup or life circumstances rather than regarding them as part of the natural course of homosexuality and encouraging the individual to resign himself to such a fate. Again, community resources may be significant in helping such an individual. Psychotherapy aimed at dealing with the individual's personality problems with a focus on issues of self-fulfilling negative concepts concerning homosexuality or internalized self-hatred will usually be indicated.

ILLNESS OR DEATH OF A LOVER. The illness or death of a lover may be particularly devastating to certain homosexual individuals. Those at highest risk would be individuals who have never been able to accept their own sexual orientation and those who are closeted and lacking in support from friends, co-workers, or family.

As noted in other situations, the need to maintain secrecy about homosexual relationships prevents the distressed individual from receiving the usual support given in times of crisis. During a serious illness families, hospitals, or physicians may prohibit or attempt to prohibit visits by anyone other than "immediate" family. If a couple is closeted or afraid of revealing their sexual orientation, the couple may be separated or at least unable to interact as a heterosexual couple might under similar circumstances. When a lover has died, the deceased person's family may knowingly or unknowingly exclude the partner from participating in funeral arrangements and activities usually associated with the bereavement period. Unfortunately, too often legal issues arise around inheritance with the surviving partner excluded from any claim to homes, property, and items to which both have financially contributed and which both have shared.

The client entering the emergency unit because of factors involving the illness or death of a lover may have a wide variety of symptoms ranging from mild anxiety to suicide attempts or psychotic disorganization. Therapeutic interventions must take into account the special circumstances that may be created because of the client's homosexuality. A supportive, understanding approach is particularly important during a time of grief and stress.

HOLIDAYS AND STRESS. The holiday period may also result in significant stress for homosexuals just as it does for many heterosexuals. Closeted individuals who have accepted the homosexual stereotype as reality or homophobic homosexuals are likely to find themselves faced with loneliness and depression. Homosexual individuals may feel alienated and lonely even among friends and family, particularly if they must keep their sexual orientation hidden. Such individuals must keep large portions of their lives a secret, thereby making the sharing of joys

241

and sorrows and a creation of real intimacy difficult if not impossible. Often there is little that one can discuss or share with the heterosexual for fear of revealing the secret of homosexuality. Innocent questions that ordinarily have the potential of strengthening and deepening relationships become threats to the secret. A question as simple as "what did you do last week?" will require censoring of the response, possibly omitting some activities, and perhaps leaving little that can be talked about. These individuals then are particularly prone to feeling isolated at times such as holidays when everyone is expected to be happy and concerned with family-oriented activities.

THE ROLE OF THE CLINICIAN

The clinician in the psychiatric emergency unit can play a significant role in disrupting long-standing self-defeating patterns within homosexuals. The internalized self-hatred and homophobia can be addressed, and education can begin. A professional, understanding approach can direct the homosexual client toward a full and rewarding life filled with positive choices rather than one limited by conformity to societal stereotypes. Those individuals who do lead productive and personally fulfilling lives but who are caught in extrinsic circumstances beyond their control will be greatly assisted by competent and professional clinicians who accept them as they are, who appreciate their individuality and their human qualities, and who make no attempt to apply their own value systems to individuals with other feelings, other behavior, and other life-styles.

Community referrals

It has been noted several times that it is appropriate for the clinician to consider referral of the homosexual client to community agencies or community groups and also to practitioners for ongoing medical or psychiatric care. Depending on the location across the country, there is a variable degree of access to useful gay organizations. Large cities often have a rich variety of organizations that can be of help to the individual

in the process of resolving some difficulty. For instance, there are groups for older gays, gay youth, parents of gays, gay parents, and married gays. There are gay rap groups, gay church groups, gay sports groups, gay travel groups, and so on. Many universities have gay campus organizations. There are now numerous professional groups such as gay physicians, gay lawyers, gay businessmen, gay airline pilots, gay mental health workers, gay psychologists, gay telephone workers, and gay clergy. These organizations and groups can aid significantly in increasing self-esteem, reducing isolation, and improve the self-image of homosexual men and women. It is advisable for every emergency facility to have a list of local gay organizations to which referrals can be made. Whenever possible, referral resources should be checked for quality before referrals are made. Homosexual individuals have often suffered from a lack of positive role models, and it is not helpful to refer a distressed individual to a deficient or poor-quality group or organization.

Individual referrals

Often it will be necessary to refer the homosexual individual to a mental health specialist for ongoing treatment. Because it is crucial that appropriate referrals be made, it is suggested that each emergency facility prepare a list of competent, knowledgeable referral sources. Care should be taken to include only individuals who are knowledgeable about current thinking and research regarding homosexual issues. Just as one would not refer a client needing medication to someone who only utilized ideas and medications popular 20 years ago, so one should not refer homosexuals to those who are unfamiliar with current concepts. It is highly recommended that mental health professionals specifically be questioned about their knowledge, ability, and willingness to work with homosexual clients. As more and more homosexual therapists make their presence known, consideration can also be given to referring clients to a homosexual clinician. This particular issue might well be discussed with the client before making a referral, and the client's wishes should be respected.

BIBLIOGRAPHY

Adelman, M.R.: A comparison of professionally employed lesbians and heterosexual women on the MMPI, Arch. Sex. Behav. 6(3):193, 1977.

American Psychiatric Association: Position statement on homosexuality and civil rights, Am. J. Psychiatry 131:497, 1974.

Bell, A.P., and Weinberg, M.S.: Homosexualities: a study of diversity among men and women, New York, 1978, Simon & Schuster, Inc.

Berzon, B., and Leighton, R., editors: Positively gay, Millbrae, Calif., 1979, Celestial Arts.

Bieber, I., and Bieber, T.: Male homosexuality, Can. J. Psychiatry 24:409, 1979.

Cass, V.C.: Homosexual identity formation: a theoretical model, J. Homosex. 4(3):219, Spring 1979.

Clark, T.R.: Homosexuality and psychopathology in non-patient males, Am. J. Psychoanal. 35:163, 1975.

Fairchild, B., and Hayward, M.: Now that you know; what every parent should know about homosexuality, New York, 1979, Harcourt Brace Jovanovich.

Freund, K., et al.: The phobic theory of male homosexuality, Arch. Gen. Psychiatry 31(4):495, 1974.

Gebhard, P.H.: Incidence of overt homosexuality in the United States and Western Europe, National Institute of Mental Health Task Force on Homosexuality: Final Report and Background Paper, Pub. No. (AMD) 76:357, Washington, D.C., 1972, Department of Health, Education and Welfare.

Gebhard, P.H., and Johnson, A.B.: The Kinsey data: marginal tabulations of the 1938-1963 interviews conducted by the Institute for Sex Research, Philadelphia, 1979, W.B. Saunders Co.

Hart, M., et al.: Psychological adjustment of non-patient homosexuals: critical review of the research literature, J. Clin. Psychiatry 39:604, 1978.

Heston, L., and Shields, J.: Homosexuality in twins, Arch. Gen. Psychiatry 18:149, 1968.

Hudson, W.W., and Ricketts, W.A.: A strategy for the measurement of homophobia, J. Homosex. 5(4):357, 1980.

Kallman, F.: Comparative twin study on the genetic aspects of male homosexuality, J. Nerv. Ment. Dis. 115:283, 1952.

Karr, R.C.: Homosexual labelling and the male role, J. Soc. Issues 34(3):73, 1978.

Kelly, J.: The aging male homosexual: myth and reality, Gerontologist 17(4):328, 1977.

Kimmel, D.: Life-history interviews of aging gay men, Int. J. Aging Hum. Dev. 10(3):239, 1979.

Kinsey, A.C., et al.: Sexual behavior in the human male, Philadelphia, 1948, W.B. Saunders Co.

Kinsey, A.C., et al.: Sexual behavior in the human female, Philadelphia, 1953, W.B. Saunders Co.

Kolb, L.: Therapy of homosexuality. In Masserman, J., editor: Current psychiatric therapies, vol. 3, New York, 1963, Grune & Stratton, Inc.

Lee, J.A.: Going public: a study in the sociology of homosexual liberation, J. Homosex. 3(1):49, Fall 1977.

Lester, D.: The relationship between paranoid delusions and homosexuality, Arch. Sex. Behav. 4:285, 1975.

Marmor, J.: Overview: the multiple roots of homosexual behavior. In Marmor, J., editor: Homosexual behavior: a modern reappraisal, New York, 1980, Basic Books, Inc., Publishers.

Meredith, R.L., and Riester, R.W.: Psychotherapy, responsibility and homosexuality: clinical examination of socially deviant behavior, Professional Psychol. 2:174, April 1980.

Mitchell, S.A.: Psychodynamics: homosexuality and the question of pathology, Psychiatry 41:254, Aug. 1978.

Morin, S.F.: Heterosexual bias in psychological research on lesbianism and male homosexuality, Am. Psychol. 32(8):629, Aug. 1977.

Pomeroy, W.B.: Homosexuality. In Weltge, R.W., editor: The same sex, Boston, 1969, The Pilgrim Press.

Shively, M.A., and De Cecco, J.P.: Components of sexual identity, J. Homosex. 3(1):41, Fall 1977.

Siegelman, M.: Parental background of male homosexuals, Arch. Sex. Behav. 3(1):3, 1974.

Socarides, C.: Some problems encountered in the psychoanalytic treatment of overt male homosexuality, Am. J. Psychother. 33:506, 1979.

Tourney, G.: Hormones and homosexuality. In Marmor, J., editor: Homosexual behavior: a modern reappraisal, New York, 1980, Basic Books, Inc., Publishers.

Tripp, C.: The homosexual matrix, New York, 1975, McGraw-Hill Book Co.

Troiden, R.R.: Becoming homosexual: a model of gay identity acquisition, Psychiatry 42:362, Nov. 1979.

Weinberg, G.: Society and the healthy homosexual, New York, 1973, Doubleday & Co., Inc.

CHAPTER 15

The client who is a member of an ethnic minority

Art Hom, M.S.W.

Danger 危 *(wei) and* *Opportunity* 機 *(ji)*—The Chinese definition of crisis **(危機)**.

The purpose of this chapter is to provide information and suggest techniques clinicians in psychiatric emergency units may use in helping ethnic minority clients. This chapter will offer (1) a brief summary of the barriers to psychotherapy, (2) the need for a cross-cultural perspective, and (3) ways psychiatric emergency units can begin to provide culturally relevant care. A method of intervention will be presented which demonstrates how various goals and techniques of crisis theory can be implemented depending on consideration of the following three variables: (1) the ethnic minority group membership plus individual differences of the client, (2) the degree of acculturation of the client into the dominant culture, and (3) the source of stress and whether it is intrapsychic or extrapsychic.

DEFINING ETHNIC MINORITY

Since the 1960s there has been a proliferation of terms used to identify various groups. Lacking clear definitions, some terms are used interchangeably, such as *ethnic group*, *minority group*, and *third world group*. The selection of terminology is often influenced by one's political beliefs and the current preferences of the group being addressed. For purposes of this chapter the term *ethnic group* will refer to people who have a shared social and cultural heritage that has been uniquely passed from one generation to another. The term *minority group* is commonly used to refer to ethnic groups whose population in the United States is relatively small in number. These groups may be low in socioeconomic status, lack political strength, and have a history of unjust treatment and oppression by the majority society. The term *third world* refers to nations not aligned with the United States or Russia; they are not industralized and are basically non-White. Non-White ethnic minority people are termed *third world group* by those who want to add a connotation of political unity to the poor, non-White groups.

Throughout history ethnic minorities have been labeled by the majority society. A person of African descent, for example, was called colored or Negro, which was based on the Latin word for black. Both of there terms came to be viewed as derogatory. During the civil rights movement of the 1960s people of African descent decided they wanted to be called Black Americans. At this same time other minority groups also became concerned about their self-identity and began to select names for themselves. Just as Negroes began calling themselves Black Americans, Orientals (Chinese, Japanese, Koreans and so on) began identifying themselves as Asian Americans, and Indians preferred to be called Native Americans. People of Spanish origin from South and Central America preferred the collective identity conveyed by the terms *Latino* and *Hispanic* to the previous custom of referring to their specific homeland (for example, Cuban or Mexican).

COMMON BARRIERS

The following case vignette will depict some of the many barriers that prevent ethnic minorities from receiving effective psychotherapy. Although the case involves a Chinese man, the difficulties are similarly experienced by most other ethnic groups and often by lower socioeconomic class Whites as well.

Case vignette #1

Mr. W is a 48-year-old recent arrival from Hong Kong who complains about a history of attacks of dizziness (*tou won* in Cantonese), insomnia, and poor appetite of several months' duration. He sought the help of a well-known internist, but a battery of comprehensive tests disclosed a normal range of findings. He was told that he had no medical illness and that his problems were mental. He was referred to a psychoanalyst who spoke to him briefly by telephone. After assessing that he could not help Mr. W, he referred him to a Chinese bilingual clinician at a psychiatric emergency unit. Mr. W was seen once but did not return again.

He complained about undergoing an expensive workup and then not receiving any treatment. He wanted an injection that could relieve him of his dizziness and other symptoms. Pleased that his new doctor spoke his language, he revealed his ideas about the cause of his illness. He felt that he was suffering a Chinese "cold" disorder, which meant that his "hot and cold" balance was out of harmony. He felt that he had overworked himself by having two jobs to support his wife, two children, an aging mother in Hong Kong, and a mentally ill sister also in Hong Kong.

This last piece of history he cautiously revealed by asking if mental illness was hereditary. He said he was concerned about his children and the possibility they may have difficulty finding marriage partners. Whenever he was questioned about his fears or about his feelings, he would quickly change the subject to his physical complaints. Beyond saying that he was feeling some depression, he could not explain or define more specifically how he felt. He denied any problems with regard to his personal relationships. When questioned specifically about any changes in his sexual interests or behavior, he reported that sex made him more tired so he had reduced the frequency. Before the end of the interview, he asked if the clinician could refer him to an herbalist.

Case vignette #1 illustrates the difficulties most ethnic clients, whether Black, Native American or Latino, may present when they appear at an emergency unit. There are marked language differences, elements of distrust, requests for concrete solutions, a prevalence of somatization, and the client's lack of "psychological mindedness" that make it problematical for most emergency clinicians to provide effective care.

Since the 1960s there has been much written about the failure of traditional psychotherapy to meet the growing needs of ethnic minorities whose representatives have become continually more vocal, demanding equal access and rights to treatment (Atkinson, 1979). Despite the growing awareness of some of the difficulties in treating ethnic minorities and the gains made in the training and hiring of ethnic minorities, the need for effective treatment methods continues. Most clinicians of all backgrounds continue to be rendered helpless by cases such as Mr. W. Worst of all, these clients remain underserved and untreated.

Miscommunication

Case vignette #1 is an example of miscommunication. Mr. W and his doctors held different views of his sickness and had conflicting expectations of the treatment. From a psychiatric perspective his problem can be diagnosed as an adjustment reaction with anxiety and depression, precipitated by his recent arrival in this country. From the client's own perspective, his problem is *tou won,* which is a culturally specific disorder based on indigenous Chinese concepts (Kleinman, 1980). This disorder is often translated to mean dizziness or vertigo. It is a common complaint of Chinese women and some Chinese men. The dizziness can be quite disabling, causing loss of wages and decreased functioning. Yet to many internists, Mr. W and others do not have "real" disorders because the tests do not reveal any organic pathology.

Avoidance of strong affects

Although the psychiatric emergency unit clinician happened to be both bilingual and experienced, he felt exasperated and helpless. Western clinical training emphasizes the technique and therapeutic value of exploring dysphoric affects. However, most clinicians will report that it is nearly impossible to get Chinese clients to talk about strong feelings, particularly toward family members; these clients prefer to name the feeling and then to describe the situation they believed caused it or its somatic and interpersonal effects (Kleinman, 1980). Their difficulty in elaborating on intrapsychic experiences can be disarming. Therefore, it could be a treatment goal to teach the language one can use to express the nuances of one's emotional life.

Somatization

It appears that one of the limits of psychotherapy for these clients is in the treatment of somatization (Kleinman, 1980). If the client's beliefs are sanctioned by their culture, as somatization is in the Chinese culture, the coping style is nearly impossible to change. Their symptoms are real and can even be the result of emotional causes, but these clients will not be persuaded to see their problems psychologically. Since they feel it is a physical illness, they see little reason to disclose personal matters, much less pay for a talking style of treatment.

Some may even argue that many clients who are not psychologically minded and who lack the resources for treatment might do better to continue handling their problems in somatic terms. By doing so, they would receive the appropriate family and social supports for somatic problems, which perhaps would not be available for psychological problems. In other words, psychological approaches to treating all somatic complaints may be culturally overvalued by helping professionals.

NEED FOR A CROSS-CULTURAL PERSPECTIVE

Case vignette #1 raises questions about the differences between indigenous Chinese concepts of illness and Western biomedical views of illness. The medical professions have a long-standing tendency to treat both medical and psychiatric healing as if healing were a totally independent, timeless, culture-free process. Kleinman (1980) and Kiev (1964) also criticize traditional psychoanalytic thinkers like Fenichel for not considering social and cultural influences while fitting a wide array of data into a single theory of human behavior.

Advocates of a holistic conception of health such as Rivers (1924), Sigerist (1951), and Kleinman (1980) have called for research to look at the relationship between culture and medicine. They are critical of the ethnocentric and reductionist view of the biomedical model, in which biological factors alone constitute the "real world" and the focus for research and treatment (Kleinman, 1980).

Medical anthropologists urge the study of primitive societies to examine the role culture plays in health care and to understand the healing process itself. Kiev (1964) found that the healer role in primitive society parallels the role of the psychiatrist, despite the absence in the former of scientific methods. The hope, the expectation, and the faith that the person has in the designated healer were felt to contribute more to therapeutic results than is ordinarily recognized in contemporary theories of psychiatry (Frank, 1974; Kiev, 1964).

Kiev (1968) further suggests that the role of the *curandero* (faith healer) in Latino folk medicine is similar to the role of psychiatrist. They both use a set of techniques designed to allay anxiety and fear and a set of beliefs that foster understanding of distressing experiences.

Fabrega (1974) compares the curer-client relationships and contrasts the "impersonal" Western characteristics, such as distance, coolness, and use of abstract concepts (jargon), to the "personal" characteristics of the *curandero,* such as closeness, shared meaning, warmth and informality, and use of everyday language. Such a comparison clearly suggests why Western therapies often are unsuccessful with Latino and other ethnic groups.

These proponents believe that all health care can be studied as a cultural system that deals with both biologic and symbolic reality of disease and illness. This reality comprises psycho-social-cultural phenomena that constitute an in-

dividual's experience of illness and also influence the science of diagnosis and treatment of illness itself. Western psychotherapy, despite its scientific basis, finds its origin in Western society and functions according to Western values and beliefs. From this perspective psychotherapy cannot simply be applied universally to ethnically different populations. For example, the technique in family therapy of encouraging the expression of suppressed anger toward one's family members reinforces a Western culturally valued coping mechanism to learn to speak out and be independent. For many ethnic minority clients this treatment technique may conflict with their culture's emphasis on self-control and the highly valued emphasis on harmonious group membership.

The need for developing a cross-cultural perspective is clear. Yet in many ways it is unclear how the clinician can compare and mediate these varied cultural perspectives. Some innovative practitioners have begun to apply the salient qualities of the *curandero* or have been challenged to seek creative methods to work with hard-to-reach clients. Even though we may learn from the study of primitive healing methods and attempt to adapt what is relevant, these "healers" lack scientific validity or the ability to treat severe emotional disorders. It would be foolish to hope that magical answers can be found in folk methods. Kiev (1968) recognizes the *curandero's* inability to treat acute schizophrenia, mania, and depression.

Although Western psychiatry is maligned by its critics for its failures, the profession must be credited with the development of humane programs and methods. The advancements in the use of both psychotherapy and biochemicals have improved the treatment and management of the severely disordered. Further advances to provide culturally relevant care are sorely needed. The remainder of the chapter will demonstrate how the crisis intervention model can be expanded to meet some of these challenges.

EXPANDING THE CRISIS MODEL

Given these many attitudes and behaviors of ethnic minorities that are barriers to traditional psychotherapy, one might wonder what possibly can be effective. The crisis intervention model has proved to be very adaptive and flexible. Clinicians need to expand this model to include identifying the clients' group membership, their level of acculturation, and any individual differences. In addition, by determining whether the sources of the stress are intrapsychic or extrapsychic, the psychiatric emergency worker can be more effective in determining the most appropriate treatment goals and methods (Fig. 15-1).

Identifying the ethnic group

Although minority groups share some common attitudes and behaviors and are culturally distinct from majority cultures, it cannot be assumed that each group is uniformly alike. It is important to identify the major ethnic group membership of the client and identify the sub-

group membership, being especially alert to any individual differences. For example, identifying a client as Latino is not sufficient, for there are many subgroups with many important differences between immigrants from Mexico, Cuba, Puerto Rico, Central America, and South America. The major differences in the manner in which different Latino groups enter the country influence their adjustment and the way help is sought (Rivera and Gonzales, 1977). When Latinos are from Puerto Rico, a U.S. territory, they enter as citizens and face far fewer immigration problems than the many Mexicans who illegally cross the U.S. border and live with the constant fear of deportation.

Central Americans who enter this country tend to be from middle-class and working class backgrounds and are able to enter through legal means. One's adjustment in this country and the manner in which help is sought depend on

Ethnic group:
(subgroups and individual differences)

	Degree of acculturation					
	TRADITIONAL		TRANSITIONAL		THIRD WORLD	
	Source of stress		Source of stress		Source of stress	
Methods / Goals	Intrapsychic	Extrapsychic	Intrapsychic	Extrapsychic	Intrapsychic	Extrapsychic
Crisis intervention						
Brief crisis treatment						

FIG. 15-1. Assessment of acculturation, source of stress, and methods of intervention.

one's class background and education level. Middle-class Central Americans would be more likely to seek help from professional medical doctors, whereas poor farm workers would be more apt to seek help from a faith healer.

Understanding the class differences in each subgroup and how they affect the manner of immigration can help clinicians recognize the various ways help is sought. For example, a well-dressed Latino man from a middle-class background in Chile who appears at a psychiatric emergency unit requesting that he see a Spanish-speaking doctor (not a female nurse) contrasts sharply with a Latino man from a lower-class background in Mexico who is brought in mute by the police. The clinicians will need to determine whether the latter client is mute because of his fear of the authorities who may deport him for illegal entry into the country or whether the client is psychologically decompensating. It is obvious that clients with immigration problems will be unlikely to seek mental health care services until they are severely ill and need to be brought in by the police.

The degree of acculturation

It is important to distinguish the degree of acculturation. After immigrants arrive, the acculturation process may spawn conflicts and uncertainties. This process may take many generations during which time two different value systems are confronted, leading to many possible resolutions. Some adapt to both cultures, blending these uniquely. Others choose to desperately preserve old ways, living in ghettoes and experiencing the wider culture as alien and threatening. Still others renounce old ways vigorously, seeking assimilation quickly. Whatever pathway is chosen, the transitional process is rarely smooth or easy.

TRADITIONAL. Ethnic groups generally consist of three basic types: traditional, transitional, and third world (Sue, 1971). The first are the traditional groups consisting of those who are foreign born, the new immigrants from Hong Kong, Puerto Rico, Southeast Asia, and so on, or those who are the least acculturated, such as those Native Americans who have never left the reser-

vation and the "down home" Blacks from the rural South. These people bring with them the traditional ethnic beliefs and practices, including those related to health.

For example, Wauneka (1962) describes the difficulty in working with Navajo patients who had contracted tuberculosis. Many Navajos are illiterate and distrust "the white man's medicine"; their language lacks the concept of contagious germs. Wauneka successfully used the public health model of prevention by patiently teaching from the Navajo's cultural perspective.

Clinicians need to be sensitive to the struggle for socioeconomic survival of traditional groups and their language and cultural differences. As previously discussed, ethnic minorities possess many attitudes and behaviors that are considered barriers to traditional psychotherapy. A method of intervention that can focus on the here-and-now external realities while supporting their social and psychological needs can be the most effective. Later in the chapter, case vignette #2 will illustrate how crisis intervention is helpful.

TRANSITIONAL. The second group includes those who are in a transitional state and tend to be the second or third generation in this country and for whom the clash of two cultures may be very sharp. Their parents are the down home folks who tend to cling to traditional beliefs, whereas these transitional persons are keenly influenced by Western education and its belief system. This group tends to have a mixed set of values. For example, American-born Chinese young adults experience considerable conflict regarding self-worth and esteem. In Chinese families self-esteem derives largely from parental approval for emotional and behavioral control. Even intellectual and artistic expression must meet the criteria for economic success and enhancement of the family's name, pride, and honor. While Westerners value economic success, they profess as well that self-growth and self-expression far outweigh familial requirements.

To intervene effectively, the clinicians need to be sensitive to this transitional group's cultural conflicts. For instance, because of the traditional Chinese influence, there will be much reluctance

249

to disclose strong affects or intimate thoughts. Yet Chinese Americans are influenced by the Western belief that, although self-disclosure is difficult, it can be therapeutic. Brief crisis treatment can be an effective method for this group. Case vignette #3 will illustrate how brief crisis treatment can be useful.

THIRD WORLD. The third group consists of ethnic minority members who do not like to be referred to as minorities but identify themselves with the third world. This is a politicized group whose members have been in the United States for many generations and who are well educated and typically middle class. These families have become acculturated to American life, yet they are not assimilated in the "melting pot" sense that is prevalent in the thinking of some Americans. In fact, that concept was more a wish than fact for many groups, although some Americans more nearly approximated this idealized concept than others. No longer is it considered ideal to give up one's past cultural background and adopt whatever the host culture provides to call oneself American. For example, the Chinese Americans hope to form an Asian-American identity by taking the best from their cultural heritage and integrating it with the best from the new country and uniting with all other third world people.

Economic survival is no longer a driving force; these people now strive for a higher quality of life for all third world people. The struggle to retain parental approval is past, while sharp conflicts between parental acceptance and self-acceptance have dimmed considerably. However, this group believes that no matter how long third world groups have lived in this country, race will influence the acculturation process and their lives.

This third world grouping is utilized more as an ideal type to complete the acculturation continuum (Sue, 1971). Those who fit this description best are the transitional persons who are well assimilated and have developed a politicized identity. They strongly believe that efforts to change social and political policy are far more relevant for the individual and society than psychotherapy. These group members, like those in the traditional group, rarely seek traditional psychotherapy. If they do, they seek out third world private practitioners. Unless there is a major life crisis where the police are involved, such as a suicide attempt, the third world client will not find it necessary to use a psychiatric emergency unit. Furthermore, Sue (1971) recommends that when third world clients do seek help, the clinicians must acknowledge the sophisticated skepticism these clients have of psychotherapy. Once these issues are addressed, brief crisis treatment can be offered.

• • •

Although grouping people into three groups can be misleading and stereotyping, it can be very helpful in making distinctions for appropriate psychiatric interventions. By assessing the clients' group membership and their levels of acculturation, clinicians can best consider clients' needs and problems and determine possible goals and methods of intervention.

The source of stress

EXTRAPSYCHIC CONFLICTS. Conflicts arising from the acculturation process can be considered extrapsychic, since they have their origin outside the person. However, members of society are influenced by society's attitudes and values, including its attitudes about ethnic minority people. How such attitudes are integrated into the personality is influenced by many internal factors. It is in the dynamic interaction between external stress and internal processing that acculturation occurs for each person (Cooper, 1979). Clinicians must attempt to distinguish where the stress originates in the process of acculturation to best help clients with their problems.

Ethnic minorities, often justifiably, tend to ascribe their problems to external sources associated with ethnic minority group membership. One must access carefully the complaints of prejudice, the effects of discriminatory practice on personality development, functioning, and coping. Most ethnic minorities are caught in a ghetto syndrome. Poor, uneducated, broken families tend to beget poor, uneducated, broken families; the cycle is self-perpetuating. Complaints by clients about unfair employment practices, unfair housing policies, and mistreatment by government bureaucracies, including police and health services, are too often real and deserve investigation.

INTRAPSYCHIC CONFLICTS. The term *intrapsychic* is used to identify the sources of the stress that arises independent of ethnic minority group membership. It must be assumed that intrapsychic conflict is the same for all people regardless of ethnicity. Although it is plausible that psychic pain is universally experienced, there remains the need for a more cultural approach to reduce the barriers to treatment. Rusk (1971) refers to three basic needs of human beings: affection, security, and significance. Any threat to meeting these needs creates cognitive confusion and emotional discomfort. For example, young students, whether White, Black, Latino or Asian, face the same anxiety and confusion when they break up with their lovers, boyfriends, or girlfriends. This would suggest similar types of intervention in helping the clients deal with the loss. However, most clients enter the unit with a mixture of problems including stress related to both intrapsychic and extrapsychic sources, which are universal as well as of ethnic origin. For example, second-generation Chinese young adult may have unique problems during the breakup of a relationship. Often traditional Chinese parents do not approve of dating or marriage until after their children, especially sons, complete college and have jobs. Rarely do they consider their children as adults until they are married. Not only is the breakup experience painful, but the loss of parental approval by dating and by the resulting poor academic performance during the crisis compound what might be an ordinary life crisis for any person.

After an assessment of the ethnic minority group membership plus individual differences of the client, the degree of acculturation of the client into the dominant culture, and the source of the stress, the clinician can begin to determine the effective method of treatment. The two most viable methods are crisis intervention and brief crisis treatment.

CRISIS INTERVENTION

According to crisis theory, clients facing an emotional situation that is too difficult for them develop maladaptive ways of coping with it. It is often possible in treatment to intervene in such a way as to alter the situation to reduce the stress or to show the clients that their reactions are maladaptive and to then direct them toward a more realistic resolution (Caplan, 1964; Lindeman, 1944; Parad, 1965). According to Malan (1976), this is done by various amounts of educating or, when possible, interpretation of the unconscious forces with the hope of effecting new growth and enabling the clients to function at a higher level than before the crisis.

Crisis intervention is an important form of brief psychotherapy. Malan (1976) and Sifneos (1967) have described the various forms of brief psychotherapy by describing a continuum consisting of (1) supportive measures such as environmental manipulation, reassurance, and drugs; (2) the teaching of new ways of dealing with emotional conflict; and (3) interpretation of unconscious forces.

Crisis intervention as defined in this chapter falls under the first category of providing supportive measures, that is, crisis support. Sifneos (1967) describes this form of treatment as best suited for the severely disturbed, because of its emphasis on drugs and the attempt at eliminating factors responsible for the present decompensation. The aim is to restore the status quo and relieve symptoms in a few weeks with frequency of visits according to need.

Crisis intervention is successful for most ethnic minority clients who are not acculturated and do not share the majority culture's language or belief in traditional psychotherapy. These clients essentially have life adjustment problems partly or largely related to socioeconomic survival. The goal is to restore their functioning and prevent further deterioration by focusing on current life changes. When these clients do enter psychiatric emergency units, they appear quite "out of place." These are clients who speak a foreign language, wear non-Western style clothing, and sometimes are accompanied by a group of non-White relatives, one of whom perhaps can speak a few words of English. Case vignette #2 illustrates this point.

Case vignette #2

The G family came to the clinic accompanying Mrs. G, who was dressed in a sari, a native garment worn by women in India. Mrs. G covered her entire head with a shawl and did not say anything in English except "sorry." Mr. G spoke through another family member and expressed his complaint that his wife had stopped cooking for the family, which included two children, ages seven and four. After explaining what difficulty he had in bringing his wife in, he apologetically demanded to have her hospitalized. The clinician ascertained that (1) the family recently arrived from India and spoke only the dialects Urdu and Punjabi, (2) they were first generation in this country, and (3) their problems were both intrapsychic and extrapsychic. Unable to speak directly to the family, the clinician arranged to have a private practitioner who could speak their language see the family without charge and work collaboratively with the clinic.

Subsequently the private practitioner and one of the clinic staff members held office visits for the family, but Mrs. G refused to attend. Further efforts were made to evaluate the family, the care of the children, and the living situation in a skid row hotel. Even with much coaxing, Mrs. G refused to cooperate with the therapist, to attend the sessions, or to comply with the carefully arrived at decision for her to take medication. The situation deteriorated rapidly. Mrs. G frequently left the hotel late at night to wander in an unsafe neighborhood. Mr. G was staying home to care for the children while jeopardizing his employment at a restaurant.

Finally, Mrs. G was involuntarily hospitalized. Although the bilingual practitioner was not a physician, he continued to treat her in conjunction with the inpatient staff. Because of her inability to speak English and her withdrawn behavior, she could not fully participate in the ward activities. However, she made some improvements in a brief 2-week period. On discharge she agreed to continue her medication and see the therapist for supportive psychotherapy.

Case vignette #2 demonstrates the application of Sifneos' first category of crisis support (1967). It consisted of a use of environmental manipulation, such as referrals to a bilingual practitioner and later to an inpatient unit; supportive measures such as home visits, private office visits, outpatient visits to the crisis clinic; and finally the use of psychotropic medications.

Although most staff members are responsive to non-English-speaking clients from foreign countries, they are quite limited by the language and different ethnic features of the clients. When a multilingual staff member can speak the client's language, the clients may appear less "out of place" and may be better evaluated in their home. The ideal crisis unit has the capacity for extensive outreach services. By having the capability of going into the home, one need not wait until the identified patient is brought to the clinic by the family or police, and treatment can begin before the problem becomes acute. Sometimes if a team can see the client early and follow through with a series of visits, they may be able to prevent further deterioration and an unnecessary hospitalization.

In addition, the psychiatric emergency unit clinician must search for strengths in the client, in the family supports, and in the community which can be brought into play. Traditionally trained clinicians have a tendency to search and recognize only the pathology. Yet this need to search for the client's strengths should not preclude the usual mental status examination and assessment to rule out psychological or organic pathology. If necessary, as case vignette #2 demonstrates, one must use psychotropic medications, alternatives to hospitalization, and hospitalization as well. For the gravely disabled, the suicidal, and the violent, careful and responsible use of all of these options can be helpful for their protection and the protection of others. When indicated, bilingual translators or staff members must follow the clients and their families through the course of inpatient care.

The crisis intervention method is effective for

the less acculturated ethnic minorities. It does require some psychic pain for clients to refer themselves or to be referred by their family. The amount of time required is minimal, as few as one or two sessions, and the cost or financial investment is offset by sliding scales based on ability to pay.

BRIEF CRISIS TREATMENT

Brief crisis treatment falls into Sifneos' second category, which consists of brief anxiety suppressive therapy and the teaching of new ways of dealing with emotional conflict (1967). This form of treatment can be either for the previously healthy client in crisis or for the severely disturbed client with a history showing character defects and precarious functioning who is, however, able to recognize the psychological nature of illness. The techniques are essentially crisis oriented, aimed at preventing the establishment of symptoms and at teaching new coping skills. Goals are to restore the status quo, to reduce symptoms, and to avoid similar situations by a series of visits lasting as long as a few months to a year.

In addition, brief crisis treatment can, when possible, include what Sifneos calls "brief anxiety-provoking therapy." This form of treatment is essentially psychodynamic, transference-oriented psychotherapy, which seeks in a brief period of time not only to relieve symptoms but also to effect personality change. According to Sifneos, this ambitious form of treatment is offered to clients who have well-defined neurotic symptoms and who have at least three of the following six criteria: (1) above average intelligence, (2) at least one meaningful relationship in their history, (3) an emotional crisis, (4) an ability to interact well with the clinician and to express feeling, (5) a motivation to work hard in the treatment, and (6) a specific chief complaint.

Depending on the ethnic minority client's level of acculturation, motivation, and source of the problem, brief crisis treatment, especially brief anxiety-suppressive therapy, can be an effective method. Ethnic minorities who are second generation or later, who speak English well, and who share some of the beliefs necessary for psy-

chotherapy (such as trusting that disclosing how one feels can be therapeutic) can be persuaded to learn from the crisis that brought them in for help. Case vignette #3 is a good example of how an initial crisis contact for a second-generation ethnic minority can develop into a brief treatment contract.

Case vignette #3

Ms. D is an attractive 22-year-old Asian American who entered a clinic, seeking a therapist to "help" her. However, during the interview she refused to give much information to the staff person and stated that she preferred to talk to the doctor, despite earnest attempts by the interviewer to initiate a working alliance. In response to the worker's questions, Ms. D would only remain silent and become tearful.

The white female interviewer felt that Ms. D was under much stress and, because of her markedly distrustful behavior, suspected that she might be paranoid. This case was quickly referred to an Asian male therapist who understood the client's difficulties with shame and in expressing herself with words.

Her initial complaints included her anxiety, her indecision about educational plans, and her difficulty in close relationships with men. Only through patient listening and gentle questioning did the therapist learn that the young woman had sought help because of her fear of "going crazy."

Very reluctantly she disclosed that her father had a history of chronic schizophrenia since she was 5 years old. Initially there was a need to be silent when she had troublesome thoughts and intense feelings. The clinician encouraged her to explore her ambivalent feelings about her father and his illness. It was learned that she had been close to her father and had felt that she was similar to him in many ways (such as physical appearance and intelligence). Since his breakdown she had feared that she too would become psychotic and had consequently withdrawn from him. As the initial anxiety subsided in the crisis contact, she gradually became able to relate her present interpersonal difficulties with men to past events and to directly link these difficulties to her relationship with her father.

The clinician, in addition, commented how she was rather remote and a little too respectful of his authority. She politely explained that she did not want to overly burden him. It was then carefully pointed out that she seemed afraid of getting too close to the therapist. She was afraid she might then experience angry feelings which she feared would overly burden him and cause him to be unavailable to her, much like her relationship with her father.

On termination of treatment after 1 year, she decided she would seek a degree in English with the goal of teaching young Asian-American students how to write and express themselves.

In practice, case vignette #3 illustrates that it is possible to treat a fairly acculturated ethnic minority person who has a defined intrapsychic conflict with a mixture of both anxiety-suppressive and anxiety-provoking forms of brief treatment. Although the client was at first resistant to treatment, after her initial anxiety was relieved she responded to the various educative and interpretative approaches. New ways of dealing with emotional conflict were learned, such as using her verbal skills to express affect toward her therapist and even her father. Gradually the client realized that she was unknowingly repeating a maladaptive pattern and that she could have more control of her life.

Although the brief treatment approaches of Sifneos (1967) and Malan (1976) are helpful, often the criteria for selection in the brief anxiety-provoking therapy discussed earlier are far too restrictive. The criteria do exclude many of the clients seen in emergency units, including the less educated, less introspective and less motivated Whites, along with a fairly wide range of ethnic minorities. Often clinicians will attempt to treat their clients with brief treatment methods even if these clients do not meet all of the

selection criteria. While many of these cases do not reach the ambitious goal of significant characterological change, the more common outcomes of symptom relief and of the beginning of character change should be considered rewarding accomplishments.

Furthermore, brief crisis treatment is a method that first requires that the psychiatric emergency unit has the staffing necessary to be able to see clients for more than one or two sessions. Many units have limited staff and office space. They are only able to do the initial assessment and then must refer the clients who want to continue in treatment to outpatient clinics. It has been my experience that many clients tend to drop out during the referral process, but with minority members the rate of attrition is far greater. Such administrative procedures as the use of a waiting list, the assignment to a different clinician, the completion of another set of registration papers, and even the change of location of office sites may constitute barriers to continuing psychotherapy. The ideal emergency unit would enable the same clinician to follow the client through a complete course of brief crisis treatment.

SUMMARY

Psychiatric emergency clinicians can offer ethnic minority clients the help of crisis intervention and brief crisis treatment, depending on the assessment of their ethnic group membership, their level of acculturation, and the nature of their psychic conflict. Provided there is a shared language, even new immigrants can often be treated with crisis intervention, while the more acculturated ethnic minorities can often do well with brief crisis treatment.

With the adoption of these techniques in the hands of well-trained clinicians, the growing commitment to provide immediate, relevant, and practical care to all members of the community can more readily be fulfilled. The recognition of the special needs of the poor and ethnic minorities is long overdue. Yet the success of this endeavor depends on the joint effort of all the professional community, including those in private practice, in community mental health, and in research.

Since most of today's briefer therapies are based on the traditional therapies, clinicians need a knowledge of and experience with the traditional long-term therapies. Traditional therapists must avoid depreciating all treatment methods that are not geared solely to long-term character change. Clinicians of all therapeutic orientations have the responsibility to sensitize themselves to the special needs of ethnic minority clients.

BIBLIOGRAPHY

Aguilera, D., and Messick, J.: Crisis intervention theory and methodology, ed. 4, St. Louis, 1982, The C.V. Mosby Co.

Atkinson, D., Morten, G., and Sue, D.W.: Counseling American minorities, Dubuque, Iowa, 1979, Wm. C. Brown Co., Publishers.

Caplan, G.: Principles of preventive psychiatry, New York, 1964, Basic Books, Inc., Publishers.

Cooper, S.: Personal communication, Oct. 1979.

Fabrega, H.: Disease and social behavior, Cambridge, Mass., 1974, Massachusetts Institute of Technology Press.

Frank, J.: Persuasion and healing, New York, 1974, Schocken Books Inc.

Hom, A., and Amada, G.: Overcoming the problem of face saving. In Amada, G., editor: Mental health on the community college campus, Washington, D.C., 1977, University Press of America.

Kiev, A., editor: Magic, faith and healing, New York, 1964, The Free Press.

Kiev, A.: Curanderismo, New York, 1968, The Free Press.

Kleinman, A.: Patients and healers in the context of culture, Berkeley, Calif., 1980, University of California Press.

Lindemann, E.: Symptomatology and management of acute grief, Am. J. Psychiatry 101:141, Sept. 1944.

Malan, D.: A study of brief psychotherapy, New York, 1976, Plenum Publishing Corp.

Parad, H.J., editor: Crisis intervention: selected readings, New York, 1965, Family Service Association of America.

Rivera, R., and Gonzales, G.: Major hispanic groups in San Francisco and their use of community mental health services: research report to San Francisco community mental health services, unpublished document, 1977.

Rivers, W.: Medicine, magic and religion, New York, 1924, Harcourt Brace Jovanovich.

Rusk, T.: Opportunity and technique in crisis psychiatry, Compr. Psychiatry 12:3, May 1971.

Sifneos, P.: Two different kinds of psychotherapy of short duration, Am. J. Psychiatry 123:1069, March 1967.

Sigerist, H.: A history of medicine, vol. 1, Primitive and archaic medicine, London, 1951, Oxford University Press, Inc.

Sue, D.W., and Sue, S.: Chinese-American personality and mental health, Amerasia J. 1:2, July 1971.

Wauneka, A.: Helping people to understand, Am. J. Nurs. 62:7, 1962.

CHAPTER 16

The client who is bereaved

Margaret Albrizio, R.N., M.S.

I don't know how much I can tell you about loss and bereavement, I should be an expert having lost a fiance by suicide, my parents and a fourteen year old brother killed by Hitler, my son, James, with leukemia, my husband dropping dead in the middle of a street in Spain and then, my son, Robert. But all I can tell you is that I am leading two lives. One on the outside trying to enjoy myself as much as possible and the inner life which is completely empty, with feelings of great bitterness and guilt . . . (From a letter written by a grieving mother whose son was interviewed by the author of this chapter before his death.)

Most people struggle through bereavement without the benefit of professional guidance. In recent years, however, experts have begun to support programs to aid this special population since the bereaved are known to be at increased risk for illness and mortality. For this reason a great deal of attention has been focused on the field of loss and bereavement. Theorists and researchers have approached these topics from a variety of perspectives. This chapter attempts to integrate some of the literature on loss and bereavement and to apply it to the psychiatric emergency setting. Emphasis is on preventative care that can support healthy coping patterns and foster an uncomplicated bereavement.

First, the concept of loss and its relationship to stress are discussed. Then the concept of death is discussed in the context of our modern technological society. Major contributors to the field, such as Freud, Lindemann, Bowlby, and Kübler-Ross, are used to illustrate the development of psychiatric theories in this area. The relationship between theories of bereavement and crisis intervention is then compared.

In this chapter the importance of incorporating health-promoting interventions for bereaved persons seen in psychiatric emergency settings is emphasized. The proposed model of the bereavement process serves as a framework to conceptualize grief rather than as a rigid structure that must be imposed on each individual griever. Each phase of bereavement is examined with attention to pertinent behaviors and issues germane to that phase, suggestions for intervention, and examples to illustrate major points.

The latter portion of the chapter briefly discusses related topics, such as those factors that affect the character of grief, the atypical grief syndrome, and the application of the bereavement model to other types of loss. Attention is then focused on family bereavement through the use of systems theory and with particular regard for childhood bereavement, the identified patient in the family, and childhood deaths. Finally, special consideration is given to the needs of the clinician when a client dies.

THE CONCEPT OF LOSS

Throughout the course of our lives individuals are subject to a continuous stream of events that result in personal loss (Speck, 1978). These range from minor and frequent events, such as the loss of a card game, to major infrequent events such as the loss of a parent or spouse. Loss is encountered from infancy, beginning with separation from the womb, to old age with the loss of physical and mental faculties. In addition, losses are often intangible, such as loss of power, of self-esteem, or of youth, or they are tangible, as in loss of a spouse.

Despite the negative emotional impact that losses often produce, they are a necessary and vital element of personal growth and development. In fact, survival is contingent on the ability to master losses, especially those that inevitably accompany each transition in life. Because loss is neither predictable nor completely avoidable, the development of coping abilities is essential.

LOSS AND ITS RELATIONSHIP TO STRESS

In 1967 Holmes and Rahe developed a questionnaire by which certain life events or changes were ranked and assigned a value according to their stress potential. Those life events that ranked highest as stressors involved substantial loss (death, divorce, relocation, job transition). The death of a spouse was ranked highest with a value of 100. The authors proposed that when the individual is faced with too many concurring stressful changes, the ability to cope is compromised and personal crisis is likely. The Holmes and Rahe scale vividly demonstrates the relationship between overwhelming stressful life events and the potential for subsequent maladaptive responses as measured by increased morbidity in the affected population. Their study revealed an 80% likelihood that an individual whose total score is 300 or more will require hospitalization within the next 24 months. These findings are validated by numerous other studies that have documented increased morbidity or mortality in persons experiencing loss and grief (Clayton, 1973; Glick et al., 1974; Maddison and Walker, 1967; Parkes, 1964, 1972; Parkes et al., 1969). This increased risk of morbidity and mortality is especially notable in the first year of bereavement. Research supports the hypothesis that if a potential crisis, such as the death of a spouse, can be anticipated, then preventative measures can be initiated to minimize or avert future difficulties. This concept of preventative intervention was proposed by Lindemann in 1944.

DEATH AS A STRESSOR

As exemplified by the Holmes and Rahe life event scale, the ability to cope is never so challenged as it is with the experience of a loss through death. When death of a family member occurs, one's sense of immortality is shaken. What can be planned for the future if life is so easily forsaken? Even when death is expected, the sudden impact of the moment creates disequilibrium, for rarely do the most careful anticipations prepare survivors for the impact of the transition from life to death (Sundow, 1967). Suddenly there is no second chance to reconciliate and no further opportunity to communicate affection or consult regarding a decision; an emotional bond is irrevocably and permanently severed. Without further explanation survivors are forced to acknowledge the finality of death in spite of its incomprehensibility. In addition, they are faced with a loss of great magnitude that comprises a myriad of subsequent stressful changes. A sense of ignorance and feelings of impotence emerge, and the survivor becomes fearful, dismayed, and often overwhelmed.

The personal struggle to comprehend and cope with death encompasses each individual in some manner at some moment in life because death has no cultural, social, or age boundaries. Death cannot be ignored indefinitely since eventually all individuals face their own death. Throughout life losses of smaller intensity familiarize almost everyone with the emotional experience of the event, but the death of a family member occurs less frequently. In summoning those coping abilities used in previous occasions, survivors are often likely to come up deficient because of the special nature of death.

Attempts to comprehend death are also reflected in culture, religion, and social custom, as evidenced by the elaborate rituals and societal role expectations that provide structure and guidance for the individual coping with a death. Perhaps if death is explained and understood, then it can be controlled, and if death is controlled, then it need not be feared. Despite all rationalization, death continues to defy comprehension.

Nevertheless, fear and preoccupation with comprehending and controlling death continue in contemporary life, particularly in Western society (Fulton, 1976). Technological advances have enabled modern societies to delay death as well as to destroy life by the use of increasingly impersonal methods of physical intervention. Furthermore, the obsessional attention to the finer details of death (clinical versus biological death) allows inattention to a more human perspective of the event itself. In addition, even though technology enables individuals to live longer, the preoccupation with averting death is often at the expense of the right to personal dignity.

With an upsurge in the awareness of human rights and the activism of the 1960s, the dilemma of impersonal death became coupled with a concern for the quality of life and both became more publicized. As a result, a reservoir of new ideas and concepts in the field of human growth and potential has developed. Recent trends in the care of the dying and the bereaved emphasize the need for improving the quality of life rather than simply prolonging it (Kübler-Ross, 1969). Death need not be an alienating or isolating experience; by improving communication, exploring the changes that occur through the dying and bereavement processes, and sharing these experiences, growth can be enhanced.

RELEVANT THEORIES IN THE DEVELOPMENT OF GRIEF MODELS

In his early work Freud (1959) described grief from an intrapsychic perspective. He postulated that mourning occurs when an individual's "energy" or libido, which has previously been attached to the object of love, is slowly relinquished. Freud conceptualized that energy is bound in one's memories and thoughts of the loved one. When a loved one dies, then this energy is freed through the process of "grief work," in which the mourner uses his free energy to liberate himself from this attachment to the loved object. When the grief work is completed, the individual is then capable of reinvesting the liberated energy toward a new attachment. The overemphasis of the libido and the disregard for the social milieu are criticisms frequently expressed by contemporary theorists regarding Freud's work.

His early contributions, however, have served to stimulate subsequent theoretical development of the relationship between the concepts of loss and depression. Furthermore, his initial notion of grief work has been greatly expanded by others who have developed a framework of therapeutic interventions used to enhance the grief work of clients seen in various settings.

In his widely quoted empirical study of 101 bereaved persons, Lindemann (1944) described the symptomatology and management of acute grief. Characteristics of the normal grief syndrome described by Lindemann include five features: (1) somatic distress marked by sighing, digestive disturbances, and feelings of weakness; (2) preoccupation with images of the deceased, for example, obsessive recollections of the death scene or frequent feelings that the deceased was present; (3) hostile reactions and irritability particularly with those relatives and friends wishing to be helpful; (4) guilt feelings associated with having neglected the deceased before the death or with not having prevented the death; and (5) loss of patterns of conduct such as an inability to attend to social or professional obligations. Lindemann also outlined some characteristics of morbid grief reactions that were distinguished from normal by the intensity, delay, or distortion of symptoms of grief. Furthermore, Lindemann discussed the nature of grief work as a process lasting 4 to 6 weeks whereby through the expression and verbalization of sorrow, anger, and guilt, the bereaved slowly detach themselves from the deceased and test new satisfactory patterns of social interactions. Glick et al. (1974) have commented that Lindemann underestimated the long-term effects of bereavement by implying that grief was a rather short-lived phenomenon. Nevertheless, Lindemann's observations conceptualized grief as a specific syndrome with distinguishable physical and emotional characteristics, which is the basis for subsequent literature in this area. He advanced the concept that early psychiatric intervention during periods of individual crisis can be an effective means of preventing later, more severe disturbances.

In his studies of childhood separations, Bowlby (1961a, 1961b) contributed significantly to the growing body of knowledge in the field of mourning. He divided the process of childhood grief into three overlapping phases. In the first phase, the child's behaviors of weeping and anger serve as adaptive mechanisms in an effort to recover the lost loved one. If the loved object (mother) cannot be summoned by these behaviors, then eventually the behaviors are extinguished and replaced by the behaviors of the second phase, disorganization. Disorganization is marked by depression, a symptom that Bowlby sees as a natural and inevitable part of life. Bowlby hypothesizes that both anger and depression are not necessarily pathological responses to loss, but rather part of the normal grief cycle. The final stage of Bowlby's grief cycle, reorganization,

is marked by the child's resumption of activities.

Bowlby contributed significant data regarding childhood responses to loss. Criticism, however, has sometimes been directed at those who have generalized these data to other age groups or settings without accounting for other variables. Despite the problems of generalizability, Bowlby has shown that responses to loss can be observed and categorized into a somewhat predictable pattern or process. In turn, elements of this general process can be utilized in conjunction with more specific knowledge of a grieving individual to anticipate needs and make appropriate therapeutic interventions that assure mental health.

In 1969, Kübler-Ross increased the general fund of knowledge on grief and illuminated psychosocial thought with a humanistic approach to the contemporary experience of dying. Based on the anticipatory stages of grief that are experienced by the dying and their families, this model emphasizes communication and human growth. From her observations, Kübler-Ross elucidated five phases of grief in the dying client: (1) denial and isolation, (2) anger, (3) bargaining, (4) depression, and (5) acceptance. These phases and the concurrent behaviors described by Kübler-Ross (1969) are quite similar to the earlier observations of Lindemann and Bowlby despite the marked differences in settings, subjects, and circumstances. For this reason, Kübler-Ross' contributions are accepted as supportive data in the general field of reactions to loss. Schneidman (1976), however, argues that grief should be regarded as a flexible process rather than the well-defined sequence of events proposed by Kübler-Ross. In spite of this criticism, Kübler-Ross' observations are invaluable tools for understanding and caring for those anticipating loss.

CRISIS THEORIES IN RELATIONSHIP TO BEREAVEMENT

Observations and concepts of bereavement have played a major role in the development of crisis theories that are used in the psychiatric emergency setting (Caplan, 1964). A crisis occurs when the individual is faced with a particular situation (problem) that is not easily resolved by the use of familiar coping mechanisms (Aquilera, 1982). Consequently, individuals sense danger and feel vulnerable, which in turn compounds their anxiety and tension, rendering them incapable of acting successfully. Aquilera outlined three variable components that contribute to this crisis situation: (1) distorted perception of the event, (2) inadequate external supports, and (3) inadequate psychological coping mechanisms. Successful crisis intervention assists individuals toward gaining the ability to alter each of these components. With successful resolution of the crisis, individuals gain an opportunity to maximize growth through the acquisition of new coping skills that can be used in future situations.

As a problem-solving model, crisis intervention is invaluable because it adapts well to and can be used in conjunction with a variety of other therapeutic modalities. Furthermore, the crisis model exemplifies the interrelationship between models of bereavement and models of crisis. For example, Hirshowitz (1973) outlined the four phases of the crisis sequence—(1) impact, (2) recoil-turmoil, (3) adjustment, and (4) reconstruction—phases that are easily comparable to the previously described grief process. The impact phase, a period of dazed shock, occurs in the first few hours to 2 days following any distressing news. During this time the individual is distractible and disoriented. In the recoil-turmoil phase, which usually lasts 1 to 4 weeks, emotions of rage, anxiety, depression, guilt, and shame may be either expressed or concealed from others. In the adjustment phase the intensity of painful feelings is diminished and the individual's time perspective moves from the past to the future. As the individual enters the reconstructive phase, problem solving and new hope emerge; the individual tests out new behaviors and forms new attachments. The interrelationship of crisis and bereavement models is easily recognized by these examples; the contributions of authors cited earlier in this chapter, particularly Lindemann, have served as the basis for the development of later crisis theories.

TYPICAL BEREAVEMENT IN THE PSYCHIATRIC EMERGENCY SETTING

Although the bereaved do not ordinarily seek psychiatric care (Clayton, 1973; Glick et al., 1974), mental health professionals in emergency settings can be particularly effective as "promoters" of positive bereavement outcomes. In the light of research that reveals increased morbidity and mortality among the bereaved (Clayton, 1973; Holmes and Rahe, 1967; Kraus, 1959; Maddison, 1968; Parkes, 1964, 1972) and particularly among young widows, appropriate mental health interventions are needed. Preventative programs that focus on facilitation of a typical bereavement process are required through all phases of bereavement. In the community, widow-to-widow programs, support groups, and specific grief counseling programs have emerged as effective "promotors." Likewise, the conjunctive services provided in emergency settings can further enhance the care of the bereaved. For example, the mental health team, in collaboration with the medical emergency team, can render valuable direct services to newly bereaved survivors of sudden deaths. In addition, since recently bereaved survivors often seek medical care for symptoms associated with the stress of bereavement (Maddison, 1968; Parkes, 1972), medical-psychiatric consultations serve as important vehicles of health-promoting (illness-preventing) activities.

Sometimes these functions in the psychiatric emergency setting which promote mental health are difficult to carry out. Unfortunately, the image of psychiatry held by both consumers and health professionals reinforces the social stigma attached to mental illness. Reinforcement of the illness model occurs on several levels. First and foremost, the psychiatric emergency team (in a community mental health system) may fail to acknowledge and promote their responsibility to primary prevention in the care of the bereaved; this lack of involvement circumvents the purpose of the modern community mental health concept that calls for care on a continuum between health and illness (Caplan, 1964). Consequently, preventative care, health promotion, and health education are often compromised, particularly in hospital settings where illness takes priority in care. Furthermore, when these functions are ignored, then conjunctive services (medical emergency teams) are likely to utilize the psychiatric emergency team for more circumscribed functions associated with responses that are considered abnormal or "sick." This attitude, in turn, reinforces a negative image of bereavement behaviors that is based on an illness model.

Survivors may resist mental health care for fear of being labeled "crazy." Consider the following examples:

Case vignette #1

A psychiatric emergency team that was not routinely involved in the care of survivors was summoned to the medical emergency area to subdue a distraught woman who refused to relinquish her dead baby. When the team arrived, Ms. R cringed in a corner holding the infant protectively while a crowd of personnel collected. The clinician dispersed the crowd and invited the woman with her baby into a quiet room, promising that the child would not be taken from her at this time. The clinician sat with her quietly as she wept and expressed her anguish and then when she was ready, she relinquished the child.

In an institution where the concept of primary prevention is poorly defined (or undefined), requests for psychiatric interventions are based on perceptions of what is thought to be an abnormal response. Ms. R, whose behavior was not necessarily abnormal (according to what is known about grief reactions), was informally labeled abnormal by the screening process that occurred in the emergency unit. Because the psychiatric emergency unit did not normally convey a health-promoting attitude or institute a preventative program, its health-promotive role in this case became distorted.

Case vignette #2

A psychiatric emergency unit clinician was called to the medical emergency unit. When the clinician introduced herself as a psychiatric nurse to the suddenly bereaved family, they immediately protested that they had no need for psychiatric care and that they were not "crazy." In subsequent introductions, the clinician avoided the stigma of the psychiatric title by identifying herself as a nurse counselor. This title appeared to carry a more positive connotation.

These two examples illustrate several factors that must be considered in the provision of mental health care for the bereaved in the emergency setting. The role of the psychiatric emergency team in assisting the bereaved will depend on (1) the philosophy of the psychiatric emergency unit toward health-promoting activities, (2) administrative support for health care activities (which may in turn depend on funding), (3) the philosophy and collaborative efforts of health professionals in adjoining health settings within the hospital and surrounding community, (4) the manner in which clinicians clarify their role to the bereaved, and (5) the bereaved individual's own perceived need for assistance. These variables may inhibit or enhance the mental health professional's overall ability to assume the variety of supportive postures that are appropriate to the needs of survivors.

THE BEREAVEMENT PROCESS: A MODEL

A synthesis of the previously cited theories of loss, crisis, and bereavement yields a model consisting of the following five stages: (1) impact, (2) shock-disbelief, (3) protest, (4) disorganization, and (5) reorganization. This model enables the clinician to conceptualize the grief process. Typically the bereaved proceeds through each stage in sequence. The initial three stages, however, emerge simultaneously and occur in the first hours and days of bereavement. During the latter stages of disorganization and reorganization, behaviors from earlier stages often resurface but usually in diminished intensity and for shorter durations of time.

Although this grief model serves as a useful tool, it is not without its limitations, since individual responses cannot be so easily compartmentalized. Mourning is a dynamic process. Within the *generalized* pattern of response the clinician will observe wide variations of *individual* response. For example, in some individuals certain stages are unobservable, totally missing, or out of sequence. In addition, the character of bereavement changes in relation to numerous intervening variables such as age, sex, relationship to the deceased, environmental supports, cultural background, and past experiences; these limitations must be considered in using the proposed model.

The length of bereavement also varies with each individual. While the acute symptoms of bereavement subside gradually over a period of weeks to months, the death of a loved one generates effects with far-reaching repercussions. In their longitudinal study of widows, Glick et al. (1974) found evidence of active grieving after a full year. Perhaps when given the chance to express themselves, these widows took advantage of an opportunity that is discouraged within their own social network of supports. One might hypothesize that although overt grieving behavior is inhibited after a period of time, bereavement continues for protracted periods in private or in the company of close friends. Furthermore, bereavement may continue indefinitely because the loss is permanent.

In the next section each stage of the bereavement process is discussed in further detail, using the following format: (1) description of the stage, (2) behaviors typically associated with the stage, (3) pertinent issues, (4) suggested interventions, (5) examples to illustrate major points, and (6) reference to research.

Stage I: Impact—"What was, is no more"

Impact is a brief yet intense period that is limited to those events immediately leading up to and including the proclamation and transmission of the news of death. Those closest to the deceased experience a sense of anxious anticipation, and their heightened sensory perceptions remain narrowly focused on thoughts related to the loved person; irrelevant stimulus information is often screened out, and these individuals appear preoccupied except in matters related to their concern for the loved one. Although death issues emerge in the survivors' consciousness,

these thoughts are quickly censored or disregarded.

The events that surround the impact stage occur with increasing frequency in health-related settings, particularly emergency units and acute care facilities. Even when death occurs outside of a health care setting, health professionals and auxilliary personnel (for example, police and ambulance drivers) are often involved as extensions of the health care system. It is therefore imperative that all health care givers acquaint themselves with the needs of the "imminently bereaved." Knowledge of this stage enables the health professional to provide effective emergency psychological care to these victims.

Despite the likelihood of involvement of health professionals during the impact stage, the bereavement literature rarely focuses on issues relevant to the emergency unit setting. The literature devoted more attention to bereavement problems occurring after the funeral when supportive relatives have dispersed and survivors are more vulnerable (Glick et al., 1974; Parkes, 1972). When anticipatory grief has been addressed, it is usually in the context of the non-emergency setting, such as care of the terminally ill on an inpatient basis.

Another shortcoming in the literature is that it offers little evidence that suggested interventions are effective, although several researchers (Glick et al., 1974; Jones, 1978) have sought the retrospective opinions of survivors as to what they perceived as helpful. Jones thought that his evidence was suggestive but inconclusive in establishing a relationship between early emergency unit care for survivors and their subsequent resolution of grief. Williams and Polak (1979) found that preventative interventions directed toward acutely bereaved families had little if any impact on subsequent adjustment. Despite this lack of evidence, experts on bereavement and crisis intervention maintain the view that early interventions facilitate healthier responses to grief (Caplan, 1964; Maddison, 1968; Raphael, 1978). The impact stage is critical because the survivor must negotiate through an unfamiliar setting, such as an emergency unit, under extreme stress and before supports are summoned; because of this vulnerability, survivors are more likely to accept those interventions provided by the crisis team. The salient facets of the impact stage and suggested interventions will be illustrated in the following discussion.

SUMMONING. Being summoned to an unfamiliar situation is often the survivor's first exposure to the possibility of death. When sufficient information has been gathered to identify surviving relatives, summoning often occurs from emergency settings by telephone. A call must be concise and must also assist the survivor in making safe, adequate plans to travel to the setting. The caller should be identified by name and should establish the relationship of the receiver to the deceased. The purpose of the call should be briefly explained and should communicate serious concern without exaggerating alarm. For example: "Hello, may I speak to Mrs. Smith. Is this Mrs. John P. Smith? My name is. . . . I am an employee of. . . . Your husband has been brought to the hospital following an auto accident. Can you come to the hospital?" At this point of impact, the recipient is often unable to comprehend because of the flood of anxiety and tension. Concerns for family members are more likely to be expressed as questions regarding their physical status rather than death per se, for example, "Is he all right?" a simple "No, it is serious" communicates reality without destroying the defenses that the survivor needs to proceed further. As a general rule, news of death need not be communicated but should not be deliberately withheld when the survivor insists on information. In addition, the caller should ascertain if the survivor is in the company of *adult* support, and the support should be identified.

The caller should also assist the receiver with arrangements for transportation and child care, obtain an estimate of the time required for travel, and establish a meeting place that is easily found in the emergency setting. A sole family member is usually cautioned against driving alone since this can be hazardous; in addition, survivors are advised to contact key support persons so that they may be accompanied rather than have to face stress alone. Although these interventions may seem simple, they are often omitted, yet they help survivors maintain order and support their coping mechanisms.

IMMINENCY OF DEATH. Often death is imminent; in such cases survivors are entitled to frequent reports and periodic supportive contacts, therefore a collaborative liaison with the health care team is essential. If it is possible and desired by the survivors, they should be given an opportunity to visit the relative receiving treatment, for this is a crucial period when potential grievers may have their last opportunity to see their relative alive. A quiet room where concerned relatives can gather affords them privacy and protection from the busy activities of the emergency area; however, relatives must also feel that they have easy accessibility to news and that they are physically close to where the person is being treated.

BREAKING THE NEWS. Although this function is traditionally assumed by the attending physician, some literature suggests that *who* imparts the news of death is not as important as *how* it is done (Jones, 1978; Kübler-Ross, 1969). Several factors must be considered in delegating this role: (1) availability, (2) comfort with the role, (3) ability to empathize, (4) ability to remain with the survivors, (5) the technical nature of the information to be shared, and (6) the practice of the institution. The attending physicians can be questioned earlier as to the degree of participation desired. In a busy emergency area where a high level of activity continues, survivors may receive better care if the attending physician enhances the efforts of a designated grief support team by being available to answer the survivors' questions.

Empathy, compassion, concern, and warmth are important attributes of the person who relays the news of death. In responses to a questionnaire, Jones (1978) found that survivors not only vividly remembered the details of being notified but that they were highly critical of staff members who seemed uncaring. Kübler-Ross (1969) emphasizes that health personnel must examine their own feelings in relation to death because often their own lack of comfort is transmitted to the survivors and interferes with their ability to convey the news.

WHO IS GIVEN THE NEWS. As a general rule, hospital staff are legally responsible for informing immediate family members of a death before informing friends. In addition, a release may be required from the family to notify other callers. Sometimes this creates tension in situations where nonrelated friends consider themselves the "family" of the deceased in the absence of close intimate ties with the biological family. Such cases must be handled individually and with good judgment, since any individual who knows the deceased is a potential griever who should be promptly informed.

Delaying the news of death creates undue strain and ambiguity for everyone, since those who know of the death are forced to play a painful charade of evasiveness with the uninformed. For example, in his sociological observations of hospital behaviors, Sundow (1967) observed discomfort among inpatient personnel who were not permitted to communicate news of death until the physician arrived. As a result, they avoided and thus alienated unsuspecting family members. In addition, nonverbal behavior may stimulate alarm and resentment in survivors who feel they are being excluded from important issues. In such situations, tensions rise and conflict between all parties can erupt.

When news is communicated, cues as to who are the key survivors is often received by the informer from the social structure demonstrated by family and friends. Immediate family members (parents, children, siblings, grandparents) are afforded additional privacy and rights to information; in crisis situations this social-familial heirarchy is usually spontaneously respected within the group. Supportive care, however, should be directed toward all grievers since silent or unobtrusive grievers may not overtly reveal their needs. For example, although members of a deceased adolescent's peer group are not afforded the same privileged communications as family members, they are psychologically vulnerable grievers who will benefit from acknowledgment of their concerns.

Stage II: Shock and disbelief— "no, that's not so, I don't believe it"

The second stage occurs simultaneously with the impact stage of grief and usually predomi-

nates for several hours or days following the news of death. The period of shock and disbelief is marked by expressions of numbness, bewilderment, a sense of unreality, frank denial, and blunted affect intermingled with outbursts of tears. This emotional response is accompanied by physical symptoms such as choking, shortness of breath, sighing, intestinal upset, and tightness in the throat, which were symptoms described by Lindemann (1944). As survivors struggle to comprehend the news, they begin an obsessional review of the events leading up to the death, which has been noted by numerous authors (Freud, 1959; Glick et al., 1974; Lindemann, 1944). Often the survivor repeats anecdotes from the life of the deceased and raises questions regarding the circumstances of death. References to the deceased at this time are often expressed as if the deceased were not dead; for example, a survivor may describe an eccentric habit that the deceased "has." Survivors often seek reassurance that the deceased felt little pain at death (Glick et al., 1974; Sundow, 1967) and that everything possible was done to save the person.

Denial is expressed in various ways by survivors. Often they demand proof of the identity of the deceased or offer alternative explanations as to the whereabouts of the deceased. Survivors speak as if the deceased were still alive and references used by health professionals that underscore reality (for example, "the body") are met with obvious displays of discomfort. Denial functions as an adaptive mechanism that cushions survivors from the full impact of this trauma, and often denial enables survivors to retain the capacity to make critical decisions despite the enormous stress on them.

ACCESS TO INFORMATION. Survivors are entitled to accurate information regarding the cause of death and medical interventions carried out. The attending physician should be prepared to give survivors a concise explanation, uncomplicated by sophisticated medical jargon. Of course, this information is best received when the physician is able to relate it in a caring, sensitive manner. Questions should be answered, and generally survivors will respect the expert's assessment that some questions are unanswerable (for example, "Would he have survived if I had discovered him sooner?"). In the busy emergency setting the details of emergency care and of the status of the deceased at arrival (that is, level of consciousness, responsiveness, ability to communicate last wishes during the final moments) become harder to retrieve as time passes. Armed with this information, survivors grasp the deceased's transition from a state of life to that of death. This valuable information enables survivors to begin the grieving process rather than becoming obsessed with unanswered questions. The clinician functions as the survivors' advocate by assisting them to obtain relevant information.

Survivors are also curious about the circumstances that occurred before the deceased's arrival in the emergency unit. Passing on erroneous or accusatory information (for example, implying fault in an auto accident) is neither helpful nor appropriate. It is therapeutic for staff to assist survivors in obtaining official reports (traffic accident reports, police reports) of investigators. Information regarding how to retrieve these documents should be written down for the survivors' reference because their short-term memory is likely to be impaired by the preoccupation with the deceased.

TIME. Survivors must absorb an incredible psychological shock in the ensuing moments and should be afforded as much time and use of a quiet room as they need. This means that those participating in grief counseling must consider their own time constraints. In the problem-solving process certain adjustments can be made for the provision of consistent supportive services. To ensure continuity, for instance, counseling can be implemented by pairs of clinicians so that if one clinician is called away, the process is not abruptly ended. Adjunctive participation of the clergy or trained volunteers is often valuable. The grief counselor need not be continuously present, and in fact, the surviving family members often require privacy even from the counselor to share their personal feelings. Quiet space also alleviates concerns that crying or expressions of grief will upset others; a separate room with a door is preferred rather than closing off a part of a large room by using curtains.

MOBILIZING SUPPORTS. Despite their shock and disbelief, survivors face the uncomfortable task of notifying other relatives and mobilizing supports. Although such functions are necessary, survivors may feel incapable of performing them and can choose the amount and level of clinician participation needed. Often the simplest tasks require the clinician's assistance (that is, recalling or finding a phone number, dialing the phone, giving directions). When the survivor is accompanied, mutual family support generates spontaneously in most cases, and this should be nurtured by the clinician. Often specific family members are designated for major supportive functions; Glick et al. (1974) found that 36% of the widows in his sample of 49 identified a brother-in-law as their principle support (this accounted for virtually all the widows whose husbands had brothers). The survivor's *perception* of family and social supports is considered a critical factor in the survivor's positive adjustment to bereavement (Maddison, 1967, 1968; Raphael, 1978). The counselor's role is important in facilitating the supportive process among family members.

VIEWING THE BODY. Evidence of the beneficial effects of viewing the body is inconclusive, although bereavement literature, in general, supports the practice. Jones found in his retrospective study that of 18 of the 26 widow respondents who viewed their husband's body, two felt distracted and uncomfortable, but all felt the experience was "the right thing to do" (1978). Glick et al. (1974) found mixed responses among widows who viewed their husband's bodies at a *wake*. A majority of widows studied wanted their husbands' bodies to appear as if they were alive and well again. Hence, there may be some merit to viewing the body of the deceased in the emergency unit before major physiological changes associated with death have taken place. Despite their distaste for it, the majority of widows in Jones' study (1978) felt that the experience of viewing the body was beneficial in helping them to confirm the reality of death. Therefore, survivors may be offered the opportunity to view the body but should not feel forced to do so.

If the staff refers to the deceased with such terms as *the body* or *it*, survivors are often visibly shaken. Although these references serve to distance the professional from the event, the survivors often perceive this as an insensitive gesture. While survivors are intellectually aware of reality, they have difficulty facing death even as they view the body. Denial may continue to emerge in the actions and behaviors of survivors (for example, comments regarding the "warmth" and "aliveness" of the deceased).

Several interventions are important in assisting survivors through the viewing. First, survivors should be informed of the condition of the body so that they are prepared for what they will see. At the survivors' request, medical support equipment may be removed, although seeing the equipment also serves to validate that the hospital team *did try* to save the deceased. Evidence of severe trauma or other unusual conditions must be transmitted to survivors; the option to abstain from viewing without provoking guilt should always be present. If the deceased has sustained disfiguring injuries, an uninjured portion of the body such as a hand can be shown.

The clinician should be present but unobtrusive during the viewing. Jones (1978) reported that all survivors in his sample favorably recalled the presence of a health care professional at this time. In addition, those survivors who were physically touched by the clinician in a compassionate manner appreciated the gesture. Similarly, expressions of emotion (crying) on the part of the clinician were not reported to be a hinderance (Jones, 1978) and were often said to be reassuring (Parkes, 1972). The clinician must keep in mind that all participants are grievers and while they can offer support to each other, often a "target" survivor (such as the spouse) becomes the focal point of interventions at the expense of others' grief.

CONCLUDING PROCESS. At some point, the family must leave. Unless there has been an extended waiting period, papers may need to be signed (insurance) and personal effects may be claimed; copies of all signed documents should be given to the survivors for their future reference (Jones, 1978). When the agency requests an autopsy, survivors often require an explanation of this procedure to dispel fears that the deceased will be mutilated or disfigured. Transportation procedures to the autopsy site or funeral home must be discussed. To transmit accurate information the clinician must know the procedures particular to the setting (agency and legal jurisdiction).

Another aspect of the concluding process is the referral. Whereas most survivors may not require further intervention, they should be offered this option in case they later feel the need. These supports facilitate the greiving process and assist individuals with many day-to-day problems initiated by the death of a family member. In many communities programs to meet the needs of the bereaved are available in the form of support groups, grief counseling programs, widow-to-widow programs, single parent groups, and special services within community-based mental health programs. The clinician can also offer a follow-up telephone call or visit.

When final arrangements are complete, documents are signed, and the deceased has been viewed, survivors often feel lost. The closing process allows the bereaved an opportunity to ask questions, and survivors may even ask for "permission" to depart (Jones, 1978). Transition to a frightened state occurs at this time, accompanied by a foreboding sense of gloom and fear of the unknown. A sense of conclusion can be accomplished by accompanying the bereaved to the exit.

After the departure the clinician and other involved staff need a period of time to discuss and analyze the events that occurred. During this concluding process staff members can express emotions and discuss the interventions. In addition, this period serves as a cushion between the experience and the other activities of the day.

Case vignette #3

Mrs. W's husband was brought to the emergency unit by ambulance after he collapsed on a sidewalk while the couple were walking to a mailbox. Both were previously widowed elderly persons who had large supportive families from their former marriages. Their own marriage of 10 years was described by Mrs. W as "boisterous and fun loving." Mrs. W sat alone in the family room at the hospital as attempts to resuscitate Mr. W continued. She had already summoned her brother-in-law and a cousin.

Mrs. W: "I can't believe it, it doesn't seem real. We stepped off the curb and I said, 'Buddy, Buddy, what's wrong?' I always call him Buddy, it's his nickname (smiles). He kept gasping and turning blue; I yelled for help."

Clinician: "Yes, I hear that it is a shock (pause). Would you like me to stay with you while you wait? (she nods agreement). I will remain in contact with the medical team so that you are kept informed."

Mrs. W: "I kept yelling for help (pause). He just went like this (demonstrating) and then he fell. We were mailing a letter to his son. We're on vacation right now, you know, and it's time to go home. We mailed the letter to tell his son when to pick us up at the airport (pause). My husband is like that, he likes things all planned ahead of time (evidence of distraction). Can you find out from the doctor, might you be able to tell me something?"

Physician is summoned and enters the room: "I'm awfully sorry, Mrs. W, but your husband couldn't survive the strain on his heart; he had a massive heart attack and died as we tried to resuscitate him. I wish I had better news for you, but we did everything we could."

Mrs. W: "Oh, no, not Buddy, we were going home, no, it can't be (tears). It's our vacation, we're all set to return home to our family, now this" (cries softly).

Mrs. W demonstrated shock and disbelief, intermingled with realistic perceptions of what had occurred. Her ability to approach reality may have been in part a result of her previous experience with conjugal bereavement. In fact, during the time preceding the news of death, Mrs. W mentioned her previous widowhood several times to the clinician although she did not question the prospects of survival for her current husband. At times, Mrs. W's statements revealed concern as to whether she had done everything she could have after he collapsed and at other times she questioned whether people had responded quickly enough to her pleas for help. This is consistent with the observations of Glick et al. (1974)

that widows of sudden death often dwell more on the facts surrounding the death, with some sense that death might have been avoided. For instance, at times, Mrs. W revealed concern as to whether she should have known something about cardiopulmonary resuscitation. She also continued reviewing their upcoming plans (even after confirmation of his death). The family continued to mourn and alternately support each other with special support directed toward the widow.

After a period of time the clinician asked: "Would you like to see your husband? He is in a special room where you won't be interrupted by staff. Each of you needs to think about what is best for yourself." (The family agreed to accompany Mrs. W.) "The staff has removed the life support equipment, but you will still see evidence of those efforts; if you feel that this will disturb you, feel free to change your mind" (all nod and enter).

Mrs. W (approaching her husband while physically supported by her brother-in-law, she touches her husband's face): "Oh, Buddy, Buddy, I know you can't hear me, but I loved you so much." (She holds his face and weeps, then composes herself.) "He is still warm." (Brother-in-law and niece stand silently and touch Mr. W's face. Cousin weeps.) After a few moments they signal that they are ready to go.

As they walk down the hall, the counselor physically touching family members, Mr. W's brother sobs and then relates sorrowfully: "I'm 84; we had such a large family, a number of my sisters have died, and now my brother." He struggles to regain composure.

What is apparent in this grief counseling experience is the lack of attention to the brother of the deceased, whose primary role became that of supporter despite his own loss. Not only was he facing another family loss, but with the loss of a sibling so close in age, he was confronted with his own mortality.

Another noteworthy aspect is the frequency

with which survivors comment on the warmth of the body. Finally, the viewing appears to function as a type of symbolic good-bye that occurs in close proximity in time to the transition between life and death.

Stage II: Protest—"Something could have been done, if only . . . "

Intermingled with emotions of the two previous phases, the powerful elements of the protest stage begin to emerge. During this stage two opposing thoughts occupy the survivor's mind: (1) the fear that something could have been done which might have prevented the death and (2) an emerging awareness that death is unalterable. This activates two dynamic emotions, hope and despair, which in turn set the stage for myriad emotions and behaviors.

Expressions of hope center around the survivor's attempts to undo the loss and effect a reunion (Bowlby, 1961b). Typical expressions such as "This shouldn't have happened" or questions regarding the exact details of the event are common. Obsessive ruminations heighten as the survivor continues to focus on any alternative in place of reality. The survivor reenacts the episode over and over, each time maintaining a glimmer of hope that the verdict might be changed. As protest progresses, searching behaviors intensify (Parkes, 1972; Bowlby, 1961b). Around each corner the survivor expects to see the deceased; strangers in the distance or with their backs turned are momentarily mistaken for the deceased and familiar noises, such as a ringing telephone, momentarily call forth the expectation that the person is still alive. The survivor gradually begins to realize that these thoughts are futile and thus hope erodes.

The clinician takes no sides in mediating the survivor's struggles between hope and despair, but functions as a supportive listener. If the clinician acknowledges the survivor's despair by encouraging socializing prematurely, the survivor will often become irritated and angry at feeling unsupported and forced to accept reality. Similarly, "jollying" the survivor in the midst of despair is met with equal distaste (Parkes, 1972). At this early stage the survivor is still struggling

to comprehend the reality, and momentary acknowledgement in the form of despair does not imply acceptance. Likewise, since the survivor's hope is often based on an unrealistic wish to recover the deceased, platitudes about a hopeful future without the person only underscore the reality of the current loss.

In summary, the protest stage repeatedly activates painful perceptions of reality which result in intermittent episodes of hope and despair (commonly observed as "pangs of grief"). Protest peaks in intensity and severity within 5 to 14 days (Parkes, 1972) as the former phase of disbelief becomes harder to maintain as a defense. Disbelief, however, continues to resurface but gradually decreases in frequency, intensity, and duration.

Evidence of the third stage of grief manifests itself in the emergency psychiatry setting in various contexts: (1) in the suddenly bereaved, (2) in recently bereaved survivors who are perceived to be experiencing difficulties with impulse control, and (3) in those who seek help for seemingly unrelated medical or psychiatric problems.

ANGER AND GUILT. Various expressions of anger and guilt emerge as the survivor faces the inability to alter the event of death. Often anger takes the form of accusations and reproaches directed toward the deceased (Bowlby, 1961b). For example, "I've told her so many times not to drive fast and to wear a seat belt!" Anger towards self takes the form of guilt, self-reproach, or in some cases suicidal ideation. An example is "I should have taught her better driving skills. It was my fault for giving her the keys." Third parties, particularly health professionals, are often common targets of the survivor's irritability for the expression of direct as well as indirect forms of aggression.

Observers differ in their opinions regarding the occurrence of anger during the bereavement process. Bowlby (1961b) believed that anger is a normal component of grief and is most often directed toward others. To Bowlby, anger serves the function of aggressively summoning back and punishing the lost love object for leaving. Glick et al. (1974) and Parkes (1972) acknowledged the presence of anger and guilt in the grief process. Glick et al. pointed out that in their sample, widows who expressed anger and guilt were more likely to have problems in recovery. Parkes suggests that these symptoms are worth monitoring since they seem to predispose the griever toward a pathological outcome. All acknowledged the difficulty of measuring the intensity and duration of these symptoms, although they agreed that in typical bereavement these symptoms diminish over time.

Survivors often inhibit expressions of anger because they recognize the irrationality of their thoughts or they fear retribution (for example, anger directed toward God may incite wrath, or anger directed at relatives will prompt them to withdraw). When the survivor or the family cannot accept the intense emotions associated with the protest stage, repression of those feelings may lead to destructive behaviors (alcohol or drug abuse, carelessness, accidents, suicide attempts) or may contribute to the exacerbation of previous medical conditions. Survivors and families alike may be relieved to learn that a certain amount of irritability, anger, and guilt is typical and is usually self-limiting. The clinician's primary responsibility is to create a safe, supportive milieu where the survivor's emotions are accepted.

Expressions of protest, such as anger, will surface in the trauma setting during the acute stage of grief on notification of death. In addition, the clinician who is cognizant of the interrelationship between presenting symptoms (physical and behavioral) and the survivor's current grief stage will contribute valuable data in the emergency unit consultative process by alerting colleagues.

IMPULSIVENESS. In an effort to avoid the traumatic emotions of grief, survivors often react impulsively. Impulsive behavior may be exhibited by sudden decisions to relocate, to change or terminate employment, and to buy or sell a house; often the survivor rationalizes the behavior; however, in many cases decisions made early in the grief process compound the stresses placed on the survivor. The Holmes and Rahe scale of life stressors (1967) vividly illustrates the potentiating negative effect of multiple changes on the individual's ability to cope. Because additional changes in the survivor's environment increase stress, major decisions and moves should be discouraged at this time. When a decision is unavoidable (for example, sale of a house to produce income), the survivor should be encouraged to seek the counsel of trusted family members or professionals. The clinician must also be aware of community programs (social welfare, financial, or legal counseling services) that are available to assist the survivor with decisions.

Erratic behavior is another type of impulsiveness the survivor may exhibit (for example, a widow who is a teetotaler is discovered tipsy by her relatives, or a previously responsible teenager receives a ticket for reckless driving). While isolated incidents may not require aggressive interventions, they should be noted as danger signals that call attention to the survivor's faltering coping abilities. By exploring these incidents and the factors that lead to the behavior, the clinician encourages survivors to "step back" and observe their own behavior. Preventative interventions at this time reinforce the survivor's responsibility to self and assist in the exploration of healthier alternatives. Finally, the survivor is provided with an avenue by which expressions of grief can be facilitated.

Case vignette #4

Mr. C was a 22-year-old man who came to a psychiatric emergency unit with a request for analgesics to help calm himself. On evaluation the clinician ascertained multiple life changes (stressors) that had precipitated the current crisis. Mr. C has sustained several recent losses: (1) he had lost his job temporarily because of a fire where he was employed, (2) he gave up his apartment because of inadequate finances, and (3) most significantly, his grandmother ("the only person who cared and understood me") had died. In addition, a history that included substance abuse as well as manic-depressive illness compounded his difficulty with stress management.

Mr. C expressed bitterness toward his parents who failed to notify him of his grandmother's death; he was unable to attend her funeral because he lacked the finances to return home, and he felt guilty about this. His parent's lack of support only intensified an already pervasive sense of isolation from his family.

Despite these major losses, Mr. C was extremely communicative, had insight regarding his problems, exhibited an understanding of his illness, and maintained several valuable supportive friendships. However, Mr. C feared he might lose control and become manic; those fears were realistic because he already suffered from a mild sleep disturbance and had on recent occasions verbally abused strangers who irritated him.

Mr. C's losses were both acknowledged and explored; his emotions were validated and encouraged. The request for analgesics, however, was deemed inappropriate and refused, but the clinician offered him the option of having lithium prescribed again if signs of hypomania persisted. On being refused his request, Mr. C stormed out angrily, claiming he could not be helped. A week later, Mr. C returned complaining of sleeping difficulties, weight loss, and irritability marked by one argument in which he verbally threatened assault but did not carry through. Mr. C discussed these symptoms further and asked to be placed on lithium. Haloperidol and lithium were administered. In the next several weeks as his lithium level reached therapeutic levels and his sleep disturbance began to resolve, the haloperidol was discontinued. At the same time Mr. C resumed his job and began exploring the family issues that had surfaced since his grandmother's death. He also successfully coped with another loss, the death of the restaurant owner for whom he worked and whom he admired. Hospitalization, which at first seemed imminent, was averted.

In this case the clinican conceptualized Mr. C's problems by using several theoretical models: crisis theory and the psychodynamics of manic-depressive illness superimposed on the bereavement model. From Mr. C's presentation the clinician was aware of multiple stressors (loss of situ-ational and financial supports, past difficulties with coping) that impinged on Mr. C's current ability to cope. Yet only when Mr. C learned of his grandmother's death did he seem to enter a spiraling course that approached a manic episode. Behaviorally and emotionally, Mr. C exhibited signs of the protest stage which were compounded by his hypomanic state.

When analgesics were denied, he angrily reproached the clinician for not caring. His refusal to discuss his current emotional condition signified a weakening of his own ability to take care of himself. Notable mental status findings were increased irritability, fear of losing control of aggressive impulses, and verbal assaultiveness toward strangers. These symptoms had intensified by his second visit, and had he not engaged in treatment, he may have warranted involuntary detention for treatment and evaluation. One can only speculate as to the extent that Mr. C's behavior was the result of his illness, but it is clear that his grandmother's death contributed significantly to the situation. Firm limit setting coupled with maintaining a safe environment in which he could express anger without condemnation and the clinician's inclusion of Mr. C in decision making all contributed to facilitation of grieving and engagement in a suitable medication regime that averted further crisis.

Stage IV: Disorganization

The fourth phase of bereavement is marked by the growing yet unacceptable realization that the deceased will never return (no matter how well the survivors behave or what "bargains" are made or how they pretend). Especially after the funeral, when social responsibilities for arrangements subside, disorganization intensifies until it overshadows earlier stages. Although the survivor is no longer occupied with obligations of the burial and supportive relatives have departed, life cannot merely be resumed. Patterns of behavior that were once automatic and organized around the deceased are lost. Lacking the focus of hopeful reunion, the individual's world is pervaded by a sense of aimlessness and emptiness. As survivors withdraw from usual patterns of activity, they may experience memory lapses, confusion, episodes of panic, physical restlessness, and difficulty concentrating (Glick et al., 1974; Bowlby, 1961b). Paranormal experiences are not unusual. The most common of these is a vague sensation of the deceased's presence; 47% of the sample taken by Glick et al. (1974) stated when questioned 13 months after their bereavement that they felt their husband's presence. A study of 227 Welsh widows and 66 widowers of varying ages (Rees, 1971) indicated that 36% experienced this phenomenon and another 14% experienced hallucinations or illusions of their dead spouse's presence. This sense of the spouse's presence seems to persist over time (Parkes, 1972).

As in previous stages, it is unlikely that the survivor's disorganization will be brought to the attention of psychiatric clinicians. More often, physical symptoms secondary to depression prompt the survivor to seek health care from general practitioners (Glick et al., 1974; Parkes, 1972). The astute health professional will use a thorough history to screen many of these casualties. A small percentage of survivors develop psychiatric emergencies because their behavior is either passively or actively self-destructive. These behaviors usually constitute an atypical grief reaction, which is discussed later in the chapter.

FEAR OF MENTAL ILLNESS. "I can't remember *who* called on the phone today or *if* anyone did, let alone *what* they said," one bereaved person was heard to lament. During disorganization the sudden change from the activities of the funeral to a normal or slow pace, combined with the absence of the deceased, leaves the survivor emotionally drained. In this void the survivor faces major role changes that refocus attention on the loss. The survivor literally "shuts down" all but the most automatic responses. Although activities may resume around them, survivors express a lack of spontaneity and vigor, complain of exhaustion, and feel as if they are merely "going through the motions." Because of the preoccupation with thoughts of the deceased, details of normal living are forgotten and confusion persists.

The clinician assumes a supportive, educative role by reminding the bereaved that their feelings are typical and usually self-limiting. The survivor benefits from those direct interventions that summon and enlist supports; the most helpful people are often those who make periodic but frequent visits and assist with daily household tasks without intruding too aggressively on the survivor's world (Parkes, 1972).

DEPRESSION. According to DSM III, the emergence of a full depressive syndrome in the context of bereavement does not constitute a mental disorder. Hence the clinical manifestations of depressive symptomatology marked by loss of interest and pleasure, dysphoric mood, sleep and appetite disturbances, feelings of inadequacy and worthlessness, and either psychomotor agitation or retardation are commonly associated with uncomplicated bereavement. Nevertheless, these symptoms can constitute major problems in the bereaved individual's course of recovery and deserve attention in the psychiatric emergency setting to prevent a more severe pathological response.

Studies cited by Epstein et al. (1975) point to the precipitation or increase in somatic conditions associated with the stress caused by conjugal bereavement. Therefore a complete physical evaluation of the bereaved person (particularly the elderly person) is urged; weight loss, sleep disturbances, and chronic physiological conditions must be monitored. Family and friends are often good resources for obtaining helpful information about the survivor's progress. Also, the tacit wish to die or frank suicidal impulses are common among survivors (Glick et al., 1974; Parkes, 1972). The risk of suicide or a suicide attempt warrants careful evaluation; clinicians, therefore, should not hesitate to broach this topic (see Chapter 8).

Although medications for sleep disturbance and anxiety are not contraindicated during bereavement, there is little evidence as to whether they aid or inhibit the process (Parkes, 1972). Because their appropriateness is questionable, if tranquilizers or sedatives are prescribed, their effects must be monitored on a regular basis. Half of Parke's widowed population took prescribed medications at some time during the first 18 months of bereavement compared with one fifth of the control group.

In summary, a range of behaviors from social withdrawal to death wishes can occur as part of a depression syndrome associated with bereavement. Behaviors that require aggressive crisis interventions (for example, suicide attempts or prolonged, unduly severe depression) often fall into the category of atypical responses. Less extreme symptoms, however, still require the clinician's attention. Early recognition of self-damaging behaviors is both desirable and necessary to prevent further development of unsatisfactory patterns of recovery. When families are educated about the grief process, they can be valuable information resources. In addition, well-informed general practitioners may note warning signals such as an increase in office visits with minor complaints, or the emergency room clinician may note an increase in suspicious accidents in the survivor's record. Certainly any increase in alcohol consumption or cigarette smoking, inattention to physical care, medication requests, or suspected drug abuse are worth exploring with the survivor. If the psychiatric emergency team actively participates in medical emergency unit activities, early screening and recognition are accomplished through the collaborative effort of both services. When these warning signals go unheeded, behaviors can intensify or become more destructive, placing added stress on the survivor's support systems (family and friends). If behaviors become unmanageable, these supports can become more cautious in their willingness to participate in treatment, thereby weakening the survivor's coping system.

Case vignette #5

Mrs. S, an 86-year-old woman, sat dejectedly outside the psychiatric emergency unit, but it was not clear that she was seeking help. For some time the staff assumed that she was waiting to be seen at a medical clinic nearby. When a clinician finally approached her, she looked up woefully and related in a quivering, high-pitched voice, "I think I'm going nuts." The clinician ushered her to a quiet room where she had little to say except, "I'm awful tired, I'd like to go to sleep, but I can't, it took all of my energy to call the taxi to bring me

here." After a long pause, she related that her husband of 35 years had died while they were on vacation. With clarity she related the painful task of visiting her husband in an unfamiliar hospital during his brief illness, her shock and despair on being informed of his death, and the struggle to arrange for his return. Now that the events had receded into the recent past, Mrs. S could not recall the data of his death nor could she recall numerous papers she had signed after having procured a lawyer. Her inability to recall the content of discussions with her lawyer became a persistent source of worry. She was preoccupied with the fear that the lawyer took advantage of her, but she refused to confront him. The clinician summoned a medical social worker who had previously established a relationship with Mrs. S, and this action comforted her. A medical appointment was arranged to monitor Mrs. S's physical status and a follow-up home visit was arranged.

At the physical examination Mrs. S was visited conjointly by the social worker and the clinician; her fears regarding the lawyer's honesty persisted, and she worried about her inability to manage her affairs. She reluctantly permitted her physician to contact the lawyer to offer his "concern and support," but Mrs. S continued to resist any active advocacy. Much to her own surprise, Mrs. S's health remained stable despite chronic cardiac problems and multiple somatic complaints. However, she remained extremely isolated and resisted home visits. The clinician continued contact through weekly phone calls and regularly scheduled medical clinic visits.

Mrs. S showed marked improvement and accepted a legal referral from a friend several months later. Her voice became spirited and she became comfortable with supportive visits from neighbors; she also began answering the many letters and cards she had received over the months.

Despite her distress, Mrs. S maintained her equilibrium initially by relying on hospital personnel who had provided her health care for many years. As she improved, she began to make social contacts with concerned neighbors and friends.

During Mrs. S's initial visit to the psychiatric clinic, the clinician listened actively to her feelings. Notable mental status findings at this time were evidence of memory loss, disorientation to date but not to person or place, impaired concentration, fleeting episodes of suicidal ideation with no plan and no past history, disturbed sleeping pattern, decreased appetite with a slight weight loss, and feelings of helplessness. This picture differed markedly from her own report and her primary physician's reports of her premorbid condition. While dementia was not ruled out, the clinician chose to focus on Mrs. S's immediate needs with the plan of monitoring her mental status over a period of time to further differentiate whether these symptoms were attributed to current stress. Her suicide potential was assessed as low based on her history and her own strong denial that she had any intention of carrying out her thoughts. The impression of low suicide potential was reassessed periodically because suicide risk can sometimes increase as the individual becomes more mobilized.

Mrs. S's first visit was extremely lengthy and allowed her time to ventilate her feelings. Advocacy was begun immediately by summoning the social worker with whom Mrs. S felt extremely close. By conclusion of the first visit she was able to remember the date of her husband's death and she had eaten a meal.

At one point after several months of contact, the clinician considered a more active intervention regarding legal advocacy because Mrs. S's concerns seemed to be impeding the grief process. She remained preoccupied with her relationship to her lawyer, and it became difficult to distinguish whether or not her concerns were of a paranoid nature because she refused to allow the clinician to intervene. However, gradually Mrs. S took her own tentative steps toward resolution when she called for a second legal opinion. To have taken charge of Mrs. S's affairs might have disturbed the therapeutic relationship because she was fiercely independent despite her insecurities. In addition, she felt equally overwhelmed

by the support that was offered; for example, she preferred phone contacts to home visits because she had to "prepare too much" for the latter. In time, Mrs. S obtained a cane ("I had always leaned on my husband"), called a second lawyer, confronted her first lawyer, chose carefully from concerned, supportive neighbors, and began paying bills. When this was accomplished, she resumed actively grieving for her husband but with a renewed sense of her own ability to cope.

Stage V: Reorganization

The fifth stage begins the uphill battle toward recovery. According to Glick et al. (1974), the widow begins recovery as early as 2 months after death. In widows, the population most often studied, failure to begin recovery within the first year of bereavement often signals continued difficulty. In the recovery stage survivors typically experience periods of renewed social interest and enthusiasm for life's activities. Awareness of the finality of death is accompanied by a more balanced and less idealistic perception of the deceased. Consequently, survivors recognize that the deceased had weaknesses as well as strengths.

Sometimes reorganization is heralded by a sudden behavioral change, for example, deciding to take a vacation, accepting a date, or acquiring a new hobby (Glick et al., 1974). On the emotional plane, reorganization is experienced in a sudden or subtle emergence of excitement about a seasonal change, in taking notice of the bustle of human activity, or in experiencing the joy of an old friendship.

Reorganization, however, is not devoid of stress. Supportive people are likely to encourage this transition both by word and by their actions, especially if reorganizational behaviors do not emerge within a socially prescribed period of bereavement. One might liken this to being "pushed out of the nest" of supportive security; it is hoped the transition is introduced gently and with respect to the individual's own inner clock. Nevertheless, many former roles require modification or abandonment, and new roles may need to be acquired. For example, the widow who has never driven may find that learning to drive aids her mobility; similarly, expectant parents whose infant dies at birth need to relinquish the parental role without having experienced it fully. Through the transition of roles the survivor identifies new problems and inadequacies that must be systematically dealt with; when solutions are found, a sense of competence and independence emerges.

Finally, relinquishing the bereavement status is not without its psychological drawbacks. The survivor often feels that this transition implies a lack of devotion or respect for the deceased, and guilt or remorse emerges in conjunction with loneliness. Renewed grieving, especially during holidays, the anniversary of death, or other special moments, often leaves survivors emotionally drained and momentarily confused about their progress. Despite the difficulties of this stage, survivors recognize their progress if events are reviewed objectively with a supportive person.

If reorganization progresses smoothly, survivors are unlikely to appear in emergency settings. However, certain crisis situations that seem irrelevant to the grieving process may prompt a survivor to seek psychiatric assistance. In addition, those who have not successfully proceeded through the stages of grief toward recovery may come to the attention of psychiatric emergency teams.

THE ANNIVERSARY OF DEATH. As the months of bereavement advance, the survivor may approach the anniversary of death with a vague sense of apprehension. Climatic and seasonal changes associated with the previous year may not consciously be associated with the death but may emerge more as subtle reminders of something disturbing. In crisis intervention settings clinicians are aware that anniversary reactions to loss can be significant precipitating events of current problems even years after the original event. Helping clients to make an association between present feelings and past events may genuinely surprise and also relieve them.

LETTING GO. To invest in new living patterns, attachment to the lost family member must recede into the background. For example, the couple whose young child died suddenly must come to terms with this loss in an effort to make a healthy adjustment to the birth of another child or to provide a secure and loving environment for remaining children. In conjugal bereavement it is common for surviving spouses to incorporate personality traits of the lost one into their own personality; this is known as identification (Glick et al., 1974; Freud, 1964; Parkes, 1972). For example, widows may adopt behaviors once characteristic of their husbands. The sense of the lost spouse's presence persists; the widow or widower may "consult" the deceased spouse in important decisions; even in such questions as remarriage, the presumed wishes of the deceased may play a significant part in making the decision. While widows may make successful adjustments in their life-styles that signify their willingness to "let go" (assume new roles or roles previously held by their husbands, develop new social ties), they may chose not to remarry. Often this decision is based on the desire to protect children from added disruption, the fear of losing newly gained independence, or the fear of experiencing another future loss. The degree to which this identification with the deceased interferes with the survivor's present life gives the observant clinician some indication of whether this adjustment is healthy.

FACTORS AFFECTING THE CHARACTER OF GRIEF

It is beyond the scope of this chapter to discuss in detail the factors that affect the process of bereavement. Nevertheless, they must be acknowledged, because they contribute to the individuality of grief reactions. Parkes divided those factors that affect the grief process into three general categories, or "determinants of bereavement outcomes": (1) antecedent, (2) concurrent, and (3) subsequent (see Parkes, 1972, Chapter IX, for elaboration on these categories.)

Although it is impossible to measure the singular effect that any one determinant exerts on the outcome of bereavement, researchers of bereavement responses have focused on several that are regarded as significant predictors of unfavorable outcomes. Poor outcomes are usually identified through morbidity and mortality because these quantitative data are both measurable and more easy to extract from records. Most studies have focused on the widow population; therefore, questions arise as to the generalization of such data.

Maddison (1967) outlined the following "suggestive factors" that most often corresponded with poor bereavement outcomes in widows: (1) widows under 45 who had dependent children, (2) evidence of preexisting marital discord, (3) evidence of previous psychopathology related to grief, (4) a prolonged death with suffering and disfigurement, (5) problem grief reactions in other family members, (6) estranged relationship with own mother or with husband's family, (7) additional problems in the immediate family, and (8) long-standing difficulties and avoiding expression of affect. Glick et al. (1974) found that initial reactions of suddenly bereaved widows are more intense and that these widows are more likely to have difficulty regaining their equilibrium; however, this point is disputed by Clayton (1973) and Maddison (1967). In Maddison's study, the most distinct determinant of bereavement outcome is the widow's perceptions of support, in other words, whether she felt that those around her were supporting her in a helpful manner. Childhood bereavement (age of bereavement as a factor) is also thought to adversely affect later psychosocial development (Bowlby, 1961a), although a cause-and-effect relationship between age and bereavement outcome is difficult to prove. Little attention has been directed toward the surviving family members of successful suicides; however, these survivors are deeply stigmatized by the event and pose special problems in the bereavement process. Several authors have commented on the detrimental effects of suicide on survivor victims (Cain, 1972; Litman, 1965; Shneidman, 1972). In these situations bereavement is characterized by extremely high amounts of shame, anger, guilt, self-blame, and disturbed self-concept (Cain, 1972).

ATYPICAL GRIEF

Because grief responses vary widely among the bereaved, it is difficult to identify a set of distinguishing characteristics that specifically connote pathology. In fact, in recent years observers of bereavement have gathered evidence that certain grief behaviors such as paranormal experiences (for example, visual and auditory hallucinations) that were previously considered abnormal, commonly occur among a significant proportion of survivors (Rees, 1971). Likewise, early observers described normal bereavement as a syndrome that occurred over a relatively circumscribed period of time lasting from 4 to 6 weeks (Lindemann, 1944). Longitudinal studies of grief (Glick et al., 1974) reveal that the more persistent nature of the bereavement syndrome does not constitute abnormality. Research on the bereavement process, however, focuses primarily on the widowed population, which makes it difficult to generalize the findings to other groups.

Since it is difficult to clearly delineate those grief behaviors that are considered pathological or abnormal, a better way of describing a bereavement syndrome that differs from the norm is the label *atypical grief*. In the literature, atypical grief reactions are distinguished from typical reactions by several general characteristics that appear singularly or in combination with each other; these are (1) a symptom that remains persistent and intense, pervades the survivor's world, and seriously interferes with living; (2) behaviors that severely affect the survivor's (or others') health or physical safety; (3) the absence of grief accompanied by rigid denial; (4) a delayed grief reaction; and (5) the survivors' lack of progress in advancing through the stages of grief. Thus atypical grief reactions are usually absent, exaggerated, or distorted grief responses.

In the psychiatric emergency setting the presence of persons exhibiting atypical grief reactions can be expected. Self-destructive behavior and in particular suicide attempts are perhaps the most common behaviors of atypical grief which require psychiatric intervention. In addition, psychiatric emergency units treat bereaved persons who are extremely regressed and inattentive to their personal care, those who exhibit problems associated with drug and alcohol abuse, and those who become frankly psychotic.

Evaluation of bereavement responses requires sensitive clinical judgments since the distinction between typical and atypical grief is rather ambiguous. The clinician can be greatly aided by a good history and collateral interviews when available as well as adequate knowledge of typical bereavement patterns. The difficulty of differentiation is made clear by Parkes (1972). In his study of widows, he notes higher, more persistent levels of self-reproach and anger in those clients who required psychiatric hospitalization following bereavement; however, no tool beyond clinical judgment was used to measure the *severity* of symptoms. In addition, Parkes points out that there is no systematic comparative data available that identifies atypical grief; furthermore, available research varies in population characteristics, time intervals used, and symptom criteria.

APPLICATION OF THE GRIEF MODEL TO OTHER TYPES OF LOSS AND LIFE CHANGES

Many of the principle components of the typical bereavement process are present in other variations of loss such as the loss of a spouse through divorce, the loss of a limb, and loss through unemployment or relocation. In most of these instances, a process of realization occurs in which initial denial or avoidance of the realization of the loss advances toward acceptance of the loss. Parkes (1972) points out that in cases of physical disfigurement such as amputation, a painful psychosocial transition takes place similar to the bereavement process identified in widowhood. He encountered alarm reactions, searching behaviors, feelings of internal loss, and also atypical grief reactions, such as chronic grief, in the amputees studied. He suggests that while more research is needed, those interventions and preventative measures thought to be helpful in counseling the bereaved might be adapted to the needs of persons experiencing other types of loss and life change.

Glick et al. (1974) also suggest that therapeutic work with children while they experience loss may assist them in easier and healthier adjustments to loss in adulthood. Early adaptations to the "little losses" that occur in early childhood provide a network of experiences that subsequently helps shape coping styles and later abilities to adjust to the loss of a loved object.

Caution must be exercised in generalizing grief theories without first researching issues germane to the particular variation of loss being studied. For example, the amputee has problems of physical mobility and body image that require special attention. In addition, establishing the meaning of a loss to the individual becomes imperative since the severity of the impact depends largely on the value placed on the loss. For example, while relocation might be regarded by one individual as an opportunity for adventure and exploration, to another person relocation signifies anxiety-producing separation from loyal friends and familiar surroundings.

In summary, while the bereavement model is applicable to other types of loss and life changes, the model is only as valuable as the clinician's knowledge of its limitations. Just as there are hazards in generalizing research of the bereavement of widowhood to other populations, so there are problems in applying the grief model to other types of loss. Societal, cultural, religious, and demographic factors must always play important roles in the use of a model that is based on research in another area of study.

FAMILY BEREAVEMENT

Currently in transition, the concept of family as the traditional nuclear family (consisting of a male parent, a female parent, and one or more children) has been challenged as being both simplistic and exclusionary of others. No matter how the family is conceptualized, it can be regarded as a system of dynamic equilibrium in which the actions of each member affect the group as a whole (Glick and Kessler, 1974). While each individual in the family has a unique personality, so does the family itself have its own personality. Family identity is usually based on close intense ties, mutual support, assumed roles, and a history of interaction. An event such as the death of a family member upsets the "homeostasis" of the family, thus creating a crisis not only for each individual but also for the family system.

According to Parkes (1972), the family as a social system chooses one of four means of adapting to the loss of a member: (1) the functions and roles of the lost member remain unaccomplished, (2) the roles and functions are divided up among one or several family members, (3) a substitute is found, or (4) the family system disintegrates. The loss of certain roles and functions varies according to the missing members' position in the family. Death of a family member not only requires psychological adjustment, but also financial, sexual, and occupational adjustments result in additional stresses. The goal of the psychiatric emergency clinician is to evoke, emphasize, and strengthen those adaptive patterns that have been used by the family in the past (Glick and Kessler, 1974).

CHILDHOOD BEREAVEMENT. Lacking the personality and intellectual development of adult family members, children have special needs that must be met for optimum adjustment to take place following a family death. As outlined by Nagy (1948), children at the age of 5 or less do not consider death irreversible but liken it to "sleeping." Between the ages of 5 and 9, death is considered a remote possibility that is more likely to occur to others, and children rationalize that extra precautions must be taken to avoid their own deaths. Between the ages of 9 and 10, the inevitability and permanence of death emerges. Adolescents typically deny that death is a pertinent issue for themselves and focus their concerns on "now" issues with a certain grandiosity of power directed toward living dangerously and beating the odds.

The clinician encountering a grieving family is obligated to guide and assist the children through their grief. To achieve this, the child's level of comprehension and the elder family members' capacity to provide appropriate information to children must be assessed. In many cases family members may avoid discussing death with children, rationalizing that youngsters are unaware of what has occurred. This attitude, while providing relief to the adult members, creates an atmosphere of apprehension and anxiety for children who are extremely sensitive to evasion and family stress levels. While inclusion of children in emergency bereavement care cannot be forced on adult family members, the parent may be relieved if support and assistance are offered in the emergency setting. The clinician must also be aware of community programs available to assist families who need further counseling. Often a follow-up call to the family to assess their needs and offer further appropriate referrals is a helpful bridge between the initial emergency contact and future problems.

The parent whose spouse has recently died poses special problems. Not only is that parent faced with the loss of a spouse, but the parent also must assist the surviving children through the bereavement process. Young children often require constant reassurance that the surviving spouse will not "disappear," that the remaining spouse is able to maintain stability, food, shelter, and the integrity of the family.

THE IDENTIFIED PATIENT. A family who is experiencing coping difficulties with the bereavement process will often come to the psychiatric or medical emergency setting with an identified patient. As the "symptom bearer," this family member may be designated as "crazy" or "sick" and is often viewed by the family as "the problem." In actuality the identified patient is often indicative of widespread disturbance in the whole family (Glick and Kessler, 1974). The psychiatric emergency clinician, mindful of this phenomenon, should treat the family as a whole rather than focus on the individual. In so doing, the clinician's interventions are more effective because the family learns that the sum total of their behaviors together have caused the problem and need treatment.

Case vignette #6

Several adult siblings of a large South American family shepherded their sister into the psychiatric emergency unit. R had broken down in tears and had not stopped crying since they had received a long-distance telephone call earlier that day notifying them of the sudden death of their oldest brother in Chile. The rest of the family remained stoic and attentive toward R. Because there were no Spanish-speaking clinicians when this family arrived, an interpreter explained that they should all return that afternoon when a Spanish-speaking clinician would be available. Their names, ages, and relationship to each other and the deceased were obtained, and the interpreter again stressed the importance of the whole family returning for the appointment. They called later in the afternoon to notify the clinic that they chose not to return that afternoon because R had fallen asleep and the family tensions had eased somewhat. A follow-up visit was arranged.

The interventions in this case were somewhat limited and inadequate because of the unavailability of a Spanish-speaking clinician. However, by simply identifying each family member rather than focusing on the identified patient and by requesting that they return as a family unit, the clinician provided this family with a rudimentary, although not explicit, lesson in family dynamics. The choice of treatment approach (that is, family versus individual), while seeming to be inconsequential, is actually a critical therapeutic decision that requires skill and deliberate thought.

CHILDHOOD DEATHS. Parents who have experienced the death of their infant or a perinatal death know that these are particularly traumatic and disturbing death events. In the case of an infant death, there is a loss of expectation and hope for the future. In addition, few familiar rituals exist in cases of childhood death; awkwardness and a sense of failure pervade.

Perinatal deaths cause special family problems. Parents have lost the tangible evidence of their ability to procreate and no memories of the infant exist. The parents have few experiences to validate their loss and mourning. In order that these qualities be minimized, the parents are offered the option to view and even hold their dead infant; the baby may be named and thus an identity affixed. Assistance with arrangements for baptism and burial is another thoughtful intervention (Lewis and Page, 1978; O'Donohue, 1978).

The sudden infant death syndrome (SIDS) is one in which an apparently healthy infant dies suddenly and the autopsy fails to identify a cause (Weinstein, 1978). Often these types of deaths precipitate questions of child neglect; parents are particularly prone to guilty remorse and are sometimes less able to rely on extended family supports. Because of the suddenness of the event as well as the role of the child as the possessor of hope for the future, SIDS deaths are particularly disturbing. Emergency supportive interventions include immediate response with life-saving measures, a nonjudgmental attitude, knowledge of supportive services available in the community, as well as the spectrum of supportive measures discussed earlier in the chapter.

THE CLINICIAN'S GRIEF OVER CLIENT SUICIDES

Much attention has been focused on the bereavement process and appropriate methods of assisting clients through this process. Considerably less research has addressed the problems incurred by the caregivers of psychiatric emergency units who are constantly exposed to human anguish and loss. Client suicides are always a possibility, yet literature rarely focuses on the clinician's reactions to such an event.

Shneidman (1972) points to several types of staff reactions to death depending on the type of ward where the death occurs. In benign wards where death is unusual, such as psychiatric, orthopedic, and obstetrics wards, death is seen as a sharp tragedy that signifies a loss of control. Typically, both administrative and professional staff members are shocked. In emergent wards (emergency rooms, intensive care units) where death is commonplace and relationships are intensified but short-lived, staff members can become overwhelmed by the psychological toll. Depression, callousness, and alcohol or drug abuse may occur. In dire wards where clients and staff struggle with poor prognosis and the dying process, staff members hesitate to become involved, knowing that their personal loss is inevitable.

In psychiatric emergency units components of both emergent and benign wards are present. Particularly when clients have been evaluated and then released, news of their suicides can create anxiety, concerns about professional competences, fear of blame, fear of press involvement, and anger directed toward family members or supervisors (Litman, 1965). Several factors contribute to these reactions: (1) the taboos surrounding suicide, (2) the unique characteristics of the therapeutic alliance, and (3) the lack of an appropriate grieving role for the staff in the psychiatric emergency setting. A client's suicide not only symbolizes rejection of values held by the psychiatric staff but may also represent to the clinician failure of self as a therapeutic tool.

In the case of a client's suicide, the unit's leaders must be sensitive to the emergence of strong feelings and must also provide a supportive atmosphere where the events leading up to the suicide can be examined nonjudgmentally. One of the most helpful means of achieving this is through the psychological autopsy (Shneidman, 1972). In a conference format the case can be examined to uncover missed cues and to better understand symptoms. The format of the psychological autopsy provides the staff with followup time to express their concerns, receive support and supervision, review the events, and explore future therapeutic alternatives. In so doing, staff members are afforded a bereavement role that does not conflict or interfere with their role as professionals; in addition, the displacement of the reaction onto others may be avoided.

SUMMARY

The literature on death, dying, bereavement, loss and life changes, and related topics is vast and expansive. Comprehensive coverage of these topics in the space limitations of this chapter is impossible, and the reader is directed to read additional references on areas not presented in detail. However, a basic understanding of the typical bereavement process and the interventions thought to be appropriate is necessary groundwork. In addition, this chapter attempted to examine issues that are of particular import to psychiatric emergency settings. Examples have been extrapolated from true situations, although names and other information are fictitious. Special attention has been focused on normal or typical bereavement since it is in the psychiatric emergency setting that program planning can be directed toward promotion of mental health and prevention of illness for the whole community.

BIBLIOGRAPHY

Aguilera, D., and Messick, J.: Crisis intervention: theory and methodology, ed. 4, St. Louis, 1982, The C.V. Mosby Co.

Bowlby, J.: Childhood mourning and its implications, Am. J. Psychiatr. 118:481, 1961a.

Bowlby, J.: Processes of mourning, Int. J. Psychoanal. 42:317, 1961b.

Cain, A.: Survivors of suicide, Springfield, Ill., 1972, Charles C Thomas, Publisher.

Caplan, G.: Principles of preventative psychiatry, New York, 1964, Basic Books, Inc., Publishers.

Clayton, P.: The clinical morbidity of the first year of bereavement: a review, Compr. Psychiatry 14:151, 1973.

Epstein, G., et al.: Research on bereavement: a selective and critical review, Compr. Psychiatry 16:537, 1975.

Freud, S.: Mourning and melancholia, collected papers (1917), New York, 1959, Basic Books, Inc., Publishers. (Edited by E. Jones.)

Freud, S.: New introductory lectures on psychoanalysis, standard edition, 1933, vol. 22, p. 3, New York, 1964, W.W. Norton & Co. (Translated and edited by J. Strachey.)

Fulton, R., editor: Death and identity, Bowie, Md., 1976, Charles Press.

Glaser, B., and Strauss, A.: Awareness of dying, Chicago, 1965, Aldine Publishing Co.

Glick, I., and Kessler, O.: Marital and family therapy, New York, 1974, Grune & Stratton, Inc.

Glick, I., Weiss, R., and Parkes, M.: The first year of bereavement, New York, 1974, John Wiley & Sons, Inc.

Hirschowitz, R.G.: Crisis theory: a formulation, Psychiatr. Annuls 12:33, 1973.

Holmes, T.H., and Rahe, R.H.: The social readjustment scale, J. Psychosom. Res. 11:213, 1967.

Jones, W.H.: Emergency room sudden death: what can be done for the survivors?, Death Education 2:231, 1978.

Kraus, A.S., and Lilienfeld, A.M.: Some epidemiologic aspects of high mortality rate in the young widowed group, J. Chronic Dis. 10:207, 1959.

Kübler-Ross, E.: On death and dying, New York, 1969, Macmillan Publishing Co.

Lewis, E., and Page, A.: Failure to mourn a stillbirth: an overlooked catastrophe, Br. J. Med. Psychol. 51(3): 237, Sept., 1978.

Lindeman, E.: Symptomatology and management of acute grief, Am. J. Psychiatry 101:141, 1944.

Litman, R.E.: When patients commit suicide, Am. J. Psychother. 19:570, 1965.

Maddison, D.: The relevance of conjugal bereavement for preventative psychiatry, Br. J. Med. Psych. **41:** 223, 1968.

Maddison, D., and Walker, W.: Factors affecting the outcome of conjugal bereavement, Br. J. Psych. **113:** 1057, 1967.

Nagy, M.: The child's theories concerning death, J. Genetic Psychiatry 73:3, 1948.

O'Donohue, N.: Perinatal bereavement: the role of the health care professional, Quality Rev. Bull. 4(9):30, 1978.

Parkes, C.: Effects of bereavement on physical and mental health: a study of the medical records of widows, Br. Med. J. 2:274, 1964.

Parkes, C.: Bereavement and mental illness, Br. J. Med. Psychol. 38:1, 1965.

Parkes, C.: The first year of bereavement, Psychiatry 33:444, 1970.

Parkes, C.: Bereavement studies of grief in adult life, New York, 1972, International Universities Press.

Parkes, C.: Benjamin, B., and Fitzgerald, H.: Broken heart: a statistical study of increased mortality among widowers, Br. Med. J. 1:740, 1969.

Public Law 88-164, Community Mental Health Centers Act of 1963, Title II, Regulations, U.S. Department of Health, Education and Welfare. U.S. Public Health Service, May 6, 1964, Statistical study of increased mortality among widowers, Br. Med. J. 1:740, 1969.

Raphael, B.: Mourning and the prevention of melancholia, Br. J. Med. Psychol. 51:303, 1978.

Rees, W.D.: The hallucinations of widowhood, Br. Med. J. 4:37, 1971.

Shneidman, E.: Postvention and the survivor victim. In Michegan, R.L. editor: International conference for suicide prevention: sixth proceedings, 1972, Edwards Bros., Inc.

Shneidman, E., editor: Death: current perspectives, Palo Alto, Calif., 1976, Mayfield Publishing Co.

Speck, P.: Loss and grief in medicine, London, 1978, Baillière Tindall.

Sundow, D.: Passing on, Englewood Cliffs, N.J., 1967, Prentice-Hall, Inc.

Weinstein, S.: Sudden infant death syndrome: impact on families and a direction for change, Am. J. Psychiatry 135(7):831, July, 1978.

Williams, W.V., and Polak, P.B.: Follow-up research in primary prevention: a model of adjustment in acute grief, J. Clin. Psychol. 35:55, 1979.

PART TWO

Management of psychiatric emergency care

WHILE PART ONE OF THIS BOOK focuses on clinical issues, Part Two examines the management and administrative components of psychiatric emergency care. Unit organization and structure must be based on the needs of the client population and should be designed to interface with other community programs. Program components and management styles may vary among units, but it is assumed that administrative decisions are uniformly influenced by the concept that services have to be unscheduled and offered around the clock. Unit management, leadership, and the multidisciplinary team are discussed in separate chapters. The final portion of this book examines how unit maintenance and functioning of psychiatric emergency care are affected by the requirements of standards of care, legal issues, the budgeting process, and interagency and intraagency collaboration.

SECTION D

Unit organization and structure

Unit organization and structure are analyzed within the context of the demands of psychiatric emergency care. Effectively meeting client needs is the basis for the organization of staffing, use of space, and extent of program differentiation.

Chapter 17, Unit Management, comprehensively reviews the major issues involved in establishing and maintaining a psychiatric emergency unit. The author emphasizes that the functioning of psychiatric emergency units is dependent on how administrators and staff define and respond to the client population, the availability of support services, type of administrative setting, physical design, and scheduling of staff from a variety of disciplines.

The importance of meeting the staff's needs is reviewed in the sections on staff training and burnout. The usefulness of workshops, in-service training, and retreats is noted, and an extensive discussion of the burnout syndrome with suggested coping strategies is provided. Other suggestions for improving staff and general unit functioning include guidelines on record keeping, documentation, use of procedures manuals, and program evaluation methodology.

Chapter 18, Leadership, points out that the key factor to improving staff and unit functioning is appropriate leadership. The chapter begins by defining leadership as the process of influencing others. The ability to influence is conceptually based on French and Raven's typology of power: reward, coercive, legitimate, referent, and expert. *Management* is differentiated from *leadership* in that the management role is described as the process of assessing a situation to determine how necessary tasks can be completed to reach goals, whereas leadership is considered the process of influencing others to achieve goals.

A review of the three major conceptualizations of leadership theories—trait, behavioral, and situational—demonstrates the complexities inherent in defining leadership and reveals the evolution of theory development in this area. Organizational determinants of leadership are discussed in the context of mechanistic (Weberian), organic (human relations), and professional models of organization. This leads to a discussion of the participative leadership style, which is recommended as the type of leadership most appropriate to psychiatric emergency settings. The chapter concludes with a description of how participative leadership can be used in decision making, staff development, and teamwork.

Chapter 19, Multidisciplinary Team Approach, presents a more thorough examination of teamwork and teams. The authors address issues of team mission and functioning. It is emphasized that members of teams should complement each other with respect to clinical skills and should be mutually supportive of each other.

The disciplinary composition of the team is examined according to ascribed roles. How nurses, psychiatrists, social workers, students, ward clerks, and administrators can work together and build cohesive ties is discussed. The authors do not recommend a single model for team building but suggest that the decision to adopt either an egalitarian operating team or a traditional hierarchically arranged team is based on personnel availability, attitudes of administrators and staff, and objectives of the program. A case vignette illustrates how two teams, one arranged in a hierarchical fashion and the other egalitarian, operate in treating the same case.

CHAPTER 17

Unit management

Zigfrids T. Stelmachers, Ph.D.

Few service institutions today suffer from having too few administrators; most of them are over-administered, and suffer from a surplus of procedures, organization charts, and "management techniques." What now has to be learned—it is still largely lacking—is to manage service institutions for performance. This may well be the biggest and most important management task for the remainder of this century (Peter F. Drucker, *The Public Interest,* 1973).

SCOPE OF PROGRAM
Definition of crisis or emergency

While starting a scientific discussion with definitions of the main concepts is an intellectually stimulating and time-honored practice, and while definitions may in some instances have practical implications, this seems to be less true of the field of crisis intervention. The main reason for this is that there are at least three principal agents who make a de facto definition of crisis: the professional, the client, and the community (police, relative, neighbor, and so on). One can readily see how the definitions may vary dramatically from agent to agent so that there is a question of whose definition is to prevail. In case of conflict, it is the community's definition that typically and ultimately determines the outcome, but the other two can obviously not be ignored. It is a well-known fact, for instance, that many clients use emergency units as medical clinics, that is, for medical problems not viewed by physicians as emergent—or even urgent. The message for a psychiatric emergency unit is that no matter how it conceptualizes *crisis* or *emergency,* clients will insist on using its services for a wide

285

variety of problems, many of which will not match the original expectations of the staff. A crisis program should be prepared for this and make the necessary allowances with regard to staffing, space, and program components. The only truly unifying concept seems to be that the services have to be *unscheduled* and be offered around the clock. To set up a walk-in, clinic-type subprogram for nonemergent clients, as some large emergency units do, is usually not practical for mental health emergency services because of their relatively small size and lack of programmatic differentiation.

Program components

A comprehensive emergency service will typically consist of several program elements that may or may not be identified as organizational units. Many of these components will represent services offered elsewhere in the community as separate and unique programs. Even though this involves some duplication of services, a generic emergency program should probably have *some* general competence in all of these areas, otherwise the client runs the risk of receiving a succession of referrals from one specialized agency to another without the benefit of definitive intervention. The availability of various specialized services in the community should, of course, influence the design of the psychiatric emergency unit. For instance, in a metropolitan area there may be a large number of social and nonestablishment-type programs utilizing a crisis intervention approach which, nevertheless, lack psychiatric expertise. In such a situation it would make sense to establish a hospital-based program specializing in psychiatric emergency care. Such a program could then provide the needed professional-medical-psychiatric backup to other community agencies for the more disturbed clients. In this way hospital-based emergency units specializing in psychiatric care frequently function as a bridge between the health center and the community, between inpatient and outpatient facilities, and between the clients at risk and their support network.

The main program elements of a psychiatric emergency unit typically are (1) crisis interven-

tion proper (for clients in stressful situations without psychiatric histories or clear-cut psychiatric symptoms); (2) psychiatric emergency treatment (for clients with diagnosable psychiatric conditions of an emergent nature); (3) emergency social service (for clients with disposition problems); (4) walk-in clinic and drop-in center (for nonemergent clients requiring evaluation); (5) hotlines (for immediate accessibility and for clients who cannot or will not come to the center personally); (6) information and referral; (7) prepetition screening and diversion (for clients considered for involuntary commitment); (8) home visits (for both on-location assessment and intervention if client is unwilling or unable to come to the center); (9) outreach services, which in particular have received much well-deserved emphasis and on which concept some crisis programs are entirely based (McGee, 1974; Polak et al., 1979); and (10) crisis homes utilized in a few of the units, that is, private homes for short-term placement of clients in emotional crises, including chronic mentally ill and acutely psychotic individuals (Brook et al., 1976). Such an arrangement can offer a safe temporary shelter and avoid unnecessary and costly hospitalization by providing treatment in a less restricted environment resembling more normal living.

Some programs will offer only one or two of these services, more comprehensive programs may contain most or all of the elements, and, of course, the emphasis and priorities regarding these elements will differ from program to program. For instance, service units designed mainly for psychiatric emergencies will emphasize that program element in their "advertising," staffing pattern, location, training, and so on, whereas crisis intervention centers will concentrate on a psychiatrically more normal population of clients whose needs are best met by a crisis intervention approach as defined by crisis theory. However, one has to recognize that this distinction is frequently of little practical value when it comes to client selection because it is made by clinicians and administrators rather than by the clients themselves, who insist on defining their own problems and choosing their facilities in a less rational and informed fashion. Perhaps the main point in all this is that there are indeed different theoretical models that influence clinical practice, whether the recipients are psychotic individuals or normal persons in emotional distress, so that the mental health professionals are well advised to be familiar with these models and apply them in a differentiated manner, that is, match them with the particular set of problems and symptoms clients bring to them. Whatever the designation of the facility, one can expect a good number of multiple-problem clients who require both crisis intervention proper and psychiatric emergency care.

Target client populations

A comprehensive psychiatric emergency unit has to be prepared to accept clients with a variety of complaints, problems, and symptoms. It will often deal with multiproblem clients who do not fit any particular category. It will treat suicidal, homicidal, or violent individuals, clients whose crisis is related to alcoholism or chemical abuse, clients who have been raped or battered, victims of incest, natural disasters, and crime, and also clients who are dying or grieving. Again, a given community may have specialized programs aimed at these various target populations, providing both advocacy as well as direct services. A comprehensive psychiatric emergency unit should not attempt to compete with these programs but instead should complement them by offering professional backup and consultation. One side contributes concentrated dedication to a select group of clients, the other side contributes a broad mental health expertise and more specialized services (such as psychotropic medications, psychotherapy, mental status examinations, and medical examination of rape victims). Such a collaboration represents a very desirable arrangement because neither side can accomplish the task alone.

ADMINISTRATIVE SETTING
Hospital

In many ways a hospital provides an ideal setting for a psychiatric emergency unit (Resnik and Ruben, 1975; Stelmachers, 1980). Hospitals are increasingly used as primary care providers.

According to the February, 1979, issue of *Hospital Physician*, hospitals have experienced a sevenfold increase in utilization of emergency and outpatient departments during a 23-year period from 1953 to 1976. Deinstitutionalization of the mentally ill has shifted the clinical burden from state hospitals to public and private general hospitals and their emergency departments. Whatever aftercare services the discharged psychiatric clients may receive in the community, sooner or later their need for medications will lead them to the local hospital. Since many emergency unit clients suffer from significant mental health problems relevant to the current crisis and since emergency departments are open around the clock, it is natural for community gatekeepers, such as the police, to think of the local hospital as the obvious recipient for people in crisis. The same is certainly true for ambulance services. Furthermore, many crisis clients require medical treatment, a good example being overdoses and other suicide attempts. Such medical treatment is readily available in hospital emergency units. Some emotionally disturbed clients require hospitalization, which also can be most easily arranged by a hospital medical staff. The law typically requires endorsement by a mental health professional for a client's involuntary hospitalization and emergency holds. Finally, many clients with unclear diagnostic status and with both emotional and physical symptoms may have to be referred back and forth several times between a medically oriented emergency unit and a psychologically oriented psychiatric emergency unit (or the medical emergency unit may choose to call a psychiatrist for consultation). This is more difficult to accomplish if the unit is located outside a hospital.

Possible drawbacks to a hospital location may be an overly medical orientation that is inappropriate for a large number of crisis clients, bureaucratic hurdles characteristic of large institutions, and the association—right or wrong—of a hospital-based program with mental illness.

Mental health center

It is now mandatory that federally funded community mental health centers offer psychiatric emergency services. Many clients who contact crisis centers are chronically mentally ill and therefore can benefit from the professional skills represented in a properly staffed mental health center. It may be more acceptable to some individuals who feel that there is less stigma attached to visiting a mental health center as compared with a hospital-based psychiatric service. On the other hand, many mental health centers lack medical or psychiatric backup which has to be arranged through cumbersome contracts with a medical facility. The availability of a psychiatric consultant 1 day a week or so (not uncommon in smaller mental health centers) is often inadequate to meet the needs of the mentally ill in emergent situations. It is certainly more immediate and clinically effective to directly administer rather than contract for psychiatric emergency services.

Freestanding

Many crisis intervention services in the United States, especially the nonpsychiatric ones, are of the freestanding type. Many pattern themselves after free clinics and suicide prevention services that developed outside formal mental health settings and in some instances were frankly antiestablishment. There is no doubt that they serve needs unmet or poorly addressed by mental health professionals. It is equally true that for the most part the traditional psychiatric institutions did not welcome these newcomers, which were viewed by them as poorly trained, unprofessional, and providing substandard treatment. The situation has changed, however, with considerable rapprochement between the two parties. Today most freestanding programs pay a dear price for their cherished autonomy: funding is a continuous problem and almost exclusive reliance on volunteers creates difficulties that will be discussed later. In the eyes of the professional community, some of these programs still lack credibility, which leads to a reluctance to make referrals. But above all, both systems deal essentially with the same client population: the mentally ill, the suicidal, the depressed, and people in a variety of emotional crises. Both sys-

tems can and should learn from each other and contribute their particular points of view and skills so there is available a continuum of care ranging from befriending (Varah, 1973) and ventilation to administration of haloperidol and hospitalization. With more sophistication regarding crisis theory among mental health professionals, there is less basis for worry that the establishment will treat people in crisis as mentally ill (unless, of course, the clients *are* mentally ill and report with psychiatric symptoms). In summary, considering the relative isolation and administrative instability of freestanding programs, they appear the least desirable.

Referral network

No unit can survive without an adequate referral network of human services. Following crisis intervention or emergency treatment, many clients still require further, more specialized or long-term attention, which a crisis center is not equipped to provide. Therefore, both formal and informal agreements with certain key agencies are an absolute necessity. Such a network would ideally include a medical emergency room, inpatient and outpatient psychiatry, detoxification and chemical dependency programs, adult and child protection units of welfare departments, the "commitment office" or a prepetition screening unit, various aftercare programs for the mentally ill (most notably community support projects), the courts and jails, specialized programs (rape, suicide, grief, victims of crime, and so on), and, perhaps most importantly, the police.

The collaboration can occur in various contexts: common case conferences about difficult multiagency clients, common teaching conferences, periodic administrative meetings, formal contracts, and personal visits. One of the most effective means of establishing a thorough understanding of each other's problems, policies, and philosophy is staff exchange. Staff from one agency can spend a day or two in another agency, perhaps even participate in the clinical activities, if appropriate and permissible.

PHYSICAL DESIGN
Location

Ideally, a psychiatric crisis center should be located on the first floor for easy access. Especially in larger institutions, it is difficult for confused, panicky, and psychotic clients to find their destination by following lengthy verbal explanations, complicated wall maps, or colored lines. If the psychiatric emergency unit is located inside a hospital, it is more important to be in close proximity to the medical emergency unit than to psychiatry services. It is desirable for the psychiatric emergency unit to have its own separate access because many, perhaps over half, of the clients will not need medical triage. Thus clients with emotional problems who first show up at the emergency unit can be directed to the crisis center, and those with medical complications entering the crisis center can be referred to the emergency unit with equal ease. Also, since most large emergency units will have holding rooms, they can be shared with the crisis program.

The crisis center should have its own waiting room located next to the receptionist's desk. Although often aggravating to the receptionist, it is important that there is someone who can keep an eye on the waiting clients and alert the clinical staff should a client attempt to leave prematurely or show signs of increasing agitation.

Interview rooms

There should be approximately one interview room for 2,000 client contacts per year, or there should be a minimum of one interview room for each line clinical staff member on the busiest shift of the day. If possible, the atmosphere and decor should be more like those of a living room than of a medical examining room. Care has to be taken, however, to avoid pieces of furniture or other objects that can be used to injure self or others. For reasons of safety each interview room should have an easily accessible alarm button connected with the main emergency unit central desk, the hospital security department, the crisis center's main waiting areas, or any other location where one can reasonably expect other people to be present who could rescue the interviewer should a dangerous situation develop. For the same reason the furniture should be arranged in such a manner that the interviewer is close to the door so that an aggressive client cannot block the exit. Finally, it is best to have all interview rooms located as close together as possible so that staff members can readily consult with each other and come to each other's assistance. During slow shifts and particularly during the night whole sections of the unit, especially unused interview rooms, can be closed off and locked to prevent clients from wandering around or off the premises (it is best to have only one open entry-exit so that clients coming and going can be closely monitored).

Observation and seclusion rooms

All emergency services will occasionally deal with clients requiring some degree of seclusion and clients who, for a variety of reasons, have to stay in the unit for long periods of time before a safe disposition can be made. Therefore, facilities should be provided that can serve this dual function.

Even though it is advisable to accept only clients who are medically cleared, it is still recommended that such clients be checked periodically by a staff member with physical assessment skills such as a nurse or physician.

Telephone rooms

It is practical to designate one room to serve as the telephone room. All publicized phone numbers should be answered in this room, and there should be a minimum of two phones so that staff members can readily communicate with each other when a call has to be traced. It is recommended that this room be in close proximity to the waiting area so that the staff can both answer phone calls and be able to see waiting or entering clients. It should be roomy enough because staff members will tend to congregate in this room unless they are interviewing a client elsewhere. The phones should ideally have an external speaker with amplification so that difficult calls can be monitored by more than one staff member.

Some psychiatric emergency units may want to protect themselves from too many calls at any given time by a backup arrangement with volunteers on call. Phones can be purchased with an add-on device that permits direct transfer of a call to a volunteer's home after sufficient screening has been done.

Conference rooms

There should be at least one multipurpose room for teaching conferences, staff meetings, shift-change meetings, group and family therapy, and finally, for the staff to retreat to from the clinical battles; the latter is not a luxury but a necessity to be recognized and officially endorsed.

STAFFING
Professional disciplines

Crisis centers utilize every conceivable mix of mental health professionals, paraprofessionals, volunteers, and students. Their selection seems to be dictated by the setting, the history of the program, availability, and budgetary considerations rather than programmatic need. Agencies with solid funding will hire professionals, whereas those operating on a shoestring budget will have to rely on paraprofessionals and volunteers with professionals providing administrative leadership, consultation, supervision, and back-up.

In any psychiatric emergency unit one may find psychiatric nurses, clinical psychologists, psychiatric social workers, psychiatrists (or psychiatric residents), chaplains, corpsmen, human service generalists, mental health workers, psychiatric technicians, chemical dependency counselors, advocates and counselors for victims of rape, incest, and battering, and lay and professional volunteers—singly or in combination. The empirical base for various types of staffing patterns is very thin and no one has convincingly demonstrated, in terms of outcome results, that one pattern is to be preferred over another.

It is difficult to single out any particular mental health discipline that is superior to the others when it comes to crisis intervention (Hankoff, 1969). The necessary skills can be found among all mental health professionals so that the final selection should be based on relevant competencies rather than professional discipline. Aside from special skills, each discipline contributes its own philosophy of mental health care, which enriches the clinical deliberations of the team and provides a desirable variety in points of view. Therefore, a multidisciplinary approach is probably the best choice.

In a medical setting, however, one must be sure to include psychiatric nurses in the team because they are unique (except for psychiatrists) in possessing mental health expertise as well as knowledge of pathophysiology and symptoms of diseases. Thus, their nursing knowledge and skills are indispensable for such functions as selecting clients in need of further examination by a physician, checking vital signs, administering medications, and—not to be forgotten—forming an easy communication bridge with other departments of the health center.

Medical or human services model

Even in a medical setting only between one third and one fourth of the clients need to see a physician. While it might be safest from a clinical standpoint to have every client medically evaluated, it is somewhat of a luxury and not very practical because of the high cost and lack of availability of medical-psychiatric time. A competent mental health professional skilled in crisis intervention is well qualified to make triage, intervention, and disposition decisions for the majority of clients with a great variety of non-psychiatric problems. Nevertheless, the crisis program should have a psychiatrist available around the clock—either located in the unit or available on relatively short notice (Glasscot et al., 1966). Because of the unpredictable nature of crisis work, such a psychiatrist can be shared with another unscheduled activity elsewhere within the agency; in a hospital the ideal combination is crisis program and in-house liaison consultation service. In their specialist role, the psychiatrists perform comprehensive psychiatric evaluations and mental status examinations, prescribe medications, or hospitalize clients if clinically indicated. Depending on their availability, preference, and program philosophy, they can function as direct service providers along with other mental health professionals or be used mainly as consultants in a more narrowly defined and specialized capacity. In the latter case the initial decision to call or not to call the psychiatrist consultant is up to the staff, and therefore it is advisable to develop a written list of criteria for requesting such consultation (Stelmachers et al., 1978). Table 17-1 represents a suggested scheme for obtaining medical clearance and psychiatric input.

Generalist or specialist roles

No matter what the particular discipline of a staff member, all members will act as mental health generalists most of the time. With the possible exception of nurses (Aguilera and Messick, 1981) the specialist function is relatively

TABLE 17-1. Criteria for requesting psychiatric-medical consultation

Condition	Description and exceptions	Recommended action
Psychosis	Psychosis chronic and individual well known to psychiatric emergency unit staff *and* no change in mental status (example: chronic psychotic client with a dispositional problem).	Use judgment.
	Psychosis associated with organic brain syndrome, alcohol or drug use.	Call emergency unit physician.
	Patient currently under a psychiatrist's care.	Obtain psychiatrist's advice and follow it. If unavailable, call psychiatric emergency unit psychiatrist.
	Not clear whether person is psychotic.	Call psychiatrist.
	All other psychotics.	Call psychiatrist.
Other severe psychopathology	Severe depression, severe anxiety attack or panic state, acute and severe hysterical episodes such as dissociative states and depersonalization (in general, all conditions requiring immediate attention and probably responsive to medication).	
	Person quickly responds to intervention.	Use judgment.
	Person does not respond to intervention or gets worse.	Call psychiatrist.
Organic brain syndrome	Psychosis associated with organic brain syndrome (OBS).	See under Psychosis.
	Nonpsychotic acute OBS.	If diagnosis relatively certain, call emergency unit physician. If not, call psychiatrist for diagnostic clarification.
	Chronic OBS *and* clinical picture stable and unchanging.	Use judgment.
Physical symptoms	Symptoms emergent or urgent (judgment regarding this to be made by staff).	Call emergency unit physician.
	Symptoms acute *and* subjective complaints of significant intensity.	Inform primary physician, receive and follow instructions. If primary physician cannot be reached, refer client to primary physician.
		If client has no primary physician, get consultation from psychiatric or medical emergency unit nurse and follow instructions. If no nurse available, contact physician or psychiatrist on call.

Continued.

TABLE 17-1. Criteria for requesting psychiatric-medical consultation—cont'd

Condition	Description and exceptions	Recommended action
	Symptoms chronic.	Use judgment.
	Client referred from emergency unit.	Make certain person has been medically cleared. If not or person still has acute physical symptoms and subjective complaints of significant intensity, refer back to emergency unit.
Suicidal risk	Risk high enough to consider either voluntary or involuntary hospitalization.	Call psychiatrist.
	Person has made a suicide attempt requiring medical treatment (regardless of suicide risk).	Call psychiatrist.
	Person has made a suicide attempt of low lethality, condition is chronic and nonpsychotic, and person is known to psychiatric emergency unit staff.	Use judgment.
	All other suicidal conditions.	Use judgment.
Homicidal threat	Threat of low potential *and* client's condition chronic and nonpsychotic *and* person is known to psychiatric emergency unit staff.	Use judgment.
	All other homicidal threats.	Call psychiatrist.
Violent behavior	Person psychotic.	See actions under Psychosis.
	Person not psychotic.	Use judgment.
Past or current treatment by psychiatrist, including past psychiatric hospitalization		Use judgment.
Patient currently on medications	Person on psychotropic medications and has somatic complaints.	Call psychiatrist.
	Person on psychotropic medications and demonstrates psychopathological symptoms.	Call psychiatrist.
	Person on psychotropic medications without somatic complaints or psychopathological symptoms.	Use judgment.
	Person on other medications.	Use judgment. If in doubt consult emergency unit physician.
Alcohol use	Episodic or habitual excessive drinking, alcohol addiction, or alcoholic deterioration.	Use judgment.
	DTs, impending DTs, Korsakoff's psychosis, alcoholic hallucinosis, alcoholic paranoid state, acute alcohol intoxication, pathological intoxication.	Call emergency unit physician.
Drug use (opiates, amphetamines, sedatives, hallucinogens, hypnotics)	Drug use.	Use judgment.
	Drug dependence.	Use judgment.
	Acute intoxication ("psychosis with drug or poison intoxication").	Call emergency unit physician.
	Overdose of opiates, sedatives, or hypnotics.	Call emergency unit physician.
	Overdose of hallucinogens or amphetamines.	Call psychiatrist.
Special conditions	Client on emergency transportation hold.	Call psychiatrist.
	Request by court for psychiatric evaluation.	Call psychiatrist.
	Request by court for evaluation, psychological evaluation, and so on.	Clarify court's intent and act accordingly. If court does not specifically request evaluation by a psychiatrist, use judgment.
	Request by a mental health professional or agency for an evaluation by psychiatrist (even if unnecessary by clinical judgment).	Honor request whenever possible.
	Request by a mental health professional or agency for hospitalization or medications.	Call psychiatrist.
	Request by client for medications, hospitalization, or evaluation by psychiatrist.	Use judgment.

minor and, where it exists, may have less to do with the professional background of the staff than with a particular area of expertise that has been independently acquired (such as geriatrics, rape, grief, or chemical dependency). In a team setting staff members will seek each other out for their known skill areas, but staff members who have worked together for longer periods of time in close proximity usually learn from each other so that everyone gradually assimilates specialized knowledge from the other team members. In a well-functioning psychiatric emergency unit with a stable staff it would be difficult to tell from observing the clinical activities of various staff members who is a social worker, nurse, psychologist, or mental health worker.

Levels of professional training

As in the case of professional disciplines, it is recommended that there be a mix of various levels of training from mental health aides and volunteers to psychiatrists and clinical psychologists with academic degrees. It would be impractical to employ personnel with a master's or doctoral degree for ventilation, reassurance, support, and handholding; it would be equally inadvisable for volunteers and staff without formal training to perform mental status examinations and diagnostic evaluations and to make decisions regarding psychiatric clients with severe psychopathology. Because of the wide variety of problems which can be expected to appear at a psychiatric emergency unit, it is best to be able to match complexity of problem with level of expertise. The trick is to make the correct matching decision early in the sequence.

Volunteers

Many psychiatric emergency programs would not be able to exist without volunteers. With diligence one can find well-qualified and dedicated volunteers, some with professional backgrounds. As more and more crisis-oriented programs compete for volunteers, however, their selection becomes a very important concern. Thorough selection procedures should be worked out, perhaps involving psychological testing and

role play, to weed out unsuitable candidates (it is not unheard of to get applications from actively psychotic individuals currently in treatment at the agency they want to work for).

Any program contemplating the use of volunteers should anticipate a relatively high turnover and the need for thorough orientation and training. To economize with the available faculty, certain lectures can be given to volunteers from several agencies as long as there are overlapping needs. In addition, there should be a procedure for evaluating the volunteers' performance on a periodic basis so that their clinical assignments fit their state of preparedness. It is almost mandatory to have a clearly assigned volunteer coordinator responsible for the recruitment, selection, training, and evaluation of all volunteers. The best recruitment is by word of mouth because it is based on the reputation the program has been able to achieve in the community. Depending on the quality of volunteers offering their services, some programs may choose to have several levels of volunteer work from clerical and receptionist duties to supervised clinical and relatively unsupervised clinical work.

Students

It is preferable for at least some of the staff members to have faculty positions at a local university or college. This way they qualify as field instructors or supervisors, and their respective professional schools are more willing to send students, both graduate and undergraduate, for practicum experience. Block placements are preferable and so is use of students with previous clinical experience because of the demanding nature of emergency work. Because of their inquisitiveness, enthusiasm, willingness to be challenged, and high motivation to learn, students are always an asset to a program, and everything should be done to create a receptive climate for them.

Scheduling

Scheduling for an around-the-clock psychiatric emergency program employing many different mental health professions is a nightmare. It requires a skilled, tough, tactful, respected, and flexible individual. Usually, the nurses have most experience with such scheduling. Scheduling is made easier with a large number of part-time staff than with a small number of full-time employees. Even at that, it is not always possible to achieve the desired mixture of professional disciplines and levels. Maximum flexibility in scheduling is advised so that staff requests can be accommodated to the fullest possible extent.

TRAINING AND STAFF DEVELOPMENT
Orientation

It is not an infrequent complaint that psychiatric emergency workers do not receive adequate preparation before being "thrown to the wolves." While it is obvious that some orientation should be given to new staff, it is less obvious that highly qualified mental health professionals still require specialized instruction in crisis intervention theory and techniques, various types of psychiatric emergencies, and such specialized topics as suicide, dangerousness, child abuse, victimology, laws pertaining to civil commitment, especially as they relate to emergency holds, use of restraints, community resources, family violence, and perhaps many others. Too often the assumption is made that a mental health professional with the proper degree should be equipped on that basis alone to deliver adequate emergency care. This is an erroneous assumption. Psychiatric emergency care is an identified area of expertise perhaps comparable to emergency medicine and family practice, both of which derive knowledge and competencies from a variety of more basic disciplines and yet represent a unique combination of skills requiring specialization and all the training that goes with it (Hoff, 1978).

In-service training

Different professionals will bring different types and levels of skills to the psychiatric emergency program. Therefore, their training needs will differ and should be tailored to their particular backgrounds. While a psychiatrist will need little instruction on psychotropic medications, all nonmedical personnel will probably profit from general familiarity with commonly administered psychoactive drugs. A mental health worker may have particular experience and skills in treating chemically dependent individuals, while psychologists and social workers may lack such training and require further instruction in that area. There obviously are topics of interest and value to everyone, but orientation and training should have built-in flexibility to accommodate individual requirements.

Since new programs develop all the time and the typical descriptions found in directories and catalogs are impersonal and lacking in relevant detail, it is a good idea to invite representatives from such programs to in-service training sessions. This serves the dual purpose of providing instruction as well as interagency liaison.

Workshops and seminars

The specialized topics for workshops and seminars lend themselves particularly well to the individual needs of different staff members described previously. One or two staff members with an identified gap in their skills or knowledge can be sent to an appropriate workshop to remedy the situation. To make most use of their experience, they can report the information gained at the workshop to other staff at the next staff meeting or in-service training session. Workshops have the additional benefit of removing line staff members from the routine drudgery and reducing chances for "shell shock."

Retreats

Retreats, scheduled once or twice a year, are an excellent time to settle administrative issues or provide intense training in a particularly vital area. They assume special importance because the staff members in an around-the-clock program seldom get together at the same time. They also offer opportunity for more personal interaction and socialization, so important as a preventive measure against burnout which will be discussed in the next section.

In conclusion, it should be clear that to provide

the proper training and staff development opportunities, budgetary sacrifices have to be made. Unlike a scheduled program, a psychiatric emergency unit has to replace staff sent to workshops, training sessions, and retreats. Temporary staff have to be trained and paid for the coverage. Former staff members, students who have graduated, and experienced volunteers can be used for this purpose, but it is the money commitment that will indicate if administration is serious about its dedication to quality professional standards.

BURNOUT
Theoretical model

Psychiatric emergency work is very stressful because of its unpredictable nature, both in terms of work load and type or problem encountered; it involves rotational shifts, high emotional intensity, and difficult-to-manage clients and occasionally will represent a certain amount of danger. Under such circumstances, it is not surprising that staff members burn out more quickly than in other settings, especially if their entire time is devoted to direct clinical service (Freudenberger, 1974).

When evaluating burnout, it is important to recognize that job stress is only one variable associated with symptoms of burnout. One has to take into account personal stress unrelated to the job, such "mediating variables" as availability of social support, and the staff member's personality, general frustration tolerance, emotional stability, and coping skill (Kessler, 1979). In this complex scheme, poor job performance is certainly related to burnout but could result from many different causes as well. It would be unwise for the organization or the individual staff members to too readily assume that certain symptoms must be job related simply because the work is known to be stressful. It is equally true, of course, that managers may tend to blame factors other than work conditions for their employees' burnout. One simply has to guard against a too simplistic or self-serving explanation of a complex phenomenon.

Burnout should not be confused with job dissatisfaction. The latter can contribute to the former but is typically caused by different factors (such as salary, technical knowledge of supervisor, job security, the supervisor's style of relating to employees, as opposed to such factors as opportunity for advancement, degree of responsibility and autonomy, and the nature of rewards for good performance).

Signs and symptoms

The symptoms signaling burnout or impending burnout are, unfortunately, unspecific and can be the result of many different causes—just like the symptoms of the delayed posttraumatic stress disorder, a clinical category that is receiving increased attention and has been included in DSM III. The following signs may be indicative of burnout: sensation of being exhausted, insomnia, depression, various physical symptoms such as headache, digestive system problems, weight loss, and shortness of breath, as well as changing moods, feelings of helplessness, increasing irritability, suspiciousness bordering on paranoia, unnecessary risk taking, rigidity, negativism, and cynicism. Burned out individuals typically spend increasing amounts of time to complete a fixed amount of work, but the quality of work and overall productivity decline dramatically. As one can see, many of these symptoms are of the type that appear after protracted stress whether produced by chronic financial worries, captivity, or a long, unhappy marriage.

Antecedents

Since most studies in the area cannot conclusively demonstrate causation, it is best to label the factors that temporally precede burnout as "antecedents." While some instruments designed to measure stress seem to be based on the assumption that certain events are equally stressful to most individuals (Holmes and Rahe, 1967), it is true that one has to take into account the individual *interpretation* of an event before one can accurately assess the degree of internal strain a given life change or condition will cause. Thus, relative inactivity may be quite relaxing to one individual but stressful to another who is energetic, and productive and enjoys challenge.

295

Another general observation is that certain individuals are less prone to burnout, other things being equal. Individuals who are less susceptible to burnout typically feel that they are in control of themselves and their environment, have a strong sense of self and purpose, are able to extract meaning from major life activities, are generally optimistic, and have no demonstrated tendency to become easily depressed. Persons especially susceptible to burnout are those who become readily overinvolved with their work or clients and those, ironically, who are particularly dedicated, idealistic, sensitive, and open. Such persons often fail to recognize their own vulnerability. A thoughtful supervisor should identify such staff members and protect them from themselves, job conditions permitting.

Because of the highly individualized way in which people react to stress and great individual differences in vulnerability, most antecedents of burnout reported in the literature are neither sufficient nor necessary to produce burnout. With this reservation in mind, here are some of the main factors associated with burnout: amount of work, opportunity for promotion, freedom to be creative, adequacy of both horizontal and vertical communication, responsibility without authority, role conflict or ambiguity, underutilization of skills, lack of clarity or consistency in organizational goals and policies, bureaucratic constraints, lack of resources and power, understimulation or overstimulation, and lack of co-worker compatibility. Rotational shifts occupy a special position because they disturb the employee's circadian rhythms and are known to cause significant physiological as well as psychological disturbances (Lanuza, 1976).

There are special problems in a psychiatric emergency setting that should be mentioned. The staff have to work day after day with very difficult clients who are assaultive, suicidal, bizarre, irrational, resistive, depressed, hopeless, chronically dependent, or involuntary, and frequently they do not improve. One typically does not have the opportunity to prepare oneself for what is to come during the next hour, both in terms of volume and type of problem or emergency. Furthermore, the helpers are supposed to be good examples of perfect mental health: tolerant, wise, and

giving; this permits less of a margin for the average amount of ignorance, ill will, and lack of patience often found in most people, including mental health profespionals. To guard against countertransference problems, mental health professionals are supposed to have good insight about their own conflicts and shortcomings so that there is less recourse to such very adaptive mechanisms as denial. Thus the clinician is quite vulnerable and sometimes falls victim to unrealistic but prevalent expectations from within and without.

Consequences

The consequences of burnout are predictable. Staff members lose interest, personal involvement, and concern for clients, which often leads to avoidance of direct contact and such substitute activities as increased frequency of staff meetings (Pines and Maslach, 1978). Some staff members withdraw and detach themselves emotionally from both clients and colleagues, as a result of which they receive less support, feedback, and outside perspective—all of which are badly needed during the prodromal stages of burnout. Other clinicians use intellectualization and compartmentalization as ways of protecting themselves from the emotional drain of direct clinical work. Even worse, some defend their own sensitivities by externalizing guilt and blame. Instead of viewing clients as sick, suffering, and in need of care, they are perceived as willfully manipulative, as having "character disorders" (meaning that they therefore cannot be anxious, depressed, or in real pain), as "hateful" people who make unreasonable demands and do their best to provoke and irritate well-meaning staff. This is not to say that difficult clients do not exist, but once burned out, clinicians seem to find more of them than before.

Coping strategies

What can individual staff members do to avoid burnout? The guiding principle should be to protect oneself against overwork, overinvolvement, and getting caught up in a messianic complex or heroic altruism. One should stay cool without becoming emotionally cold, that is, not defend oneself by becoming tough and insensitive. To remain effective, a clinician has to retain some vulnerability, otherwise genuineness and empathy suffer. Staff members may also choose to reduce their time commitment, even if it involves financial sacrifices. The same can be accomplished by taking more frequent leaves of absence if acceptable to the management. If everything fails, psychiatric emergency workers should change jobs before burnout occurs, or if possible, change duties and activities within the same job. They can take up special projects of interest as long as they are compatible with the goals of the organization—even if the rewards are only intrinsic ones. Finally, it may be wise to develop sources of satisfaction outside work, be they recreational, social, familial, or spiritual.

A small group atmosphere and peer support are some of the best antidotes against burnout. Since staff in psychiatric emergency units work under most trying circumstances and in close proximity to each other, they have to rely on each other's judgment and it helps if they are personally compatible and have a social life extending beyond work hours. No amount of administrative skills can match the support clinicians get from the understanding of co-workers who are all subjected to the same hardships and can truly appreciate the strain experienced by all professionals in crisis intervention.

Many of the strategies outlined will be less successful without the tacit or expressed approval of the management. Regular assessment of staff satisfaction is very advisable. It communicates to the line staff management's concern for their well-being, and it provides the administrator with specific information regarding areas of discontent. Such discontent should be openly discussed at staff meetings or retreats so that corrective action can be taken, if feasible. It is recommended that the management permit liberal leaves of absence and the greatest possible flexibility in scheduling to accommodate individual needs. It is very beneficial to staff morale to engage the staff in continued education activities such as sending as many staff members as possible to relevant workshops and seminars. To make the job more varied and interesting, cer-

tain assignments and responsibilities can be rotated among qualified staff. The starting of new programs or subprograms always has a certain vitalizing effect on the organization because it produces new tasks and an opportunity for creativity in planning and implementation. Staff should be given maximum autonomy in setting goals for themselves and making independent treatment decisions and clinical dispositions. This should be limited only by the individual staff member's own skill level and certain bureaucratic constraints that dictate that only designated professionals with academic degrees can perform more specialized clinical activities (hospital admission, psychological testing, administration of medications, and legal holds). Above all, a good administrator will do everything possible to provide staff members with opportunity for continued growth. This may include encouraging promising clinicians to leave when they have achieved their full potential, even though they are valuable to the organization. Finally, it is said that one of the most telling precursors of staff burnout is the loss of the leader's charisma (Freudenberger, 1974). Therefore, program directors should prevent their own burnout by periodic changes in their own job description, which means that they either have to leave or redefine their job. To finish on a positive note, one can perhaps view burnout as a valuable symptom of organizational decay. While disruptive, it signals—if identified in time—that something needs to be done, that the program itself may be in need of some crisis intervention.

RECORDS AND MISCELLANY
Clinical records

Since a significant number of psychiatric emergency unit clients are chronic, that is, they reappear from time to time or are actually scheduled for a certain number of return visits, it is best to establish a cumulative file for them instead of using the usual "emergency room sheet." Even for unscheduled sporadic emergency care, it is useful to have a record that can be consulted each time the client comes in. If the psychiatric emergency unit is a part of a larger agency, such as a hospital, one should consider keeping the crisis file separate from the hospital records because of the higher degree of confidentiality it deserves. For those clients who already are registered as hospital clients and receive their medical care from the hospital, one can send a brief abstract from the crisis file to the hospital chart so that the primary care provider can learn about the crisis visits, even though some clinically sensitive material has been deleted.

It is probably advisable to use a problem-oriented rather than diagnosis-oriented approach because the frequently hurried and incomplete evaluations done in emergency situations do not lend themselves to arriving at a respectable diagnostic formulation. Also, as stated before, many clients will not have psychiatric problems nor exhibit psychiatric symptoms. Consequently, applying a psychiatric diagnosis to various problems of living would seem inappropriate, and probably undesirable from the client's point of view.

The record should contain clearly identified sections dealing with problems of particular importance. This would include the degree of dangerousness to oneself or others, the application of legal holds, the use of medications or restraints, placing the clients in holding rooms, and perhaps an indication of the level of overall functioning or impairment. Corresponding to each problem, the record should contain a statement about the treatment or disposition provided. Finally, it is very useful to have a section of the record reserved for follow-up instructions and the results of follow-up. Many follow-up activities cannot be accomplished by the staff member who saw the client. To make sure that the necessary information and instructions are communicated to staff on the next shifts, it is not sufficient to rely on verbal report during shift change meetings. The follow-up note itself will give an indication to what extent the client has complied with treatment suggestions or referral. It will also show whether further intervention is necessary. It is important to record the names and phone numbers of all professionals and agencies currently providing services to the client. Staff members unfamiliar with a particular client can readily contact these valuable sources of information should another emergency arise.

Finally, it is practical to separate the more lengthy narrative data base from the face sheet, which should only contain the most essential clinical information that can be easily scanned without having to read the entire record. See Fig. 17-1 for an example of a face sheet used at the Hennepin County Medical Center in Minneapolis.

Fees

Emergency services by their very nature are expensive because staffing patterns have to be geared to peak performance, which at times results in considerable "down time." And production of revenues is a serious concern for the administration. On the other hand, a comprehensive psychiatric emergency program will provide services for which it is difficult, if not impossible, to charge the client. For the most part, this involves all the hotline contacts and information and referral activities. It is also difficult to establish reasonable charges because of the very nature of emergency evaluation and treatment, which is often provided by several staff members over a considerable period of time but interrupted by other activities. Many of the clients may be indigent and without medical insurance, so that sending a bill can be a futile gesture. A considerable number of clients are brought to psychiatric emergency units against their wishes and would not be inclined to pay for services they did not request. Finally, many emotionally disturbed individuals are further aggravated by an investigation of their financial background, ability to pay, and so on, especially it if occurs early in the sequence or even before they have received any clinical attention. Because of all this, the administration may consider not charging any fees at all, or charging only nominal fees. Another possibility is to charge only for certain services, such as psychiatric consultation, home visits, or scheduled repeat visits. In either case many programs follow the practice of charging differentially for regular (usually meaning shorter) and intensive or extended visits.

HENNEPIN COUNTY MEDICAL CENTER
CRISIS INTERVENTION CENTER DATE / / | TIME: ___ a.m. p.m. | HCMC No.: | CIC No.:

Name: _____
    (last)   (first)   (middle)

Address: _____
    (street)

_____
    (city)   (state)   (zip)   (phone)

Relative: _____
    (name)   (relation)

_____
    (address)   (phone)

Referral Source: _____

B.D.: _____ (age)
Sex: Male Female
Marital Status:
    Sg. M D W Sp.
Race: _____
Religion: _____
Aid: YES NO
Program:
Worker:
Phone No.:

PRIOR CIC RECORD: YES NO
HCMC PATIENT: YES NO
HCMC PS PATIENT: YES NO
  Current: _____
  Previous: _____
PREVIOUSLY ON IPS: YES NO
OTHER MH RX YES NO
  Current: _____
  Previous: _____

ABILITY TO PAY:
  GAMC _____
  MEDICARE I.D. # _____
  MED. ASSIST. # _____
  PRIVATE INS. CO. Yes _____ No _____

LIST OF PROBLEMS

PROGRAM ELEMENTS
1. Suicide Phone
2. Crisis Phone
3. Walk-in
4. Home Visit
5. Child Abuse Phone
6. Other
_____ (specify)

SERVICE PROVIDED
1. Evaluation Only
2. Referral Only
3. Crisis Intervention
4. Interven. and Ref.
5. Consultation
6. Crisis Treatment
7. Other
_____ (specify)

● P1 _____
● P2 _____
● P3 _____

INCAPACITATION/DISTURBANCE:
1. Non-Emergent
2. Mild
3. Moderate
4. Severe

SUICIDE POTENTIAL:
(SHORT TERM) (LONG TERM)
1. None   1. None
2. Low   2. Low
3. Moderate   3. Moderate
4. High   4. High

DANGER TO OTHERS:
1. None
2. Low
3. Moderate
4. High

HOLD:
1. None
2. Transportation
3. 72-Hour
4. Both 2 & 3

SUMMARY OF HOW PROBLEMS WERE HANDLED
● P1 _____
● P2 _____
● P3 _____

► MEDICATIONS: _____ (signed) / (title)
_____
(signed) (title)

INSTRUCTIONS TO FOLLOW-UP STAFF: _____

FOLLOW-UP ACTION BY CIC: _____

C R I S I S   C E N T E R

CRISIS CENTER — MEDICAL RECORDS

FIG. 17-1. Form used by the Crisis Intervention Center of the Hennepin County Medical Center.

Resource file

Because every psychiatric emergency unit is relying heavily on referrals to other agencies, it is essential to keep a comprehensive and regularly updated resource file. Larger metropolitan areas have a myriad of agencies with only peripheral relevance to emergency programs. It is more important to identify the usually much smaller number of agencies involved in most of the referrals to and from the unit. The typical description of agencies in directories and catalogs is incomplete, inaccurate, out of date, or overly grandiose. For the most important programs, therefore, a more personalized and thorough information-gathering process is recommended. One staff member can be assigned as liaison person to these programs. This staff member can either periodically visit them or invite their representatives to make a presentation about their program to the psychiatric emergency unit staff. All this information should be recorded so that it becomes available to staff members not present during the presentation.

To the extent that clients with psychiatric symptoms are involved in the referral, it is useful fo have a file of private practitioners, especially psychiatrists, in the community. Information can be obtained, by way of a questionnaire, regarding each therapist's preferences (adolescents only, outpatients only, specialization in family therapy, and so on), hospital admission privileges, and general readiness to accept clients from the psychiatric emergency unit. The politically dictated practice of giving out three randomly selected names from the yellow pages or professional directories is ill advised for psychiatrically emergent clients. Such clients demand immediate attention and cannot wait for a leisurely disposition, nor should they be referred to therapists not used to dealing with emergencies. Unless the client expresses a particular preference for a therapist, agency, or hospital, referrals should be made to care providers who are skilled in treating emergency cases and known by past history to readily accept them and respond quickly to the request for services. Depending on the information the unit has gathered from past experience with various professionals and agencies, one should be careful to point out to the client that a referral need not imply endorsement.

Procedure manual

It is helpful to collect all policies, procedures, and other useful information in one manual. This material lends itself readily to orientation of new staff members, students, and volunteers and can be consulted by other staff as needed. Suggested content areas include the following:
1. All important phone numbers.
2. A general program description, including goals and objectives, job descriptions for the various professional disciplines and volunteers, and content of orientation and training programs.
3. Policies and procedures—methods of triage of clients, eligibility criteria, role of the team leader, criteria for home visits, guidelines for scheduling staff, provisions for transporting clients, and perhaps standing orders or algorithms for various clinical conditions.
4. Records and phone system—explanation of the record system, what information to collect, how to record it, how to trace phone calls, how to record on the various phone and walk-in logs, how to use a problem oriented approach, and so on.
5. Safety and security—protocols for handling violent clients, use of mechanical and chemical restraints, when and how to write incident reports, under what circumstances security guards should be involved.
6. Medical issues—criteria for consulting a psychiatrist, a list of available psychotropic medications, admission criteria for hospitalization, and how to recognize medical problems for nonmedical staff members.
7. Legal issues. It is essential to have on record all forms for various legal holds, all pertinent sections from state laws regulating involuntary commitment, emergency hospitalization, confidentiality, privacy and privileged communication, reportable offenses, issues of competence, and consent to treatment, and the clinical obligations to various types of court referrals. Additional

material is needed in those states having statutes regarding child abuse, abuse of vulnerable adults, emancipated minors, and Good Samaritan laws. It is prudent to have some guidelines about the disposal of weapons and illegal drugs found on clients; the same applies to all search and seizure activities, whether performed by clinical staff or security officers.

8. Program evaluation—if the unit has a program evaluation component, all the forms and procedures involved in evaluation should be explained in this section.

This list of content areas is by no means inclusive and some portions may be irrelevant to a number of psychiatric emergency programs. The content should fit the particular program are the setting within which it operates.

DATA COLLECTION AND PROGRAM EVALUATION
What data to collect

Apart from data required for reporting purposes to funding agencies, the psychiatric emergency unit should collect the data they are interested in—and no more. There seems to be a general tendency to collect every possible piece of information just in case someone should want to do research on some esoteric topic or another. This leads to very unwieldy data collection systems that are unfocused, do not lend themselves to utilization for management purposes, are difficult to implement, and sometimes discourage administrators from doing any data collection at all. This would be unfortunate because an ongoing data collection system is an excellent tool for observing trends over time which have implications for programming and staffing.

These are some of the content areas from which an agency could choose those most relevant to its program: brief demographic data, prior contact with the unit, referral source, prior and current psychiatric care, current social and health agency involvement, general psychiatric impression, initial problem, type of contact (outreach, phone, walk-in), professional discipline of the principal intervenor, service provided (psychotherapy, type of medication, hospitalization, and

so on), clinical disposition, and number of interventions for each crisis.

For any ongoing data collection—and program evaluation—it is most efficient and timesaving to utilize data bank cards if a computer and a programmer-consultant are readily available. This makes it possible to have regular quarterly or annual printouts with all the desired cross tabulations and overtime comparisons.

Administrative program evaluation

Administrative program evaluation, sometimes called "structural" program evaluation, is aimed at the administrative efficiency of an entire program and its overall impact on the community. The content of administrative goals can vary widely from the time clients have to wait before they receive services, to program visibility in a community, staff satisfaction, regular revision of the procedures manual, capability to train students, recruitment and retention of quality volunteers, and number of home visits per period of time (Lund, 1972). Clinical and administrative program evaluation can be combined: a programmatic goal of the center might be to achieve a certain degree of client satisfaction or attainment of treatment objectives in aggregate form (Beaulieu and Baxter, 1974), that is, at least 80% of clients should be satisfied with the services received and after a three-month period at least 60% should meet treatment goals set at first contact.

When administrative goals are planned, it is advisable to involve persons outside the psychiatric emergency program in the planning process. Each agency has to meet the frequently differing and sometimes contradictory expectations from various "audiences" (consumer, funder, administrator, staff). Inclusion of such outsiders also minimizes the possible criticism that the unit conveniently set easy, parochial, or profession-dominated goals, The same is true for the follow-up evaluation: individuals external to the agency should participate in assessing to what extent the administrative goals have been met. The method to be used for such administrative evaluation can be either straightforward "management by objectives" (Spano and Lund, 1973) or "goal attainment scaling" (Kiresuk and Sherman, 1968).

The benefits of such evaluation are (1) staff knowledge about goals serves as a motivator to achieve along the lines indicated by the goals; (2) such evaluation enhances staff morale because it indicates administration's interest in a well-functioning program and the welfare of its clients and staff; (3) evaluation provides a convenient time frame to remind the program director of things to accomplish; and (4) evaluation results in corrective feedback to administration regarding program deficiencies that require some action.

Clinical program evaluation: outcomes and process

Most psychiatric emergency units that conduct any program evaluation concentrate on *process* measures. The crisis intervention field has relied heavily on volunteers who had to be specially selected and trained and whose performance was closely scrutinized because they lacked the traditional degrees and credentials. Also process evaluation is easier to accomplish than outcome evaluation. Thus it is not surprising to find process measures heavily emphasized in the American Association of Suicidology standards (McGee, 1976).

The typical process criteria, such as empathy, warmth, and genuineness, have a rather unclear relationship to outcome. They certainly should not be accepted as measures of clinical effectiveness before further study. Not faring much better are other proposed process variables (personal involvement of staff with the agency, ability to secure communication with a suicide caller, evidence that a plan of action has been developed, and so on). This is not to say that peer review of the quality of a clinical interview is irrelevant to outcome or is an unproductive activity. It simply means that such evaluation schemes are difficult to make objective and quantified so that they can be meaningfully related to outcome data.

Outcome evaluation is probably the preferred method to choose if the unit has adequate resources to accomplish it (a minimum of 2% of the overall budget will typically be needed to do a decent job). A variety of methods are available for such an undertaking: client satisfaction measures (Larsen et al., 1979), the already-mentioned goal attainment scaling (Stelmachers et al., 1972), symptom reduction, pretreatment and posttreatment behavior comparisons, interprogram comparisons, and comparisons of one type of intervention against another within the same program. All of them have shortcomings when applied in a crisis setting. Many crisis services, especially hotlines, permit or even encourage anonymity of their clients, which makes follow-up and research nearly impossible. A large number of crisis clients are transients or otherwise rather mobile individuals with unstable life patterns who are quite difficult to locate. Typically there is a larger sample loss among them as compared with regular mental health center populations. The regression toward the mean effect is probably larger because the emergent nature ot the client's condition tends to produce more extreme initial scores, which can only change in one direction, namely, go down. Since the intervention is characteristically quite brief and hardly ever aimed at personality restructuring, the expected effects of such an intervention are rather minimal and also are under the strong influence of factors extraneous to the crisis intervention. This makes it harder to attribute changes to the treatment received. Clients in emergency situations are often too disturbed, psychotic, or confused to meaningfully participate in goal setting and treatment planning. A good number of them cannot even remember the contact and therefore cannot provide any feedback regarding their views of the intervention. The client satisfaction measures, too, become dubious indicators of treatment quality when applied to involuntary, resistive, and uncooperative clients.

The recommendations follow naturally from the problems listed earlier. Intervention goals should be few and simple, that is, appropriate to the amount of intervention provided. The follow-up period should be short (in most instances no longer than 1 month) because a few emergency visits can hardly be expected to produce lasting changes that will still be manifest 1 year later.

While outcome research is to be preferred, an agency should not neglect process evaluation if it is more readily available. As a matter of fact, it would seem desirable to use more than one evaluation method, whatever its nature, because none are universally accepted and most are poorly intercorrelated (Stelmachers, et al., 1977). Zusman (1969) states that ". . . in psychiatry, there are many ways in which a patient can get better. Usually after treatment a patient is better in some areas and unchanged in others. A useful outcome measure thus depends on ability to measure separately changes in a number of areas . . ."

A final note of caution: the more sophisticated evaluation studies present the least evidence for specific treatment effects directly attributable to crisis intervention (Stelmachers, 1975). Most of the observed change and "improvement" seems to be the result of a combination of regression toward the mean and "nonspecific treatment effects." Perhaps these nonspecific effects should receive more attention so that we can capitalize on them through a better understanding of how and under what circumstances they have most influence. Despite all the limitations of methodology, psychiatric emergency programs would be well advised to employ *some* evaluation scheme, no matter how limited or simple. One author concludes that " . . . performance may improve temporarily as a result of enhanced motivation induced by the attention of the investigator" (Bigelow and Ciarlo, 1976). Erickson (1975) comments: "Granting that attention-placebo is powerful in its effects, it would seem useful for hospital units to approach their task with a set to change and innovate." He goes on to say that " . . . carefully formulated innovations carried out by staff excited about the potential in what they are doing improves outcome."

Audits

Audits are an added tool for quality control, typically used in health care settings. Essentially, an audit is an "evaluation of medical care in retrospect through analysis of clinical records" (Lembcke, 1956). Audits can be process or outcome oriented, retrospective or concurrent; they can focus on diagnosis, problem, or a particular treatment modality. There can be spot audits or ongoing audits, and the a priori standards can be set for general adequacy of clinical care or for services that are specific to a professional discipline. Review can be done by committee or individual staff members permanently assigned to that position or by rotating responsibility among several peers. The heart of any audit is the development of objective criteria against which clinical activity can be monitored. In addition, there has to be a mechanism for identifying variance with standards and provision for corrective action if there is no acceptable explanation for the deviation. There are publications describing the audit process in great detail which should be of considerable help to an administrator (see, for instance, the PEP Primer for Psychiatry issued by the Joint Commission on Accreditation of Hospitals).

Program evaluation: tool for management and education

Program evaluation can be used for both management and education, but the program director and the staff should be clear about its purpose from the start. If evaluation is to be used as an administrative tool for performance evaluation of individual staff members, it naturally will be more threatening and therefore lead to more resistance. This would be especially true if staff members would be rated "outstanding" or "adequate" in their personnel files depending on the clinical outcomes they produce in their clients. It would be even more true if promotions—or lack of them—would be closely tied to clinical outcome results. If, on the other hand, evaluation is used as a feedback mechanism and learning experience, staff members will probably be much more accepting of having their practice scrutinized. Results for individual staff members may or may not be available to the program director, but if they are, the staff should be informed very clearly about what the program director intends to do with the data. For instance, staff members may not object to the notion of instituting workshops and seminars on certain topics to overcome certain weaknesses discovered in the evaluation process which seem to exist in a large number of staff members and could be corrected by a focused educational effort in those areas.

However the results are applied, one can expect that some of them will lead to change and that change per se is often threatening to staff members used to doing things in a certain way. Such resistance should be anticipated, openly discussed, and dealt with constructively before it can wreck the most well-intentioned attempt to make a program accountable.

SUMMARY

Psychiatric emergency programs are receiving more and more well-deserved attention by the national institutes and professional associations and organizations. Psychiatric emergency work is difficult but challenging and exciting for both the staff and administrators, but more information is needed to prevent disillusionment and burnout. There are many theoretical, programmatic, and organizational models to choose from and to improve. The whole field, despite tremendous progress during the last 10 to 15 years, cries for innovative approaches, more research, and greater knowledge transfer. Clinicians need to know more about the differential effects, that is, outcome results, of various types of treatment approaches for the same behavioral emergencies. To accomplish that a better system for classifying both type and severity of an emergency is required (in particular, the chronically emergent high utilizers of psychiatric emergency units deserve special attention). Unfortunately, clinicians really do not know what constitutes good or even acceptable care of, for example, an acute psychotic episode, homicidal threats, or panic states in a way comparable to medical emergencies, such as cardiac arrest. The existing algorithms for the assessment and treatment of various psychiatric emergencies are too crude and schematic to be of any practical use; they mostly just adorn bulging procedures manuals to impress outside reviewers. Not only are standards of care lacking and tools to measure clinical performance inadequate, but ignorance of the cost-effectiveness of various procedures is equally

disturbing. Are 2-hour ventilation and handholding sessions with psychiatric technicians equivalent to a 15-minute incisive and directive therapeutic intervention by a psychiatrist? Are both better than either of them applied singly? For what conditions? And so the questioning goes.

At this time the best clinicians can do is to use a broad-spectrum approach: be familiar with and utilize a wide variety of treatment techniques from a wide variety of professional disciplines and apply them in a reasonable, commonsense (but also rather indiscriminate) fashion to a wide variety of multiple-problem clients.

Finally, there is a need for rapprochement between various scientific fields and organizational entities. Crisis theorists and stress researchers must get together with experts in suicidology, victimology, psychopharmacology, and thanatology because knowledge from these fields is crucial to designing and conducting an effective psychiatric emergency service. It is not necessary to wait for the development of more solid crisis or stress theories before one can start teaching and applying the considerable empirical knowledge accumulated in such content areas as domestic violence, dangerousness, grief, sexual assault, and natural disasters. Just as emergency medical technicians need better training in general principles of mental health and psychiatric emergencies, mental health professionals require more knowledge in these disparate fields of science.

On the public policy level, it would be desirable to have better collaboration between such organizations as the American Association of Suicidology, National Institute of Mental Health (Section on Disaster Assistance and Emergency Mental Health), the Community Mental Health Center System, the National Organization for Victims Assistance, the American Psychiatric Association (Task Force on Emergency Care), the Emergency Medical Services System (Section on Behavioral Emergencies), and probably many others. The ultimate dream would be to achieve an enlightened and informed public policy, a unified organizational support system, and an integrated theoretical and empirical knowledge that would be disseminated to the practitioners who in turn would apply scientifically validated intervention strategies to various types of well-defined emergency conditions in a rational and discriminating manner.

BIBLIOGRAPHY

Aguilera, D., and Messick, J.: Crisis intervention: theory and methodology, ed. 4, St. Louis, 1982, The C.V. Mosby Co.

Beaulieu, D.E., and Baxter, J.: Evaluation of the adult outpatient program, Hennepin County Mental Health Services, PEP Report, Minneapolis, 1969-1973, chap. 9, 1974.

Bigelow, D.A., and Ciarlo, J.A.: The impact of therapeutic effectiveness data on community mental health center management, Eval. Studies Rev. Ann., volume 1, 1976.

Brook, B., et al.: Community families as alternatives in psychiatric hospital intensive care, Hosp. Community Psychiatry 27(3):195, 1976.

Erickson, R.C.: Outcome studies in mental hospitals: a review, Psychol. Bull. 82:4, 1975.

Freudenberger, H.J.: Staff burn-out, J. Soc. Issues 30(1):159, 1974.

Glasscote, R.M., et al.: The psychiatric emergency: a study of patterns of service, The Joint Information Service of the American Psychiatric Association and the National Association for Mental Health, Washington, D.C., 1966, p. 45.

Hankoff, L.D.: Emergency psychiatric treatment: a handbook of secondary prevention, Springfield, Ill., 1969, Charles C Thomas, Publishers.

Hoff, L.: People in crisis: understanding and helping, Reading, Mass. 1978, Addison-Wesley Publishing Co., Inc., p. 266.

Holmes, T., and Rahe, R.: The social readjustment rating scale, J. Psychosom. Res. 11:231, Aug. 1967.

Kessler, R.C.: A strategy for studying differential vulnerability to the psychological consequences of stress, J. Health Soc. Behav. 20:100, June 1979.

Kiresuk, T.J., and Sherman, R.E.: Goal attainment scaling: a general method for evaluating comprehensive community mental health programs, Community Ment. Health J. 4:443, 1968.

Lanuza, D.M.: Circadian rhythms of mental efficiency and performance, Nurs. Clin. North Am. 11(4):583, Dec. 1976.

Larsen, D.L., et al.: Assessment of client/patient satisfaction: development of a general scale, Evaluation and Program Planning 2:197, 1979.

Lembcke, P.A.: Medical auditing by scientific methods, J.A.M.A. 162:646, 1956.

Lund, S.H.: Administrative evaluation of a crisis intervention center, National Institute of Mental Health, Grant No. 5 RO1 MN 1678902, 1972.

McGee, R.K.: Crisis intervention in the community, Baltimore, 1974, University Park Press, p. 85.

McGee, R.K., editor: Evaluation criteria for the certification of suicide prevention and crisis intervention programs, official publication of the American Association of Suicidology, 1976.

PEP primer for psychiatry, performance evaluation, procedure for auditing and improving patient care, Joint Commission on Accreditation of Hospitals, 1975.

Pines, E., and Maslach, C.: Characteristics of staff burnout in mental health settings, Hosp. Community Psychiatry 29:233, 1978.

Polak, P.R., Kirby, M.W., and Deitchman, W.S.: Treating acutely psychotic patients in private homes, New Directions for Mental Health Services 1:49, 1979.

Resnik, H.L.P., and Ruben, H.L.: Emergency psychiatric care, Bowie, Md., The Charles Press, Inc., 1975.

Spano, R.M., and Lund, S.H.: Management by objectives in a hospital-based social service unit, National Institute of Mental Health, Grant No. 5 RO1 MH 1678904, 1973.

Stelmachers, Z.T.: Crisis intervention: quo vadis? unpublished paper, 1975.

Stelmachers, Z.T.: Mental health crisis intervention programs, The changing role of the hospital: options for the future, Chicago, 1980, American Hospital Association, p. 211.

Stelmachers, Z.T., Lund, S.H., and Meade, C.J.: Hennepin County Crisis Intervention Center: evaluation of its effectiveness, Fall 1972.

Stelmachers, Z.T., Ellenson, G.M., and Baxter, J.: Quality control system of a crisis center: method and outcome results, unpublished study, 1977.

Stelmachers, Z.T., Baxter, J.W., and Ellenson, G.M.: Auditing the quality of care of a crisis center, Suicide and Life-Threatening Behav. 8(1):18, Spring 1978.

Varah, C.: The samaritans in the 70's, London, 1973, Constable & Co., Ltd.

Zusman, J., and Ross, E.R.: Evaluation of the quality of mental health services, Arch. Gen. Psychiatr. 20:352, March, 1969.

CHAPTER 18

Leadership

Rebecca Partridge, R.N., M.S.
Jacquelyne G. Gorton, R.N., M.S., C.S.

> *Leadership, the power of individuals to inspire cooperative personal decision by creating faith; faith in common understanding, faith in the probability of success, faith in the ultimate satisfaction of personal motives*
> (Barnard, 1938, p. 259).

Although the concept of leadership has received considerable attention by researchers over the last 50 years, there remains a feeling among many that it is an unexplainable phenomenon. Among health care professionals, successful and inept leaders are easily recognized, but the determinants of success or failure often remain undetected. Since few clinicians involved with psychiatric emergency care receive any formal preparation in leadership, this chapter will offer a theoretical and practical framework that may be helpful to those seeking or finding themselves in leadership roles.

Leadership is most often defined as the ability to influence others. Natemeyer (1978, p. 165) states: "Leadership is generally defined as the process of influencing the activities of others toward the accomplishment of organizational goals, where power is the resource that enables a leader to actually influence others."

The concept of power is essential to leadership. Power is the mechanism of influencing the behavior of others. French and Raven (1959) described five types of power: reward, coercive, legitimate, referent, and expert. *Reward power* is based on the leader's ability to grant perquisites for the desired behavior. *Coercive power* is engendered through the expectation of or the enactment of punishment if the attempt to influence is resisted. *Legitimate power* is based on internalized values that convey an obligation to accept the leader's authority because of a role, code, or standard. *Referent power* is based on psychological identification with the leader. *Expert power* is based on the perception that the leader possesses special knowledge.

The leader's ability to reward and coerce is exercised through the use of real and symbolic measures. Financial incentives, such as salary increases, are the most common type of material rewards, and conversely, withholding a raise is the most common type of financial punishment. Symbolic rewards are manifest through the receipt or denial of praise, prestige, and other vestiges of social acceptance.

In addition to this differentiation between the concepts of leadership and power, another important distinction should be made before embarking on a review of leadership theories—the difference between leadership and management. Koontz (1961) describes "the semantics jungle" that exists in the literature dealing with leadership and management. Some authors use the words interchangeably and others invent idiosyncratic definitions. In this chapter, the term *management* will be used to refer to the role as described by Levitt (1976, p. 73):

> Management consists of the rational assessment of a situation and the systematic selection of goals and purposes (what is to be done?); the systematic development of strategies to achieve these goals; the marshalling of the required resources; the rational design, organization, direction, and control of these activities required to attain the selected purposes.

The term *leadership* will be used in this chapter to describe "the process of influencing the activities of an organized group is its efforts toward goal setting and goal achievement" (Stogdill, 1959, p. 20). In practice there is considerable overlapping between management and leadership, but an analytical distinction can be made. Perhaps the most concise way of distinguishing between leadership and management is to remember that management positions are always assigned whereas positions of leadership *may* be assumed.

Conceptualizations of leadership can be grouped into three major categories: *trait* theories, *behavioral* theories, and *situational* theories. The sequencing of these categories portrays the evolution of leadership theories.

TRAIT THEORIES

As far back as the ancient Greeks and Romans, it was thought that leaders were born—not made. Aristotle believed that the world was divided into leaders and followers: "from the hour of their birth, some are marked out for subjection, others for rule." In 1535 in his handbook for princes, Machiavelli contended that courage, conviction, pride, and strength were traits important to leadership (1952).

Originally, this thinking took form in the *great man theory* of leadership, which held that certain people were in possession of "natural" leadership abilities and were, therefore, destined to rise out of any situation to become leaders (Carlyle, 1907). Later the emphasis shifted from individual destiny to the traits possessed by the individual.

The *trait theory* emerged as a possible explanation for leadership. A trait can be defined as an "enduring attribute of a person that appears consistently in a variety of situations" (Kimble et al., 1974, p. 298). According to this theory, "leaders distinctively possess such traits as intelligence, emotional maturity, perseverance, tact, faith, dominance, courage, insight, and so on and on" (Merton, 1969, p. 2614). These traits were thought to be inherited, so successful leaders were observed and analyzed in an attempt to discover more about the traits they possessed.

Davis (1972, p. 103) has summarized the following traits that apear to be relevant for successful organizational leadership:

1. *Intelligence.* Leaders are usually slightly more intelligent than their followers. But, a successful leader is usually not extremely more intelligent than the followers.
2. *Social maturity and breadth.* Leaders tend to be self-assured, confident, mature, emo-

tionally stable and have diverse interests.
3. *Inner-motivation and achievement drives.*
Leaders are usually intrinsically motivated
and achievement oriented.
4. *Human relations attitudes.* Leaders tend to
be empathetic, considerate, and respectful
of their followers.

Although there is considerable face validity in
descriptions like these, research efforts have repeatedly failed to yield conclusive eivdence supporting them. Lengthy lists of traits have been
generated, but more often than not, the findings
were contradictory and confusing. "Similar to the
trait theories of personality, the trait approach to
leadership has provided some descriptive insight
but has little analytical or predictive value"
(Luthans, 1977, p. 440). On the whole, the trait
theory of leadership has been a failure. However,
the evidence that disproved this theory served as
the impetus for the development of behavioral
leadership theories.

BEHAVIORAL THEORIES

The legacy of the trait theory of leadership
served as the antecedent to the recognition of several constructs on which behavioral theories of
leadership are based. First, it became obvious
that if traits were identified, they might be
learned by others who did not naturally acquire
them. And second, it became clear that the trait
theory ignored the unique characteristics of the
followers.

Social scientists studying leadership began to
shift their emphasis from what a leader *is* to what
a leader *does*. The "behavioral leadership theory
differs from trait theory in that behavior can be
observed" (Moloney, 1979, p. 23).

Generally regarded as the seminal work on
leadership behavior is the research conducted in
the late 1930s by Kurt Lewin, Ronald Lippitt,
and Ralph K. White (1939). The study was designed to examine patterns of aggressive behavior among 10-year-old boys. The results revealed that when exposed to three types of leader
behavior, authoritarian, democratic, and laissez-
faire, the subjects overwhelmingly preferred the
democratic leader. The three kinds of leader behavior were defined as follows:

1. *Authoritarian*—all determination of policy
made by leader
2. *Democratic*—all policies a matter of group
discussion and decision, encouraged and assisted by the leader
3. *Laissez-faire*—complete freedom for group
or individual decision without any leader
participation

The effect of the autocratic leader was paradoxical; the leader's behavior caused frustration
among the group members, and they exhibited
either aggression or apathy. However, on the
whole the behavior of the laissez-faire leader
resulted in the greatest amount of aggression
among the subjects.

It is important to remember that although this
research made a tremendous contribution to the
field, it has often been cited to erroneously pro-
mulgate the democratic leadership style as the
ideal for all situations. It is inappropriate to in-
discriminately generalize these findings that are
based on data collected more than 40 years ago
on preadolescent boys in volunteer hobby clubs.
By today's standards, the research design of this
study is unsophisticated and open to criticism.
But even with its shortcomings, this study, more
than any other, is viewed as the salient work in
the field of leadership.

The focus on leader behavior persists, but it
has been partially supplanted by the situational
leadership theories. These grew out of the recognition that attention to the leader's behavior and
the follower's characteristics was not sufficient to
explain the phenomenon of leadership. To these
two variables was added a third—the situation.

SITUATIONAL THEORIES
Tannenbaum and Schmidt's continuum of leadership behavior

As pointed out earlier, the research by Lewin,
Lippitt, and White had often unwisely been used
to justify the claim that democratic leadership
is the one style that is best. Tannenbaum and
Schmidt refuted this notion in 1958 with the
proposition that a continuum of leadership behavior exists. The most current version of their
continuum of leadership behavior is shown in
Fig. 18-1 (Tannenbaum and Schmidt, 1973).

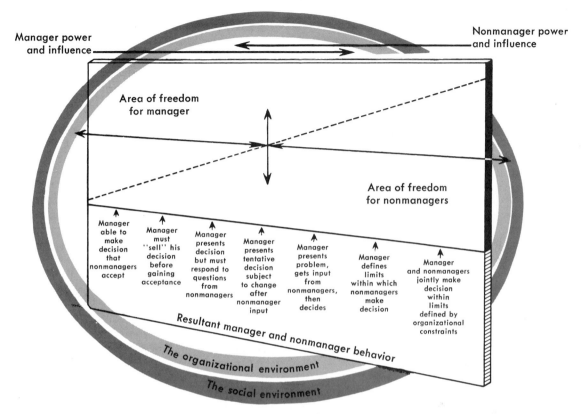

Manager power and influence

Nonmanager power and influence

Area of freedom for manager

Area of freedom for nonmanagers

| Manager able to make decision that nonmanagers accept | Manager must "sell" his decision before gaining acceptance | Manager presents decision but must respond to questions from nonmanagers | Manager presents tentative decision subject to change after nonmanager input | Manager presents problem, gets input from nonmanagers, then decides | Manager defines limits within which nonmanagers make decision | Manager and nonmanagers jointly make decision within limits defined by organizational constraints |

Resultant manager and nonmanager behavior

The organizational environment

The social environment

FIG. 18-1. Tannenbaum and Schmidt's continuum of leader behavior.

Reprinted by permission of the Harvard Business Review. Exhibit from "How to Choose a Leadership Pattern" by Robert Tannenbaum and Warren H. Schmidt (May-June 1973). Copyright © 1973 by the President and Fellows of Harvard College; all rights reserved.

At the left end of the continuum is the autocratic leadership style, in which the manager makes decisions that are accepted by nonmanagers. At the far right is the other extreme, the democratic style with the manager and nonmanagers jointly making decisions. The laissez faire style is not included because it is basically viewed as an abdication of the leadership role.

The Tannenbaum and Schmidt framework has gained enormous acceptance primarily because the concept of selecting a leadership style acknowledges the unique characteristics and preferences of individuals. Three areas must be considered when selecting a leadership style: the *leader,* the *followers,* and the *situation.* Forces in the leader include the leader's personal value system, confidence in followers, leadership inclinations, and tolerance for ambiguity. Forces in the followers include their need for independence, readiness to assume responsibility, tolerance for ambiguity, interest in the problem, understanding and identification with the organizational goals, knowledge and experience, and expectations with regard to sharing in the decision-making process. The key to successful leadership lies in the development of "a climate of mutual confidence and respect, in which people tend to feel less threatened by deviations from normal practice, which in turn makes possible a higher degree of flexibility in the whole relationship" (Tannenbaum and Schmidt, 1973, p. 16). Forces in the situation include the type of organization, its value and traditions, the amount of time available, and the nature of the problem to be solved.

Even though seven clearly identifiable leadership styles are available in this framework, it is inappropriate for a leader to be so erratic as to use all of them. Followers will become confused and frustrated with such an array of behavior. Indeed, it is essential to let the followers know exactly what they can expect from their leader in a given situation and it would be prudent to maintain a degree of consistency with regard to the types of leadership styles utilized.

Fiedler's contingency theory

Fiedler's approach is also among the most widely known; he contends that successful leadership performance is *contingent* on how favorable the situation is to the leader. He defines three variables on which leadership effectiveness is dependent, or contingent: leader-member relationship, the nature of the task, and the power of the leader's position.

Methods have been devised to assess each factor. Questionnaires are used to determine the group member's feelings about the leader. The task is rated on four factors: "decision verifiability—the degree to which the correctness of the solution can be demonstrated; goal clarity—the degree to which the desired outcome is clearly stated; goal path multiplicity—the number of possible methods for performing the task; and solution specificity—the degree to which there is more than one correct solution" (Fiedler, 1965, p. 14). Finally, position power is determined by possession of a special rank or title and by the ability to promote or demote. There are eight possible combinations of these three variables, as shown in Table 18-1.

Leader control is necessary if the staff is highly emotional, insecure, or in a crisis situation (Moloney, 1979, pp. 27, 30). Nondirective, permissive leadership is appropriate for groups whose members are autonomous and function at a high level of expertise. Fiedler's main point (1972, p. 456) is that a leader may perform "well in one sit-

uation but not in another" depending on how the leader's knowledge, skills, intelligence, and personality interact with situational variables, including type of group, task, time stipulations, complexity, and duration.

Fiedler's findings (1965, p. 15) suggest that "managing, controlling, directive leaders tend to be most effective in situations which are either very favorable for them or which are relatively unfavorable. In contrast, non-directive, permissive, considerate leaders tend to perform best in situations of intermediate difficulty." In addition to Fiedler, there are a number of other contemporary theorists investigating the situational variables of leadership (Hersey and Blanchard, 1977; House, 1971; Reddin, 1970; and Stogdill, 1974). But whatever theoretical approach a leader chooses, it must be flexible to meet the requirements of different situations, the needs of followers, and the leader's abilities. The successful leader realizes that there is no one best style.

ORGANIZATIONAL DETERMINANTS OF LEADERSHIP

A brief discussion of organizational theory may help to elucidate the role of leadership in an organizational context. Hospitals have a strong bureaucratic heritage that influences the organizational structure of contemporary health care facilities. Litwak (1961) provides a useful

Table 18-1. Fiedler's contingency model of leadership effectiveness

Leader-member relations	Task structure	Leader position-power
Good	Unstructured	Strong
Poor	Unstructured	Strong
Good	Structured	Strong
Poor	Structured	Strong
Good	Unstructured	Weak
Poor	Unstructured	Weak
Good	Structured	Weak
Poor	Structured	Weak

From Moloney, M.M.: Leadership in nursing, St. Louis, 1979, The C.V. Mosby Co.; modified from Fiedler, F.: Admin. Sci. Q. **17**(4):455, 1972.

framework for understanding organizational structures, which can be employed here to illustrate the situational nature of leadership.

The characteristics of traditional bureaucracies (Weber, 1946) are well known; they are rule governed, hierarchical, impersonal, task specific, and usually very efficient when faced with circumscribed predictable tasks.

This type of bureaucratic structure is *mechanistic* and can be contrasted against the *organic* system associated with the human relations approach. "The organic form is appropriate to changing conditions, which give rise constantly to fresh problems and unforseen requirements for action which cannot be broken down or distributed automatically arising from the functional roles defined within a hierarchic structure" (Burns and Stalker, 1961, p. 121). The organic organizational system recognizes expert knowledge of the participants and allows for a network structure of control; tasks are mutable and seen in the total situation of concern.

Litwak (1961) adds a third model, which is a partial synthesis of the traditional Weberian bureaucratic (mechanistic) model and the human relations (organic) model—it is the professional model. He presents seven characteristics that vary to a greater or lesser extent among the three models of bureaucracy (Weberian, human relations, and professional):

1. Appointments based on merit.
2. Impersonal relations
3. A priori specification of job authority
4. Hierarchical authority
5. Separation of policy and administrative decisions
6. General rules
7. Specialization

Appointments based on merit occur extensively in all three models, but many (including the authors of this chapter) would argue that traditional Weberian bureaucracies sometimes allow seniority to outweigh merit in appointment decisions. The other six characteristics occur extensively in the Weberian model (mechanistic) and minimally in the human relations model (organic) with a partial integration of the polarities occurring in the professional model. The key feature of the professional model is that it allows the "inclusion of contradictory forms of social relations" (Litwak, 1961, p. 181), that is, it allows elements of the mechanistic and organic systems to coexist in the same organizational entity. Therefore, the professional model seems the most appropriate vehicle for portraying and analyzing the situational determinants of leadership in psychiatric emergency units.

Litwak (1961, p. 182) described the professional model as follows:

> . . . most efficient where the job requires dealing with both uniform and nonuniform events or with social skills as well as traditional areas of knowledge; e.g., situations requiring standardized administrative tasks and great professional autonomy—large hospitals, large graduate schools, large research organizations—and situations requiring both knowledge of administrative details as well as high interpersonal skills—large social work agencies or psychiatric hospitals.

Psychiatric emergency units engage in activities that are both mechanistic and organic. For example, legal protocol for involuntarily holding a person brought to the unit by the police is quite mechanistic and must be followed exactly, whereas the assessment and treatment process is an organic activity requiring professional judgment and interpersonal skills.

Where the organic and mechanistic systems interface, there is the potential for conflict. To minimize conflict, *mechanisms of segregation* are utilized; Litwak mentions four: (1) *Role separation* refers to the designation of certain employees to deal with specific tasks. For example, the administrator of a psychiatric emergency unit may handle many of the mechanistic functions (such as budgeting and staffing), thereby giving the clinicians more time to pursue the organic activities related to direct client care. (2) *Physical distance* can be used as a mechanism of segregation. Perhaps the most dramatic example is the psychiatric emergency unit that is geographically separate from a hospital. Less obvious but equally illustrative is the psychiatric emergency unit that, although located in a hospital, has a separate entrance so that clients may enter without

311

being subjected to the mechanistic bureaucracy imposed in most medical emergency unit admission procedures. (3) *Transferral occupations* are those in which one is required to work in both mechanistic and organic areas. The administrator who also functions as a clinician is a good example. Another familiar example is the rotation of qualified staff members who as temporary supervisors of the psychiatric emergency unit assign cases to their colleagues. The dilemma of transferral positions is that the person must "switch areas of work from one set of social relations to another without contaminating the atmosphere of either" (Litwak, 1961, p. 183). (4) *Evaluation procedures* may serve as mechanisms of segregation. As the organizational structure is periodically assessed and redesigned, the organic and mechanistic systems may be redefined or altered. For example, procedures for securing informed consent for treatment and medications need to be evaluated periodically and altered to reflect recent legal decisions. The new policy may dictate adherence to a strict informed-consent protocol (mechanistic), whereas the previous policy allowed for the use of considerable professional discretion (organic).

Another way to characterize the essence of the mechanistic and organic systems is through decision analysis. Simon (1960) has pointed out the essential difference between "routine" and "critical" decisions. Routine decisions are not really decisions at all because the conclusions are foregone—they are already prescribed by an established set of criteria which feeds into the outcome. Critical decisions, however, are not programmed in advance; they are the result of "much stirring about, deliberation, discussion, (and) often vacillation" (Burns and Stalker, 1961, p. 115). Mechanistic systems utilize routine decisions, whereas organic systems require that critical decisions be made. Participative leadership is appropriate to organizational settings, such as psychiatric emergency units, which incorporate elements of both mechanistic and organic systems. The following discussion will focus on participative leadership, but the topic of decision-making strategies will be resumed later in this chapter.

PARTICIPATIVE LEADERSHIP AND DECISION MAKING

It is well known that professional employees have a distaste for autocrats. Writing in 1926, long before participative leadership came into vogue, Follet argued against "the giving of orders" to employees. She favored a situational approach that encouraged participation of all those involved.

> One *person* should not give orders to another *person,* but both should agree to take orders from the situation . . . the essence of scientific management (is) the attempt to find the law of the situation. With scientific management, the managers are as much under orders as the workers, for both obey the law of the situation.

When employees dealing with nonuniform tasks are allowed the freedom to make their own decisions, there is a high correlation between motivation and productivity (Pelz, 1960). A collegial environment that fosters consultation and "positive emotional involvement" is likely to be the most productive social environment in a psychiatric emergency unit. Studies of inpatient psychiatric units "involving professions whose chief technical tools are social, suggest that greatest efficiency requires some positive emotional involvement" (Litwak, 1961, p. 180).

Psychiatric emergency staff members are quite familiar with clinical decision making and they are often accustomed to considerable autonomy in this regard. All health care professions utilize a decision-making process that includes data collection, diagnosis, planning, intervening, and evaluating, and this process is appropriate for nonclinical decisions as well.

"Almost no decision made in an organization is the task of a single individual" (Burns and Stalker, 1961, p. 115). Since the definition of a problem molds the outcome of the decision-making process, it is important to avoid having definitions made in the narrow perspective of just one person as often occurs with autocratic leadership. Objectivity is fostered when all relevant persons participate. All those directly affected by a decision should have the opportunity to influence the outcome. Participation is particularly important in situations where it is crucial that staff members implement a decision (MacCrimmon and Taylor, 1975).

Regardless of the level of participation of staff, the leader will generally be held responsible for the quality of the decisions. Criteria that can be used to assess the quality of decisions include the collection of factual, relevant, objective data; documentation of how the decision evolved; the defensibility; acceptability; and beneficial results. Participative leadership that encourages staff involvement in decision-making processes will increase the likelihood that these criteria will be met.

Defensibility of a decision is a critical factor. Decisions made regarding psychiatric emergency care (for example, the decision to hospitalize a client) are contextual, but they are often judged by persons unfamiliar with the context (such as the family) or at a later point in time (as is the case with utilization review). The process leading to important decisions should be documented in writing so that the details will be available later if it becomes necessary to justify or defend a decision. Also, documentation is useful in the evaluation process.

Schein (1969, p. 53) describes six types of group decision making: (1) *Decision by lack of response,* which is what happens quite often when one person makes a suggestion, but before any discussion occurs, another suggestion is made, causing the first person to feel his idea "plopped." (2) *Decision by authority rule* occurs when there is a power structure that allows the leader to decide after listening to the group discussion. (3) *Decision by minority,* also quite common, gives the group members the impression they were "railroaded" into a particular decision. This occurs when discussion is cut off before dissenting views are presented or when a powerful person dominates the discussion. (4) *Decision by majority rule* is familiar to all. It is most often achieved by voting. Although a very popular method of group decision making, it does have some disadvantages. It produces opposing coalitions and a win-lose atmosphere that may hinder future decision making, and it does not take into account the degree of support or rejection held by

the individual group members. (5) *Decision by consensus* is achieved when there is a clear sense in the group that most members favor a certain decision and the opposing members feel that they have had sufficient opportunities to influence the group. (6) *Decision by unanimous consent* is obtained when everyone agrees on a decision. The last two methods, consensus and unanimous consent, are particularly time consuming but are useful in making decisions that will require a high degree of compliance from the group members.

Problem solving and decision making are inextricably intertwined. Literature on the subject does not consistently differentiate between them. Some authors identify decision making as a subset of problem solving. They describe decision making as focusing on evaluation and choice among alternatives, whereas they see problem solving as encompassing the entire process of problem formulation, creation of alternatives, and information processing which results in choice. Others view problem solving as a subset of decision making. For the purposes of this chapter, decision making will be considered a generic term incorporating problem solving. Since decision analysis and modeling make up a complex field, this chapter will present only two relatively simple approaches that have proven applicability to health care settings. The two decision-making models discussed here are the Bernhard-Walsh model (1981) and the Claus-Bailey model (Bailey and Claus, 1975).

The Bernhard-Walsh model is simple and quick, so it is appropriate for most common problems encountered in psychiatric emergency settings. It consists of the following six steps:

1. Identify parameters of the decision situation.
2. Establish characteristics of the ideal solution.
3. List possible solutions.
4. Choose the best solution.
5. Implement the decision.
6. Evaluate results of decision.

This model is efficient and can be used for most problems and decisions in psychiatric emergency programs. Its main weakness occurs in step 4 with the subjective weighing of possible solutions against the characteristics of the ideal solution. However, the degree of subjectivity can be reduced if the leader includes staff participation to determine characteristics of the ideal solution and to weigh the potential solutions. Individuals in the group can check each other's objectivity and reasoning, whereas one decision maker without the benefit of such monitoring would be more likely to make biased or poorly based choices.

The Claus-Bailey model is suitable when major decisions need to be made or complex problems need to be solved. The 10 steps of this model are as follows:

1. Identify overall needs, purposes, goals.
2. Define the problem.
3. Compare constraints, capabilities, resources, claimant groups.
4. Specify approach to problem solution.
5. Write behavioral objectives and performance criteria.
6. List alternative solutions.
7. Analyze options.
8. Choose best alternative based on decision rules.
9. Control and implement decisions.
10. Evaluate effectiveness of action.

More detailed information on how to apply these models is available in the works of Bailey and Claus (1975) and Bernhard and Walsh (1981). No matter which model is used, a standard framework for problem solving and decision making can be applied to a variety of situations in psychiatric emergency care.

PARTICIPATIVE LEADERSHIP AND STAFF DEVELOPMENT

Participative leaders can utilize decision models to expand staff members' understanding of the evaluation process, clinical arena, and organizational theory. Participative leadership enhances staff motivation and participation. There is abundant documentation showing that if the staff has the opportunity to engage in decision making, then positive results occur. Examples of such studies date from the early Western Electric studies (Roethlisberger and Dickson, 1939) to the work by Coch and French (1948) and more recently Guest (1962). Staff members who participate in making policies are more likely to be enthusiastic about their work than are those who have little opportunity to engage in policy making (Kramer, 1970; Kramer and Baker, 1971).

For example, the leader of one psychiatric emergency unit developed a program for staff development as a result of applying a decision model to the problem of staff dissatisfaction. The leader of the problematic unit utilized a participative leadership style and met with the dissatisfied staff members to hear their complaints and to assess the situation. The staff agreed to form a committee that would follow the steps of a decision model and the guidelines of decision making as their leader encouraged. These basic guidelines should be followed whenever major decisions are to be made: The leader encourages the staff to (1) review relevant literature, (2) experiment with several systems or methods, (3) seek advice, (4) become familiar with experiences of other psychiatric emergency units or other mental health care providers, (5) compare their biases against standards and philosophies, (6) evaluate consequences over time and on the entire community, (7) pilot test the plan, if possible, and (8) follow up with an evaluation of outcomes (Arndt and Huckabay, 1980, p. 128). Using these guidelines the staff acquired new information from the literature and gained skill in an analytical method of decision making.

The staff development program that evolved was successful. All staff members participated and reported that they were pleased with the benefits of the learning experience on a personal and professional level. Scheduling was arranged so that each person could have time off the unit to work on special projects. The topics of the projects were selected in consultation with the leader. To participate in the program, staff members had to select a topic or experience that was related to psychiatric emergency work and agree to be on call through use of a beeper system while off the unit. The projects were often organized into written reports or verbal presentations. One hour a week was reserved for these presentations, and continuing education credit was awarded when appropriate.

Staff development in the clinical arena was provided by reports, demonstrations, and the application of theory and special techniques. Topics included the psychiatric emergency treatment of victims of abuse, clients with self-inflicted wounds, and clients who attempt to manipulate staff. At these meetings, staff members had an opportunity to exchange ideas and discuss possible changes in their roles. In addition, staff members working on projects related to consultations and teaching experiences often would engage other staff members in their work, which promoted teamwork and interdisciplinary collaboration.

This comprehensive staff development program was created by staff members who were dissatisfied with their job. In this case a participative leader showed concern over their discomfort and worked with them in creating a solution that not only alleviated their dissatisfaction, but also enriched their performance. The staff development program continues to be a success because the entire group practices the principles of participative leadership—encouragement of members to choose their own projects, involvement of members in project presentation, and encouragement of honest objective feedback about the project (Bernhard and Walsh, 1981, p. 49).

PARTICIPATIVE LEADERSHIP AND TEAMWORK

Inherent in the philosophy of teamwork is the belief that all members have the right to be entrusted with responsibility, to be given authority to act, and to be accountable for their actions (Douglass, 1980, p. 99). This philosophy of teamwork is especially pertinent to the operation of psychiatric emergency units that use teams in which members evaluate client problems and are responsible for decisions regarding how these problems can be resolved. A smoothly functioning team is necessary so that team members devote their skills and energy to the often complex process of making appropriate assessments and justifiable interventions. If the team does not work well, for example, if members are not aware of each other's tasks or are not motivated to work,

then the team's ability to provide therapeutic care is substantially diminished. For a team to work effectively, a leadership style that promotes utilization of member expertise and accountability as well as intergroup communication and collaboration is required. The psychiatric emergency unit leader's task is to adopt a leadership style that will foster the functioning of a highly coordinated, highly motivated team whose members agree on how to work together.

When team members participate in the decision making regarding how the team is organized and how the work is assigned, the team becomes cohesive, supportive, and highly efficient (Arndt and Huckabay, 1980, p. 125A). Since participative leadership encourages and assists staff members in group discussion and decisions regarding policies and procedures that affect them, this leadership style is most effective in promoting teamwork. If the leader assumes authority for defining the team's goals and how the work is to be distributed, then often the team members resist assuming assignments, do not work up to capacity, and experience low morale. Laissez faire leadership of teams often results in confusion over identifying goals and unclear definition of member responsibility, which can result in a team splintered by independent and disconnected member activity (Arndt and Huckabay 1980, p. 126; Moloney, 1979, p. 23). The participative leader who solicits input from team members about how their functions are planned, implemented, and evaluated, unites the members in the goal formulation process and motivates them to work by meeting their needs of personal worth and approval.

Participative leaders of psychiatric emergency units can involve staff in decisions affecting their work at general staff meetings or with small teams who work together on each shift. The leader can ask the team members which clients they prefer to work with instead of making arbitrary assignments based on the leader's assessment of staff abilities and client needs. Team members tend to choose what they can do best whether it is working with specific clients, for example, the John Doe who necessitates "detective work" to obtain a history, or being in charge of triage. By involving team members in discussions and decisions about work distribution, the leader recognizes and utilizes each member's talents, abilities, and interests to form a united team ready for the challenge of handling psychiatric emergencies. By encouraging team discussions and decision making, the leader is also providing an atmosphere of openness and acceptance in which staff members have the opportunity to direct their own destinies and to work together to make wise decisions. Team members support one another and their leader because they have all engaged in determining the objectives of care and who is responsible for meeting these objectives. Participative leaders who show respect for each individual's abilities by encouraging open discussion and decision making regarding the organization and functioning of psychiatric emergency programs foster highly cohesive motivated teams that work very effectively and efficiently.

SUMMARY

In this chapter the concept of leadership has been defined as the process of influencing others. The ability to influence is based on five types of power: reward, coercive, legitimate, referent, and expert. *Management* was differentiated from *leadership* in that *management* was described as the process of assessing a situation to determine how necessary tasks could be completed to reach goals whereas *leadership* was described as the process of influencing the activities of others to achieve goals.

A review of the three major conceptualizations of leadership—trait, behavioral, and situational theories—was provided to demonstrate the complexities inherent in defining leadership and to reveal the evolution of thought in this domain.

The organizational determinants of leadership were discussed in the context of mechanistic (Weberian), organic (human relations), and professional models of organization (Litwak, 1961). This led to a discussion of the participative leadership style, which is thought to be the type of leadership most appropriate to psychiatric emergency settings. The chapter concludes with a discussion as to how a participative leadership style can be used in decision making, staff development, and teamwork.

BIBLIOGRAPHY

Arndt, C., and Huckabay, L.M.D.: Nursing administration, St. Louis, 1980, The C.V. Mosby Co.

Bailey, J.T., and Claus, K.E.: Decision making in nursing, St. Louis, 1975, The C.V. Mosby Co.

Barnard, C.I.: The functions of the executive, Cambridge, Mass., 1938 and 1968, Harvard University Press.

Bernhard, L.A., and Walsh, M.: Leadership: the key to the professionalization of nursing, New York, 1981, McGraw-Hill Book Co.

Burns, T., and Stalker, G.M.: The management of innovation, London, 1961, Travistock Publications Ltd.

Carlyle, T.: On heroes, hero-worship, and the heroic in history, 1907, Houghton Mifflin Co.

Coch, L., and French, J.R.P.: Overcoming resistance to change, Hum. Relations, p. 512, Aug. 1948.

Davis, K.: Human behavior at work, ed. 4, New York, 1972, McGraw-Hill Book Co., p. 103.

Douglass, L.M.: The effective nurse leader and manager, St. Louis, 1980, The C.V. Mosby Co.

Fiedler, F.C.: Leadership—a new model, Discovery 26: 12, April 1965.

Fiedler, F.C.: The effects of leadership training and experience: contingency model interpretation, Admin. Sci. Q 17:453, 1972.

Follet, M.P.: The giving of orders. In Metcalf, H.C., editor: Scientific foundations of business administration, Baltimore, 1926, The Williams & Wilkins Co.

French, J.R.P., and Raven, B.: The bases of social power, In Cartwright, D.: Studies in social power, Ann Arbor, Mich., 1959, Institute for Social Research.

Guest, R.H.: Organizational change: the effect of successful leadership, Homewood, Ill., 1962, Dorsey Press.

Hersey, P., and Blanchard, K.H.: Management of organizational behavior: utilizing human resources, ed. 3, Englewood Cliffs, N.J., 1977, Prentice-Hall, Inc.

House, R.J.: A path-goal theory of leader effectiveness, Admin. Sci. Q. 16:321, 1971.

Kimble, G.A., Garmezy, N., and Zigler, E.: General psychology, ed. 4, New York, 1974, The Ronald Press Co., p. 298.

Koontz, H.: The management theory jungle, Academy of Management J., p. 174, Dec. 1961.

Kramer, M.: Role conception of baccalaureate and success in hospital nursing, Nurs. Res. 19(5):428, 1970.

Kramer, M., and Baker, C.: The exodus: can nursing afford it? J. Nurs. Admin 1(3):15, 1971.

Levitt, T.: Management and the post industrial society, The Public Interest, p. 73, Summer 1976.

Lewin, K., Lippitt, R., and White, R.K.: Patterns of aggressive behavior in experimentally created social climates, J. Soc. Psychol. 10:271, 1939.

Litwak, E.: Models of bureaucracy which permit conflict, Am. J. Soc. 67:177, Sept. 1961.

Luthans, F.: Organizational behavior, ed. 2, New York, 1977, McGraw-Hill Book Co.

MacCrimmon, K.R., and Taylor, R.N.: Decision making and problem solving. In Dunnette, M.D., editor: Handbook of industrial and organizational psychology, Chicago, 1975, Rand McNally & Co.

Machiavelli, N.: The prince, New York, 1952, The New American Library, Inc.

Merton, R.K.: The social nature of leadership, Am. J. Nurs. 69:2614, 1969.

Moloney, M.M.: Leadership in nursing, St. Louis, 1979, The C.V. Mosby Co.

Natemeyer, W.E.: Classics of organizational behavior, Oak Park, Ill., 1978, Moore Publishing Co.

Pelz, D.C.: Conditional effects in relationship of auton-omy and motivation to performance (mimeographed), Aug. 1960.

Reddin, W.J.: Managerial effectiveness, New York, 1970, McGraw-Hill Book Co.

Roethlisberger, F.J., and Dickson, W.J.: Management and the worker, Cambridge, Mass., 1939, Harvard University Press.

Schein, E.H.: Process consultation: its role in organization development, Reading, Mass., 1969, Addison-Wesley Publishing Co., Inc.

Simon, H.A.: The new science of management decision, New York, 1960, New York University Press.

Stogdill, R.M.: Individual behavior and group achievement, New York, 1959, Oxford University Press.

Stogdill, R.M.: Handbook of leadership, New York, 1974, The Free Press.

Tannenbaum, R., and Schmidt, W.H.: How to choose a leadership pattern, Harvard Business Rev. pp. 162, 166, May-June 1973.

Weber, M.: Essays in sociology, New York, 1946, Oxford University Press.

CHAPTER 19

The multidisciplinary team approach

Barry B. Perlman, M.D.
Arthur H. Schwartz, M.D.

For a team to exist, there must be more than a variety of providers: each provider must function as a sub-unit of a whole in a synergistic relationship (Parker, 1972, p. 9).

A multiplicity of missions requires that a multidisciplinary team staff the psychiatric emergency unit. If one were to ask emergency unit personnel what their task was, the responses would be wide ranging. Beyond the treatment provided for acute psychotic decompensations and life-threatening situations, there are a host of functions, including support for the deinstitutionalized persons with chronic mental problems, work with families in crisis, counseling for rape and assault victims, and social interventions for the homeless. It is patently obvious that such divergent demands on the staff require expertise in many areas. For example, social interventions with the homeless require an intimate working knowledge of community and governmental support systems. The alleviation of the psychological pain experienced by the rape victim may be best accomplished by women who are not psychiatrists or psychologists. The use of people who by their professional identity would not stigmatize the victim as requiring help for mental illness facilitates ventilation and enables the traumatized individual to find relief. In an acute psychotic break, the need for psychopharmacological intervention can best be provided by psychiatrists with expertise in this area.

These clear-cut examples do not do justice to the clinical complexities encountered in the day-to-day operation of a psychiatric emergency unit. Often, even the most seemingly pedestrian of cases requires the joint efforts of team members in order that biopsychosocial needs may be met (Engel, 1977).

Not only do the team members complement each other with respect to clinical skills (though they have been known to compete), but of equal importance, they offer support to each other in the face of unrelenting stress. The stress relates both to the nature of the work and to the staff's reaction to the problems and tensions in which they are continuously immersed. Specifically, the need to see many people for and about whom critical decisions and dispositions must be made results in a trying workday. In addition, the severity of the psychopathology presented by many individuals drains the nurturing capacity of the staff. Even a closely knit, mutually supportive team is not immune from the phenomenon of burnout, but without a cohesive team, burnout is assured. Witnessing the psychological demoralization of a colleague is a severe stressor in and of itself.

Clearly, the rigorous demands of a professional life spent in a psychiatric emergency unit require personnel with considerable maturity, interpersonal skills, and flexibility. The draining nature of the job is best handled when those assigned to it have chosen this area of professional activity, rather than when, as so often happens, assignment is made as the price of institutional and departmental entrance. Younger professionals are often forced to "pay their dues" in this fashion.

Interpersonal facility is important in a closely intermeshed team functioning in a situation akin to that of a ship's crew. In addition, this skill is necessary when dealing not only with the individuals in need of care but with agitated, frightened, and not uncommonly, hostile relatives. Maturity enables the staff to empathize without overidentifying with the situations encountered. Practically, a good sense of humor may be important for staff morale, and effective defense against the barrage of human tragedy, and a significant clue in choosing personnel who will adapt to an emergency setting.

Finally, flexibility is a crucial staff attribute because of the highly variable manner in which people ask for help and in which solutions to their problems must be addressed. A rigid individual who needs a nonvarying external environment in which to work may be incapacitated in an emergency unit situation.

THE COMPOSITION OF THE TEAM

The composition of psychiatric emergency unit and crisis teams has been shown to be fairly consistent across institutions (Lieb et al., 1973; Talbott, 1976). The staffing pattern of the psychiatric emergency service of The Mount Sinai Hospital in New York City, which registered 3,500 individual visits in 1979, is representative of patterns found in large, urban, voluntary teaching hospitals. During the 5-day workweek the service is staffed by:

1 psychiatrist-director, full-time
1 hospital administrator, part-time
1 clerk-registrar, full-time
1 psychiatric nurse clinician, full-time
1 psychiatric social worker, full-time
1 psychiatric social worker, half-time
1 chief resident, ⅛- to ¼-time
5 psychiatric residents, 1 day each
5 supervising psychiatrists, 1 afternoon a week each

Evening and weekend coverage is provided by a postgraduate, third-year resident on call in the hospital.

In nonteaching institutions different patterns of coverage emerge based on the distribution of diagnoses seen and on the institution's commitment to psychiatric care. For example, a community hospital offering inpatient psychiatric care may have a small full-time psychiatric nursing and social work staff in the emergency unit. Night coverage could be provided by a rotation of the psychiatric attending staff or by psychiatrists specifically hired for this function.

At hospitals without psychiatric departments, coverage may be provided through regional agreements. For example, Westchester County in

New York State has a mobile psychiatric emergency team composed of a psychiatrist and a psychiatric technician. This team functions by handling crises either in homes or in the emergency units of hospitals without special psychiatric units. In other community hospitals without psychiatric departments per se, contractual agreements are often made between the state department of mental health and private counseling agencies to provide emergency psychiatric "backup" to the emergency unit on a 24-hour basis. Often state funding provides monies for private groups to provide this service. Generally, an on-call setup is most compatible for these smaller general hospital settings.

THE DISCIPLINES

Critical to the functioning of any emergency unit anticipating the handling of psychoses is the psychiatrist. By virtue of both clinical and legal considerations the psychiatrist remains the linchpin of an effectively functioning delivery system. As a consequence of their training, psychiatrists should bring to the team expertise in psychopharmacology, a knowledge of dynamic processes, and a familiarity with crisis intervention and family therapy. Most important, psychiatrists must possess clinical diagnostic acumen. Individuals seen on any given day may range across the diagnostic spectrum, and cases may include character pathology, major depressive episodes with manifest suicidal behavior, acute psychotic episodes, including schizophrenia and mania, and organic mental syndromes, including toxic psychoses. To differentiate between these categories, the psychiatrist must be able to sharply focus the interview so as to gather pertinent historical and mental status data. The need to be aware of medical problems and the ability to perform brief neurological examinations may be crucial in the recognition of neurological disorders presenting as psychiatric syndromes. Examples include encephalopathies and subdural hematomas. Koranyi (1979) has documented the extent to which medical problems seen in a psychiatric clinic are misdiagnosed as psychosomatic. The psychiatrist is best able to represent the team in dealing with other medical colleagues because of the common training they share in medicine.

The psychiatrist has often been the designated leader of the team because of traditional hospital hierarchical considerations. Even in situations where the designated leader is someone other than the psychiatrist, other team members may expect such leadership. As Bernard and Ishiyama (1960) have pointed out, leadership is most effective when assigned roles are capable of being achieved. The leader in the emergency unit must possess an activist temperament to put into effect the rapid clinical decisions called for by the acute nature of the problems confronted. A psychiatrist appointed to such a position ought not be one who is most comfortable with a laid-back, nondirective approach. While within the group the leadership may not always rest with the psychiatrist for any particular problem, within an institutional or hospital setting the psychiatrist is usually held accountable by the organization for the performance of the emergency unit team (Rubin and Beckhard, 1972).

The importance of psychiatric nurse clinicians in the emergency unit is readily apparent when one considers the breadth of their task. Bridging the gap between the social and medical focuses, nurses are called on to be responsible for triage of individuals, to do initial screenings, to act as teachers and consultants for their counterparts in other areas of the emergency unit, to administer medication, and to monitor those retained in holding areas or quiet rooms. In such situations they must assess physical and behavioral variables. As nurses expand their areas of expertise in addition to the aforementioned primary functions, a focus on intrafamilial stress and the effects of illness on family relationships becomes a major thrust in their work.

As opposed to the surgical nurse who has a clearly demarcated function in the operating room, the psychiatric nurse, along with all other mental health professionals, must struggle with the ambiguity that attends blurred roles (Rubin and Beckhard, 1972). This ambiguity presents problems for the nurse in several ways. First, since nurses are members of a traditionally feminine and support-oriented profession, internal stresses may be produced when long-time practitioners are expected to assume positions of equality and perhaps even leadership with professionals to whom they had formerly been subservient. Second, as nurses assume enlarged clinical responsibility, there often is uncertainty about their accountability for making decisions in spheres where they formerly had an implementary role. These problems cannot be ascribed to nurses alone. Rather, in a complementary fashion, other professional groups, particularly physicians, are faced with redefining their expectations of the nurses beside whom they work. For example, in some team situations where the nurse is a clinical constant, part-time physicians may have to adjust to being subordinate. An additional factor may come into play in the years ahead as the number of women in medicine and particularly in psychiatry increases. Over one fourth of U.S. medical students currently are women (Division of Educational Measurement and Research). While this change has occurred in medicine, nursing has remained an essentially female profession. The traditional female-nurse, male-physician hierarchy is being strikingly altered.

A nurse who is to play a major role in the psychiatric emergency unit ought to have a master's degree (M.A., M.S., M.N.) in psychiatric nursing. Inpatient experience, during which there is the opportunity to deal with acute psychotic emergencies in a better controlled situation, is an invaluable part of the preparation for subsequent emergency psychiatric work. An equally important experience would be past work as a staff R.N. in an emergency unit. This environment can be totally alien and threatening without some previous familiarity. Emergency psychiatric nursing has become, in essence, a subspecialty of psychiatric nursing.

Social workers, as a consequence of their expertise in community resources and intrafamilial problems, have emerged as an important component of the emergency team. If the psychiatric emergency unit functions on a triage basis, then those problems falling to the social worker often entail the issue of the interaction between illness and the environment. Homeless individuals, often with associated psychopathology, exemplify this type of problem. Even if someone requires medication for psychopathology, the major therapeutic focus of the team may lie in the realm of that person's relation to the community and family. Even when confronted with the extreme symptomatology of schizophrenia, work and social functioning have been shown to be of ciritcal importance in outcome (Strauss and Carpenter, 1975, p. 9).

If the system in a particular emergency unit allocates admissions assignments to each team member in rotation regardless of the client's problem, then the social worker, at least initially, would function no differently than any other team member. Such a team arrangement draws the special expertise available from other disciplines into play where necessary to assist the primary clinician and thereby ensures well-balanced clinical care. The personal network a competent social worker creates with counterparts at other agencies serves to soften the hard edge by which relations between institutions are often marked.

Although certain traditional areas of expertise and legally specified boundaries demarcate the professional responsibilities of nursing and social work, functionally there is considerable blurring. Competent members of both disciplines are able to perform many of the same tasks. This interchangeability will become increasingly possible as nursing education lengthens and as the professional standards rise so that more nurses will have bachelor's and master's degrees. Currently, only 20% of all registered nurses have a B.S. and less than 5% have an M.S. Formerly registered nurses with only 3 years of hospital training were ill prepared to assume functions now routinely performed by their better-educated colleagues in social work. In most cases even the psychiatrist is unable to bring any further interpersonal and psychotherapeutic expertise to bear on the clinical problems. As in the nursing field, social work remains a primarily feminine discipline, and as a result, many of the problems confronted by nurses in dealing with psychiatrists pertain. Kane (1975, p. 21) has stated that, "Some professions are associated with a particular sex or social class, making it difficult to judge whether the professional or personal attributes most explain behavior."

321

Despite extensive training and considerable skill, the psychologist brings no unique professional expertise to the emergency unit team. While individual psychologists may be excellent in this setting, the special skills that result from their training are better applied in either inpatient or outpatient clinic settings. For example, psychological testing, a valuable tool for cognitive and psychodynamic assessment, is not a procedure that can be undertaken during the brief time the individuals spend in the emergency unit. The skills psychologists possess can add depth to the understanding of human beings but are best applied when continuing work will be undertaken.

The other skills necessary for competent functioning in the emergency unit are those already possessed by the other disciplines. The fact that clinical psychologists, who might be considered for an emergency unit position, are likely to hold a doctoral degree means that a higher salary scale for essentially similar services would be required. This extra expenditure of the health care dollar if often hard to justify.

The title of psychiatric emergency unit clerk does not do justice to the responsibility of the position. In designating that the position be filled by a clerk, the institution fails to appreciate the many skills required for the post. For example, the clerk must have good telephone skills and the ability to convey a feeling of stability, kindness, and interest as the first member of the team with whom the public has contact. Additionally, the minor administrative requirements of the position necessitate a tactful demeanor and efficiency. For these reasons the person holding this job ought to be designated a registrar and selected from among better qualified individuals than ordinarily apply for the position of clerk.

At the hub of the admissions procedure for many psychiatric units is the psychiatric registrar. In this capacity the registrar must be able to deal firmly, yet politely, with unit clerks, staff psychiatrists, and private psychiatrists seeking to admit clients to the hospital. It is obvious that such a position exposes the registrar to pressure and requires intuitive administrative skills. If the community surrounding the hospital is largely bilingual, a registrar fluent in both languages will be a great asset. Clearly, it would be best if all of the team members were bilingual but this, unfortunately, is rarely possible. It has been shown that, given the opportunity, Spanish-speaking individuals will seek out Hispanic psychiatrists (Nagelberg, 1980). In addition to a shared language, cultural affinity with the population to be served ought to be looked for when selecting the registrar. Such a registrar can help the team shepherd those in need of care through an often alien institutional system.

In assigning administrative responsibility for the emergency unit, it is clear that in most instances a full-time administrator is not warranted. Therefore it is best to make the psychiatric emergency unit one component of an administrator's responsibility. Depending on the infrastructure of the institution, it may be better for the administrator to be linked horizontally with other ambulatory services or vertically with the department of psychiatry. In this way, an able person can be recruited and the position can be used as a career springboard.

To a greater degree than is true for the other team members, the administrator must come to terms with a split in allegiance. Responsible both for implementing and revising the psychiatric program and for carrying out the hospital's mandates, both fiscal and programmatic, the administrator may be torn by conflicting mission and loyalties. For example, at a time of fiscal retrenchment the hospital may ask the administrator to economize, whereas the program requires expansion for the improvement of clinical service. Unfortunately, the decision as to which way the administrator tilts is often dependent on the hierarchical structure in which promotions take place. In this respect, community mental health centers have an advantage over general hospitals in that there is generally no separation of administrative and clinical agendas.

This position is usually filled by entrance-level administrators who would be expected to advance either within the institution or by moving to another setting. It should be recognized that it is preferable to have administrative turnover rather than saddling the unit with someone who reaches the peak of a career in this slot. This admonition protects against the operation of the "Peter principle" at this level (Peter and Hull, 1969). Quality more than compensates for turnover. This principle of personnel management is critical not only for administrators but for each discipline represented within the team. Despite the anxiety and disruption attendant on the team's support of upward job mobility, individual morale and esprit de corps are enhanced by it over time.

The selection of an administrator means scouting for a person with interpersonal, budgetary, and managerial skills. Confronting the challenge of extracting maximum productivity from workers whose jobs are defined by contracts between the union and the hospital, the administrator must display flexibility in the interpretation of the rules in order to gain the cooperation of the nonprofessional staff. The budgetary area is where the administrator makes the most vital contribution to the team and is the arena in which the split of allegiance is most likely to manifest itself. Creative administration enables the team to develop programs, to have some funds for books and journals and to send representatives to appropriate educational forums both to contribute and to learn.

In hospitals where training programs exist, the emergency unit is often an integral part of the clinical experience in psychiatry. For medical students the emergency unit provides a theater in which the student may serve as the primary interviewer, learn to rapidly diagnose a wide range of psychopathological conditions, and gain skill in handling crises. The emergency unit experience may thus be the most useful experience in preparing the future physician, regardless of the specialty eventually chosen, for work with emotionally upset individuals.

Psychiatric residents complicate the life of the team. On-line work in the emergency unit is a requisite of every psychiatric residency program. As a consequence, the permanent staff members of the unit often have to deal with physicians who resent participation. An additional kink in the system resulting from this requirement is that the resident psychiatrist may be expected to assume a position of authority in a situation in which his clinical skills are the least developed. In addition, it is hard to maintain group cohesiveness when residents rotate through the unit and when the assigned may spend only part of a workweek in the emergency area. The special attention and supervision showered on the residents may foster feelings of resentment within the team. Many of the same issues surround the rotation through the psychiatric emergency unit of social work and nursing students.

Having identified the members of the team, we must now address the manner in which they interdigitate to form a group. Merely bringing people together or giving them a shared task is not necessarily sufficient for the formation of a working group. To call a group of people a team does not make it one. The molding of individuals from disparate disciplines into a coherent team with shared goals is an ongoing process. This process requires that the attention of the team members focus both on the clinical care that must be delivered and on the internal workings of the group. The self-conscious absorption with the group becomes a necessary component in each individual's expenditure of daily energy.

Over a period of time while individuals work together, a bond can be formed between them so that a team truly emerges. This bond requires time to develop and must be continually cultivated if it is to flourish. Except in the exceptional circumstance where a service is being started, most workers fill an open slot in an ongoing team. In such a situation the first period of working together is one in which the institutionally defined jobs are redefined to accommodate the particular skills and personalities of the actual workers. Just as a muscial conductor can place his imprint on a musical score, so the team members are continually reinterpreting their roles within the bounds of legal and institutional constraints. Whenever a new member enters, the process of definition is reactivated. If, for example, a psychiatrist who possessed considerable family evaluative and therapeutic skills replaced a colleague not schooled in these areas, the equilibrium of the team might be disrupted. Competition could ensue with the social worker or nurse who heretofore had been seen as possessing the term's expertise in this area. Like the movements of tectonic plates, the substitution of one group member for another has consequences for team organization, leadership, communication, morale, interpersonal relations, and task assignment. The group must assimilate a new person with a different personality and work style. The flow of information may be altered until other individuals have assessed to what extent the replacement can be trusted, whereas the replacement must overcome the barriers of previously existing group norms and the feelings the group had for the team member who departed. As with the expression of grief in any group situation, the remaining members wrestle with feelings of anger about having been abandoned and resentment toward the new individual for not being precisely like the replaced colleague. Clearly, much of the process of giving up the ties to the person who has left and accepting the newcomer is unconscious and needs to be uncovered through the communicative patterns of the team.

In the handling of clinical responsibilities the setting often dictates the manner in which the team functions. In a hospital in which a permanent staff is attached to the psychiatric emergency unit and in which an educational mission is not primary, several possibilities exist for evaluations and dispositions. The composition of the emergency unit staff must be appropriate to the kinds of problems encountered in that emergency unit. For example, in a receiving hospital into which police bring disturbed individuals, it can be anticipated that the concentration of severe psychopathology will be great and the psychiatric needs of the team will be magnified. An emergency unit located in an area in which large numbers of recent immigrants reside will be faced with the problems of families under stress, both internally and with respect to the interface with the new society and the institutions of that society. It has been shown that migration to a new country is associated with an increased prevalence of psychological disturbance, which has been attributed to the tendency of disturbed individuals to migrate and to the disruptive aspects of the migration itself (Kuo, 1976; Mezey, 1960; Odegaard, 1932). Schleifer et al. (1979) have shown that the stressfulness of migration correlates with the level of reported success in adjusting to the new life situation. Therefore social

workers would be vital to an emergency unit confronting such problems, and additional social work lines might be added fo foster the delivery of comprehensive services.

Random crises occurring in any community may suddenly place enormous demands on the psychiatric emergency unit. In such circumstances, exemplified by the aftermath of the Coconut Grove fire in Boston (Lindemann, 1944) or the great Ohio flood (Erikson, 1976), the psychiatric team may have to quickly integrate additional personnel from each of the disciplines to ensure that an appropriate level of care is provided.

A case example will serve to illustrate the way in which the team functions.

Case vignette #1

A Chinese college student was brought to a psychiatric emergency unit by her roommate, who had noticed increasingly bizarre behavior over the previous week. After she was registered, the unit psychiatrist was called to see her. He noted paranoid ideation, blocking of thoughts, agitation, pressured speech, some inappropriate affect manifested by silly laughter, and the possibility of auditory hallucinations. After consulting with the student, he suspected that the precipitating stress might have been her parents' disapproval of her continuing relationship with an Occidental boyfriend. To gather more information about this possible precipitant and to establish the groundwork for crisis intervention, the psychiatrist asked the team social worker to join him in the assessment of the situation by gathering more information from the roommate. That discussion confirmed the importance of the intrafamilial dispute raging about the boyfriend. A decision was made to bring the disturbed woman's parents into the emergency unit. Contact was made with them by the social worker. While awaiting the arrival of the parents, the student was placed in a quiet setting with minimal stimulation. During this time the nurse clinician assigned to the team established rapport and observed a decline in bizarre behavior. Vital signs were taken. With the arrival of the parents the social worker and psychiatrist met with them and obtained information that confirmed and elaborated their basic hypothesis. A brief interdisciplinary discussion led to the formulation of the following plan. The student would be medicated with neuroleptic drugs and an attempt would be made by the social worker to intervene intensively with the young woman and her family.

The student was able to return to the dormitory with her roommate who had agreed to watch over her, understanding that emergency unit personnel would be available on a 24-hour basis. Unfortunately, during the night the student's behavior deteriorated once again and she was returned to the emergency unit. Hospitalization was felt to be unavoidable. Continued medication in the ward as well as the use of family intervention led to a resolution of the crisis.

In this case the emergency unit psychiatrist directed the manner in which the members of the other disciplines collaborated; this exemplifies the way care is structured when hierarchical relations among professions prevail (Ducanis and Golin, 1979, p. 16).

This case might have been handled somewhat differently if a nonhierarchical structure existed. Had intake assignments been made in a rotational fashion, the nurse clinician might have been the first team member to meet the student. After gathering relevant data, the nurse would have had to call in the psychiatrist for medication and might have asked for assistance in mental status evaluation. Depending on that particular nurse's experience and skills in working with families, the nurse might have seen the family or asked for social work assistance.

An alternative way to structure the team in a psychiatric emergency unit would be to specifically assign discrete tasks based on expertise of each member. In the case vignette when it was elicited that the family conflict was central, the social worker would have been designated team leader for this particular case. The social worker would have called in other disciplines as needed, for example, the psychiatrist for medication. As long as hospitals remain primarily hierarchical, it may be difficult to operationally realize such a model.

Regardless of model, conflict will exist within every team. However, its manifestations will differ depending on the structural model. Experienced consultants underscore the importance of making conflicts manifest lest they subliminally distort working relations (Fry et al. 1974, p. 39). The leader must have the ability to absorb criticism and permit staff dissension without feeling threatened. The physician's expectation of preeminence in a medical setting aids in this process. Members of other disciplines traditionally subservient to the physician may find it more difficult when placed in positions of leadership to negotiate the process of conflict resolution.

It should be recognized that the size of the group has been reported to have a bearing on team cohesiveness. Kane (1975) has reported that small groups mesh best and create an atmosphere within which group democracy can be expected to flourish. It is asserted that the advantages of a democratic process to a group include such things as the ability to function during transition periods between leaders, greater job satisfaction, and enhanced job productivity. Furthermore, shared values and norms facilitate the development of a sentient group. On the other hand, as group size increases, more stress impinges on the leader but the opportunity for an individual to lead is magnified.

Although lip service is often paid to the concept of a "leaderless" group and these groups have been described in the literature, in fact, leaders emerge in any group setting (Astrachan et al., 1967). Depending on the situation or the issue, various people will take the lead at different times. This accounts for the feelings of liberation and autonomy associated with these so-called leaderless groups (Yalom, 1970, p. 323). Kane (1975, p. 28) has referred to the myth of the leaderless group. In a smoothly operating team, expertise with a particular problem ought to define who assumes the lead with respect to the particular clinical issue. Teamwork is the essence rather than a rigid notion of team. To the extent that a democratic structure facilitates a fluidity of roles, it may be the preferred model. Democracy and fluidity do not, however, imply that a unanimity of thinking is necessary. In fact, if the group finds overwhelming agreement among the members, it should serve as a warning that individual members may be adbicating personal responsibility in the face of group pressure (Rae-Grant and Marcuse, 1968).

Pines and Kafry (1978) have made the observation that when work is shared, as with working units such as those described, the pressures of the assigned work load are eased. As a result there is less work tedium and less likelihood that the phenomenon of staff "burnout" will occur. Factors that foster the formation of a closely knit team include geographical propinquity, minimizing the use of esoteric jargon, and maximizing intrateam communication. Each discipline has evolved a vocabulary which, beyond clinical utility, serves to set its members apart from others and reinforce their sense of shared professional identity. For example, psychiatrists refer to people who seek their help as *patients* whereas social workers usually refer to these same individuals as *clients*.* Although a shared vocabulary is important for the optimum functioning of the group, it must be recognized that an eradication of professional differences is not the aim. The assumption of the vocabulary and approach of another discipline may merely lead to professional conformity and potentially the loss of a unique clinical perspective. In hospitals that include the psychiatric emergency unit within the general emergency department it is most

efficient, though rarely feasible, if each of the members of the team has an office in that location so as to facilitate ready participation in the provision of care. In mental health centers, which lack a formal emergency unit, it is of substantial importance that task rather than discipline determine the allocation of space.

Weekly team meetings also are a place in which practical problems confronted by team members can be addressed. They also provide a forum for the resolution of interpersonal friction that arises within the team. The kinds or practical problems that can profitably be brought to such a meeting include difficulties individual team members are having with segments of the institution external to the psychiatric emergency unit. The team member responsible for that particular set of relations will then be able to negotiate a resolution of the conflict on behalf of the unit. Personnel problems that may be addressed include staff productivity and feelings that responsibilities are not equitably distributed. Other situations do not lend themselves to resolution within the group. For example, the matrix pattern of responsibility may make it difficult for the institutionally designated leader of the team to assess the performance of staff members of different disciplines with respect to their institutionally mandated responsibilities (Beckhard, 1972). In such situations the team leader must develop links to the professional person who heads the other disciplines represented on the team. It may only be through such a collaboration that appropriate quality control can be exercised. In a reciprocal fashion, team members in conflict with the leader may be able to seek a redress of grievances by

---

*A controversy currently exists about when to identify those in need of health care as *patients* or when the term *client* would be more appropriate. The authors of this chapter take the position that *patient* is the best designation for individuals who are grossly disorganized or who may show the manifestations of substance abuse, or for those whom current research has identified important potential biological markers and for whom somatic treatments will determine much of the therapeutic outcome. The term is also best used for individuals requiring hospitalization. This concept is embedded in the reasoning of the President's Commission on Mental Health (1978, p. 163) when they refer

to the "chronically mentally ill patient." The term *client* is acceptable in situations in which a person solicits help for a variety of problems faced in everyday living and in which there is little evidence of profound biological aberrations. Generally, a psychotherapeutic approach is used with the client expected to be an equal participant in the interactional process. Much of the dispute about the use of *client* or *patient* has unfortunately emerged along disciplinary lines with social workers preferring clients and physicians patients. In this book, by editorial decision, only the term *client* will be used. The authors of this chapter have chosen to avoid the use of either term.

having the leader of their discipline speak on their behalf to the team leader and, where that does not suffice, to their supervisor. Fry and Miller (1974) have identified the ability to turn to supervisors as an important safety valve that contains pressures that could not otherwise be dealt with effectively.

In situations in which the same members of the team are not present in the emergency unit on a daily basis, as is the case when residents or others are assigned for given days, it may be useful for members of the unit to gather at the start of each day to anticipate potential problems. At such a meeting the availability of beds within the institution would be discussed as well as the availability of outpatient treatment slots in various outpatient clinics. If no beds are available, the team could prepare a plan for dealing with those requiring acute management before arranging for interinstitutional transfer. The team would assign a specific liaison person to alert potential receiving institutions, thus facilitating the flow of work throughout the day. It should be realized that in such a situation, where staff is not constant, cooperative staff relations rather than a team functioning as an organic whole is the best that can be achieved.

Another function of import to workers within the unit is in-service education. A primary goal of such education is to decrease the lag time between the learning and the application of new attitudes, skills, and knowledge. In this regard certain topics are best taught within the context of the team, whereas others are best addressed in teaching conferences held within each of the departments represented on the team. The kind of material that is most amenable to on-site teaching includes case material and topics relevant to the day-to-day management of the mentally ill and their families who are seen in the psychiatric emergency unit. Thus the handling of a violent individual is best taught at the unit level. In contrast, the subject of violence as an academic topic, including the root causes of violence, might be discussed most satisfactorily at a departmental level. People from outside the institution with expertise in particular areas can be brought in at the departmental or institutional level to enrich the teaching program. A

further point to be made relevant to the handling of violence is the relation of the emergency unit team to the institution's security personnel. Although security guards are not technically members of the team, it is often wise to have the same guards assigned to respond to psychiatric crises. In this way they actually complement the team and over time they come to appreciate the special problems involved in dealing with disturbed behavior in contrast to criminal behavior. The process of educating the security force should not be left to the mental health professionals alone, but rather, in situations where a sophisticated police department is available, their expertise should be sought as well.

The emergency unit mission naturally extends itself into crisis management. Depending on the availability of staff, either the emergency unit personnel themselves or others assigned to this task by the institution can be made available to follow individuals for short periods of time on an intensive basis until either the crisis is resolved or a suitable long-term disposition can be made. Appropriate for crisis work are those situations dealing with external life stresses such as the death of a loved one, individuals on the verge of psychotic decompensation, generational disputes that threaten the integrity of the family unit, as well as the problems of rape victims and the battered. The most significant contribution of the crisis team is in averting psychiatric hospitalization with its attendant disruptions and stigma. As in the case of the emergency unit, the crisis personnel should operate as a team (Lieb et al., 1973, p. 15). When well functioning, such teams are capable of reaching out into homes and places of employment. In this way the firsthand observational material of interactive phenomena becomes the primary data on which the team bases its evaluative and intervention strategies.

While the team approach has many advantages, some of which have been described in this chapter, a uniformly positive attitude does not exist. A few authors have spelled out the caveats associated with the team model. Indeed, group-focused preoccupation has been reported as a danger lest too much time be wrested from the final goal of delivery of psychiatric care. Rubin and

Beckhard (1972) have raised the question of whether the expenditure of energy on the reversal of "naturally" occurring leadership roles is truly worhthwhile. Rae-Grant and Marcuse (1968, p. 4) have stated that "the myth that the total team is effectively discharging responsibility for a given patient may mask the fact that no one fully accepts responsibility or feels himself to be ultimately accountable for what happens." Thus they feel that a certain anonymity may come to exist within the team which manifests as irresponsibility and that the mirroring of each other's opinions often mitigates against a thoughtful consideration of the problem. As an example, they point to the generational conflicts that may arise when one team member sees the parents while another sees the children. The individual team members seeing only a segment of the problem may incorrectly overidentify with the people they are treating.

SUMMARY

This chapter has addressed issues of team mission and functioning. Teams have much to offer, but those working within them must be aware of the pitfalls as well. No definitive data exist to establish whether a given institution should adopt an egalitarian team or a traditional hierarchical team for its emergency unit. Rather, the decision must be based on the personnel available, the attitudes intrinsic to the institution, the objectives of the program, and the experiences described by others facing similar problems.

BIBLIOGRAPHY

Astrachan, B.M., et al.: The unled patient group as a therapeutic tool, The Int. J. Group Psychother. 17:178, 1967.

Beckhard, R.: Organizational issues in the team delivery of comprehensive health care, Milbank Mem. Fund Q. 50:287, 1972.

Bernard, S.E., and Ishiyama, T.: Authority conflicts in the structure of psychiatric teams, Soc. Work 5:77, 1960.

Division of Educational Measurement and Research, American Association of Medical Colleges: 1980-1981 Fall Enrollment Survey, Washington, D.C., 1981.

Ducanis, A.J., and Golin, A.K.: The interdisciplinary health care team, Germantown, Md., 1979, Aspen Systems Corp.

Engel, G.: The need for a new medical model: a challenge for biomedical science, Science 196:129, 1977.

Erikson, K.T.: Loss of communality at Buffalo Creek, Am. J. Psychiatry 133:302, 1976.

Fry, L.J., and Miller, J.P.: The impact of interdisciplinary teams on organizational relationships, Sociol. Q. 15:417, 1974.

Fry, R.E., Lech, B.A., and Rubin, I.: Working with the primary care team: the first intervention In Wise, H., et al., editors: Making health teams work, Cambridge, Mass., 1974, Ballinger Publishing Co.

Kane, R.A.: The interprofessional team as a small group, Soc. Work Health Care 1:19, 1975.

Koranyi, E.K.: Morbidity and rate of undiagnosed physical illnesses in a psychiatric clinic population, Arch. Gen. Psychiatry 36:414, 1979.

Kuo, W.: Theories of migration and mental health: an empirical testing on Chinese Americans, Soc. Sci. Med. 10:297, 1976.

Lieb, J., Lipsitch, I.I., and Slaby, A.E.: The crisis team, New York, 1973, Harper & Row, Publishers.

Lindemann, E.: Symptomatology and management of acute grief, Am. J. Psychiatry 101:141, 1944.

Mezey, A.G.: Psychiatric aspects of human migrations, Int. J. Soc. Psychiatry 5:245, 1960.

Nagelberg, S., et al.: Providers and receivers in the private psychiatric Medicaid system, Am. J. Psychiatry 137:690, 1980.

Odegaard, O.: Emigration and insanity, Acta Psychiatry Neurol. Suppl. 4, 1932.

Parker, A.W.: The team approach to primary health care, Neighborhood Health Center Seminar Program, monograph series no. 3, Berkeley, Calif., 1972, University of California Extension.

Peter, L.F., and Hull, R.: The Peter principle, New York, 1969, William Morrow & Co., Inc.

Pines, A., and Kafry, D.: Occupational tedium in social services, Soc. Work 23:499, 1978.

President's Commission on Mental Health: Report of the Task Panel on Community Support Systems, vol. 2, Washington, D.C., 1978, U.S. Government Printing Office.

Rae-Grant, Q.A.F., and Marcuse, D.J.: The hazards of teamwork, Am. J. Orthopsychiatry 38:4, 1968.

Rubin, I.M., and Beckhard, R.: Factors influencing the effectiveness of health teams, Milbank Mem. Fund Q. 50:317, 1972.

Schleifer, S.J., et al.: A study of American immigrants to Israel utilizing the SRRQ, J. Psychosom. Res. 23:247, 1979.

Strauss, J.S., and Carpenter, W.T.: The key clinical

dimensions of the functional psychoses. In Freedman, D.X., editor: Biology of the major psychoses. Res. Publ. Assoc. Res. Nerv. Ment. Dis. **54:**9, 1975.

Talbott, J.A., and Monroe, R.A.: The organization of psychiatric emergency services. In Glick, R.A., et al., editors: Psychiatric emergencies, New York, 1976, Grune & Stratton, Inc.

Yalom, I.D.: The theory and practice of group psychotherapy, New York, 1970, Basic Books, Inc., Publishers.

Unit maintenance and functioning

Ongoing unit maintenance and functioning are frequently altered by the enforcement of standards, changes in the law, restrictions of the budget, and the effort required to continue interagency and intraagency collaboration. For example, as a result of the mandates of informed consent laws, interviewing techniques had to be changed and additional forms had to be completed to demonstrate clients' agreement with treatment planning. The chapters in this section offer information and advice that will guide in the development and evaluation of unit policies and procedures and will enhance compliance with the multitude of regulations, recommendations of accrediting bodies, and fiscal-legal requirements.

Chapter 20, Standards of Care, explains the rationale for standards, reviews existing standards, describes recent efforts to construct standards, and predicts trends for implementation of standards. The author contends that standards are needed to foster safe and adequate care and ideally should be written by people with clinical experience. Existing standards are divided into three categories: practice standards, program and facility standards, and payment standards. The discussion of the relevance of standards to psychiatric emergency care demonstrates that, unfortunately, terminology and requirements are often vague and not helpful.

The author describes recent efforts by collaborating organizations, such as the American Psychiatric Association, Emergency Department Nurses' Association, and Joint Review Committee for Accreditation of Paramedic Training Programs, to construct standards. The standards for psychiatric emergency care in a hospital emergency department, for psychiatric emergency care services in community mental health centers, for the emergency component of a state mental hospital, and for categorization of psychiatric emergency services are listed. The chapter concludes with a prediction that standards will be written more precisely, appropriately, and comprehensively and will eventually be part of state mental health codes and legislation.

In Chapter 21 the legal implications of psychiatric emergency work are extensively discussed. The chapter begins with a review of how the law has affected care delivery through the work of client advocates, judicial involvement, and legislative reaction. Then the most common legal questions that arise in emergency settings are discussed: commitment procedures; competency; informed consent; seclusion, restraint, and forcible medication; confidentiality; and accuracy and adequacy of documentation.

The second half of Chapter 21 focuses on clinicians' concerns and rights. Information of how emergency staff are protected under due process of law is given for the situations related to assault and litigation. The author concludes that the current trend toward conservative treatment is the result of large numbers of unresolved legal issues in psychiatric emergency care.

In Chapter 22, specific and comprehensive information regarding the budgetary process is clearly and cleverly presented. The author emphasizes that the goal of a budget is to reflect the philosophy and orientation of the emergency program and should incorporate sound management, planning, and fiscal abilities. Specific strategies of budgeteering are elaborated on by detailed and practical explanations of such budgeting building blocks as accrual basis accounting, cost-benefit analysis, and the components of an operating budget.

The latter portion of Chapter 22 highlights methods for justification of a budget and for securing funding resources. Some of the budgeting methods explained include simple regression technique, demand analysis, and multiple regression analysis. Other budgeting techniques are offered for the specific aim of breaking even (break-even analysis), for planning staffing needs, and for the larger goal of completing a fiscal analysis of income, expense, and service units. Finally, practical guidelines are given for soliciting funding and dealing with the politics and marketing aspects of resource procurement.

Chapter 23, Interagency and Intraagency Collaboration, points out that conflicts exists within and between mental health agencies. Ways to reduce the harmful effects of conflict between psychiatric emergency units and other agencies are addressed. The need for collecting accurate and detailed information regarding clients' problems is vividly portrayed with case vignettes. Then practical suggestions are offered regarding how to obtain this information for the history, referral, and follow-up. Other approaches to resolve system inadequacies, such as "dumping," competition, and inadequate phone and written communication, include interventions by administrators and use of intraagency and interagency meetings for training, consultation, and treatment planning.

The second half of Chapter 23 focuses on soliciting community support and building a positive liaison with police. The author recommends that people in the community who have traditionally intervened in crises (clergy, firemen, police), should be involved in the planning of emergency programs and that participation in these planning meetings can be used to gain support and publicity for the efforts of the emergency staff. Helpful and detailed information is given on developing collaboration with important community members. Developing a liaison with the police is suggested to alleviate common frustrations associated with police-client agency contact. The author concludes this chapter with a discussion of how psychiatric emergency unit staff members can realistically determine the unit's image and focus.

CHAPTER 20

Standards of care

Gail M. Barton, M.D., M.P.H.

Historically a variety of practices, rituals, and instinctive responses were used in the treatment of psychiatric problems. Treatment methods have consisted of trephining as evidenced in prehistoric skulls, of commanding out the demons as described in the Bible, and of shackling people in jails and poorhouses as depicted in the art of the Reformation, and of whirling people on chairs or dunking people in creeks as was common in the days of the "father of psychiatry," Benjamin Rush. Some reasonable ideas such as sending the psychotic into homes of a town as occurred in Gheel in the 1600s again are being used (in the 1950s it was the general practice to commit all clients to state mental hospitals).

Recently psychiatric emergency care has changed drastically. Psychotropic medications make outpatient care much more possible, community mental health centers have sprung up since the Mental Health Act of 1963, general hospitals have added psychiatric wards, and emergency departments in hospitals have become the accepted place to go when an emergency is perceived by the client, the relatives, or members of the community such as the police or clergy. Admissions to state mental hospitals in the majority of instances now are voluntary rather than commitments. In this era of relative enlightenment, standards have been written and are being developed to guide the practice of psychiatric emergency care givers.

Webster defines *standard* as something established by authority, custom, or general consent as a model or example. (Webster, 1977). It is a measure for judging value, extent, or quality.

DEFINITION OF PSYCHIATRIC EMERGENCY

The American Psychiatric Association (APA) has drafted a definition of a psychiatric emergency as a situation that includes an *acute* disturbance of thought, behavior, mood, or social relationship which requires *immediate* intervention as defined by the client or family or social unit (Barton, 1978a).

The Emergency Medical Services (EMS), The American College of Emergency Physicians (ACEP), and the American Medical Association (AMA) all use the term *behavioral* instead of *psychiatric*. *Behavioral* refers to an obvious activity directed outward as a manifestation of either medical or psychiatric problems. Since it does not clearly include the possibility of a disturbance of cognition or mood, this author and the APA Task Force found it too restrictive compared to *psychiatric*. Undoubtedly, the other organizations chose *behavioral* to encompass persons within their purview in a context that seemed less stigmatizing and more normalizing than *psychiatric*.

Traditionally the recipients of services in a setting under medical control have been referred to as *patients,* and often the recipients of services in health care settings not under medical control have been referred to as *clients*. The use of *patient* or *client* has come to have political ramifications. This issue is especially highlighted in the discussion of standards.

WHY STANDARDS FOR PSYCHIATRIC EMERGENCY CARE ARE NEEDED

The dangers associated with operating without standards for psychiatric emergency care are great. Clinicians would be left to provide whatever level and kind of care they are willing and able to do. People with psychiatric problems are perceived by many in the emergency care field as misfits in the emergency care situation as well as in society. They require someone to talk with them to understand their problems; no obvious wound or protruding bone reveals their distress. Without standards, a rushed triage nurse might not take the temperature of a confused elderly man or might miss a key piece of information which could quickly facilitate identification of the infection that is overwhelming him. A harried emergency physician might lavage a suicidal person's stomach and discharge the person "home" to a single room in a local flophouse without ever knowing what support system is available, if any, to change the stresses that converged to precipitate the suicide attempt. An inadequate facility, such as a small crowded unit with no privacy in which to evaluate clients, might well mean the person will not reveal the real cause for concern. Without standards limiting the number of hours worked by a psychiatric resident, the client could be in the hands of a professional who is too tired to accurately analyze the complexities of possible drug interactions.

Who should write standards?

The common practice of having standards written by persons who are not actually practicing in the clinical area of psychiatric emergency care can lead to some strange non sequiturs: "The majority of *applicants* arriving at a hospital emergency service are in a state of crisis" (Joint Commission on Accreditation of Hospitals, 1979b, p. 13—emphasis added). No one working in an emergency department or community mental health center would ever use the word *applicant* for a person seeking emergency assistance. Those who are employed to develop standards for various state agencies often have worked their way up through the civil service or other similar bureaucracy, often changing from one agency or department to another as they move up. Experience in the clinical field may not be required. Therefore, it is necessary for clinicians and community representatives to be involved in the development and review of standards.

The vacuum created by the absence of standards has given legislative (and judicial) bodies free rein to set up rules and regulations. State mental health codes, including commitment regulations, are examples of this source of standards that must guide emergency personnel in handling psychiatric cases.

EXISTING STANDARDS

The preceding paragraphs have only hinted at the fact that there are different kinds of standards that relate to psychiatric emergency services. It is time to make them explicit. There are standards written by practitioners evolving from their provision of clinical services. Another kind are practice standards often written by state agencies such as the licensure office, and by professional organizations providing recognition of competence to qualified members (Nelson, 1979). There are also program and facility standards. These are often written by state departments of mental health, public health, and safety.

Payment standards are written as a contract agreement by the subscriber and the health insurance provider. They often limit benefits to certain diagnostic entities, restrict reimbursement for care for certain lengths of time, and designate which professionals can be providers of different types of care (Nelson, 1979).

Standards of the Joint Commission on Accreditation of Hospitals (JCAH)

The Joint Commission on Accreditation of Hospitals was created in 1951 as an independent, nonprofit organization that accredits hospitals who voluntarily request JCAH review. It originally focused only on hospital accreditation, but as the community mental health centers and other programs such as those for the mentally retarded, drug abusers, and alcoholics developed, it expanded its accrediting sphere. In 1978 it attempted to consolidate the accreditation process and standards to eliminate contradictions from one setting to another and duplication of accreditation efforts. An important fact that

has a bearing on emergency psychiatry in this regard is that the APA is not yet a sponsoring organization of JCAH even though the APA has applied to be one. At the moment APA input in writing standards is through lower level advisory committees only. This makes them reactive rather than proactive in writing the standards. Additionally, surveyors in the field are hired by JCAH. They are not necessarily clinicians—their background, like that of those penning the standards, may very likely be in educational psychology.

The Consolidated Standards for Child, Adolescent, and Adult Psychiatric, Alcoholism, and Drug Abuse Programs offer very little reference to emergency services per se. The most specific reference is Section 25.2.2h, which specifies that the pharmacist should keep and maintain approved antidotes and other emergency drugs in the pharmacy and inpatient care areas (JCAH, 1979a). Consultation services, such as to the police, are "optional" as are "outreach" efforts designed to help clients who might not be able to come in when experiencing an emergency. There are sections on safety, sanitation, and community disaster planning which offer more detail than those relating directly to provision of emergency services.

In the JCAH Community Mental Health Service Programs Manual (JCAH, 1979b), there is a section entitled "The Service Functional Area," which seems to relate to persons who have a psychiatric emergency. They are described as "persons in acute states of crisis" and "applicants arriving at a hospital emergency service—in a state of crisis." The section identifies eight service functions including "identification" and "crisis stabilization." *Screening* is part of the identification and is described as "the initial assessment of an applicant's role performance and role-support system"; it also determines "the individual's related degree of penetration into the system." (JCAH, 1979b, p. 13). As can be seen, a translator may be required to interpret these standards in the workplace to give guidance to the health care professional. One such translation might be "Talk to the clients, find out who their friends and family are, and then make decisions about the kind of care that can be provided that fits the problems and the setting." There is a subsection entitled "Crisis Stabilization Services," which provides definitions for *crisis care, crisis support, temporary residence, crisis intervention* and *temporary sponsorship* (JCAH, 1979b, p. 16). A translation into terms more familiar to clinicians converts those terms into statements relating to having 24-hour, short-term, acute-care beds either in a hospital or a community mental health center inpatient unit and having residential as well as outreach team and foster care capabilities. There is brief mention of a "balanced service system" concept on which the philosophical framework is based. It is supposed to be a "systematic response," which provides needed services. Services are to be built on client assets and provided in the "least restrictive environments" in a variety of settings. There is another section that relates to citizen participation in the development of "the system's responsiveness to citizen needs."

The section on staff development states that "a total reliance on the discipline-oriented staffing structure is no longer adequate for the existing mental health system. . . . Work is defined in terms of what has to be done rather than which disciplines exist to do the work . . . the education and training process must instill in staff a critical capacity and a desire to try innovative and creative approaches in the performance of their tasks" (JCAH, 1979b, p. 38). Unfortunately, that passage does not specify what disciplines should be represented, what academic or clinical background is necessary, or how these professionals might effectively work together in complementary roles.

The JCAH Accreditation Manual for Hospitals (JCAH, 1980) has a section entitled "Emergency Services." The standards themselves are somewhat general in nature: "Standard 1: There shall be a well defined plan of emergency care based on community need and the capabilities of the hospital." Within the interpretation that follows, four levels of hospitals are mentioned, with level 1 being the most comprehensive. Both levels 1 and 2 are expected to have "inhouse capability to manage physical and related emotional problems on a definitive basis." The section does not quite get to the point of saying that there should

be a capability to treat people with a purely emotional problem unconnected to a physical problem! Staff coverage is also left somewhat open—to be "determined by the medical staff in accordance with clinical competence and privileges." The emergency department director is expected to establish guidelines for how "specially trained personnel" will prioritize who sees the physician and when. The staff is expected to have training and educational programs including "recognition and attention to psychological and social needs of the patients and facilities." The standards also stipulate that there be written policies about such issues as confidentiality and protocols on problems such as rape and child abuse. Also, the staff is expected to be able to manage drug and alcohol problems, the emotionally ill, and "the difficult to manage." Overall, the standards are extremely vague and not too helpful in clinical programming, facility planning, or staff training and qualifications.

Standards of the National Institute of Mental Health (NIMH)

Perhaps in response to the confusion and vagueness in terminology of the JCAH's standards, another set of standards by a federal agency interested in psychiatric care emerged. In 1977, NIMH produced the National Standards for Community Mental Health Centers (NIMH, 1977) in response to the JCAH's earlier version of principles of accreditation of community mental health service programs (JCAH, 1976).

Hartman and Allison (1978) prepared a paper comparing the JCAH and NIMH standards. The NIMH set used terminology more familiar to clinicians, such as *clients* rather than *consumers* and *service coordinators* instead of *case managers*. It was more realistic in its ordering of treatment modalities: JCAH expected restraints to be used only after seclusion failed—not taking into account the fact that the majority of community mental health center (CMHC) staff members have never seen a seclusion room, let alone have one in their facility. It is a rare CMHC that even has restraints available. The NIMH version was more concerned with substance in the program: NIMH requires a written plan on how the emergency services will be available 24 hours a day. JCAH requires the service but not a written plan. Otherwise, the two sets are fairly similar: neither are very specific about emergency services other than 24-hour crisis intervention availability.

The production by JCAH of the August, 1979, version of CMHC standards only exaggerated the differences in language and moved it even further from a medically understandable and compatible model. It left more CMHCs comfortable with the NIMH specific guidelines for delivering services to emergencies.

Thus far a collaborative organizational approach to standards (JCAH) and a federal agency approach (NIMH) have been explored. Now a professional association's standards will be examined.

Standards of the American Medical Association

The American Medical Association has drafted a set of guidelines relating to hospital emergency capabilities. The latest version, which is still in draft form (AMA, 1980), has a section entitled "Behavioral Emergencies." It discusses a proposal to sort "behavioral patients" according to their diagnosis into different levels of capability hospitals. The flaw in this plan is that the diagnoses of behavioral patients are usually not clear until *after* they have been examined (rather than at the triage desk). The guidelines list the types of personnel that should be available based on the range of care offered by the facility's emergency department. It also states how available the type of personnel should be: physically present 24 hours a day, on call, or promptly available from inside or outside the hospital. The AMA plan also describes the types of services, equipment, laboratory, quality assurance, research, and training that are appropriate in three different categories of a hospital. The current draft (AMA, 1980) shows much merit but also has some major flaws such as suggesting that a psychoanalyst is essential but leaving out the special capabilities of rape counseling, domestic violence counseling, child abuse counseling, substance abuse management, clergy, and security

services. The equipment list is needlessly long. A simple reference to a general emergency room capability would be sufficient. It also mentions a "psychiatric intensive care unit," which as a concept may bear consideration, but in fact just do not exist (a very rare exception could prove the rule). The standards for laboratory services need to be expanded to include the procedures for obtaining blood and urine levels of toxic substances, alcohol and lithium levels, EEG tracings, and CT scans. Revised drafts are expected shortly. The Michigan Department of Public Health (MDPH) has revised the AMA draft guidelines thoroughly and logically (MDPH, 1980).

Standards of Blue Cross/Blue Shield (BC/BS)

An example of a third-party payment provider producing standards relating to psychiatric emergencies is Blue Cross/Blue Shield. It is expected that third-party carriers such as BC/BS will attempt to define what a psychiatric emergency is through the reimbursement schedules. For instance, in some guidelines enacted by Michigan BC/BS (Michigan BC/BS, 1980) a depressed person is not covered when seen in the emergency department but a manic depressive is, a drug reaction is covered but an overdose is not, an anxiety reaction is covered, but a situational reaction is not. The use of a differential diagnosis list seems to slip certain diagnostic categories into the reimbursable side of the ledger. The logic for the BC/BS exclusions is hard to fathom.

EFFORTS BY COLLABORATING ORGANIZATIONS TO CONSTRUCT STANDARDS

A number of professional organizations united by overlapping aims and memberships have been developing sets of guidelines for clinical management. The organizations have included the APA, the ACEP, the Emergency Department Nurses Association (EDNA), and the Joint Review Committee for Accreditation of Paramedic Training Programs (JRC). Each has focused on different aspects of the task of writing standards, and each has shared their expertise with one another.

There is no one set of guidelines that all of these organizations have yet approved—they are still in draft form as are the AMA guidelines for categorization. Even so, other organizations such as the EMS and the Department of Transportation (DOT), which produces paramedic training guidelines, have asked for input. Both the AMA and JCAH have received the current draft as well as correspondence from the APA about their own drafts and how they might be improved.

The collaborating organizations used the Delphi technique as the method of developing standards. This method was implemented in the manner described here. A draft of standards was initially written by the APA Task Force on Emergency Care Issues. This Task Force was composed of psychiatrists, clinicians, and educators, who mailed their version out to emergency facilities and departments of mental health across the country. Responses were then requested of the recipients of the draft. Their suggestions were integrated into a succeeding draft that was further commented on by EDNA, ACEP, the Michigan Department of Mental Health (MDMH), and the MDPH. The initial and then succeeding drafts were made available to anyone who wanted them with the stipulation that the receiving facilities try out the standards and return comments about them to the APA Task Force.

Most responses have been favorable and have resulted in the drafting of a set of documents now entitled "Proposed Standards for a Mental Health Component of a Hospital Emergency Department" (Barton, 1979c), , "Proposed Guidelines for a Comprehensive Community Mental Health Center Emergency Services Unit" (Barton, 1979a), and "Proposed Standards for the Emergency Services Component of a State Hospital" (Barton, 1979b). There are some supplemental guidelines for rural care as well (Barton, 1979e).

The drafts of standards for both the CMHCs and the general hospitals are currently being further tested in Michigan through the use of a survey instrument to determine the level of compliance for each standard at each facility. The survey is being sponsored by Michigan ACEP, Michigan Psychiatric Society (MPS), the MDMH,

and the MDPH. Preliminary results from the general hospitals indicate compliance with a great many of the standards, especially by the surburban hospitals. Rural hospitals have more trouble complying with staffing, facility, and program standards. Urban hospitals have the problem of clients waiting for long time periods before being seen, although they do have qualified and trained staff doing the evaluation and treatment (Barton, 1981). Tentative plans to extend this survey nationwide are under way. Further refinement of these guidelines for standards can then be accomplished.

Guidelines for psychiatric emergency care in hospital emergency departments

The guidelines focus primarily on care, but some relate to professional training and qualifications, some to facilities, and one to payment. The guidelines in draft form as of December, 1980 state as follows:

1. There shall be a telephone which shall be answered 24 hours a day.
2. The 24-hour telephone shall have a number which is advertised in the phone book, by community posters, by agency notification and by public information efforts.
3. There shall be an outreach team which shall go out to a psychiatric emergency when called upon by the telephone response staff.
4. There shall be a 24-hour walk-in service for a psychiatric emergency evaluation, intervention and disposition.
5. No patient shall be refused for lack of funds to pay for the services.
6. There shall be mental health professionals assigned to the telephone, outreach and walk-in services.
   a. There shall be a designated director of the psychiatric emergency component.
   b. There shall be a psychiatrist at least at the postgraduate year (PGY) II level assigned 24 hours a day.
   c. There shall be a registered nurse assigned 24 hours a day.
   d. There shall be a master's level social worker assigned 24 hours a day.

e. Mental health workers may be assigned to fulfill staff functions 24 hours a day under the supervision of one of the above professionals.

7. Staff assigned to the psychiatric component of the hospital emergency department shall show documented evidence of training in psychiatric emergency care.

a. This documentation may include description of professional training experiences, professional credentials, licensure, in-service orientation, in-service education and continuing education.

b. Staff without documentation of psychiatric emergency care experience shall be under the direct supervision of staff who have such documented experience.

8. There shall be a policy and procedures manual which includes psychiatric emergency care protocols for the staff's reference.

9. Patients with mental health emergencies shall be triaged within 5 minutes of entering the emergency department.

10. Patients shall always have their vital signs taken and recorded at triage.

11. Initial signs and symptoms shall be brought to the immediate attention of a medical professional at the time of triage so that prioritization in the context of other emergency department cases can be made and so that consideration about contacting psychiatric/mental staff can be decided at once.

12. Recordkeeping for the general emergency department shall include a psychological assessment section so that components can be evaluated as to relevant signs and symptoms, if any, and if so, whether they need immediate attention.

13. A log shall be kept of all psychiatric emergency calls, walk-ins and accompanied cases. This log shall include:

a. The nature of the call
b. Identification information about the caller
c. Time and date
d. Recommendations made

e. Patient/caller's intentions
f. Actions taken/planned

14. There shall be a written plan and set of policies that assures protection of a patient's rights. Forms and information concerning this assurance shall be routinized into each patient's records.

15. Psychiatric emergency care shall include evaluation, intervention and disposition:

a. *Evaluation* shall include assessment of the client's mental status, medical status as it relates to presenting symptoms, medication status, the family/job/housing situation and therapy status.

b. *Intervention* shall include the potential for face-to-face counseling for patient and family, and medication initiation, monitoring and detoxification, if needed.

c. *Disposition* shall include the capacity to arrange medical consultation and hospitilization, voluntary and involuntary psychiatric hospitalization, respite care placement, out-patient care, home visits, aftercare, day treatment, drug or alcohol programming, problem pregnancy help, spouse or child abuse help, children's services, adolescent services, geriatric services, services for the mentally retarded and social services as needed.

16. There shall be pharmaceutical and psychiatric emergency reference texts immediately available in the evaluation area.

17. There shall be written sharing of information between the emergency department and the disposition facility at least within 24 hours of transfer of the case but preferably, immediately.

18. Instructions for outpatient, follow-up services shall be written and given to the individual and/or family. They should at least include location, phone number, agency name, date of appointment.

19. There shall be written transfer agreements between the emergency department and the inpatient dispositional facilities.

20. There shall be 24-hour access to the in-patient dispositional facilities.

21. There shall be transportation protocols to the dispositional facilities.
22. There shall be a list of the dispositions for use by the emergency department staff.
23. No psychiatric emergency visit shall take longer than 18 hours for the patient from arrival in the emergency department to disposition.
24. There shall be a separate room/area available to evaluate and intervene with a psychiatric emergency patient.
    a. A room/area which respects the patient and family's dignity and privacy.
    b. A room/area which is designed to protect the patient, staff and other person's safety in the emergency department.
    c. A room/area which is contiguous to medical staff and medically equipped, should those services be needed immediately.
    d. The room/area should be equipped with a telephone, a desk, several chairs, an examining bed with side rails and restraints.
    e. There must be a room available to provide a secure, safe, locked, secluded, quiet environment.
    f. There must be provision in the emergency department for the patient's basic needs, including:
       1. Toileting
       2. Protection of property, including valuables
       3. Washing
       4. Nourishment
25. There shall be neuroleptic medication and other supplies deemed necessary by the nursing staff immediately available.
26. There shall be neurological, neurosurgical, medical, surgical, pathological, pharmacological and radiological consultation services immediately available.
27. There shall be laboratory services immediately available for body fluid testing and screening should these services be necessary.
28. There shall be social work/nursing staff to immediately involve the family or others who come with the patient for:

a. Information gathering
b. Coordination of the intervention with patient's family, lifestyle, current treatment
c. Crisis intervention with any of them where the need evolves while in the emergency department
d. Disposition planning with their needs considered
e. Primary prevention activities if time and circumstances permit.

29. There should be consideration for basic needs of family and significant others while they are in emergency department with the patient.
30. There shall be a staff person in the emergency department who is designated the case manager and synthesizer as well as one who is the designated authority with regard to each case.
31. The ongoing therapist, facility or clinic who has the patient in active treatment will be contacted by the emergency department staff in the process of the evaluation, whenever possible.
32. There shall be lists of available translators for the emergency department staff should they require language assistance to do their evaluation.
33. There shall be periodic testing of the psychiatric component of the emergency department to assess its accessibility, availability, effectiveness and efficacy.
34. There shall be regular, documented meetings of the emergency department staff to discuss administrative, supervisory, training, programmatic and client management issues.
35. There shall be documented liaison with the community being served.
    a. There shall be a citizen's advisory forum.
    b. There shall be written materials available to the public describing services.
    c. Emergency department staff shall be participants in community education efforts concerning emergency care and psychiatric emergency care issues.
36. There shall be a written plan to coordinate

with other agencies in the event of a disaster.

    a. This shall include coordination with a State plan.

    b. This shall include disaster preparedness training of staff.

37. Psychiatric emergency care services of emergency departments shall be certified periodically.

    a. Departments of Public Health will usually include this certification along with their certification of emergency departments.

    b. Psychiatric emergency care service components of emergency departments may be certified as "comprehensive" if they can show evidence of substantial compliance with the above standards.

    c. Designations of lesser degree than comprehensive will include: "general," "basic," or "unclassified" to indicate what level of limited capability they function as a psychiatric service component to an emergency department (AMA, 1980).

Guidelines for psychiatric emergency care in CMHCs

These guidelines are completely parallel to those of the emergency department. They carefully include reference to medical screening and capability to arrange for hospital emergency care if the center is separate from a hospital (Barton, 1979a).

Guidelines for psychiatric emergency care in a state mental hospital

The standards for the state mental hospital include much of the above standards. They also include close collaboration with local CMHCs and local general hospitals so that clients are not shuffled and lost among them. Written agreements between the different agencies to facilitate client flow are also emphasized. Medical and surgical consultations with hospitalization or the availability of consultants is stressed as well (Barton, 1979b).

CATEGORIZATION OF PSYCHIATRIC EMERGENCY SERVICES

Another form of standards, called categorization of emergency care services, has emerged. It is similar in its resulting statements as to what each facility should have, but it also includes a method of formalizing interrelationships.

Drafts dealing with categorization were compiled with much assistance to APA from ACEP, MDMH, and MDPH, and from previous AMA proposals. The APA draft describes categorization as follows: "Categorization of emergency services and facilities is being done on a national, state and regional level in order to facilitate emergency health care" (Barton, 1978a). Categorization should allow the development of an information base on what types and range of services are available at any one hospital. It could provide the basis for determining what services need to be upgraded in a region to obtain definitive care for any type of emergency. It could provide the information needed for an ambulance driver or any individual to choose which hospital could manage a particular problem and to what degree the severity of a problem could be managed.

Three ways to categorize, according to the two organizations (AMA and EMS) who have been most involved in the development of the scheme, are by horizontal, vertical, and circular grading.

HORIZONTAL. In horizontal categorization hospitals are graded according to the comprehensiveness of the emergency services provided. The entire spectrum of emergency service care would be categorized in the horizontal subclassification of *comprehensive;* a middle range of services would be considered *general;* a limited range would be considered *basic.* Another category, "major," had been placed between the categories "comprehensive" and "general" but has been dropped as superfluous. Designation of levels I, II, III, and IV has also been used to describe the decreasing comprehensiveness of emergency services (JCAH, 1980).

VERTICAL. Hospitals also can be graded vertically according to the specialty care capability and resources in selected critical care areas. Those having the most comprehensive, definitive treatment capabilities at least through the acute phase are considered *centers;* those able to manage cases from emergency through acute care but with more limited expertise and resources are considered *units;* those managing emergency care and acute care on an even more limited basis are considered *programs.* Many facilities might not even gain a vertical categorization label if their available resources are not geared toward a particular critical care area.

CIRCULAR. Circular categorization specifies the capability a region has to coordinate its emergency services and specialty care facilities.

Some emergency services, such as first aid provided by staff members from a sheriff's department, may not fall within this current schema. To create a system of care for their clientele, it is advised that staff members from these services identify where each level of care is available and develop ways to achieve access. This may require writing transportation agreements, service agreements, holding arrangements, and so on.

The categorization drafts which resulted from the Collaborative-APA effort actually are a refinement and restatement of the guidelines for standards for emergency departments provided earlier. Differences in the facilities' services would be seen in levels of staffing and how fast a response time would be expected. The vertical categorization also would differ in how elaborately a ward or unit would be staffed, how extensive a treatment program would be available, and how broad a range of client problems and age groups would be served.

PROTOCOLS FOR HANDLING SPECIFIC PSYCHIATRIC EMERGENCIES

Another result of the Collaborative-APA effort was construction of samples of protocols that focused on specific psychiatric problems. The one following is an example of a protocol for child abuse (Barton, 1979d).

Child abuse protocol

A. *Legal aspects*
1. Consider that there are legal and psychological responsibilities in this emergency care situation.

2. Purpose of laws:
   a. To identify children who are being abused for their protection and treatment.
   b. Recording of incidence and accumulation of statistics to demonstrate magnitude of problem.
3. Mandatory reporting in all but Alaska, Missouri, New Mexico, North Carolina, Texas, Washington. In these latter states reports may be made but are not required.
4. Who reports: the M.D. most often.
5. What:
   a. Serious physical injury(s) inflicted by other than accidental means by a parent or other person responsible for child's care.
   b. No report required for child who is dead, except in Arkansas (coroner's report) or Tennessee (undertaker's report) and now Illinois. Siblings thus are still vulnerable to similar fate in these states.
   c. Malnutrition now reported in Illinois, New Mexico and South Dakota.
6. To whom: varies by state.
7. Immunity clauses in all states except Minnesota, Oregon, and Wisconsin to allow M.D. reporting the alleged abuse without threat or fear of civil or criminal proceeding as result of the reporting. M.D. liable for prosecution if doesn't report.
B. *Prehospital phase of child abuse treatment*
1. Airway, breathing, circulation restoration if needed.
2. Assessment of extent of injuries.
3. Immobilization of fractures.
4. History taking, description of environment identification of witnesses, significant others.
5. Transport.
C. *Emergency Department Phase of Child Abuse Treatment*
1. Airway, breathing, circulation restoration.
2. Assessment of extent of injuries—use trauma/rape protocols.

3. Laboratory and X-ray examination.
4. History from relatives, neighbors, teachers.
5. With index of suspicion high, file abuse report.
6. Admit child.
7. Confront parents with impressions.
8. Provide counseling referral to parents.
9. Notify social service to consider evaluation of home situation especially in regard to siblings.

There are other sample protocols on such topics as drug intoxication, violence, restraints, and commitment available from the APA. It is the intent of the Collaborative-APA effort that these protocols will stimulate local psychiatric emergency care providers to systematize the handling of these cases. It is hoped they will add their own protocols to the samples and that these will be reflective of an optimal handling of such cases and not a reduction of the level of care to whatever the person on call feels like providing at the time.

There has been some degree of controversy about the development and use of detailed protocols for specific problems. Some critics have felt the cookbook approach will decrease creativity, set up the staff for malpractice if a step isn't followed, or slow down the speed of psychiatric emergency care delivery. Those who favor protocols believe that protocols will provide better, more thorough care, will lessen the likelihood of malpractice suits, will provide more assurance that the staff is acting appropriately, and will provide actual measures of quality assurance.

TRENDS

The goal of those who write standards is to improve the form and substance of emergency care. The Collaborative-APA effort is attempting to move such standard-setting bodies as JCAH, AMA, DOT, EMS, and NIMH toward more precise, appropriate, and comprehensive standards in psychiatric emergency care. Hard work and persistence at the national level of the collaborating organizationa may pay off—only time will tell. Greater effort to get many of these standards into state mental health codes and into legisla-tion may require a gigantic grass-roots effort by knowledgeable providers and community representatives. Otherwise the inertia in a ponderous health care system already plodding along providing a mediocre-to-poor level of care to a vulnerable population may persist.

ACKNOWLEDGMENTS

The author would like to take this opportunity to name the members of the APA Task Force on Psychiatric Emergency Care Issues who shared their thoughts in the meetings through which evolved the many drafts penned by her. Stephen Soreff, M.D.; Andrew Slaby, M.D.; John Petrich, M.D.; and Clotilde Bowen, M.D.; active consultants were: Bonnie Fauman, M.D.; Michael Fauman, M.D., Ph.D.; Betsy Comstock, M.D.; Paul McClelland, M.D.; Lucy Ozarin, M.D.; Elinor Walker; Kenneth Pitts, M.D.; Judith Jacobs, D.P.H.; Marion Fane; J. Michael Foxworth, M.D.; and residents Raul Gomez, M.D., and John Friedman, M.D.

BIBLIOGRAPHY

American Medical Association: Categorization of hospitals, Chicago, 1976, The Association.

American Medical Association, Commission on Emergency Medical Services: Behavioral emergencies, draft of guidelines for the categorization of hospital emergency capabilities, Chicago, Aug. 1980, The Association.

Barton, G.: Categorization scheme proposal for psychiatric emergency care settings, draft developed with the Task Force on Emergency Care Issues for the American Psychiatric Association, Washington, D.C. 1978a.

Barton, G.: Working draft of definition developed for Task Force on Psychiatric Emergency Care Issues for the American Psychiatric Association, Washington, D.C., 1978b.

Barton, G.: Proposed guidelines for a comprehensive community mental health center emergency services unit, draft developed with the Task Force on Psychiatric Emergency Care Issues for the American Psychiatric Association, Washintgon, D.C., 1979a.

Barton, G.: Proposed standards for the emergency services component of a state hospital, draft developed with the Task Force on Psychiatric Emergency Care Issues for the American Psychiatric Association, Washington, D.C., 1979b.

Barton, G.: Proposed standards for a mental health component of a hospital emergency department, draft developed with the Task Force on Psychiatric Emergency Care Issues for the American Psychiatric Association, Washington, D.C., 1979c.

Barton, G.: Sample protocols for psychiatric emergencies, drafts developed with the Task Force on Psychiatric Emergency Care Issues for the American Psychiatric Association, Washington, D.C., 1979d.

Barton, G.: Rural psychiatric emergency care, draft developed with the Task Force on Psychiatric Emergency Care Issues for the American Psychiatric Association, Washington, D.C., 1979e.

Barton, G.: A comparison of standards with clinical psychiatric emergency settings in Michigan: a preliminary study, speech given at University of Michigan, Ann Arbor, March 1981.

Hartman, K., and Allison, J.: A comparison of NIMH standards for CMHC's and JCAH's principles for accreditation of CMH service programs, Lincoln, Neb., April 1978, Department of Public Institutions.

Joint Commission on Accreditation of Hospitals: Consolidated standards: for child, adolescent, and adult psychiatric, alcoholism and drug abuse programs, Chicago, 1979a, The Commission.

Joint Commission on Accreditation of Hospitals: Principles for accreditation of community mental health service programs, Chicago, 1976, The Commission.

Joint Commission on Accreditation of Hospitals: Prin-ciples for accreditation of community mental health service programs, Chicago, Aug. 1979b, The Commission.

Joint Commission on Accreditation of Hospitals: Accreditation manual for hospitals, Chicago, 1980, The Commission.

Michigan Blue Cross/Blue Shield: List of diagnoses covered by Michigan Blue Cross/Blue Shield, Lansing, Mich., 1980.

Michigan Department of Public Health, Division of Emergency Medical Services, Planning and Evaluation Section: Draft of behavioral criteria for categorization, Lansing, Mich., 1980, The Department.

National Institute of Mental Health: National standards for community mental health centers, Rockville, Md., 1977, The Institute.

Nelson, S.H.: Standards affecting mental health care: a review and commentary, Am. J. Psychiatry 136(3): 303, March 1979.

Ware, J.R.: The sayings of Confucius: the teachings of China's greatest sage—a translation, New York, 1955, The New American Library, Inc.

Webster's new collegiate dictionary, Springfield, Mass., 1977, G & C Merriman Co.

White, K.: Expert witnesses can shape standards of care, Mich. Medicine 80:67, Feb. 1981.

CHAPTER 21

Legal issues

Michael J. Rice, R.N., M.S.N.

The argument that societal intervention is appropriate when the individual is suffering from conduct described as a combination of dangerousness and mental illness, asks psychiatry and psychiatrists to do exactly what they have been most castigated for allegedly doing—namely being agents of the establishment (Peszke, 1975, pg. 76. Courtesy Charles C Thomas, Publishers, Springfield, Ill.)

IMPACT OF THE LAW

At no time in the history of mental health has the law had such a dramatic impact on care delivery as it does today. Within the last decade approximately two thirds of the state legislatures have rewritten their mental health laws (Ennis, 1978). Most of the state mental health statutes have incorporated changes that have limited the powers of mental health professionals and have reinforced client's right safeguards (Ennis, 1978). However, no area of mental health law has protected fewer of the client's rights or provided fewer safeguards than those areas that cover emergency psychiatric care (Ennis and Siegel, 1973).

The fact that psychiatric emergency care laws have not been altered to provide more client's rights safeguards is noteworthy in relation to recent judicial actions. State supreme courts have been requested to hand down decisions on cases questioning such issues as the legality of commitment statutes and the right of involuntary clients to refuse medications. Although few of the recent court cases directly address psychiatric emergency problems, they provide definite implications for the practice of psychiatric emergency care.

The court rulings and altered legislation are in response to the need for clearly defined client civil liberties. Groups such as the Network Against Psychiatric Assault and the American Civil Liberties Union (ACLU) and even legislated client advocacy boards have defined their view of mental clients' rights. These definitions are often in conflict with the viewpoint held by mental health professionals. The resultant legal clashes have had a dramatic effect on mental health care. For example, judicial rulings in the *Rennie vs. Klein* case have raised serious questions about the right of an involuntary client to refuse psychotropic medications (Roth, 1979). Court actions such as the Rennie decision have caused mental health professionals to examine the treatment approaches that they may use in psychiatric emergency care situations.

Emergency care clinicians also face the job of defining the legal boundaries of their practice according to two types of law, statutory and decisional. Statutory law is law that is passed by a state or federal legislative body (Creighton, 1970). Statutory law is often enacted through a regulatory agency such as the Department of Health. This regulatory agency enforces the statutory law through the establishment and publication of codes defining the practice guidelines of the statute. These codes, although often called regulatory or administrative laws, are only extensions of the original statute and not laws themselves. When the statutory law has an effect on the rights of individuals, it is frequently taken to the judicial system for constitutional clarification. The decision of the court on the issue is called decisional law (Willig, 1970). The decisional law, because of its constitutional foundation, is then the final guideline for those people affected by the original statute.

Recently the judicial system has established new decisional laws on psychotropic drug use and treatment approaches, which have constitutionally clarified sections of statutory mental health laws. It is anticipated that as the client advocate segments of society continue to push for further definitions of client's rights, psychiatric emergency care will be redefined. The impact of new laws on care delivery will require psychiatric emergency clinicians to become more aware of decisional and statutory law as well as the attitude of society toward the care of the mentally ill.

Client advocates

With the passage of new mental health legislation in the late 1960s, and an increased consumer awareness of psychiatric care, many people became concerned about the rights of the mentally ill. This concern was manifested in the formation of several client's rights activist groups. The viewpoint of these advocates has been that the civil and constitutional rights of the mental client outweigh the rights of the state in the treatment process. Unfortunately, mental health professionals have been cast as opponents of client's rights (Hoffman and Dunn, 1976). This is largely a result of the mental health professionals' role in supporting and enacting those state laws mandating involuntary detention and treatment.

Judicial involvement

Judicial involvement in mental client's rights began in 1966 when the District of Columbia Court of Appeals heard the case of *Rouse v. Cameron*. This was the first case that recognized the right of the involuntary committed mental client to treatment. In a landmark decision, the Court of Appeals ruled that all clients had a right to receive an individual treatment plan and periodic reevaluation of that treatment plan (Stone, 1975).

The next landmark case occurred in the Alabama Supreme Court in 1971. The Alabama Court heard the *Wyatt v. Stickney* case, which dealt with the conditions of the state mental hospitals in Alabama (Stone, 1975). The case was built on the fundamental right of all people under the Constitution to receive humane treatment. This right was upheld by the court, and in 1972 the court enforced its ruling. The court defined for the State of Alabama the standards of care that all people had the right to receive in Alabama hospitals (Stone, 1975).

Perhaps the most publicized case of this type was *O'Connor v. Donaldson.* On June 26, 1975, the U.S. Supreme Court ruled on the case, stating that a person who is not dangerous and can care for himself cannot be hospitalized without being treated (Reinert, 1979). The ruling held strong implications of liability for practicing mental health professionals. This court's ruling recognized that a mental health professional who violated a person's constitutional right to freedom was liable for damages (Clayton, 1976).

Legislative reaction

The court decisions on mental client's rights did not go unnoticed by the state legislatures. Many of the legislatures were already under pressure from client advocates to include client's rights safeguards in their mental health acts. The resulting mental health legislation contained some radically altered concepts. The most noted mental health act was California's Lanterman-Petris-Short Act of 1969. The LPS Act formalized a number of rights, including (1) limitations on the length of time a person could be held involuntarily in a psychiatric facility; (2) a judicial review of all involuntary cases; (3) an ongoing mechanism for the treatment, supervision, and placement of gravely disabled clients, and (4) encouragement of the use of all the available community mental health service agencies. The LPS Act also limited the type of client who could be involuntarily detained to those who were suicidal, homicidal, or gravely disabled.

The LPS Act was particularly significant because of the treatment limitations and client's rights safeguards that it gave to mental health professionals. Recently, new provisions for utilization review and advocacy review boards have been added to the California Welfare and Institutions Code, of which the LPS Act is a part. These provisions allow the state to utilize client rights review boards to systematically review the care delivered to all involuntarily detained patients.

PSYCHIATRIC EMERGENCY CARE

The field of psychiatric emergency care is a relatively new subspecialty of mental health which grew out of the need to provide care for the many psychosocial problems that confronted staffs of the emergency departments in general hospitals (Peszke, 1975). Because the field is new, it has not yet standardized its unique nomenclature and procedures. Some of these terms may soon require a legal definition. Terms like *emergency hospitalization, emergency commitment,* and *involuntary commitment* are often used interchangeably when referring to the same procedure but may refer to different procedures as defined within the state mental health statutes.

Psychiatric emergency procedures

Psychiatric emergency care procedures are basically those procedures used to allow for the apprehension and detention of persons who require immediate care and evaluation (Brooks, 1974). Most state mental health statutes include the categories of emergency detention, emergency evaluation, and emergency commitments in the section relating to psychiatric emergency care. The emergency procedures provide few, if any, client's rights safeguards and involve the least amount of administrative paperwork (Ennis and Siegel, 1973). Psychiatric emergency procedures may be initiated by the police, health officers, or a court judge. However, a court hearing is required by only 14 states before authorization of the emergency procedure (Brooks, 1974).

The psychiatric emergency procedures are intended to facilitate the hospitalization of the mentally ill under dire circumstances. Unfortunately, there is a serious question as to the validity of the application of these emergency procedures. The ACLU argues that the emergency procedures are used for most involuntary admissions, thereby denying the client the right to a court hearing (Ennis and Siegel, 1973). The ACLU also states that the abuse of the emergency procedures has resulted in the emergency procedure becoming the standard procedure for hospitalization (Ennis and Siegel, 1973). Their argument is supported by the statistics on New York City which show that the emergency procedure was used for 99% of all involuntarily hospitalized clients (Ennis and Siegel, 1973). This fact raises grave questions about the definition of

347

the emergency for which the mentally ill are hospitalized.

VOLUNTARY VERSUS INVOLUNTARY STATUS

Social reaction to the mentally ill has gone from one extreme to the other. In the 18th century, society held a concerned but uninvolved attitude toward the mentally ill. Although the mentally ill were cared for in a custodial manner, they were often viewed as a source of entertainment for the public (Mora, 1975). Not until the advent of the concepts of civil liberties and democracy did social attitudes become more paternalistic. In the 19th century, society began to pressure the state to assume a role in carrying out society's good intentions toward the mentally ill. It was during this time that the first involuntary commitment laws were enacted.

As governmental agencies assumed a more paternal approach, some people became increasingly concerned about the need for expedient treatment of the mentally ill. Often parents, family, and friends would approach the judicial system to commit the mentally ill for treatment. However, in the 1960s new mental health legislation radically altered the focus of society's paternalistic attitude. Social emphasis was placed on the mentally ill client's civil liberties rather than on their need for treatment. This emphasis on client's rights resulted in many legal battles between client's right activists and mental health professionals. Often the mental health professionals found themselves facing adversarial courts that expounded on the rights of the mentally ill (Treffert and Krojeck, 1976). The judicial systems' rapid response to the client's rights issue was unprecedented in the history of the law (Ennis, 1978).

The state legislatures also responded to the client's rights issues and quickly rewrote their mental health statutes. These new mental health acts specified for the first time the types of clients who could be committed to a psychiatric facility. The commitment clauses of the mental health acts for the 50 states vary greatly and not all support the concept of due process as a safeguard for the client's civil rights (Brooks, 1974).

Emergency commitment criteria

Almost all state statutes have provisions that define the criteria for emergency commitment in terms of whether or not the client is (1) a danger to self; (2) a danger to others; or (3) unable to provide or obtain food, shelter, and clothing. The causal factor for these categories must be "due to mental illness." The presence of mental illness, however, does not have to be diagnosed by a mental health professional in all states. Some state mental health statutes, like New York's, state that the emergency commitment procedure may be initiated by anyone (Brooks, 1974).

The "danger to self" category was intended to provide for the treatment of a person who had expressed the intent, or exhibited an overt act, which would result in great bodily harm or death. Basically, this category is used to cover two types of clients: (1) the potential suicide and (2) the person who, as the result of an acute mental illness, is unable to protect himself from physical harm (Brooks, 1974).

There is little difficulty in diagnosing potentially suicidal clients and appropriately hospitalizing them according to law. There is, however, controversy about the use of the danger to self category for mentally incapacitated clients. Typical examples of this second type of client are young adult schizophrenics who, because of their mental illness, unknowingly place themselves in dangerous situations (Seigel et al., 1978). Psychiatric evaluations of this type of client often vary. While many staff members see the clients as passively dangerous to themselves, others feel that they are more in need of treatment but too ill to seek it (Brooks, 1974). What the controversy does suggest is that the definition of danger to self may need further clarification to be applied to the severely disorganized client.

Psychiatric emergency care staff have found the "danger to others" category the most difficult to define. The concept of dangerousness is difficult to define and few statutory definitions are of benefit (Brooks, 1974). The primary problem facing psychiatric emergency care staff in the use of this category is determining whether or not the danger to others is a result of an acute mental illness. California's LPS Act (Section 5003) clearly specified that: "This part (section) shall not be construed to repeal or modify laws relating to the commitment of mentally disordered sex offenders and mentally disordered criminal offenders" (California Department of Mental Health, 1979, p. 1). The difficulty in making the distinction between the mentally ill criminal who is dangerous and the mentally ill client may be the result of mental health professionals' lack of experience working with the criminal population rather than any deficiency in clinical skills.

A second major problem with the danger to others category lies in the controversy about mental health professionals' ability to predict dangerousness. Civil libertarians, such as members of the ACLU, contend that the mental health professionals' ability to predict dangerousness is at best very poor. The ACLU cites the Operation Baxtrom report on violence prediction as an instance where almost 100% of the psychiatrists' predictions of dangerousness were wrong (Ennis and Siegel, 1973).

Obviously, the problems involved in using the danger to others category are complex and come with no easy answers. Even California's LPS Act allows for involuntary hospitalization of only those who are imminently dangerous but offers little in terms of a more concrete definition (Brooks, 1974). The psychiatric emergency care staff may have to rely on a rational judgment of the risks of releasing the client versus the benefits of treating the client when using the danger to others category.

The criteria for the "gravely disabled" category have also posed problems for the psychiatric emergency care staff. California's LPS Act defined the gravely disabled as follows: "The condition in which a person, as the result of a mental disorder, is unable to provide for his basic personal needs of food, clothing or shelter" (California Department of Mental Health, 1979, p. 4).

Historically these are the persons who have been involuntarily committed. The gravely disabled client is often stereotyped as elderly, chronically ill, and needing treatment. There have been many variations in the definition of the gravely disabled criteria. Perhaps the most significant was the U.S. Supreme Court opinion in

the *O'Connor v. Donaldson* case. The Supreme Court ruled that persons could not be involuntarily hospitalized if they could rely on family or friends to provide food, shelter, and clothing (Clayton, 1976).

In practice, clients have been labeled as gravely disabled when their behavior did not indicate the use of the homicidal or suicidal categories. It is not uncommon to see the displaced elderly, the indigent, and the culturally maladjusted admitted to the hospital as gravely disabled. These people seldom have a mental illness but have been brought to the hospital when more appropriate social services could not be found.

Emergency commitment procedures

Emergency commitment procedures vary from state to state. Ten states have no emergency commitment statute but use common law as a rationale for the emergency care of the mentally ill (Brook, 1974). The general format for these emergency commitment procedures is that a police officer or a designated mental health professional may initiate the emergency procedure for the purpose of evaluation or detention. This emergency commitment procedure may be enacted only if the client has exhibited behaviors indicating a danger to self or others or is incapable of obtaining food, shelter, and clothing. The time limits allowed for the emergency detention range from 24 hours in Georgia to 30 days in Oklahoma (Brooks, 1974). The average period for emergency detentions usually is 3 to 7 days.

The use of a temporary detention period in conjunction with emergency commitment for evaluation varies from one state statute to the next. Hypothetically, emergency commitment procedures allow a client to be "detained" only until admission to a hospital can be scheduled (Brooks, 1974) These emergency detentions often occur without allowing the client the right to a hearing. Several states have tried to cover the legalities of the emergency detention by establishing separate emergency detention procedures. Currently, 27 state statutes allow temporary detention periods that are used for both evaluation and treatment (Brooks, 1974).

349

Prior judicial hearing

Emergency commitment procedures do not usually require that a judicial review be held before the initiation of the procedure. The states with statutes that do not require a probable cause hearing for emergency commitment have encountered difficulties because of the 1972 Wisconsin ruling in the case of *Lessard v. Schmidt.* This case focused on the client's right to a due process hearing before any commitment proceeding. The Wisconsin court concurred, stating that any person has the constitutional right to be present at their mental health commitment hearing (Kopolow, 1978). It is clear that the Lessard ruling requires all mental health professionals to carefully evaluate the issues of emergency hospitalization and the client's right to a prior judicial hearing (Kopolow, 1978).

Notification of rights

Client notification of rights is one of the most neglected procedural issues of psychiatric emergency care. Notification of rights is often withheld even in states whose statutes do provide for notification (Brooks, 1974). Furthermore, in states where nonjudicial commitment is possible, the mental health statutes seldom make reference to the client's right to prior notification (Kittrie, 1971).

Mental health professionals often state that notification is anxiety producing and that this is a rationale for not notifying clients of their rights (Kittrie, 1971). Some legal writers also argue that the client's interests are protected more when notification is withheld. However, client advocates feel that no situation could be more traumatic than an emergency commitment (Kittrie, 1971) and that notification should be a formal procedure that could be enforced by the courts (Ennis and Siegel, 1973).

The judicial system has not as yet ruled on the client's right to notification in emergency commitment situations. There is, however, a court case that has direct implication for notification of rights in *any* commitment procedure. In the *Suzuki v. Quisenberry* case in Hawaii, a federal judge ruled that the state mental health commitment law was unconstitutional because it lacked the procedures necessary for adequate notification of client's rights (Ennis, 1978). From this it may be inferred that it is illegal to withhold notification of a client's rights in any emergency commitment procedure.

California's Welfare and Institutions Code is one of the few state statutes requiring that clients be notified of their rights in an emergency commitment procedure. The California statute emergency commitment notification procedure is detailed and complex. At the time of a client's apprehension, the authorized official or mental health professional is required to read the following statement:

> "My name is _____ . I am a (position) with (name of agency). You are not under criminal arrest, but I am taking you for examination by mental health professionals at (name of facility). You will be told your rights by the mental health staff" (California Department of Mental Health, 1979, p. 10).

If clients are apprehended at their residence, then the following statement must also be read:

> "You may bring a few personal items with you which I will have to approve. You can make a phone call and/or leave a note to tell your friends and/or family where you have been taken" (California Department of Mental Health, 1979, p. 10).

Once the client arrives at the emergency evaluation facility, the psychiatric emergency care staff often repeat this information. It is usually repeated because there is concern that detaining personnel may not have made the required statement during the apprehension of the client. The psychiatric emergency care staff are also responsible for giving the client a form that adheres to the following format:

> "My name is _____ . My position is _____ . You are being placed into the psychiatric facility because it is our professional opinion that as a result of mental disorder, you are (criteria for emergency commitment). We feel this is true because (facts on which allegation is based). You will be held for a period up to 72 hours. This does not include weekends or holidays. Your 72-hour period begins (date and time)" (California Department of Mental Health, 1979, p. 10).

After completing the notification, emergency care staff members are required to complete a record of advisement. There are situations, such as overdoses, when the emergency staff cannot notify clients of their rights. When notification cannot be accomplished, then the staff must keep a record of the reason that notification was not completed. Notification of rights must then be done at the earliest possible date and recorded.

Obviously, even with California's detailed notification procedure, not all clients receive notice of their rights. The strength of any law rests in the hands of those who apply it. The psychiatric emergency care staff members of any state, regardless of statute provisions, bear the ethical and legal responsibility for notifying clients of their rights.

INFORMED CONSENT OF MEDICATION USE

The prescription and administration of medications have long been solely at the discretion of physicians and nurses. Both physicians and nurses have promulgated that education, research, and clinical experience have provided them with a unique expertise concerning medications. Surprisingly, recent court rulings and client advocate stances have radically altered the administration of psychoactive agents, even in psychiatric emergency care areas.

Many client advocates, including former mental clients, feel that physicians and nurses have at times used psychotropic medications not only for treatment but also as punishment when the clients refuse to comply with the staff's demands (Brooks, 1974). Client's rights advocates additionally argue that the mentally ill are not adequately informed as to the possible hazards of receiving psychotropic medications (Flynn, 1979). The client's rights advocates feel that all clients treated with psychotropic medications should be informed of all the side effects of the drugs, such as tardive dyskinesia (an irreversible neurological condition that can cause twitching of facial and skeletal muscles).

The problem of informed consent for medication use has sparked a large controversy in the area of psychiatric emergency care. The core issue facing emergency care mental health professionals is, "Is it moral or humane to withhold medication that would improve the quality of a client's life in the interest of protecting his civil rights?" Many physicians and nurses do not think it is in the client's best interest to withhold medicinal treatment. They maintain that full disclosure of the potential side effects of the medications would frighten clients more than it would reassure them. The issue is one of balancing the benefits of medication with the risks of adequately informing the client.

Informed consent

Informed consent has a wide range of definitions. Fundamentally, *informed consent* means that a client consents to medical treatment knowing both the benefits and the possible risks of that treatment. The concept first became an issue in the United States in 1914 in the case of *Schloendorff v. New York Hospital* (Fine, 1977). Since that time, there has been growing concern about informed consent procedures, which has peaked within the last decade, largely as a result of several court cases that have had a major impact on health care in the United States.

The first modern landmark court ruling on informed consent was the *Cobbs v. Grant* case in 1972. The California Supreme Court ruled that a physician must inform the patient adequately from a legal standpoint and not from a medical standpoint (Fine, 1977). The ruling further specified that the client must be informed of any potential risks and the possible alternatives to a proposed procedure.

For psychiatric emergency areas the *Cobbs v. Grant* ruling presents an awkward dilemma. Are acutely psychotic clients competent enough to give legal informed consent? Many psychiatric emergency clinicians argue that informed consent cannot be obtained from psychotic clients because their psychosis has rendered them incompetent. However, the judicial system does not concur with this argument.

The judicial system feels that the presence of a mental illness does not imply that a person is mentally incompetent (Brotman, 1978). The courts state emphatically that incompetency can only be determined by the court, a process that may take several weeks. This is because the court often solicits testimony from several expert witnesses to establish grounds for a decision on a person's competency (Brotman, 1978).

The implications for psychiatric emergency care are clear. Only in life-threatening emergencies can the informed consent procedures be waived. Psychiatric emergency staff members cannot ignore the informed consent procedures when a person enters the unit with a mental illness, regardless of the client's suspected incompetence.

Informed consent for involuntary clients

The problem of informed consent presents the psychiatric emergency care staff with a difficult problem when faced with emergency commitments. The primary difficulty centers on the use of psychotropic medications without informed consent. Unfortunately, the guidelines are nebulous and vague for the emergency care staff faced with the problem.

The first court case on the informed consent of an involuntary client was the landmark *Rennie v. Klein* case of 1978 in New Jersey. Rennie had been diagnosed as having a manic depressive illness. The mental health staff wanted to treat him with varying doses of fluphenazine and chlorpromazine for homicidal behavior. Mr. Rennie refused treatment and through his attorney obtained two court injunctions that prohibited the staff from administering the medications. The court's final decision on the case was that involuntary clients have the right to refuse medications (Roth, 1979).

The right of an involuntary client to refuse medication was also reinforced by the U.S. District Court of Appeals in Massachusetts in the 1979 case of *Rogers v. Okin* (Herrington, 1979). The court ruled that on the basis of the First Amendment an involuntary client had the right to refuse drug treatment in order to be free of involuntary mind control (Herrington, 1979). Similar court cases that could place strict limits on the use of psychotropic drugs are pending in many states (Campbell, 1978).

The majority of psychiatric emergency care

staff members usually feel secure giving medications without obtaining informed consent. Often they rely on the doctrine that informed consent is not required by the law in emergency situations (Foster, 1978). However, in light of the Rennie and Rogers decisions, the use of medications in emergency care situations should be reevaluated. The question now is, "Who decides when an emergency exists?" (Flynn, 1979). Do emergency care staff members or the courts decide? Presently no clear answer exists.

THE LEAST RESTRICTIVE ALTERNATIVE

Clients who have been brought to the psychiatric emergency unit have had a number of their rights denied. Even more of the clients' rights are denied if they become threatening or assaultive and are placed in seclusion or restraints. The psychiatric emergency care staff members resort to such restrictive modes of management because of their clinical and legal responsibilities. Such clinical actions are now being evaluated according to the "least restrictive alternative" concept.

The least restrictive alternative concept has several definitions, but basically it implies that clients should be managed in a fashion that will restrict the fewest number of their rights. The concept first appeared in the 1966 *Lake v. Cameron* case. Ms. Lake was an elderly, confused woman who was committed to St. Elizabeth's Hospital in Washington, D.C. Her attorney filed suit in District Court, stating that she could be managed in an environment that restricted fewer of her rights (Brooks, 1974). Ms. Lake died before a less restrictive alternative was arranged. However, the concept of the "new client right" had been born and was reinforced in other court cases. In 1973 another District of Columbia court used the least restrictive alternative concept as a basis for ruling in the *Dixon v. Weinberger* case. The court concurred with the client's request stating that clients have a legal right to be confined in the least restrictive environment available (Kopolow, 1978).

As support for the least restrictive alternative concept grew, the judicial system began to utilize it as a basis for justifying rulings. In 1976 the

Alabama Supreme Court ruled in the case of *Wyatt v. Stickney* that, even when using medications, mental health professionals should attempt to achieve treatment goals through the use of the least restrictive alternative (Harvis, 1979). This ruling implies that the psychiatric emergency staff must use the lowest level of medication possible to treat the client.

The seclusion or restraint alternative

The psychiatric emergency staff must use seclusion or restraints on clients to prevent staff or client injury from violent client attacks. Legally emergency care staff members are obligated to protect clients from harm or self-injury. This use of both seclusion and restraints must be reevaluated in light of the least restrictive alternative concept.

The process of seclusion has definitions that range from social isolation to involuntary confinement. The California Welfare and Institutions Code (Title IX) defines seclusion as "the involuntary placement of an individual in a locked room." The California Code also states that seclusion cannot be used as punishment or in lieu of a less restrictive treatment alternative (California Department of Mental Health, 1979). These statutory guidelines require that the mental health staff investigate and use less restrictive treatment modalities before resorting to the use of seclusion. Clearly, anyone who violates the statutes is legally liable to the client for any infringement of the client's rights.

Although the definition of *restraints* is not as clear, it is safe to assume that the concept of the least restrictive alternative also applies. The application of either cloth (soft) or leather restraints cannot be punitive or be substituted for a less restrictive intervention.

CONFIDENTIALITY

The concept of maintaining a client's confidence has been considered sacred in even the briefest psychotherapeutic contacts. This presents psychiatric emergency staff members with difficulties, as they are often contacted by the police, secret service investigators, family, friends, and employers who wish to locate the client or to be kept informed about a client's condition. On the reverse side, the issue of confidentiality has also caused psychiatric emergency staff members much frustration when they attempt to obtain information about a client from past therapists and treatment facilities. The confidentiality of a client is always maintained except when the therapist is required to breach a confidence by law or if the client's life is in imminent danger (Brooks, 1974). Recently, however, court cases regarding client confidentiality versus social rights to know have created problems in providing treatment.

Social versus client needs

The issue of society's rights to know versus client's confidentiality was first highlighted in the *Tarasoff v. University of California Regents* case in 1976. In this case a client told his therapist that he had plans to harm a woman readily identifiable as Ms. Tarasoff. The therapist was concerned but let the client leave. The therapist later discussed the case with a supervisor and contacted the campus police, although no effective action was taken (Brooks, 1974).

Ms. Tarasoff was killed by the client, and her parents instituted the lawsuit. The therapist's attorney argued that the therapist could not have contacted anyone without breaching confidentiality, which was illegal. However, the court ruled that when a specific person is in danger, a breach of client confidentiality is not only allowed but is required to protect the interests of the third party. The court further ruled that the therapist had an obligation to notify the intended victim and the police of the client's threat.

This California Court of Appeals ruling caused much consternation among mental health professionals. The court had in essence stated that a psychotherapist was legally obligated to breach a client's confidence under certain circumstances. Those circumstances were defined as the threat of danger to a third person not involved in the therapeutic process.

Such a breach of client confidentiality was not recommended by the California Court of Appeals in the 1977 *Bellah v. Greenson* case. In this case a disturbed young woman made plans to commit suicide. Before the issue could be resolved in therapy, the client followed through with her suicide plans and died. Her parents subsequently brought suit against the therapist, stating that when a life was at risk, the therapist had an obligation to breach the client's confidentiality. The court, however, disagreed and ruled that, although the therapist is required to breach confidentiality to communicate the risk of an assault on a third party, the therapist is not required to do so when there is a risk of the client's inflicting self-harm (California Court of Appeals, 1977).

State regulation

The concept of confidentiality is mentioned in the ethical codes of most mental health disciplines. It is not, however, covered in all state statutes. Presently only 36 states and the District of Columbia have statutes on physician-client confidentiality (Barton and Sanborn, 1978a). The number of states having confidentiality statutes is significant when considering the use of client confidentiality in court. The strength of a confidentiality stance in any court depends on the language of the state statute. Unfortunately, many of these confidentiality statutes are too vague to be of value (Barton and Sanborn, 1978a).

Many mental health professionals are confused or unaware of the legal aspects of confidentiality privileges. First, confidentality is a privilege. It is a statutory grant made to individuals who are at risk of having their privacy invaded (Barton and Sanborn, 1978a). As previously noted, not all states have legislation that grants the privilege of confidentiality. Furthermore, the privilege of confidentiality is a client's privilege and not the psychotherapist's privilege (Grossman, 1978). It should, however, be noted that although it is not a therapist's privilege, the ethical codes of all health professions uphold the need to maintain a client's confidence. Finally, it must be understood that often the judicial system has taken the stance that there are circumstances when society's constitutional rights to know override the client's privilege of confidentiality (Grossman, 1978).

THE MEDICAL RECORD: THE SIGNIFICANCE OF DOCUMENTATION

The initiation of documenting care is generally credited to Phillipe Pinel during the French Revolution (Mora, 1975). Today, accurate documentation holds many of the keys to relieving mental health professionals' anxiety regarding the legal requirements for emergency care. With the increased incidence of lawsuits and legal inquiries into client's rights, the medical record has become a legal document that can be used as evidence in legal procedures (Streiff, 1975).

Documentation of rights

The medical record is the emergency care staff's written account of the care delivered to a client from the time of admission to discharge. With the current emphasis on client's rights, the psychiatric emergency clinician can use the record to document admission status, notification of rights, and attempts to use less restrictive treatment alternatives.

Some states, such as California, have legislated the basic informational content on client's rights that is to be documented in the chart by the psychiatric emergency staff (see section on emergency commitment). Whatever the method of documentation used, the emergency care staff is required to document if emergency detention holds were applied, who initiated the hold, and whether the advisement was completed.

The type and amount of documentation necessary for an emergency commitment varies according to the guidelines of the state's mental health statutes (see emergency commitment procedures). There are, however, some constants that should be included on all involuntary hold forms placed in the chart.

The emergency detention or "hold" form should include the following information:

1. The statutory title of the hold and the mental health statutes relating to the hold.
2. The name and address of the client being detained.
3. The conditions on which the client was apprehended for evaluation (behavior noted and allegations).

4. The category under which the client was apprehended (suicidal, homicidal, or gravely disabled) and verification that notification has occurred.
5. The signature of the persons who apprehended the client and an address or phone number where they can be contacted.
6. The initial observations and evaluation of the psychiatric emergency clinicians.
7. The category under which the hold will be continued (suicidal, homicidal, or gravely disabled).
8. The signature and title of the emergency staff members who authorized the hold.
9. The address of the facility where the hold is initiated.

The form used (Fig. 21-1) should include a carbon copy that will be placed in the emergency chart to verify the conditions on which the hold was instituted.

Because of the controversy about a client's notification of rights (see emergency commitment procedures section), the psychiatric emergency care staff should also include a form verifying the notification of a client's rights. Each notification of psychiatric emergency detention form should include the following information:

1. Client's name and address.
2. The name and professional title of the emergency care staff member initiating the hold.
3. The notification statement (Fig. 21-2).
4. The official name of the psychiatric emergency facility where the hold was instituted.
5. The mental health statute and relevant statute codes that authorize the emergency detention.
6. The category (suicidal, homicidal, or gravely disabled) under which the client is being detained.
7. The rationale for applying the hold (based on allegations and observations of suicidal, homicidal, or gravely disabled behavior).
8. The time period during which the client may be held on the emergency hold.
9. Statement if the emergency detention may lead to further hospitalization.

10. The time and date that the emergency detention was initiated.
11. The signature of the client (if possible).
12. The signature of the emergency staff member notifying the client of the hold.

The Notice of Emergency Psychiatric Detention form (Fig. 21-2) should include a carbon copy that can be placed in the chart to document that notification was completed by the staff.

As a result of the client's condition, the psychiatric emergency staff may not be able to formally notify the client of the conditions under which the emergency detention was instituted. In these circumstances the psychiatric emergency staff should document that notification was not completed. If a form is used (Fig. 21-3), it should include the following:

1. Title of form.
2. Emergency facility's title.
3. Statement that notification of emergency psychiatric detention has not occurred.
4. Client's full name.
5. Client's address.
6. Reason notification was not completed.
7. Category under which the client is being held.
8. Name and title of emergency staff who completed the form.
9. Date form was completed.
10. Phone number at which staff member can be contacted.

If clients are later transferred to an inpatient unit, then copies of the Psychiatric Emergency Detention, the Notice of Psychiatric Emergency Detention, and the Record of Incomplete Notification should accompany them.

Consent to treatment

It is difficult to identify even general guidelines for documenting consent to treatment. This is because it is a futile exercise to attempt to legally define standards of informed consent (Barton and Sanborn, 1978b). If the consent is obtained, then psychiatric emergency care staff members are faced with the problem of justifying in the charts the validity of consent from a psychotic person. Since staff members might be taken into court, documentation of informed

Psychiatric Emergency Detention

(State Mental Health Statute and Code)

Under the provisions of (State Mental Health Code) emergency
evaluation and/or detention at   (name of emergency facility) is
requested for (client's name) currently residing at (address,
city, and state)   This request is being made based on the
following information:

> (Allegations and observations of person apprehending the
> client.)

For these reasons I/we believe that the above named should be
held for evaluation/treatment because as the result of a mental
illness, they are (check categories): Dangerous to self_____
Dangerous to others_____Gravely disabled _____. I/we have____
have not_____notified the above named person of the reasons for
emergency detention.

Name_____ Phone number _____ Date ___/___/___

(To be completed by emergency facility)

Through evaluation/observation the following facts have been
obtained:

For these reasons, I believe that the above named person is in
need of evaluation/treatment at   (facility)   for a period not
to exceed (statute time limit) without a prior judicial hearing.
In my evaluation the person is, as the result of a mental illness:
Dangerous to self____Dangerous to others____Gravely disabled____.

The hold shall begin at ___(hour)__ on _____(date)_____.

Name_____ Title _____ Facility _____

_____ Phone number _____ Date _____

FIG. 21-1. Psychiatric emergency detention form.

```
                Notice of Psychiatric Emergency Detention
                  (State Mental Health Statute and Code)


Client's Name _____ Address _____


My name is  (first and last name) . I am a      (job title)

with _____ (facility) _____ .  You are not under arrest, but

are being detained for examination/treatment by the mental health

staff at ___ (facility) _____ pursuant to the state mental health

law ___ (title of law and related sections) ___ .  You are being de-

tained because it is our professional opinion that as a result of

mental illness, you are likely to:

                    (Check categories applicable)

                    Harm yourself _____

                    Harm others _____

                    Be unable to provide/obtain

                    food, shelter, and clothing____

We feel this is true because of ___ (allegations by community/police

and observations by emergency staff) _____


_____

You may be held for a period of ___ (statute limits) ___ at which time

you may either be released or detained further until a judicial

review is held if you so request.  Your initial detention begins

_____ (date) _____ at _____ (time) _____ .


Signature of client _____ (name) _____

Signature of person presenting hold notice _____ (name and title) ____
```

FIG. 21-2. Notification of psychiatric emergency detention form.

Record of Incomplete Notification Emergency Detention Rationale

_____(facility)_____

Notification of psychiatric emergency detention according to
(state mental health statute) had not been completed for

      Client _____(first and last name)_____

      Residing at _____(address, city, and state)_____

Notification has not been completed for the following reasons:

Because of the client's mental illness resulting in his/her being
Dangerous to self _____ Dangerous to others _____ Gravely disturbed _____
he/she will be detained pursuant to _____(mental health statute)_____

Name _____

Title _____

Date _____

Phone number _____

FIG. 21-3. Form for incomplete notification of psychiatric emergency detention.

consent can be viewed as a self-serving effort on the part of the staff (Chayet, 1976). The problem is highlighted by pending cases in which clients are claiming that they did not give consent before receiving psychotropic medications.

Psychiatric emergency clinicians also face two major problems in obtaining consent to treatment: (1) the controversy over whether consent can be obtained from psychotic persons and (2) the quality of the consent given by clients of other cultures. The issue of obtaining consent from violent clients is easily answered by accurate descriptive documentation of the behavior as a rationale for treatment. These cases are true "emergencies" and can be documented as such, along with the names of available witnesses.

The problem of obtaining signed consent to treatment from clients who do not speak or read English is a common occurrence in large metropolitan psychiatric emergency care facilities. The ACLU recommends that admission materials given to the client should be written in a language that the client can easily understand (Ennis and Seigle, 1973). The psychiatric emergency facility that deals with multiple cultures should maintain a supply of forms that have been translated into the languages of the persons that it serves.

The record in court

The increasing number of malpractice and client's rights lawsuits have given the medical record increased importance in judicial proceedings. In many instances the courts view the record as the true representation of a given set of circumstances (Streiff, 1975). Once a medical record is admitted into court as evidence, it cannot be corrected or added to through cross-examination (Streiff, 1975). Therefore, the information in the chart must be accurate and clear so that misconceptions are not drawn by the court. Psychiatric emergency clinicians should remember that the medical record may be used either as evidence against them or for their protection, depending on its content.

The courts realize that most mental health professionals cannot recall all of the care given

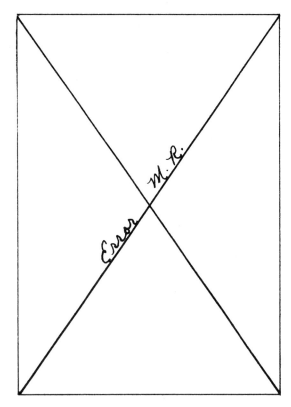

FIG. 21-4. Legally acceptable method for noting error of whole page.

to a particular client (Streiff, 1975). In these circumstances the medical record can be used to help the mental health staff review the circumstances in which they cared for the client. Since psychiatric emergency staff members see a large number of clients and cannot be expected to remember the details of each case, it is important that the record be legible and accurate. If the notes are illegible, then extraction of relevant information is difficult or impossible.

How the correction of charting errors is handled is important. It is not uncommon to see areas in the chart that have been scribbled over or that are covered with typewriter correction fluid. Not only do these corrections make reviewing the record difficult, but they may jeopardize the validity of the entire record in court.

359

If the validity of the chart is in question, then the testimony of the mental health staff may also be questioned, particularly if the testimony is based on a review of the medical record. If it can be demonstrated that the record is inaccurate and is not representative of the true situation, it will not be allowed in court as evidence (Streiff, 1975).

Charting errors can be dealt with in a manner which is legal and does not damage the validity of the record in court. Errors that involve a word or sentence should have a line drawn through them and should be labeled "error" with the writer's initials in the space above the deletion. When several sentences or the whole page is involved, the page should have an X through it and be labeled "error" along with the writer's initials (Fig. 21-4).

PSYCHIATRIC EMERGENCY CLINICIANS' FEARS AND RIGHTS
Assaults

All mental health professionals who work in psychiatric emergency care areas face the risk of assault. This problem frequently creates fantasies and fears that are often worse then the reality. Psychiatric emergency clinicians should recognize that they also have rights and are protected under the due process of the law.

All psychiatric emergency staff members will inevitably be confronted by an assaultive client. How prepared they are to cope with the assault will depend on experience and training in the management of assaultive behavior. Emergency staff members should never take a verbal or physical assault personally. Often the assault is not caused by the staff member's interventions. Frequently the assault is the result of circumstances over which the staff member has no control. Although the emergency clinician may receive the brunt of a client's rage, it is usually the result of transference, a response to internal stimuli, or a psychotic loss of control; it is a plea for help. In these situations the staff can greatly reduce the potential for injuries through the use of teamwork to subdue and manage the client.

Unfortunately, there are situations when the assault is personally directed at a specific staff member. This frequently happens with clients who have some form of personality disorder or are seeking drugs. When assaults occur, psychiatric emergency care staff members do have avenues of recourse open to them under the due process of the law. Psychiatric emergency care staff members may proceed along both the hospital policy guidelines and through the judicial system to ensure protection of their rights. If they have any questions about their rights or the steps for legal action, they should contact the hospital administration and the local district attorney.

Hospital support

If psychiatric emergency staff members are assaulted and injured, they should receive a physical examination and medical treatment as soon as possible. This should immediately be followed by completion of the appropriate employee injury forms. Usually if these steps are completed in accordance with the policy of the employing agency, workman's compensation insurance will reimburse the costs of the medical treatment. When the proper procedure is followed, no difficulty will arise in obtaining reimbursement from the insurance carrier.

Psychiatric emergency care staff members can also investigate the use of disability insurance to minimize the loss of pay when they are the victims of an assault. The cost for short-term disability insurance varies geographically, but the cost is relatively small. This form of insurance coverage usually provides some supplemental income for a set period of time if they are unable to return to work. Some policies pay up to 75% of the staff member's monthly income for as long as 6 months if necessary.

Finally, the emergency care clinician can check with the hospital security staff or the administrators to see if there is a hospital committee that deals with the problem of staff assaults. Usually these committees work on the reduction or elimination of staff assaults through various mechanisms. In addition to developing policy and improving security systems, many such committees teach courses to the staff on how to avoid being assaulted.

Legal support

The concept of prosecuting assaultive clients was once considered a ludicrous and ineffective mechanism to cope with assaults. However, the concept is beginning to be accepted by the staff of many psychiatric emergency care facilities. This procedure is not commonly used and cannot be applied to all assaultive clients. It is used primarily to assist the emergency staff to cope with the habitual criminals who frequently claim mental illness to avoid prosecution in other areas.

There has been some difficulty in utilizing this approach, and at best it is arduous for the assaulted staff member. The best procedure is to have a hospital representative contact the local district attorney to discuss the issue and set up procedural guidelines. Once this is accomplished, a hospital policy can be written which details how the procedure should be initiated.

To press charges of assault or battery will require the assaulted psychiatric emergency staff member to spend a fair amount of time in the district attorney's office. Staff members who use this procedure frequently become frustrated with the lack of speed with which the judicial system operates.

LITIGATION

The possibility of being involved in a malpractice suit is a fear of many psychiatric emergency clinicians. Each year the number of mental health professionals taken to court seems to increase dramatically. Although fear of litigation should be the cause for some concern, it is not cause for panic. In general, psychiatric care is considered to be a low-risk specialty (Barton and Sanborn, 1978c). There are, however, some identified areas where psychiatric emergency clinicians are at some risk. These areas are (1) improper commitment, (2) death, (3) drug reactions, (4) unauthorized release of information, (5) suicide, and (6) improper treatment (Trent, 1978).

Malpractice insurance

Malpractice cases result when psychiatric emergency staff are obliged to provide care, the care is not provided or provided inappropriately, and the client suffers harm as a direct result. (Perry, 1978). Aside from knowledge of one's legal rights and professional responsibilities, malpractice insurance is one of the more favored forms of personal liability protection. Unfortunately, while the number of malpractice cases is increasing, the number of malpractice insurance carriers is diminishing (Barton and Sanborn, 1978). However, malpractice insurance is still available and psychiatric emergency staff members are urged to carry some personal malpractice insurance. The names of companies offering malpractice insurance may be obtained by contacting the state branches of the professional associations. Many types of malpractice coverage are available, but they usually include two forms of coverage within a policy: per case coverage and per annum coverage. It is important when reviewing the potential policy to notice the maximum coverage of both the per annum and per case clauses. For example, if a policy has a $10,000 per case maximum and a $30,000 per annum maximum, the most that the insurance company will pay for damages on any one case is $10,000. The most that the insurance company will pay for damages in a year is $30,000 regardless of the number of claims made against the policyholder. If the court's suggested damage settlement against the policyholder exceeds either amount, then the policyholder is liable for the difference.

Most malpractice policies have strict guidelines that the policyholder must follow if a suit is filed. These guidelines are usually in the "small print" section, but if the guidelines are not followed, then the insurance carrier may void the policy. Usually, the content of these sections deals with the actions that the policyholder should take when notified of a pending malpractice suit. The content of these procedural clauses varies and should be closely reviewed before selecting the policy.

Respondent superior

Psychiatric emergency staff in supervisory positions should be aware of the legal concept of respondent superior. For practical purposes, the *respondent superior* concept means that supervisors are responsible for the actions of a subordinate even if they are not physically present (Willig, 1970). For example, if a psychiatric emergency staff member allowed an acutely suicidal person to leave the hospital and the person committed suicide, then the supervisor may also be named as a co-defendant in a malpractice suit. Although the concept extends the responsibility of the act, it does not negate the responsibility of the staff member who committed the act. The concept of respondent superior is one of the primary reasons that employing agencies carry malpractice insurance.

Psychiatric emergency staff members often experience a false sense of security when they are told that the employing agency carries malpractice insurance. This does not mean that the employing agency's insurance covers the liability for the employees' actions. Only about 2% of the hospitals in the United States have malpractice insurance that covers the individual staff member (Creighton, 1970). Usually, if the employing agency carries malpractice insurance, it is for its own protection from the respondent superior concept and not for the protection of the employee.

Protective procedures

Attorneys are viewed with some suspicion by mental health professionals (Brodsky, 1974). However, when staff members learn that they are involved in a pending lawsuit, attorneys rapidly become invaluable allies. Representation by an attorney in litigation proceedings is essential. Most mental health professionals are unfamiliar with the language of the courtroom and frequently become confused, contradictory witnesses on the stand (Brodsky, 1974). The use of an attorney will provide both support and equal representation in the courtroom.

If a psychiatric emergency clinician is informed of a malpractice suit, then both the malpractice insurance company and a personal attorney should be contacted. These representatives should be informed of all the available facts about the case. The attorneys will often provide the clinician with suggestions for further actions

and proceed with preparing a defense. Under no circumstances should clinicians speak with anyone about the case unless their personal attorney is present. Clinicians should also never speak with the attorney of the plaintiff except through their attorney. Initially, psychiatric emergency care clinicians being charged with a malpractice allegation should sit down and document everything they can about the client's case. This information should be turned over to the defending attorney who will use it to gather evidence for the defense.

THE ERA OF DEFENSIVE PSYCHIATRIC EMERGENCY CARE

The increased number of legal issues in psychiatric emergency care has resulted in a trend toward conservative treatment. Frequently, psychiatric emergency clinicians feel that it is safer to use a restrained approach to care delivery. This attitude has dramatically affected the clinicians' approach to dealing with involuntary cases, medication consent, and the client's rights issues. It is not uncommon to hear the psychiatric emergency clinician comment that it is legally safer to let the courts decide an issue of a client's care rather than assuming the responsibility themselves.

This attitude is the direct result of legislation that dictates guidelines for practice which are later ruled unconstitutional by the judicial system. It is significant to note that the attitude of many emergency care clinicians regarding current legal issues of care is one of frustration and impotence. This may be because the majority of mental health professionals involved in providing emergency care have not taken an active role in defining or accepting the ethical-legal problems involved in the delivery of care to their clients. The present emergency care delivery problems will not dissipate until the psychiatric emergency care clinicians have become involved in the process of establishing new legislation for ethical-legal standards of care. It would be beneficial for both the mental health professionals and the client's rights activists to begin a dialogue on the medicolegal factors of psychiatric emergency care before the enactment of new mental health legislation. This dialogue should not be held for the purpose of the self-preservation of either group but rather for the maintenance of the delivery of quality emergency care.

BIBLIOGRAPHY

Barton, W., and Sanborn, C.: Confidentiality. In Barton, W., and Sanborn, C., editors: Law and the mental health professions, New York, 1978a, International Universities Press.

Barton, W., and Sanborn, C.: Fiction at interface. In Barton, W., and Sanborn, C., editors: Law and the mental health professions, New York, 1978b, International Universities Press.

Barton, W., and Sanborn, C.: Malpractice. In Barton, W., and Sanborn, C., editors: Law and the mental health professions, New York, 1978c, International Universities Press.

Brodsky, S.: Buffalo Bill's defunct now: vulnerability of mental health professionals to malpractice. In Barton, W., and Sanborn, C., editors: Law and the mental health professions, New York, 1978, International Universities Press.

Brooks, A.: Law, psychiatry and the mental health system, Boston, 1974, Little, Brown & Co.

Brotman, S.: Opinions on Rennie versus Klein, Civil Action No. 77-2624, December 12, 1978, U.S. District Court of New Jersey.

Brown, M., and Fowler, G.: Psychodynamic nursing, Philadelphia, 1971, W.B. Saunders Co.

California Court of Appeals: *Bellah v. Greenson,* Civ. 39770, First District, Division 2, October 5, 1977.

California Department of Mental Health: California Mental Health Services Act, Sacramento, 1979, California Health and Welfare Agency.

Campbell, L.: Psychotropic drug use periled, San Francisco Med. **52:**7, July 1978.

Chapman, A.H., and Almeida, E.: The interpersonal basis of psychiatric nursing, New York, 1972, G.P. Putnam's Sons.

Chayet, N.: Informed consent of the mentally disabled: a failing function, Psychiatr. Ann. **6:**6, June 1976.

Clayton, T.: O'Connor versus Donaldson: impact in the states, Hosp. Community Psychiatry **27**(4):272, 1976.

Creighton, H.: Law every nurse should know, Philadelphia, 1970, W.B. Saunders Co.

Ennis, B.: Judicial involvement in public practice. In Barton, W., and Sanborn, C., editors: Law and the mental health professions, New York, 1978, International Universities Press.

Ennis, B., and Seigel, L: The rights of mental patients, New York, 1973, Avon Books.

Fine, A.: Informed consent in California, The West. J. Med. **127:**2, August 1977.

Flynn, W.: Psychotropic drugs and informed consent, Hosp. Community Psychiatry **30**(1):51, 1979.

Foster, H.: Informed consent of mental patients. In Barton, W., and Sanborn, C., editors: Law and the mental health professions, New York, 1978, International Universities Press.

Grossman, M.: Right to privacy versus the right to know. In Barton, W., and Sanborn, C., editors: Law and the mental health professions, New York, 1978, International Universities Press.

Harvis, B.: The mental patient has the right to refuse treatment, Leg. Aspects Med. Pract., vol. 7, January 1979.

Herrington, B.S.: U.S. Court of Appeals upholds drug refusal right, Psychiatr. News **15:**23, December 7, 1979.

Hoffman, B. and Dunn, R.: Guaranteeing the right to treatment, Psychiatr. Ann., vol. 6, June 1976.

Joint Commission on Mental Health: Action on mental health, New York, 1961, Basic Books, Inc., Publishers.

Kittrie, N.: The right to be different, Baltimore, Md., 1971, The Johns Hopkins University Press.

Kopolow, L.: Patients' rights and psychiatrists' practice. In Barton, W., and Sanborn, C., editors: Law and the mental health professions, New York, 1978, International Universities Press.

Mora, G.: Historical and theoretical trends in psychiatry. In Freedman, A., Kaplan, H., and Sadack, B., editors: Comprehensive textbook of psychiatry, Baltimore, 1975, The Williams & Wilkins Co.

Perry, S.: Managing to avoid malpractice, J. Nurs. Admin. **8**(8):43, 1978.

Peszke, M.: Involuntary treatment of the mentally ill, Springfield, Ill., 1975, Charles C Thomas, Publisher.

Reinert, R.E.: A note on the meaning of the Donaldson decision, Hosp. Community Psychiatry **30**(8):563, 1979.

Roth, L.: Judicial action report, Psychiatr. News **15:** 3, February 2, 1979.

Seigel, A., Hegland, K., and Wexler, D.: Implementing a new commitment law in the community: practical problems for the professional. In Barton, W., and Sanborn, C., editors: Law and the mental health professions, New York, 1978, International Universities Press.

Stone, A.A.: Overview: the right to treatment—comments on the law and its impact, Am. J. Psychiatr. **132:**1125, November 1975.

Streiff, C., editor: Nursing and the law, Rockville, Md., 1975, Aspen Systems Corp.

Treffert, D., and Krojeck, R.: In search of a sane commitment statute, Psychiatr. Ann., vol. 6, June 1976.

Trent, C.: Psychiatric malpractice insurance. In Barton, W., and Sanborn, C., editors: Law and the mental health professions, New York, 1978, International Universities Press.

Willig, S.: The nurses guide to law, San Francisco, 1970, McGraw-Hill Book Co.

Yolles, S.: Community psychiatry 1963-1974, J. Operational Psychiatry 2:2, 1975.

Zwerling, I.: The impact of the community mental health movement on psychiatric practice and training, Hosp. Community Psychiatry 27(4):258, 1976.

CHAPTER 22

Budgeteering

Leo S. Shea, Ph.D.

*So advantage is had
From whatever is there
But usefulness rises
From whatever is not.*
                    Lao-Tzu

BUDGETARY PROCESSES

Consider the person in crisis. The person usually feels helpless and hopeless. Programs, like individuals, respond to the dangers and opportunities presented by change in a wide-ranging, sometimes hazardous manner.

The director of a psychiatric emergency care program may resemble that person in crisis. Perhaps the director feels like the passive recipient of an expense budget that somehow is determined by the Inbox from Mount Olympus. Or under an impossible deadline, the director, frantically pulling together pieces of data, may feel more like the camel awaiting that fateful straw. Other directors may feel perplexed at the monotonous, irritating regularity with which fiscal planning and management require them to confront people and paper to keep the money flowing.

As in crisis intervention, however, fiscal planning and management are both an art and a science. Thus a program's budget can be approached in an active, planful manner, drawing from its quirks, dangers, opportunities, and delights. A competent crisis intervention specialist and a competent budgeteer have much in common.

Each wants to widen vision, attend to inner and outer strengths, enhance active coping strategies, develop informed action plans, and evaluate the efficacy of plans put into action.

The psychiatric emergency care program's operating budget is a metaphorical translation of its experiences, needs, dreams, and wishes. The budget reflects the philosophy and practices of the emergency program. One look is very telling. The operating budget is a great deal more than a mere quantitative fiscal summary. For instance, it speaks directly to how objectives are to be translated into action as well as to the nature and scope of crisis services that can be delivered. As such it reflects the parent organization's influences: where does the program fit along the priorities of treatment modalities? Then, too, the various political, economic, auditing, managerial, and planning trends must be considered. And, finally, has the community had an impact?

Like a fire department, the psychiatric emergency care program must be available around the clock each day of the year. This fact poses particular fiscal challenges. Of certain importance is the necessary above-average-capacity staffing frequently encountered to meet this basic mission. Since the bulk of a psychiatric emergency care program's expense budget is reserved for salaries and staff benefits, it is especially important that the innovative budgeteer finds creative ways to reduce this expense, by both cost-reduction and income-generating measures. The seemingly apparent solution, to add staff, is certainly not always the answer.

Decreasing expenses and increasing income require careful planning. The goal is to ensure competent, effective interventions at the least possible cost to the community. Toward this end, focus must not only be placed on reducing the cost of delivering a unit of service but also on reducing the cost to the community for the crises that never happened. To draw out the analogy a bit, the community wants competent, effective fire departments. For fiscal management purposes one must, therefore, view both the cost per fire and the cost associated with the fires that never occurred.

Budgeteering can become a valuable management planning tool. For instance, a budget can be exceptionally helpful in pointing out the alternatives available when one plans the distribution of usually scarce resources. In this regard, planful budgeteering can have a positive ripple effect by, for instance, strengthening weak program, organizational, and community ties. Precisely because of the way by which a budget coordinates and addresses interdependencies, a budget can indicate where dovetailing of services is necessary. Frequent consideration of the various opportunities to pair (as well as to pare) is essential. After all, if it were not for the clinicians in the psychiatric emergency care program, there would be an unknown number of additional clinicians in some other clinical service.

Every management tool has a variety of applications. At the least an operating budget should be a melding of sound management, planning, and fiscal abilities. Integrating these skills into the budget should permit the following:

1. Evaluation of the program's need, demand, benefit, cost, scope, and significance
2. Facilitation of the program's operations
3. Facilitation of short-term and long-term program plans

There are a number of concrete functions that each budget serves. These functions form the periodic vital signs of the program. Of course, the functions most persons are familiar with are those of periodically reporting income and expenses. For an informed, realistic review of the program, however, the budgeteer must also have periodic statistical data—data that address retrospective, current, and prospective progress toward objectives. The informed budgeteer wants to say something articulate about the program. To make a thorough budget report, one should compare income, expense, and statistics with philosophy, practice, and alternatives.

Historical budgeting influences

Many political, economic, management, and accounting trends have had an enormous historic influence on the budgeting process. In-depth overviews of these influences are offered in Hyde and Shafritz (1978) and Wildavsky (1974). Far from having an arbitrary, haphazard development, budgeting processes have become increasingly refined and exactingly more valuable as planning methods.

Until about the first World War, budgeteering did not offer managers sufficient, adequate data with which to evaluate their operation's processes, general efficacy, and planning. Increasingly scarcer resources, greater competition, and industrialization made it essential for successful managers to do more than simply hold departments or individuals responsible for expenditures. Generations of Scrooges and Bob Cratchits had provided extensive methods by which to classify expenditures and income. But this retrospective, red-and-black focus alone was no longer adequate. Something more than mere accountability was needed.

Roughly coinciding with World War I, both government and industry became interested in looking ahead. Prospective budgeting techniques that involved predictions were developed. Line-item budgeting alone could no longer suffice. Through a process commonly called "program budgeting" (Macleod, 1971), government and industrial management had enhanced their budgets with forward vision. Like the ancient god Janus, budgeteers could now simultaneously look backward and forward.

By the 1960s performance-based budgeting processes became the vogue. Utilizing such fiscal management techniques as cost-benefit analysis, managers wanted ways of assessing the effectiveness and impact of their programs. To do this evaluation, they began using systems analysis, 5-year forecasts, and strategic budgetary planning procedures. In 1965, President Johnson mandated the use of the Planning Programming Budgeting Systems (PPBS) approach for all federal agencies. PPBS incorporated each of the performance-based techniques (Schick, 1966).

As a result of ever-shrinking tax bases, phenomena such as Proposition 13 and the development of consumer awareness, and the seemingly impossible expansion of government regulations, a new criterion was added to budgetary processes: relevance. Zero-base budgeting (Cheek, 1977) was introduced by President Carter in an attempt to add in this dimension of relevance. The name zero-base budgeting is derived from an underlying question regarding the very life of a program; the immortality of each program is brought into question. Programs must not only be accountable, effective, prospective, and impactful, they must also demonstrate their relevance, starting from "zero," as it were. Comprehensible decision packages, each tied to a price and a long-range objective, are also developed in this system. The benefits of each package are weighed against alternative methods and the costs that would accrue if the package were not implemented. While this latest budgeting process brings a valuable focus on the margin of change from year to year, some questions have been raised about the assumptions underpinning the zero-base budgeting procedure (see Hyde and Shafritz, 1978).

These are some of the salient influences on general budgeting procedures. Add to these fiscal management influences the impactful changes unfolding in the health care system. The various machinations of health economics have profoundly influenced what types of health care are available at what cost and what might be available in the future (Fuchs, 1974). Emergency mental health services have long been seen as providing an essential service that could be either very expensive or inexpensive (McGee, 1967). Emergency mental health service delivery took hold as a widely utilized clinical service (NIMH, 1976a, 1977) so quickly that many general hospitals were providing these services early in the service's evolution (NIMH, 1973b). It is well documented that mental health service delivery is changing from a primary interest in inpatient service to a chief focus on outpatient services (NIMH, 1977). Getting even more specific, the rapidly increasing trend toward using the psychiatric emergency program as a mental health system entry point for both acute and chronic clients has profound budgetary ramifications (Gerson and Bassuk, 1980).

Despite the difficulties associated with assessing treatment outcome for society, client, and clinician (Strupp, Hadley, and Gomes-Schwartz, 1977), consistent pressure has been exerted to have mental health services reimbursed by private and governmental insurance plans (President's Commission on Mental Health, 1978). The

National Institute of Mental Health (NIMH) has long advocated the removal of financial barriers to securing mental health services; they even take it a step further by recommending the elimination of cost controls: "Mental health services should be at the same rate as for other types of health services" (1973a, p. 112). Today health care system politics are also influencing such general potential resources as national health insurance and health maintenance organizations (Falkson, 1980).

What can be drawn from the history of these various influences on budgeteering? Whatever form a budget takes, it must do more than just account for the outflow of money. A budget must also demonstrate the program's need, impact, relevance, effectiveness, and planfulness. To accomplish this justification for the program's existence, the program must be able to show that it is accomplishing its mission, that is has thoughtful cost-reduction mechanisms in place, that it is flexibly anticipating demand for service in an informed manner, that it is capable of capitalizing on changes that will result in greater efficiency, reduced costs, and increased income, and that the services provided are the services needed.

Basic budgeting building blocks

To be healthy, the organization with which a psychiatric emergency care program is affiliated must possess a structure that promotes cooperation, participation, and an effective delivery of services. The policies and procedures should be well conceptualized and defined. Thus the organization's management and its table of organization should actively catalyze participation by appropriately delegating authority and responsibility for fiscal matters. The greater the vitality of the organization, the greater the level of involvement each program has in the fiscal management and planning process. The healthy organization's managers will be actively using the fiscal data to make decisions (Drucker, 1974) based on the past and on the direction where the data suggest a specific program and the organization are to head. This structural integrity is necessary for all psychiatric emergency care programs,

regardless of whether they are based in mental health centers (Smith and Sorensen, 1974) or in general hospitals (Herkimer, 1972).

Although excellent basic budget guides exist (Gross, 1974; Houck, 1979), some of the factors in making budgets bear emphasis or clarification. A psychiatric emergency care program must be able to obtain, store, and retrieve relevant statistical and fiscal data. To do this successfully, a program's organizational structure should provide adequate administrative facilities, support, and procedures. As will be shown, such information as income, expenses, types and level of service demand, and demographic data about the area served will be critical components of the program's operating budget. Without these data, a program will be seriously handicapped in its evaluation and planning aspects.

Assuming adequate administrative organizational supportive services, including participation in the fiscal process, exist, the next provision needed is a fiscal time frame. Typically an organization will establish its own fiscal year and require that its programs work within this framework for budgeting purposes. It is common for organizations and programs to endure the frustrations of contending with the varying fiscal years of a variety of income sources. Although the parent organization may have a July-through-June fiscal year, the fiscal years for federal, state, local, and private income sources may each be quite different—a major reason for being planful.

A budget should be spread out over a fiscal year in a strategic manner. The budgeteer must knowingly anticipate fluctuations in income, expenses, service demand, or other factors known to influence the program's operation. Such strategy is best carried out at the program level, which means that the psychiatric emergency care program must be viewed as a "responsible cost center" (Gross, 1974), that is, a psychiatric emergency care program director is accountable to the organization for the program's operating budget. This arrangement has positive effects on program management by, at the very least, sharpening staff awareness of costs and income and facilitating program-level fiscal evaluation and planning.

Characteristically, psychiatric emergency care programs receive a fixed budget usually based on historical demand for services. This type of budget is called a "fixed" or "appropriations" budget. There are many disadvantages to this type of budget. For example, it may mistakenly assume an even one-twelfth distribution of income, expense, or demand over the fiscal year, thus not adequately accounting for new trends or seasonal fluctuations. Of course, it is also important to note that the upper limit cannot be exceeded in a fiscal year.

A more dynamic method of budgeting is found in the "flexible" and "step" budgets (see Houck, 1979). Presupposing solid statistical data, this variable budgeteering allows for establishing a basic budget and then different budgets are added to (or in some cases deleted from) the basic budget at predetermined levels of service delivery over a realistic time frame. Obviously, to successfully use this dynamic form of budgeting, a psychiatric emergency care program must be able to pinpoint costs, income, and service demand with some assuredness.

Ideally the program's budget should reflect the organization's use of accrual basis accounting rather than cash basis accounting. The latter system, like one's checkbook, is simply a recording of the flow of cash as received and expenses as incurred. Cash basis accounting is inadequate since it only reflects the actual present income and expenses. For effective fiscal management, something is missing. The organization also needs an awareness of the outstanding income and expenses as well. The accrual basis accounting system associates income and expenses with the period of time in which they are incurred, thereby presenting managers with a more accurate picture of the organization's health. For any given period accrual basis accounting can show the balance between accounts payable (unpaid bills and money owed) and accounts receivable (money and services due).

Another good reason to use an accrual system is that outside auditors will issue an unqualified statement to organizations using this system (Gross, 1974); a qualified statement would mean that the organization does not observe generally accepted accounting principles.

The organization's administrative staff can be of enormous help by maintaining accurate fiscal records for the psychiatric emergency care program. Double-entry bookkeeping is the superior system because of its high accuracy and intrinsic self-balancing aspects. In this bookkeeping system there are at least two entries for every transaction; for each entry there is at least one offsetting entry.

Some organizations within which a psychiatric emergency care program may be located have other valuable fiscal tools. For example, there may be an organizational chart of accounts, which is simply a coded numbering system for the various accounts or items in the organization—a sort of budgeteering Dewey decimal system (see American Hospital Association, 1976). Or the organization may have salary matrices and demographic data that may greatly facilitate the program's fiscal planning and management.

Whatever the organization's fiscal policies and procedures, they should be simple, accurate, flexible, and evaluative. They should be readily understood by anyone with an average intelligence, interest, and the willingness to spend the time learning them. There should be no doubt about the accuracy and consistency of the fiscal and supporting statistical data. Because contingencies abound and because, despite our most rigorous efforts, predictions are apt to be inaccurate, a psychiatric emergency care program budget must be flexible and adaptable. This permits the keeping of fiscal crises in a creative rather than destructive vein. Finally, the fiscal policies and procedures should enhance evaluation so the program can consider efficiency, relevance, and effectiveness and judge whether it is accomplishing its mission and whether it can do more.

Costs

Before considering elaborations of a program's operating budget, the psychiatric emergency care budgeteer must become familiar with the varieties and behaviors of costs.

At the broadest level a psychiatric emergency care program imposes and is affected by three types of costs. Providing psychiatric emergency care services incurs the costs associated with operating the program. Staff salaries, supplies, and other operating costs would not be generated if the program did not exist. At a less concrete level, opportunity costs are generated by the program's existence. These costs address what ripple effects along the continuum of opportunities are created by the program's existence. Earlier, for example, it was mentioned that because the psychiatric emergency care program exists, there can be fewer clinicians in another program. In cost-benefit analysis or systems analysis this opportunity cost is referred to as opportunity foregone, a sort of ecological borrow-from-Peter-to-pay-Paul notion. Finally, there are social costs, which are costs such those imposed (consciously or not) on the public as the result of management decisions, for instance, the social costs of not having a full-time psychiatric emergency care program. Typically social costs are measured in quanta of lives or suffering, when they can be measured at all. Of course, this aspect of social costs raises an important question: one measures operating costs by dollars, but what is the unit of measure for suffering or life? Various attempts are made to standardize the measurement by placing dollar values on life, disability, and mental illness (see NIMH, 1975), but one is left with a lingering doubt about the successfulness of these attempts.

At the program level the budgeteer is concretely confronted with direct and indirect costs. Direct costs are controllable costs, in that a program director can manage some degree of direct control over them. Direct costs such as salaries, rent, and staff development costs comprise the bulk of a psychiatric emergency care program's expense budget. On the other hand, indirect costs are those costs that are noncontrollable, such as the program's share of the organization's administrative costs. Since the administration of an organization is an essential supportive service, each of the income-generating cost centers share in the administrative cost. Some have advocated that inflation should be built into a budget as a form of indirect cost (for example, Drucker, 1974, p. 210).

A competent crisis intervention specialist is skilled at identifying types of behavior. A competent budgeteer knows it is equally important to understand the behavior of costs. An excellent way to classify cost behavior is by viewing the effects that service delivery has on them. For the purposes of psychiatric emergency care program budgeting, three behaviors are focused on. The budgeteer wishing more detailed analysis is referred to Houck (1979).

Some costs appear quite independent of the amount of service delivered. These can be classified as "fixed costs." Fixed costs include such items as costs associated with facilities and basic program salaries.

"Variable costs," on the other hand, positively correlate with the amount of service provided, as Fig. 22-1 illustrates. The greater the amount of service, the greater the variable costs. A good ex-

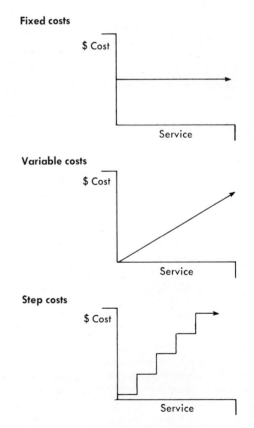

FIG. 22-1. Behavior of fixed, variable, and step costs compared with demand for service.

ample of variable costs is offered in the case of a program that provides extensive home-visit service. The more home visits, the greater the costs associated with providing this type of service, such as travel reimbursements.

There also are combination fixed and variable costs—costs that are constant for a certain range of service demand, dropping or increasing from that range as the demand drops or increases. These costs are graphically referred to as "step" or "step-variable" costs. Clinical staffing, when associated with service demand, is an example of a step cost. The number of clinical staff members hinges on the range of service demand. Because the clinical staffing salaries and benefits usually account for about 80% of a psychiatric emergency care program's expense budget, one must be quite careful about these step costs.

The program operating budget

A program's operating budget actually consists of three budgets: statistical, expense, and income budgets. Regardless of whether they are estimated or actual budgets, the psychiatric emergency care program needs these three budgets for sound fiscal planning and management. The fully informed, innovative program will find it helpful (not burdening) to have both actual and estimated versions of the three operating budget components on a regular basis.

STATISTICAL BUDGET. The rationale for a current and prospective statistical budget should be remarkably clear. The relevant, effective, and efficient psychiatric emergency care program wants to be ahead of its service demand, to move innovatively on types and methods of service delivery, to ensure targeted populations are being served, to discover populations not being served, to develop cost-reduction and income-generation mechanisms, to determine costs for various services, and to have data available with which to make realistic interpretations of the income and expense budgets. The organization should be helpful toward these ends by providing a vehicle for accurate, timely data collection. Such practical automated methods as Management Information Systems (MIS) have gained wide acceptance as facilitators in this process

(see Hargreaves et al., 1974; Smith and Sorensen, 1974). Using an automated MIS routine may save by reducing the dollar costs associated with manual tabulation and the psychological and pragmatic costs related to inaccuracies.

Sometimes statistical data gathering becomes too complex a task. This not only is costly (in both fiscal and psychological senses of the term) but tends to promote inefficiency. Gathering data that no one will use is patently useless. Care needs to be given so that data are instructive. The statistical budget needs to be parsimonious and actively used. Suggested budget data for a psychiatric emergency care program are included in Table 22-1. The data should be computed on a monthly basis and also summarized in yearly totals.

One of the key statistical budget components for fiscal planning and management purposes is a standardized unit of measurement for service delivered. It is especially helpful for this standardized service unit to be reflective of that critical variable—time. Since most psychiatric emergency care programs provide an array of crisis intervention services, the program may find it of value to compare these units by type of service delivered (for example, comparing face-to-face interviews with telephone services) or by location of services (comparing home visits with visits to emergency room, mental health center, police station, and so on). Such comparisons will uncover highly useful trend and utilization patterns for the budgeteer. Staffing and purchasing can be more efficiently planned by use of the statistical budget. The examples that follow in this chapter use a standardized service unit based on 15 minutes of service. Consistent with MIS systems, units are rounded to the closest 15-minute interval (a 10-minute contact is counted as one unit, a 48-minute contact as three units, and contact of an hour and 25 minutes as six units).

With a statistical budget and a standardized service unit, a program budgeteer has a method for converting service time into expense dollars. An organizational salary matrix (Fig. 22-2) is helpful when comparing service units of the entire clinical staff. This matrix helps clarify by allowing the budgeteer to make dollar value comparisons by skill level.

TABLE 22-1

STATISTICAL BUDGET FORMAT FOR (month or year)
(_____ Days-_____ Contacts-_____ Clients)

| | Projected | Actual |

Time of contacts
Day of week (list Sunday through Saturday)
Time of day (divide 24-hour period into useful subdivisions, e.g., 4-hour blocks)
Length of contact (use service units 1, 2, 3, 4, 5, etc.—see text)

Location of contacts (list all relevant locations such as ER, CMHC, police department, home visits, telephone)

Demographic data
Age (use relevant ranges)
Sex
Referral sources (list)
Principal diagnosis (list)
Census area (list)

Suicide data
History of attempt
Ideation (no plan)
Ideation (with plan)
Attempt (list methods)
Completions (list methods)
Survivor interventions
Psychological autopsies

Hospitalizations (may want to list specific hospitals)
Voluntary
Involuntary

Consultations
Clinicians
Private practitioners
(List others—court, police, schools, etc.)

Client frequencies
_____ clients made 1 contact
_____ clients made 2 contacts
_____ clients made 3 contacts
Etc.

Title		$ Ranges[1]					
		1[2]	2	3	4	5	N[3]
Psychiatrist:	Staff						
	Resident						
	Intern						
Psychologist:	Staff, Ph.D.						
	Staff, M.A.						
	Intern						
Psychiatric social worker:	Staff, M.S.W.						
	Intern						
Psychiatric nurse:	Staff, M.S.						
	Staff, B.S.N.						
	Staff, R.N.						
	Student						
Secretary							
Receptionist							
Etc.							

FIG. 22-2. A salary matrix. Fiscal planning and management are facilitated by using the organization's salary matrix, particularly for computing expense budget forecasts or reviewing the cost of service provided by types of clinicians. Ranges may vary from locked in, fixed amounts per year of experience to more variable amounts based on merit reviews (in which case yearly averages may be the best estimate). Other staff titles may exist (for example, program director, clinical team leader, mental health aide, suicidologist, counselor).
[1]Each block usually represents dollar figures of gross salary.
[2]Usually the basic starting salary with minimal or no experience.
[3]Usually the upper limit. Sometimes a modest increase is allowed beyond this limit to account for cost-of-living increases.

The accuracy, relevance, and utility of the statistical budget are matters for continuous concern. The budgeteer also needs to ensure that the data are being properly interpreted. An amusing, valuable book addressing the proper interpretation and presentation of statistical data was written by Huff (1954).

EXPENSE BUDGET. The second budget within a program's operating budget is the expense budget. Even a casual glance at a psychiatric emergency care program's expense budget will sharply reveal that the program's expenses cluster into three broad categories: salaries and benefits, operating expenses, and share of organizational costs. The following list illustrates the items most frequently found in psychiatric emergency care program expense budgets. Of special note is the high percentage of the expense budget set aside for salaries and benefits. It is quite common for this portion of the expense budget to range in the vicinity of 80% of the total expense budget. It is imperative to figure in costs associated with *all* benefits (including such less obvious ones as educational leave, professional development costs, and tuition reimbursements). Be sure to include any vacant positions, on-call or overtime pay, and vacation relief.

Program expense budget items[1]

Salaries and benefits
  Clinical salaries[2]
  Clerical salaries
  Fringe benefits
  FICA tax
  Unemployment taxes
  Student stipends
  Professional consultant(s) (and other contracted services)
  Workman's compensation insurance
  Professional liability insurance
  Professional development
Operation
  Professional materials
  Medication vouchers
  Dues and subscriptions
  Advertising and printing
  Books
  Mileage
  Meals
  Telephone
  Postage
  Office supplies
  Office machine maintenance
  Office equipment
  Furniture
  Maintenance
  Utilities
  Rent (or mortgage, depreciation, and so on)
  Miscellaneous (fund raising, special projects, and so on)
Program net expenses (sum of above)
Administrative pro rata (and other cost sharing)
Total expense budget (sum of Program Net Expenses and all cost sharings)

Other expenses related to the ongoing operation of the program comprise the next largest portion of a total expense budget. Many of these expenses are variable costs so they are quite sensitive to the service demand fluctuations. Thus it is particularly valuable to ensure enough budget flexibility so that predictably heavy seasonal or cyclical demands can be accommodated. By doing this, the budgeteer allows for possible cost reductions through the use of anticipated bulk supply purchases or, at the least, ensures that adequate income is available during peak demand periods. Any expenses for special projects such as fund raising or bulk mailings should be included in this portion of the expense budget.

The last section of a program's expense budget reflects the program's prorated share of other organizational costs. Through this sharing of costs, organizations spread the expenses of non-income-generating cost centers between programs. For example, in mental health centers administrative services are cost shared; in hospitals such cost centers as the housekeeping and pharmacy services are also cost shared.

INCOME BUDGET. The third (and oftentimes sorely neglected) budget component of a psychiatric emergency care program's operating budget is the income budget. The following list illustrates a typical psychiatric emergency care program's income budget. All possible income sources are listed in this budget, usually differentiated between those specifically earmarked for the psychiatric emergency care program and those not earmarked for the program. The budgeteer should include all income-producing activities, including consultations to courts, schools, police, and other agencies; paid educational endeavors; and psychotherapeutic, diagnostic, or counseling services. Usually psychiatric emergency care clinicians can do a fair amount of income-generating work that greatly reduces the cost of the crises that never happened.

Program income budget items[1]

Earmarked income
  Client fees
  Consultation fees
  Blue Cross/Blue Shield insurance

---

[1]Figures for expected and actual expenditures for each month, for the fiscal year, and for the fiscal year to date should be provided.
[2]On-call pay differential should be included.

---

[1]Figures for expected and actual income for each month, for the fiscal year, and for the fiscal year to date should be provided.

Other insurance

Medicaid

Other organizational or local, state, or federal sources (specify)

Total earmarked income

Nonearmarked income

City

County

State

Division of (Mental Health, Public Health, and so on)

NIMH grant

Other grants (specify)

United Way (or other federated funding sources)

Other sources

Total nonearmarked income

Gross income (sum of all above)

Adjustments

Contractual discounts

Client discounts

Insurance discounts

Bad debt rate

A number of variables impact on this budget. Of paramount importance is demand—but demand for reimbursable services is the best way to express the point here. Certainly demand variations will affect what income is possible in a given period. However, this variance becomes more critical when fluctuations are experienced in reimbursable service areas. It is one thing to experience a shift in telephone contacts (nonreimbursable) and quite another to experience that shift in direct-service client contacts. To approach the income budget with confidence, the budgeteer must have an accurate statistical budget. Another significant variable is that the income budget directly hinges on the assumptions that realistic client charges are possible and that there is a solid collection rate.

Notice that the preceding list contains certain anticipated deductions from the gross income figure. Subtracting contractual, client, and insurance discounts adds to the accuracy of the program's income budget. To further contribute to its accuracy, an additional adjustment for the bad debt rate is made. This latter adjustment is usually a subjective deduction that is based on historical patterns, which makes keeping track

of this rate especially valuable. Ideally the organization can provide these data. If not available and an estimate is needed, be conservative. Use a ball-park figure that is on the high side (that is, a larger deduction). In a program heavily involved in involuntary commitment procedures, for example, it may safely be assumed that almost all of these clients will not pay for this particular service. The budgeteer may want to include a modest third-party income figure based on knowledge of prevailing front-end deductibles, the percentage of clients with insurance or Medicaid, and the like. Each of these adjustments to the gross projected income figure should assist the budgeteer in zeroing in on the income reality for the program over that particular time frame. Keeping track of the income sources and the adjustments over the years will greatly facilitate income budgeteering.

JUSTIFICATION OF THE BUDGET

The effective budgeteer has a number of fiscal planning and management resources from which to draw. The thoughtful budgeteer must build on a solid foundation and must also have a well-conceptualized blueprint for the future. The building blocks for a program's foundation are the various historical facts shaped in the past and the present operating budget components. Clinical trends, competition, and funding source decisions form the mortar. The blueprint is elaborated on and located in the program and organization's goals and strategies. The operating budget translates these influences into dollars, the bricks in the psychiatric emergency care program's metaphor. Like any metaphor, the budget should help draw the program's translation of treatment and operation philosophy into fresh angles of vision. These crisp insights can provide clues for imaginative, innovative unfoldings for new client, clinician, or community services as well as additional income-generation or cost-reduction alternatives.

Forecasting service demand

One of the most practical methods by which the program's budget can be justified is by developing the ability to predict the expected psychiatric emergency care demand. It is of comfort to know that there are concrete ways of making these predictions. After all, a prudent budgeteer does not want to rely on star-chamber or metaphysical techniques or wholly emotional appeals or to awkwardly advocate the bigger-is-always-better thought process. Even neophyte psychiatric emergency care programs can make reasoned estimates by surveying the service demand presented to other agencies in the community. A data-oriented baseline is necessary.

Being able to make demand forecasts based on accurate historical data certainly adds confidence to all involved. Further, such forecasts enhance the fiscal planning and management of the program. For instance, the budgeteer can use these data to develop a step budget for the addition of staff members, basing each step on a thoughtful elaboration of service demand capacity per clinician. By extrapolation such staffing forecasts can also be extended to clerical staffing requirements. Of course, one needs to also consider the costs associated with salaries and benefits by clinician skill level and profession.

A straightforward manner of prediction is offered by a statistical method possessing a variety of math anxiety–inducing aliases (such as "least squares method," "line of best fit," or "simple regression method"; see Alder and Roessler, 1964, pp. 158-167). Actually, the statistical technique is quite easy to compute right in the office.

Suppose a psychiatric emergency care program experienced the pattern of service demand illustrated in Fig. 22-3. How could the program's budgeteer forecast the next year's demand? Clearly, an increasing trend is noted. However, there is enough variation in the absolute differences between each succeeding pair of years that the budgeteer may wish to derive some confidence from determining the line that best fits the data from all 5 years and then project that line one point (that is, 1 year) further. This is precisely what the simple regression technique allows one to do.

Simplifying the basic statistical formula (Alder and Roessler, 1964, p. 161) to meet the needs of the psychiatric emergency care program budgeteer results in the following computational process (a completed example is offered in Table 22-2):

1. Prepare a table large enough for five columns of data. Enter the year and corresponding total of service units for each

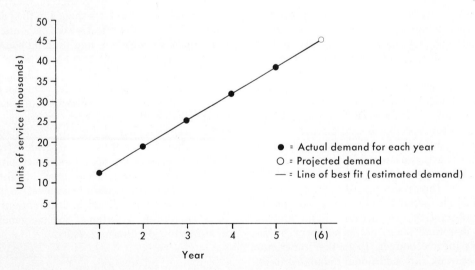

FIG. 22-3. Scatter diagram for service demand over 5 years. "Line of best fit" is extended to sixth (projected) year through the simple regression technique. See text for specifics. Note the differences between actual and estimated demand.

year in columns one and two, respectively (oldest year in top row). The example offered in Table 22-2 reflects the prediction of a sixth year's demand based on 5 years of service.

2. Determine and enter the appropriate column three values (including sign) from the matrix provided in Table 22-2. Compute and enter the square of each of these values in column four.

3. Multiply columns two and three and enter the product in column five (include sign).

4. Total columns two, four, and five. Record each column sum beneath each column.

5. Divide the total of column two by the number of years. Record this average beneath the column total.

6. Divide the sum of column five by the sum of column four. Record the answer beneath the sum of column five (this is the yearly adjustment figure referred to later).

7. Prepare another table, this time with provision for four columns (see Table 22-3).

8. Enter the year and the average service demand for the total period studied in the first and second columns.

9. Multiply the result of step six (yearly adjustment figure) above by each year's respective column three value (including sign) from Table 22-2. Record the product for each year in column three.

10. Add each year's column two and column three entries (observe signs). Enter each sum in column four.

11. The above computations yield the various coordinates (points on the graph) that describe the "line of best fit" (that is, the solid line in Fig. 22-3).

12. To determine the forecasted demand for the next year, multiply the yearly adjustment figure (from step six above) by the absolute number of years that the projected year is from the middle year. (NOTE: When data analysis on an even number of years is being computed, divide the num-

TABLE 22-2. Simple regression example for 5 years' data: part I

		Columns		
1	2	3	4	5
1977	12,640	−2	4	−25,280
1978	16,940	−1	1	−16,940
1979	25,040	0	0	0
1980	29,780	+1	1	+29,780
1981	35,370	+2	4	+70,740
Totals:	119,770		10	58,300
Average:	23,954	Yearly adjustment figure:		5,830

Column 3 value matrix[1]

Total number of data years	Enter following values for each year (oldest year = year 1)						
	Year 1	Year 2	Year 3	Year 4	Year 5	Year 6	Year 7
3	−1	0	+1				
4	−3	−1	+1	+3			
5	−2	−1	0	+1	+2		
6	−5	−3	−1	+1	+3	+5	
7	−3	−2	−1	0	+1	+2	+3

From Ferguson, G.A.: Statistical analysis in psychology and education, New York, 1971, McGraw-Hill Book Co.
[1]For values beyond 7 years, consult a statistics text for a table of coefficients of orthogonal polynomials, using the linear dimension (see Ferguson, 1971, p. 463).

TABLE 22-3. Simple regression example for 5 years' data: part II

		Columns	
1 Year	2 Data average	3 (Column 3 value)(Yearly adjustment)	4 Best fit trend point[1]
Data years			
1977	23,954	+ (−2)(5830)	= 12,294
1978	23,954	+ (−1)(5830)	= 18,124
1979	23,954	+ (0)(5830)	= 23,954
1980	23,954	+ (+1)(5830)	= 29,784
1981	23,954	+ (+2)(5830)	= 35,614
Projected year(s)			
1982	23,954	+ (3)(5830)	= 41,444
1983	23,954	+ (4)(5830)	= 47,274
1984	23,954	+ (5)(5830)	= 53,104

From Ferguson, G.A.: Statistical analysis in psychology and education, New York, 1971, McGraw-Hill Book Co.
[1]Plot these points on the same graph on which actual demand data are plotted (see example in Fig. 22-3).

ber of years by 2, then add 0.5 to the result: thus for 4 years, use 2.5; for 6 years, use 3.5; and so on). Next, add this product to the average derived from step five. This yields the projected service demand for the year ahead. Note that 2-year and 3-year projections can also be computed.

Progressive (increasing) demand trends result in relatively more vertical lines; regressive (decreasing) demand trends yield relatively more horizontal best-fit lines. Be certain that appropriate procedures are followed when graphing demand data (see Huff, 1954). Placing demand (service units) along the vertical axis and years along the horizontal axis is recommended.

Despite the computational ease and wide acceptance of the regression technique, there are two important limitations to keep in mind when using the technique. It must be recalled that this technique generalizes a year's worth of data into one point. It cannot address seasonal or monthly fluctuations. Also by using historical data, it retains a retrospective focus; by itself, it has no way of figuring in any significant local trends or influences not reflected in the past demand data. A second limitation is that the technique only utilizes one variable, gross demand. The consequence here is that it will be insensitive to such other variables as changes in procedures, staffing, manner or methods of delivering service, competition, and vacation periods.

The best method for the presentation of seasonal or monthly demand trends is to compare the monthly data on a year-by-year basis. These data can then be compared with data of the last 3 years, for example. Table 22-4 reflects an example of demand data for 5 years. A psychiatric emergency care program may use these data or a collapsed version such as that presented in Table 22-5 to add additional staff during peak demand times or to plan vacation or other leave times. Note that using this method will provide monthly averages for each year as well as the relative percentage of demand contributed by each month in each year.

When the budgeteer desires or needs a more sophisticated analysis of many variables, the statistical technique called *multiple regression analysis* should be used. A particularly practical guide for this technique is offered in Cohen and Cohen, 1975. This more sophisticated analysis permits the budgeteer to examine the influences of a number of variables (for example, the number of clinicians, the number of contacts per clinician, time and place of contacts, population trends and demographics, and the unemployment

TABLE 22-4. Monthly demand analysis for 5 years

	1977		1978		1979		1980		1981	
	N^1	$\%^2$	N	%	N	%	N	%	N	%
January	850	6.725	1,160	6.848	1,640	6.550	2,410	8.093	3,200	9.047
February	860	6.804	1,050	6.198	1,960	7.827	2,090	7.018	2,760	7.803
March	1,020	8.070	1,380	8.146	1,800	7.188	2,280	7.656	3,300	9.330
April	780	6.171	1,210	7.143	1,630	6.510	2,530	8.496	3,150	8.906
May	1,140	9.019	1,430	8.442	1,930	7.708	2,400	8.059	3,070	8.680
June	1,340	10.601	1,420	8.383	2,270	9.065	2,080	6.985	2,500	7.068
July	1,040	8.228	1,640	9.681	2,240	8.946	2,690	9.033	3,230	9.132
August	1,100	8.703	1,440	8.501	2,470	9.864	2,930	9.839	3,840	10.857
September	920	7.278	1,490	8.796	1,910	7.628	2,540	8.529	2,810	7.945
October	1,250	9.889	1,540	9.091	2,270	9.065	2,560	8.596	2,750	7.775
November	1,220	9.652	1,490	8.796	2,580	10.304	2,610	8.764	2,630	7.436
December	1,120	8.861	1,690	9.976	2,340	9.345	2,660	8.932	2,130	6.022
Totals	12,640	100.001	16,940	100.001	25,040	100	29,780	100	35,370	100.001
Monthly averages	1,053.3		1,411.7		2,086.7		2,481.7		2,947.5	

[1]The total number of service demand units each month.
[2]The percentage of the yearly total demand for service. (For comparison purposes, one-twelfth equals 8.333%.)

rate). Most computer centers or systems have canned multiple regression programs, which enormously facilitate the use of this more complex technique (see Nie et al., 1975).

Aiming to break even

Are fees, grants, and other income sufficient to meet the psychiatric emergency care program's expense budget? Just how much is enough? Can the psychiatric emergency care program lower costs, raise income, increase activity, or effect some combination of strategies toward each of these goals? Can the program break even? How much does demand have to fall before significant loss occurs? The cost accounting method that addresses these questions best is called *break-even analysis* (Tucker, 1963).

To accomplish break-even analysis, the budgeteer needs to know the program's fixed and variable costs and the income per unit of service. Fig. 22-4 depicts a break-even graph. Assume that the Somewhere Psychiatric Emergency Care Program knows that they have a total program expense budget of $200,000, of which $160,000 are fixed costs, and $40,000 are variable costs. Assume, too, that the Somewhere Program uses a system of 15-minute standardized service units, that it can charge $15 per service unit, and that each unit can be tagged with a total of $10 income from all income sources after adjusting for bad

debts and discounts. The Somewhere Program is averaging 16,000 units of service a year. Given this information, the program's budgeteer computes the break-even point by first subtracting the variable cost per unit from the total service charge per unit (in this example: $2.50 from $15, leaving $12.50). Next, the budgeteer divides this difference into the total fixed cost ($160,000 ÷ $12.50 per unit), which results in the total number of units needed to break even (12,800).

The Somewhere Psychiatric Emergency Care Program is apt to operate well in the black. The budgeteer may, as a result, assess the opportunity to replace staff (for example, place the psychiatrist on an on-call basis, replaced by a less costly, equally income-generating psychologist) or to add staff (and associated new income opportunities). For example, the budgeteer may wonder whether a $25,000 psychologist could be added safely or whether the on-call premium rate could be increased by $25,000. The budgeteer knows that an additional 17% needs to be added on to this salary to account for various fringes and benefits. This brings the total cost for that psychologist to $29,250. By adding this figure to the total fixed program costs, the budgeteer accomplishes the computations in the previous paragraph and discovers that the psychologist could be added ($189,250 ÷ $12.50 = 15,140 units to break even) or that the on-call rate could

TABLE 22-5. Monthly demand analysis collapsed for 3 years

	1979	*1980*	*1981*	*Totals*	*Percent*
January	1,640	2,410	3,200	7,250	8.039
February	1,960	2,090	2,760	6,810	7.551
March	1,800	2,280	3,300	7,380	8.183
April	1,630	2,530	3,150	7,310	8.105
May	1,930	2,400	3,070	7,400	8.205
June	2,270	2,080	2,500	6,850	7.595
July	2,240	2,690	3,230	8,160	9.048
August	2,470	2,930	3,840	9,240	10.245
September	1,910	2,540	2,810	7,260	8.050
October	2,270	2,560	2,750	7,580	8.404
November	2,580	2,610	2,630	7,820	8.671
December	2,340	2,660	2,130	7,130	7.906
Totals	25,040	29,780	35,370	90,190	100.002
				(÷ 36) =	
Averages	2,086.7	2,481.7	2,947.5	2,505.3	

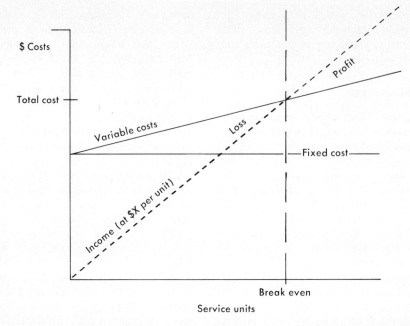

$ Costs

Total cost

Variable costs

Loss

Profit

Fixed cost

Income (at $X per unit)

Break even

Service units

FIG. 22-4. The general graphic format for a break-even analysis. Note that psychiatric emergency care programs have relatively high fixed costs, thus break-even points will also be relatively high.

be increased ($185,000 ÷ $12.50 = 14,800 units to break even).

Given these break-even analyses, the budgeteer has the delightful dilemma of assessing which decision is most justified. In assessing this justification, the budgeteer can address such valuable issues as enhancement of the scope or nature of the emergency care delivery system (for example, the psychologist may be able to do needed community agency consultations) as well as provision of additional time or funding so that work loads could be reduced or salaries increased or, at the least, costs associated with staff turnover, burnout, and poor morale reduced.

Planning staffing needs: in search of a full-time equivalent

Psychiatric emergency care programs, like any demand service, are predictably unpredictable. In addition, they must be available 24 hours every day of the year. Regardless of the partic-

ular program model, it seems reasonable to assume that most staff members are employed on a 40-hour per week basis. Although there are 52 weeks in a year and thus 2,080 paid hours, no one expects to work every one of those hours. So, certain benefit hours must be deducted from this gross figure. With good fiscal management practices in mind, the budgeteer deducts all benefit hours from each employee's total. Typically this means subtracting at least holidays, vacation days, and sick days to be certain of adequate staffing. Suppose that a psychiatric emergency care program offers 10 holidays, 20 vacation days, and 15 sick days to an employee each year. This results in a deduction of 360 benefit hours needing deduction from the total, $(10 \times 8) + (20 \times 8) + (15 \times 8) = 360$, leaving a working figure of 1,720 hours per employee (2,080 − 360).

There are 8,760 hours in 1 year. This means that to simply cover each hour of the day each day of the year, 5.093 full-time equivalent clinicians are needed at a minimum (8,760 ÷ 1,720).

Of course, this assumes a lot already. For instance, on the one hand, it would be much more cost-effective in rural or low-demand areas to pay clinicians on an incident fee basis with one clinician covering for an entire week; on the other hand, this also assumes that only one client will be in contact with a clinician in any given hour, which is far from the case in urban, high-demand emergency services. Furthermore, given the scope of a psychiatric emergency care program, the budgeteer must consider the deleterious effects of stress, tension, morale, and sleep deprivation that will probably take some toll, given the affectively loaded clientele served by a psychiatric emergency care program's clinicians.

Fig. 22-5 offers a method for a psychiatric emergency care program wishing to assess how many full-time equivalent clinicians are needed to meet the program's demand for service. Hours have been converted into the standardized 15 minutes that equal one unit. The method assumes a floor of 25% of available time devoted to client contacts and a ceiling of 50%. From a cost and income view, this means that each clinician should be spending between 25% and 50% of available work hours in client activities, consultations, and the like. The balance of available time is perceived of as time to be used for dicta-

tion, travel, professional development, nonreimbursable consultation and education activities, and so on. Of course, the elasticity of deciding when to add (or subtract) an additional clinician and the actual implementation are related to the numerous variables affecting each psychiatric emergency care program. A safe guiding rule, though, is the 50% ceiling. When each clinician (or full-time equivalent) has reached this ceiling, it is time to step up by one full-time equivalent; when each clinician (or full-time equivalent) has consistently remained at a less than 33% level of client contacts, the opportunity exists to decrease the staff by one full-time equivalent (or to deploy the staff in another manner).

Other pragmatic justification methods

One extremely valuable, practical operating budget justification tool is the fiscal analysis of a psychiatric emergency care program along the dimensions of income, expense, and service units. Table 22-6 gives a format for presentation of this analysis. This analysis enables the program budgeteer to assess the cost of the crisis services as well as the cost of the in between time, which can be viewed as the cost of the crises that never happened. When data are available, a 5-year analy-

TABLE 22-6. A suggested format for 5-year fiscal analysis of psychiatric emergency care program

Analysis format	First year	Second year	Third year	Fourth year	Most recent year
Income generated[1]					
Expected					
Actual					
Direct expense[2]					
Service units[3]					
Clinical staff FTEs[4]					
Income per FTE					
Expense per FTE					
Service units per FTE					
Income per service unit					
Expense per service unit					
Expense per nonservice unit[5]					

[1]Income from all earmarked sources.
[2]Excludes indirect expenses.
[3]Use standardized service unit.
[4]FTE = full-time equivalent (see text).
[5]Nonservice units are those units found when subtracting the units accounted for in footnote 3 from the total possible units based on the number of FTEs.

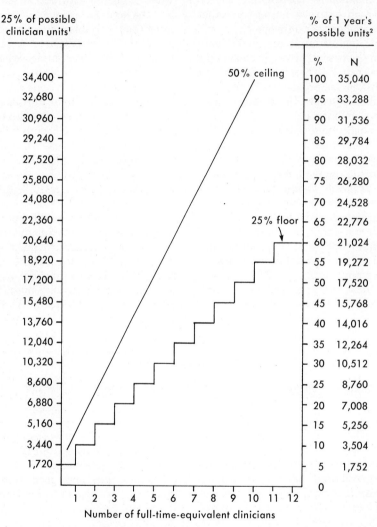

FIG. 22-5. A suggested method for determining the number of full-time equivalent clinicians needed based on step demand.

[1]Computed at rate of each clinician available for 1,720 hours (see text); one unit =15 minutes.

[2]Provided for comparison. Total of 35,040 units per 365-day year.

sis is especially useful for the effective psychiatric emergency care program. Plotting the income, expense, and service unit data on a graph is a useful way to depict 5-year trends.

The fiscal analysis may readily reflect cost reductions effected by, for example, using less costly staff members for nonreimbursable activities such as telephone interventions or triaging of psychiatric emergencies.

A highly visible and accessible psychiatric emergency care program tests the strength of the program and that of the organization with which it is affiliated. This testing forces the need for frequent clarification of mission, objectives, values, costs, and benefits. A great deal of the strength behind this test of vitality rests in the simple fact that the more available a service is, the more apt it is to be used (NIMH, 1976c, p. 6).

It is, however, extremely important to be relevant. One clear measure of relevancy is found through an exacting analysis of the statistical budget, especially from the angle of *need* (services clients are assumed to require) versus *demand* (services clients want). A comprehensive, accurate statistical budget is particularly valuable in demonstrating that a psychiatric emergency care program is serving the emergency demand in the program's area. Although this suggestion sounds blatantly obvious, many deficiencies have been easily demonstrated by essentially using statistical budget data (see NIMH, 1976a) and comparing these data along such census tract information as percentage of the population in poverty or along the rural versus urban dimension. Attention should also be given when justifying the budget to ensure that the program's service is in keeping with area health services plans and is not duplicating other psychiatric emergency care services in the area (for example, providing walk-in emergency psychiatric service when there already is an adequate provision of such service to the area; see NIMH, 1973b, 1977). On the other hand, one does not want to be chiefly serving clients from another area (NIMH, 1976b). Remember too that an effective budgeteer should be "prospective": know where the psychiatric emergency care program is going, not only where it has been. To do this well, a budgeteer interested in budget justification must show how the psychiatric emergency care program is integrated into the community's mental health care delivery system and planning as well as the program's specific operation, planning, and financing.

Another viewpoint that analysis of the statistical budget reveals is what is *not* being accomplished. Again, a comparison of the statistical data against the area's vital statistics, census data, and resources will help. Is the program effectively intervening with the chronic psychiatric emergency care clients? How does the program's environment or method(s) of service delivery need changing?

Applying systems theory to analyze the mix between the populations served and the matching of services to the demand is also of practical value to a planful psychiatric emergency care budgeteer (see Marmor, 1975). Does the analysis reflect that the program is playing an active, effective role in the mixture of the area's treatment modalities and programs? A budgeteer will want to keep (or gain) a perspective on the specific, relevant targeted populations; the range of the program's relevant services; and the proper evaluation of the program's services. Is the clinical staff being effectively mobilized? Are other kinds of staff or resources called for? Is there adequate staffing for continuity of care? How far is continuity carried (for example, does it include survivors of suicides, accidents, and other victims)? Is there opportunity to do both person-oriented and population-oriented interventions? Preventive clinical work? Consultation and education services for other health care or human service agencies or professionals?

Further questions good systems theory application can raise for a budgeteer are: What is the global fiscal impact of the psychiatric emergency care program on the organization? On the community's quality of life? Is it cost absorbing (for example, by using front-end deductibles) or cost creating (for example, by reducing the length of stay for hospitalizations or outpatient services)? Does it seem to enhance consumer education and awareness of mental health services as well as their appropriate uses? Is the program acting as a fixed, coordinated referral or entry point? What does the analysis suggest for organizational-level fiscal plans? For the area's health care system? What is the impact on peer standards review committees, local tax bases, the nurturance of other local health services and facilities, and community advisory boards?

Cost-benefit analysis (Levin, 1975; Rothenberg, 1975) is an excellent potential justification technique with which a psychiatric emergency care program budgeteer can weigh the various opportunities gained or lost as a result of the existence of the program. As mentioned earlier, there are both benefits and costs incurred by the program which extend far beyond that which can be easily translated into dollars. It is especially difficult to measure such costs to all concerned brought on by mental illness, disability, or death. On the other hand, it is reasonable to assume that the nature and amount of effective care available in a community will reduce these costs and benefit the general quality of life, life satisfaction, or hopefulness existing in the community. A community with relevant, effective resources is an empowered, healthier community.

Nevertheless, imperfect substitute measures exist. Budgeteers wishing to use cost-benefit analysis to support their program's budget must strive to include each cost and benefit along the relevant dimensions associated with the program's effect on clients, clinicians, the organization, the community, and other agencies. Exactly what are the consequences of providing and not providing the services? Such analysis highlights the broad interdependencies in the program's network, as strongly suggested in the mere sketching out of an influence matrix (Fig. 22-6).

Sometimes a budgeteer may want to justify the program based on comparisons with other psychiatric emergency care programs. There are many functional variances between different psychiatric emergency care program models of operation. So a budgeteer must approach a comparison analysis cautiously. Some of the concrete variables that may confound or otherwise influence program comparisons are as follows: (1) there may be functional differences in how psychiatric emergency care services are offered. For example, is the program staffed wholly by physi-

cians or is there a reasoned, planful mix of clinical staff? Does the program include such extra-site activities as home visitation or agency on-site consultation? Does the program include a high-volume demand for nonreimbursable services such as telephone intervention? (2) Salary levels will differ across the country (even within professions). (3) The availability and cost of facilities and equipment (such as telephone services and radio pagers) may vary significantly from region to region, which is perhaps of particular importance along the rural-urban dimension. (4) The laws and practices relative to service reimbursement vary from state to state. (5) Hospital bylaws determining who can be on the staff and what kind of privileges they might have vary from hospital to hospital. (6) The continuity or intensity of emergency service varies from area to area (and so may the nature of the demand). (7) The opportunities for sharing or contracting services may also vary significantly.

One last, but very valuable, budget justification centers on validation of the program by special outside groups. Obtaining national recognition by becoming certified by the American Association of Suicidology* or being otherwise successfully evaluated (for example, by the Joint Commission on the Accreditation of Hospitals or NIMH) adds important credibility to a program's operation and thus to its budget.

FUNDING RESOURCES

Fiscal stasis is not just inadequate; it may also prove to be suicidal. Psychiatric emergency care programs require funding from a variety of sources to survive and flourish. In many parts of the country a demand-based service, such as a psychiatric emergency care program, may never be able to pay its keep. So grant income becomes even more critical. An array of funding resources also permits program flexibility. A principal, beneficial outcome of such flexibility is allowing the clinical staff to remain focused on targeted populations instead of spending huge amounts of precious clinical time beating around the funding resource bushes.

---

*Central office: 2459 South Ash, Denver, Colo. 80222.

		Clients	Staff	Organi-zation	Community	Other agencies
Client time	Cost					
	Benefit					
Staff	Cost					
	Benefit					
Other operation	Cost					
	Benefit					
Community resources	Cost					
	Benefit					
Other agencies	Cost					
	Benefit					

(Etc.)

FIG. 22-6. Brief example of a cost-benefit influence matrix associated with a psychiatric emergency care program. Refer to Levin, 1975, and Rothenberg, 1975, for detailed cost-benefit analysis methodological considerations. "Other agencies" might include each of the other public and private-sector mental health care providers, social service agencies, educational facilities, and so on.

To continuously develop and actively elaborate on the smorgasbord of funding resources is a key function of a psychiatric emergency care program budgeteer. Taking useful advantage of the knowledge of local or organizational grantspersons can greatly facilitate this function. One must know how to complete a specific grant, to meet the source's criteria (for example, certain targeted populations, areas, or services), and to apply to the correct source. When such grant specialists are not available and when local fund-ing is sought, program budgeteers must roll up their sleeves.

To the extent possible, local-level funding opportunities should be used, for it is precisely at the local level that needs and demands can be best identified by persons familiar with the local area's prevailing social and economic conditions. The local level is also often the testing ground for the program's track record. Trust and credit do need to be earned. Thus the program's budgeteer needs to be planful, deliberate, and active, and the entire program needs to be credible. The opportunities for in-house cost sharing and the allocation of nonearmarked organizational income must be explored. Further, given that the well-armed budgeteer has much of the necessary budgetary justification data in hand, the budgeteer may also be exploring the possibilities of sharing service delivery—either together with or through contractual arrangement—with other programs and agencies in the locale. Such cost of service sharings may lead to substantial cost reductions or income advantages as well as improved service delivery.

An array of multiple funding resources also promotes vitality by reducing program reliance on any single funding source. An unfortunately common example may be found in the emergency service program of a comprehensive community mental health center that is relying solely on NIMH grant income. That program's fiscal passivity may have significant ripple effects on the delivery of its services. A more active budgeting stance has been advocated for some time now from both the private (Macleod, 1971) and the public (Sorensen and Phipps, 1972) sectors.

Other opportunities may be present within the clinical staff's competencies. A particularly skillful consultant or educator may have had a profoundly positive impact on the local citizenry, for example. That clinician's skillfulness is apt to be recognized and remembered. Also a program may have received favorable press reports as the result of helpful interventions in a local disaster or other newsworthy crisis. The public relations work and marketing skills of the organization and of the particular psychiatric emergency care program may greatly facilitate the harvesting of local funding opportunities.

A program budgeteer will also want to take advantage of other local resources that have the effect of reducing costs or increasing income. Such methodological options as matching funds, in-kind donations, and innovative donation possibilities (for example, yearly pledges with monthly payments) are valuable general resources. A budgeteer might approach smaller funding resources with specific needs, such as professional grant-writing or fund-raising skill or consultation, volunteer time, pledges for cash or

materials, bulk purchasing rates or discounts, data processing contributions, public relations services and advertisements, marketing advice, and printing, postage, and clerical time; the list is endless. Businesses or business groups may be particularly impressed by an informed presentation of exactly how the sought-after resources will affect expenses, income, and service delivery. Even a well-heeled psychiatric emergency care program (if one actually exists) will need to attend to this appropriate use of local resources to reduce the cost associated with those crises that never occurred (stated from another somewhat different angle, to reduce the costs associated with going from on-call to in-place).

Some specific resources

Fortunately, a psychiatric emergency care program budgeteer has a vast number of reference materials available for identifying and gaining access to potential funding resources. For instance, immediately available are the local telephone company's "yellow pages." Paradoxically, the telephone book is so heavily utilized in the delivery of psychiatric emergency care services that it is sometimes overlooked as a fiscal resource. Perhaps no better compendium of local funding resources exists. The state capital's telephone directory may also be especially helpful in identifying government-level prospects. Telephone books can identify the following potential resources for a program budgeteer: local, county, state, and federal agencies; local or regional foundation representatives; large and small businesses; retailers; unions; social, civic, fraternal, veteran, and special interest groups and associations; health and social service organizations; and charitable or federated funding resources.

Grant seeking is a specialized art. A budgeteer must first sort through the forest of possibilities. A superb starting point for such orientation is offered in Howard Hillman's "the art of winning" series (1975, 1977, 1980). The local, organizational, or state library may offer such important grant resources as the *Federal Register* and *The Foundation Directory*. As the Hillman books point out, there are governmental, corporate, and foundation grant resources located throughout the United States. So regardless of where a psychiatric emergency care program may be located, access to grant source materials is available. The skillful use of these resources, however, hinges on timeliness (for example, a program's budgeteering efforts may not match the timing of the particular resources's fiscal calendar).

When a budgeteer has a well-conceptualized action plan and an informed capability of presenting program needs, it is valuable to contact specific funding prospects in both public and private sectors to obtain the relevant informational booklets and application materials. Often prospective funding resources are very willing to consult and offer guidelines, advice, and valuable grant preparation clues.

Some effort must be made to weigh the use of federated funding resources such as the United Way. A budgeteer must balance the potential income from these resources with the costs associated with obtaining the grant. Some of these agencies, for instance, do not allow a recipient to do other types of local fund raising. Others may permit additional local fund raising only after obtaining approval. There are other costs, albeit somewhat more covert. For example, one must also figure in the costs associated with any federated funding resource's promotional activities that can take up much staff time. However, federated resources may sharply reduce fund raising costs by offering a convenient dispersal point for the area's charitable contributions.

The budgeteer who wants to invite community participation in the nurturance and growth of the psychiatric emergency care program will need to focus on developing multiple, specific needs requests and then attempt to match these needs with appropriate funding sources. This process may be income oriented, as in seeking cash, or expense oriented, as in seeking services or consultations. Inviting community participation has the effect of cementing the community's investment at both tangible and intangible levels.

POLITICS OF FUNDING

Is the psychiatric emergency care program salable? Has it developed, implemented, and evaluated itself so that a credible, successful track record can be presented? Or has the prospective psychiatric emergency care program been thoughtfully planned, carefully drawing from the experiences of other programs? Does the funding request package have a reasonable price tag? Does the primary salesperson know the program as well as the prevailing funding resource trends?

Marketing and stating the case

Know the market. That sounds simple, but just as budgeteering is both an art and science, so is marketeering. Thus it is especially vital to understand the market's needs, limits, expectations, and roles. The public and private sectors may differ enormously along these dimensions. Bringing the budget to either sector for funding, however, requires consideration of a number of successful marketeering practices. Again, the Hillman books (1975, 1977, 1980) may prove to be valuable tools for the budgeteer turned salesperson (also refer to Dermer, 1975, for foundations information, and Mirkin, 1972, for local fund raising tips).

Not the least of the important variables to consider when marketeering is one's attitude. Most of us fall somewhere between the grace of a swan and the brute force of a pile driver. When marketing the program, one must convey confidence, commitment, and a positive outlook. Being careful about one's attitude adds confidence to the presented case. Neither histrionics nor SWAT team tactics bring credibility to the program. An attitudinal or behavioral style of this sort will probably reflect a lack of respect for the funding resource's values. No one appreciates overkill or oversell.

Before proceeding to specific markets, the budgeteer should develop a funding budget and timetable. Then the budgeteer should stick to them (within reason). Get to know and figure in the strategic time frames, fiscal years, and so on, of each potential funding source so requests are submitted on time. Doing this will help keep a perspective while working out the alternatives. Action plans for the funding request should be clearly spelled out in a realistic, innovative manner. Allow time to get things done; it is highly unlikely, for instance, that one meeting with a prospective funding source will suffice. An active budgeteer will want to develop a fund-seeking calendar that covers 2 to 3 years. It is of course possible (and suggested) to use the fund-raising budget, the calendar, and the alternatives as objective measures of how well one is doing.

Information helps. A psychiatric emergency care program budgeteer must develop a clear, concise, persuasive sales line. This sales line should be written down in a fashion that avoids extremes in terms of claims, design, presentation, and general emotional tone. Also it is important to be brief and to the point. Grant finders and fund raisers call this brief sales line a case statement. The psychiatric emergency care program's case statement may also be useful for general reference and public relations endeavors. Being succinct enhances the probability of the case statement being read (or heard, as the case may be). Be sure to address what makes the psychiatric emergency care program special, valuable, unique, needed, and used. Outline the program's needs, the needs for change, and the criteria underlying strategies for change.

Involvement helps. Most crisis intervention specialists know that one great way to mobilize constructive problem solving and commitment in another is by inviting involvement and participation. Invite participation and mobilize mutual problem solving by eliminating dualistic comments (such as "we" versus "they") and substituting an invitational mood ("us," "let's," and so on). Invite questions. Questions offer the opportunity to clarify the program even further. In other words, it is quite possible for a program's budgeteer to squelch any possible misinterpretations by dovetailing involvement and information sharing.

Another approach to involvement is to have a few (remember: no overkilling) influential, knowledgeable supporters contribute to any written or personal presentations. Be sure to include someone who can speak to fiscal aspects of the psychiatric emergency care program as well. Such support shows local commitment and impact and may persuasively address the entire continuum resulting from the program's service delivery—from dollars to lives to the community's quality of life. Certainly such support will vastly influence the credibility of a psychiatric emergency care program's case.

Guidance helps. People need maps to understand the whys and wherefores of a psychiatric emergency care program—especially since the program's statistics are apt to reflect some affectively laden material, such as the number of completed suicides, attempted suicides, rapes, battered spouses and children, and psychoses. Anyway, how does one stop other human beings from killing themselves? Should one? Being specific and clear in the presentation of the program's ways, means, funding requests, and operating methods will go a long way. The fund agents may know nothing about crisis or suicide intervention. Being available and accessible to them will help by reducing uncertainties and any ambiguities.

Being credible, committed, and competent helps. It is not wise to assume that because a funding request was made, the request by itself will speak to these issues. Instead, a planful budgeteer will outline the clinical competencies within the program. After all, it is important for a prospective fund source to know that the program will be able to do the job. Although good fiscal planning and management strongly urge a budgeteer to look forward and backward, it is usually a good marketing strategy to present the case with a "now" orientation. Use the statistical past and the short-run future as a framework within which the program's relatively immediate needs are painted. Informative data help best when they are realistically framed and add clarity to the program's needs or needs for change. Presenting a credible, committed, and competent fiscal management picture is of particular help in supporting and clarifying the criteria guiding a psychiatric emergency care program's strategies.

Modest tooting of the horn helps. If the program has earned distinctions or has otherwise been singled out, share that recognition. For example, a psychiatric emergency care program may have been evaluated by consultants outside of the agency or national-level certification groups, such as the American Association of Suicidology.

How to ask

If a psychiatric emergency care program does not ask, the program will not receive. So the task is to make the best possible presentation of the program with as much data and clarity as possible on one hand, while moderating overzealousness, dramatics, and data deluge on the other.

It is a good general strategy to meet the prospective funding resource in person. Doing this cultivates needed contacts and helps clarify the resource's needs, values, expectations, and requirements. Being present conveys a responsive commitment and places some pressure on the prospective resource. Attending carefully to this latter aspect is essential; while optimism is important, tactlessness is self-destructive. Face-to-face meetings are especially important when a program seeks substantial funding. Not only does it pay to meet the persons behind the resource, but they may have a need to meet the program personnel or budgeteer.

Another helpful general strategy involves the setting of financial goals. A budgeteer should present realistic, data-based needs, modestly aimed somewhat higher in the case of funding appeals to the general public or individuals. It is far, far better to fall short of a higher goal. However, a budgeteer must be much more precise with government, corporate, and foundation grant requests. It is also important to note that Internal Revenue Service tax-exempt status is required for most corporate, foundation, and individual grants.

A budgeteer should especially spell out any evaluation-based or assessment-based innovations and programming changes as well as present programming. By doing so, a psychiatric emergency care program's budgeteer shares with the potential funding resource an openness to evaluation and a spirit of continuously planful management.

Regardless of whether the funding request is fully accomplished in person or in writing, there are some general guidelines that a psychiatric emergency care program budgeteer can follow. More specific suggestions are offered in the references cited earlier. The following boxed material lists a number of potentially valuable guidelines. For detailed funding request guidelines, see Hillman (1975, 1977, 1980), Dermer (1975), and Mirkin (1972).

Guidelines for funding requests

Develop a realistic 2-year or 3-year fund-raising budget and time line. Stick to them.

Be well armed with statistical, fiscal, and performance data, presenting these data in a clear, easy-to-understand, thorough manner.

Be modest, accurate, confident, and committed.

Know your market—know their fiscal years, time lines, expectations, and values. Meet each prospective fund resource.

Demonstrate, without outlandishness, the program's competence (or potential competence).

Show the program's concern about relevance and effectiveness.

Have an optimistic, confident, tactful manner and attitudinal set.

Develop a 25-words-or-less case statement.

Develop an effective one-page or two-page program summary.

Focus on potential opportunities (as opposed to gripes and problems).

Invite participation, a sense of working shoulder-to-shoulder.

Inform prospective resources of the program's operating methods, techniques, and evaluation-based changes. Present a brief organizational model so the resource sees where the program fits and who will be responsible for the funds.

Tell what is needed and why from them.

Develop realistic expectations of the results and share them.

Mention any special distinctions.

Gather and use supporting statements or presenters (including someone versed in fiscal matters).

Demonstrate local impact and demand.

Do not use flashy or expensive paper, slides, brochures, or presentations.

Be realistic but innovative.

Aim the sight a little higher for public or individual appeals; be more precise with government, corporate, and foundation grant requests.

SUMMARY

A psychiatric emergency care program's budget is a metaphorical expression of that program's translation of crisis intervention philosophy into action. As the quote at the beginning of the chapter suggests, advantage and utility are simultaneously present. A psychiatric emergency care program budgeteer can apply the various fiscal management and planning tools offered in this chapter to reduce costs, increase income, and measure program relevance and demand. A program's operating budget is not one but three budgets: statistical, expense, and income budgets. Each offers the budgeteer valuable fiscal assessment and planning opportunities. Each points in its particular way to what is there and what is not there so that the budgeteer can pair and pare. The aim is to provide competent, innovative, flexible psychiatric emergency care services at the least possible cost to the community. Diversification of clinician activities yields greater income potential, reduces costs, and softens the effects of stress, burnout, poor morale, and sleep deprivation. To achieve this goal, continuous informed fiscal evaluation is essential. A program must reduce the costs of psychiatric emergency care services as well as the costs associated with the crises that never happened. Further, budgeteers must not allow their programs to become too dependent on any one funding source. Such stasis is suicidal. Multiple sources of funding and diversification of psychiatric emergency care clinical income-generating activities are to be planfully cultivated. Participation in program budgeteering is encouraged as it offers a wide range of benefits. Psychiatric emergency care program costs and benefits are to be gauged by the program's effects on the various client, organization, health care, community, and economic interdependencies. Systems theory is particularly valuable in viewing the ripples created by a psychiatric emergency care program's existence.

A psychiatric emergency care program's human and organizational successes form the ledger from which others will assess the program's debits and credits. Through planful retrospective and prospective application of sound management practices, a psychiatric emergency care program can show those auditors that "the bottom line" involves much more than dollars alone. There are many lives on the balance sheet, too.

BIBLIOGRAPHY

Alder, H.L., and Roessler, E.B.: Introduction to probability and statistics, San Francisco, 1964, W.H. Freeman & Co.

American Hospital Association: Chart of accounts for hospitals, Chicago, 1976, The Association.

Cheek, L.M.: Zero-base budgeting comes of age, New York, 1977, American Management Association.

Cohen, J., and Cohen, P.: Applied multiple regression/correlation analysis for the behavioral sciences, Hillsdale, N.J., 1975, Lawrence Erlbaum Associates.

Dermer, J.: How to raise funds from foundations, New York, 1975, Public Service Materials Center.

Drucker, P.: Management: tasks, responsibilities and practices, New York, 1974, Harper & Row, Publishers.

Falkson, J.L.: HMOs and the politics of health system reform, Chicago, 1980, American Hospital Association.

Ferguson, G.A.: Statistical analysis in psychology and education, New York, 1971, McGraw-Hill Book Company.

Fuchs, V.R.: Who shall live?, New York, 1974, Basic Books, Inc., Publishers.

Gerson, S., and Bassuk, E.: Psychiatric emergencies: an overview, Am. J. Psychiatry 137:1, 1980.

Gross, M.J.: Financial and accounting guide for nonprofit organizations, New York, 1974, Ronald Press.

Hargreaves, W.A., et al.: Management information systems for mental health centers, San Francisco, 1974, National Institute of Mental Health.

Herkimer, A.G.: How accounting will serve the manager of the future, Chicago, 1972, Hospital Financial Management Association.

Hillman, H., and Abarbanel, K.: The art of winning foundation grants, New York, 1975, Vanguard Press, Inc.

Hillman, H.: The art of winning government grants, New York, 1977, Vanguard Press, Inc.

Hillman, H.: The art of winning corporate grants, New York, 1980, Vanguard Press, Inc.

Houck, L.D.: A practical guide to budgetary and management control systems, Lexington, Mass., 1979, Lexington Books.

Huff, D.: How to lie with statistics, New York, 1954, W.W. Norton & Co., Inc.

Hyde, A.C., and Shafritz, J.M., editors: Government budgeting: theory, process, politics, Oak Park, Ill., 1978, Moore Publishing Co.

Lao-Tzu: The way of life, New York, 1955, The New American Library, p. 63. (Translated by R.B. Blakney.)

Levin, H.M.: Cost effectiveness analysis in evaluation research, In Guttentag, M., and Struening, E.L., editors: Handbook of evaluation research, vol. 2, Beverly Hills, Calif., 1975, Sage Publications, p. 89.

Macleod, E.K.: Program budgeting works in nonprofit institutions, Harvard Business Review **49**:46, 1971.

Marmor, J.: The relationship between systems theory and community psychiatry, Hosp. Community Psychiatry **26**:807, 1975.

McGee, R.K.: Planning emergency treatment services for comprehensive community mental health centers, Gainesville, Fla., 1967, University of Florida.

Mirkin, H.R.: The complete fund raising guide, New York, 1972, Public Service Materials Center.

National Institute of Mental Health: Financing mental health care in the United States, DHEW Publishing No. (HSM) 73-9117, Washington, D.C., 1973a, U.S. Government Printing Office.

National Institute of Mental Health: Directory of general hospitals providing walk-in emergency mental health services, DHEW Publishing No. (HSM) 73-9022, Washington, D.C., 1973b, U.S. Government Printing Office.

National Institute of Mental Health: The cost of mental illness—1971, DHEW Publishing No. (ADM) 76-265, Washington, D.C., 1975, U.S. Government Printing Office.

National Institute of Mental Health: A study of deficiencies and differentials in the distribution of mental health resources in facilities, DHEW Publishing No. (ADM) 79-517, Washington, D.C., 1976a, U.S. Government Printing Office.

National Institute of Mental Health: Services to the mentally disabled of metropolitan community mental health center catchment area, DHEW Publishing No. (ADM) 76-373, Washington, D.C., 1976b, U.S. Government Printing Office.

National Institute of Mental Health: Services to the mentally disabled of selected catchment areas in Eastern New York state and New York City, DHEW Publishing No. (ADM) 76-372, Washington, D.C., 1976c, U.S. Government Printing Office.

National Institute of Mental Health: Psychiatric services and the changing institutional scene, 1950-1985, DHEW Publishing No. (ADM) 77-433, Washington, D.C., 1977, U.S. Government Printing Office.

Nie, N.H., et al.: SPSS: Statistical package for the social sciences, New York, 1975, McGraw-Hill Book Co.

Perlman, R.: Consumers and social services, New York, 1975, John Wiley & Sons, Inc.

President's Commission on Mental Health, vol. II: report of the task panel on cost and financing, Stock No. 040-000-00391-6, Washington, D.C., 1978, U.S. Government Printing Office.

Rothenberg, J.: Cost-benefit analyses: a methodological exposition. In Guttentag, M., and Struening, E.L., editors: Handbook of evaluation research, vol. 2, Beverly Hills, Calif., 1975, Sage Publications, p. 55.

Schick, A.: The road to PPB: the states of budget reform, Public Admin. Rev. **26**:243, 1966.

Smith, T.S., and Sorensen, J.E., editors: Integrated management information systems for community mental health centers, Rockville, Md., 1974, National Institute of Mental Health.

Sorensen, J.E., and Phipps, D.W.: Cost-finding and rate-setting for community mental health centers, DHEW Publishing No. (HSM) 72-9138, Washington, D.C., 1972, U.S. Government Printing Office.

Strupp, H.H., Hadley, S.W., and Gomes-Schwartz, B.: Psychotherapy for better or worse, New York, 1977, Jason Aronson, Inc.

Tucker, S.W.: The break-even system: a tool for profit planning, Englewood Cliffs, N.J., 1963, Prentice-Hall, Inc.

Wildavsky, A.: The politics of the budgetary process, Boston, 1974, Little, Brown & Co.

CHAPTER 23

Interagency and intraagency collaboration

Gail Pisarcik, R.N., M.S., C.S.

Collaboration implies a sharing of planning and action, with joint responsibility for (the) outcome (Brill, 1976).

INTERAGENCY COLLABORATION: HISTORY, REFERRAL, AND FOLLOW-UP

Team and interagency collaboration in the delivery of any human service is important, but never more so than between the psychiatric emergency care unit and other resources, given the enormous responsibilities and need of the acute psychiatric crisis situation. At the time that clients arrive in the psychiatric emergency unit, they may be in extreme and urgent need that has grown over a period of time. They will only be seen for a matter of minutes or hours during which much is expected. Collaboration at this time of contact with clients and their social and professional community presents a unique opportunity to effect significant intervention at a particularly vulnerable and malleable moment in their life—one in which a referral might finally be accepted or social relationships modified. Without the collaboration of social supports and other agencies and professionals, the work of the psychiatric emergency staff would be critically limited.

History

Clients may be complete strangers who are unable or unwilling to give important histories. Even with clients who do give a history, an objective and professional perspective is invaluable in making dispositional decisions. How these decisions are influenced is suggested by the following examples: (1) A client minimizes the significance of a cut wrist, saying that it was sustained accidently. In talking with the primary therapist, the clinician learns of past near-lethal suicide attempts and a current crisis. (2) A client with psychotic symptoms is having trouble articulating a request in the medical emergency department, appears very disorganized, and is referred to the psychiatric emergency unit. A local facility is able to report that this behavior represents the client's baseline functioning, that this person generally manages quite well, and that the client may have come to the hospital seeking reassurance regarding a history of high blood pressure. The call also provides the name and number of the person who runs the halfway house where the client resides. (3) A client expresses suicidal ideation after a family argument. A call to an outpatient facility reveals that in the past a supportive stay with a relative has helped greatly to relieve the anxiety. (4) A client who is directly and indirectly demanding hospitalization is found to have detrimentally regressed during previous hospitalization. The clinician learns that the treatment plan is to avoid hospitalization with a short course of high doses of medication accompanied by more intensified follow-up from the usual treatment agency.

Depending on state laws and institutional and individual policies, some facilities may be reluctant to divulge information without the client's consent. This becomes an appreciable problem when written consent is required. This may be the case with facilities that treat problems related to drug addiction and occasionally with private psychiatric hospitals. At times the facility will concede to offering information with the consent of the client by telephone. When this is not possible, limited information might be obtained. The clinician should keep in mind exactly what information is absolutely essential, as opposed to what information would be optimal. For example, the psychiatric emergency unit clinician may need to know the client's primary care giver, medications, or date of last hospitalization. Other facility records may include names and numbers of family members or the address of the client so that hospitalization can be made in the appropriate catchment area. When seeking background information, clinicians should state hospitalization is being seriously considered so that the staff at the appropriate facility may share information that may lead to an alternative disposition.

The psychiatric emergency unit clinician gradually becomes a supersleuth in many respects, combing through papers and clothing of psychotic persons to find dates of previous psychiatric or medical appointments, recent entries in bank books, receipts, or pictures on driver's licenses, which might indicate a time of higher functioning and give clues to the acuity of the illness. Phone numbers on scraps of papers and the landlord's name given by a police officer are often avenues to more information. Unfortunately, persons with severe illness who are least able to articulate their situation are often also without social ties or references. For some of the more disturbed persons of a community, the most comprehensive source of information may lie within the mental health system.

Experienced clinicians will often call the local state mental hospital, other psychiatric facilities, and nursing homes in their effort to find information about a person. It may happen that a client with a functional or organic psychosis or other impairment has simply wandered away from an institution. The most likely facilities, of course, are those in close proximity to the psychiatric emergency unit. Obtaining simple information as to whether a person is currently under care in the particular setting is usually not a problem. Agencies and resources other than psychiatric and medical facilities, such as the missing persons division of the police department, may be helpful and should also be explored. Alphabetically indexed 5 by 8-inch cards have been used in one busy unit to keep brief, accessible notes on all clients seen by that service. In addition to standard formal records, each visit is recorded with a short, systematized note on this card (others may be attached). The advantages of this system are that it allows for easy access (unlike chart retrieval systems); it can include informal observations, thoughts, and diagnostic possibilities; and it can include extremely helpful phone numbers of professional and institutional contacts, both for information gathering and for collaboration on disposition. It can also include treatment plans and information from important care givers which will help the staff to be more consistent with the overall treatment plan, thus alleviating the need for frequent calls to different institutions about the same client. The cards provide a place to note calls to the unit in anticipation of a possible visit from a client currently in crisis. Instructions, requests, and background information are recorded and easily passed on to the care giver who always checks the cards before seeing any client.

Referral

A majority of clients seen by the psychiatric emergency unit will be referred for follow-up or on an as-needed basis. Referrals will be made to public hospitals (including city, state, federal, and veterans); private psychiatric inpatient hospitals or units in general hospitals; partial hospitalization programs; psychiatric and counseling outpatient services; and alcoholic and drug detoxification centers. Referrals may be to telephone contacts such as a suicide prevention center or a crisis hot line. Occasionally, referrals will even include places providing day labor, jobs, day care for children, or even inexpensive or free sources of food and lodging. Familiarity with different sources of payment—Medicare, Medicaid, private insurance, and self-payment—is necessary, as is a knowledge of what type of insurance facilities require.

The psychiatric emergency unit must run smoothly and efficiently to provide appropriate care. Mechanisms for referral, like those of history gathering, must be in place. The appropriate time for exploring resources for an abused child or psychotic individual is not at 3 o'clock on a Saturday morning. A written resource book of referrals which is problem-oriented and periodically updated will ensure the best referral sys-

tem. Each resource should be accompanied by referral procedures, and informal notations should be made about how helpful the resource has been to staff and clients referred there and how frequently and readily referrals were accepted. Ideally, clinicians should be familiar with the receiving agency. Visits to those places where referrals are most frequently made is wise for many reasons. A staff visit promotes more appropriate referrals, allows for a more adequate and familiar orientation of client needs, and serves to initiate and encourage personal relationships with colleagues and to improve communication between agencies' staff members.

Clients often have many and varied needs. Shorn of extended family, neighbors, friends, and hometown and left to the isolation our society seems to foster, they may be unable to survive the assaults of unemployment, cutoffs of welfare checks, death, or infidelity. Clients' problems may be labeled as psychiatric for lack of other appropriate titles or availability of help. It may have little to do with psychiatry per se, but the anguish of clients who are in need may be more psychiatric than medical or surgical. Clients may, in fact, develop psychiatric symptoms or illnesses when more basic needs are not met. It is not uncommon for persons to come to the psychiatric emergency unit with primary problems of shelter, food, or finances and secondary anxiety or other symptoms. The referral "repertoire" will necessarily include very basic information about what is available in the area for most effective crisis intervention. It should be self-evident that, despite the pressure of time, the temptation to make expedient but inappropriate referrals should be avoided.

Follow-up

It is important for clinicians to seek follow-up of clients. Clinicians' skills are enhanced when they see a somewhat larger picture than the limited "slice of life" that is presented in the emergency situation. The efficacy of referrals and subsequent inherent problems can be appreciated. Also, an attempt at collaboration through follow-up manifests concern for both clients and the other agencies' staff members who may have been hurriedly dealt with during the urgency of the moment. Follow-up may give clinicians information that will be helpful if and when the client returns. Follow-up may be thought of as a luxury in a busy psychiatric emergency setting, but advantages such as reduced recidivism may result in an administrative policy for just such efforts. Follow-up is just one aspect of interagency collaboration. There are many others that are very relevant to client care.

PROBLEMS OF INTRAAGENCY COLLABORATION
"Dumping"

There is tremendous pressure to provide for clients who report to the unit in terribly urgent, often compromised situations. Clinicians possess the knowledge and experience to determine what should optimally be done for clients and what they absolutely need as a bare minimum of intervention. Unfortunately, the mental health system may not be able to provide either. Often there are wide gaps in systems. Problems stemming from specialization of srevices and deinstitutionalization are at the root of some intraagency cases of dumping. A syndrome not unique to the psychistric field, dumping involves getting rid of difficult or problematic clients by sending them to another facility or service for assessment and treatment. Clients who are dumped usually include those who are chronic treatment failures, who are old and debilitated, unmanageable, abusive and belligerent, or transient, and who may lack financial or interpersonal resources. In instances of dumping, the question of responsibility for the care of a particular client arises, with everyone disowning that responsibility.

The dumping syndrome is as undesirable as it is common, particularly in urban settings. The medical health system, as well as the mental health system, is guilty of fostering and then participating in this phenomenon. For the very undesirable, diagnostically uninteresting client without resources, entry into an inpatient setting usually is not easy. In determining a client's primary problem (for example, is senility a psychiatric or a medical problem?) or in deciding the client's catchment area (is it where he lived the

last 10 days or where he lived the previous 6 months?), there is sometimes no clear-cut answer, and discussion could continue forever. Even families sometimes engage in dumping senile, debilitated, or psychotic relatives at an emergency unit or psychiatric emergency unit without any information at all.

The implications of dumping are obvious. Clients' care suffers, and staff negativity and anger are often conveyed to clients who become victims of the situation. Although written policies are not a panacea, they can provide a helpful framework. Rotational systems by which facilities and different services within facilities accept or perform certain services for transient, poor, or otherwise "undesirable" clients should be written and, more importantly, enforced. With increasing numbers of older clients and incidence of psychiatric illness seemingly rising, there may well be a need to address this problem in more detail at each psychiatric emergency unit.

Overspecialization of services can be frustrating for psychiatric emergency clinicians. A number of clients are both suicidal and alcoholic, but in some areas detoxification centers are forbidden to take persons who are suicidal risks (they feel that they are not equipped to deal with this problem), psychiatric hospitals are discouraged from taking alcoholic persons (not being able to care for someone who may experience delirium tremens), and medical hospitals are reluctant to take persons with either problem since there is not a delineated, treatable medical diagnosis. Given the fact that the buck stops with the psychiatric emergency unit and given the need for an inpatient setting in some situations, there is a tendency to emphasize the appropriate problem to a particular agency and to minimize or omit other problems. Many clinicians may rationalize their distortion of client problems by their belief that the end justifies the means. Concomitant with the specialization of resources is the sometimes complicated method of referral which may all but preclude a psychiatric emergency unit referral.

A tremendous gap in most systems is apparent with somewhat psychotic persons who are quite sick, and, though not committable in the strictest sense, are so disturbed as to preclude them from

395

desiring, arranging for, or keeping appointments for outpatient treatment. Halfway house and structured living arrangements are not immediately accessible as a rule, and such resources are limited. The availability of beds in state mental hospitals is declining as a result of the trend toward de-institutionalization. The reluctance of psychiatrists to commit persons to mental facilities against their will is also increasing as individual and class-action lawsuits increase. These trends have enormous implications for psychiatric emergency treatment of clients. Interaction with public facilities such as state mental hospitals may be difficult because of such realities as poor staffing and large numbers of admissions. These facilities are often asked to admit those clients without resources who frequently are seen in the psychiatric emergency unit.

Unfortunately staff members at such facilities often discourage or refuse admissions because their institutions are currently operating at or above capacity. At the same time, a large number of clients are being prematurely discharged from these institutions to accommodate the requests for admission. These clients eventually come to the psychiatric emergency unit in need of readmission. Add to this vicious circle the rather common reluctance of on-call clinicians at admitting facilities to accept the responsibility for a client who they will have to "work-up," and the problems become more exaggerated. While solutions are *not* quite so obvious, there are certainly approaches that can help the situation.

The answer to larger and chronic problems are best sought at a higher administrative level. Directors of psychiatric emergency units should be advising their mental health department and legislators about the problems of individuals and groups of clients. They should use statistical data and clinical experience to help bring about changes in "the system." They can also have regular dialogue with heads of inpatient and outpatient resources to prevent problems from arising and handle ones that concern clients (for example, responsibility for cost of transportation of clients across county lines.) Situations occasionally occur in which there is a problem or disagreement between agencies which reaches an impasse. Channels that are created for just such problems should be used. Most hospital and psychiatric services have backup systems of more experienced administrative persons who can, when called, interact with their counterparts in other institutions. Clarification of the problem and decision as to responsibility for the client can often be done more easily by those somewhat removed from the scene. In this way the problem is resolved by those who are not embroiled in the situation, and persons affecting policy changes are made aware of the urgency and difficulty of problems.

Again, written guidelines, agreements, policies, rules, and regulations may not completely alleviate misunderstandings and problems between agencies, but they can provide an invaluable context in which to begin to resolve problems and build working relationships. This is particularly true in large metropolitan settings where the bureaucracy and lack of accountability can become overwhelming and discouraging. Exact relationships should be spelled out and responsibilities delineated so that some accountability is built into the system and gaps in that responsibility can be assessed and, it is hoped, closed.

A grass-roots, personal approach to intra-agency referrals is also advantageous. It is useful to identify oneself as an individual and a colleague working with a peer at the other end of the telephone line. This works particularly well when individuals at different agencies work the same shift consistently or have occasion to call frequently. Personal familiarity promotes a sense of responsibility and accountability. Frequent personal communication also tends to foster empathy for the other's situation. The value of a sense of humor and a friendly tone of voice cannot be underestimated. When the defensive lines are removed, collaboration can develop, much to the clients' benefit. It is not wise to be deceptive in any one particular case, because this distortion can jeopardize future collaborative efforts. A facility that has been sent an inappropriate referral will view future referrals with suspicion for some time to come. A positive understanding between staffs of different agencies facilitates objective communication instead of emotional reactions. Rather than overreacting in response to a suspected dump, staff members who have previously collaborated can ask for clarification. Negative confrontation merely invites retaliation and the fulfillment of preconceived negative opinions. Each phone encounter should be approached freshly. The clinician should keep in mind that misunderstandings may be just that, for example, an inappropriate transfer may be the result of a genuine lack of familiarity with the correct channels. Clarity, honesty, and cooperation are the basic tools for building strong collaborative ties between psychiatric emergency units and other agencies.

When certain problems arise, intraagency groups may best deal with them. Intraagency meetings can be arranged to develop comprehensive treatment plans for particularly problematic or high-utilization clients. These meetings can determine which agency has primary responsibility, plan consistent approaches, and tackle seemingly unanswerable problems regarding the client's care.

Competition

In addition to interagency dumping, there is the problem of interagency competition. Competition may occur when more than one comparable service or agency performs similar functions and offers comparable services. While competition may provide for a healthy rivalry and thereby upgrade care, it may more likely create an atmosphere of noncooperation to the possible detriment of clinical care.

Economics may be the basis for problems with intraagency collaboration and may be at the root of competition and conflict. Political and administrative factors should also be considered when introducing a program that will cause a shift in client flow. For example, the development of a center to treat Spanish-speaking clients in one city requires planning and collaboration to effect referrals from all other facilities. There may be a conflict of interest within the same facility that is delivering the service. These concerns may be at variance with the initiation and success of alternative and more effective or creative services and are problems that may preclude the success of

those services. Planning, foresight, and compromise are key factors in reducing unhealthy competition.

Phone and written communication

Clinicians and professionals from other mental health agencies may never have occasion to see each other. Yet their interdependence demands interaction. Accurate and thorough written and phone communication will often be the route to effective working relations and optimal care of clients. A phone call to a facility before transferring or referring a client is not an amenity but a necessity. It is also imperative that professional talk to professional to facilitate worthwhile dialogue—the sharing and clarification of thoughts and expectations. An identified voice on the other end of the line decreases the isolation and potential hostility of staff members from different institutions. Clinicians at referring and accepting facilities may be involved in the care of the client, and work on the case may overlap shifts, involving still more professionals. It is, therefore, important to note and pass on specific names and concerns that have already been discussed to ensure accountability of continuity of care. Informal requests might be made during the call (for example, the receiving clinician may request that a client be transported as soon as possible or that the client receive medication before transfer.)

Written communication is also vital. Beyond legal ramifications and issues of unsafe care inherent in the lack of adequate documentation on transfer, referring documents can provide immense information to personnel at a receiving facility. Ambulance records, police forms, nurses' notes, record of prescribed and administered medications, and a medical workup should all be sent, along with the names and phone numbers of persons closest to or most knowledgeable about the client. Agencies receiving this communication will often assume ongoing responsibility for care of the client. Lack of phone and written communication can foster hostility among psychiatric staff members who, when under stress from the demands of emergency work, can quickly displace their anger and frustration. Thus phone and written communication are the basic means of building collaboration.

BUILDING COLLABORATION

The 1963 Community Mental Health Centers Act provided that emergency psychiatric treatment be included as one of the five essential services in all federally funded community mental health centers (Public Law 88164). The impetus for this requirement followed a basic shift in orientation in the delivery of mental health services from large, centralized state mental hospitals to treatment in community-based alternatives (Joint Commission on Mental Health and Mental Illness, 1961). As a result of this new orientation to mental health care, the census of clients in mental hospitals in this country declined 65% from 1955 to 1978 (approximately 366,000 people) (Bassuk and Gerson, 1978). The discharge of these clients has seldom been accompanied by the development of adequate alternative sources of treatment (Slovenko and Luby, 1974), and given the trend toward briefer periods of hospitalization, emergency facilities have assumed a greater and greater role in the care of psychiatric clients. The proliferation of psychiatric emergency units has increased the demand for such services among those who formerly neglected their emotional problems (Nemiah, 1968).

If psychiatric emergency units are to absorb the weight of this expanded role and contain and define the acute crisis, as well as direct clients to longer term resources, the complex interaction of many resources is needed. These include individual, group, couple, and family outpatient services, day treatment facilities, medication programs, halfway houses, temporary housing, boarding homes, sheltered workshops, rehabilitation programs, emergency financial aid resources, visiting nurses' associations, senior citizens' activities, Meals-on-Wheels, and homemaker services. Still other agencies may be needed when more unusual situations occur (for example, psychotic persons, with no social supports, who are in need of hospitalization but are accompanied by their child or pet).

Certain services are crucial to providing comprehensive care for clients, such as medical backup to rule out organic causes for the client's condition or to treat urgent physical problems, a source of medication and commitment petitions, and some provision of physical safety for client and clinician. An emergency unit can provide for these needs and is often a comprehensive and expedient setting in which to practice emergency psychiatry. However, alternative arrangements may meet certain needs. One collaborative arrangement between a community psychiatric emergency unit and a police department allows clinicians to occasionally see clients (who may be in danger of losing control) right at the police station.

It seems that most effective collaborative systems are built on a mutual need. An example is one mental health system in Massachusetts which includes an emergency service in the community and one in the emergency department of a large general hospital interface. The former offers respite beds where clients can be held for short periods pending disposition and can also place clients in the homes of families in the community (on a 3-hour notice). The emergency department service, on the other hand, can offer the facilities and resources of a general hospital setting with holding beds for clients needing more intensive observation.

The staff of an emergency unit which needs and respects the services of the psychiatric emergency clinician will be more likely to allow the clinician to use that unit. A willingness of the psychiatric emergency clinician to be available and helpful will enhance the cooperation of the staff in the emergency unit. Effective collaboration might produce the need for staff privileges in a particular emergency unit. Such privileges are no longer reserved for physicians alone. This may require careful elaboration of responsibility and legalities. In one hospital that was reluctant to allow nonphysician clinicians from the local psychiatric emergency unit to see clients in their emergency unit because of a concern for liability, an agreement was worked out in which those clinicians would come to the emergency unit and collaborate with the staff for the express purpose of facilitating *disposition* rather than *treatment* per se. Likewise, other agencies may want to extend privileges for specific services, at least during an initial period in which trust is being built. Credibility may be enhanced by the willingness of psychiatric emergency unit staff members to see those clients who are not able to pay. Mutual projects may also create a helpful alliance. Mutual in-service training, consultation, and informal invitations to receptions might help.

There may be resistance from the community and other sources to a new psychiatric emergency unit. Some concerns will be more concrete than others. Questions will arise such as, "Who are these people?" "Are they competent?" "Will we lose access to hospital beds?" "Will we lose control?" People need to find out that problems can be dealt with flexibly and that there is room for some overlap.

The nature of the interface between the psychiatric emergency unit and the community will vary. Ths suicide telephone counselling service will have a different relationship with the community than the private consultant team, the large urban emergency department psychiatrist service, or the team affiliated with a state hospital. What remains constant is the fact that clients are helped considerably more when efforts are coordinated. The support of the administration of different services coupled with written agreements and a system of accountability ensure this coordination and allow the participating agencies to be responsive to the needs of clients. Regular meetings between agencies that consistently interface provide a useful format and forum for planning and troubleshooting. It may be desirable to set up a system of site visits that provide increased familiarity and cooperation. The staff might work with particular groups such as schools, churches, the elderly, and minority members to determine the community needs relative to psychiatric emergency care. These groups are also sources of community support and publicity for the psychiatric emergency unit.

ELICITING COMMUNITY SUPPORT AND PUBLICITY

How community support is elicited will depend on the size and character of the community and the existing services. Those who have provided crisis intervention to date should be included in the planning for new comprehensive services. Who is called on in a crisis? Is it the clergy, police, firemen, visiting nurses, or designated leaders in the community? One study identified a group of informal care givers—local people to whom residents turned for help and advice in the East Harlem community. These informal care givers included clergy, social club owners, spiritualists, and merchants. Results suggested that formal human service agencies should increase efforts to locate and work with community care givers (Leutz, 1977). People in crisis are most likely to call a familiar number such as 911, the local hospital emergency unit, or the state mental hospital. It is most important to recognize these resources. Channels for follow-up and problem solving can be planned. Such innovative programs as one in North Dakota has promoted a mental health training course for students in beauty colleges as well as for alcoholic beverage handlers (Wheeler and Miller, 1973).

Support can be initially requested on an administrative level. Meetings can include sharing of information and planning. Educational lectures or workshops can be offered with a twofold purpose. Such programs can better prepare initial responders to know how to give preprofessional care and can also disseminate information about what the psychiatric emergency unit has to offer clients and the community.

Publicity can help to elicit support and inform the public about the psychiatric emergency unit. Information should be aimed at the media that will reach the people who will support or use the service. Newspapers can print feature stories on the unit. Whenever a new person is hired or a program started, a newspaper article can remind the public of the care provided by the staff of the psychiatric emergency unit. Informal newsletters or church bulletins can let people know as well. Radio and television may also do feature stories. Public messages (for example, a feature on holiday depression in December) can be designed to directly solicit clients or explain services. Pamphlets and posters can also be used. It may be useful to designate one person to be responsible for community liaison, consultation, and education. This staff member should become familiar with and be known to the community at large.

NEED FOR LIAISON WITH POLICE

An important component of the community is the police department, and liaison with this agency deserves special consideration. Police currently provide the only free, mobile crisis intervention service available to the public 24 hours a day. The police are used, particularly by the poor, in the way that family physicians and clergy are used by the middle class—as the first source of help in time of need. It is estimated that 85% of all calls to urban police departments are calls for help in crisis situations such as family disturbances, rape, adolescents beyond parental control, or runaways (Everstine et al., 1977). This very important role of the police in crisis intervention cannot be ignored and should be integrated into the psychiatric emergency unit system of a community.

Police and emergency psychiatric clinician roles and responsibilities may overlap. In urban areas, in particular, there will be frequent situations in which it is unclear whether the actions of a person are criminal or psychiatric.

Case vignette #1

Police brought to the psychiatric emergency unit a person who was suspected of setting a fire in an apartment building. Although obviously quite disturbed, his behavior in the psychiatric emergency unit did not meet the criteria of the commitment laws of the state involved, so it was not possible to impose an involuntary commitment. The state mental hospital refused to accept this person for evaluation because the potential for arson would constitute a danger to others. Police were unable to arrest him because of lack of sufficient evidence. The "creative disposition," which was a result of police and clinician collaboration, was to have him arrested for loitering and disturbing the peace. A letter written by the clinician, to be given to the judge the next morning, explained the need for

hospitalization and requested that the court commit him to a state mental hospital equipped to care for dangerous persons. Medication and referral plans were made in the event that the client-prisoner was not hospitalized the next day.

A liaison with the police is necessary to effect the safety of the clinicians and clients from time to time. Although police should not be used as "baby-sitters" or "bouncers," their help is often invaluable and their service should be used discriminately. Administrative policies prohibiting firearms in client care areas may be unpopular. Arrangements in which they are left at a reception desk with an administrator or held by one officer for the others should be planned.

Police officers and clinicians have much in common. They are often serving clients who may be demanding, exhausting, and unable to extend positive feedback. Both are subject to burnout and need as much peer and administrative support as possible. Clinicians work in a tremendously emotion-draining and stressful environment that serves a large number of difficult and needy clients. Police officers frequently deal with situations that also are very intense and complex but with the additional burden of constant personal danger. Both find themselves trying to fill huge gaps in "the system" and facing problems they can do little about. There is, however, an enormous potential for increased efficacy with coordination and cooperation between the two. This cooperation will depend on police training and orientation. This potential can best be realized by input early in the police recruit's training and an understanding by clinicians of the philosophy and orientation of police.

Police training and orientation

The background of police and clinicians is important to the understanding of possible differences in philosophy and orientation. The police officer is trained to protect the community at large and to advocate for the rights of the citizens of that community. The psychiatric clinician is taught to advocate for the particular individual designated as *client* and to treat individual needs as the paramount concern. An important function of the police is to investigate, determine if a crime has been committed, and attribute blame. The psychiatric clinician learns not to blame but to accept and set limits on clients' behavior. It is with great effort that no blame is assigned to clients. Rather, behavior and its determinants are evaluated, help is offered, and in the case of antisocial clients, limits are set.

Police are trained to deal primarily with normal people who can communicate understandably and expeditiously. While they may have training in crisis intervention, they usually do not have a good appreciation of severe psychiatric illness and how to deal with persons exhibiting unusual behavior. They may be frustrated when they "don't get anywhere" with such persons. Clinicians deal with many clients who are not "acting normal" and may tend to minimize the abnormality of a client who seems very bizarre. Police may interpret such responses to clients as a lack of concern or desire to do anything for the client.

Police may allot an hour or half hour to a particular call and may become frustrated and impatient if it takes longer to learn the details of the case and finish their report. Clinicians are more accustomed to spending time with clients, appreciate the client's communication problem, and have the skills, medication, and milieu to effect better communication.

The fact that a large proportion of the calls that police receive are for work that comes under the heading of crisis intervention may not be very acceptable to those officers who resent doing "social work" and want to do "police work." Sometimes litigation by a client against a police officer may involve a psychiatric emergency staff member. Police officers may be protectively self-defensive, even when dealing with helping professionals. For example, information gathering by clinicians may be perceived by police officers to be critical of their actions, and therefore cooperation may be reduced. Such problems may be overcome with the use of both formal and informal systems that increase collaboration.

Use of formal and informal systems to increase collaboration with police

Increased collaborative efforts may be effected by having police and clinicians "walk a mile in each other's shoes." This concept has worked well for others. For example, emergency department nurses and emergency medical technicians have observed each other functioning in their respective environments with very positive results. Clinicians and police might benefit by spending an 8-hour period observing each other at work to increase the understanding of each other's role.

Orientation for both the police and the psychiatric emergency staff is necessary and should be instituted formally and informally. In addition, formal presentations at the Police Academy promote cooperation and convey respect for the entire police department. Education should familiarize each group with the other's role and philosophy as well as provide helpful information that can be used by members of the other field. The inclusion of an informal educative effort will encourage discussion and the reduction of some problems that might otherwise arise. Instruction of police officers by mental health professionals has been shown to be effective in changing attitudes toward mentally ill clients and in enabling officers to distinguish between mental illness and other behavior, thereby increasing interest in and sympathy for psychiatric problems (Janua, 1980). Even such topics as holds and restraints used with emotionally disturbed clients (as opposed to those for criminals) may be covered.

Some police departments are beginning to regularly assign officers to a particular district to enable them to know and better serve those areas. When this is the case, clinicians may want to work with those particular police assigned to their areas, sharing information and building a working relationship.

Some of the most effective relationships are built through informal contact. A cup of coffee offered and shared can do much for increasing collaboration. Mutual recognition, respect, and sharing of information are also enhanced in this way. Referrals will increase, and there will be willingness to work together if each encounter is a positive one. When an institution is made up of individuals familiar to one another, barriers

401

lessen. Collaboration can also be enhanced on an individual basis by telephoning to inform officers about the disposition or identity of a client they transported to the unit. Such behavior may enhance care of clients in the future.

A supportive response from police may be very important to those in crisis. While society views the support of the mental health clinician as part of the professional's responsibility, a positive attitude demonstrated by police may be viewed as support from someone who symbolizes strength and protection and, therefore, may be very reassuring.

If police can be positive forces, they can also be seen in a negative light as well. They may become the objects of paranoid delusions or projected hostility and may produce fear and intense anger in some clients. Police officers intervening in family disturbances calls frequently become targets of displaced aggression, especially in cases of battered wives, child abuse, and incest. An abrasive relationship between the police and the community can be an explosive precipitant of grievance, tension, and disorder. In a study of violence involving police, Toch (1968) concluded that violence is frequently triggered by persons in authority because they allow themselves to fit into preconceived stereotypes that can engender negative reactions and contribute to acting out behaviors during a crisis.

Officers may have anger of their own to displace. They may lack expertise, feel threatened, or be anxious; react hastily, irrationally, or in stereotypical fashion; or resort to instant arrest, treat disputants like children, intimidate with power plays, or use suppressive force in deterring possible violence (Barocas, 1973). Clinicians can formally and informally teach police that it is best not to take sides in family disputes but rather to listen and refer. Police dealing with family disputes should be aware of feelings, biases, and personal experiences that may influence their responses.

Police interface with the client and the psychiatric emergency unit

Recognition and respect are attitudes that can be subtly expressed and that mean a great deal.

Police sometimes feel "used" by the community at large. In the psychiatric emergency setting, police may be used inappropriately as bodyguards when there is a period of danger, only to be summarily dismissed when the danger has passed. Police may understandably question the sincerity of professionals who are sensitive to the feelings of others only when those others are clients. While clinicians are advocates primarily for the client at hand, respect given to police will facilitate the development of rapport between clinicians and the police. Demeaning an officer for suspected negative treatment of a client may only serve to promote more negative treatment of future clients. Efforts at understanding the other's role and the use of proper channels for questions may be more useful.

A difficult problem arises when police have expended much time and effort, often risking great personal harm, to forcibly remove a person from their environment, only to see them released shortly thereafter. Misunderstandings can be prevented by explanations of the limitations of the psychiatric emergency unit in hospitalizing or containing clients. In explaining those limitations, an analogy can be made between the mental health system and the legal system in that both are imperfect and both err on the side of protecting the rights of the individual. Just as police are frustrated with the judicial system, clinicians are often frustrated with the mental health system. The police know of many persons in the community they believe should be contained, just as psychiatric clinicians know of many clients who are quite disturbed yet are not in inpatient settings. If these frustrations are shared rather than taken out on each other, relationships can be enhanced and a camaraderie promoted.

Certain problems in communication are more common than others and should be guarded against. For example, clinicians may appear critical, questioning officers' reports of the client's behavior, minimizing the severity of the situation, and maintaining an "I'll wait and see myself" attitude. Regardless of the root of this negativity, the fact remains that police input is often very accurate and probably represents basic indicators of the client's impairment. Clients' demeanor frequently changes in the formal setting of the psychiatric emergency unit, many times for the better. They may have been removed from a possibly intense or unsafe environment and given a chance to "cool off" or "regroup" during their transportation to the unit. The officers' account, then, can be helpful in determining the entire picture and is not a discounting of the clinicians' ultimate responsibility of diagnosis and disposition that is based on interview, observation, and evaluation. Psychiatric emergency work is unquestionably enhanced by collaborative efforts with police and others.

Collaborative effort with the police and other community resources in which each enhances the other's work can improve the care of clients as well as improve morale. Efforts toward this collaboration are certainly worthwhile and an endeavor appropriately assumed by a mental health service.

The following approaches in the clinical situation will help the interface with police:

- Approach police with respect and courtesy.
- Acknowledge difficulties in getting client to hospital.
- At arrival of police, determine time frame of officers.
- Ascertain who called police (if anyone called), exactly what the problematic behavior consisted of, and why the client was brought to this facility.
- Ask for any documents completed by police or others, such as an involuntary hold.
- If police are behaving inappropriately toward clients (for example, laughing) diplomatically explain that the client's behavior is really beyond their control.

With the police, as with the community at large, the image of the unit is an important consideration, with implications for ultimate efficacy.

DETERMINING THE IMAGE OF THE PSYCHIATRIC EMERGENCY UNIT

The image of the unit will be considerably influenced by its affiliations and administrative ties. For example, the unit that is an integral part or extension of a larger institution will carry the image of that particular institution. Funding will also affect image. If funding for the unit is provided by public sources, clients may see it as more accessible to the poor. If funding is provided by community groups or individuals, more responsiveness to the funding source may be expected.

Despite the fact that some facets cannot be changed, there are many ways in which the psychiatric emergency unit can determine its image and focus. The purpose and mandate of the unit must be determined early in its operation. For example, the Psychiatric Emergency Team in Los Angeles and the Mobile Emergency Service Unit of Santa Clara perform emergency psychiatric evaluations to decide the question of hospitalization, while a third agency, the Emergency Treatment Center of Northern California, "backs up" 10 police departments and has as its focus on-site help and continuity of follow-up care (Everstine et al., 1977).

The psychiatric emergency unit will develop its image as people learn what it can and cannot do. Precedents are set, particularly when a need is met that no one else will address. For example, the psychiatric emergency unit that provides transportation to a client on one occasion may be called on when that need arises any other time in the future. While a certain amount of flexibility is desirable, the psychiatric emergency unit cannot become all things to all people. It is important to set realistic expectations for what the unit can consistently do.

How clients see and use the unit will depend on such factors as their experience with mental health systems, their own neediness, and their psychological makeup. A potential problem with any service that is as expedient as the psychiatric emergency unit usually is, is that it may begin to replace other more appropriate services for the client. The unit may serve those clients who overuse the unit, for example, clients may attempt to use psychiatric emergency units as outpatient clinics instead of keeping appointments at clinics as referred. The basis for this frequent use may be the fault of the system at large because of poor liaison between referral agencies or because of a reduction in services. It may also be the result of the extent of the client's problems or may have to do with the fact that an alliance and even transference with the unit is being created that might better be taking place in a more comprehensive, ongoing facility. Clinicians need to be aware of their own countertransference when they repeatedly interview clients who do not follow through with referrals. All clinicians need to learn why certain clients overuse unit services and then appropriately intervene.

The units' image will be influenced by every encounter each individual clinician has with clients. The person answering the phone and initially taking information will also be important to the public relations of the unit and must be as sensitive and helpful as the rest of the staff. Each staff member that the client comes in contact with *is* the psychiatric emergency unit and must realize that clients may be extremely vulnerable during a crisis and need much support.

Clinicians find themselves caught in the middle of a conflict involving issues of individual's rights, the rights of society, and legal and psychiatric considerations. Restrictions on psychiatric treatment against the client's will and limited and delineated, rather than global, denial of civil rights are the trend. Clients who are unwilling to be seen or treated yet seem distressed or disturbing to others may require the equally undesirable dispositional choices of involuntary hospitalization or unsupervised release. A situation may arise in which health professionals may be able to keep clients against their will but not be able to medicate them. Clinicians must make difficult decisions, often under such stressful conditions as the threat of a lawsuit by an agitated client.

Monitoring of helping professions by outsiders is becoming more prevalent. Consumers have come increasingly involved in the direction and review of mental health services, and they question commitment, physical restraint, and forcing of medications in particular. Some services will have consumer input inherent in a board of directors or client rights advisory service composed of people drawn from the community. Others may choose to create an advisory board to help guide the staff and heighten their awareness of the needs of the community as a whole. The persis-

tent shortage of resources and mental health personnel demands that the psychiatric emergency and other services be innovative to effectively serve more people. Consumers and community members can point to the particular community's needs. They can also be used to solicit funds from city budgets or private sources to maintain the unit or obtain such things as furniture for the unit. A community advisory board can be invaluable to the unit or other adjunctive mental health service. Members who are an integral part of the community are trusted more than "professionals" when explaining to other members the purpose, philosophy, and logistics of the psychiatric service and dispelling myths and overcoming resistance at a grass-roots level.

SUMMARY

Interagency and intraagency collaboration is a necessity, not a luxury. The psychiatric emergency unit is a pivotal service but must articulate with many other facets of a particular mental health system and the community at large to be effective. Efforts directed toward collaboration are really efforts toward better care for clients.

ACKNOWLEDGMENTS

The author would like to acknowledge helpful conversations with Linda Achber, R.N., and police officers John Noyes and Edward C. Donovan.

BIBLIOGRAPHY

Barocas, H.A.: Urban policemen: crisis mediators or crisis creators? Am. J. Orthopsychiatry **43**:632, July 1973.

Bassuk, E.L., and Gerson, S.: De-institutionalization and mental health services, Sci Am. **238**:46, 1978.

Brill, N.: Teamwork: working together in the human services, Philadelphia, 1976, J.B. Lippincott Co., p. 21.

Everstine, D.S., et al.: Emergency psychology: a mobile service for police crisis calls, Fam. Process **16**(3):281, Sept. 1977.

Janua, S.S., et al.: Training police officers to distinguish mental illness, Am. J. Psychiatry **137**:2, Feb. 1980.

Joint Commission on Mental Health and Mental Illness: Action for mental health, New York, 1961, Basic Books, Inc., Publishers.

Leutz, W.N.: The informal community caregiver: a link between the health care system and local residents, Am. J. Orthopsychiatry, p. 678, July 1977.

McGough, L.S., and Carmichael, W.C.: The right to treatment and the right to refuse treatment, Am. J. Orthopsychiatry, p. 307, April 1977.

Nemiah, J.C.: Help! (editorial), Am. J. Psychiatry **124:** 1698, 1968.

Slovenko, R., and Luby, E.: From moral treatment to railroad out of the mental hospital, Bull. Am. Acad. Psychiatry Law, 2:223, 1974.

Toch, H.: Violent men, Chicago, 1968, Aldine Publishing Co.

Wheeler, R., and Miller, H.: A mental health education program for North Dakota's beverage handlers and beauty colleges (mimeograph), Bismarck, N.D., 1973, North Dakota Mental Health Association.

Index

A

Abscess and seizures, 56
Absence seizures, generalized, 52
Abstraction, assessment of, 42
Abuse
  alcohol, 163-169
    diagnostic criteria for, 164
  amphetamine, 169-171
    patterns of, 169
  barbiturate, 171-175
    diagnostic cirteria for, 172
    patterns of, 171-172
  of children
    physical, 195
    potential for, assessment of, 16-17
    sexual, 195-199
  cocaine, 169
  hallucinogen, 175-176
  heroin, 176
  opiate, 176-177
  opioid, patterns of, 176-177
  phencyclidine, 177-179
    patterns of, 177-178
  sedative-hypnotic, diagnostic criteria for, 172
  substance
    by child, 192-193
    client with problem with, 161-179
      general approaches to, 162-163
      guidelines for assessment and treatment of, 163
    definition of, 162
    multiple, 162
Accidents, cerebrovascular, 38-39
Accounting
  accrual basis, 369
  cash basis, 369
Accrual basis accounting, 369
Acculturation, degree of, determination of, 249-250
ACEP; see American College of Emergency Physicians
Acetohexamide and alcohol, 166
Activity, psychomotor, assessment of, 19

Addison's disease, 35, 38
Adjustment disorders, differential diagnosis of, 93
Administrative program evaluation, 301-302
Administrative settings for psychiatric emergency unit, 287-288
Administrative support services in budget, 368
Administrator, 322-323
Adolescent; see Child; Teenager
Adrenal cortex
  hyperfunction of, 37-38
  hypofunction of, 38
Adrenal disorders, 37-38
α-Adrenergic blocker and alcohol, 166
Adrenocorticosteroids, organic mental disorders induced by, 35-36
Advocates, client, 346
Affect
  assessment of, 19-20
  disturbances of
    in borderline condition, 102
    in schizophrenic disorders, 72
  self-destructive impulses or actions without significant disturbances of, 92
  strong, avoidance of, by ethnic minorities, 246
Affective disorder
  atypical, 86, 88
  biogenic amines and, 88
  bipolar, 86-87
  chemotherapy for, 98-99
  client with, 86-99
  clinical presentation of, 89-91
  depressed type of, 87
  differential diagnosis of, 92-94
  etiology of, 88-89
  genetics and, 88
  hallucinogen, diagnostic criteria for, 176
  interview technique for client with, 94-97
  major, 86-87
  manic type of, 87
  mixed type of, 87

Affective disorder—cont'd
  other specific, 86, 87-88
  psychodynamics of, 88-90
  psychotherapy for, 97-99
  treatment of, 97-99
  unipolar, 87
Affective illness versus thought disorder, 90
Affective type of partial seizures, 54-55
Age and suicidal behavior, 127
Aggravated assault
  frequency of, 139
  versus homicide, 139-140
Aggression, 150-151
  and frustration, 150, 151
  Pavlov's theory of conditioning and, 150
Aging homosexual, 241
Agitation
  assessment of, 19
  psychomotor, 90
Akinetic mutism, description of, 30
Alcohol
  methyl, 165
  tolerance to, 164
  use of, and assessment of person in crisis, 18
  withdrawal from, 164
Alcohol abuse, 163-169
  diagnostic criteria for, 164
  and suicide, 128-129
Alcohol amnestic disorder, 168-169
Alcohol dependence, diagnostic criteria for, 164
Alcohol-drug reactions, signs of, 165-166
Alcohol hallucinosis, 167-168
Alcohol idiosyncratic intoxication, diagnostic criteria for, 165
Alcohol intoxication, 164-165
Alcohol-sensitizing agents, 165
Alcohol withdrawal, 164, 167
Alcohol withdrawal delirium, 168
Alcohol withdrawal seizures, 56-57
Alcoholic epilepsy, 56-57
Alcoholism, 18
  definition and diagnosis of, 163-164
  and seizures, 56-57
Aldomet; *see* Methyldopa
Alexia, 42
Alienation in borderline client, 102
Alkaloids, belladonna, causing organic mental disorders, 35
Alliance between client and clinician, developing, in crisis intervention, 6-7
Alzheimer's disease, 31
  and seizures, 56
AMA; *see* American Medical Association
Ambivalent cry for help, 124-125

"Ambulatory schizophrenia," 101
American Association of Suicidology, 384
American Civil Liberties Union, 346
American College of Emergency Physicians, 334, 337, 338, 341
American Medical Association, 334, 338, 341
  Standards of, 337
American Psychiatric Association, 337, 338, 341
  definition of psychiatric emergency, 334
  Task Force on Emergency Care Issues, 338
Amines, biogenic; *see* Biogenic amines
Amitriptyline
  and alcohol, 166
  for depression, 88
  organic mental disorders induced by, 35
  and seizures, 64
Amnesic syndrome, 33-34
Amnestic disorder
  alcohol, 168-169
  from barbiturates or similarly acting sedatives or hypnotics, 174-175
Amobarbital for affective disorders, 98-99
Amphetamine
  delusional disorder from, diagnostic criteria for, 171
  properties of, 169-170
  use of, screening for, 18
Amphetamine abuse, 169-171
Amphetamine intoxication
  diagnostic criteria for, 171
  and seizures, 56, 58
Amphetamine precipitated psychotic reaction, 171
Amphetamine psychosis, 58, 169, 170, 171
  treatment of, 34
Amphetamine toxicity, acute, 170-171
Amytal; *see* Amobarbital
Analgesics and alcohol, 165
Aneurysm, ruptured, 39
"Angel dust"; *see* Phencyclidine
Anger
  in borderline clients, 102
  in survivor, 268-269
Anhedonia in borderline client, 102
Anniversary of death, effect of, on survivor, 274
Anoxic conditions and seizures, 56
Antabuse; *see* Disulfiram
Anticoagulants and alcohol, 165
Anticonvulsant drugs, 62-63
  and alcohol, 166
  for generalized tonic-clonic seizures, 51
  intoxication with, and seizures, 56
  for posttraumatic seizures, 57
  and psychiatric complications, 65-66
  psychotropic effects of, 66
  toxicity with, and seizures, 65-66

Antidepressants
  for affective disorders, 98
  and alcohol, 166
  and biogenic amines, 88
  for dementia, 32
  tricyclic
    and biogenic amines, 88
    causing organic mental disorders, 35
    and seizures, 64-65
Antihistamines and alcohol, 166
Antihypertensives and alcohol, 166
Anti-infective agents and alcohol, 166
Antipsychotic agents
  and alcohol, 166
  and epilepsy, 62-63
Anxiety
  of clinician provoked by client, 14
  in crisis state, 5-6
  respiratory alkalosis, hyperventilation caused by, 36-37
"Anxiety-provoking therapy, brief," 253, 254
APA; *see* American Psychiatric Association
Aphasia
  motor, 41
  sensory, 41
Appearance, assessment of, 19
Appropriations budget, 369
Apresoline; *see* Hydralazine
Arguments as cause of homicidal behavior, 138-139
Arithmetical ability, assessment of, 42
Arrest, cardiorespiratory, seizures after, 56
Arteriosclerotic thrombosis, cerebral, 38
Arteriovenous malformation and seizures, 56
Arylcyclohexylamine intoxication, diagnostic criteria for, 178
Aseptic meningitis, 39
Asian Americans, 245
"As-if personality," 101
Aspirin and alcohol, 165
Assault
  aggravated
    frequency of, 139
    versus homicide, 139-140
  behaviors related to, continuum of, 151-152
  definition of, 149
  fears and rights of clinician regarding, 360
Assault cycle, 153-154
Assaultive behavior
  in child or adolescent, 201
  client with, 149-159
    assessment of, 154-155
    crisis management of, 155-158
    medication and physical containment for, 158-159
  by client in uproar, 157-158

Assaultive behavior—cont'd
  by fearful client, 156
  by frenzied client, 156-157
  stages of, 153-154
Assertive behavior, 211
Assessment, framework for, 14-15
Assessment process, 13-23
Assistance for client with substance abuse problem, 162-163
Astrocytoma, 39
Atabrine; *see* Quinacrine
Atarax; *see* Hydroxyzine
Ativan; *see* Lorazepam
Atropine poisoning, 35
Attention, disorder of, delirium as, 30-31
Attorney, representation by, in litigation proceedings, 362
Atypical affective disorder, 86, 88
Atypical grief, 275-276
Atypical psychosis, differential diagnosis of, 75
Auditory hallucinations
  in schizophrenic disorders, 72
  with seizures, 53
Audits, 303
Aura for generalized tonic-clonic seizures, 50
Authoritarian leader, 308
Automatisms with seizures, 53-54
Autopsy, psychological, 279
Aventyl; *see* Nortriptyline
Avitaminosis producing mental disturbances, 36

B
Background Interference Test to test for brain damage in elderly person, 46
Bacterial meningitis, 39
Barbiturate(s)
  action of, 172
  and alcohol, 166
  amnestic disorder from, 174-175
Barbiturate abuse, 171-175
  diagnostic criteria for, 172
  patterns of, 171-172
Barbiturate dependence, diagnostic criteria for, 174
Barbiturate intoxication, 172
Barbiturate overdoses
  diagnosing and treating, critical nature of, 172-174
  treatment of, 173
Barbiturate withdrawal and seizures, 57
Barbiturate withdrawal delirium, 174
Battered women, interventions with, 213-218
Battering of women, 211-218
BC/BS; *see* Blue Cross/Blue Shield
Behavior(s)
  related to assault, continuum of, 151-152

Behavior(s)—cont'd
  assaultive
    in child or adolescent, 201
    client with, 149-159
  assertive, 211
  of borderline clients, 103
  disoriented or disorganized, and suicide risk, 129
  erratic, in bereavement process, 269
  homicidal, client with, 138-147
  impulsive, in bereavement process, 269-270
  leadership, Tannenbaum and Schmidt's continuum of, 308-310
  self-destructive, in child, 199-201
  suicidal; *see* Suicidal behavior; Suicide
Behavioral, 334
Behavioral syndrome of epilepsy, 61-62
Behavioral theories of leadership, 308
Belladonna alkaloids causing organic mental disorders, 35
Bellah v. Greenson, 353-354
Bender Gestalt Visual-Motor Test, 44, 45-46
  to test for brain damage in elderly person, 46
Benzodiazepine sedatives for amphetamine toxicity, 170
Benzodiazepine withdrawal and seizures, 57
Benzodiazepines and alcohol, 166
Bereaved client, 256-279
  crisis intervention for, 259-260
  depression in, 271-273
  fear of mental illness in, 271
Bereavement
  childhood, 275, 277
  crisis theories in relationship to, 259-260
  family, 276-278
  by homosexual client, 241
  length of, 262
  in psychiatric emergency setting, typical, 260-261
  uncomplicated, 93-94
Bereavement process
  disorganization stage in, 270-273
  impact stage in, 262-264
  model for, 261-274
  protest stage in, 268-270
  reorganization stage in, 273-274
  shock and disbelief stage in, 264-268
  suicide and, 275
Beriberi, 36
Bernhard-Walsh decision-making model, 313-314
Biogenic amines
  and affective disorders, 88
  antidepressant medications and, 88
  depression and, 88
  mania and, 88
Biologic sex, 228

Bipolar affective disorders, 86-87
Bisexual; *see* Homosexual
Bizarre posturing, assessment of, 19
Black Americans, 245
Blood alcohol levels, signs of, 164
Blue Cross/Blue Shield, Standards of, 337
Borderline clients
  behavior of, 103
  countertransference with, 114-116
    coping with, 116
  environment of, assessing, 117-118
  hospitalization of, 119-120
  interview with, 118
  medication for, 118-119
  object relations in, 102-103
  psychotherapy with, 107
  sense of self of, 103-104
  structural interview for, 110-112
  suicidal behavior of, 116-117
  therapeutic alliance with, 118
  treatment considerations for, 117-121
  treatment plan for, 118-121
Borderline conditions
  assessment and diagnosis of, 110-113
  client with, 100-122
    interview with, 113-117
  crisis in, 106-110
  description of person with, 101-104
  developmental perspective of, 104-106
  differential diagnosis of, 112-113
  disturbances of affect in, 102
  historical roots of, 101
Borderline development, 105-106
Brain
  infections of, 39-40
  tumors of, 39
Brain damage in elderly persons, testing for, 46
Brain disorders, organic; *see* Organic brain disorders
Brain syndrome, organic
  with mania, differential diagnosis of, 90
  mixed, 35
Break-even analysis, 379-380
"Brief anxiety-provoking therapy," 253, 254
Brief crisis treatment for ethnic minority client, 253-254
Brief reactive psychosis, 75
Budget, 365-390
  appropriations, 369
  basic building blocks of, 368-369
  challenges regarding, 366
  comparison analysis of, 384
  cost-benefit analysis of, 384, 385
  expense, 373-374
  and fiscal year, 368

Budget—cont'd
  fixed, 369
  flexible, 369
  income, 374-375
  justification of, 375-384
  operating, 371-375
  statistical, 371-373
  step, 369
  support services in, 368
  systems theory and, 383-384
Budgetary processes, 365-375
Budgeteering, 365-390
  influences on, 366-368
Budgeting
  performance-based, 367
  program, 367
  zero-base, 367
Budgeting influences, historical, 366-368
Budgeting Systems, Planning Programming, 367
Bureaucracy
  mechanistic, 311
  organic, 311
  professional, 311
Bureaucratic models, 311
Burnout
  antecedents of, 295-296
  consequences of, 296
  coping strategies for, 296-297
  signs and symptoms of, 295
  theoretical model for, 295

C

Caffeine intoxication and seizures, 56
Calcium carbimide and alcohol, 165
Cannabis delusions, 34
Carbamazepine
  as anticonvulsant, 66
  for generalized tonic-clonic seizures, 51
  for psychomotor epilepsy, 56
Cardiorespiratory arrest, seizures after, 56
Care
  emergency, psychiatric; *see* Psychiatric emergency care
  standards of, 333-343
Case statement, 388
Cash basis accounting, 369
Catatonic schizophrenic, differential diagnosis of, 91
Catatonic type of schizophrenia, 74
Categorization of psychiatric emergency services, 341-342
Central nervous system stimulants and alcohol, 166
Centrencephalic seizures, 52
Cerebral arteriosclerotic thrombosis, 38
Cerebral beriberi, 36

Cerebral infarction and seizures, 56
Cerebral palsy and seizures, 56
Cerebrovascular accidents, 38-39
Cerebrum, reticulum cell sarcoma of, 39
Change, social, and violence, 150
Charting errors, legally acceptable method for noting, 359-360
Chemotherapy for affected disorders, 98-99
Child
  assaultive behavior in, 201
  as client
    in emergency room, parental involvement in, exceptions to, 192-194
    referral of, 203
  community supports for, utilization of, 202-203
  as danger
    to others, 201
    to self, 199-201
  emergency care of, 185-204
  emotionally abandoned, 202
  and family violence, 213, 216
  interview techniques with, 191-192
  physical abuse of, 195
  self-destructive behavior in, 199-201
  sexual abuse of, 195-199
  substance abuse of, 192-193
  as victim, 195-199
Child abuse, potential for, assessment of, 16-17
Child abuse protocol, 342-343
Childhood bereavement, 275, 277
Childhood deaths, 278
Childhood grief, 259
"China white," 176
Chloral hydrate
  for affective disorders, 98
  and alcohol, 166
Chloramphenicol and alcohol, 166
Chlordiazepoxide
  and alcohol, 166
  withdrawal from, and seizures, 57
Chloromycetin; *see* Chloramphenicol
Chlorpromazine
  and alcohol, 166
  for amphetamine intoxication, contraindication of, 58
  for PCP overdose, 179
  and seizures, 62
Chlorpropamide and alcohol, 166
Chorea, Huntington's, 32, 34
  and seizures, 56
Circular categorization of psychiatric emergency services, 342
Clarification
  in crisis intervention, 11
  in interview with borderline client, 111

Claus-Bailey decision-making model, 314
Clearance, medical, before psychiatric evaluation, 30
Clerk, psychiatric emergency unit, 322
Client
  anxiety in clinician provoked by, 14
  and clinician, alliance between, developing, in crisis
     intervention, 6-7
  in crisis
    previous level of functioning of, 8-10
    resources for, 8
    significant others of, 8
  definition of, 326
  gathering information from, in crisis intervention,
     7-10
  history of, and crisis intervention, 7-8
  with organic disorder, 29-47
  seeking psychiatric emergency care, 13-14
  with seizure disorder, 49-66
  use of term, 334
Client advocates, 346
Client versus social needs regarding confidentiality,
    353-354
Client's rights, law and, 346
Clinic, psychiatric emergency, staff in, 3-4; *see also* Psy-
    chiatric emergency unit
Clinical program evaluation, 302-303
Clinical records, 297-298, 299
Clinician
  anxiety of, provoked by client, 14
  and client, alliance between, developing, in crisis in-
    tervention, 6-7
  grief of, over client suicides, 278-279
  psychiatric nurse, 320-321
Closed injuries of head, 40
Cobb v. Grant, 351
Cocaine
  abuse of, 169
  use of, screening for, 18
Coercive power, 306-307
Cognitive type of partial seizures, 54
Collaboration
  building, 398-399
  interagency and intraagency, 392-404
  with police, informal and formal systems for, 401-402
Coma, 30
Coma-vigil, 30
Combat neurosis, 5
"Coming-out process" of homosexual client, crisis in,
    238-242
Commitment
  emergency; *see* Emergency commitment
  involuntary, of homicidal client, 145-146
Communication
  phone and written, interagency, 397-398

Communication—cont'd
  with schizophrenic people, setting up, 77-79
Community mental health centers
  NIMH guidelines for, 336-337
  psychiatric emergency care in, guidelines for, 341
  standards for, drafts of, 338
Community Mental Health Centers Act of 1963, 398
Community support(s)
  for child, utilization of, 202-203
  and publicity, eliciting, 399-400
Comparison analysis of budget, 384
Competency, 351-352
Competition, interagency, 397
Complaint, initial, 17
Computerized tomography scan in diagnosis of demen-
    tia, 32
Concussion, 40
Conditioning, Pavlov's theory of, and aggression, 150
Conference rooms for unit, 290
Confidentiality
  legal issues regarding, 353-354
  of relationship between clinician and homicidal cli-
    ent, 145
Conflict, bureaucratic, minimizing, 311-312
Confrontation in interview with borderline client,
    111
Confusion about boundaries of self in schizophrenic dis-
    orders, 72
Consciousness
  assessment of, 20
  levels of, 30
Consciousness-raising groups, 208, 210
Consent
  informed; *see* Informed consent
  to treatment, documentation of, 355, 359
Consolidated Standards for Child, Adolescent, and
    Adult Psychiatric, Alcoholism, and Drug
    Abuse Programs, 335
Consultation, psychiatric-medical, criteria for request-
    ing, 291-292
Contingency theory of leadership, Fiedler's, 310
Continuum of leadership behavior, Tannenbaum and
    Schmidt's, 308-310
Conversion reaction, psuedoepileptic, 59-61
Coping ability, previous, determination of, 7-8
Coping devices and suicidal behavior, 128
Cortex, adrenal
  hyperfunction of, 37-38
  hypofunction of, 38
Corticosteroid intoxication and seizures, 56
Cost(s), 369-371
  direct, 370
  fixed, 370
  indirect, 370

Cost(s)—cont'd
  opportunity, 370
  social, 370
  step, 371
  step-variable, 371
  variable, 370-371
Cost-benefit analysis of budget, 384, 385
Coumadin; *see* Warfarin
Counteridentification, projective, with borderline client, 116
Countertransference, 96-97
  with borderline client, 114-116
    coping with, 116
  coping with, by clinicians, 116
Court, medical record in, 359-360
Cretinism, 37
Cries for help by suicidal client, 124-125
Crisis
  assessment of, framework for, 14-15
  client in
    previous level of functioning of, 8-10
    resources for, 8
    significant others of, 8
  definition of, 4-5, 285-286
  emotional concept of, 5
  physical disorders contributing to, 18
  precipitating event for, 7
  and suicidal behavior, 128
  susceptibility to, 8
Crisis center; *see* Psychiatric emergency unit
Crisis intervention, 3-12
  alliance between client and clinician in, developing, 6-7
  for bereaved client, 259-260
  for ethnic minority client, 251-253
  gathering information from client in, 7-10
  history of client and, 7-8
  history of interest in, 5
  outcome of, 12
  pitfalls in, 11-12
  problem solving in, 10-11
  techniques of, 6-11
Crisis management of assaultive client, 155-158
Crisis model for ethnic minority clients, expanding, 247-251
Crisis state, 4-5
  characteristics of, 5-6
  client in, recognition of, 5-6
Crisis teams, composition of, 319-320
Crisis theories in relationship to bereavement, 259-260
Crisis treatment
  brief, for ethnic minority client, 253-254
  empathy in, 6-7
  outcome of, 12

Crisis treatment—cont'd
  pitfalls in, 11-12
Critical decisions, 312
Cross-cultural perspective for dealing with ethnic minority clients, need for, 246-247
Curandero, 247
Cushing's syndrome, 37-38
Cyclothymic disorder, 87
Cyclothymic personality, differential diagnosis of, 90

D
Dalmane
  for affective disorders, 98
  and alcohol, 166
Danger
  to others, emergency commitment because of, 348-349
  to self, emergency commitment because of, 348
Dangerousness, potential for, assessment of, 15-17
Darvon; *see* Propoxyphene hydrochloride
Darvon-D; *see* Propoxyphene napsylate
Data collection, 301
DBI; *see* Phenformin hydrochloride
Death; *see also* Loss
  anniversary of, effect of, on survivor, 274
  childhood, 278
  parental, and depression, 89
  as stressor, 257-278
Decision(s)
  critical, 312
  defensibility of, 313
  routine, 312
Decision making
  group, types of, 313
  participative leadership and, 312-314
  and problem solving, 313
Decision-making models, 313-314
Decisional law, 346
Defensive psychiatric emergency care, 362-363
Deficiency, thiamine, amnesia from, 168
Degenerative disorders and seizures, 56
Déjà vu with seizures, 54
Delirium, 30-31
  alcohol withdrawal, 168
  barbiturate withdrawal, 174
  course of, 31
  etiology of, 31
  febrile, 31
  symptoms of, 30-31
  treatment of, 31-32
Delirium tremens, 56-57, 168
Delusion(s)
  assessment of, 20
  cannabis, 34

Delusion(s)—cont'd
  in schizophrenic disorders, 71
Delusional disorder
  from amphetamine or similarly acting sympathomi-
      metics, diagnostic criteria for, 171
  hallucinogen, diagnostic criteria for, 176
  substance-induced, in schizotypal personality, 76-
      77
Delusional syndrome, organic, 34
Dementia, 31-33
  course of, 31-32
  depression accompanying, 33
  determination of, 30
  diagnosis of loss of memory in, 32
  etiology of, 32
  laboratory tests to diagnose, 32
  multiinfarct, 39
  nutritional, 36
  presenile, 31
    and seizures, 56
  senile, 31, 32
    and seizures, 56
    treatment of, 32-33
  symptoms of, 31
Democratic leader, 308
Denial in bereavement process, 264
Depakene; *see* Valproic acid
Dependence
  alcohol, diagnostic criteria for, 164
  barbiturate, diagnostic criteria for, 174
  sedative-hypnotic, diagnostic criteria for, 174
  substance, 162
Depersonalization with seizures, 54
Depressed clients, interviews with, 96
Depressed type of affective disorder, 87
Depression
  in bereaved client, 271-273
  and biogenic amines, 88
  in borderline client, 102
  chemotherapy for, 98-99
  in crisis state, 5-6
  with dementia, 33
  methyldopa and, 88
  parental death and, 89
  phencyclidine induced, 178
    treatment of, 179
  reserpine and, 88
  sadness without, 92-93
  versus schizophrenia, 91
  and suicidal behavior, 128
  in widows, 93
Depressive episode
  clinical presentation of, 90-91
  differential diagnosis of, 91

Depressive illness, major, 87
DES: *see* Diethylstilbestrol
Desipramine
  for depression, 88
  and seizures, 64
Detention, temporary, 349
Detention form, psychiatric emergency, 354-355, 356
  notification of, 357
Development
  borderline, 105-106
  normal, 104-105
Developmental disorders and seizures, 56
Dexedrine; *see* Dextroamphetamine and alcohol
Dextroamphetamine and alcohol, 166
Diabetes mellitus, 38
Diabinese; *see* Chlorporpamide
Diagnosis, formal, in emergency room, 17-22
Diazepam
  and alcohol, 166
  for homicidal client, 146
  for phencyclidine overdose, 178, 179
  for senile dementia, 32
Diazepam withdrawal and seizures, 57
Diazoxide for phencyclidine overdose, 178
Diethylstilbestrol to prevent pregnancy, 220
Dilantin; *see* Phenytoin
Direct costs, 370
Disability insurance, 360
Disease
  Addison's, 35, 38
  Alzheimer's, 31
    and seizures, 56
  Jakob-Creutzfeldt's, 31
  neoplastic, and seizures, 56
  Parkinson's, 32
  Pick's, 31, 32
  Sturge-Weber, and seizures, 56
  vascular, and seizures, 56
  venereal, in teenager, 193-194
  Wernicke's, 168
Disorganization stage in bereavement process, 270-273
Disorganized behavior and suicide risk, 129
Disorganized type of schizophrenia, 74
Disoriented behavior and suicide risk, 129
Distance, physical, as mechanism of segregation, 311-
    312
Disulfiram and alcohol, 165
Dixon v. Weinberger, 352
Documentation
  of care, significance of, 354-359
  of client's rights, 354-355
  of consent to treatment, 355, 359
Dollard and Miller, stimulus-response theory of per-
    sonality of, and aggression, 150-151

Doriden; *see* Glutethimide

Doxepin
  and alcohol, 166
  organic mental disorders induced by, 35
  and seizures, 64

"Dreamy state" with seizures, 54

Drug abuse and suicide, 128-129

Drug-induced psychosis, 18-19

Drug-induced states and seizures, 56, 57-58

Drugs; *see* specific drug

"Dumping," 395-397

Dying client, grief in, stages in, 259

Dymelor; *see* Acetohexamide

Dysarthria, 41

Dyskinesia, tardive, 351

Dyslexia, 42

Dysphagia, 41

Dysthymic disorder, 87-88

E

EDNA; *see* Emergency Department Nurses Association

Education
  For client with substance abuse problem, 162-163
  in-service, 327

Ego psychology, 89

Elavil; *see* Amitriptyline

Elderly, brain damage in, testing for, 46

Electroencephalogram
  in diagnosis of dementia, 32
  in evaluation of seizures, 50

Electrolyte disturbances, 36-37

"Emancipated minor," 187, 188

Embolic phenomena and seizures, 56

Embolism, 38

Emergency
  definition of, 285-286
  psychiatric, 334
    protocols for handling, 342-343

Emergency care, psychiatric; *see* Psychiatric emergency care

Emergency commitment
  criteria for, 348-349
  documentation of circumstances surrounding, 354-355
  prior judicial hearing for, 350
  procedures for, 349

Emergency Department Nurses Association, 337, 338

Emergency departments, hospital, psychiatric emergency care in, guidelines for, 338-341

Emergency detention, 349

Emergency detention form, psychiatric, 354-355, 356
  notification of, 357

Emergency Medical Services, 334, 338, 341

Emergency medication for schizophrenic disorders, 80

Emergency psychiatric nursing, 321

Emergency room, formal diagnosis in, 17-22

Emergency unit; *see* Psychiatric emergency unit

Emigration and schizophrenic disorders, 71, 73

Emotional crisis, concept of, 5

Emotionally abandoned children, 202

Empathic listening, 7

Empathy
  in crisis treatment, 6-7
  in interview of client with affective disorder, 94-95

Emptiness in borderline client, 102

EMS; *see* Emergency Medical Services

Encephalitis, 39-40
  and seizures, 56

Encephalopathy
  hypertensive, and seizures, 56
  lead, and seizures, 56
  Wernicke's, niacin deficiency in, 36

Endocrine disturbances, 37-38

Epilepsy; *see also* Seizures
  alcoholic, 56-57
  antipsychotic medications, and, 62-63
  behavioral syndrome of, 61-62
  forms of, 50-56
  "idiopathic," 56
  local causes of, 56
  and pseudoepilepsy, differential diagnosis of, 60
  psychomotor, 52-56
    clinical features of, differentiating it from psychiatric disorders, 55-56
  and psychotropic medications, 62-65
  schizophreniform psychosis of, 58-59
    valproic acid for, 66
  systemic causes of, 56
  temporal lobe, characteristics of person with, 62-63

Equanil; *see* Meprobamate

Erratic behavior in bereavement process, 269

Ethchlorvynol and alcohol, 166

Ethionamide and alcohol, 166

Ethnic groups, 245; *see also* Ethnic minority

Ethnic minority, 244-245
  client who is member of, 244-255
    avoidance of strong affects by, 246
    brief crisis treatment for, 253-254
    common barriers to, 245-246
    crisis intervention for, 251-253
    crisis model for, expanding, 247-251
    degree of acculturation of, 249-250
    need for cross-cultural perspective when dealing with, 246-247
    somatization by, 246
    stress for, source of, 250-251

Ethnic minority group, identifying, 248-249

Ethosuximide
    for generalized absence seizures, 52
    for seizures, 51
Evaluation
    outcome, 302
    process, 302
    program; *see* Program evaluation
    psychiatric, medical clearance before, 30
Evaluation procedures as mechanism of segregation, 312
Examination
    mental status, 43-44
    neurological, 41-42
Expense budget, 373-374
Expert power, 307
Exploitation of women, 210-211; *see also* Violence against women
Extrapsychic conflicts by ethnic minority clients, 250-251

F

Face sheet for clinical records, 298, 299
Facility standards, 335
Family and friends, availability of, in crisis, 22
Family bereavement, 276-278
Family interview, 190-191
Family violence, child and, 213, 216
Fear(s)
    of mental illness in bereaved client, 271
    of psychiatric emergency clinicians, 360-361
Fearful client, assaultive behavior by, 156
Febrile delirium, 31
Fees, 298
Feminist therapy, 210
Fiedler's contingency theory of leadership, 310
File, resource, 300
Films, x-ray, of skull in diagnosis of dementia, 32
Fiscal analysis of psychiatric emergency care program, 381, 383
Fiscal year, budget and, 368
"Fits"; *see also* Epilepsy; Seizures
    rum, 56, 167
    uncinate, 53
Fixed budget, 369
Fixed costs, 370
Flagyl; *see* Metronidazole
Flashbacks, 176
Flexible budget, 369
Flexibility of staff members, 319
Fluphenazine, 63
    and seizures, 62
Fluphenazine hydrochloride for mania, 98
Flurazepam for senile dementia, 32
Follow-up, 394-395

Formal diagnosis in emergency room, 17-22
"Free basing," 169
Freestanding psychiatric emergency units, 288
Frenzied client, assaultive behavior by, 56-57
Friends and family, availability of, in crisis, 22
Fructose for alcohol intoxication, 165
Frustration and aggression, 150, 151
Full-time equivalent, 380-381
    determining, 382
Fulvicin; *see* Griesofulvin
Functioning
    level of, previous, of client in crisis, 8-10
    and maintenance of unit, 330-404
Funding, politics of, 387-389
Funding requests, guidelines for, 389
Funding resources, 384-387
Furazolidone and alcohol, 166
Furoxone; *see* Furazolidone

G

Gay; *see* Homosexual client
Gay groups, value of, 238
Gender identity, 228
Gender identity conflict, 228
Gender identity disorder, 228
General knowledge, assessment of, 41-42
Generalized absence seizures, 52
Generalized tonic-clonic seizures, 50-52
Genetic factors in schizophrenic disorders, 73
Genetic theories of homosexuality, 230
Genetics and affective disorders, 88
Gesture, suicidal, 132-134
Glioblastoma multiforme, 39
Glutethimide and alcohol, 166
Grand mal seizures, 50-52
Grant seeking, 385-387
"Gravely disabled client," emergency commitment of, 349
Great man theory of leadership, 307
Grief
    atypical, 275-276
    character of, factors affecting, 274-275
    childhood, 259
    of clinician over client suicides, 278-279
    in dying client, stages in, 259
Grief model
    application of, to the losses and life changes, 276
    development of, relevant theories in, 258-259
Grief reactions, differential diagnosis of, 93, 94
Grief syndrome, characteristics of, 258-259
Grief work, 258-259
Grifulvin; *see* Griseofulvin and alcohol
Griseofulvin and alcohol, 166
Group decision making, types of, 313

Guanethidine and alcohol, 166
Guilt in survivor, 268-269

H

Hallucinations
    alcoholic, 167-168
    assessment of, 20
    in schizophrenic disorders, 72
    with seizures, 53
Hallucinogen(s)
    abuse of, 175-176
    psychotic reactions to, 176
    use of, patterns of, 175
Hallucinogen affective disorder, diagnostic criteria for, 176
Hallucinogen delusional disorder, diagnostic criteria for, 176
Hallucinogen hallucinosis, diagnostic criteria for, 175-176
Hallucinogenic toxicity, 175
Hallucinosis
    alcohol, 167-168
    hallucinogen, diagnostic criteria for, 175-176
Haloperidol
    for amphetamine psychosis, 58
    for amphetamine toxicity, 170
    for homicidal client, 146
    for mania, 98
    for phencyclidine overdose, 179
    for psychosis with epilepsy, 63
    for senile dementia, 33
Hazard and suicidal behavior, 128
Head injury, 40-41
Head trauma and seizures, 56
Health, mental, of women, 208-210
Hearing, judicial, prior, for emergency commitment, 350
Hebephrenic schizophrenia, 74
Help, cries for, by suicidal client, 124-125
Hemorrhage
    from head injuries, 40-41
    hypertensive, 38-39
    intracerebral, and seizures, 56
Heredity and affective disorders, 88
Heroin abuse, 176, 177; *see also* Opiate abuse
Heterosexual bias, 236-237
Heterosexuality, Kinsey's seven-point scale of, 229
High-lethality suicide attempts, multiple, 128
Hispanic, 245
Historical budgeting influences, 366-368
History
    of client and crisis intervention, 7-8
    of current disorder, 17
    importance of, 393-394

History—cont'd
    patient, taking, 17
    psychiatric
        past, ascertaining, 17-18
        and suicidal behavior, 128
Holidays and stress for homosexual client, 241-242
Holmes and Rahe scale, 257
Homicidal behavior
    arguments as cause of, 138-139
    assessment of, 140-144
    client with, 138-147
        intervention with, 144-147
        involuntary commitment of, 145-146
        pharmacological agents for, 146
        physical control for, 146-147
    origins of, 140
    potential for, determining, 143-144
Homicidal individual, profile of, 138, 139
Homicide versus aggravated assault, 139-140
Homophobia, 236-237
Homosexual client, 227-242
    aging, 241
    clinical presentation of, 237-242
    crises in "coming out" by, 238-242
    evaluation and treatment issues regarding, 234-237
    fear of exposure by, 241
    holidays and stress for, 241-242
    identity development of, 233-234
    and illness or death of lover, 241
    married, 240-241
    stereotypes of, 232
Homosexual orientation, origin of, 230-231
Homosexual relationship, breakup of, 237-238
Homosexuality
    incidence of, 229-230
    Kinsey's seven-point scale of, 229
    and psychopathology, 231-232
    research on, 229-232
    theories of, 230-231
Horizontal categorization of psychiatric emergency services, 341
Hormonal theories of homosexuality, 230
Hormone, thyroid, for hypothyroidism, 37
Hospital(s)
    general, standards for, drafts of, 338
    mental, state, psychiatric emergency care in, guidelines for, 341
    as setting for psychiatric emergency unit, 287
Hospital emergency departments, psychiatric emergency care, in, guidelines for, 338-341
Hospital support of clinician, 360
Hospitalization
    of borderline client, 119-120

Hospitalization—cont'd
of person in crisis, 23
of schizophrenic client, decision regarding, 82-84
of suicidal client, 131
Human relations bureaucratic model, 311
Human services model for unit, 290-291
Humor of staff members, 319
Huntington's chorea, 32, 34
and seizures, 56
Hydralazine and alcohol, 166
Hydroxyzine
and alcohol, 166
for homicidal client, 146
Hyperfunction of adrenal cortex, 37-38
Hyperglycemia, 38
Hypertensive encephalopathy and seizures, 56
Hypertensive hemorrhage, 38-39
Hyperthyroidism, 37
Hyperventilation, respiratory alkalosis, caused by
anxiety, 36-37
Hypocalcemia and seizures, 56
Hypofunction of adrenal cortex, 38
Hypoglycemia, 38
and seizures, 56
Hypoglycemic agents and alcohol, 166
Hypomagnesemia and seizures, 56
Hypomania, differential diagnosis of, 90
Hyponatremia, pathological water intoxication with,
and seizures, 56
Hypothyroidism, 37
Hysterical seizures, 60
Hysteroepilepsy, 60

I

Iatrogenic agents causing organic mental disorders, 35
Iatrogenic hypothyroidism, 37
Ideation, suicidal
assessment of, 129-131
intervention in, 131-132
staff response to, 132
Identification by widowed spouse, 274
"Identified patient," child as, 185-186
Identity
gender, 228
sexual, 227-229
Identity development of homosexual client, 233-234
"Idiopathic epilepsy," 56
Idiopathic seizures, 50
Idiosyncratic intoxication, alcohol, diagnostic criteria
for, 165
Illness
affective, versus thought disorder, 90
depressive, major, 87
mental, fear of, in bereaved client, 271

Illusions with seizures, 53
Image of psychiatric emergency unit, determining, 403-
404
Imipramine
and alcohol, 166
for depression, 88
organic mental disorders induced by, 35
and seizures, 64
Impact stage in bereavement process, 262-264
Impulses, self-destructive, without significant distur-
bance of affect, 92
Impulsiveness in survivor, 269-270
Impulsivity in borderline client, 103
Income budget, 374-375
Incompetency, 351-352
Incomplete notification of psychiatric emergency deten-
tion, form for, 355, 358
Indirect costs, 370
Infarction, cerebral, and seizures, 56
Infection(s)
of brain, 39-40
cerebral, and seizures, 56
Information, gathering, from client in crisis interven-
tion, 7-10
Informed consent
definition of, 351
for involuntary clients, 352
of medication use, 351-352
INH; *see* Isoniazid
Initial complaint, 17
Injury, head, 40-41
In-service education, 327
In-service training, 294
Insight, assessment of, 42
Insurance
disability, 360
malpractice, 361
Intellectual functioning, assessment of, 20-21
Interagency collaboration, 392-395
Interagency competition, 397
Interagency and intraagency collaboration, 392-404
International League Against Epilepsy, 50
Interpersonal facility of staff members, 319
Interpretation
in crisis intervention, 11-12
in interview with borderline client, 111
Intervention, crisis; *see* Crisis intervention
Interview
with borderline client, 118
with client with borderline condition, 113-117
dont's in, 96
with manic clients, 95
moralizing in, 96
with seriously depressed clients, 96

Interview—cont'd
structural, for borderline clients, 110-112
Interview rooms for unit, 289
Interview technique
for children, 191-192
for client with affective disorder, 94-97
Intoxication
alcohol, 164-165
idiosyncratic, diagnostic criteria for, 165
amphetamine, and seizures, 56, 58
from amphetamine or similarly acting sympathomimetics, diagnostic criteria for, 171
arylcyclohexylamine, diagnostic criteria for, 178
barbiturate, 172
as medical emergency, 30
opiate, diagnostic criteria for, 177
phencyclidine
diagnostic criteria for, 178
and seizures, 56, 57-58
sedative-hypnotic, diagnostic criteria for, 172
water, pathological, with hyponatremia and seizures,
56
Intraagency collaboration, problems of, 395-398
Intraagency and interagency collaboration, 392-404
Intracerebral hemorrhage and seizures, 56
Intrapsychic conflict by ethnic minority clients, 250-
251
Involuntary clients, informed consent for, 352
Involuntary commitment of homicidal client, 145-
146
Involuntary hold forms; *see* Psychiatric emergency
detention form
Involuntary versus voluntary commitment, 348-351
Irritation of clinician with client, 97
Ismelin; *see* Guanethidine
Isolation and suicidal behavior, 129
Isoniazid and alcohol, 166

J
Jakob-Creutzfeldt disease, 31
Jamais vu with seizures, 54
JCAH; *see* Joint Commission on Accreditation of Hos-
pitals
Job dissatisfaction, 295
Joint Commission on Accreditation of Hospitals, 338,
384
Accreditation Manual for Hospitals, 336
Community Mental Health Service Programs Man-
ual, 335-336
Standards of, 335-336
Joint Review Committee for Accreditation of Paramed-
ic Training Programs, 337
JRC; *see* Joint Review Committee
Judgment, assessment of, 42

Judicial hearing, prior, for emergency commitment,
350
Judicial involvement in mental client's rights, 346-347

K
Ketamine, 177
Kinsey's seven-point scale of homosexuality or hetero-
sexuality, 229
Knowledge, general, assessment of, 41-42
Korsakoff's syndrome, niacin deficiency in, 36

L
Laboratory examinations of person in crisis, 18
Laboratory tests to diagnose dementia, 32
Laissez-faire leader, 308
Lake v. Cameron, 352
Lanterman-Petris-Short Act of 1969, 347, 348, 349
"Latent psychosis," 101
Latino, 245
Law
decisional, 346
impact of, 345-347
mental health, 345-363
changes in, 347
psychiatric emergency care; see Legal issues
and rights of clients, 346
statutory, 346
Lead encephalopathy and seizures, 56
Leader
authoritarian, 308
democratic, 308
laissez-faire, 308
psychiatrist as, 320
"Leaderless group," myth of, 325
Leadership, 306-316
definition of, 306, 307
and management, differences between 307
organizational determinants of, 310-312
participative
and decision making, 312-314
and staff development, 314-315
and teamwork, 315-316
and power, differences between, 306-307
theories of
behavioral, 308
Fiedler's contingency, 310
situational, 308-310
trait, 307-308
Leadership behavior, continuum of, Tannenbaum and
Schmidt's, 308-310
Learned disorder, schizophrenia as, 73-74
"Least restrictive alternative" concept, 352-353
Legal implications of suicidal behavior, 125-126
Legal issues, 345-363

Legal support of assaulted psychiatric emergency clini-
    cian, 361
Legally acceptable method for noting errors in medical
    record, 359-360
Legitimate power, 307
Leptomeningitis, 39
Lesbian; *see* Homosexual client
Lesions, space-occupying, 39
Lessard v. Schmidt, 350
Lethality assessment, 126
Liaison with police, need for, 400-403
Librium; *see* Chlordiazepoxide
Life changes, application of grief model to,
    276
Life events, research on, as these relate to schizophren-
    ic exacerbations, 79
Life-style and suicidal behavior, 128
"Line of best fit," 376
Listening, empathic, 7
Lithium
    and seizures, 56, 63-64
    toxicity from, signs and symptoms of, 64
Lithium carbonate for mania, 98
Litigation, 361-362
Living arrangements and suicidal behavior, 127
Lorazepam
    for homicidal client, 146
    withdrawal from, seizures and, 57
Loss; *see* also Death
    application of grief model to, 276
    concept of, 257
    relationship of, to stress, 257
    responses to, 258-259
LPS Act; *see* Lanterman-Petris-Short Act of 1969
LSD, 175; *see* also Hallucinogens
Lumbar puncture in diagnosis of dementia, 32
Lupus erythematosus and seizures, 56

M

Maintenance and functioning of unit, 330-404
Major affective disorder, 86-87
Major depressive illness, 87
Major tranquilizers
    for mania, 98
    for senile dementia, 32
Malpractice insurance, 361
Malpractice suit, 361-362
Management and leadership, differences between, 307
Mania
    acute, differential diagnosis of, 75-77
    and biogenic amines, 88
    chemotherapy for, 98-99
    organic brain syndromes with, differential diagnosis
        of, 90

Mania—cont'd
    versus schizophrenia, 90
Manic clients, interview with, 95
Manic episode
    clinical presentation of, 89-90
    differential diagnosis of, 90
Manic type of affective disorders, 87
Marketeering, 387-388
Married homosexual, 240-241
Maturity of staff members, 319
Mechanistic bureaucracy, 311
Medical clearance before psychiatric evaluation, 30
Medical model for unit, 290-291
Medical record, 354-359
    in court, 359-360
    error in, legally acceptable method for noting, 359-
        360
Medical students, 323
Medication; *see* also specific drug
    antidepressant; *see* Antidepressant drugs
    antipsychotic, and epilepsy, 62-63
    for assaultive client, 158-159
    for borderline client, 118-119
    emergency, for schizophrenic disorders, 80
    for homicidal client, 146
    informed consent for use of, 351-352
    psychotropic, and epilepsy, 62-65
    right of client to refuse, 352
Meetings, team, 326-327
Mellaril; *see* Thioridazine
Memory, assessment of, 42
Meningioma, 39
Meningitis
    aseptic, 39
    bacterial, 39
    and seizures, 56
    viral, 39
Meningoencephalitis, 39
Mental client's rights, judicial involvement in, 346-347
Mental disorders, organic
    assessment for, 17, 18
    substance-induced, 35-36
Mental health of women, 208-210
Mental health centers
    community
        NIMH guidelines for, 336-337
        psychiatric emergency care in, guidelines for, 341
        standards for, drafts of, 338
    as setting for psychiatric emergency unit, 287-288
Mental health laws, 345-363
    changes in, 347
Mental hospitals, state, psychiatric emergency care in,
    guidelines for, 341
Mental illness, fear of, in bereaved persons, 271

Mental status examination, 43-44
  categories in, 19-21
Mentally ill, rights of, 345-363
Meprobamate and alcohol, 166
Mescaline, 175; *see also* Hallucinogens
Metabolic-nutritional states and seizures, 56
Methadone, 176, 177
  overdose of, treatment of, 177
Methanol poisoning, 165
Methyl alcohol, 165
Methyldopa
  and alcohol, 166
  and depression, 88
Methylene dioxyamphetamine, 175; see also Hallucino-
    gens
Methylphenidate, psychotic reaction to, 171
Methyprylon and alcohol, 166
Metronidazole and alcohol, 166
Migration, stressfulness of, 324
Miltown; *see* Meprobamate
Minor, "emancipated," 187, 188
Minor tranquilizers for senile dementia, 32
Minority, ethnic; *see* Ethnic minority clients
Minority group, 245; *see also* Ethnic minority clients
Miscommunication and ethnic minorities, 246
Mixed organic brain syndrome, 35
Mixed type of affective disorder, 87
Monoamine oxidase and biogenic amines, 88
Monoamine oxidase inhibitors and alcohol, 166
Moralizing in interview, 96
Morphine abuse, 177; *see also* Opiate abuse
Motion, disturbances of, in schizophrenic disorders, 72
Motivation in schizophrenic disorders, 72
Motor aphasia, 41
Multidisciplinary team approach, 318-328
Multiinfarct dementia, 39
Multiple sclerosis and seizures, 56
Multiple substance abuse, 162
Murder; *see also* Homicidal behavior
  frequency of, 139
  potential for, determining, 143-144
Mutism, akinetic, 30
Mysoline; *see* Primidine
Myxedema, 37

N

Naloxone for opiate overdose, 177
Narcan; *see* Naloxone
National Commission on the Causes and Prevention of
    Violence, 150
National Institute of Mental Health, 384
  Standards for, 336-337
National Standards for Community Mental Health
    Centers, 336

Native Americans, 245
Navane; *see* Thiothixene
Neoplastic disease and seizures, 56
Network Against Psychiatric Assault, 346
Neuroleptics
  for borderline client, 119
  and epilepsy, 62-63
  for schizophrenic disorders, 80
  and seizures, 56
Neurological examination, 41-42
Neurological variables in schizophrenic disorders, 73
Neuropsychiatric disorders associated with seizures,
    56-58
Neurosis, combat, 5
Neurosyphilis and seizures, 56
Niacin deficiency, 36
NIMH; *see* National Institute of Mental Health
Nitroglycerin and alcohol, 166
Noctec; *see* Chloral hydrate
Noludar; *see* Methyprylon
Norepinephrine and affective disorders, 88
Norpramin; *see* Desipramine
Nortriptyline
  and alcohol, 166
  for depression, 88
Notification
  of psychiatric emergency detention, incomplete, form
      for, 355, 358
  of psychiatric emergency detention form, 355, 357
  of rights in emergency commitment, 350-351
Nurse, psychiatric, 320-321
  in unit, 290
Nursing, psychiatric, emergency, 321
Nutritional dementias, 36

O

Object relations in borderline client, 102-103
Objective countertransference with borderline client,
    114
Objectivity of clinician, loss of, 97
OBS; *see* Organic brain syndrome
Observation rooms for unit, 289
Obtundation, 30
Occupations, transferral, as mechanism of segregation,
    312
O'Connor v. Donaldson, 347, 349
Olfactory hallucinations with seizures, 53
Oligodendroglioma, 39
Open injuries of head, 40
Operating budget, 371-375
Operation Baxtrom report, 349
Opiate abuse, 176-177
Opiate intoxication, diagnostic criteria for, 177
Opiate overdose, diagnosis and treatment of, 177

Opiates and alcohol, 165
Opioid abuse, patterns of, 176-177
Opportunity costs, 370
Organic brain disorder
  client with, 29-47
  definition of, 29
Organic brain syndrome
  with mania, differential diagnosis of, 90
  mixed, 35
  sedative-hypnotics for, contraindication of, 98
Organic bureaucracy, 311
Organic delusional syndrome, 34
Organic mental disorder
  assessment for, 17, 18
  substance-induced, 35-36
Organic personality syndrome, 34-35
Organization and structure of unit, 283-328
Organizational determinants of leadership, 310-312
Orientation
  police, 400-401
  to unit, 294
Orinase; *see* Tolbutamide
Others, danger to, emergency commitment because of,
  348-349
Outcome evaluation, 302-303
Overdose(s)
  barbiturate
    diagnosing and treating, critical nature of, 172-174
    treatment of, 173
  opiate, diagnosis and treatment of, 177
  sedative-hypnotic, treatment of, 173
Overidentification, avoiding, 97
Overnight hospitalization of borderline client, 119
Overspecialization of services, 395
Oxazepam withdrawal and seizures, 57

P

Palsy, cerebral, and seizures, 56
Pancreatic disorders, 38
Panic in crisis state, 5-6
Paranoia, 75
Paranoid disorders, differential diagnosis of, 75
Paranoid personality disorder, differential diagnosis of,
  75
Paranoid type of schizophrenia, 74
Parental death and depression, 89
Parental involvement with child client, exceptions to,
  192-194
Parkinson's disease, 32
Paroxysmal activity in EEG in evaluation of seizures,
  50
Partial seizures with complex symptomatology, 52-56
  signs and symptoms of, 53-56
  treatment of, 56

Participative leadership
  and decision making, 312-314
  and staff development, 314-315
  and teamwork, 315-316
Past psychiatric history, ascertaining, 17-18
Pathological water intoxication with hyponatremia and
  seizures, 56
Pathology, borderline; *see* Borderline conditions
Patient
  definition of, 326
  use of term, 334
Patient history, taking, 17
Pavlov's theory of conditioning and aggression, 150
Payment standards, 335
PCP; *see* Phencyclidine
Pellagra, 36
Penicillin to prevent venereal disease after rape, 220
Penicillin intoxication and seizures, 56
Pentazocine abuse, 177
Perceptions, assessment of, 20
Perceptual disturbances in schizophrenic disorders,
  72
Perchloroethylene; *see* Tetrachloroethylene
Performance-based budgeting, 367
Permission to intervene with child patient without pa-
  rental knowledge, 187-190
Personal countertransference with borderline client,
  114-116
Personal resources and suicidal behavior, 128
Personality
  "as-if," 101
  borderline, 100-122; *see also* Borderline conditions
  cyclothymic, differential diagnosis of, 90
  schizotypal, substance-induced delusional disorder
    in, 76-77
  stimulus-response theory of, of Dollard and Miller
    and aggression, 150-151
Personality disorders
  differential diagnosis of, 93
  paranoid, differential diagnosis of, 75
Personality syndrome, organic, 34-35
Personality traits of epileptic individuals, 61-62
Pertofrane; *see* Desipramine
Petit mal seizures, 52
Peyote, 175; *see also* Hallucinogens
Pharmacological agents for homicidal client, 146
Phencyclidine, 175; *see also* Hallucinogens
  elimination of, from body, 179
  use of, screening for, 18-19
Phencyclidine abuse, 177-179
Phencyclidine induced depression, 178
  treatment of, 179
Phencyclidine intoxication
  diagnostic criteria for, 178

Phencyclidine intoxication—cont'd
  and seizures, 56, 57-58
Phencyclidine-precipitated psychotic episodes, 178
  treatment of, 179
Phencyclidine toxic psychosis, 177
  treatment of, 179
Phencyclidine toxicity
  acute, 177
  treatment of, 178-179
Phenformin hydrochloride and alcohol, 166
Phenobarbital
  and alcohol, 166
  for generalized tonic-clonic seizures, 51
Phenobarbital substitution and withdrawal technique
    for barbiturate abuse, 174
Phenothiazines
  for amphetamine psychosis, 34
  for mania, 98
  and seizures, 62
Phentolamine
  and alcohol, 166
  for amphetamine toxicity, 170
Phenytoin
  and alcohol, 166
  for generalized tonic-clonic seizures, 51
  for psychomotor epilepsy, 56
  and seizures, 65
Phenytoin "toxicity," 65
Philosophical implications of suicidal behavior, 125-126
Phone communication, interagency, 397-398
Physical abuse of children, 195
Physical containment of assaultive client, 158-159
Physical control of homicidal client, 146-147
Physical design of unit, 289-290
Physical disorders contributing to psychiatric crisis, 18
Physical distance as mechanism of segregation, 311-
    312
Physician-client confidentiality, 354
Physiological variables in schizophrenic disorders, 73
Physostigmine
  for atropine poisoning, 35
  for tricyclic antidepressant – induced organic mental
      disorders, 35
Pick's disease, 31, 32
Placidyl; *see* Ethchlorvynol
Planning, treatment, 22-23
Planning Programming Budgeting Systems, 367
Poisoning
  atropine, 35
  methanol, 165
Police
  collaboration with, formal and informal systems for,
      401-402
  liaison with, need for, 400-403

Police interface with client and psychiatric emergency
    unit, 402-403
Police training and orientation, 400-401
Politics of funding, 387-389
Postconcussive syndrome, 57
Posturing, bizarre, assessment of, 19
Power, 306
  coercive, 306-307
  expert, 307
  and leadership, differences between, 306-307
  legitimate, 307
  referent, 307
  reward, 306
Practice standards, 335
Precipitating event for crisis, 7
Pregnancy, teenage, 194
Presenile dementia, 31
  and seizures, 56
Primidone
  for psychomotor epilepsy, 56
  for seizures, 51
Principle, Von Domarus, 77
Problem solving
  in crisis intervention, 10-11
  and decision making, 313
Procedures manual, 300-301
Process evaluation, 302
Professional bureaucracy, 311
Professional bureaucratic model, 311
Professional organizations, efforts of, to construct stan-
    dards, 337-341
Professional training, levels of, in unit, 293
Program budgeting, 367
Program evaluation
  administrative, 301-302
  clinical, 302-303
  as tool for management and education, 303-304
Program operating budget, 371-375
Program standards, 335
Projective counteridentification with borderline client,
    116
Prolixin; *see* Fluphenazine hydrochloride
Propoxyphene hydrochloride
  and alcohol, 165
  overdose of, 176, 177
Propoxyphene napsylate, overdose of, treatment of, 177
Protest stage of bereavement process, 268-270
Protocol
  child abuse, 342-343
  for handling specific psychiatric emergencies, 342
Protriptyline and seizures, 64
Pseudodementia, 30, 91
Pseudoepilepsy and epilepsy, differential diagnosis of,
    60

Pseudoepileptic conversion reaction, 59-61
"Pseudoneurotic schizophrenia," 101
Pseudoretardation, 44
  determination of, 30
Pseudoseizures, 59-61
Pseudotumor cerebri, 39
Psilocybin, 175; *see also* Hallucinogens
Psychiatric, 334
Psychiatric complications, anticonvulsants and, 65-66
Psychiatric disorders and seizures, 58-62
Psychiatric emergencies
  common, 24
  definition of, 334
  protocols for handling, 342-343
Psychiatric emergency care
  clients seeking, 13-14
  in community mental health centers, guidelines for, 341
  defensive, 362-363
  demand for, forecasting, 375-379
  difficulty of, 3-4
  in hospital emergency departments, guidelines for, 338-341
  legal issues in, 347-348
  management of, 281-404
  practice of, 1
  standards for
    authorship of, 334-335
    existing, 335-337
    need for, 334-335
  in state mental hospital, guidelines for, 341
  theoretical basis of, 2-23
Psychiatric emergency care laws; *see* Legal issues
Psychiatric emergency care program, fiscal analysis of, 381, 383
Psychiatric emergency clinician
  assaulted
    hospital support of, 360
    legal support of, 361
  assaults on, 360
  fears and rights of, 360-361
Psychiatric emergency detention form, 354-355, 356
  notification of, 357
Psychiatric emergency procedures, legal issues in, 347-348
Psychiatric emergency services, categorization of, 341-342
Psychiatric emergency unit
  administrative setting for, 287-288
  bereavement in, 260-261
  composition of, 319-320
  conference rooms for, 290
  data collection in, 301
  image of, determining, 403-404

Psychiatric emergency unit—cont'd
  interview rooms for, 289
  levels of professional training in, 293
  location of, 289
  maintenance and functioning of, 330-404
  management of, 285-305
  medical or human services model for, 290-201
  observation rooms for, 289
  organization and structure of, 283-328
  orientation to, 294
  physical design of, 289-290
  police interface with client and, 402-403
  professional disciplines involved in, 290
  program of
    components of, 286-287
    scope of, 285-287
  program evaluation of, 303-304
    administrative, 301-302
    clinical, 302-303
  psychiatric nurses in, 290
  psychiatrists in, 290-291
  records and miscellany of, 297-301
  referral network for, 288
  scheduling for, 293-294
  schizophrenic client's experience in, 70-71, 79-82
  seclusion rooms for, 289
  staff in, 3-4
  staffing of, 290-294
  students in, 293
  target client populations for, 287
  telephone rooms for, 289-290
  training and staff development on, 294-295
  volunteers in, 293
  waiting room for, 289
Psychiatric emergency unit clerk, 322
Psychiatric evaluation, medical clearance before, 30
Psychiatric history
  past, ascertaining, 17-18
  and suicidal behavior, 128
Psychiatric-medical consultation, criteria for requesting, 291-292
Psychiatric nurse clinicians, 320-321
  in unit, 290
Psychiatric nursing, emergency, 321
Psychiatric registrar, 322
Psychiatric residents, 323
Psychiatrist, 320
  as team leader, 320
  in unit, 290-291
Psychodynamic theories of homosexuality, 230-231
Psychodynamics of affective disorders, 88-89
Psychological autopsy, 279
Psychological intervention with homicidal client, 144-145

Psychological testing, 44-46
Psychologists, 322
Psychology
  ego, 89
  self, 89
Psychomotor activity, assessment of, 19
Psychomotor agitation, 90
Psychomotor epilepsy, 52-56
  clinical features of, differentiating it from psychiatric disorder, 55-56
Psychomotor retardation, 90
Psychomotor type of partial seizures, 53-54
Psychopathology and homosexuality, 231-232
Psychosensory type of partial seizures, 53
Psychosis
  amphetamine, 58, 169, 170, 171
    treatment of, 34
  atypical, differential diagnosis of, 75
  brief reactive, 75
  drug-induced, 18-19
  "latent," 101
  schizophreniform, of epilepsy, 58-59
    valproic acid for, 66
  steroid, 37-38
  toxic, phencyclidine, 177
    treatment of, 179
Psychotherapy
  for affective disorders, 97-99
  wirh borderline clients, 107
"Psychotic character," 101
Psychotic episodes, phencyclidine-precipitated, 178
  treatment of, 179
Psychotic reaction
  amphetamine precipitated, 171
  from hallucinogens, 176
Psychotropic effects of anticonvulsants, 66
Psychotropic medications
  and epilepsy, 62-65
  informed consent for use of, 351-352
  and seizures, 56
Public Law 88164, 398
Publicity, eliciting, 399-400

Q

Quinacrine and alcohol, 166

R

Race and suicidal behavior, 127
Rape, 218-224
Rape crisis group, 222
Rape trauma syndrome, 221-222
Raped women, intervention with, 219-224
Rapist, 219
Rauwolfia alkaloids and alcohol, 166

Reaction(s)
  alcohol-drug, signs of, 165-166
  conversion, pseudoepileptic, 59-61
  grief, differential diagnosis of, 93, 94
  psychotic
    amphetamine precipitated, 171
    from hallucinogens, 176
Reactive psychosis, brief, 75
Reading ability, assessment of, 42
Record(s)
  clinical, 297-298, 299
  medical, 354-359
    in court, 359-360
    error in, legally acceptable method for noting, 359-360
  and miscellany of unit, 297-301
Referent power, 307
Referral, 394
  of child client, 203
  of homosexual client, 242
  of schizophrenic client, 83-84
Referral network for psychiatric emergency unit, 288
Refugee status and schizophrenic disorders, 71, 73
Registrar, psychiatric, 322
Regitine; *see* Phentolamine
Relabeling for client with substance abuse problem, 162-163
Relationships, homosexual, breakup of, 237-238
Relevancy of psychiatric emergency program, 383
Renal failure and seizures, 56
Rennie v. Klein, 346, 352
Reorganization stage in bereavement process, 273-274
Requests, funding, guidelines for, 389
Reserpine and depression, 88
Residents, psychiatric, 323
Residual type of schizophrenia, 74-75
Resistant cries for help, 125
Resource file, 300
Resources
  availability of, assessment of, 22
  for clients in crisis, 8
  funding, 384-387
Respiratory alkalosis hyperventilation caused by anxiety, 36-37
Respondent superior, 361-362
Restraints, legal issues regarding use of, 353
Retardation, psychomotor, 90
  assessment of, 19
Reticulum cell sarcoma of cerebrum, 39
Retreats, 294
Reward power, 306

Rights
  client's
    documentation of, 354-355
    and law, 346
    to refuse medications, 352
  of mental client, judicial involvement in, 346-347
  of mentally ill, 345-363
  notification of, in emergency commitment, 350-351
  of psychiatric emergency clinicians, 360-361
Ritalin; *see* Methylphenidate
Rogers v. Okin, 352
Role separation as mechanism of segregation, 311
Rouse v. Cameron, 346
Routine decisions, 312
"Rum fits," 56, 167
Ruptured aneurysm, 39

S
Sadness without depression, 92-93
Salary matrix, 373
Sarcoma, reticulum cell, of cerebrum, 39
Scale, Holmes and Rahe, 257
Scan, CT, in diagnosis of dementia, 32
Scanning speech, 41
Scatter diagram for service demand, 376
Scheduling for unit, 293-294
Schizoaffective disorder, differential diagnosis of, 75
Schizoaffective schizophrenia, differential diagnosis of, 90
Schizophrenia; *see also* Schizophrenic disorders
  "ambulatory," 101
  catatonic type of, 74
    differential diagnosis of, 91
  versus depression, 91
  disorders similar to, requiring differential diagnosis, 75-77
  disorganized type of, 74
  and epilepsy, 58-59
  hebephrenic, 74
  as learned disorder, 73-74
  versus mania, 90
  paranoid type of, 74
  "pseudoneurotic," 101
  residual type of, 74-75
  schizoaffective, differential diagnosis of, 90
  undifferentiated type of, 74
Schizophrenic clients
  emergency unit problems with, 79-82
  experience of, in psychiatric emergency facility, 70-71
  hospitalization of, decision regarding, 82-84
  referral of, 83-84
  setting up communication with, 77-79

Schizophrenic disorders; *see also* Schizophrenia
  client with, 70-84
  confusion about boundaries of self in, 72
  current classification of, 71-73
  delusions in, 71
  differential diagnosis of, 75-77
  disturbances of affect in, 72
  disturbances of motion in, 72
  etiological factors in, 71
  general presentation of self in, 72
  genetic factors in, 73
  impairment of sensory function in, 73
  manifestations of, 71-72
  modes of thinking in, 71-72
  motivation in, 72
  onset of, 72-73
  perceptual disturbances in, 72
  physiological and neurological variables in, 73
  predisposing factors to, 73
  sociological variables in, 73
  types of, and diagnostic criteria, 74-75
  withdrawal in, 72
Schizophrenic exacerbations, research on life events as these relate to, 79
Schizophreniform disorder, differential diagnosis of, 75
Schizophreniform psychosis of epilepsy, 58-59
  valproic acid for, 66
Schizotypal personality, substance-induced delusional disorder in, 76-77
Schloendorff v. New York Hospital, 351
Sclerosis
  multiple, and seizures, 56
  tuberous, and seizures, 56
Scopolamine causing organic mental disorders, 35
Screening tests of person in crisis, 18
Seclusion, legal issues regarding use of, 353
Seclusion rooms for unit, 289
Security guards, 327
Sedatives for senile dementia, 32
Sedatives-hypnotics
  abuse of, diagnostic criteria for, 172
  for affective disorders, 98
  and alcohol, 166
  amnestic disorder from, 174-175
  dependence on, diagnostic criteria for, 174
  intoxication from, diagnostic criteria for, 172
  overdose of, treatment of, 173
Seizure disorder, client with, 49-66
Seizures; *see also* Epilepsy
  alcohol withdrawal, 56-57, 167
  centrencephalic, 52
  generalized absence, 52
  generalized tonic-clonic, 50-52

Seizures—cont'd
  grand mal, 50-52
  hysterical, 60
  idiopathic, 50
  lithium and, 63-64
  neuropsychiatric disorders associated with, 56-58
  partial, with complex symptomatology, 52-56
  petit mal, 52
  psychiatric disorders and, 58-62
  temporal lobe, 52-56
  tricyclic antidepressants and, 64-65
Self
  confusion about boundaries of, in schizophrenic disorders, 72
  danger to, emergency commitment because of, 348
  general presentation of, in schizophrenic disorder, 72
  sense of, in borderline client, 103-104
Self-destructive behavior; *see also* Suicide
  of borderline clients, 116-117
  in child, 199-201
Self-destructive impulses or action without significant disturbances of affect, 92
Self-destructiveness in borderline client, 103
Self-image of women, changes in, 207-208
Self psychology, 89
Semicoma, 30
Seminars, 294
Senile dementia, 31, 32
  and seizures, 56
  treatment of, 32-33
Sense of self of borderline client, 103-104
Sensory aphasia, 41
Sensory function, impairment of, in schizophrenic disorders, 73
Separation-individuation, process of, 104-105
Serax; *see* Oxazepam
Serotonin and affective disorders, 88
Service demand
  forecasting, 375-379
  scatter diagram for, 376
Services, overspecialization of, 395
Sex
  biologic, 228
  and suicidal behavior, 127
Sex-role, social, 228
Sexual abuse of child, 195-199
Sexual identity, 227-229
Sexual orientation, 228
Shock-disbelief stage in bereavement process, 264-268
Significant others
  of client in crisis, 8
  and suicidal behavior, 128
Simple stroke, 38
Sinequan; *see* Doxepin

Situational theories of leadership, 308-310
Skull, x-ray films of, in diagnosis of dementia, 32
Slums of urban area, living in, and schizophrenic disorders, 73
Social change and violence, 150
Social versus client needs regarding confidentiality, 353-354
Social costs, 370
Social sex-role, 228
Social workers, 321
Socialization of women, 206-208
Socioeconomic factors and suicidal behavior, 127
Somatic symptoms in crisis state, 5-6
Somatization by ethnic minority clients, 246
Space-occupying lesions, 39
Specific affective disorders, other, 86, 87-88
Speech
  assessment of, 20
  scanning, 41
Speech disorders, assessment of, 41
Staff in psychiatric emergency clinic, 3-4
Staff development
  participative leadership and, 314-315
  in psychiatric emergency unit, 294-295
Staff members, qualities of, 319
Staff response to suicidal behavior, 132, 134
Staffing of unit, 290-294
Staffing needs, planning, 380-381
Standards
  of American Medical Association, 337
  of Blue Cross/Blue Shield, 337
  of care, 333-343
  definition of, 334
  efforts by collaborating organizations to construct, 337-341
  facility, 335
  of Joint Commission on Accreditation of Hospitals, 335-336
  of National Institute of Mental Health, 336-337
  payment, 335
  practice, 335
  program, 335
  of psychiatric emergency care
    authorship of, 334-335
    existing, 335-337
    need for, 334-335
State mental hospital, psychiatric emergency care in, guidelines for, 341
State regulation of confidentiality, 354
Statistical budget, 371-373
Statutory law, 346
Stelazine; *see* Trifluoperazine
Step budget, 369
Step costs, 371

Step-variable costs, 371
Steroid psychosis, 37-38
Steroids, organic mental disorders induced by, 36
Stimulants, central nervous system, and alcohol, 166
Stimulus-response theory of personality of Dollard and Miller and aggression, 150-151
Stress
  for ethnic minority client, source of, 250-251
  for homosexual client, 241-242
  of migration, 324
  relationship of, to loss, 257
  and team support, 319
Stressor, death as, 257-258
Stroke, 38-39; *see also* Cerebrovascular accidents
  and seizures, 56
  simple, 38
  stuttering, 38
Structural interview for borderline clients, 110-112
"Structural" program evaluation, 301
Structure and organization of unit, 283-328
Students in unit, 293
Stupor, 30
Sturge-Weber disease and seizures, 56
Stuttering stroke, 38
Substance abuse
  by child, 192-193
  clients with problem with, 161-179
    general approaches to, 162-163
    guidelines for assessment and treatment of, 163
    definition of, 162
    multiple, 162
Substance dependence, 162
Substance-induced delusional disorder in schizotypal personality, 76-77
Substance-induced organic mental disorders, 35-36
Sudden infant death syndrome, 278
Suicidal behavior
  alcohol and drug abuse and, 128-129
  chronic, 134-136
  client with, 124-136
    clinical characteristics of, 128
    hospitalization of, 131
  coping devices and, 128
  crisis and, 128
  demographic data concerning, 127
  depression and, 128
  diagnosis of, 129-134
  hazard and, 128
  high-risk factors in, 128-129
  isolation and withdrawal and, 129
  legal and philosophical implications of, 125-126
  life-style and, 128
  personal resources and, 128
  psychiatric history and, 128

Suicidal behavior—cont'd
  significant others and, 128
  staff response to, 132, 134
Suicidal character, 134-136
Suicidal client, emergency commitment of, 348
Suicidal gesture, 132-134
Suicidal ideation, 129-132
Suicidal threats, 129-132
Suicide; *see also* Self-destructive behavior
  and bereavement process, 275
  by borderline client, 116-117
  by child, 200-201
  client, grief of clinician over, 278-279
  potential for, assessment of, 16
  right to commit, 126
Suicide attempt, 132-134
  multiple high-lethality, 128
Suicide plan, 128
Suicide risk, general assessment of, 126-129
Sulfonamides and alcohol, 166
Sulfonylurea drugs and alcohol, 166
"Sundown syndrome," 32
Support, community, eliciting, 399-400
Suzuki v. Quisenberry, 350
Symbolic abilities, assessment of, 42
Symbolic cry for help, 125
Sympatholytic drugs and alcohol, 166
Sympathomimetics
  delusional disorder from, diagnostic criteria for, 171
  intoxication from, diagnostic criteria for, 171
Syndrome
  amnesic, 33-34
  behavioral, of epilepsy, 61-62
  borderline, 100-122; *see also* Borderline conditions
  Cushing's, 37-38
  dumping, 395-397
  grief, characteristics of, 258-259
  Korsakoff's, niacin deficiency in, 36
  organic brain
    with mania, differential diagnosis of, 90
    mixed, 35
  organic delusional, 34
  organic personality, 34-35
  "postconcussive," 57
  rape trauma, 221-222
  stuttering stroke, 38
  sudden infant death, 278
  "sundown," 32
  traumatic, 40-41
  Wernicke-Korsakoff, and dementia, 32
  withdrawal
    characteristics of, 162
    and seizures, 56, 57
Systems theory and budget, 383-384

T

Taking over for client with substance abuse problem, 162-163

Tannenbaum and Schmidt's continuum of leadership behavior, 308-310

Tardive dyskinesia, 351

Target client populations for psychiatric emergency unit, 287

Tasaroff v. University of California Regents, 353

TCAs; *see* Tricyclic antidepressants

Team
   cohesiveness of, 325
   conflict within, 325
   crisis, composition of, 319-320

Team approach, multidisciplinary, 318-328

Team meetings, 326-327

Team support and stress, 319

Teamwork, participative leadership and, 315-316

Teenager; *see also* Child
   pregnancy in, 194
   venereal disease in, 193-194

Tegretol; *see* Carbamazepine

Telephone rooms for unit, 289-290

Temporal lobe epilepsy, characteristics of person with, 62-63

Temporal lobe seizures, 52-56

Temporary detention, 349

Temposil; *see* Calcium carbimide

Tension in crisis state, 5

Test
   Background Interference, to test for brain damage in elderly person, 46
   Bender Gestalt Visual-Motor, 44, 45-46
      to test for brain damage in elderly person, 46
   laboratory, to diagnose dementia, 32
   screening, of person in crisis, 18

Testing
   for brain damage in elderly persons, 46
   psychological, 44-46

Tetrachloroethylene and alcohol, 166

Tetracycline to prevent venereal disease after rape, 220

Theory(ies)
   of conditioning, Pavlov's, and aggression, 150
   crisis, in relationship to bereavement, 259-260
   in development of grief models, 258-259
   of homosexuality, 230-231
   of leadership
      behavioral, 308
      Fiedler's contingency, 310
      situational, 308-310
      trait, 307-308
   of personality, stimulus-response, of Dollard and Miller and aggression, 150-151
   systems, and budget, 383-384

Therapeutic interaction between clinician and borderline client, 113-117

Thiamin deficiency, 36
   amnesia from, 168

Thinking, modes of, in schizophrenic disorders, 71-72

Thioridazine and seizures, 62

Thiothixene for mania, 98

Third world group, 245; *see also* Ethnic minority group

Thorazine; *see* Chlorpromazine

Thought contents, assessment of, 20

Thought disorder versus affective illness, 90

Thought process, assessment of, 20

Threatened violence, clinician and, 95-96

Threats, suicidal, 129-132

Thrombosis, 38

Thyroid disorders, 37

Thyroid hormone for hypothyroidism, 37

Tics, assessment of, 19

Tofranil; *see* Imipramine

Tolazamide and alcohol, 166

Tolbutamide and alcohol, 166

Tolerance
   to alcohol, 164
   definition of, 162

Tolinase; *see* Tolazamide

Tonic-clonic seizures, generalized, 50-52

Toxic conditions and seizures, 56, 57-58

Toxic psychosis, phencyclidine, 177
   treatment of, 179

Toxic states and seizures, 56

Toxicity
   amphetamine, acute, 170-171
   anticonvulsant, and seizures, 65-66
   causing assaultive behavior, 155
   hallucinogenic, 175
   lithium, signs and symptoms of, 64
   phencyclidine, acute, 177
      treatment of, 178-179
   phenytoin, 65

Training
   in-service, 294
   police, 400-401
   professional, levels of, in unit, 293
   and staff development in psychiatric emergency unit, 294-295

Trait theories of leadership, 307-308

Tranquilizers
   for homicidal client, 146
   major
      for mania, 98
      for senile dementia, 32
   minor, for senile dementia, 32

Transferral occupation as mechanism of segregation, 312

Transient hallucinosis from alcohol withdrawal, 167-168

Transsexual, 228

Transvestite, 228

Trauma

head, and seizures, 56

seizures after, 57

Traumatic syndrome, 40-41

Treatment

consent to, documentation of, 355, 359

crisis; *see* Crisis treatment

Treatment planning, 22-23

Trecator; *see* Ethionamide

Tremors

alcohol withdrawal, 167

assessment of, 219

Tricyclic antidepressants

and biogenic amines, 88

causing organic mental disorders, 35

and seizures, 56, 64-65

Trifluoperazine, 63

for homicidal client, 146

and seizures, 62

Tuberous sclerosis and seizures, 56

Tumors of brain, 39

U

Uncinate fits, 53

Uncomplicated bereavement, 93-94

Undifferentiated type of schizophrenia, 74

Unheeded cry for help, 125

Unipolar affective disorders, 87

Unit; *see* Psychiatric emergency unit

Uproar, client in, assaultive behavior by, 157-158

V

Valium; *see* Diazepam

Valproic acid, 63

as anticonvulsant, 66

Variable costs, 370-371

Vascular disease and seizures, 56

Vasodilators and alcohol, 166

Venereal disease in teenager, 193-194

Vertical categorization of psychiatric emergency services, 341-342

Victim, child as, 195-199

Violence; *see also* Assaultive behavior; Homicidal behavior

family, child and, 213, 216

potential for, assessment of, 15-17

social change and, 150

social context of, 150

threatened, clinician and, 95-96

Violence—cont'd

against women, 205-225

attitudes of staff members toward, 224

Viral meningitis, 39

Vistaril; *see* Hydroxyzine

Visual hallucinations with seizures, 53

Vivactil; *see* Protriptyline

Voluntary versus involuntary commitment, 348-351

Volunteers in unit, 293

Von Domarus principle, 77

W

WAIS; *see* Wechsler Adult Intelligence Scale

Warfarin and alcohol, 165

Water intoxication, pathological, with hyponatremia and seizures, 56

Weberian bureaucratic model, 311

Wechsler Adult Intelligence Scale, 44

interpretation of scores on, 45

to test for brain damage in elderly persons, 46

Wechsler Intelligence Scale for Children, Revised Form, 44

Wernicke-Korsakoff syndrome and dementia, 32

Wernicke's disease, 168

Wernicke's encephalopathy, niacin deficiency in, 36

Widows, depression in, 93

Wife abuse, 211

Withdrawal

alcohol, 164

delirium from, 168

diagnostic criteria for, 167, 168

barbiturate

delirium from, 174

and seizures, 57

benzodiazepine, and seizures, 57

definition of, 162

in schizophrenic disorders, 72

and suicidal behavior, 129

Withdrawal seizures, alcohol, 56-57

Withdrawal syndrome

characteristics of, 162

and seizures, 56-57

Women

battered, interventions with, 213-218

battering of, 211-218

changes in attitudes of, 207-208

exploitation of, 210-211

mental health of, 208-210

raped, interventions with, 219-224

self-image of, changes in, 207-208

socialization of, 206-208

violence against, 205-225

attitudes of staff members toward, 224

Workshops, 294

Writing ability, assessment of, 42
Written communication, interagency, 397-398
Wyatt v. Stickney, 346, 353

X

X-ray films of skull in diagnosis of dementia, 32

Z

Zarontin; *see* Ethosuximide
Zero-base budgeting, 367